SOCIAL SECURITY T
THE LEGISLATIC

VOLUME III:
ADMINISTRATION,
ADJUDICATION AND
THE EUROPEAN DIMENSION

AUSTRALIA
LBC Information Services
Sydney

CANADA and USA
Carswell
Toronto

NEW ZEALAND
Brooker's
Auckland

SINGAPORE and MALAYSIA
Sweet & Maxwell Asia
Singapore and Kuala Lumpur

SOCIAL SECURITY TRIBUNALS LEGISLATION 2000

General Editor
David Bonner, LL.B., LL.M.

VOLUME III: ADMINISTRATION, ADJUDICATION AND THE EUROPEAN DIMENSION

Commentary by
Robin White, M.A., LL.M.
Professor of Law, University of Leicester
Deputy Social Security Commissioner

Mark Rowland, LL.B.
Social Security Commissioner

Consultant Editor
Child Poverty Action Group

LONDON
SWEET & MAXWELL
2000

Published in 2000 by
Sweet & Maxwell Limited of
100 Avenue Road, Swiss Cottage,
London NW3 3PF
(http://www.sweetandmaxwell.co.uk)
Computerset by Wyvern 21 Ltd, Bristol
Printed in England by
Clays Ltd, St. Ives plc

No natural forests were destroyed to make this product.
Only farmed timber was used and re-planted.

A catalogue record for this book is
available from the British Library

ISBN 0 421 824 808

All rights reserved. Crown Copyright Legislation is reproduced under the terms of Crown Copyright Policy Guidance issued by HMSO.

No part of this publication may be reproduced or transmitted, in any form or by any means, or stored in any retrieval system of any nature without prior written permission, except for permitted fair dealing under the Copyright, Designs and Patents Act 1988, or in accordance with the terms of a licence issued by the Copyright Licensing Agency in respect of photocopying and/or reprographic reproduction. Application for permission for other use of copyright material including permission to reproduce extracts in other published works shall be made to the publishers. Full acknowledgment of author, publisher and source must be given.
Application for permission for other use of copyright material controlled by the publisher shall be made to the publishers. Material is contained in this publication for which publishing permission has been sought, and for which copyright is acknowledged. Permission to reproduce such material cannot be granted by the publishers and application must be made to the copyright holder.

Commentators have asserted their moral rights under the copyright, Designs and Patents Act 1988 to be identified as the authors of the commentary in this Volume.

CHILD POVERY ACTION GROUP

The Child Poverty Action Group is a charity, founded in 1965, which campaigns for the relief of poverty in the United Kingdom. It has a particular reputation in the field of welfare benefits law derived from its legal work, publications, training and parliamentary and policy work, and is widely recognised as the leading organisation for taking test cases on social security law.

CPAG is therefore ideally placed to act as Consultative Editor to this 3-volume work—**Social Security: Legislation 2000**. CPAG is not responsible for the detail of what is contained in each volume, and the authors' views are not necessarily those of CPAG. The Consultant Editor's role is to act in an advisory capacity on the overall structure, focus and direction of the work.

For more information about CPAG, its rights and policy publications or training c ourses, its address is 94 White Lion Street, London, N19PF (telephone: 020 7837 7979—website: http//www.cpag.org.uk).

FOREWORD

I very much welcome this edition of social security and related legislation in the new three volume format. Together they will be an indispensable guide for all those who work in our tribunals—tribunal members, administrators, representatives, and, of course, the parties themselves. The 1998 Act and subsequent regulations, which did so much to affect the way we work, have been fully assimilated into the text. No tribunal service could be better served, and I warmly welcome this edition.

August 2000   His Honour Judge Michael Harris
President of the Appeals Service

PREFACE

Administration, Appeals and the European Dimension is Volume III of a new three volume series, *Social Security: Legislation 2000*. The companion volumes are: Bonner, Hooker and White, *Volume I: Non Means Tested Benefits*, and Wood, Wikeley, Bonner and Poynter, *Volume II: Income Support, Jobseeker's Allowance, Tax Credits and the Social Fund*. These volumes bring together in a more user-friendly, non-duplicative manner material formerly covered in Bonner, Hooker and White, *Non-Means Tested Benefits: The Legislation;* and Rowland, *Medical and Disability Appeal Tribunals: The Legislation*. Those familiar and well-respected works had formed the standard works of reference for social security tribunals and practitioners.

Each of the volumes in *Social Security: Legislation 2000* provides a legislative text, clearly showing the form and date of amendments, and commentary up to date to April 10, 2000.

Administration, Appeals and the European Dimension consolidates material which was previously found in *Bonner, Mesher* and *Rowland* in so far as it concerns administration and appeals. It also includes a more detailed treatment of European Community Law than was formerly contained in *Bonner*, and deals with the European Convention on Human Rights whose provisions may be relied upon in proceedings before the tribunals under the Human Rights Act 1998. In addition to the presentation of primary materials, the volume includes commentary on those materials, which will assist tribunals in their interpretation and application in cases coming before them.

The entry into force of the Human Rights Act 1998 on October 2, 2000 is sure to bring before tribunals a number of new arguments about the compatibility of both fundamental features of the benefit system and its administration as well as more detailed points relating to particular aspects of particular benefits. The commentary to the Human Rights Act 1998, and to the provisions of the Convention to which direct reference can be made before decision makers, tribunals, the Commissioners and the courts and set out in Schedule 1 to the Act, tries to focus on issues likely to be faced in the social security jurisdiction rather than to offer a comprehensive account of the Convention regardless of the context in which questions arise.

More so than ever, the task of converting three separate works into a more user-friendly arrangement of material as well as revising and updating the legislative text and commentary, has required considerable flexibility on the part of the publisher and a great deal of help from a number of sources, including input on the content and structure of this volume from CPAG as advisory editor to the series.

Preface

To maximise space for explanatory commentary we have provided lists of definitions only where the commentary to the provision is substantial, or where reference to definitions is essential for a proper understanding of the provision. Users of this book should always check whether particular words or phrases they are called on to apply or interpret have a particular meaning ascribed to them in legislation. Generally, the first or second regulation in each set of regulations contains definitions of key terms (check the 'Arrangement of Regulations' at the beginning of each set for indication of the subject matter covered by each regulation). There are also definition or 'interpretation' sections in each of the Acts (check the 'Arrangement of Sections' at the beginning of each Act for an indication of the subject matter covered by each section or Schedule).

In the past, users of 'Bonner', 'Mesher and Wood' and 'Rowland' have provided valuable comments which have invariably been helpful to us in ensuring that the selection of legislative material for inclusion and the commentary on it reflect the sort of difficulties encountered in practice, and they have helped shape the content of each of those works. We would very much welcome comment on the volumes in this new series. Please write to the General Editor of the series, David Bonner, Faculty of Law, The University, Leicester LE1 7RH, who will pass on any comments received to the appropriate commentator.

Our gratitude must also go to the President of the Appeals Service, Judge Harris and his staff for continuing the tradition of help and encouragement.

Mark Rowland
Robin White
August 2000

CONTENTS

	Page
Forword	vii
Preface	ix
Using this book and finding other sources of information	xiii
Table of Cases	xix
Table of Social Security Commissioner's Decisions	xxvii
Table of European Directives	xxxi
Table of European Regulations	xxxiii
Table of European Treaties and Conventions	xxxv
Table of Abbreviations	xxxvii

PART I
STATUTES

	Para.
Social Security Administration Act 1992	1.1
Social Security (Recovery of Benefits) Act 1997	1.179
Social Security Contributions (Transfer of Functions, etc.) Act 1999	1.254
Social Security Act 1998	1.265

PART II
EUROPEAN COMMUNITY LAW

European Communities Act	2.1
Extracts from the EC Treaty	2.16
Council Regulation (EEC) No. 1408/71	2.44
Council Regulation (EEC) No. 574/72	2.107
Council Directive 79/7	2.118

PART III
HUMAN RIGHTS LAW

Human Rights Act 1998	3.1

PART IV
STATUTORY INSTRUMENTS

		Paras
1979/628	The Social Security (Claims and Payments) Regulations 1979	4.1
1987/1968	The Social Security (Claims and Payments) Regulations 1987	4.13
1999/3108	The Social Security (Claims and Information) Regulations 1999	4.189
1999/1495	The Social Security Commissioners (Procedures) Regulations 1999	4.208
1999/991	The Social Security and Child Support (Decisions and Appeals) Regulations 1999	4.242
1982/1408	The Social Security (General Benefit) Regulations 1982	4.380
1976/615	The Social Security (Medical Evidence) Regulations 1976	4.424
1988/664	The Social (Payments on Account, Overpayments and Recovery) Regulations 1988	4.441
1997/2205	The Social Security (Recovery of Benefits) Regulations 1997	4.481

	Page
Index	629

Using this book and finding other sources of information

Introduction

This book is not designed as an introduction to, or general textbook on, the law relating to social security. Inevitably some familiarity with the social security system has been assumed. It may though help readers who are not already experts to have some information about the kinds of material covered in this book and referred to in the commentary. Given the speed of change in social security, it is also valuable to have some indication of useful sources of information about current developments.

Social security law: primary sources and the status of the commentary in this book

Social security law consists of *Acts of Parliament*, also known as statutes or primary legislation, *Regulations*, also known as statutory instruments or delegated legislation, and of *decisions of the Social Security Commissioners* (referred to as 'the Commissioners') and of *the courts*. The precise mixture of the three sources differs from benefit to benefit.

This book contains an up-to-date text of the principal statutes and the key regulations relevant to the work of the appeal tribunals under the jurisdiction of The Appeals Service (TAS) and of the Social Security Commissioners, and of those who appear before them. The commentary on those provisions aims to throw light on the statutory provosions or regulations and to show, where they are any, how the decisions of the Commissioners and the courts interpret and apply those provisions. The focus in decision making, however, must always remain on the actual words of the statutory rule or regulation as applied by decisions of the Commissioners and the courts. The commentary merely reflects the opinion of the commentator on what actually is the law contained in those sources.

Although some aspects of this note are designed particularly to be help to those readers who are not lawyers, it also contains important information for lawyers. Later, it explains a little more about the nature of some of the sources, particularly Commissioners' decisions. It begins by giving guidance on finding the particular provision you require in a statute and in a set of regulations.

Using this Book

Finding a particular section in a statute

Suppose you wanted to find section 71 of the Social Security Administration Act 1992. Sometimes the word 'section' is abbreviated to 's.'; so you could refer to s.71 of the Social Security Administration Act 1992.

To find this provision, you can use the contents pages to find where provisions of the Social Security Administration Act 1992 are printed. You can also use the running heads at the top of each page; the header on the left hand page gives the name of the Act while the header on the right hand page gives the year and chapter number (abbreviated 'c.') as well as the section dealt with on that page. The chapter number simply indicates the order in the Parliamentary year of the statute; the Social Security Administration Act 1992 is chapter 5, meaning that it was the fifth statute to be passed in the 1992 Parliamentary session.

After the text of the section comes a note of the amendments made to the provision, reference to relevant definitions, and the commentary which appears under the heading GENERAL NOTE. Where the section is re-enacted in consolidating legislation, that is, legislation drawing together all the amendments made over time in a new statute, the derivation, or source, of the provision is also given so that you can see where the provision originally appeared. This can be helpful in considering any decisions of Commissioners or the courts on the earlier form of the provision.

Finding a particular regulation

Suppose you wanted to find regulation 3 of the Social Security and Child Support (Decisions and Appeals) Regulations 1999. Sometimes the word 'regulation' is abbreviated to 'reg.'; so you could refer to reg. 3 of the Social Security and Child Support (Decisions and Appeals) Regulations 1999.

To find this provision, use the contents pages to find the Social Security and Child Support (Decisions and Appeals) Regulations 1999. Then move forward within the regulations until you find the one you want. Again the running headers at the top of each page will assist you. The header on the right hand page gives the statutory instrument number, that is the year of publication and the number, as in S.I. 1999 No. 991, indicating that these regulations were the 991st set of regulations made in the 1999 Parliamentary session.

As with statutes, after the text of the regulation comes a note of the amendments made to the provision, reference to relevant definitions, and the commentary which appears under the heading GENERAL NOTE. Where the regulation is re-enacted in consolidating regulations, that is, legislation drawing together all the amendments made over time in a new set of regulations, the derivation, or source, of the provision is also given so that you can see where the provision originally appeared. This can be helpful in considering any decisions of Commissioners or the courts on the earlier form of the provision.

Using this Book

Commissioners' decisions

Both reported and unreported decisions of Commissioners are important sources of guidance on the interpretation and application of legislation relating to social security benefits and their administration. Where relevant, these are binding on both decision-makers and on tribunals. The binding nature of Commissioners' decisions is discussed below. Most appears are heard by a single Commissioner, though the Chief Commissioner does occasionally direct that cases of special importance should be heard by three Commissioners sitting together. This is known as a Tribunal of Commissioners.

Each Commissioner's decision is given a file number in the Office of the Social Security and Child Support Commissioners, which is a unique identification number. So Commissioner's decision *CU/23/1992* is the 23rd case on unemployment benefit registered in 1992. The letters 'CU' indicate that the decision is that of a Commissioner (C) and that the benefit in question is unemployment benefit (U).

From 1995, there has been a change of approach, reflecting computerisation. The system of numbering consecutively within benefits in a particular year ceased. The lettering system remains the same, but the number after the first stroke, as in *CU/7328/1995*, indicated that this was the 7328th case on any benefit registered since the beginning of 1995. The system of consecutive numbering from the beginning of 1995 ran until the start of 1997. From 1997 cases have been registered consecutively by number within a calendar year without a separate range of numbers for each benefit.

Some decisions are starred and are referred to as starred decisions. All this means is that the Commissioner who made the decision thinks that it might raise a point of general importance and should be circulated to other Commissioners to see whether the decision would receive widespread support among the Commissioners. The Chief Commissioner decides whether any particular decision is to be reported. The decision will then be renumbered with the initial letter 'R' for 'reported' and will receive a new reference. So *R(S)3/90* is the third reported decision in 1990 on sickness or invalidity benefit. It has become customary to indicate that a decision is that of a Tribunal of Commissioners by adding the letter 'T' in brackets after the reference, as in *R(I)12/75(T)*. Reported decisions were published by the Stationary Office and are available in nearly all tribunal venues. They can be consulted in many libraries, in offices of the Benefits Agency, and at the offices of the Commissioners in London and Edinburgh. The publication of bound volumes currently ends with the 1989 to 1990 volume. Unreported decisions may be consulted at the offices of the Commissioners in London and Edinburgh.

The system of reporting described above is currently under review, and there may be changes. Criticisms were expressed of the reporting arrangements by the Select Committee on Social Security in its conclusions following its enquiry into the work of the Commissioners.

Although the Chief Commissioner has directed that so far as possible decision-makers and tribunals should refer to reported decisions only,

Using this Book

the legal position is that all decisions of individual Commissioners have equal weight. A decision of a Tribunal of Commissioners binds individual Commissioners, unless they are satisfied that there are compelling reasons for not following it. Tribunals of Commissioners are free to depart from previous decisions both of individual Commissioners and of earlier Tribunals of Commissioners: *R(U)4/88*. Decision-makers and tribunals must follow a decision of a Tribunal of Commissioners in preference to a decision of an individual Commissioner. Where a reported and an unreported decision of an individual Commissioner conflict, the practice has developed of following the reported decision since the fact of reporting indicates that the decision has the support of a majority of Commissioners. If these rules do not resolve a conflict between Commissioners' decisions, then decision-makers and tribunals are free to choose which of the conflicting decisions to follow. No preference is accorded *per se* to the later decision. Where either the decision-maker or a claimant intends to rely on an unreported decision, a copy of the unreported decision should be presented to the tribunal. In the case of the decision-maker, a copy should be included in the appeal papers, and in the case of the claimant, courtesy requires that notice should be given to the decision-maker of an intention to rely on the unreported decision. This could avoid an adjournment to enable the decision-maker to consider the impact of the unreported decision.

The reporting of decisions is slow. For this reason, considerable reliance is placed by representatives on publications such as the *Journal of Social Security*, the *Journal of Social Welfare and Family Law*, *Legal Action*, *The Law Society's Gazette*, the *Disability Rights Bulletin*, and *CPAG's Welfare Rights Bulletin* for early information and comment on new decisions. The following websites contain Commissioners' decisions:
http://www.hywels.demon.co.uk/commrs/ and
http://www.courtservice.gov.uk/tribunals/ossc_frm.htm

Decisions of the courts

Though unravelling the precise legal position of court decisions is somewhat complex, it is not clear that decision-makers, tribunals and Commissioners are bound by decisions of the Divisional Court of the Queen's Bench Division when a judicial review has been pursued: see *CS/253/1990*, and the Court of Appeal when cases go to appeal from the Commissioners or following a judicial review. Note, however, that in *CSBO* v *Leary*, reported as an appendix to *R(SB)6/85*, it was confirmed that decisions of the Divisional Court dealing with questions arising from actions of the old Supplementary Benefit Appeal Tribunals under the statutory right of appeal before 1980 do not bind the Commissioners.

Decisions of the House of Lords bind all courts (except the House of Lords itself), the Commissioners and the tribunals.

In joined cases *CIS/16992/1996*, *CIS/2809/1997* and *CFC/1587/1997* (starred as 100/97), a Commissioner concludes that a single Commis-

Using this Book

sioner is not bound by a decision of a single High Court judge given on judicial review but is bound by a decision of a Divisional Court (that is, two or more High Court judges sitting together).

What does it mean to say that a case is binding

Reference to decisions being binding means that where a similar point is raised in a later case before an adjudicating authority bound by the decision, that adjudicating authority must accept the interpretation of the law contained in the decision. So a Commissioner's decision explaining what a term in a particular regulation means, lays down the definition of that term in much the same way as if the term had been defined in the regulations themselves. The decision may also help in deciding what the same term means when it is used in a different set of regulations, provided that the term appears to have been used in a similar context.

Appeals to the Commissioners are now available only on points of law, but before April 1987 appeals were available on points of fact as well as law. Care should be taken in reading older decisions to appreciate that some were concerned with fact rather than law, though the reported decisions invariably contain points of general application. Relevant decisions of the Commissioners and the courts are explained in the commentary to the statutory provisions in this volume, together with guidance on their significant for decision-making in the tribunals. Users of the book should remember that it is the decision itself which is binding and not the explanation of it in the commentary; that is merely the opinion of the commentator.

European Community Law

The European Community is part of the European Union. European Community Law affecting social security is covered in this volume.

The European Union has two courts: the Court of Justice of the European Communities, and the Court of First Instance. Decision-makers, tribunals and Commissioners are under a duty by reason of Article 10 (ex 5) of the EC Treaty to apply decisions of the Luxembourg courts, where relevant to cases before them, in preference to other authorities binding on them.

Decisions of the Court of Justice of the European Communities come in two parts: the Opinion of the Advocate General and the decision of the Court. It is the decision of the Court which is binding. The Court is assisted by hearing the Opinion of the Advocate General before itself coming to a conclusion on the issue before it. The Court does not always follow its Advocate General. Where it does, the Opinion of the Advocate General often elaborates the arguments in greater detail than the single collegiate judgment of the Court. No dissenting judgments appear in reports from the Court of Justice.

Decisions of the Luxembourg courts are available on the world wide web at http://www.curia.eu.int/

Using this Book

The Strasbourg Court

The Court of Human Rights in Strasbourg is quite separate from the Luxembourg courts and serves a different purpose. The work of the Court and the impact of the Human Rights Act 1998 on social security are discussed later in this volume.

Judgments of the Court of Human Rights are made by majority, and separate concurring or dissenting judgements are included with the decision of the majority where the Court is not unanimous.

Decisions of the Court of Human Rights are available on the world wide web at http://www.echr.coe.int/

Official guidance

The law has been translated into a more civil servant friendly format. Prior to the decision making and appears changes made by the Social Security Act 1998, guidance on benefits and their administration was set out in the thirteen volume *Adjudication Officers Guide (AOG)* published by the Stationery Office. This has now been replaced by a twelve volume *Decision Makers Guide (DMG)*. This is available on the world wide web at http://www.dss.gov.uk/hq/pubs/dmg/

The coverage of the DMG is as follows:

Volume 1	Decision making and appears
Volume 2	International subjects
Volume 3	Subjects common to all benefits
Volume 4	Jobseeker's Allowance and Income Support
Volume 5	Jobseeker's Allowance and Income Support
Volume 6	Jobseeker's Allowance and Income Support
Volume 7	Jobseeker's Allowance and Income Support
Volume 8	Working Families' Tax Credit/Disabled Person's Tax Credit
Volume 9	Children's Benefits
Volume 10	Benefits for Incapacity, Disability and Maternity
Volume 11	Industrial Injuries Benefits
Volume 12	Widows Benefits and Retirement Pension

It should be noted that the DMG is not binding on tribunals and Commissioners; it is internal guidance for the use of decision makers within the Department.

Unofficial guidance

There is a large number of guides. CPAG's *Welfare Benefits Handbook*, published annually each Spring, is unrivalled as a practical and comprehensive introduction from the claimant's viewpoint.

TABLE OF CASES

Achterberg-te Riele v. Sociale Verzekeringsbank Amsterdam (C–48/88) [1989] F.E.C.R. 1963; [1990] 3 C.M.L.R. 323, ECJ 2.121
Adoui (Rezguia) v. Belgium (C–115/81) [1982] E.C.R. 1665; [1982] 3 C.M.L.R. 631, ECJ 2.33
Airey v. Ireland (No.1) (A/32) (1979-80) 2 E.H.R.R. 305, ECHR 3.66
Allen v. Allen [1986] 2 F.L.R. 265; [1986] Fam. Law 268, CA 1.100
Arcaro, Criminal Proceedings against, (C-168/95) [1997] All E.R. (EC) 82; [1997] 1 C.M.L.R. 179; [1998] En v. L.R. 39, ECJ 2.212
Atlanta Fruchthandelsgesellschaft mbH v. Bundesamt fur Ernahrung und Forstwirtschaft (C–465/93) [1996] All E.R. (E.C.) 31; [1996] 1 C.M.L.R. 575, *The Times*, November 29, 1995, ECJ 2.41

Baron v. Secretary of State for Social Services *The Times*, March 25, 1985, CA .. 4.343
Beaney (Deceased); *sub nom.* Beaney v. Beaney [1978] 1 W.L.R. 770; [1978] 2 All E.R. 595; 121 S.J. 832, Ch D 1.61
Beate Reibold v. Bundesanstalt fur Arbeit (C–216/89) [1990] E.C.R. I-4163 .... 2.91
Bergemann v. Bundesanstalt fur Arbeit (C–236/87) [1988] E.C.R. 5125; [1990] 1 C.M.L.R. 525, ECJ 2.91
Bestuur van de Nieuwe Algemene Bedrijfsvereniging v. Warmerdam-Steggerda (C–388/87) [1989] E.C.R. 1203; [1991] 2 C.M.L.R. 86, ECJ 2.91
Bestuur van de Sociale Verzekeringsbank v. Cabanis-Issarte (C–308/93) [1996] 2 C.M.L.R. 729, ECJ 2.48
Black v. Doncaster MBC [1999] 1 W.L.R. 53; [1998] 3 All E.R. 631; [1998] P.I.Q.R. Q139; (1998) 95(29) L.S.G. 27; (1998) 142 S.J.L.B. 199; *The Times*, July 14, 1998; *The Independent*, June 29, 1998 (C-.S.), CA 1.250
Bland v. Chief Supplementary Benefit Officer [1983] 1 W.L.R. 262; [1983] 1 All E.R. 537; (1983) 127 S.J. 53, CA 1.313
Bramhill v. Chief Adjudication Officer (C–420/92) [1995] 2 C.M.L.R. 35, ECJ . 2.132

Caisse Regionale d'Assurance Maladie (Lille) v. Diamente Palermo (Toia) (C-237/78) [1979] E.C.R. 2645; [1980] 2 C.M.L.R. 31, ECJ 2.50
Campus Oil Ltd v. Minister for Industry and Energy (C–F72/83); *sub nom.* Campus Oil Ltd v. Minister for Industry and Energy (No.2) [1984] E.C.R. 2727; [1984] 3 C.M.L.R. 544, ECJ 2.39
Carlin v. United Kingdom (1997) App. No.27537/95, ECHR 3.86
Centre Public d'Aide Sociale, Courcelles v. Lebon (C–316/85) [1989] 1 C.M.L.R. 337; *The Times*, September 9, 1987, ECJ 2.33
Charles v. Hugh James Jones & Jenkins [2000] 1 All E.R. 289; [2000] Lloyd's Rep. P.N. 207; *The Times*, December 22, 1999, CA 1.300
Chief Adjudication Officer v. Foster [1993] A.C. 754; [1993] 2 W.L.R. 292; [1993] 1 All E.R. 705; [1993] C.O.D. 259; (1993) 137 S.J.L.B. 36; *The Times*, February 1, 1993; *The Independent*, February 2, 1993; *The Guardian*, January 29, 1993, HL 1.309
Chief Adjudication Officer v. Sherriff (1995) 92(22) L.S.G. 41; (1995) 139 S.J.L.B. 131; *The Times*, May 10, 1995, CA 1.61
Chief Adjudication Officer v. McKiernon, unreported, July 8, 1993 .... 0.00
Chief Supplementary Benefit Officer v. Leary [1985] 1 W.L.R. 84; [1985] 1 All E.R. 1061; (1984) 81 L.S.G. 3596; (1984) 128 S.J. 852, CA 1.65
CILFIT Srl v. Ministro della Sanita (Minister of Health) (C–283/81) [1982] E.C.R. 3415; [1983] 1 C.M.L.R. 472, ECJ 2.41
Clarke v. United Kingdom (1997) App. No. 27011/95, ECHR 3.86

Table of Cases

Colchester Estates (Cardiff) v. Carlton Industries Plc [1986] Ch. 80; [1984] 3 W.L.R. 693; [1984] 2 All E.R. 601; (1984) 271 E.G. 778; (1984) 81 L.S.G. 2699, Ch D 1.309
Commission of the European Communities v. Belgium (No.1); sub nom. Public Employees, Re (No.1) (C-149/79) [1980] E.C.R. 3881; [1981] 2 C.M.L.R. 413, ECJ 2.33
Commission of the European Communities v. Belgium; sub nom. Unemployed Heads of Households, Re (C-229/89) [1993] 2 C.M.L.R. 403; [1991] I.R.L.R. 393, ECJ 2.125
Commission of the European Communities v. Germany (C-205/84) [1986] E.C.R. 3755 .... 2.33
Commock v. Chief Adjudication Officer (1990) 87(14) L.S.G. 47, CA 1.60
Confédération des Syndicats Médicaux v. France (1986) 47 D.R. 225 .... 3.20
Cornwell v. United Kingdom *The Times*, May 10, 2000, ECHR 3.81
Cotter v. Minister for Social Welfare (C-377/89); McDermott v. Minister for Social Welfare [1991] 3 C.M.L.R. 507; [1991] I.R.L.R. 380, ECJ 2.12
Cowan v. Tresor Public (C-186/87) [1989] E.C.R. 195; [1990] 2 C.M.L.R. 613; *The Times*, February 13, 1989, ECJ 2.33
Coyne v. United Kingdom *The Times*, October 24, 1997, ECHR 3.64

De Cubber v. Belgium (Investigating Judge) (A/86) (1985) 7 E.H.R.R. 236, ECHR 3.65
De Moor v. Belgium (A/292-A) (1994) 18 E.H.R.R. 372, ECHR 3.64
Decker v. Caisse de Maladie des Employes Prives (C-120/95) [1998] All E.R. (E.C.) 673; [1998] 2 C.M.L.R. 879; (1999) 48 B.M.L.R. 32, ECJ 2.78
Delaney v. Delaney (1990) [1990] 2 F.L.R. 457; [1991] F.C.R. 161; [1991] Fam. Law 22; (1990) 154 J.P.N. 693, CA 1.100
Deumeland v. Germany (A/120) (1986) 8 E.H.R.R. 448, ECHR 3.62, 3.64
Di Paolo v. Office National de l'Emploi (C-76/76) [1977] E.C.R. 315; [1977] 2 C.M.L.R. 59, ECJ 2.90, 2.91
Dombo Beheer BV v. Netherlands (A/274-A) (1994) 18 E.H.R.R. 213, ECHR 3.64
Drake v. Chief Adjudication Officer (C-150/85) [1987] Q.B. 166; [1986] 3 W.L.R. 1005; [1986] 3 All E.R. 65; [1986] 3 C.M.L.R. 43; (1987) 84 L.S.G. 264; (1986) 130 S.J. 923, ECJ 2.121, 2.123
Duggan v. Chief Adjudication Officer *The Times*, December 19, 1988, CA 1.64

Emmott v. Minister for Social Welfare; Emmott v. Attorney General (C-208/90) [1991] 3 C.M.L.R. 894; [1993] I.C.R. 8; [1991] I.R.L.R. 387, ECJ 2.12
Engel v. Netherlands (No.1) (A/22) (1979-80) 1 E.H.R.R. 647, ECHR 3.69
Ettl v. Austria (A/117) (1988) 10 E.H.R.R. 255, ECHR 3.68
Evans v. Secretary of State for Social Services [1993] P.I.Q.R. P370; *The Times*, September 14, 1993; Independent, September 17, 1993, CA 4.343

Fedje v. Sweden (A212-C) (1994) 17 E.H.H.R. 14 3.64 .... 3.65
Feldbrugge v. Netherlands (A/99) (1986) 8 E.H.R.R. 425, ECHR 3.62, 3.65
Findlay v. United Kingdom (1997) 24 E.H.R.R. 221; *The Times*, February 27, 1997; *The Independent*, March 4, 1997, ECHR 3.64
Firma Foto-Frost v. Hauptzollamt Lubeck-Ost (C-314/85) [1988] 3 C.M.L.R. 57; *The Times*, December 30, 1987, ECJ 2.41
Firma Rheinmuhlen-Dusseldorf v. Einfuhr- und Vorratsstelle fur Getreide und Futtermittel; sub nom. Rheinmuhlen-Dusseldorf v. EVST (C-166/73) [1974] E.C.R. 33; [1974] 1 C.M.L.R. 523, ECJ 2.39
Foster v. British Gas Plc (C-188/89) [1991] 1 Q.B. 405; [1991] 2 W.L.R. 258; [1990] 3 All E.R. 897; [1990] 2 C.M.L.R. 833; [1991] I.C.R. 84; [1990] I.R.L.R. 353; *The Times*, July 13, 1990, ECJ 2.10
Francovich v. Italy (C-6/90) [1991] E.C.R. I-5357; [1993] 2 C.M.L.R. 66; [1995] I.C.R. 722; [1992] I.R.L.R. 84; *The Times*, November 20, 1991, ECJ 2.12
Franklin v. Chief Adjudication Officer *The Times*, December 29, 1995, CA 1.62

Gaygusuz v. Austria (1997) 23 E.H.R.R. 364, ECHR 3.81, 3.86
Gillow v. United Kingdom (A/109) (1989) 11 E.H.R.R. 335; *The Times*, November

Table of Cases

29, 1986, ECHR 3.8179
Gimenez Zaera v. Instituto Nacional de la Seguridad Social (C-126/86) [1989] 1 C.M.L.R. 827, ECJ 2.18
Golder v. United Kingdom (A/18) (1979-80) 1 E.H.R.R. 524, ECHR 3.66
Graham v. Secretary of State for Social Security); *sub nom.* Secretary of State for Social Security v. Graham (C-92/94 [1995] All E.R. (E.C.) 736; [1995] 3 C.M.L.R. 169; [1996] I.C.R. 258; *The Times*, September 25, 1995; *The Independent*, October 9, 1995 (C-.S.), ECJ 2.130
Gray v. Adjudication Officer (C-62/91) [1992] 2 C.M.L.R. 584, ECJ 2.84
Gul v. Regierungsprasident Dusseldorf (C-131/85) [1986] E.C.R. 1573; [1987] 1 C.M.L.R. 501, ECJ 2.33

Höfner v. Mactrotron [1991] E.C.R. I-2010 .... 2.33
Harrison's Settlement, Re; *sub nom.* Harrison v. Harrison [1955] Ch. 260; [1955] 2 W.L.R. 256; [1955] 1 All E.R. 185; 99 S.J. 74; *The Times*, December 22, 1954, CA 4.347
Hassall v. Secretary of State for Social Security [1995] 1 W.L.R. 812; [1995] 3 All E.R. 909; [1995] R.T.R. 316; [1995] P.I.Q.R. P292; (1995) 92(8) L.S.G. 41; (1995) 139 S.J.L.B. 57; *The Times*, December 26, 1994; *The Independent*, December 16, 1994, CA 1.1861.206
Hodgson v. Armstrong [1967] 2 Q.B. 299; [1967] 2 W.L.R. 311; [1967] 1 All E.R. 307; 110 S.J. 907, CA 4.37
HP Bulmer Ltd v. J Bollinger SA (No.2) [1974] Ch. 401; [1974] 3 W.L.R. 202; [1974] 2 All E.R. 1226; [1974] 2 C.M.L.R. 91; [1974] F.S.R. 334; [1975] R.P.C. 321; 118 S.J. 404, CA 2.39
Hughes v. Chief Adjudication Officer (C-78/91) [1992] 3 C.M.L.R. 490; [1993] 1 F.L.R. 791; [1993] Fam. Law 477; *The Independent*, July 23, 1992; Financial *The Times*, August 4, 1992, ECJ 2.123
Hulley v. Thompson [1981] 1 W.L.R. 159; [1981] 1 All E.R. 1128; 125 S.J. 47, DC 1.100

Insurance Officer v. McCaffrey [1984] 1 W.L.R. 1353; [1985] 1 All E.R. 5; (1985) 82 L.S.G. 203; (1984) 128 S.J. 836, HL 1.4, 1.13, 4.19s2
Ireland v. United Kingdom (A/25) (1979-80) 2 E.H.R.R. 25, ECHR 3.55
Irish Creamery Milk Suppliers Association v. Ireland (C-36/80) [1981] 2 C.M.L.R. 455, ECJ 2.39

Jackson v. Chief Adjudication Officer (C-63/91); Cresswell v. Chief Adjudication Officer [1993] Q.B. 367; [1993] 2 W.L.R. 658; [1993] 3 All E.R. 265; [1992] 3 C.M.L.R. 389; [1993] Fam. Law 477; *The Times*, October 22, 1992, ECJ 2.123, 4.23
Johnson v. Chief Adjudication Officer (No.1) (C-31/90) [1993] Q.B. 252; [1991] 3 C.M.L.R. 917, ECJ 2.121
Johnson v. Chief Adjudication Officer (No.2) (C-410/92) [1995] All E.R. (E.C.) 258; [1995] 1 C.M.L.R. 725; [1995] I.C.R. 375; [1995] I.R.L.R. 157; *The Times*, December 26, 1994; Financial *The Times*, December 20, 1994, ECJ ... 2.12
Jones v. Chief Adjudication Officer [1994] 1 W.L.R. 62; [1994] 1 All E.R. 225; (1993) 137 S.J.L.B. 188; *The Times*, July 22, 1993, CA 1.62
Jones v. Department of Employment [1989] Q.B. 1; [1988] 2 W.L.R. 493; [1988] 1 All E.R. 725; (1988) 85(4) L.S.G. 35; (1987) 137 N.L.J. 1182; (1988) 132 S.J. 128; (1988) 85 L.S.G. 35, CA 1.318
Jones v. Secretary of State for Social Services; *sub nom.* R. v. National Insurance Commissioner, Ex p. Hudson; R. v. National Insurance Commissioner, Ex p. Jones; R. v. National Insurance Commissioner, Ex p. Lloyd-Jones [1972] A.C. 944; [1972] 2 W.L.R. 210; [1972] 1 All E.R. 145; (1971) 116 S.J. 57, HL . 1.366
JS (A Minor) (Declaration of Paternity), Re [1981] Fam. 22; [1980] 3 W.L.R. 984; [1980] 1 All E.R. 1061; (1980) 10 Fam. Law 121; 124 S.J. 881, CA 4.68
JW Teuling-Worms v. Bedrijfsvereniging voor de Chemische Industrie; *sub nom.* Teuling v. Bedrijfsvereniging voor de Chemische Industrie (C-30/85) [1988] 3 C.M.L.R. 789, ECJ 2.125

Table of Cases

Keegan v. Ireland (A/290) [1994] 3 F.C.R. 165; (1994) 18 E.H.R.R. 342, ECHR 3.66
Klass v. Germany (A/28) (1979-80) 2 E.H.R.R. 214, ECHR 3.20
Knightley v. United Kingdom (1997) App. No.28778/95, ECHR 3.63
Knoch v. Bundesanstalt fur Arbeit (C-102/91), unreported, July 8, 1992, ECJ 2.91
Kohll v. Union des Caisses de Maladie (C-158/96) [1998] 2 C.M.L.R. 928, ECJ 2.78
Krafft and Rougeot v. France (11543/85) (1990) 65 D.R. 51 3.81
Kraska v. Switzerland (A/254-B) (1994) 18 E.H.R.R. 188, ECHR 3.64

Lang v. Devon General [1987] I.C.R. 4; (1986) 83 L.S.G. 2653; (1986) 136 N.L.J. 893, EAT 4.37
Lawrie-Blum v. Land Baden-Wurttenberg (C-66/85) [1987] 3 C.M.L.R. 389; [1987] I.C.R. 483, ECJ 2.33
Leigh v. United Kingdom (1984) 38 D.R. 74 3.20
Levin v. Secretary of State for Justice; *sub nom.* Levin v. Staatssecretaris van Justitie (C-53/81)[1982] E.C.R. 1035; [1982] 2 C.M.L.R. 454, ECJ 2.18, 2.33
Lloyd v. McMahon [1987] A.C. 625; [1987] 2 W.L.R. 821; 85 L.G.R. 545; [1987] R. v. R. 58; (1987) 84 L.S.G. 1240; (1987) 137 N.L.J. 265; (1987) 131 S.J. 409; [1987] 1 All E.R. 1118; [1987] 27 R. v. R. 58, HL 4.350
Lombardo v. Italy (A/249-B) (1996) 21 E.H.R.R. 188, ECHR 3.63

M v. United Kingdom and Ireland (1986) 47 D.R. 27 3.53
MB v. United Kingdom (1994) 77-A D.R. 42 3.20
McCaffery v. Datta [1997] P.I.Q.R. Q64, CA 1.215
María Martínez Sala v. Freistaat Bayern [1998] E.C.R. I-2691 2.23
Marleasing SA v. La Comercial Internacional de Alimentacion SA (C-106/89) [1990] E.C.R. I-4135; [1993] B.C.C. 421; [1992] 1 C.M.L.R. 305, ECJ 2.21
Massa v. Italy (A/265-B) (1994) 18 E.H.R.R. 266, ECHR 3.63, 3.67
Meyers v. Adjudication Officer (C-116/94) [1995] All E.R. (E.C.) 705; [1996] 1 C.M.L.R. 461; [1995] I.R.L.R. 498; *The Times*, July 19, 1995; *The Independent*, September 11, 1995 (C-.S.), ECJ 2.123
Mitchell v. Laing 1998 S.C. 342; 1998 S.L.T. 203; 1998 S.C.L.R. 266; 1997 G.W.D. 40-2035; *The Times*, January 28, 1998, 1 Div 1.213, 1.249
Molenbroek v. Bestuur van de Sociale Verzekeringsbank (C-226/91) November 19, 1992, ECJ 2.125
Müller v. Austria (1975) 3 D.R. 25 0.00
Mulvey v. Secretary of State for Social Security 1997 S.C. (H.L.) 105; 1997 S.L.T. 753; 1997 S.C.L.R. 348; [1997] B.P.I.R. 696; 1997 G.W.D. 11-488; *The Times*, March 20, 1997, HL 1.87, 1.166

National & Provincial Building Society v. United Kingdom [1997] S.T.C. 1466; (1998) 25 E.H.R.R. 127; 69 T.C. 540; [1997] B.T.C. 624; [1998] H.R.C.D. 34; *The Times*, November 6, 1997, ECHR 3.85
National Assistance Board v. Parkes; *sub nom.* Stopher v. National Assistance [1955] 2 Q.B. 506; [1955] 3 W.L.R. 347; [1955] 3 All E.R. 1; 99 S.J. 540, CA 1.100
Neale v.Bingle (1996) 96(3) Q.R. 7, CC (Slough) 1.186
Nielsen v. Denmark (1986) 46 D.R.55 3.20
Norris and National Gay Federation v. Ireland (1984) 44 D.R.132 3.20

Ophelia, The [1916] 2 A.C. 206, PC 1.63

Page v. Chief Adjudication Officer *The Times*, July 4, 1991, CA 1.57
Partridge v. Adjudication Officer (C-297/96) [1998] 3 C.M.L.R. 941; *The Times*, July 2, 1998, ECJ 2.58
Perry v. Chief Adjudication Officer [1999] 2 C.M.L.R. 439; *The Times*, October 20, 1998; *The Independent*, October 21, 1998, CA 2.52
Petroni v. Office National des Pensions pour Travailleurs Salaries (C-24/75) [1975] E.C.R. 1149, ECJ 2.37
Pinna v. Caisse d'Allocations Familiales de la Savoie (C-41/84) [1986] E.C.R. 1; [1988] 1 C.M.L.R. 350, ECJ 2.37
Piscitello v. Instituto Nazionale della Previdenza Sociale (C-139/82) [1984] 1 C.M.L.R. 108, ECJ 2.56

Table of Cases

Plewa v. Chief Adjudication Officer [1995] 1 A.C. 249; [1994] 3 W.L.R. 317; [1994] 3 All E.R. 323; (1994) 91(30) L.S.G. 32; (1994) 138 S.J.L.B. 152; *The Times*, July 9, 1994; *The Independent*, July 29, 1994, HL 1.51
Posthuma van Damme v. Oztuerk (C-280/94) unreported, February 1, 1996, ECJ 2.121
Poyser and Mills Arbitration, Re; *sub nom* Poyser v. Mills [1964] 2 Q.B. 467; [1963] 2 W.L.R. 1309; [1963] 1 All E.R. 612; 107 S.J. 115, QBD 4.343
Pressos Compania Naviera SA v. Belgium (A/332) (1996) 21 E.H.R.R. 301, ECHR 3.85
Pretore di Salo v. Persons Unknown; *sub nom.* Criminal Proceedings against a Person or Persons Unknown (C-14/86) [1989] 1 C.M.L.R. 71; *The Times*, June 20, 1987, ECJ 2.39
Pretto v. Italy (A/71) (1984) 6 E.H.R.R. 182, ECHR 3.64

R. v. Adjudication Officer, Ex p. Golding; *sub nom.* R. v. Secretary of State for Social Security, Ex p. Golding [1996] N.P.C. 107, CA 4.188
R. v. Bouchereau (C-30/77) [1978] Q.B. 732; [1978] 2 W.L.R. 251; [1981] 2 All E.R. 924; [1978] E.C.R. 1999; (1978) 66 Cr. App. R. 202; [1977] 2 C.M.L.R. 800; 122 S.J. 79; [1978] 2 W.L.R. 250; (1977) 66 Cr. App. R. 202; (1977) 122 S.J. 79, ECJ 2.33
R. v. Deputy Industrial Injuries Commissioner Ex p. Moore [1965] 1 Q.B. 456; [1965] 2 W.L.R. 89; [1965] 1 All E.R. 81; 108 S.J. 1030, CA 1.304
R. v. International Stock Exchange of the United Kingdom [1993] Q.B. 534; [1993] 2 W.L.R. 70; [1993] 1 All E.R. 420; [1993] B.C.L.C. 834; [1993] B.C.C. 11; [1993] 2 C.M.L.R. 677; (1994) 6 Admin. L.R. 67; [1993] C.O.D. 236; *The Times*, November 2, 1992; *The Independent*, November 24, 1992, CA 2.39
R. v. Medical Appeal Tribunal Ex p. Gilmore; *sub nom.* Gilmore's Application, Re [1957] 1 Q.B. 574; [1957] 2 W.L.R. 498; [1957] 1 All E.R. 796; 101 S.J. 248, CA 1.318
R. v. Saunders (Vera Ann) (C-175/78) [1980] Q.B. 72; [1979] 3 W.L.R. 359; [1979] 2 All E.R. 267; [1979] E.C.R. 1129; [1979] 2 C.M.L.R. 216; 123 S.J. 674, ECJ 2.33
R. v. Secretary of State for Health, Ex p. Richardson (C-137/94) [1995] All E.R. (E.C.) 865; [1995] 3 C.M.L.R. 376; [1996] I.C.R. 471; *The Times*, October 27, 1995; *The Independent*, November 17, 1995, ECJ 2.123, 2.130
R. v. Secretary of State for Social Security, Ex p. Cullen [1997] C.O.D. 405; *The Times*, May 16, 1997, CA 4.55, 4.138
R. v. Secretary of State for Social Security, Ex p. Equal Opportunities Commission (C-9/91) [1992] 3 All E.R. 577; [1992] 3 C.M.L.R. 233; [1992] I.C.R. 782; [1992] I.R.L.R. 376; *The Times*, August 19, 1992; *The Independent*, September 14, 1992 (C-.S.), ECJ 2.130
R. v. Secretary of State for Social Security, Ex p. Moore *The Times*, March 9, 1993; *The Independent*, April 12, 1993, CA 4.374
R. v. Secretary of State for Social Security, Ex p. Sarwar [1997] 3 C.M.L.R. 648, CA 4.444
R. v. Secretary of State for Social Security, Ex p. Smithson (Florence Rose) (C-243/90) [1992] 1 C.M.L.R. 1061, ECJ 2.123
R. v. Secretary of State for Social Security, Ex p. Sutton (C-66/95) [1997] All E.R. (E.C.) 497; [1997] 2 C.M.L.R. 382; [1997] C.E.C. 1110; [1997] I.C.R. 961; [1997] I.R.L.R. 524; *The Times*, April 25, 1997, ECJ 2.128, 3.26
R. v. Secretary of State for Social Security, Ex p. Taylor; R. v. Secretary of State for Social Security, Ex p. Chapman [1997] B.P.I.R. 505; [1996] C.O.D. 332; *The Times*, February 5, 1996, QBD 1.87
R. v. Secretary of State for Social Security, Ex p. Taylor (C-382/98) [2000] All E.R. (EC) 80; [2000] 1 C.M.L.R. 873; [2000] C.E.C. 3; *The Times*, January 25, 2000, ECJ 2.130
R. v. Secretary of State for Social Services, Ex p. Britnell; *sub nom.* Britnell v. Secretary of State for Social Services [1991] 1 W.L.R. 198; [1991] 2 All E.R. 726; (1991) 135 S.J. 412; *The Times*, March 15, 1991; *The Independent*, April 4, 1991, HL 1.65
R. v. Secretary of State for Social Services, Ex p. Child Poverty Action Group [1990]

Table of Cases

2 Q.B. 540; [1989] 3 W.L.R. 1116; [1989] 1 All E.R. 1047; (1989) 86(41) L.S.G. 41; (1989) 133 S.J. 1373; *The Times*, October 10, 1988; *The Independent*, October 24, 1988 (C-.S.); *The Independent*, October 11, 1988; *The Guardian*, October 12, 1988, CA 4.51

R. v. Secretary of State for the Home Department, Ex p. Nelson *The Independent*, June 2, 1994, QBD 4.55

R. v. Secretary of State for Transport Ex p. Factortame Ltd [1990] 2 A.C. 85; [1989] 2 W.L.R. 997; [1989] 2 All E.R. 692; [1989] 3 C.M.L.R. 1; [1989] C.O.D. 531; (1989) 139 N.L.J. 715; *The Times*, May 19, 1989; *The Independent*, May 26, 1989; Financial Times, May 23, 1989; *The Guardian*, May 25, 1989; Daily Telegraph, June 5, 1989, HL 2.9, 2.12

R. v. Secretary of State for Transport, Ex p. Factortame (No.2) [1991] 1 A.C. 603; [1990] 3 W.L.R. 818; [1991] 1 All E.R. 70; [1991] 1 Lloyd's Rep. 10; [1990] 3 C.M.L.R. 375; (1991) 3 Admin. L.R. 333; (1990) 140 N.L.J. 1457; (1990) 134 S.J. 1189, HL 4.444

R. v. Social Fund Inspector, Ex p. Ledicott *The Times*, May 24, 1995, QBD 1.382

R. v. Social Fund Officer, Ex p. Hewson, unreported, transcript CO 1132/92, QBD 1.381

R. v. Social Security Commissioner, Ex p. Snares [1997] C.O.D. 403, QBD .. 2.13, 4.444

R. v. West London Supplementary Benefits Appeal Tribunal Ex p. Clarke [1975] 1 W.L.R. 1396; [1975] 3 All E.R. 513; 119 S.J. 743, DC 1.98

R. v. Secretary of State for Social Security, Ex p. Taylor [1999] E.C.R. 2.123

R. v. Secretary of State for Social Security, unreported, July 31, 1997, QBD 4.444

Raad van Arbeid v. Brusse (C-101/83) [1984] E.C.R. 2223; [1985] 2 C.M.L.R. 633, ECJ 2.71

Ramrath v. Ministre de la Justice; *sub nom.* Ramrath v. Minister of Justice (C-106/91) [1995] 2 C.M.L.R. 187; [1992] 3 C.M.L.R. 173; *Financial Times*, May 27, 1992, ECJ 2.33

Raulin v. Minister van Onderwijs en Wetenschappen (C-357/89) [1994] 1 C.M.L.R. 227, ECJ 2.33

Ravnsborg v. Sweden (A/283-B) (1994) 18 E.H.R.R. 38, ECHR 3.69

Reformed Church of X v. The Netherlands (1497/62) (1962) 5 Y.B. 286 .... 3.76

Reyners v. Belgium, (C-2/74) [1974] E.C.R. 631; [1974] 2 C.M.L.R. 305, ECJ .. 2.33

Rijksdienst voor Arbeidsvoorziening v. van Gestel (C-454/93) [1996] 1 C.M.L.R. 437; (1996) 93(20) L.S.G. 31, ECJ 2.71

Ringeisen v. Austria (No.1) (A/13) (1979-80) 1 E.H.R.R. 455, ECHR 3.62

Robins v. United Kingdom (1998) 26 E.H.R.R. 527; *The Times*, October 24, 1997, ECHR 3.64

Ruiz-Mateos v. Spain (A/262) (1993) 16 E.H.R.R. 505, ECHR 3.64

Salesi v. Italy (A/257-E) (1998) 26 E.H.R.R. 187, ECHR 3.62, 3.64

Schouten and Meldrum v. Netherlands (A/304) (1995) 19 E.H.R.R. 432, ECHR 3.62

Schuler-Zgraggen v. Switzerland (A/263) [1994] 1 F.C.R. 453; (1993) 16 E.H.R.R. 405; *The Times*, October 21, 1993, ECHR 3.26, 3.62, 3.64

Secretary of State for Social Security v. Thomas; *sub nom.* Thomas v. Chief Adjudication Officer (C-328/91) [1993] Q.B. 747; [1993] 3 W.L.R. 581; [1993] 4 All E.R. 556; [1993] 3 C.M.L.R. 880; [1993] I.C.R. 673; [1993] I.R.L.R. 292; *The Times*, April 5, 1993, ECJ 2.130

Secretary of State for Social Services v. Solly [1974] 3 All E.R. 992, CA ... 1.54, 1.116

Shallow v. Shallow [1979] Fam. 1; [1978] 2 W.L.R. 583; [1978] 2 All E.R. 483; 121 S.J. 830, CA 1.100

Sharples v. Chief Adjudication Officer [1994] 1 All E.R. 225, CA 0.00

Simmenthal SpA v. Amministrazione delle Finanze dello Stato (No.3)(C-70/77) [1978] E.C.R. 1453; [1978] 3 C.M.L.R. 670, ECJ 2.41

Smith v. Cosworth Casting Processes Ltd (Practice Note) [1997] 1 W.L.R. 1538; [1997] 4 All E.R. 840; [1997] P.I.Q.R. P227; (1997) 94(10) L.S.G. 31; (1997) 141 S.J.L.B. 66; *The Times*, March 28, 1997, CA 1.313

Snares v. Adjudication Officer (C-20/96) [1997] All E.R. (E.C.) 886; [1998] 1 C.M.L.R. 897; *The Times*, December 10, 1997, ECJ 2.58

Sporrong and Lonnroth v. Sweden (A/52) (1983) 5 E.H.R.R. 35, ECHR 3.85

Steen v. Deutsche Bundespost (C-332/90) [1992] 2 C.M.L.R. 406, ECJ 2.33

Table of Cases

Steenhorst-Neerings v. Bestuur van de Bedrijfsvereniging voor Detailhandel, Ambachfen en Huisvrouwen (C-338/91) [1993] E.C.R. I-5475; [1995] 3 C.M.L.R. 323; [1994] I.R.L.R. 244, ECJ 2.12
Stevens v. United Kingdom, unreported, September 9, 1998, ECHR 3.63
Sulak v. Turkey (1996) 84 D.R.101 .... 3.88
Swaddling v. Adjudication Officer (C-90/97) [1999] All E.R. (EC) 217; [1999] 2 C.M.L.R. 679; [1999] C.E.C. 184; [1999] 2 F.L.R. 184; [1999] Fam. Law 382; *The Times*, March 4, 1999, ECJ 2.52
Szrabjer v. United Kingdom (19970 App. No. 270004/95, ECHR 3.86

Telemarsicabruzzo SpA v. Circostel [1993] E.C.R. I-393; *The Times*, February 10, 1993; *Financial Times*, February 12, 1993, ECJ 2.41
Testa v. Bundesanstalt fur Arbeit, Nuremberg (C-41/79); [1981] E.C.R. 1979; [1981] 2 C.M.L.R. 552, ECJ 2.88
Tyrer v. United Kingdom (A/26) (1979-80) 2 E.H.R.R. 1, ECHR 3.55

Union Nationale des Entraineurs et Cadres Techniques Professionnels du Football (UNECTEF) v. Heylens (C-222/86) [1989] 1 C.M.L.R. 901;*The Times*, October 26, 1987, ECJ 2.33
Union Royale Belge des Societes de Football Association (ASBL) v. Bosman; *sub nom.* Royal Club Liegois SA v. Bosman; Union des Associations Europeennes de Football (UEFA) v. Bosman (C-415/93) [1996] All E.R. (EC) 97; [1996] 1 C.M.L.R. 645; [1996] C.E.C. 38; *The Times*, January 17, 1996, ECJ 2.33

Van Breedam v. Belgium F(1989) 62 D.R.109 .... 3.81
Von Colson and Kamann v. Land Nordrhein-Westfahlen (C-14/83) [1984] E.C.R. 1891; [1986] 2 C.M.L.R. 430, ECJ 2.21

Wadey v. Surrey CC (No.2) [1999] 1 W.L.R. 1614; [1999] 2 All E.R. 334; [1999] P.I.Q.R. Q128; (1999) 96(4) L.S.G. 38; (1999) 143 S.J.L.B. 20; *The Times*, January 8, 1999; *The Independent*, December 17, 1998, CA 1.129
Waldemar Fellinger v. Bundesanstalt fTr Arbeit, Nürnberg (C-67/79) [1980] E.C.R. 535; [1981] 1 C.M.L.R. 471, ECJ 2.86
Webb v. EMO Air Cargo (UK) Ltd (C-32/93) [1994] Q.B. 718; [1994] 4 All E.R. 115; [1994] 2 C.M.L.R. 729; [1994] I.C.R. 770; [1994] I.R.L.R. 482; (1994) 144 N.L.J. 1278; *The Times*, July 15, 1994; Financial Times, July 19, 1994; *The Guardian*, July 23, 1994, ECJ 3.10
White v. Chief Adjudication Officer [1986] 2 All E.R. 905; (1986) 83 L.S.G. 1319; (1986) 130 S.J. 448, CA 1.313, 4.241
Wirth v. Landeshauptstadt Hannover (C-109/93), unreported, December 7, 1993, ECJ 2.33
Willis v. United Kingdom (36042/97), unreported 3.81
Wisely v. John Fulton (Plumbers) Ltd (No.1) 1998 Rep. L.R. 91; 1998 G.W.D. 19-991, OH 1.219

X v. Netherlands (A/91) (1986) 8 E.H.R.R. 235, ECHR 3.76
X v. Austria (1962) 5 Y.B. 238 .... 3.20
X v. United Kingdom (1970) 30 CD 70 .... 3.64
X v. United Kingdom (1970) 13 Y.B. 892 .... 3.85
X Association v. Sweden (1982) 28 D.R. 204 .... 3.20, 3.64

TABLE OF SOCIAL SECURITY COMMISSIONER'S DECISIONS

C 6/1999(CR(S)) 1.186	CIS 5/1992 .... 4.461
CA 303/1992 .... 1.61	CIS 136/1992 .... 1.65
CA 171/1993 .... 4.55	CIS 137/1992 .... 1.65
CCR 41993 .... 1.186, 1.206	CIS 442/1992 .... 1.65
CCR 5336/1995 .... 1.186	CIS 545/1992 .... 1.61
CCR 2127/1999 .... 1.186	CIS 734/1992 .... 1.55
CCS 910/1999 .... 4.239	CIS 759/1992 .... 4.28
CCS 2064/1999 .... 4.352	CIS 812/1992 .... 4.113
CDLA 913/1994 .... 4.444, 2.13	CIS 102/1993 .... 1.62
CDLA 14895/1996 .... 4.65	CIS 251/1993 .... 4.76
CDLA 15961/1996 .... 1.304, 4.20	CIS 332/1993 .... 1.55
CDLA 16902/1996 .... 1.309	CIS 501/1993 .... 2.39
CDLA 3680/1997 .... 4.339	CIS 645/1993 .... 1.59
CDLA 4110/1997 .... 4.346	CIS 26/1994 .... 1.50
CDLA 1389/1997 .... 4.346	CIS 145/1994 .... 1.62
CDLA 5793/97 .... 4.343	CIS 288/1994 .... 4.188
CDLA 1347/1999 .... 4.325	CIS 459/1994 .... 4.61
CDLA 2934/1999 .... 1.300	CIS 674/1994 .... 1.62
CDLA 4102/1999 .... 1.309	CIS 757/1994 .... 1.59
CDLA 4734/1999 .... 1.281, 1.300	CIS 783/1994 .... 4.76
CDLA 5413/1999 .... 4.343	CIS 856/1994 .... 4.76
CF 26/1990 .... 1.59	CIS 1642/1994 .... 4.113
CF 3532/1997 .... 1.64	CIS 451/1995 .... 1.52
CG 2112/1988 .... 1.62	CIS 5206/1995 .... 4.188
CG 65/1989 .... 1.54	CIS 7009/1995 .... 4.138
CG 662/1998 .... 1.62	CIS 12016/1996 .... 4.138
CG 1567/1998 .... 1.62	CIS 12022/1996 .... 1.55
CI 141/1987 .... 4.347	CIS 12025/1996 .... 1.60
CI 636/1993 .... 4.343	CIS 12032/1996 .... 1.61
CI 105/1998 .... 1.366	CIS 13742/1996 .... 1.56, 1.64
CI 1327/1998 .... 4.313	CIS 14025/1996 .... 1.60
CI 4781/1998 .... 4.313	CIS 15146/1996 .... 4.188
CIB 13368/1996 .... 2.130	CIS 619/1997 .... 1.56, 1.64
CIB 3013/1997 .... 4.346	CIS 771/1997 .... 2.39
CIB 668/1998 .... 4.343	CIS 1055/1997 .... 1.52
CIB 4497/1998 .... 1.309, 4.343	CIS 2498/1997 .... 1.59
CIB 213/1999 .... 1.304	CIS 3899/1997 .... 4.76
CIS 734/1982 .... 1.55	CIS 610/1998 .... 4.85
CIS 254/1989 .... 4.75	CIS 1721/1998 .... 4.85
CIS 8/1990 .... 4.23	CIS 2057/1998 .... 4.82, 4.85
CIS 156/1990 .... 1.62	CIS 2132/1998 .... 4.343
CIS 159/1990 .... 1.64	CIS 2447/1998 .... 1.64
CIS 359/1990 .... 1.62	CIS 3749/1998 .... 4.85
CIS 375/1990 .... 4.23	CIS 3994/1998 .... 4.85
CIS 616/1990 .... 1.88	CIS 4437/1998 .... 4.352
CIS 620/1990 .... 4.75	CIS 5117/1998 .... 1.58
CIS 222/1991 .... 1.64	CIS 5848/1999 .... 1.59
CIS 465/1991 .... 4.138	CJSA 13/1998 .... 4.85
CIS 625/1991 .... 1.78	CJSA 3121/1998 .... 4.85
CIS 638/1991 .... 4.113	CJSA 3994/1998 .... 4.84

Table of Social Security Commissioner's Decisions

CJSA 4840/1998	2.121	R(A) 4/1989	4.325
CP 1074/1997	4.68	R(A) 2/1990	4.259
CS 175/1988	4.28, 4.37	R(A) 2/1994	2.123
CS 156/1990	1.62	R(A) 1/1995	1.61
CS 62/1992	4.75	R(CR) 1/1995	1.186
CS 366/1993	1.65	R(CR) 1/1996	1.186
CSB 53/1981	1.65	R(FC) 2/1990	1.309
CSB 966/1985	1.60	R(FC) 2/1990	2.13
CSB 64/1986	1.64	R(I) 1/1951	4.397
CSB 727/1987	1.59	R(I) 69/1953	4.397
CSB 790/1988	1.62	R(I) 81/1953	4.397
CSB 1093/1989	1.52	R(I) 93/1953	4.397
CSB 329/1990	1.62	R(I) 56/1954	4.259
CSB 83/1991	1.65	R(I) 35/1955	4.397
CSB 18/1992	1.62	R(I) 35/1957	4.397
CSB 108/1992	1.58	R(I) 35/1958	4.397
CSB 168/1993	4.113, 4.138	R(I) 18/1961	4.343
CSB 61/1995	4.138	R(I) 30/1961	4.343
CSB 15394/1996	4.350	R(I) 4/1965	1.304
CSB 574/1997	4.350	R(I) 1/1969	4.397
CSB 790/1998	1.62	R(I) 14/1974	4.347
CSB 1272/1999	1.52	R(I) 3/1975	4.261
CSCR 746/1987	1.201	R(I) 12/1975	1.309, 1.318
CSCR 1/1995	1.206	R(I) 2/1983	4.106
CSCR 3/1995	1.201	R(I) 2/1988	4.259
CSCS 1/1995	1.199	R(I) 1/1990	4.307
CSDLA 5/1995	4.325	R(I) 4/1991	4.313
CSDLA 90/1998	4.339	R(I) 5/1994	4.343
CSDLA 303/1998	4.350	R(IS) 5/1991	4.113
CSDLA 71/1999	4.352	R(IS) 7/1991	4.127
CSDLA 505/1999	1.309	R(IS) 5/1992	1.65
CSDLA 536/1999	4.217	R(IS) 11/1992	1.63
CSDLA 551/1999	4.343	R(IS) 4/1993	4.51
CSDLA 737/1999	1.308	R(IS) 9/1993	1.309
CSDLA 868/1999	1.308	R(IS) 14/1995	4.175, 4.188
CSG 357/1997	1.65	R(IS) 2/1996	1.52
CSIB 596/1999	1.309	R(IS) 2/1998	4.76
CSIB 611/1999	1.308, 1.309	R(IS) 11/1999	1.309, 1.304, 4.127, 4.343, 4.352
CSIB 973/1999	3.23	R(IS) 15/1999	1.309
CSIS 45/1990	1.52	R(M) 6/1986	4.343
CSIS 48/1992	4.28, 4.37	R(P) 2/1957	4.383
CSIS 61/1992	4.86	R(P) 3/1993	4.127
CSIS 66/1992	4.27	R(P) 1/1996	2.131
CSIS 7/1994	1.64	R(S) 7/1956	4.106
CSIS 98/1994	4.188	R(S) 9/1956	4.383
CSIS 99/1994	4.76	R(S) 1/1963	4.19
CSIS 134/1994	4.77	R(S) 2/1963	4.127
CSIS 137/1994	4.77	R(S) 1/1971	4.383
CSIS 8/1995	1.65	R(S) 6/1978	4.76
CSIS 174/1996	1.52	R(S) 8/1979	4.383
CSS 33/1990	1.60	R(S) 8/1985	1.313
CSS 35/1995	4.77	R(S) 4/1986	4.75, 4.76
CSSB 621/1988	1.52	R(S) 3/1989	4.239
CSSB 316/1989	1.52	R(S) 5/1989	4.77
CSSB 517/1989	1.52	R(S) 3/1990	4.75
CSSB 6/1995	1.54, 1.116	R(S) 1/1992	4.75
CSU 3/1991	1.58	R(S) 2/1993	2.39
CSU 13/1992	4.127	R(S) 1/1996	1.309
CU 94/1994	4.19	R(S) 2/1998	1.304
R(A) 1/1972	4.343	R(SB) 9/1084	4.20
R(A) 4/1981	4.259		

Table of Social Security Commissioner's Decisions

R(SB) 3/1981 .... 1.64
R(SB) 21/1982 .... 1.54, 1.59, 1.61, 1.64, 1.65, 1.116
R(SB) 12/1983 .... 1.313
R(SB) 23/1983 .... 1.54
R(SB) 28/1983 .... 1.57, 1.59, 1.116
R(SB) 29/1983 .... 4.51
R(SB) 34/1983 .... 1.55
R(SB) 43/1983 .... 1.53
R(SB) 52/1983 .... 1.309
R(SB) 54/1983 .... 1.60
R(SB) 9/1984(T)   4.21, 4.29, 4.82, 4.113
R(SB) 18/1984 .... 1.88
R(SB) 20/1984 .... 1.65
R(SB) 25/1984 .... 4.106
R(SB) 36/1984 .... 1.60
R(SB) 40/1984 .... 1.59, 1.62, 4.110
R(SB) 6/1985 .... 1.65
R(SB) 9/1985 .... 1.57, 1.58, 1.65
R(SB) 10/1985 .... 1.60, 1.65
R(SB) 15/1985 .... 1.65
R(SB) 18/1985 ..... 1.57, 1.58, 1.78, 1.58
R(SB) 28/1985 .... 1.81
R(SB) 11/1986 .... 1.65
R(SB) 15/1987 ..... 1.60, 1.61, 1.62, 1.64
R(SB) 8/1988 .... 4.113
R(SB) 5/1989 .... 4.19
R(SB) 8/1989 .... 4.37
R(SB) 13/1989 .... 1.64
R(SB) 1/1990 .... 1.309
R(SB) 3/1990 .... 1.58, 1.62, 1.64
R(SB) 5/1990 .... 4.113
R(SB) 6/1990 .... 1.60
R(SB) 1/1991 .... 1.65
R(SB) 2/1991 .... 1.58
R(SB) 3/1991 .... 1.65
R(SB) 4/1991 .... 1.50
R(SB) 6/1991 .... 2.39
R(SB) 7/1991 .... 1.52
R(SB) 1/1993 .... 4.27
R(SB) 1/1994 .... 4.138
R(U) 9/1960 .... 4.19
R(U) 2/1979 .... 4.19
R(U) 7/1983 .... 4.19
R(U) 4/1986 .... 2.91
R(U) 4/1988 .... 1. 309, 1.318
R(U) 3/1989 .... 4.239

TABLE OF EUROPEAN DIRECTIVES

Note. Page references in bold indicate that the particular Article is recited in full.

1964	64/221	[1963–64] O.J. Spec. Ed. 117 .... 2.33
		Arts 5–9 .... 2.33
1968	68/369	[1968–69] O.J. Spec. Ed. 485 .... 2.33
1973	73/148	[1973] O.J. L172/14 2.33
1976	76/207	[1976] O.J. L39/40 Art. 1(2) 2.118, 2.123
1978	79/7	[1979] O.J. L6/24 .. 2.19, 2.42, 2.118, 2.121
		Art. 1 .... **2.119**
		Art. 2 .... **2.120**
		Art. 3 ...... 2.121, **2.122**
		(1) 2.123

Art. 4 ...... **2.124**, 2.125
  (1) 2.125
Art. 5 .... **2.126**
Art. 6 ...... **2.127**, 2.128
Art. 7 .... **2.129**
  (1) 2.134
    (a) 2.130
    (c) 2.131
    (d) 2.132
Art. (2) **2.134**
Art. 8 .... **2.134**
Art. 9 .... **2.136**
Art. 10 .... **2.137**
1989 89/48 [1989] O.J. L19/16 . 2.33
1992 92/51 [1992] O.J. L209/25 2.33

TABLE OF EUROPEAN REGULATIONS

Note. Page references in bold indicate that the Article is recited in full.

1971 Reg. 1408/71	O.J. L149/2 ...	2.37, 2.44, 2.84, 2.88, 2.107, 2.118, 2.121
	Title I	2.45
	Title II	2.63
	Title III	2.51, 2.57, 2.73 et seq.
	Art. 1	**2.45**, 2.46
	Art. 2	**2.47**
	Art. 3	**2.49**
	Art. 4	**2.51**
	(1)	2.45, 2.53
	(a)–(h) ...	2.57
	(2)	2.45, 2.53
	(2a)	2.45, 2.53, 2.57
	Art. 5	**2.53**, 2.58
	Arts 6–9	2.54
	Art. 7(2c)	2.49
	Art. 8(1)	2.49
	Art. 10	**2.55**, 2.57, 2.123
	(a)	2.52, **2.56**, 2.57
	Art. 11	2.59
	Art. 12	**2.60**, 2.61, 2.91, 2.109
	(2)	2.109
	(3)	2.109
	(4)	2.109
	Arts 13–16	2.70
	Art. 13	**2.62**
	(2)(a)	2.64
	(b)	2.65
	Arts 14–17	2.62
	Art. 14	**2.64**
	a	**2.65**
	(2)	2.68
	(3)	2.68
	(4)	2.68
	b	2.66
	c	2.62, **2.67**, 2.109
	d	**2.68**
	e	2.68
	f	2.62, 2.109
	(2)	2.67
	(3)	2.67
Art. 17		**2.70**
a		**2.72**
Art. 18		**2.73**, 2.77
Art. 19		**2.74**, 2.76
(1)		2.76
(2) ...		2.76, 2.77
Art. 20		2.75
Art. 21		**2.76**
Art. 22		**2.77**, 2.78
a		2.79
b		2.79
Art. 23		**2.80**
Art. 24		**2.81**
Arts 25–66a		2.82
Art. 41		2.60
Art. 43(2)		2.60
(3)		2.60
Art. 46		2.60
a		2.109
b		2.109
c		2.109
Art. 50		2.53, 2.60
Art. 51		2.60
Art. 57(5)		2.60
Art. 60(1)(b)		2.60
(29)(b)		2.60
Art. 67		**2.83**, 2.84, 2.91
Art. 68		**2.85**
(1)		2.86
Art. 69		2.84, **2.87**, 2.88, 2.90, 2.91, 2.113
(1)		2.89
(c)		2.113
(2)		2.88
Art. 70		2.88, **2.89**
Art. 71		2.84, 2.88, **2.90**, 2.91
(1)(a)		2.91
(a)(i)		2.91
(ii) ..		**2.83**, 2.91, 2.94
(b)		2.91
(i) ...		2.83, 2.91
(ii) ..		2.83, 2.91, 2.94

Table of European Regulations

a 2.92	Annex II 2.45, 2.51,
Art. 72 .... **2.93**,	2.56, 2.57,
2.94, 2.99	2.104, 2.105
a **2.94**	Annexes III–VIII 2.106
Art. 73 ...... **2.95**, 2.97,	Annex III 2.49
2.98, 2.114	Annex VI 2.96
Art. 74 ...... **2.96**, 2.97,	Annex VII 2.67
2.98, 2.114	1972 Reg. 574/72 .... 2.107
Art. 75 .... **2.97**	Art. 7 .... **2.109**
Art. 76 .... **2.98**	Art. 8 .... **2.110**
a 2.99	a **2.111**
Arts 77–85 .... 2.100	Art. 9 .... 2.112
Art. 77 ..... 2.53, 2.114	a **2.112**
Art. 78 ..... 2.53, 2.114	Art. 10 .... **2.114**
Art. 86 .... **2.101**	a **2.115**
Art. 87 .... **2.102**	b–122 ..... 2.116
Art. 88–98 .... 2.103	Art. 15(3) 2.115
Art. 97 ...... 2.45, 2.53	Annexes 1–11 .... 2.117
Art. 98 .... 2.68, 2.89	Annex 8 .... 2.115
Annex I 2.45, 2.104	1997 118/97 [1997] O.J. L28/4 ... 2.44
	1997 1290/97 [1997] O.J. L176/1 . 2.45
	1998 1606/98 [1998] O.J. L209/1 2.45,
	2.51, 2.62,
	2.68, 2.110
	1999 307/99 [1999] O.J. L307/99 2.45,
	2.47, 2.55

EUROPEAN TREATIES AND CONVENTIONS

Note. Page references in bold indicate that the particular Article is recited in full.

1950 European Convention on
    Human Rights ..... 3.1 et seq.
    Art. 1 .... 3.2, 3.81
    Art. 2 .... 3.2, **3.52**
    Art. 3 .... 3.2, **3.54**
    Art. 4 .... 3.2, **3.56**
    Art. 5 .... 3.2, **3.58**, 3.59
        (3) 3.91
        (5) 3.26, 3.27, 3.91
    Art. 6 .... 3.2, **3.60**, 3.61, 3.62,
        3.64, 3.66, 3.67, 3.69
        (1) 3.2, 3.62, 3.64
    Art. 7 .... 3.2, **3.70**
    Art. 8 ....
    .... 3.2, **3.71**, 3.72, 3.73, 3.81
    Art. 9 .... 3.2, 3.36, **3.75**
    Art. 10 .... 3.2, **3.77**
    Art. 11 .... 3.2, **3.78**
    Art. 12 .... 3.2, **3.79**
    Art. 13 .... 3.2, 3.26
    Art. 14 ....
    .... 3.2, 3.73, **3.80**, 3.81, 3.86
    Art. 15(1) 3.91
        (3) 3.91
    Art. 16 .... 3.2, **3.82**
    Art. 17 .... 3.2, **3.83**
    Art. 18 .... 3.2, **3.84**
    Art. 26 .... 3.2
    Art. 27(2) 3.2
    Art. 31 .... 3.2
    Art. 32 .... 3.49
    Art. 34 .... 3.8, 3.17, 3.19,
        3.20, 3.23
    Art. 35 .... 3.8
    Art. 41 . 2.128, 3.24, 3.26, 3.64
    Art. 46 .... 3.2, 3.49
    Art. 54 .... 3.49
    First Protocol ... 3.2, 3.49, 3.93
    Art. 1 .... 3.2, 3.73, 3.80,
        3.84, 3.85, 3.86
    Art. 2 .... 3.2, 3.39, **3.87**, 3.91
    Art. 3 .... 3.2, **3.87**
    Sixth Protocol
    Art. 1 .... 3.2, 3.49, 3.90
    Art. 2 .... 3.2
    Sched. 2 .... 3.90
    Sched. 3 .... 3. 90
    Ninth Protocol 3.7
    Eleventh Protocol 3.8,
        3.20, 3.49
    Art. 11 .... 3.49
1951 Geneva Convention on the
    Status of Refugees Art. 1   2.45
1957 Rome Treaty (EC Treaty formerly EEC Treaty) 2.4
1992 Maastricht Treaty on European Union 2.4
1999 Amsterdam Treaty amending both the EC Treaty and the Treaty on European Union 2.4, 2.8, 2.118, 2.121, 2.123
    Title IV 2.17
    Art. 2 (ex2) 2.16, 2.17, 2.18
    Art. 3 (ex 3) 2.16, 2.17, 2.18, 2.33
    Art. 4 .... 2.16
    Art. 5 (ex 3b) 2.18
    Art. 10 (ex 5)   2.11, 2.20, 2.123
    Art. 12 (ex 6) 2.22, 2.50
    Art. 13 (ex 6a) 2.24
    Art. 14 (ex 7a) 2.25
    Art. 15 .... 2.25
    Art. 17 (EX 8) 2.26
    Art. 18 (ex 8a) 2.27, 2.33
    Art. 19 (ex 8b) 2.28
    Art. 20 (ex 8c) 2.29
    Art. 21 (ex 8d) 2.30
    Art. 22 (ex 8e) 2.31
    Art. 26 .... 2.25
    Art. 39 (ex 48) 2.23, 2.32, 2.34
    Art. 39–55 (ex 48–66) 2.33
    Art. 39(2) (ex 48(2)) 2.50
        (3) (ex 48(3)) 2.33
        (4) (ex 48(4)) 2.33
    Art. 40 (ex 49) 2.34
    Art. 41 (ex 50) 2.35
    Art. 42 (ex 51) 2.36, 2.37
    Art. 45 (ex 55) 2.33
    Art. 46(1) (ex 56(1)) 2.33
    Art. 47(2) 2.25
    Art. 48 (ex58) 2.33
    Art. 49 .... 2.25

Art. 55 (ex 66) 2.33	Art. 195 .... 2.30
Art. 80 .... 2.25	Art. 226 (ex 169) 2.10
Art. 93 .... 2.25	Art. 234 (ex 177) 2.13, 2.38
Art. 95 .... 2.25	Art. 235 .... 2.118
Art. 141 (ex 119) 2.118	Art. 249 (ex 189) 2.8, 2.10
Art. 177 .... 2.40	Art. 251 . 2.22, 2.27, 2.34, 2.36
Art. 190(4) 2.28	Art. 308 (ex 235) 2.42
Art. 194 .... 2.30	

TABLE OF ABBREVIATIONS USED IN THIS SERIES

Adjudication Regulations	Social Security (Adjudication) Regulations 1986
All E.R.	All England Law Reports (Butterworths)
AO	Adjudication Officer
AOG	HMSO, *Adjudication Officer's Guide*
Attendance Allowance Regulations	Social Security (Attendance Allowance) Regulations 1991
Blue Books	HMSO, *The Law Relating to Social Security Vols. 1–11*
CBA 1975	Child Benefit Act 1975
CPAG	Child Poverty Action Group
CAO	Chief Adjudication Officer
CSO	Child Support Officer
Claims and Payments Regulations 1979	Social Security (Claims and Payments) Regulations 1979
DAT	Disability Appeals Tribunal
Claims and Payments Regulations 1987	Social Security (Claims and Payments) Regulations 1987
C.M.L.R.	Common Market Law Reports
Commissioners Procedure Regulations	Social Security Commissioners (Procedure) Regulations 1999
Computation of Earnings Regulations 1978	Social Security Benefit (Computation of Earnings) Regulations 1978
Computation of Earnings Regulations 1996	Social Security Benefit (Computation of Earnings) Regulations 1996
Decisions and Appeals Regulations 1999	Social Security and Child Support (Decisions and Appeals) Regulations 1999
Dependency Regulations	Social Security Benefit (Dependency) Regulations 1977
DLA	Disability Living Allowance
DMA	Decision-making and Appeals
DMG	HMSO, *Decision Maker's Guide*
Disability Working Allowance Regulations	Disability Working Allowance (General) Regulations 1991
DPTC	Disabled Persons Working Tax Credit
DWA	Disability Working Allowance
E.C.R.	European Court Reports

Table of Abbreviations used in this Series

EHRR	European Human Rights Reports
Eur. L. Rev	European Law Review
Family Credit Regulations	Family Credit (General) Regulations 1987
General Benefit Regulations	Social Security (General Benefit) Regulations 1982
HASSASSAA 1983	Health and Social Services and Social Security Adjudication Act 1983
Hospital In-Patients Regulations	Social Security (Hospital In-Patients) Regulations 1975
Income Support Regulations	Income Support (General) Regulations 1987
IB Regulations	Social Security (Incapacity Benefit) Regulations 1994
I.L.J.	Industrial Law Journal
IWA	Social Security (Incapacity for Work) Act 1994
IW (General) Regulations	Social Security (Incapacity for Work)(General) Regulations 1995
IW (Transitional) Regulations	Social Security (Incapacity for Work)(Transitional) Regulations 1995
Invalid Care Allowance Regulations	Social Security (Invalid Care Allowance) Regulations 1976
JSA Regulations	Jobseeker's Allowance Regulations 1996
JSA (Transitional) Regulations	Jobseeker's Allowance (Transitional) Regulations 1996
J.S.W.L.	Journal of Social Welfare Law
JSWFL	Journal of Social Welfare and Family Law
JSSL	Journal of Social Security Law
MAT	Medical Appeal Tribunal
Maternity Benefit Regulations	Social Security (Maternity Benefit) Regulations 1975
Medical Evidence Regulations	Social Security (Medical Evidence) Regulations 1976
Ogus, Barendt and Wikeley	A. Ogus, E. Barendt and N. Wikeley, *The Law of Social Security* (4th ed., Butterworths, 1995)
Overlapping Benefits Regulations	Social Security (Overlapping Benefits) Regulations 1979
Overpayments Regulations	Social Security (Payments on account, Overpayments and Recovery) Regulations 1988
Persons Abroad Regulations	Social Security Benefit (Persons Abroad) Regulations 1975
Persons Residing Together Regulations	Social Security Benefit (Persons Residing Together) Regulations 1977
Prescribed Diseases Regulations	Social Security (Industrial Injuries) (Prescribed Diseases) Regulations 1985

Table of Abbreviations used in this Series

Recoupment Regulations	Social Security (Recoupment) Regulations 1990
RMO	Regional Medical Officer
SDA	Severe Disablement Allowance
Severe Disablement Allowance Regulations	Social Security (Severe Disablement Allowance) Regulations 1984
SMP	Statutory Maternity Pay
SSA 1975	Social Security Act 1975
SSA 1980	Social Security Act 1980
SSA 1985	Social Security Act 1985
SSA 1986	Social Security Act 1986
SSA 1988	Social Security Act 1988
SSA 1989	Social Security Act 1989
SSA 1998	Social Security Act 1998
SS (No. 2) A 1980	Social Security (No. 2) Act 1980
SSAT	Social Security Appeal Tribunal
SSHBA	Social Security and Housing Benefits Act 1982
SS (MP) A 1977	Social Security (Miscellaneous Provisions) Act 1977
SSP	Statutory Sick Pay
SSPA 1975	Social Security Pensions Act 1975
SSCBA 1992	Social Security Contributions and Benefits Act 1992*
SSAA 1992	Social Security Administration Act 1992*
SSCPA 1992	Social Security Consequential Provisions Act 1992
USI Regulations	Social Security (Unemployment, Sickness and Invalidity Benefit) Regulations 1983
White Paper	Jobseeker's Allowance, Cm. 2687 (October, 1994)
Widow's Benefit and Retirement Pensions Regulations	Social Security (Widow's Benefit and Retirement Pensions) Regulations 1979
Wikeley, Annotations	N. Wikeley, *Annotations to Jobseekers Act 1995 (c.18), Current Law Statutes Annotated (1995)*
W.L.R.	Weekly Law Reports

*Where the context makes it seem more appropriate, these could also be referred to as Contributions and Benefits Act 1992, Administration Act 1992

PART I

STATUTES

Social Security Administration Act 1992

(1992 c.5)

ARRANGEMENT OF SECTIONS

PART I

CLAIMS FOR AND PAYMENTS AND GENERAL ADMINISTRATION OF BENEFIT
SECTION

Necessity of Claim

1. Entitlement to benefit dependent on claim.
2. Retrospective effect of provisions making entitlement to benefit dependent on claim.

Widowhood benefits

3. Late claims for widowhood benefit where death is difficult to establish.
4. Treatment of payments of benefit to certain widows.

Claims and payments regulations

5. Regulations about claims for and payments of benefit.

Community charge benefits etc.†

6. *Omitted.*
7. Relationship between community charge benefits† and other benefits.

†*Unreliable heading. (Council tax benefit replaced community charge benefits w.e.f. 1.4.93.)*

Industrial injuries benefit

8. Notification of accidents, etc.
9. Medical examination and treatment of claimants.
10. Obligations of claimants.

Disability working allowance

11. Initial claims and repeat claims.

The social fund

12. Necessity of application for certain payments.

Child benefit

13. Necessity of application for child benefit.

Statutory sick pay

14. Duties of employees etc. in relation to statutory sick pay.

Statutory maternity pay

15. Duties of women etc in relation to statutory maternity pay.

Payments in respect of mortgage interest etc.

15A. Payment out of benefit of sums in respect of mortgage interest etc.

Emergency payments

16. Emergency payments by local authorities and other bodies.

PART II

ADJUDICATION

17.–70. *Repealed.*

PART III

OVERPAYMENTS AND ADJUSTMENTS OF BENEFIT

Misrepresentation etc.

71. Overpayments—general.
71ZA. Overpayments out of social fund.

Jobseeker's allowance

71A. Recovery of jobseeker's allowance: severe hardship cases.

Misrepresentation etc. (continued)

72. Special provision as to recovery of income support.

Adjustments of benefits

73. Overlapping benefits—general.
74. Income support and other payments.
74A. Payment of benefit where maintenance payments collected by Secretary of State.

Housing benefit

75. *Omitted.*

Community charge benefits†

76. *Omitted.*
77. *Omitted.*

†*Unreliable heading. (Council tax benefit replaced community charge benefits w.e.f. 1.4.93.)*

Social fund awards

78. Recovery of social fund awards.

Northern Ireland payments

79. Recovery of Northern Ireland payments.

Adjustment of child benefit

80. Child benefit—overlap with benefits under legislation of other member States.

PART IV

RECOVERY FROM COMPENSATION PAYMENTS

81–104. *Repealed.*

Social Security Administration Act 1992

Part V

Income Support and the Duty to Maintain

105. Failure to maintain—general.
106. Recovery of expenditure on benefit from person liable for maintenance.
107. Recovery of expenditure on income support: additional amounts and transfer of orders.
108. Reduction of expenditure on income support: certain maintenance orders to be enforceable by the Secretary of State.
109. Diversion of arrested earnings to Secretary of State—Scotland.

Part VI

Enforcement

110.–121. *Omitted.*

Part VII

Provision of Information

Inland Revenue

122. *Omitted.*

Persons employed or formerly employed in social security administration or adjudication

123. *Omitted.*

The Registration Service

124. Provisions relating to age, death and marriage.
125. Regulations as to notification of deaths.

Personal representatives—income support and supplementary benefit

126. Personal representatives to give information about the estate of a deceased person who was in receipt of income support or supplementary benefit.
126A. *Omitted.*

Housing benefit

127. *Repealed.*

Community charge benefits

128. *Repealed.*

Expedited claims for housing and council tax benefit

128A. *Repealed.*

Statutory sick pay and other benefits

129. Disclosure by Secretary of State for purpose of determination of period of entitlement to statutory sick pay.
130. Duties of employers—statutory sick pay and claims for other benefits.

Statutory maternity pay and other benefits

131. Disclosure by Secretary of State for purpose of determination of period of entitlement to statutory maternity pay.
132. Duties of employers—statutory maternity pay and claims for other benefits.

Maintenance proceedings

133. Furnishing of addresses for maintenance proceedings, etc.

PART VIII

ARRANGEMENTS FOR HOUSING BENEFIT AND COMMUNITY CHARGE BENEFITS† AND RELATED SUBSIDIES

134.–140. *Omitted.*

PART IX

ALTERATION OF CONTRIBUTIONS ETC.

141.–149. *Omitted.*

Part X
Review and Alteration of Benefits

150.–154. *Omitted.*

Part XI

Computation of Benefits

155. Effect of alteration of rates of benefit under Parts II to V of Contributions and Benefits Act.
155A. Power to anticipate pensions up-rating order.
156. Up-rating under section 150 above of pensions increased under section 52(3) of the Contributions and Benefits Act.
157. Effect of alteration of rates of child benefit.
158. Treatment of excess benefit as paid on account of child benefit.
159. Effect of alteration in the component rates of income support.
159A. Effect of alteration of rates of a jobseeker's allowance.
160. Implementation of increases in income support due to attainment of particular ages.
160A. Implementation of increases in income-based jobseeker's allowance due to attainment of particular ages.

Part XII

Finance

161.–166. *Omitted.*
167. The social fund.
168. Allocations from social fund.
169. Adjustments between social fund and other sources of finance.

Part XIII

Advisory Bodies and Consultation

170.–176. *Omitted.*

Part XIV

Social Security Systems Outside Great Britain

Co-ordination

177. Co-ordination with Northern Ireland.

Reciprocity

178. Reciprocal arrangements with Northern Ireland—income-related benefits and child benefit.
179. Reciprocal agreements with countries outside the United Kingdom.

(1992 c. 5)

PART XV

MISCELLANEOUS

Travelling expenses

180. *Omitted.*

Offences

181. *Omitted.*
182. *Omitted.*

National Insurance Numbers

Industrial injuries and diseases

182c. Requirement is apply for National Insurance Number
183. *Omitted.*
184. *Omitted.*

Workmen's compensation etc.

185. *Omitted.*

Supplementary benefit etc.

186. Application of provisions of Act to supplementary benefit etc.

Miscellaneous

187. Certain benefit to be inalienable.
188. *Omitted.*

PART XVI

GENERAL

Subordinate legislation

189. Regulations and orders—general.
190. Parliamentary control of orders and regulations.

Social Security Administration Act 1992

Supplementary

191. Interpretation—general.
192. Short title, commencement and extent.

SCHEDULES:

1. Claims for benefit made or treated as made before 1st October 1990.
2.–9. *Omitted.*
10. Supplementary benefit etc.

PART I

CLAIMS FOR AND PAYMENTS AND GENERAL ADMINISTRATION OF BENEFIT

Necessity of claim

Entitlement to benefit dependent on claim

1.2

1.—(1) Except in such cases as may be prescribed, and subject to the following provisions of this section and to section 3 below, no person shall be entitled to any benefit unless, in addition to any other conditions relating to that benefit being satisfied—
  (a) he makes a claim for it in the manner, and within the time, prescribed in relation to that benefit by regulations under this Part of this Act; or
  (b) he is treated by virtue of such regulations as making a claim for it.
[²(1A) No person whose entitlement to any benefit depends on his making a claim shall be entitled to the benefit unless subsection (1B) below is satisfied in relation both to the person making the claim and to any other person in respect of whom he is claiming benefit.
  (1B) This subsection is satisfied in relation to a person if—
  (a) the claim is accompanied by—
    (i) a statement of the person's national insurance number and information or evidence establishing that that number has been allocated to the person; or
    (ii) information or evidence enabling the national insurance number that has been allocated to the person to be ascertained; or
  (b) the person makes an application for a national insurance number to be allocated to him which is accompanied by information or evidence enabling such a number to be so allocated.
  (1C) Regulations may make provision disapplying subsection (1A) above in the case of—
  (a) prescribed benefits;
  (b) prescribed descriptions of persons making claims; or
  (c) prescribed descriptions of persons in respect of whom benefit is claimed,

or in other prescribed circumstances.]

(2) Where under subsection (1) above a person is required to make a claim or to be treated as making a claim for a benefit in order to be entitled to it—
  (a) if the benefit is a widow's payment, she shall not be entitled to it in respect of a death occurring more than 12 months before the date on which the claim is made or treated as made; and
  (b) if the benefit is any other benefit except disablement benefit or reduced earnings allowance, the person shall not be entitled to it in respect of any period more than 12 months before that date,
except as provided by section 3 below.

(3) Where a person purports to make a claim on behalf of another—
  (a) for an attendance allowance by virtue of section 66(1) of the Contributions and Benefits Act; or
  (b) for a disability living allowance by virtue of section 72(5) or 73(12) of that Act,
that other shall be regarded for the purposes of this section as making the claim, notwithstanding that it is made without his knowledge or authority.

(4) In this section and in section 2 below "benefit" means—
  (a) benefit as defined in section 122 of the Contributions and Benefits Act;
[[1](aa) a jobseeker's allowance;] and
  (b) any income-related benefit.

(5) This section (which corresponds to section 165A of the 1975 Act, as it had effect immediately before this Act came into force) applies to claims made on or after 1st October 1990 or treated by virtue of regulations under that section or this section as having been made on or after that date.

(6) Schedule 1 to this Act shall have effect in relation to other claims.

AMENDMENTS

1. Jobseekers Act 1995, Sched. 2, para. 38 (October 7, 1996).
2. Social Security Administration (Fraud) Act 1997, s.19 (December 1, 1997).

DERIVATION

Social Security Act 1975, s.165A.   1.3

DEFINITIONS

  "the 1975 Act"—see s.191.
  "claim"—*ibid.*
  "disablement benefit"—*ibid.*
  "the Contributions and Benefits Act"—*ibid.*
  "income-related benefit"—*ibid.*
  "prescribe"—*ibid.*

GENERAL NOTE

Subsection (1)
  The general rule is that there cannot be entitlement to benefit unless a claim   1.4
is made for it. Section 1 applies to claims made on or after October 1, 1990.
Sched. 1 deals with earlier claims.

The introduction of the predecessor of s.1 was precipitated by the decision of the House of Lords in *Insurance Officer v. McCaffrey* [1984] 1 W.L.R. 1353 that (subject to an express provision to the contrary) a person was entitled to benefit if he met the conditions of entitlement even though he had not made a claim for that benefit. Claiming went to payability, not entitlement. This was contrary to the long-standing assumption of the DSS and was corrected with effect from September 2, 1985.

Section 3, which is excluded from the operation of s.1, deals with late claims for widow's benefits where the death of the spouse is difficult to establish.

Subsection (1A)–(1C)

1.5 These provisions were inserted by s.19 of the Social Security Administration (Fraud) Act 1997 and came into force on December 1, 1997. The effect of subss. (1A) and (1B) is to impose an additional condition of entitlement to benefit where subs. (1)(a) applies (*i.e.* in the normal case). A claimant will not be entitled to benefit unless when making a claim he provides a national insurance (NI) number, together with information or evidence to show that it is his, or provides evidence or information to enable his NI number to be traced, or applies for a NI number and provides sufficient information or evidence for one to be allocated to him. This requirement for an NI number applies to both the claimant and any person for whom he is claiming, except in prescribed circumstances (subs. (1C)). See reg. 2A of the Income Support Regulations, and the Jobseeker's Allowance Regulations, for who is exempt and note the different dates from which this requirement bites for these benefits.

Subsection (2)

1.6 This provision imposes an overall limit of 12 months to the entitlement to benefit before the date of claim. Not all benefits are caught by subs.(1) and there is a further exclusion in para. (b). Reg. 19 of and Sched. 4 to the Claims and Payments Regulations impose the ordinary time-limits for claiming and since April 1997 allow the limits in the cases of income support, JSA, family credit and disability working allowance to be extended for a maximum of three months only in tightly defined circumstances. The test of good cause has been abandoned. Where there is such an extension, the claim is then treated as made on the first day of the period for which the claim is allowed to relate (reg. 6(3)). Although the drafting is not at all clear, the reference in subs.(2) to the 12-month limit from the date on which the claim is made or is treated as made seems to make the limit start from the date fixed by reg. 6(3). However, reg. 19(4) prevents an extension of the time-limit for the benefits covered by reg. 6(3) leading to entitlement earlier than three months before the actual date of claim. But the restriction seems to stem from that regulation and not from s.1(2), or the earlier forms set out in Sched. 1.

Note that from April 1997 the time limit for claiming social fund maternity and funeral payments is three months (Claims and Payments Regulations, reg. 19(1) and Sched. 4, paras. 8 and 9) and there is no longer any provision allowing claims for these payments to be made outside this time limit.

Subsection (3)

1.7 Subs. (3) deals with a particular situation which may arise in connection with claims to attendance allowance and disability living allowance. In general, there is no objection to claims being made by someone on behalf of another person, though the Department will require a clear indication that the agent is acting with the express authority of the person claiming.

Subsection (5)

1.8 There were a number of different versions of the section from which this section is derived and subs (5) indicates that this section is limited to claims made on or after October 1, 1990. Schedule 1 sets out the earlier variations of the section. In many cases concerning claims to benefit care will need to be taken to apply the law as at the date of the claim. There is a particular risk of error where appeals are being reheard after the considerable delays inherent in successful appeals. Obviously, as time goes by this risk will diminish and eventually disappear.

Retrospective effect of provisions making entitlement to benefit dependent on claim

2.—(1) This section applies where a claim for benefit is made or treated as made at any time on or after 2nd September 1985 (the date on which section 165A of the 1975 Act (general provision as to necessity of claim for entitlement to benefit), as originally enacted, came into force) in respect of a period the whole or any part of which falls on or after that date.

(2) Where this section applies, any question arising as to—
(a) whether the claimant is or was at any time (whether before, on or after 2nd September 1985) entitled to the benefit in question, or to any other benefit on which his entitlement to that benefit depends; or
(b) in a case where the claimant's entitlement to the benefit depends on the entitlement of another person to a benefit, whether that other person is or was so entitled,

shall be determined as if the relevant claim enactment and any regulations made under or referred to in that enactment had also been in force, with any necessary modifications, at all times relevant for the purpose of determining the entitlement of the claimant, and, where applicable, of the other person, to the benefit or benefits in question (including the entitlement of any person to any benefit on which that entitlement depends, and so on).

(3) In this section "the relevant claim enactment" means section 1 above as it has effect in relation to the claim referred to in subsection (1) above.

(4) In any case where—
(a) a claim for benefit was made or treated as made (whether before, on or after 2nd September 1985, and whether by the same claimant as the claim referred to in subsection (1) above or not), and benefit was awarded on that claim, in respect of a period falling wholly or partly before that date; but
(b) that award would not have been made had the current requirements applied in relation to claims for benefit, whenever made, in respect of periods before that date; and
(c) entitlement to the benefit claimed as mentioned in subsection (1) above depends on whether the claimant or some other person was previously entitled or treated as entitled to that or some other benefit,

then, in determining whether the conditions of entitlement to the benefit so claimed are satisfied, the person to whom benefit was awarded as mentioned in paragraphs (a) and (b) above shall be taken to have been

1.9

entitled to the benefit so awarded, notwithstanding anything in subsection (2) above.

(5) In subsection (4) above "the current requirements" means—
(a) the relevant claim enactment, and any regulations made or treated as made under that enactment, or referred to in it, as in force at the time of the claim referred to in subsection (1) above, with any necessary modifications; and
(b) subsection (1) (with the omission of the words following "at any time") and subsections (2) and (3) above.

DERIVATION

Social Security Act 1975, s.165B.

DEFINITIONS

"the 1975 Act"—s.191.
"benefit"—see s.1(1).
"claim"—see s.191.
"claimant"—*ibid*.

GENERAL NOTE

There are a number of benefits where entitlement can depend on whether a person was entitled to a benefit at some earlier date (*e.g.* on reaching pensionable age). While the predecessor of s.1 clearly governed such questions from September 2, 1985, onwards, it was arguable that in relation to earlier dates the *McCaffrey* principle (see note to s.1(1) above) had to be applied. *R(S) 2/91* decided that that argument was correct. The predecessor of s.2 was inserted by the Social Security Act 1990 to reverse the effect of that decision and to do so retrospectively back to September 2, 1985.

The form of s.2 is complex and the retrospective effects are difficult to work out. It only applies to claims made or treated as made on or after September 2, 1985 (subs.(1)). Thus very late appeals or very long good causes for late claim might not be affected. Then on any such claim if a question of entitlement at any other date arises (including dates before September 2, 1985) that question is to be decided according to the principle of s.1 as it was in force at the relevant time (subs.(2)). The only exception to this is that if for any period benefit has been awarded following a claim, that beneficiary is to be treated as entitled to that benefit even though under the current requirements he would not be (subs.(4)).

Widowhood benefits

Late claims for widowhood benefit where death is difficult to establish

3.—(1) This section applies where a woman's husband has died or may be presumed to have died and the circumstances are such that—
(a) more than 12 months have elapsed since the date of death (whether he died, or is presumed to have died, before or after the coming into force of this section);
(b) either—

(i) the husband's body has not been discovered or identified or, if it has been discovered and identified, the woman does not know that fact; or
(ii) less than 12 months have elapsed since she first knew of the discovery and identification of the body; and
(c) no claim for any of the widowhood benefits, that is to say—
(i) widow's benefit,
(ii) an invalidity pension under section 15 of [¹the Social Security Pensions Act 1975], or
(iii) a Category A retirement pension by virtue of subsection (5) of that section,

was made or treated as made in respect of the death by the woman before 13th July 1990 (the coming into force of section 6 of Social Security Act 1990, which inserted in the 1975 Act section 165C, the provision of that Act corresponding to this section).

(2) Where this section applies, notwithstanding that any time prescribed for making a claim for a widowhood benefit in respect of the death has elapsed, then—
(a) [²in any case falling within paragraph (b)(i) of subsection (1) above, where it has been decided under section 8 of the Social Security Act 1998 that the husband had died or is presumed to have died; or]
(b) in any case falling within paragraph (b)(ii) of subsection (1) above where the identification was made not more than 12 months before the woman first knew of the discovery and identification of the body,

such a claim may be treated as made at any time before the expiration of the period of 12 months beginning with the date on which that [² decision] was made or, as the case may be, the date on which she first knew of the discovery and identification.

(3) If, in a case where a claim for a widowhood benefit is made or treated as made by virtue of this section, the claimant would, apart from subsection (2) of section 1 above, be entitled to—
(a) a widow's payment in respect of the husband's death more than 12 months before the date on which the claim is made or treated as made; or
(b) any other widowhood benefit in respect of his death for a period more than 12 months before that date,

then, notwithstanding anything in that section, she shall be entitled to that payment or, as the case may be, to that other benefit (together with any increase under section 80(5) of the Contributions and Benefits Act).

AMENDMENTS

1. Pensions Schemes Act 1993, Sched. 8 (February 2, 1994).
2. Social Security Act 1998, Sched. 7 (September 6, 1999).

DERIVATION

SSA 1975, s.165C, as amended.

1.11

Social Security Administration Act 1992

Treatment of payments of benefit to certain widows

1.12 **4.** In any case where—
(a) a claim for widow's pension or a widowed mother's allowance is made, or treated as made, before 13th July 1990 (the date of the passing of the Social Security Act 1990); and
(b) the Secretary of State has made a payment to or for the claimant on the ground that if the claim had been received immediately after the passing of that Act she would have been entitled to that pension or allowance, or entitled to it at a higher rate, for the period in respect of which the payment is made,

the payment so made shall be treated as a payment of that pension or allowance, and, if and to the extent that an award of the pension or allowance, or an award at a higher rate, is made for the period in respect of which the payment was made, the payment shall be treated as made in accordance with that award.

DERIVATION

1.13 SSA 1990, s.21(1) and Sched. 6, para. 27(2).

Claims and payments regulations

Regulations about claims for and payments of benefit

1.14 **5.**—(1) Regulations may provide—
(a) for requiring a claim for a benefit to which this section applies to be made by such person, in such manner and within such time as may be prescribed;
(b) for treating such a claim made in such circumstances as may be prescribed as having been made at such date earlier or later than that at which it is made as may be prescribed;
(c) for permitting such a claim to be made, or treated as if made, for a period wholly or partly after the date on which it is made;
(d) for permitting an award on such a claim to be made for such a period subject to the condition that the claimant satisfies the requirements for entitlement when benefit becomes payable under the award;
(e) [³ for any such award to be revised under section 9 of the Social Security Act 1998, or superseded under section 10 of that Act, if any of those requirements are found not to have been satisfied;]
(f) for the disallowance on any ground of a person's claim for a benefit to which this section applies to be treated as a disallowance of any further claim by that person for that benefit until the grounds of the original disallowance have ceased to exist;
(g) for enabling one person to act for another in relation to a claim for a benefit to which this section applies and for enabling such a claim to be made and proceeded with in the name of a person who has died;
(h) for requiring any information or evidence needed for the deter-

mination of such a claim or of any question arising in connection with such a claim to be furnished by such person as may be prescribed in accordance with the regulations;

(i) for the person to whom, time when and manner in which a benefit to which this section applies is to be paid and for the information and evidence to be furnished in connection with the payment of such a benefit;

(j) for notice to be given of any change of circumstances affecting the continuance of entitlement to such a benefit or payment of such a benefit;

(k) for the day on which entitlement to such a benefit is to begin or end;

(l) for calculating the amounts of such a benefit according to a prescribed scale or otherwise adjusting them so as to avoid fractional amounts or facilitate computation;

(m) for extinguishing the right to payment of such a benefit if payment is not obtained within such period, not being less than 12 months, as may be prescribed from the date on which the right is treated under the regulations as having arisen;

(n) [^{3}...]
(nn) [^{2}...]
(o) [^{3}...]

(p) for the circumstances and manner in which payments of such a benefit may be made to another person on behalf of the beneficiary for any purpose, which may be to discharge, in whole or in part, an obligation of the beneficiary or any other person;

(q) for the payment or distribution of such a benefit to or among persons claiming to be entitled on the death of any person and for dispensing with strict proof of their title;

(r) for the making of a payment on account of such a benefit—
  (i) where no claim has been made and it is impracticable for one to be made immediately;
  (ii) where a claim has been made and it is impracticable for the claim or an appeal, reference, review or application relating to it to be immediately determined;
  (iii) where an award has been made but it is impracticable to pay the whole immediately.

(2) This section applies to the following benefits—

(a) benefits as defined in section 122 of the Contributions and Benefits Act;

[^{1}(aa) a jobseeker's allowance;]

(b) income support;
(c) [^{4} working families' tax credit];
(d) [^{4} disabled persons tax credit];
(e) housing benefit;
(f) any social fund payments such as are mentioned in section 138(1)(a) a or 2) of the Contributions and Benefits Act;
(g) child benefit; and
(h) Christmas bonus.

(3) The reference in subsection (1)(h) above to information or evid-

ence needed for the determination of a claim includes a reference to information or evidence required by a rent officer under section 121 of the Housing Act 1988.

(4) Subsection (1)(n) above shall have effect in relation to housing benefit as if the reference to the Secretary of State were a reference to the authority paying the benefit.

(5) Subsection (1)(g), (i), (l), (p) and (q) above shall have effect as if statutory sick pay and statutory maternity pay were benefits to which this section applies.

AMENDMENTS

1. Jobseekers Act 1995, Sched. 2, para. 39 (October 7, 1996).
2. Social Security Act 1998, Sched. 6, para. 5(1) (May 21, 1998). This amendment applies from May 21, 1998 until s.21(2)(d) of the 1998 Act comes into force.
3. Social Security Act 1998, Sched 8. (July 5, 1999)
4. Tax Credits Act 1999, Sched. 1 (October 5, 1999)

DERIVATION

1.15   Subss. (1) and (2): Social Security Act 1986, s.51(1) and (2).

DEFINITIONS

"the Contributions and Benefits Act"—see s.191.
"prescribed"—*ibid.*

6 *Omitted.*

1.16   *Community charge benefits, etc.*

Relationship between community charge benefits and other benefits

1.17   **7.**—(1) Regulations may provide for a claim for one relevant benefit to be treated, either in the alternative or in addition, as a claim for any other relevant benefit that may be prescribed.

(2) Regulations may provide for treating a payment made or right conferred by virtue of regulations—

(a) under section 5(1)(r) above; or
(b) under section 6(1)(r) to (t) above,

as made or conferred on account of any relevant benefit that is subsequently awarded or paid.

(3) For the purposes of subsections (1) and (2) above relevant benefits are—

(a) any benefit to which section 5 above applies; and
(b) [¹council tax benefit].

AMENDMENT

1. Local Government Finance Act 1992, Sched. 9, para. 13 (April 1, 1993).

DERIVATION

Social Security Act 1986, s.51B. 1.18

DEFINITIONS

"claim"—see s.191.
"prescribed"—*ibid.*

GENERAL NOTE

Subsection (1)
See Claims and Payments Regulations, Sched. 1. 1.19

Subsection (2)
See the Social Security (Payments on account, Overpayments and Recovery) Regulations, regs. 5 to 8. 1.20

Industrial injuries benefit

Notification of accidents, etc.

8. Regulations may provide— 1.21
(a) for requiring the prescribed notice of an accident in respect of which industrial injuries benefit may be payable to be given within the prescribed time by the employed earner to the earner's employer or other prescribed person;
(b) for requiring employers—
   (i) to make reports, to such person and in such form and within such time as may be prescribed, of accidents in respect of which industrial injuries benefit may be payable;
   (ii) to furnish to the prescribed person any information required for the determination of claims, or of questions arising in connection with claims or awards;
   (iii) to take such other steps as may be prescribed to facilitate the giving notice of accidents, the making of claims and the determination of claims and of questions so arising.

DERIVATION

SSA 1975, s.88. 1.22

GENERAL NOTE

The regulations made under this section are the Claims and Payment Regulations 1979, regs 24 and 25. The provisions of the regulations are, of course, significant in trying to ensure that the adjudicating authorities have access to a record of the circumstances surrounding an industrial accident, and the opportunity to put questions to the employer. Entries in the accident book are not always illuminating, but it is in the interests of the employees that they give the fullest possible contemporaneous account of the accident, particularly where its effects may be slow to emerge (as, sometimes, in head or back injuries).

Medical examination and treatment of claimants

1.23   9.—(1) Regulations may provide for requiring claimants for disablement benefit—
   (a) to submit themselves from time to time to medical examination for the purpose of determining the effect of the relevant accident, or the treatment appropriate to the relevant injury or loss of faculty;
   (b) to submit themselves from time to time to appropriate medical treatment for the injury or loss of faculty.

   (2) Regulations under subsection (1) above requiring persons to submit themselves to medical examination or treatment may—
   (a) require those persons to attend at such places and at such times as may be required; and
   (b) with the consent of the Treasury provide for the payment by the Secretary of State to those persons of travelling and other allowances (including compensation for loss of remunerative time).

DERIVATION

1.24   SSA 1975, s.89.

DEFINITIONS

"medical examinations," "medical treatment": see s.191.

GENERAL NOTE

The regulations referred to are the Claims and Payments Regulations 1979, reg. 26.

Obligations of claimants

1.25   10.—(1) Subject to subsection (3) below, regulations may provide for disqualifying a claimant for the receipt of industrial injuries benefit—
   (a) for failure without good cause to comply with any requirement of regulations to which this subsection applies (including in the case of a claim for industrial death benefit, a failure on the part of some other person to give the prescribed notice of the relevant accident);
   (b) for wilful obstruction of, or other misconduct in connection with, any examination or treatment to which he is required under regulations to which this subsection applies to submit himself, or in proceedings under this Act for the determination of his right to benefit or to its receipt,
or for suspending proceedings on the claim or payment of benefit as the case may be, in the case of any such failure, obstruction or misconduct.

   (2) The regulations to which subsection (1) above applies are—
   (a) any regulations made by virtue of section 5(1)(h), (i) or (l) above, so far as relating to industrial injuries benefit; and
   (b) regulations made by virtue of section 8 or 9 above.

   (3) Regulations under subsection (1) above providing for disquali-

fication of the receipt of benefit for any of the following matters, that is to say—
  (a) for failure to comply with the requirements of regulations under section 9(1) or (2) above;
  (b) for obstruction of, or misconduct in connection with, medical examination or treatment, shall not be made so as to disentitle a claimant to benefit for a period exceeding 6 weeks on any disqualification.

DERIVATION

SSA 1975, s.90(2)–(4) as amended.   1.26

GENERAL NOTE

In *R(S)9/51* it was held that a deeply held personal conviction that a claimant's religious beliefs require him or her to refuse to have a medical examination amounted to good cause for refusal to do so. Mere prejudice or distaste for the process will not alone suffice. But the decision did go on to point out the possible consequential difficulties of meeting the burden of proof for entitlement to benefit if the refusal to submit to a medical examination resulted in their being no, or little, medical evidence available. Much would depend on the cogency of the other evidence available which might be sufficient to establish incapacity without full medical evidence. See also *CSIS/065/1991* discussed in the annotations to reg. 2 of the Medical Evidence Regulations.

[¹Disabled person's tax credit]

Initial claims and repeat claims

11.—(1) In this section—   1.27
"Initial claim" means a claim for a [¹disabled person's tax credit] made by a person—
  (a) to whom it has not previously been payable; or
  (b) to whom it has not been payable during the period of 2 years immediately preceding the date on which the claim is made or is treated as made; and
"repeat claim" means any other claim for a [¹disabled person's tax credit].
  (2) On an initial claim a declaration by a claimant that he has a physical or mental disability which puts him at a disadvantage in getting a job is conclusive, except in such circumstances as may be prescribed, that for the purposes of section 129(1)(b) of the Contributions and Benefits Act he has such a disability (in accordance with regulations under section 129(3) of that Act).
  (3) If—
  (a) a repeat claim is made or treated as made not later than the end of the period of 8 weeks commencing with the last day of the claimant's previous award; and
  (b) on the claim which resulted in that award he qualified under section 129(2) of the Contributions and Benefits Act by virtue—

(i) of paragraph (a) of that subsection; or
(ii) of there being payable to him a benefit under an enactment having effect in Northern Ireland and corresponding to a benefit mentioned in that paragraph,

he shall be treated on the repeat claim as if he still so qualified.

AMENDMENT

1. Tax Credits Act 1999, Sched. 1 (October 5, 1999)

DERIVATION

1.28 Social Security Act 1986, s.27B(1) to (3).

DEFINITION

"the Contributions and Benefits Act"—see s.191.

GENERAL NOTE

Section 11 supplies some special rules under which some parts of the qualifications for a disabled person's tax credit are deemed to be satisfied.

Subsection (1)

1.29 An initial claim is one made by a person who has never been entitled to a disabled person's tax credit or whose last week of entitlement was more than two years before the date of claim. Any other claim is a repeat claim.

Subsection (2)

1.30 On an initial claim a claimant's declaration, on the elaborate self-assessment claim form, that he has a disability which puts him at a disadvantage in getting a job is conclusive. This general rule does not apply if the claim itself contains indications to the contrary or the decision-maker has before him evidence pointing to the contrary (Disability Working Allowance (General) Regulations, reg. 4).

Subsection (3)

1.31 This provision applies to claimants who have been awarded disability working allowance on the basis that they were entitled to higher rate short-term incapacity benefit, long-term incapacity benefit, severe disablement allowance or income support, housing benefit or council tax benefit with the disability premium or pensioner premium for disability or any Northern Ireland equivalent (see Contributions and Benefits Act, s.129(2)(a) and (4) and Disability Working Allowance Regulations, reg. 7). When such an award expires and the repeat claim is made within eight weeks, the claimant is deemed to satisfy the requirement. Thus if a claimant initially qualifies on this ground and continues to satisfy the other conditions of entitlement, awards may continue indefinitely.

The social fund

Necessity of application for certain payments

1.32 **12.**—(1) A social fund payment such as is mentioned in section 138(1)(b) of the Contributions and Benefits Act may be awarded to a person only if an application for such a payment has been made by him or on his behalf in such form and manner as may be prescribed.

(2) The Secretary of State may by regulations—
(a) make provision with respect to the time at which an application for such a social fund payment is to be treated as made;
(b) prescribe conditions that must be satisfied before any determination in connection with such an application may be made or any award of such a payment may be paid;
(c) prescribe circumstances in which such an award becomes extinguished.

DERIVATION

Social Security Act 1986, s.33(1) and (13). 1.33

DEFINITIONS

"the Contributions and Benefits Act"—see s.191.
"prescribed"—*ibid.*

GENERAL NOTE

Subsection (1)
This provision applies to the "ordinary" social fund, not to maternity payments or cold weather payments. See the Social Fund (Applications) Regulations. 1.34

Subsection (2)
See the Social Fund (Miscellaneous Provisions) Regulations. 1.35

Child benefit

Necessity of application for child benefit

13.—(1) Subject to the provisions of this Act, no person shall be entitled to child benefit unless he claims it in the manner, and within the time, prescribed in relation to child benefit by regulations under section 5 above. 1.36

(2) Except where regulations otherwise provide, no person shall be entitled to child benefit for any week on a claim made by him after that week if child benefit in respect of the same child has already been paid for that week to another person, whether or not that other person was entitled to it.

DERIVATION

CBA 1975, s.6. 1.37

GENERAL NOTE

There is a general bar on receiving child benefit if it has already been paid to someone else in respect of the same child even though that other person was not entitled to it.

The rules relating to claims for and payments of child benefit are now to be found in the Claims and Payments Regulations 1987.

See notes to reg. 14A of the Child Benefit (General) Regulations 1976 for an escape route from the application of the rule in subs. (2).

Statutory sick pay

Duties of employees etc. in relation to statutory sick pay

1.38 14.—(1) Any employee who claims to be entitled to statutory sick pay from his employer shall, if so required by his employer, provide such information as may reasonably be required for the purpose of determining the duration of the period of entitlement in question or whether a period of entitlement exists as between them.

(2) The Secretary of State may by regulations [¹ made with the concurrence of the Inland Revenue] direct—
- (a) that medical information required under subsection (1) above shall, in such cases as may be prescribed, be provided in a prescribed form;
- (b) that an employee shall not be required under subsection (1) above to provide medical information in respect of such days as may be prescribed in a period of incapacity for work.

(3) Where an employee asks an employer of his to provide him with a written statement, in respect of a period before the request is made, of one or more of the following—
- (a) the days within that period which the employer regards as days in respect of which he is liable to pay statutory sick pay to that employee;
- (b) the reasons why the employer does not so regard the other days in that period;
- (c) the employer's opinion as to the amount of statutory sick pay to which the employee is entitled in respect of each of those days,

the employer shall, to the extent to which the request was reasonable, comply with it within a reasonable time.

AMENDMENT

1. Transfer of Functions Act 1999, Sched. 3 (April 1, 1999).

DERIVATION

1.39 SSA 1981, s.17(2)–(3).

Statutory maternity pay

Duties of women, etc., in relation to statutory maternity pay

1.40 15.—(1) A woman shall provide the person who is liable to pay her statutory maternity pay—
- (a) with evidence as to her pregnancy and the expected date of confinement in such form and at such time as may be prescribed; and
- (b) where she commences work after her confinement but within the maternity pay period, with such additional information as may be prescribed.

[¹(1A) Any regulations for the purposes of subsection (1) above must be made with the concurrence of the Inland Revenue.]

(2) Where a woman asks an employer or former employer of hers to provide her with a written statement, in respect of a period before the request is made, of one or more of the following—
  (a) the weeks within that period which he regards as weeks in respect of which he is liable to pay statutory maternity pay to the woman,
  (b) the reasons why he does not so regard the other weeks in that period, and
  (c) his opinion as to the amount of statutory maternity pay to which the woman is entitled in respect of each of the weeks in respect of which he regards himself as liable to make a payment,
the employer or former employer shall, to the extent to which the request was reasonable, comply with it within a reasonable time.

AMENDMENT

1. Transfer of Functions Act 1999, Sched. 3 (April 1, 1999)

DERIVATION

SSA 1986, s.49 and Sched. 4, paras 6 and 7.

[¹Payments in respect of mortgage interest etc.

Payment out of benefit of sums in respect of mortgage interest etc.

15A.—(1) This section applies in relation to cases where—
  (a) mortgage interest is payable to a qualifying lender by a person ("the borrower") who is entitled, or whose partner, former partner or qualifying associate is entitled, to income support [² or an income-based jobseeker's allowance]; and
  (b) a sum in respect of that mortgage interest is or was brought into account in determining the applicable amount for the purposes of income support [² or an income-based jobseeker's allowance] in the case of the borrower or the partner, former partner or qualifying associate;
and any reference in this section to "the relevant beneficiary" is a reference to the person whose applicable amount for the purposes of income support [² or an income-based jobseeker's allowance] is or was determined as mentioned in paragraph (b) above.

(2) Without prejudice to paragraphs (i) and (p) of section 5(1) above, regulations may, in relation to cases where this section applies, make provision—
  (a) requiring that, in prescribed circumstances, a prescribed part of any relevant benefits to which the relevant beneficiary is entitled shall be paid by the Secretary of State directly to the qualifying lender and applied by that lender towards the discharge of the liability in respect of the mortgage interest;
  (b) for the expenses of the Secretary of State in administering the

making of payments under the regulations to be defrayed, in whole or in part, at the expense of qualifying lenders, whether by requiring them to pay prescribed fees or by deducting and retaining a prescribed part of the payments that would otherwise be made to them under the regulations or by such other method as may be prescribed;
(c) for requiring a qualifying lender, in a case where by virtue of paragraph (b) above the amount of the payment made to him under the regulations is less than it would otherwise have been, to credit against the liability in respect of the mortgage interest (in addition to the payment actually made) an amount equal to the difference between—
    (i) the payment that would have been so made, apart from paragraph (b) above; and
    (ii) the payment actually made;
and, in any such case, for treating the amount so credited as properly paid on account of benefit due to the relevant beneficiary;
(d) for enabling a body which, or person who, would otherwise be a qualifying lender to elect not to be regarded as such for the purposes of this section, other than this paragraph;
(e) for the recovery from any body or person—
    (i) of any sums paid to that body or person by way of payment under the regulations that ought not to have been so paid; or
    (ii) of any fees or other sums due from that body or person by virtue of paragraph (b) above;
(f) for cases where the same person is the borrower in relation to mortgage interest payable in respect of two or more different loans; and
(g) for any person of a prescribed class or description who would otherwise be regarded for the purposes of this section as the borrower in relation to any mortgage interest not to be so regarded, except for the purposes of this paragraph;
but the Secretary of State shall not make any regulations under paragraph (b) above unless he has consulted with such organisations representing qualifying lenders likely to be affected by the regulations as he considers appropriate.

(3) The bodies and persons who are "qualifying lenders" for the purposes of this section are—
(a) any authorised institution, within the meaning of the Banking Act 1987, to which section 67 of that Act applies (companies and partnerships which may describe themselves as banks etc),
(b) any building society incorporated under the Building Societies Act 1986,
(c) any body or person carrying on insurance business, within the meaning of the Insurance Companies Act 1982,
(d) any county council, district council, islands council or London Borough Council,
(e) the common Council of the City of London,
(f) the Council of the Isles of Scilly,
(g) any new town corporation,

and such bodies or persons not falling within the above paragraphs as may be prescribed.

(4) In this section—

"mortgage interest" means interest on a loan which is secured by a mortgage of or charge over land, or (in Scotland) by a heritable security, and which has been taken out to defray money applied for any of the following purposes, that is to say—
  (a) acquiring any residential land which was intended, at the time of the acquisition, for occupation by the borrower as his home;
  (b) carrying out repairs or improvements to any residential land which was intended, at the time of taking out the loan, for occupation by the borrower as his home;
  (c) paying off another loan; or
  (d) any prescribed purpose not falling within paragraphs (a) to (c) above;

but interest shall be regarded as mortgage interest by virtue of paragraph (c) above only to the extent that interest on that other loan would have been regarded as mortgage interest for the purposes of this section had the loan not been paid off;

"partner" means—
  (a) any person to whom the borrower is married and who is a member of the same household as the borrower; or
  (b) any person to whom the borrower is not married but who lives together with the borrower as husband and wife, otherwise than in prescribed circumstances;

and "former partner" means a person who has at some time been, but no longer is, the borrower's partner;

"qualifying associate", in relation to the borrower, means a person who, for the purposes of income support [²or an income-based jobseeker's allowance], falls to be treated by regulations under Part VII of the Contributions and Benefits Act [² or (as the case may be) under the Jobseekers Act 1995,] as responsible for so much of the expenditure which relates to housing costs (within the meaning of those regulations) as consists of any of the mortgage interest payable by the borrower, and who falls to be so treated because—
  (a) the borrower is not meeting those costs, so that the person has to meet them if he is to continue to live in the dwelling occupied as his home; and
  (b) the person is one whom it is reasonable, in the circumstances, to treat as liable to meet those costs;

"relevant benefits" means such of the following benefits as may be prescribed, namely—
  (a) benefits, as defined in section 122 of the Contributions and Benefits Act;
[²(aa) a jobseeker's allowance;]
  (b) income support;

"residential land" means any land which consists of or includes a dwelling.

(5) For the purposes of this section, regulations may make provision—

(a) as to circumstances in which residential land is or is not to be treated as intended for occupation by the borrower as his home; or

(b) as to circumstances in which persons are to be treated as being or not being members of the same household.]

AMENDMENTS

1. Social Security (Mortgage Interest Payments) Act 1992, s.1(12) and Sched., para. 1 (July 1, 1992; the equivalent amendment to the Social Security Act 1986 came into force on March 16, 1992).
2. Jobseekers Act 1995, Sched. 2, para. 40 (October 7, 1996).

DEFINITION

1.43 "Contributions and Benefits Act"—see s.191.

GENERAL NOTE

Section 15A authorises the regulations which set out the meat of the scheme for direct payment to lenders of the element of housing costs in income support, and from October 7, 1996, income-based JSA, to cover mortgage interest and supplies some basic definitions. The main provisions are in Sched. 9A to the Claims and Payments Regulations.

Emergency payments

Emergency payments by local authorities and other bodies

1.44 **16.**—(1) The Secretary of State may make arrangements—
(a) with a local authority to which this section applies; or
(b) with any other body,
for the making on his behalf by members of the staff of any such authority or body of payments on account of benefits to which section 5 above applies in circumstances corresponding to those in which the Secretary of State himself has the power to make such payments under subsection (1)(r) of that section; and a local authority to which this section applies shall have power to enter into any such arrangements.

(2) A payment under any such arrangements shall be treated for the purposes of any Act of Parliament or instrument made under an Act of Parliament as if it had been made by the Secretary of State.

(3) The Secretary of State shall repay a local authority or other body such amount as he determines to be the reasonable administrative expenses incurred by the authority or body in making payments in accordance with arrangements under this subsection.

(4) The local authorities to which this section applies are—
(a) a local authority as defined in section 270(1) of the Local Government Act 1972, other than a parish or community council;
(b) the Common Council of the City of London; and
(c) a local authority as defined in section 235(1) of the Local Government (Scotland) Act 1973.

(1992 c.5, s.16)

DERIVATION

Social Security Act 1988, s.8.   1.45

PART II

ADJUDICATION

GENERAL NOTE

The entirety of Part II of the Social Security Administration Act 1992 is repealed by the Social Security Act 1998 in order to give effect to the policy proposals outlined in the Government's Consultation Paper, *Improving Decision Making and Appeals in Social Security*, Cm 3328. The theme of the proposals is to modernise the administration of the social security system. The emphasis is placed on simplifying organisational structures, defining responsibilities and streamlining procedures. The Consultation Paper points to 13 different types of decision-maker involved in the determination of claims to benefit. In particular, the split between adjudication officers' and Secretary of State's decisions is criticised for causing confusion for both Departmental staff and claimants, especially where one individual officer is simply acting in different capacities. The lack of a right of appeal from Secretary of State decisions creates further anomalies.   1.46

The proliferation of decision-makers at the appeals level is also seen as inflexible and cumbersome. The distinctive jurisdictions of Social Security Appeal Tribunals, Disability Appeal Tribunals, Medical Appeal Tribunals, Child Support Appeal Tribunals and Vaccine Damage Tribunals are felt to impose rigid, categorical boundaries. The rectification of manifest errors in tribunal decisions requires a ponderous trek to the Commissioners.

The remedial measures, however, go far beyond those necessary to tackle complexity and delay. Greater managerial control is the order of the day. Thus, the division between adjudication officer's and Secretary of State's decisions is resolved by abolishing adjudication officers and having all decisions on and in relation to claims taken in the name of the Secretary of State by decision makers. In this way, the prerogative of adjudication officers' to "act independently of Agency Managers, Chief Executives and Ministers when making decisions", which is evidently treated by the Consultation Paper as a problem, is bluntly terminated. Similarly to disappear are the Chief Adjudication Officer, who is responsible for monitoring and promoting standards of administrative decision-making, and the Central Adjudication Service, which serve as a source of relatively policy-free guidance on the interpretation and application of the law. At the appeals level, the clock is turned back 15 years, to before the days of the Independent Tribunal Service (and its precursor, the Office of the President of Social Security Appeal Tribunals). The administration of the appeals system is to revert to the Department through the mechanism of an appeals agency headed by a Chief Executive accountable to the Minister. The ITS as such will be replaced by The Appeals Service—a dualistic body comprising the appeals agency and a judicial arm headed by a President.

The transition from the old administrative and tribunal arrangements to the new has been phased in benefit by benefit during the course of 1999: The timetable is:—

June 1, 1999:	Child Support
July 5, 1999:	Disablement Benefit
	Reduced Earnings Allowance
	Retirement Allowance
	Child Benefit & Guardians Allowance

Social Security Administration Act 1992

September 6, 1999:   Incapacity Benefit
                              Severe Disablement Allowance
                              Retirement Benefit
                              Widows Benefit
                              Maternity Allowance
October 5, 1999:   Family Credit renamed working families' tax credit
                              Disability Working Allowance renamed disabled person's tax credit
October 18, 1999:   Jobseeker's Allowance
                              Disability Living Allowance
                              Attendance Allowance
                              Invalid Care Allowance
November 29, 1999:   All other benefits, including:—
                              Income Support and social fund payments

On and from each transition date all claims or pending appeals in relation to the particular benefit converted on that date will be dealt with under the new arrangements. A series of commencement orders will give effect to the transitional measures.

However, the intended simplification of responsibility for decision-making fragments with the introduction of the Social Security Contributions (Transfer of Functions, etc.) Act 1999, which moves responsibility for deciding most of the contribution questions vested in the Secretary of State by s.17 Social Security Administration Act 1992 to the Board of Inland Revenue with corresponding rights of appeal to the tax appeal Commissioners.

PART III

OVERPAYMENTS AND ADJUSTMENTS OF BENEFIT

Misrepresentation etc.

Overpayments—general

1.47

71.—(1) Where it is determined that, whether fraudulently or otherwise, any person has misrepresented, or failed to disclose, any material fact and in consequence of the misrepresentation or failure—

(a) a payment has been made in respect of a benefit to which this section applies; or

(b) any sum recoverable by or on behalf of the Secretary of State in connection with any such payment has not been recovered,

the Secretary of State shall be entitled to recover the amount of any payment which he would not have made or any sum which he would have received but for the misrepresentation or failure to disclose.

[1(2) Where any such determination as is referred to in subsection (1) above is made, the person making the determination shall [2 in the case of the Secretary of State or a tribunal, and may in the case of a Commissioner or court]—

(a) determine whether any, and if so what, amount is recoverable under that subsection by the Secretary of State, and

(b) specify the period during which that amount was paid to the person concerned.]

(3) An amount recoverable under subsection (1)(above is in all cases recoverable from the person who misrepresented the fact or failed to disclose it.

(4) In relation to cases where payments of benefit to which this section applies have been credited to a bank account or other account under arrangements made with the agreement of the beneficiary or a person acting for him, circumstances may be prescribed in which the Secretary of State is to be entitled to recover any amount paid in excess of entitlement; but any such regulations shall not apply in relation to any payment unless before he agreed to the arrangements such notice of the effect of the regulations as may be prescribed was given in such manner as may be prescribed to the beneficiary or to a person acting for him.

(5) Except where regulations otherwise provide, an amount shall not be recoverable under [³. . .] regulations under subsection (4) above unless—

(a) the determination in pursuance of which it was paid has been reversed or varied on an appeal or [² has been revised under section 9 or superseded under section 10 of the Social Security Act 1998]; and

(b) it has been determined on the appeal or [² under that section] that the amount is so recoverable.

[⁴(5A) Except where regulations otherwise provide, an amount shall not be recoverable under subsection (1) above unless the determination in pursuance of which it was paid has been reversed or varied on an appeal or [² has been revised under section 9 or superseded under section 10 of the Social Security Act 1998].]

(6) Regulations may provide—

(a) that amounts recoverable under subsection (1) above or regulations under subsection (4) above shall be calculated or estimated in such manner and on such basis as may be prescribed;

(b) for treating any amount paid to any person under an award which is subsequently determined was not payable—

   (i) as properly paid; or

   (ii) as paid on account of a payment which it is determined should be or should have been made,

   and for reducing or withholding any arrears payable by virtue of the subsequent determination;

(c) for treating any amount paid to one person in respect of another as properly paid for any period for which it is not payable in cases where in consequence of the subsequent determination—

   (i) the other person is himself entitled to a payment for that period; or

   (ii) a third person is entitled in priority to the payee to a payment for that period in respect of the other person, and for redu-

cing or withholding any arrears payable for that period by virtue of the subsequent determination.

(7) Circumstances may be prescribed in which a payment on account by virtue of section 5(1)(r) above may be recovered to the extent that it exceeds entitlement.

(8) Where any amount paid is recoverable under—
  (a) subsection (1) above;
  (b) regulations under subsection (4) or (7) above; or
  (c) section 74 below,
it may, without prejudice to any other method of recovery, be recovered by deduction from prescribed benefits.

(9) Any amount recoverable under the provisions mentioned in subsection (8) above—
  (a) if the person from whom it is recoverable resides in England and Wales and the county court so orders, shall be recoverable by execution issued from the county court or otherwise as if it were payable under an order of that court; and
  (b) if he resides in Scotland, shall be enforced in like manner as an extract registered decree arbitral bearing a warrant of execution issued by the sheriff court of any sheriffdom in Scotland.

[5(10A) Where—
  (a) a jobseeker's allowance is payable to a person from whom any amount is recoverable as mentioned in subsection (8) above; and
  (b) that person is subject to a bankruptcy order,
a sum deducted from that benefit under that subsection shall not be treated as income of his for the purposes of the Insolvency Act 1986.

(10B) Where—
  (a) a jobseeker's allowance is payable to a person from whom any amount is recoverable as mention in subsection (8) above; and
  (b) the estate of that person is sequestrated,
a sum deducted from that benefit under that subsection shall not be treated as income of his for the purposes of the Bankruptcy (Scotland) Act 1985.]

(11) This section applies to the following benefits—
  (a) benefits as defined in section 122 of the Contributions and Benefits Act;
[6(aa) subject to section 71A below, a jobseeker's allowance;]
  (b) [7. . .], income support;
  (c) [8working families' tax credit];
  (d) [8disabled person's tax credit];
  (e) any social fund payments as are mentioned in section 138(1)(a) or (2) of the Contributions and Benefits Act; and
  (f) child benefit.

AMENDMENTS

1. Social Security (Overpayments) Act 1996, s.1(2) (for determination made after July 24, 1996).

2. Social Security Act 1998, Sched. 7 (July 5, 1999).

3. Social Security (Overpayments) Act 1996, s.1(3) (for determinations made after July 24, 1996).

4. Social Security (Overpayments) Act 1996, s.1(4) (for determinations made after July 24, 1996).
5. Jobseekers Act 1995, s.32(1) (October 7, 1996)
6. Jobseekers Act 1995, Sched. 2 (October 7, 1996)
7. Jobseekers Act 1995, Sched. 3 (October 7, 1996)
8. Tax Credits Act 1999, Sched. 1 (October 5, 1999).

DERIVATION

Social Security Act 1986, s.53   1.48

GENERAL NOTE

Regulations
The regulations referred to in this section are the Overpayments Regulations.   1.49

Limitation periods
Arguments that overpayments are not recoverable because of the application of   1.50
the limitation periods applicable to the recovery of debts in actions before the
courts are destined to fail. In *R(SB)5/91* the Commissioner said,

> "The plain fact is that section 9(1) of the Limitation Act 1980 simply has no application to proceedings before the adjudicating authorities. But when the amount of the overpayment has been *finally* determined by them, as in this case it is by my decision (unless it is proposed to take the matter on appeal to the Court of Appeal) then, and then only, for the purposes of recovery of the overpayment by action in the Courts, time begins to run." (para. 7).

In *CIS/026/1994* the claimant sought a review of the overpayment decision on the grounds that the Secretary of State was no longer able to seek recovery of the overpaid benefit because more than six years had passed and any action in a court would be barred by the operation of s.9(1) of the Limitation Act 1980, and that this constituted a relevant change of circumstances. The overpayment was at the time of the application being recovered at the rate of £5.00 per week from the claimant's retirement pension. The Commissioner regarded the applications as wholly misconceived (as had the tribunal). The Commissions confirmed that, so far as relevant to social security payments, "the Limitation Acts take away only the remedy by action or by set-off and that they leave the right otherwise untouched. The social security adjudicating authorities are not concerned with and have no jurisdiction in respect of remedies by action or set-off." (para. 5).

When does s.71 apply?
The predecessor to the section replaced the misrepresentation/non-disclosure   1.51
test formerly contained in s.20 of the Supplementary Benefits Act 1976 which applied to supplementary benefit and the due care and diligence test in s.119 of the Social Security Act 1975 which applied to non-means tested benefits. Following a series of cases, it has been finally established by the House of Lords in *Plewa v. Chief Adjudication Officer* [1994] 2 W.L.R. 317 that where the overpayment spans periods before and after April 6, 1987 (the date s.53 of the Social Security Act 1986 came into force) the relevant test prior to April 6, 1987 must be applied to the overpayment in respect of that period, and the new test applied to the period starting on April 6, 1987. Only where the whole of the period of the overpayment is on or after April 6, 1987 is the new test alone applied to the issue of recoverability.

The requirement for revision on review

1.52 The first requirement in overpayment cases is for a variation of the decision awarding benefit to be made either on review, supersession or appeal. Without such a variation, there is no power to recover overpayments: s.71(5). The only exception to this rule is found in reg. 12 of the Overpayments Regulations (see below). Tribunals usually deal with cases where there has been a revision of the initial determination on review. However, a common ground upon which appeals to the Commissioner concerning overpayment decisions have succeeded is the failure of the tribunal to consider whether grounds for review within s.71(5) exist: see *R(SB)7/91*. In a number of unreported decisions (*CSSB/621/ 1988*, *CSSB/316/1989*, *CSSB/517/1989* and *CSIS/118/1990*), Commissioners exhort tribunals to remember that revision on review is a prerequisite to recovery under s.71. Where the overpayments span a number of years, every decision over that period must be identified and revised on review before the overpayment is recoverable: see para. 6 of *CSIS/45/1990*.

In *CIS/451/1995* the Commissioner held that the section generally requires that the review of entitlement and the determination that there has been a recoverable overpayment must generally happen at the same time. The Social Security (Overpayments) Act 1996 has amended s.71 to reverse the effect of that decision. There is still a requirement that there must have been a review of benefit entitlement and a decision that there is a recoverable overpayment, but these need not take place at the same time.

In *CIS/1055/1997* the Commissioner holds that the determination referred to is a recovery determination (and not an entitlement determination). The new provisions apply to recovery determinations made after July 24, 1996 regardless of the date of any entitlement determination (including the entitlement determination which resulted in there having been an overpayment of benefit). In *CSIS/174/1996* the Commissioner indicated that in his view the determination must be that of an adjudication officer and could not be a decision of a tribunal correcting an earlier omission. The Commissioner considers that best practice is for the review decision itself to be put before the tribunal and not simply a summary of it in the written submission to the tribunal. This is considered essential where the claimant puts in issue any of its terms.

In *CSB/1272/1989* the Commissioner considers whether a tribunal could use its powers to determine questions first arising in the course of the appeal to correct a failure by an adjudication officer to review the award of benefit as required by what was then s.53(4) of the Social Security Act 1986. That decision attracted some cautionary comments in *CSB/1093/1989*. The issue is now largely academic since the power to determine questions first arising in the course of the appeal has not been re-enacted in the Social Security Act 1998. There will be little alternative but to set aside any decision where there has not been a review as required by the section.

The nature of the evidence which an adjudication officer was expected to produce to demonstrate that there has been a review as considered in *R(IS)2/ 96*. The Commissioner holds that a computer print-out is not sufficient by itself to establish that a review has taken place (though it might, if the output is intelligible and records that a proper determination had taken place), since there must be some human interaction with the computer to convert computer-based information into a review decision. The Commissioner notes that the computer print-out in issue in the case was, by itself, unintelligible. However, verbal evidence to interpret the print-out, or submission of a copy of a letter informing the claimant of the decision which contained sufficient detail might suffice to show that there had been a review and revision of entitlement. Failure to provide such evidence would mean that the adjudication officer had failed to meet the burden of proof in overpayment cases.

The test to be applied
The test laid down in subs. (1) requires a number of conditions to be satisfied. Where:

1.53

(a) any person

(b) whether fraudulently or otherwise

(c) misrepresents, or

(d) fails to disclose

(e) a material fact

(f) and this results in an overpayment of benefit for any period

the amount of the overpayment is recoverable from the person misrepresenting or failing to disclose that material fact.

It is for the Department to prove on the balance of probabilities the facts which justify the recovery of the overpayment: *R(SB)43/83*. Appeals involving overpayments require fastidious attention to the facts which are often hotly disputed. In such disputes having regard to where the burden of proof lies is particularly important.

Any person
The person making the misrepresentation of failing to disclose need not be the claimant. It can be anyone. In *R(SB)21/82* recovery was sought from the claimant's wife; and in *R(SB)23/83* it was the claimant's personal representative. It had been made clear in *Secretary of State for Social Services v. Solley* [1974] 3 All E.R. 922 that recovery from the estate of a deceased person was possible. However, tribunals are not the place in which which objections to liability by the executor on the grounds, for example, that the estate has already been distributed are to be resolved. Those are matters concerning a decision to pursue recovery (which were reserved under the old adjudication system for the Secretary of State) rather than liability for the overpayment, and may need adjudication in court: *CSSB/006/1995*.

1.54

Non-disclosure by someone other than the claimant requires some clear evidence of responsibility on that person to disclose information. In *R(SB)21/82* the Commission said that the non-disclosure must have occurred "in circumstances in which, at least, disclosure by the person was reasonably to be expected."

In *CG/065/1989* the adjudication officer had sought recovery (in addition to recovery from the claimant) from two solicitors who had acted for the claimant. The Commissioner advises that where recovery is sought from more than one party, a tribunal should deal with the recoverability of the overpayment from each of the parties covered by the adjudication officer's decision. It will not be enough to decide only that the overpayment is recoverable from the claimant.

Appointees
Special considerations can arise where recovery is sought from an appointee. The authorities on the liability of an appointee are in some disarray and there are conflicting decisions of the Commissioners.

1.55

In *CG/065/1989*, a case concerning recovery from solicitor appointees, the Commissioner contemplated recovery being available from both the claimant and any appointee. In *CIS/734/1992* the Commissioner held that there could be no recovery from the claimant by reason of the appointee's misrepresentation or failure to disclose, but there could be recovery from the appointee. In *CIS/332/1993* the acts of the appointee, when acting as such, are treated as acts of the claimant and so recovery is only available from the claimant (or the claimant's estate) and not the appointee (paras. 22–24). Reliance is placed, in part, on an analogy with the situation in *R(SB)34/83,* which concerned a failure to disclose material facts by a receiver appointed by the Court of Protection, and where the resulting overpayment was recoverable from the claimant's estate rather than from the receiver personally. The Commissioner notes that the decision in *CIS/734/1992,* which was predicated on the claimant's lack of capacity because of his mental state, meant that it would be inappropriate to impute to him any failure to disclose or misrepresentation of the appointee. But is it, of course, of the essence of an appointment that the claimant is for some reason unable to act. Are distinctions based on physical and mental capacity appropriate when reg. 33 of the Claims and Payments Regulations under which such appointments are made speaks of the appointee exercising any right to which the claimant may be entitled? The Commissioner acknowledges that the matter is one of extreme difficulty.

In *CIS/12022/1996 (starred as 99/97)* a different Commissioner describes the distinction between a person in their capacity as appointee and in their personal capacity as "puzzling and metaphysical". In upholding the decision of a tribunal that an overpayment was recoverable from an appointee who was the mother of the claimant and had failed to disclose increases in the claimant's savings, the Commissioner appears to differ from the view that the capacity in which a person acts affects the person from whom the overpayment is recoverable.

There is logic in both positions. The first Commissioner is making the point that an appointee's acts are those of the claimant who is unable to act for himself or herself. If a person is acting as appointee, then the recovery should be from the claimant. The second Commissioner reflects the realities of daily life by noting that a person in the position of appointee will almost certainly not make clear distinctions in the capacity in which they are dealing with the Department. If they should have disclosed something such as an increase in savings, then recovery can be sought from them as well as from the claimant.

Since there is a difference between two Commissioners, tribunals are free to follow whichever of these two decisions they prefer.

A useful article on the appointee system can be found at Lowery, R and Lundy, L, "The Social Security Appointee System" [1994] J.S.W.F.L. 313.

Overpayments involving spouses

1.56 In *CIS/619/1997 (starred as 40/98)* the Commissioner follows *CIS/13742/1996 (starred as 15/98)* in holding that s.71 requires a review of the claims of both husband and wife before reg. 13 of the Overpayments Regulations can be used to offset benefit payable to one spouse against an overpayment that is recoverable from the other spouse. Tribunals faced with such cases should have regard to these two decisions in dealing with an appeal before them. The Commissioner also questions the propriety of inclusion in papers relating to the wife's appeal of details concerning the husband where she had maintained throughout that she was living separately from her husband. He suggests that there might be breach of confidentiality in relation to the husband's affairs, and appears to urge that such cases may be ones in which consideration would need to be given to disclosure of the husband's affairs to the tribunal as distinct from disclosure to the claimant. He recognises that this in turn gives rise to issues touching on the requirement to provide a fair hearing from the claimant and of natural justice.

Whether fraudulently or otherwise

1.57 The wording makes clear that there is no need to prove any fraudulent intent. Wholly innocent mistakes by claimants can result in recoverable overpayments: *R(SB)28/83; R(SB)9/85;* and *R(SB)18/85.* Innocent misrepresentations are easy to imagine. But it may be better to think of non-fraudulent failures to disclose rather than innocent failures, since non-disclosures involve some breach of a duty to disclose. In *R(SB)28/83* it was suggested that the duty to disclose extends to matters relevant to the claim to benefit which a person with reasonable diligence would have been aware.

This interpretation of the section is confirmed by the Court of Appeal in *Page and Davis v. Chief Adjudication Officer*, published as a supplement to *R(SB)2/92*, where Dillon LJ said:

> "The whole burden of the phrase 'whether fraudulently or otherwise' must be ... that it is to apply even if the misrepresentation is not fraudulent, in other words, if it is innocent. No other construction makes any sense, in my view, of this particular subsection."

Misrepresents
Misrepresentation is founded on positive and deliberate action: *R(SB)9/85*, and may be oral or in writing, or even in some cases arise from conduct such as the cashing of a giro-cheque. As noted above the reason why the statement represented to the Department is incorrect is irrelevant. If a statement has been made, whether written or oral (*R(SB)18/85*) which is untrue, it is a misrepresentation whatever the explanation for the incorrect information proffered. A misrepresentation in a written document may be qualified by an oral statement; it is often asserted by claimants that the form does not accurately reflect everything that was said. While generally claimants bear responsibility for the contents of forms, if it is accepted that an oral qualification has not been properly noted, this may preclude the written representation from being a misrepresentation: *R(SB)18/85*.

1.58

A written misrepresentation may also be qualified or modified when that written communication is read in conjunction with other written communications which should be before the decision-maker in making the decision which resulted in the overpayment of benefit: *R(SB)2/91*, paras 10–13. In such cases, it goes without saying that careful findings of fact are vital. Tribunals should call for originals (or clear copies) of statements signed by persons which are claimed to be the misrepresentation on which an overpayment decision is founded.

Rather more complex than cases where a claimant argues that they have qualified the contents of a misrepresentation in some way in completing the form on which the claim is based are those cases where the claimant argues that they have qualified the contents of a current claim by information contained in an earlier claim. These situations are much less likely to lead to the overpayment not being recoverable. So in *CSB/108/1992* a claimant, who misrepresented that he did not have an army pension believing that it was not relevant to a claim to supplementary benefit and who sought to rely on statements which appear to have been made by him in connection with claims for unemployment benefit and sickness benefit, did not succeed in escaping a liability to repay overpaid supplementary benefit. The Commissioner indicated that the contemporaneity of the oral qualifications was crucial.

In *R(SB)3/90* the Commissioner holds that there can still be a misrepresentation of a material fact even where there has been an earlier disclosure of that fact (para. 11). Although disclosure prevents any recovery of an overpayment based on the failure to disclose head, a misrepresentation by declaration on a claim form that a claimant had no money coming in when superannuation payments from a former employer were in payment, receipt of which had previously been disclosed, overrides that disclosure. The Commissioner specifically states that the Department is entitled to rely on statements in the current claim form and is under no duty to check back to see whether those statements are consistent with earlier disclosures. So it remains incumbent on claimants to be meticulous in their completion of claim forms even after a course of dealing with the Department.

CSU/03/1991 adds a gloss to *R(SB)3/90*. *CSU/03/1991* was a case in whch two forms had been submitted by the claimant containing conflicting information about the claimant's pension position. When he initially claimed unemployment benefit, he disclosed on Form UB461 the correct amount of his pension expressed as a weekly amount, but a few days later he erred in recording on Form UB81(PEN) the pension as £293.75 per *year* rather than per *month*. The claimant's argument was that in considering his claim the adjudication officer should have had both documents before him or her, that this would have indicated the error and no overpayment would have resulted. The adjudication officer sought to argue that he or she was not required to check back to see whether any inconsistent information was given in earlier documents. The Commissioner held that something had clearly gone wrong in the Department; both documents should have been before the adjudication officer in determining this claim and the adjudication officer could not rely on *R(SB)3/90* as the basis for recovering the overpayment of benefit which resulted from the adjudication officer's reliance on the incorrect figure on the Form UB81(PEN).

In *CIS/5117/1998*, starred as 77/99, the Commissioner addresses the question of the extent to which silence can constitute a misrepresentation. The claim form for income support had been completed by an officer of the Department, and read back to him. The form indicated that the claimant was married and living with his wife. None of the questions about his wife, and in particular about her earnings or other income, had been answered. The tribunal found as a fact that the claimant had not been asked questions about his wife's earnings or other income by the Department's officer. An overpayment decision went on appeal to the tribunal which found that there had been no misrepresentation or failure to disclose in the circumstances of this case. The adjudication officer appealed. The Commissioner upheld the tribunal; the only substantial issue was whether or not the claimant made a misrepresentation by his silence when he made the claim on which the award of income support was based.

The Commissioner concludes that *R(SB)18/85* applied to this case. The claimant answered all the questions put to him by the officer of the Department, and the form was not read over to the claimant in its entirety. In these circumstances, says the Commissioner, the claimant's "misrepresentation" that the information on the form was complete "was qualified by the fact that he had supplied all the information for which he had been asked" in circumstances where the officer had given him no opportunity to answer the relevant questions about his wife's earnings, gave no indication that such matters might be material to benefit entitlement, and did not read back the entries on the claim form to confirm their correctness.

The facts of this case are unusual, and appear to represent a failure by the Department to follow its own recommended procedures. But, where such unusual circumstances are established, the claimant's silence does not amount to a misrepresentation. In so far as *CIS/645/1993* suggests that silence as to material facts known to the claimant amounts to a misrepresentation, that decision must be read as referring to a deliberate decision to say nothing on a matter known to be material.

Failure to disclose

1.59 The notion of a failure to disclose of more open-ended that than of a misrepresentation. The case law is complicated and can be confusing. The person failing to disclose must know (or at some time have known—forgetfulness will not excuse non-disclosure: *R(SB)21/82*, para. 20(4)) some fact which is withheld.

(1992 c.5, s.71)

It should always be remembered that failure to disclose "necessarily imports the concept of some breach of obligation, moral or legal—*i.e.* that non-disclosure must have occurred in circumstances in which ... disclosure by the person in question was reasonably to be expected": *R(SB)21/82*, but note that this was a case involving disclosure by someone other than the claimant.

It may, however, be that a person's mental state may be such that he or she cannot be expected to know of a relevant fact, such as an increase in his or her assets. This was hinted at in *R(SB)40/84*. In *CSB/727/1987* the Commissioner held that a person claiming supplementary benefit who disclosed in the application for the benefit that she was owed child benefit and one parent benefit in the circumstances where she had made it "abundantly clear that she regarded it as being due to her and that it would be received in due course" could not reasonably be expected to disclose the start of the payment of that benefit. The resulting overpayment of supplementary benefit was not recoverable. The Commissioner used the analogy of the duty of full disclosure which exists in insurance law. Where sufficient information is given on the claim form to put the Department on notice about the anticipated receipt of resources, it may be unnecessary to disclose the actual receipt of those resources.

See also comments on *CIS/5848/1999* below.

Tribunals are frequently presented with arguments on behalf of claimants that disclosure in the circumstances could not reasonably be expected. A question which often attaches to the consideration of this question is the standard by which reasonableness should be measured. In *CF/026/1990* the Commissioner provides valuable guidance on this point. The appeal concerned an overpayment of child benefit which arose when the claimant's daughter began to receive income support in her own right. The tribunal found that the claimant suffered from learning and reading difficulties and did not fully understand the ramifications of the social security system. The tribunal also found that the claimant was aware that her daughter was receiving income support. The Commissioner begins his consideration of the question of when disclosure can reasonably be expected by reminding tribunals that *R(SB)21/82*, which is frequently cited in support of the proposition that that disclosure might reasonably be expected, was a case concerning recovery from someone other than the claimant. Nevertheless, he accepts that the question may be relevant when the issue relates to a failure to disclose by the claimant, though the issue should be firmly located in the context of the possibility of recovery even where there is a wholly innocent failure to disclose. The key finding is in paragraph 11 of the decision:

> "In this case, as to the claimant's near illiteracy and the family's educational difficulties, I consider that in deciding whether or not there is a failure to disclose by the claimant the test must be *objective*. It must be asked whether, given the claimant's knowledge of the receipt of income support, a reasonable man or woman would have considered that it was material. If so, then there would be a duty to disclose even on the part of the claimant, who, considered subjectively, might not have the necessary education or literacy to realise that disclosure should be made."

Perhaps somewhat controversially, a different Commissioner found in *CIS/757/1994* that the test of whether disclosure could reasonably be expected by a mentally handicapped claimant who knew that her daughter had been taken into care by the local authority had to be determined objectively without regard to her mental capacity. Any harshness could be mitigated by a decision of the Secretary of Stte not to enforce the right to recover the overpaid benefit.

Non-disclosure of assets is likely to be more important in cases involving income-related benefits. It has been held that where the fact not disclosed in ownership of assets and the person failing to disclose is not the owner of them, the Department must prove knowledge by that person of ownership of the assets: *R(SB)21/82* and *R(SB)28/83*.

Disclosure to whom and the continuing duty to disclose

1.60   The obligation to disclose is a continuing obligation to take reasonable steps to ensure that the adjudication officer (now decision-maker) is in possession of all information relevant to the benefit claimed: *R(SB)54/83*. Real difficulties have arisen in the supplementary benefit and income support contexts as to whether disclosure to the unemployment benefit office where supplementary benefit or income support is issued constitutes disclosure to the Department. It is now clear that this issue is one of fact for the tribunal: *R(SB)36/84* and *R(SB)10/85* impliedly approved by the Court of Appeal in *Commock v. Chief Adjudication Officer*, decision of December 1, 1989 reported as an appendix to *R(SB)6/90*. There are suggestions in *R(SB)54/83* at para. 16 that the duty is to disclose to the benefit section responsible for the administration of the particular benefit. But it may be argued that in a unified system of adjudication, disclosure to any adjudication officer constituted good disclosure to the Department as a whole. Whether that remains the case under the system established under the Social Security Act 1998 remains to be seen: the separation of issues relating to benefit may prove to be problematic in a number of contexts.

The following approach is suggested on the basis of the existing authorities, especially *CSB/966/1985* and *R(SB)15/87*:

(a) A personal disclosure to an officer in the local office administering the award of benefit is complete disclosure and absolves the person from further disclosure even if it is not acted on by the department and the claimant continues to receives benefit or suffers no reduction in benefit: *R(SB)15/87*. Subsequent statements when signing for benefit are not misrepresentations because the representation made is that there has been no change subsequent to the disclosure. This proposition is approved by the Commissioner in *CIS/14025/1996*, para. 6. The words of the Commissioners in *R(SB)15/87* sell out exactly who the officer should be to whom the disclosure is made:

"We accept that a claimant cannot be expected to identify the precise person or persons who have the handling of the claim. His duty is best fulfilled by disclosure to the local office where his claim is being handled whether in the claim form or otherwise in terms that make sufficient reference to his claim to enable the matter disclosed to be referred to the proper person. If he does this, it is difficult . . . to visualise any circumstances in which a further duty to disclose the same matter can arise. In the case of a [supplementary benefit or income support] claimant required to be available for employment who is directed . . . to deliver or send his claim to the relevant unemployment benefit office for onward transmission to the department, disclosure on the claim form submitted must also be regard as fulfilling the duty."

But disclosure to the Post Office where benefit is collected will not amount to disclosure to the Department: *CSS/33/1990*, para. 6.

(b) A continuing obligation to disclose will exist where a claimant (or someone acting on the claimant's behalf) has disclosed to an officer of the Department either not in the local office or not in the section of that office administering the benefit. Such disclosure will initially be good disclosure provided that the claimant acted reasonably in thinking that the information would be brought to the attention of the relevant officer. But if subsequent events suggest that the information has not reached that officer,

(1992 c.5, s.71)

then it might well be considered reasonable to expect a claimant to disclose again in a way more certain to ensure that the information is known to the relevant benefit section. How long it will be before a subsequent disclosure is required will vary depending on the particular facts of each case."

The above paragraph is approved by the Commissioner in *CIS/14025/1996*, para. 6. He notes that in such circumstances it is the practice of the Department to expect a further disclosure after the second payment following the first disclosure, and says he would "not cavil with such an approach", though each case must be considered on its own facts. The stronger the claimant's belief that the information would be passed to the adjudication officer (or now decision-maker), the longer it is reasonable to wait before a second disclosure is made.

(c) The disclosure need not be in writing though it will normally be reduced to written form in the Department and signed by the person making the disclosure: see reg. 32 of the Claims and Payments Regulations. Nor need it be made by the claimant in person. Where the information is proffered by someone acting on behalf of the claimant, it must be reasonable for that person to act as the claimant's delegate (this should be presumed if the claimant has asked to delegate to act) and it must be made clear that the delegate is acting on behalf of the claimant and in connection with the claimant's claim to benefit. Note that there are suggestions in para. 29 of *R(SB)15/87* that the disclosure may well be complete even if the information was given in the course of some entirely separate transaction if (1) the information was given to the relevant benefit office, (2) the claimant knew the information had been given, and (3) it was reasonable for the claimant to believe it was unnecessary for him to take any action himself. Casual or incidental disclosure is not good enough. Careful findings of fact will be needed because it seems quite common for the delegate to be also at the office in connection with his or her own claim to benefit. What remains unclear is whether such delegated disclosure removes the continuing obligation to disclose. The matter may depend on findings of fact about the delegated disclosure. The clearest evidence that the information has been disclosed dull and in connection with the claimant's claim to benefit at the relevant local office would certainly justify a conclusion that the disclosure was complete and would relieve the claimant of any continuing obligation to disclose just as if the disclosure had been made personally.

In *CIS/14025/1996*, para. 7, the Commissioner comments as follows on this proposition:

"Finally Bonner implies that it might be different in certain circumstances, depending on the dicta in para 29 . . . of *R(SB)15/87*. That paragraph however concerns the disclosure *on behalf of* another person. Thus disclosure may be made *on behalf of* the claimant:

(a) if the information was given to the relevant office;

(b) the claimant knew that the information had been given and;

(c) it was reasonable for the claimant to believe that it was unnecessary for him to take any action himself.

That does not, in my view, go to the adequacy of the disclosure made; it only goes to whether disclosure by one person can be said to have

41

been disclosure on behalf of another. In this context disclosure, as it were, by chance of 'casual or incidental' is not disclosure on behalf of a claimant. While I have relied on the general principles set out in Bonner above, I dissent from the particular view expressed concerning para 29 of *R(SB)15/87*."

(d) There appears to be a difficulty over written disclosures posted to the Department. Can the claimant rely on something akin to the presumption that a posted letter arrives in the ordinary course of post contained in s.7 of the Interpretation Act 1978 unless the contrary is proved. This is probably a case where the continuing obligation to disclose exists because subsequent events may indicate that the potal disclosure has not been effective. The difficulty relates to issues of evidence and proof: must the Department rebut the presumption that the letter was delivered or can they simply say that they have no record of receipt and that it is for the claimant to ensure that his or her disclosure arrives? The former will probably be more difficult than the latter since it would be proper to inquire as to the incidence of letters going stray after arriving at the Department.

In *CIS/5848/1999* the Commissioner addresses the issue of when *separate* notifications of circumstances to the Secretary of State are required. The scenario is a familiar one. A claimant, with children, claimed income support for herself and her children; unusually she was not in receipt of child benefit when she claimed income support but she also claimed that benefit. When she claimed that benefit she disclosed that she was also an income support claimant. Income support was paid without deduction of child benefit. The overpayment which resulted from this came to light about six months later; the Commissioner says, "the probable explanation is either a belated putting-together of information already in the possession of the Secretary of State in different places in the department's records, or a belated realisation, on the part of those responsible for calculating her income support, of the significance of the information they already had." The appeal tribunal upheld an overpayment decision. The adjudication officer's case was based upon a failure to disclose receipt of payments of child benefit. The claimant argued, and the Commissioner found on the balance of probabilities, that the claimant's child benefit award was duly communicated by the child benefit centre to the officials concerned with calculating her income support entitlement. That says Commissioner was sufficient to dispose of the appeal in favour of the claimant; their failure to recalculate the benefit was not caused by the claimant's lack of a separate notification of the same piece of information.

The Commissioner goes on to argue that a person cannot be said to fail to disclose a fact which the recipient of the information, the Secretary of State, already knows. Two key paragraphs read:

"22. . . . it does not seem to me that it should be regarded as a foregone conclusion in favour of the Secretary of State in all such cases nowadays that the responsibility must always be on the claimant to ensure that each one of possibly numerous different sets of officials or agents dealing with his or her social security affairs on behalf of the Secretary of State is made *separately* aware of material information. The normal position under the general law is that actual knowledge on the part of a large organisation such as a business or a government department is established by the due submission of information in written form to *any* relevant arm of that organisation, without there having to be repeated separate acts of "disclosure" to each other arm that is or may be concerned with the same piece of knowledge.

23. I do not for my part find it obvious why a different principle should

now apply in determining whether multiple or repeated notifications of the same information, to different people all acting in the name of and on behalf of the same Secretary of State, should be held to be necessary before the Secretary of State can be said to have knowledge of that information for the purposes of s.71. Particularly now that the operations of the department and indeed government itself are being made increasingly monolithic, and with the enormous advances over the last twenty years in systems for the storage and rapid retrieval and dissemination of information without the need for separate pieces of paper to be carried between offices, it seems to me that the answers to what is 'reasonably required of the claimant' in any particular case must reflect current, not past, conditions, That well established, practical and flexible test remains applicable, but what is said in the older cases about separate notification to different offices should I think be read in the context of the system as it then was, widely diffused with many local and other offices each depending on their own paper records and dealing with separate aspects of 'insurance' and 'welfare' benefit systems which used to be more clearly differentiated from each other, under different primary legislation with different entities responsible. The questions remains what is reasonable, but the answers given then may not necessarily hold good now."

This decision is, unsurprisingly, controversial and a direction has been given for a Tribunal of Commissioners to hear four appeals in October 2000 to determine whether this (and another smilar case *CIS/2498/1997*) are correctly decided or whether the traditional responsibility for separate disclosure is required by s.71.

Mental capacity
As noted above, questions of mental capacity have been raised both in relation to misrepresentations and failures to disclose. The issue is not without difficulty even though some basic guidance is contained in the case law reported above. 1.61

CSB/1093/1989 explores in some detail issues concerning mental capacity in overpayments cases. The particular question addressed was the extent to which claimants are entitled to escape the normal consequences of material misrepresentations by contending that they were mentally incapacitated at the time when they signed the relevant document.

The case concerned an overpayment of supplementary benefit which had arisen when, over a period of six months, the claimant misrepresented that her son was still a member of the family for benefit purposes when he had left school and had undertaken a Youth Training Scheme. It was argued on behalf of the claimant that her mental condition, combined with effects of anti-depressant drugs, was such that she could not be held responsible for putting her signature to the declarations in connection with the benefit claim. There is a discussion of the possibility of pleading *non est factum* (that the mind did not go with the pen with the result that the signature is to be treated as not having been made). The Commissioner stresses the narrow nature of the defence of *non est factum* and the difficulty of applying the doctrine to the realities of a modern social security system. The Commissioner indicates at paras 17 and 18 that he believes that the case of *Re Beaney, deceased* [1978] 1 W.L.R. 770, which was not concerned with social security at all, might be of assistance to tribunals. Mrs Beaney was an old lady whose health had been deteriorating for some time. She executed a transfer of a house to her eldest daughter in circumstances where all parties present at the signing of the document, including a solicitor who was an old friend of Mrs Beaney's late husband, thought that she understood what she was doing. Medical evidence, however, was that she had advanced senile dementia and her mental state was such that she could not have understood what she was doing. The two younger children sought a declaration that the transfer was void for want of capacity. The judge stated in his judgment that the degree or extent of understanding required in respect of any instrument is relative to the particular transaction which it is to effect. The more trivial the transaction, the lower the requisite degree of understanding. The Commissioner indicates that regard must be had to this test and that the key question is whether a claimant at the time of signing realised that he or she was signing a document in connection with a claim to benefit which could result in the payment of benefit. If the answer is negative, then s.71 cannot be applied to that claimant.

In difficult cases all the evidence will need to be considered over the period under review. So lucid letters written by the claimant about benefit in the relevant period will be relevant evidence of capacity. The most important evidence will be that of expert medical witnesses, whose views are to be preferred, as in *Re Beaney*, to the views of witnesses who are without medical qualifications.

In *Chief Adjudication Officer v. Sheriff*, Court of Appeal, May 4, 1995, *The Times*, May 10, 1995 was an appeal from a Commissioner's decision in *CIS/ 545/1992*. The Court of Appeal concluded that, even where a receiver has been appointed by the Court of Protection, a claimant who signs a claim form for benefit is capable of making a misrepresentation as to the facts upon which payment of benefit is based. Nor can such a person defeat a claim to repayment of overpaid benefit by arguing that he or she lacked capacity to make a representation. Nourse L.J. said:

> "If the representor need not know of the material fact misrepresented, I cannot see why should make any difference if she does not know that she is making a representation. That no doubt would make the misrepresentation more innocent. But it would not take it outside s.53(1) [now s.71(1)]. So that can be no ground for saying that the misrepresentation was not made by the claimant."

Millett LJ put it even more bluntly:

> ". . . it does not avail a recipient of benefit from whom the Secretary of State seeks repayment of benefit on the ground that he misrepresented a material fact to deny that he had mental capacity to make the representation."

The claimant's mental capacity may, however, be taken into account in considering whether it was reasonable to expect disclosure of a material fact: *CA/ 303/1992* (to be reported as *R(A)1/95*), where the test was said to be whether a reasonable man would have thought it was material to disclose the knowledge in question. The distinction made in *CA/303/1992* was that questions of mental capacity were said to be relevant only to the question of whether or not the claimant knew the fact which is was argued should have been disclosed. But once it is established that the claimant's mental capacity was sufficient for them to "know" the material fact, then mental capacity ceased to be relevant to the question of the duty to disclose. This does not appear to be consistent with the statements in *R(SB)40/84* suggesting that mental capacity is relevant both to knowledge of the material fact and the reasonableness of any failure to disclose.

The Commissioner in *CIS/12032/1996* has sought to reconcile this line of decision. In paragraph 16 he said:

> "I received detailed oral legal argument . . . on the extent to which, if at all, a claimant's mental state could show that there was no 'failure' to disclose. Among Commissioners' decisions cited to me were *R(SB)21/82*, paras 4(2), 13(1) and 19(5), *R(SB)40/84*, para. 11(1) and Appendix para 1 and *CA/303/ 92*, to be reported as *R(A)1/95*. In so far as the last of those decisions appears

(1992 c.5, s.71)

to state that mental state is never relevant to 'failure', then I consider that is inconsistent with earlier reported decisions, one of which *R(SB)40/84* does not appear to have been cited to the Commissioner. However, in so far as the earlier reported decisions do admit the relevance of mental state to 'failure' to disclose, I conclude, after a close examination of them, that such state is only relevant where it renders the claimant *wholly incapable* of appreciating the need to disclose the material fact of which he knows (see *e.g. R(SB)21/82*, para. 13(1)—psychotic chronic schizophrenia and *R(SB)40/84*—possible senility of 80 year old). Anything less will not suffice. I leave it to the new tribunal to decide whether the claimant's own and medical evidence in this case shows such a state of mind. Clearly, cogent evidence is needed, when the non-disclosure was of a comparatively elementary fact, not an esoteric one."

Material fact
The fact misrepresented or not disclosed must be "material". This will usually be determined by consideration of issues of causation (see below). But it seems right that a representation by a claimant that he or she is entitled to benefit, being a question of law, should only be treated as a material fact in so far as it amounts to a representation that the circumstances justifying the award of the benefit have not changed: see *CIS/156/1990* discussed below. However, if a claimant who made a representation that they were entitled to benefit when they *knew* they were not, such a representation would become a misrepresentation of fact since the claimant knew the representation of entitlement to be untrue.

1.62

In *R(SB)3/90* the Commissioner holds that there can still be a misrepresentation of a material fact even though there has been an earlier disclosure of that fact (para. 11) (discussed above).

However, where the misrepresentation in issue is the result of the signing of a declaration to the effect that the claimant has reported any fact affecting payment, great care will need to be taken by tribunal in considering whether there are good grounds for recovery. In *CSB/790/1988* the Commissioner held that the declaration made, for example, each time a person receives payment from a payment book is simply a declaration that the claimant had reported facts she understood should be reported as a result of reading the instructions in the order book. The declaration was held merely to guard against failure to disclose material facts and was of no assistance on the issue of misrepresentation. The key passage in the Commissioner's decision reads:

"The declaration on the order books . . . is as follows:
'I declare that I have read and *understand* all the instructions in this order book, that I have *correctly* reported any fact which could affect the amount of my payment and that I am entitled to the above sum.' (my emphasis).
What was the representation made in that declaration? It seems to me that it was no more than that the claimant had reported any fact she understood should be reported, as a result of reading the instructions, and imports the claimant's belief as to whether or not she had already informed 'the issuing office' of her child benefit. It was a representation as to what she believed. . . . The point turns on what was actually represented and not whether the representation was innocent or otherwise." (para. 10).

Two cases from Northern Ireland (where the requirements for recovery of overpayments are the same), *CI/89(WB)* and *C2/89(CB)*, concerned the receipt of child benefit for a child who had left school in circumstances where the claimant was not aware of this. Recovery was sought in reliance on a misrepresentation alleged to have been made when the claimant signed the order book to the effect that her circumstances had not changed. The Commissioner in Northern

Ireland refused to accept that such a declaration could be converted into a misrepresentation of material fact. The Commissioner says that "a misrepresentation of material fact must be just that". So it will be important for tribunals to ask themselves what material fact has been misrepresented by the signing of a particular statement. These decisions get perilously close to saying that declarations made to the best of a person's knowledge and belief do not amount to misrepresentations. Again tribunals will need to take considerable care not to jump to the conclusion that the circumstances in which a misrepresentation is made are not relevant to the issue of recovery under s.71. Decisions should also be clear as to the exact nature of the material fact the subject of the misrepresentation.

In *CIS/359/1990* the Commissioner considered *CSB/790/1988* and in paras 7 and 8, after quoting paragraph 10 of the earlier decision, said of it:

"I regret that I have to disagree with that restricted interpretation. I do not see how it could be said that the declaration was qualified and limited to what the claimant *believed* she had to disclose. Such a construction, it seems to me, is wholly artificial and at variance with the plan words of the declaration. A claimant who signs such a declaration specifically avers that he has 'correctly reported any fact which could affect the amount of my payment. . . .' In other words, he specifically warrants that the factual position is as he has reported it. There is no qualification such as 'as far as I am aware'. In fact, the claimant does even further and declares 'I am entitled to the above sum.'

Now, it could be said that the requirement that a claimant sign a declaration as all embracing as that asserting entitlement to the relevant sum, without which he will not be paid, is wholly unfair, particularly having regard to the technical issues sometimes involved; but so long as this requirement is imposed, and as long as the claimant in each case signs the undertaking, he is, in my judgment caught. Unless and until the Secretary of State removes this all embracing provision, each claimant will in practice be representing, not only that all material facts have been correctly reported, a not unreasonable requirement, but that he is entitled to the sum shown on the order, and if he is not, he will be guilty of a misrepresentation."

This decision warrants two comments. First, it is in conflict with *CSB/790/1988*. Both are decisions of Commissioners sitting alone. In such circumstances it is open to decision makers and tribunals to choose which they prefer and there is no obligation to prefer the later decision. Secondly, the Commissioner in *CIS/359/1990* does not address the question of whether a representation in the form "I am entitled to the above sum" is a representation of a material fact. There is a strong argument that such a representation is a representation of law and not of material fact, since entitlement depends on matching the facts to the statutory conditions of entitlement. The claimant can be expected to know about changes of fact affecting his or her circumstances, but cannot be expected to know how those facts interact with the often complex statutory conditions of entitlement.

The precise scope of the declaration attested by a signature to a declaration in the following terms accordingly remains unclear:

"I have read and understand all the instructions in this order book, that I have correctly reported ANY facts which could affect the amount of my payment and that I am entitled to the above sum."

In *CS/156/1990* the Commissioner states explicitly that a declaration that a person is entitled to a sum of benefit cannot amount to a misrepresentation of a material fact because entitlement is a matter of law and not of fact (para. 5).

The particular circumstances may, however, make the presentation of an order containing such a declaration a misrepresentation of a material fact as when a person who is not the claimant presents the order for encashment. That amounts to a representation that the presenter is the person to whom the order book relates or who has the authority of the beneficiary to seek the encashment of the order.

CIS/102/1993 supports the view both that a representation "I am entitled to the above sum" is a representation of law and not of fact, and that there can be a representation of a material fact by conduct where a person continues to cash orders in an order book knowing that their entitlement to benefit has been reviewed in order to withdraw it.

In *CSB/329/1990* the Commissioner was faced with a situation in which an elderly Asian who spoke little English continued to sign orders to the effect that there had been no change in his circumstances when two non-dependants had moved into his home. The Commissioner says,

"It seems to me to be beyond all question that there *was* a misrepresentation in this case. I am well aware of the Northern Ireland cases to which the claimant's representative referred at the appeal tribunal hearing. Those cases are not, of course, in any way binding upon me. I have never been disposed to follow them. They cannot be reconciled with well-known decisions of the United Kingdom Commissioners." (para. 5).

The significance of this form of declaration has now been considered by the Court of Appeal in *Jones v. Chief Adjudications Officer* [1994] 1 All E.R. 225. The majority of the Court of Appeal considered that every time a person signs a declaration in this form, they make a representation that there are no new facts known to them at the time which affect the amount of their benefit but which they have not reported. That representation is limited to disclosure of material facts known to the applicant, but Dillon L.J. goes further to say that the representation is not further limited "to what a reasonable man would think would affect the amount of the payment."

The dissenting judge, Evans L.J., *obiter*, confirms that a declaration of entitlement (". . . and that I am entitled to the above sum") cannot be a misrepresentation since it is a representation of law and not of a material fact.

The appeal in the case of *Sharples v. Chief Adjudication Officer* [1994] 1 All E.R. 225 (heard together with the *Jones* appeal) was much more straightforward. There, Sharples had signed a declaration containing the sentence "As far as I know, the information on this form is true and complete." Since the material fact which affected his benefit entitlement was not known to him—the inheritance by his partner of insurance policies—he was protected by the qualification to the declaration he had signed.

In *CP/34/1993* and *CIS/145/1994* the Commissioner holds that where a claimant signs an order book confirming that all material facts have been reported, it does not matter that a relevant fact is not at the time known to the claimant. The effect of the declaration is to convert what would be a failure to disclose a material fact if it was known into a misrepresentation, where it is the error of fact rather than the knowledge of it which is crucial. The appeal from *CIS/145/1994* under the name *Franklin v. Chief Adjudication Officer*, The Times, December 29, 1995, has now ruled that an income support claimant who declared that she had correctly reported any fact which could affect the amount of her benefit was not guilty of a misrepresentation for failing to report facts which were not known to her. The *Franklin* decision follows the *Jones* case, which held that the representation made on signing an order book was limited to facts known to the representor at the time. In other words, it was a representation that the claimant had reported any facts known to them which might affect their benefit entitlement. This view is followed by the Commissioners in *CSB/18/1992* and *CIS/674/1994*. In the latter decision, a distinction was made between responses to specific questions, where ignorance of the true facts does not prevent recovery on the grounds of misrepresentation, and responses to non-specific questions where knowledge of the true facts is a prerequisite to the making of a misrepresentation.

A further limitation on the ambit of the representation made by signing the declaration on a payable order is suggested, *obiter*, by the Commssioner in *CG/662/1998*, *CG/1567/1998* and *CG/2112/1998*. In these cases, an indefinite award of invalid care allowance had been made to the claimant in respect of care for a person who had been awarded a disability living allowance for a fixed period. Contrary to the instruction at the back of the order book, the claimant had not reported the non-renewal of the disability living allowance and an overpayment of invalid care allowance had occurred. The Commissioner decides on the basis of the majority decision in *Jones* that by signing the order book declaration, the claimant had misrepresented that he had correctly reported any fact that could affect the amount of benefit payable. The relevant fact was the ending of the award of the disability living allowance *and* its non-replacement. However, he went on to suggest that the representation made by signing the declaration was limited not only to facts known to the claimant, as in *Jones*, but also to facts that had not already been reported on the signatory's behalf or otherwise. But this as subject to the conditions set out in para. 29 of *R(SB)15/87*, namely that "(a) the information was given to the relevant benefit office; (b) the claimant was aware that the information had been so given; and (c) in the circumstances it was reasonable for the claimant to believe that if was unnecessary for him to take any action himself." In his view these conditions had to be strictly applied. Thus, on the facts of these cases, while the existence of *accurate* information in the computer system might be enough to satisfy (a) (it was accepted that the ICA Unit both knew that disability living allowance had been awarded for a fixed term and had the means of knowing (through the Benefits Agency's computer records) that a renewal claim had not been successful to the required extent), (b) was not satisfied because the claimant could not have known, at the time he signed the order book, whether or not the information was accurate. In addition (c) was not met because the Benefits Agency was perfectly entitled to ask the claimant to report facts as a means of checking the accuracy of information held on computer and the fact that the Agency apparently did not use the computer at all in these circumstances did not make it reasonable for the claimant not to follow the instruction in the order book. The view expressed by the Commissioner is *obiter* and did not assist the claimant in this case but might apply on other facts. For example, if the claimant could show that he knew that the appropriate benefit office had the correct information, it might well be reasonable for him to take no further action, depending on the particular circumstances of the case.

Missing documents

1.63 Arguments concerning missing documents are often raised in appeals concerning overpayments. *R(IS)11/92* now provides detailed guidance on the principles to be applied in such cases. In this case the Commissioner confronts what he describes as "a certain mythology" building up around the old prize case *The Ophelia* [1915] P. 192 and [1916] 2 A.C. 206. *The Ophelia* concerned the practice of "spoliation of documents" that is the deliberate destruction of documents and the presumption that the contents of the documents destroyed by their holder are contrary to their claims. The case has been relied upon before a number of tribunals to found an argument that where the Department has destroyed documents they hold, the contents of those documents are to be presumed to be helpful to the claims made by claimants.

(1992 c.5, s.71)

The Commissioner at paragraph 23 reviews the evidence before him concerning the "weeding" of files. The information in that paragraph is no more than the Commissioner's findings of fact in the case on the evidence given to him and should not be taken as reflecting universal practice. In every case, it will be important for tribunals to hear some evidence on what the practices adopted in the particular office having the conduct of the claim. What does seem clear, however, is that there is a general practice of weeding files after 18 months of documents which appear no longer to have relevance to any current claim.

The Commissioner then turns his attention to the implications of the doctrine of spoliation in *The Ophelia* for tribunals and states a number of important propositions:

- The case seems to have passed out of current thinking (para. 28). *The Ophelia* is not a binding authority, but is only of persuasive authority. It is, however, not to be lightly disregarded if the principle it enshrines accords with common sense in the social security jurisdiction (para. 29).

- The assertion that *The Ophelia* supports the proposition that documents which have been destroyed by the Department must be presumed to support the claimant's case is mythology. Spoliation had a technical meaning and is not the same as simple destruction. The key distinction is between deliberate destruction of documents *with the intention of destroying evidence*, and the deliberate destruction of documents *where there is no such intention*. Adverse presumptions come into place only in the former context (para. 30).

- There is no such thing as "*The Ophelia* principle"; it is merely a case illustrating the application of a principle of evidence applicable in the prize jurisdiction. The underlying principle, however, remains good law. Reliance on the rule that destroyed documents must be construed against the destroyer of those documents depends on the establishment of some reprehensible act or omission by the destroyer (paras 31 and 32).

The Commissioner goes on to note that that where documents have been destroyed, then tribunal will need to rely on secondary evidence concerning the contents of the destroyed documents; such evidence might be oral or written. Tribunals can, of course, admit any evidence which they regard as relevant and helpful.

The Commissioner summarised his conclusion on *The Ophelia* in Appendix III of the decision; paragraphs (3) and (4) bear quotation:

"(3) The strong presumptions which are to be drawn against a party who destroys documents *only* fall to be drawn where the documents were destroyed with the intention of destroying evidence. (The intention to destroy evidence will, of course, be almost impossible to establish where the destroying party is aware of copies of the destroyed documents). Where there is no such intention, the only detriment to which the destroying party lays himself open is the loss of the corroboration which the documents might have afforded him.

(4) Accordingly, in the social security jurisdiction *no* presumptions fall to be drawn where the Department of Social Security has destroyed documents with the intention of clearing storage space or simply because no point can be seen in retaining such documents."

Tribunals should have regard to where the burden of proof lies in cases with a history. In overpayments cases, it is for the decision maker to show that the grounds for recovering any overpayment exist. This in turn general required the

Causation

1.64 Under section 71 the overpayment must be "in consequence of the misrepresentation or failure to disclose" and so there must be a clear causal connection between the misrepresentation or failure to disclose and the overpayment: *R(SB)3/81*, *R(SB)21/82* and *R(SB)15/87*. So, for example, if a clear finding of fact could be made that an overpayment was the result of an administrative error by the Department unconnected with any misrepresentation or failure to disclose, there would be no causal link between the misrepresentation or failure to disclose and the overpayment, which would not be recoverable. But it seems that failure of an administrative procedure for notification between benefit sections will not break the chain of causation: *CSB/64/1986*. Arguments that a breakdown of internal communication between parts of the Department have been met with the consistent arguments that the test of causation is whether, if the claimant had disclosed or not misrepresented a material fact, the Secretary of State would have made payment of the benefit. If the answer is that he would not, then the necessary causal connection is made: *R(SB)3/90* and *Duggan v. Chief Adjudication Officer*, appendix to *R(SB)13/89*. But if it can be shown that the inter-office communication system did operate but was not then used to initiate any reviews, there would be a break in the chain of causation: *R(SB)15/87* and *CIS/159/1990* and *CSIS/7/1994*. See also *CIS/5899/1999* discussed in relation to the obligation to disclose material facts.

The scope of *Duggan* where there has been an error or neglect by an adjudication officer is discussed in *CIS/2447/1998*. The claimant stated on her income support claim form in November 1993 that her partner was not working. In October 1995 it came to light that he had always been in full-time work. The claimant's income support award had been reviewed in March 1994 following the birth of her son. It was argued that any overpayment after that review resulted not from the misrepresentation on the claim form but from the adjudication officer's negligence. This was because the adjudication officer had failed to identify any basis for the claimant's continued entitlement to income support after that time. She was no longer exempted from the condition of being available for work on the ground of pregnancy and she was not a single parent. The tribunal rejected this argument, holding that the circumstances were not distinguishable from those in *Duggan*. The Court of Appeal's decision in that case was closely related to its particular facts. It had not laid down a general rule that, whatever the extent or nature of the error by an adjudication officer, it did not remove the causative effect of some earlier failure to disclose or misrepresentation by a claimant. All the circumstances of the case had to be looked at. For example, if in the present case, the claimant had later told the income support office that she had won £10,000 and the adjudication officer had mistakenly determined that that did not affect entitlement to income support, the continued payment of benefit could not be said to have as even one of its causes the initial misrepresentation that her partner was not in full-time work. However, the actual facts of this case did not fall into that category. The information that her baby had been born would not on its own have inevitably led to to the conclusion that entitlement to income support would cease. Even though the claimant might have become a person required to be available for work, her entitlement to income support would only have ceased if she had, for example, refused to make herself available for work. The adjudication officer's failure to investigate such issues was an additional, but not the sole, cause of the overpayment and, as such, did not break the chain of causation between the initial misrepresentation and the overpayment. As had been noted in *CF/3532/1997* adjudicating bodies have no jurisdiction to apportion responsibility for overpayments between a number of parties on the basis of a number of causes of the overpayment. This is, however, something the Secretary of State might take into account in determining whether to seek recovery of all or part of a recoverable overpayment.

An example of an error by the adjudication officer which did exonerate the claimant can be found in *CIS/222/1991*. The Commissioner holds that if the claimant's answers on the claim form were plainly inconsistent and ambiguous, this put the adjudication officer on notice to investigate the position. If this was not done, any overpayment was not recoverable as it was due to error on the part of the Department rather than a misrepresentation by the claimant. Here the information *on the claim form* should have triggered investigation by the adjudication officer, but the adjudication officer chose not to resolve those conflicts before awarding benefit.

Note that if income support is paid while a claimant is waiting for a decision on entitlement for another benefit and arrears of the other benefit are paid for this period, any excess income support cannot be recovered under this section, since it does not result from a failure to disclose. But section 74 and the Overpayments Regulations will operate to allow the excess to be deducted from the arrears of the other benefit or recovered from the recipient.

The situation dealt with in *CIS/13742/1996* is a particular illustration of the fact that the overpayment has to result from the misrepresentation or failure to disclose. The claimant and her partner (who were now separated) had each claimed benefit as single people while they were living together as husband and wife (and had thus been paid more benefit in total than that to which they would have been entitled had they claimed as a couple). The adjudication officer decided that the total amount of the overpayment was recoverable from the claimant. However the Commissioner holds that this was incorrect. Any overpayment to the partner was not due to any action or failure to act on the part of the claimant but due to the fact that he had held himself out as a single person. Thus the claimant was not the cause of the overpayment to the partner and as a result recovery of any such overpayment could not be sought from her. But had the claimant herself been overpaid benefit? From November 21, 1983 the claimant could have claimed benefit in respect of herself and her family (up to November 21, 1983 the claim could only have been made by her partner). Thus if the claimant could show that such a claim would have been successful, there would be no question of an overpayment because she would have received less benefit than she was entitled to. If, however, she could not have qualified as the claimant for the family, she would be liable to repay *all* the benefit that she had received in the relevant period. The Commissioner did, however, comment that in his view it would be inequitable for the Secretary of State to require her to repay more than the amount of the actual excess benefit paid.

The question of recovery of an overpayment from one member of a couple where both had been claiming income support separately was also considered in *CIS/619/1997*. The Commissioner agrees with *CIS/13742/1996* that unless there had been a review of the decision awarding benefit to the other member of the couple (in this case the husband), the overpayment, and any offset against it under the Overpayments Regulations could only be considered in connection with the claimant's own claim. It was therefore incumbent on the tribunal to ascertain the position on the husband's claim (which they had not done).

The amount of the overpayment
It is for the adjudicating authorities to determine the amount of the overpayment. 1.65

In *CS/366/1993* the Commissioner gives advice on the level of proof of payment of a benefit recovery of which is being sought. This is an issue which can come up in overpayment appeals, when a claimant either directly or indirectly puts in issue whether they have ever received the money which the adjudication officer, or now decision maker, says is recoverable. The Commissioner reminds tribunals that the burden of proof is on the balance of probabilities. Where there is evidence of entitlement to and payment of benefit, that may be sufficient to show that the benefit was paid. It certainly is in the absence of any challenge by the claimant. Equally, no higher burden will lie with the adjudication officer if the claimant does not adduce evidence that he or she did not receive the benefit, but simply asked the adjudication officer to prove that the benefit was paid.

A schedule showing how the overpayment is calculated is normally included in the appeal papers, but great care must be taken in simply adopting these, especially if there is any variation of the decision under appeal. The tribunal may, for example, find that an overpayment is recoverable for a different period. This will affect the amount recoverable. The need for tribunals to state expressly the sum which is recoverable and how it is calculated was stressed in *R(SB)9/85*. This advice was repeated in *R(SB)11/86* where the Commissioner helpfully approves the practice of leaving a difficult recalculation to the adjudication officer *provided that* it is made clear that the claimant or the adjudication officer may refer the matter back to the tribunal in the event of any particular difficulty or disagreement arising. The approach tribunals should adopt is to recalculate benefit in the light of the facts as found by them to determine the amount of the overpayment: *R(SB)20/84* and *R(SB)10/85(T)*. In *R(SB)11/86* it was held that underpayments of benefit during the relevant period could be taken into account, but in relation to non-means tested benefits, at least, this may need to be qualified in the light of reg. 13 of the Overpayments Regulations.

A controversial question under the pre-April 1987 law was how far it was possible to take account of underpayments of benefit against the overpayment. Reg. 13(b) of the Overpayments Regulations provides that from the gross amount of the overpayment is to be deducted any additional amount of income support which should have been awarded on the basis of the claim as originally presented or with the addition of the facts misrepresented or not disclosed. This allows a somewhat more extensive set-off than under the old law. *CSIS/8/1995* holds that reg. 13 makes it mandatory for an adjudication officer to consider the question of a possible underpayment of benefit of income support when calculating the overpayment. A tribunal must also consider the question of any offset before it reaches a decision on the recoverability of the overpayment; it cannot merely decide that an overpayment is recoverable and then refer the question of any offset back to the adjudication officer: *CSG/357/1997*.

R(IS)5/92 confirms that the reg. 13(b) deduction from the amount of the overpayment is not limited to the period after the beginning of the overpayment but can go back to the date of claim. In addition, *CSIS/8/1995* points out that the overpayment may relate to an entirely different benefit. Again, there need be no connection between the respective periods. But the examination of the additional amount which would have been payable must be based on the claim as originally presented, or with the addition of the material facts misrepresented or not disclosed. In *R(IS)5/92* the Commissioner construes "claim as presented" in reg 13(b) as including facts that would be discovered by "any reasonable enquiry . . . prompted by the claim form." This is applied in *CIS/136/1992* to require the adjudication officer to consider an award of income support on hardship grounds. *CIS/137/1992* points out that reg. 13 is concerned with deductions from an overpayment and so only comes into play after the overpayment had been calculated. The review which results in a decision as to the amount of benefit that ought to have been paid is therefore to be carried out without any fetter being imposed by reg. 13.

Another problem now dealt with by regulations arises when the misrepresentation or failure to disclose is of capital resources. If it emerged that a claimant who had been in receipt of income support or family credit for a few years throughout had capital of £1.00 over the limit, it would be most unfair to require repayment of the whole amount of benefit. If the capital had been properly taken into account, so that benefit was not initially awarded, the capital would immediately have been reduced below the limit in order to provide for living expenses. So the Commissioner applied the "diminishing capital" principle: *CSB/53/1981, Chief Supplementary Benefit Officer v. Leary*, appendix to *R(SB)6/85* and *R(SB)15/85*. The position is now governed by reg. 14 of the Overpayments Regulations. This provides for the reduction of the figure of capital resources at quarterly intervals from the beginning of the period of the overpayment period by the amount overpaid in income support or family credit in the previous quarter. No other reduction of the actual amount of capital resources is allowed: reg. 14(2). Under the Commissioners' approach the notional reduction had to be made week by week. It will be considerably easier to make the calculation at 13 week intervals, but the tendency will be for smaller reductions of the overpayment to be produced.

It is for the decision maker to prove the existence of the amount of capital taken into account in calculating an overpayment: *R(SB)21/82*. Here, sums had suddenly appeared in building society accounts and there was no evidence where they had come from. The Commissioner commends the adoption of a lower figure of overpayment rather than a higher one based on the assumption that the capital assets had not been possessed before any evidence existed about them. The Commissioner in *R(SB)43/83* agrees strongly on the burden of proof, but points out that if the person concerned was alive and failed to give any proper explanation of the origin of such sums, adverse inferences could be drawn against them, enabling the adjudication officer to discharge the burden of proof. He goes on to hold that the estate of a deceased person should be in the same position. Therefore, a heavy responsibility devolved on the executor to make every reasonable enquiry as to the origin of the money. But if after such efforts there was no evidence where the money came from from the burden of proof on the adjudication officer would not have been discharged.

Care needs to be taken by tribunals in the way in which matters relating to the amount of the overpayment are handled. As noted above, *R(SB)11/86* helpfully approved the practice of giving directions for the recalculation of the overpayment, while making it clear that either party is free to return to the tribunal for a determination by the tribunal of any disputed issue. *CSB/083/1991* illustrates how things can go wrong. A tribunal concluded that there had been a recoverable overpayment but went on to say, "The amount of overpayment is therefore recoverable. Actual amount to be rechecked, and this matter is therefore adjourned."

The claimant took issue with the decision on recoverability and appealed to the Commissioner who held that the determination of the tribunal did not constitute a decision and consequently the Commissioner was without jurisdiction. It is unclear whether a decision which followed more closely the guidance in *R(SB)11/86* would constitute a decision. On the one hand, all the ingredients to convert the directions into a decision would be present, but on the other, the possibility of the parties returning to the tribunal suggests that there is not yet a final determination of all the relevant issues before the tribunal. A claimant who continued to dispute the recoverability of any overpayment is not in a good position to agree a recalculation of the overpayment. Those receiving applications for leave to appeal in such cases may need to consider carefully whether there is a full decision of the tribunal which will attract a right of appeal.

In *CIS/442/1992* the Commissioner reminds tribunals of the proper procedure to follow when the calculation of the amount of the overpayment is initially left for determination by the parties. Where reference back to the tribunal is necessary, then that reference should be to the same tribunal which dealt with the issue of liability (para. 5). Should it prove necessary to refer the case back to a differently constituted tribunal, then both the issue of liability and the issue of calculation will need to be considered at the adjourned hearing (para. 7). A different tribunal should only hear the case if satisfied that it is not practicable to reconvene the original tribunal (para. 7).

An argument was raised that s.53(1A) of the SSA 1986 (now s.71(2) of the Administration Act) outlawed the practice of remitting the calculation of the amount of the overpayment in the manner set out in *R(SB)11/86*. The Commissioner concludes that this argument is misplaced and that the new subsection did nothing to disturb "the existing practice of remitting matters of quantification" (para. 8).

In *R. v. Secretary of State for Social Security, ex parte Britnell* [1991] 1 W.L.R. 198, the House of Lords held that the power in reg. 20 of the Overpayments Regulations to apply the recovery provisions of s.71 to any amount recoverable under any enactment repealed by the Social Security Act 1986 as if it was an amount recoverable under s.71 was valid and wide enough to encompass recovery of overpaid unemployment benefit in 1973–74 from a subsequent entitlement to supplementary benefit.

Note that in certain circumstances duplicated benefit may be recovered from a benefit due in another Member State of the European Union: *R(SB)1/91* and *R(SB)3/91*.

Automated credit transfers

1.66 Subsection (4) provides an independent ground for recovering overpayments resulting from the use of payments to a bank account or other similar account. Recovery will only be available if the claimant received, before agreeing to such method of payment, notice in the form specified in reg. 11 of the Overpayments Regulations. These overpayments arise most often in cases of child benefit.

Tax credits: substitution of subsections (8)–(9)

1.67 Section 71(8)–(9) is, with effect from October 5, 1999, by virtue of s.2 and Part IV, paragraph 10 of Schedule 2 to the Tax credits Act 1999 to be read as follows in any case where the overpayment was made in respect of tax credits:

"(8) An amount recoverable under subsection (1) above in any year of assessment—

(a) Shall be treated for the purposes of Part VI of the Taxes Management Act 1970 (collection and recovery) as if it were tax charged in an assessment and due and payable;

(b) Shall be treated for the purposes of section 203(2)(a) of the Income and Corporation Taxes Act 1988 (PAYE) as if it were an underpayment of tax for a previous year of assessment.

(8A) Where—

(a) An amount paid in respect of a claim is recoverable under subsection (1) above; and

(b) A penalty has been imposed under section 9(1) of the Tax Credits Act 1999 (penalties for fraud etc.) on the ground that a person fraudulently or negligently made an incorrect statement or declaration in connection with that claim, the amount shall carry interest at the rate applicable from the date on which it becomes recoverable until payment.

(9) The rate applicable for the purposes of subsection (8A) above shall be the rate from time to time prescribed under section 178 of the Finance Act 1989 for those purposes."

A useful book
A detailed guide on overpayment is P Stagg, *Overpayments and Recovery of Social Security Benefits*, Legal Action Group, 1996, ISBN 0 905 09973 7

1.68

[¹ Overpayments out of social fund

71ZA.—(1) Subject to subsection (2) below, section 71 above shall apply in relation to social fund payments to which this section applies as it applies in relation to payments made in respect of benefits to which that section applies.

1.69

[²(2) Section 71 above as it so applies shall have effect as if the following provisions were omitted, namely—
  (a) in paragraph (a) of subsection (5) and subsection (5A), the words "reversed or varied on an appeal or";
  (b) in paragraph (b) of subsection (5), the words "appeal or"; and
  (c) subsections (7), (10A) and (10B).]
(3) This section applies to social fund payments such as are mentioned in section 138(1)(b) of the Contributions and Benefits Act.]

AMENDMENTS

1. Social Security Act 1998, s.75(1) (October 5, 1998).
2. Note that until ss.9, 10 and 38 of the 1998 Act come into force, subs. (2) is substituted by para. 8 of Sched. 6 to the Act.

GENERAL NOTE

Section 75(2) of the Social Security Act 1998 provides that s.71ZA applies to social fund overpayment decisions made on or after October 5, 1998.

1.70

[¹Jobseekers's allowance

Recovery of jobseeker's allowance: severe hardship cases

71A.—(1) Where—
  (a) a severe hardship direction is revoked; and
  (b) it is determined by an adjudication officer that—
    (i) whether fraudulently or otherwise, any person has misrepresented, or failed to disclose, any material fact; and
    (ii) in consequence of the failure or misrepresentation, payment of a jobseeker's allowance has been made during the relevant period to the person to whom the direction related,
an adjudication officer may determine that the Secretary of State is entitled to recover the amount of the payment.
  (2) In this section—

1.71

"severe hardship direction" means a direction given under section 16 of the Jobseekers Act 1995; and

"the relevant period" means—
  (a) if the revocation is under section 16(3)(a) of that Act, the period begining with the date of the change of circumstances and ending with the date of the revocation; and
  (b) if the revocation is under section 16(3)(b) or (c) of that Act, the period during which the direction was in force.

(3) Where a severe hardship direction is revoked, the Secretary of State may certify whether there has been misrepresentation of a material fact or failure to disclose a material fact.

(4) If the Secretary of State certifies that there has been such misrepresentation or failure to disclose, he may certify—
  (a) who made the misrepresentation or failed to make the disclosure; and
  (b) whether or not a payment of jobseeker's allowance has been made in consequence of the misrepresentation or failure.

(5) If the Secretary of State certifies that a payment has been made, he may certify the period during which a jobseeker's allowance would not have been paid but for the misrepresentation or failure to disclose.

(6) A certificate under this section shall be conclusive as to any matter certified.

(7) Subsections (3) and (6) to (10) of section 71 above apply to a jobseeker's allowance recoverable under subsection (1) above as they apply to a jobseeker's allowance recoverable under section 71(1) above.

(8) The other provisions of section 71 above do not apply to a jobseeker's allowance recoverable under subsection (1) above.]

AMENDMENT

1. Jobseekers Act 1995, s.18 (October 7, 1996).

GENERAL NOTE

1.72 Section 16 of the Jobseekers Act 1995 enables the Secretary of State to direct that a person under the age of 18 is to qualify for JSA in order to avoid severe hardship. The direction may be revoked on the ground of change of circumstances (s.16(3)(a)) or on the ground that the young person has failed to pursue an opportunity, or rejected an offer, of training without good cause (s.16(3)(b)) or on the ground that mistake as to or ignorance of a material fact led to the determination that severe hardship would result if JSA was not paid (s.16(3)(c)). A special provision is needed for recovery in cases of misrepresentation or failure to disclose because the revocation of the direction is not a review which can found action under s.71 and it appears that it does not enable the decision on entitlement to JSA to be reviewed for any period before the date of the revocation. Although the determination is made by the adjudication officer under subs. (1), the Secretary of State's certificate is conclusive on almost every issue (subs. (3) to (6)). The provisions of s.71 about the mechanics of recovery apply.

Special provision as to recovery of income support

1.73 72.—[1. . .]

(1992 c.5, s.72)

AMENDMENT

1. Repealed by Jobseekers Act 1995, Sched. 3 (October 7, 1996).

Overlapping benefits—general

73.—(1) Regulations may provide for adjusting benefit as defined in section 122 of the Contributions and Benefits Act [¹, or a contribution-based jobseeker's allowance] which is payable to or in respect of any person, or the conditions for [² receipt of that benefit] where—
  (a) there is payable in his case any such pension or allowance as is described in subsection (2) below; or
  (b) the person is, or is treated under the regulations as, undergoing medical or other treatment as an in-patient in a hospital or similar institution.

(2) Subsection (1)(a) above applies to any pension, allowance or benefit payable out of public funds (including any other benefit as so defined, whether it is of the same or a different description) which is payable to or in respect of—
  (a) the person referred to in subsection (1);
  (b) that person's wife or husband;
  (c) any child or adult dependent of that person; or
  (d) the wife or husband of any adult dependant of that person.

(3) Where but for regulations made by virtue of subsection (1)(a) above two persons would both be entitled to an increase of benefit in respect of a third person, regulations may make provision as to their priority.

[³(4) Regulations may provide for adjusting—
  (a) benefit as defined in section 122 of the Contributions and Benefits Act; or
  (b) a contribution-based jobseeker's allowance,
payable to or in respect of any person where there is payable in his case any such benefit as is described in subsection (5) below.]

(5) Subsection (4) above applies to any benefit payable under the legislation of any member State other than the United Kingdom which is payable to or in respect of—
  (a) the person referred to in that subsection;
  (b) that person's wife or husband;
  (c) any child or adult dependent of that person; or
  (d) the wife or husband of any adult dependant of that person.

AMENDMENTS

1. Jobseekers Act 1995, Sched. 2, para. 49(2)(a) (June 11, 1996)
2. Jobseekers Act 1995, Sched. 2, para. 49(2)(b) (June 11, 1996)
3. Jobseekers Act 1995, Sched. 2, para. 49(3) (June 11, 1996)

DERIVATION

SSA 1975, s.85 as amended.

GENERAL NOTE

See the Hospital In-Patients Regulations and Overlapping Benefits Regulations.

Income support and other payments

74.—(1) Where—
  (a) a payment by way of prescribed income is made after the date which is the prescribed date in relation to the payment; and
  (b) it is determined that an amount which has been paid by way of income support [¹or an income-based jobseeker's allowance] would not have been paid if the payment had been made on the prescribed date,

the Secretary of State shall be entitled to recover that amount from the person to whom it was paid.

(2) Where—
  (a) a prescribed payment which apart from this subsection falls to be made from public funds in the United Kingdom or under the law of any other member State is not made on or before the date which is the prescribed date in relation to the payment; and
  (b) it is determined that an amount ("the relevant amount") has been paid by way of income support [¹or an income-based jobseeker's allowance] that would not have been paid if the payment mentioned in paragraph (a) above had been made on the prescribed date,

then—
  (i) in the case of a payment from public funds in the United Kingdom, the authority responsible for making it may abate it by the relevant amount; and
  (ii) in the case of any other payment, the Secretary of State shall be entitled to receive the relevant amount out of the payment.

(3) Where—
  (a) a person (in this subsection referred to as A) is entitled to any prescribed benefit for any period in respect of another person (in this subsection referred to as B); and
  (b) either—
    (i) B has received income support [¹or an income-based jobseeker's allowance] for that period; or
    (ii) B was, during that period, a member of the same family as some person other than A who received income support [¹ or an income-based jobseeker's allowance] for that period; and
  (c) the amount of the income support [¹or an income-based jobseeker's allowance] has been determined on the basis that A has not made payments for the maintenance of B at a rate equal to or exceeding the amount of the prescribed benefit,

the amount of the prescribed benefit may, at the discretion of the authority administering it, be abated by the amount by which the amounts paid by way of income support [¹or an income-based jobseeker's allowance] exceed what it is determined that they would have been had A, at the time the amount of the income support [¹or an income-based jobseeker's allowance] was determined, been making payments for the maintenance of B at a rate equal to the amount of the prescribed benefit.

(1992 c.5, s.74)

(4) Where an amount could have been recovered by abatement by virtue of subsection (2) or (3) above but has not been so recovered, the Secretary of State may recover it otherwise than by way of abatement—
   (a) in the case of an amount which could have been recovered by virtue of subsection (2) above, from the person to whom it was paid; and
   (b) in the case of an amount which could have been recovered by virtue of subsection (3) above, from the person to whom the prescribed benefit in question was paid.

(5) Where a payment is made in a currency other than sterling, its value in sterling shall be determined for the purposes of this section in accordance with regulations.

AMENDMENT

1. Jobseekers Act 1995, Sched. 2, para. 50 (October 7, 1996).

DERIVATION

Social Security Act 1986, s.27.

1.77

DEFINITION

"prescribed"—see s.191.

GENERAL NOTE

Most of this section was originally, in substance, s.12 of the Supplementary Benefits Act 1976. There are changes in form from the old s.12, but the overall aim is the same, to prevent a claimant from getting a double payment when other sources of income are not paid on time. This is an important provision, which is often overlooked. It now extends to income-based JSA as well as to income support.

Subsection (1)

Prescribed income is defined in reg. 7(1) of the Social Security (Payments on account, Overpayments and Recovery) Regulations 1988 ("the Overpayments Regulations") as any income which is to be taken into account under Part V of the Income Support (General) Regulations or Part VIII of the Jobseeker's Allowance Regulations. The prescribed date under reg. 7(2) is, in general, the first day of the period to which that income relates. If as a result of that income being paid after the prescribed date, more income support or income-based JSA is paid than would have been paid if the income had been paid on the prescribed date, the excess may be recovered. Note that the right to recover is absolute and does not depend on lack of care on the claimant's part, or on the effect of this section having been pointed out. That approach is confirmed in *CIS/625/1991*, where the Commissioner rejected the argument that there had to be an investigation of what an adjudication officer would in practice have done if the income had been paid on time. An example would be where a claimant has not been paid part-time earnings when they were due and as a result has been paid income support on the basis of having no earnings. Once the arrears of wages are received, the excess benefit would be recoverable. Late payment of most social security benefits is covered in subss. (2) and (4), but can also come within subs. (1). For instance, if a claim is made for child benefit and while a decision is awaited income support is paid without any deduction for the amount of the expected child benefit, then if arrears of child benefit are eventually paid in full

1.78

(*i.e.* the abatement procedure of subs. (2) does not work) the "excess" income support for the period covered by the arrears is recoverable under subs. (1) or (4).

It is essential that the dates on which prescribed income was due to be paid and on what dates due payments would have affected income support entitlement should be determined *(R(SB) 28/85* and *CIS/625/1991)*.

Subsection (2)

1.79   Prescribed payments are listed in reg. 8(1) of the Overpayments Regulations and include most social security benefits, training allowances and social security benefits from other E.C. countries. As under the excess income support or JSA. If the abatement mechanism breaks down, the Secretary of State may recover the excess under subs. (4). Under s.71(8)(c), amounts may be recovered by deduction from most benefits.

Subsection (4)

1.80   See notes to subss. (2) & (3).

Subsection (5)

1.81   *R(SB) 28/85* had revealed problems in valuing a payment of arrears in a foreign currency which might cover quite a long period during which exchange rates varied. This provision authorises regulations to be made to deal with the conversion. See reg. 10 of the Payments Regulations, which appears to require the actual net amount received to be taken into account, reversing the effect of *R(SB) 28/85*.

[1 Payment of benefit where maintenance payments collected by Secretary of State

1.82   **74A.**—(1) This section applies where—

(a) a person ("the claimant") is entitled to a benefit to which this section applies;

(b) the Secretary of State is collecting periodical payments of child or spousal maintenance made in respect of the claimant or a member of the claimant's family; and

(c) the inclusion of any such periodical payment in the claimant's relevant income would, apart from this section, have the effect of reducing the amount of the benefit to which the claimant is entitled.

(2) The Secretary of State may, to such extent as he considers appropriate, treat any such periodical payment as not being relevant income for the purposes of calculating the amount of benefit to which the claimant is entitled.

(3) The Secretary of State may, to the extent that any periodical payment collected by him is treated as not being relevant income for those purposes, retain the whole or any part of that payment.

(4) Any sum retained by the Secretary of State under subsection (3) shall be paid by him into the Consolidated Fund.

(5) In this section—

"child" means a person under the age of 16;

"child maintenance", "spousal maintenance" and "relevant income" have such meaning as may be prescribed;

"family" means—

(a) a married or unmarried couple;

(b) a married or unmarried couple and a member of the same household for whom one of them is, or both are, responsible and who is a child or a person of a prescribed description;

(c) except in prescribed circumstances, a person who is not a member of a married or unmarried couple and a member of the same household for whom that person is responsible and who is a child or a person of a prescribed description;

"married couple" means a man and woman who are married to each other and are members of the same household; and

"unmarried couple" means a man and woman who are not married to each other but are living together as husband and wife otherwise than in prescribed circumstances.

(6) For the purposes of this section, the Secretary of State may by regulations make provision as to the circumstances in which—

(a) persons are to be treated as being or not being members of the same household;

(b) one person is to be treated as responsible or not responsible for another.

(7) The benefits to which this section applies are income support, an income-based jobseeker's allowance and such other benefits (if any) as may be prescribed.]

AMENDMENT

1. Child Support Act 1995, s.25 (October 1, 1995).

GENERAL NOTE

See reg. 2 of the Social Security Benefits (Maintenance Payments and Consequential Amendments) Regulations 1996 for definitions of "child maintenance", "spousal maintenance" and "relevant income" and regs 3 to 5 for other points of interpretation.

Where maintenance payments are being collected on behalf of an income support or income-based JSA claimant or any member of the family, s.74A provides for part or the whole of those payments to be retained by the Secretary of State, in which case they will be disregarded for the purpose of calculating the claimant's benefit. See regs 55A and 60E of the Income Support Regulations and regs. 119 and 127 of the Jobseeker's Allowance Regulations.

1.83

75.–77. *Omitted.*

1.84

Social fund awards

Recovery of social fund awards

78.—(1) A social fund award which is repayable shall be recoverable by the Secretary of State.

1.85

(2) Without prejudice to any other method of recovery, the Secretary of State may recover an award by deduction from prescribed benefits.

(3) The Secretary of State may recover an award—

(a) from the person to or for the benefit of whom it was made;

(b) where that person is a member of a married or unmarried couple, from the other member of the couple;
(c) from a person who is liable to maintain the person by or on behalf of whom the application for the award was made or any person in relation to whose needs the award was made.

[¹(3A) Where—
(a) a jobseeker's allowance is payable to a person from whom an award is recoverable under subsection (3) above; and
(b) that person is subject to a bankruptcy order,

a sum deducted from that benefit under subsection (2) above shall not be treated as income of his for the purposes of the Insolvency Act 1986.

(3B) Where—
(a) a jobseeker's allowance is payable to a person from whom an award is recoverable under subsection (3) above; and
(b) the estate of that person is sequestrated,

a sum deducted from that benefit under subsection (2) above shall not be treated as income of his for the purposes of the Bankruptcy (Scotland) Act 1985.]

(4) Payments to meet funeral expenses may in all cases be recovered, as if they were funeral expenses, out of the estate of the deceased, and (subject to section 71 above) by no other means.

(5) In this section—

"married couple" means a man and woman who are married to each other and are members of the same household;

"unmarried couple" means a man and a woman who are not married to each other but are living together as husband and wife otherwise than in circumstances prescribed under section 132 of the Contributions and Benefits Act.

(6) For the purposes of this section—
(a) a man shall be liable to maintain his wife and any children of whom he is the father; and
(b) a woman shall be liable to maintain her husband and any children of whom she is the mother;
(c) a person shall be liable to maintain another person throughout any period in respect of which the first-mentioned person has, on or after 23rd May 1980 (the date of the passing of the Social Security Act 1980) and either alone or jointly with a further person, given an undertaking in writing in pursuance of immigration rules within the meaning of the Immigration Act 1971 to be responsible for the maintenance and accommodation of the other person; and
(d) "child" includes a person who has attained the age of 16 but not the age of 19 and in respect of whom either parent, or some person acting in place of either parent, is receiving income support [² or an income-based jobseeker's allowance].

(7) Any reference in subsection (6) above to children of whom the man or the woman is the father or mother shall be construed in accordance with section 1 of the Family Law Reform Act 1987.

(8) Subsection (7) above does not apply in Scotland, and in the application of subsection (6) above to Scotland any reference to children

of whom the man or the woman is the father or the mother shall be construed as a reference to any such children whether or not their parents have ever been married to one another.

(9) A document bearing a certificate which—
(a) is signed by a person authorised in that behalf by the Secretary of State; and
(b) states that the document apart from the certificate is, or is a copy of, such an undertaking as is mentioned in subsection (6)(c) above,

shall be conclusive of the undertaking in question for the purposes of this section; and a certificate purporting to be so signed shall be deemed to be so signed until the contrary is proved.

AMENDMENTS

1. Jobseekers Act 1995, s.32(2) (October 7, 1996).
2. Jobseekers Act 1995, Sched. 2, para. 51 (October 7, 1996).

DERIVATION

Subss. (1) to (3): Social Security Act 1986, s.33(5) to (7).   1.86
Subs. (4): 1986 Act, s.32(4).
Subs. (5): 1986 Act, s.33(12).
Subss. (6) to (9): 1986 Act, ss.26(3) to (6) and 33(8).

DEFINITION

"prescribed"—see s.191.

GENERAL NOTE

Subsections (1) to (3)
These provisions give the framework for recovery of social fund loans. See   1.87
the Social Fund (Recovery by Deductions from Benefits) Regulations 1988.

Income support and JSA are prescribed benefits for the purposes of subs. (2) (reg. 3(a) and (c) of the Social Fund (Recovery by Deductions from Benefits) Regulations). In *Mulvey v. Secretary of State for Social Security* (March 13, 1997), the House of Lords held that where deductions were being made from benefit under subs. (2) when the claimant was sequestrated (the Scottish equivalent of a declaration of bankruptcy), the Secretary of State was entitled to continue to make the deductions. If that were not so, the gross benefit would become payable to the claimant, who would thus gain an immediate financial advantage from sequestration, a result which Parliament could not have intended.

"Prior to sequestration the [claimant] had no right to receive by way of income support more than her gross entitlement under deduction of such sum as had been notified to her by the [Secretary of State] prior to payment of the award by the [Secretary of State]. This was the result of the statutory scheme and she could not have demanded more. The [Secretary of State's] continued exercise of a statutory power of deduction after sequestration was unrelated thereto and was not calculated to obtain a benefit for him at the expense of other creditors. The only person who had any realistic interest in the deductions was the [claimant] from which it follows that the [Secretary of State] was not seeking to exercise any right against the permanent trustee." (Lord Jauncey)

Social Security Administration Act 1992

The view of the Inner House of the Court of Session was thus approved. See the notes in the 1996 edition for the earlier decisions in *Mulvey*.

English bankruptcy law is not the same as Scottish sequestration law. However, in *R. v. Secretary of State for Social Security, ex p. Taylor and Chapman, The Times*, February 5, 1996, Keene J. reached the same conclusion as the Inner House in *Mulvey* in relation to the effect of s.285(3) of the Insolvency Act 1986 in these circumstances. The deductions in *Chapman* were not being made under subs. (2) but from the claimant's retirement pension under s.71(8) in order to recover an overpayment of income support, but it was accepted that the position was the same in both cases. Keene J. rejected a submission by the Secretary of State that the operation of s.285(3) was precluded in this situation, but held that it did not prevent the deductions under subs. (2) and s.71(8) being made. The Secretary of State was not seeking to go against "the property of the bankrupt" within the terms of s.285(3) as the claimants' entitlement under the 1992 Act was to the net amount of benefit. In *Mulvey* (above) Lord Jauncey said this about the contrary argument:

> "Even more bizarre would be the situation where overpayments obtained by fraud were being recovered by deduction from benefits. On sequestration the fraudster would immediately receive the gross benefit. It is difficult to believe that Parliament can have intended such a result."

Note that s.32 of the Jobseekers Act 1995 amends both ss.78 and 71 to provide that amounts deducted under subs. (2) or s.71(8) from JSA payable to a bankrupt person are not to be treated as income for the purposes of the Insolvency Act 1986 and the Bankruptcy (Scotland) Act 1985 (in effect giving preference to the DSS over other creditors, although the House of Lords in *Mulvey* rejected such a comparison).

Subsection (4)

1.88 Subs. (4) contains an important provision for the recovery of any payment for funeral expenses out of the estate of the deceased. Reg. 8 of the Social Fund Maternity and Funeral Expenses (General) Regulations lists sums to be deducted in calculating the amount of a funeral payment. These include assets of the deceased which are available before probate or letters of administration have been granted. The old reg. 8(3)(a) of the Single Payments Regulations required the deduction of the value of the deceased's estate, but since it might take some time for the estate to become available, the provision in subs. (4) is preferable.

The funeral payment is to be recovered as if it was funeral expenses. Funeral expenses are a first charge on the estate, in priority to anything else (see *R(SB) 18/84*, paras. 8 and 10, for the law in England and Scotland). *CIS/616/1990* decides that the right to recover is given to the Secretary of State. The adjudication officer (and the tribunal) has no role in subs. (4).

The only other method of recovery is under s.71, which applies generally where there has been misrepresentation or a failure to disclose and does depend on a review of entitlement by an adjudication officer followed by a determination of an overpayment.

Subsections (6) to (9)

1.89 See the notes to s.105.

Northern Ireland payments

Recovery of Northern Ireland payments

1.90 **79.** Without prejudice to any other method of recovery—

(a) amounts recoverable under any enactment or instrument having effect in Northern Ireland and corresponding to an enactment or instrument mentioned in section 71(8) above shall be recoverable by deduction from benefits prescribed under that subsection;
(b) amounts recoverable under any enactment having effect in Northern Ireland and corresponding to section 75 above shall be recoverable by deduction from benefits prescribed under subsection (4) of that section; and
(c) awards recoverable under Part III of the Northern Ireland Administration Act shall be recoverable by deduction from benefits prescribed under subsection (2) of section 78 above and subsection (3) of that section shall have effect in relation to such awards as it has effect in relation to such awards out of the social fund under this Act.

DERIVATION

Para. (a): Social Security Act 1986, s.53(7A).
Para. (b): 1986 Act, s.29(8).
Para. (c): 1986 Act, s.33(8A).

1.91

DEFINITIONS

"the Northern Ireland Administration Act"—see s.191.
"prescribed"—*ibid.*

Child benefit—overlap with benefits under legislation of other member States

80. Regulations may provide for adjusting child benefit payable in respect of any child in respect of whom any benefit is payable under the legislation of any member State other than the United Kingdom.

1.92

DERIVATION

CBA 1975, s.4A.

1.93

PART IV

RECOVERY FROM COMPENSATION PAYMENTS

GENERAL NOTE ON PART IV

Part IV has been repealed with effect from October 6, 1997 by the Social Security (Recovery of Benefits) Act 1997 (c.27), which re-enacts the provisions of Part IV with significant amendments. It applies to all compensation schemes in respect of any accident, injury or disease settled on or after October 6, 1997. Two sets of implementing regulations have been promulgated: the Social Security (Recovery of Benefits) Regulations 1997 (S.I. 1997 No. 2205) and the Social Security (Recovery of Benefits) (Appeals) Regulations 1997 (S.I. 1997 No. 2237). The relevant primary and secondary legislation can be found in this volume.

1.94

Social Security Administration Act 1992

PART V

INCOME SUPPORT AND THE DUTY TO MAINTAIN

Failure to maintain—general

1.95 **105.**—(1) If—
  (a) any person persistently refuses or neglects to maintain himself or any person whom he is liable to maintain; and
  (b) in consequence of his refusal or neglect income support [¹or an income-based jobseeker's allowance] is paid to or in respect of him or such a person,
he shall be guilty of an offence and liable on summary conviction to imprisonment for a term not exceeding 3 months or to a fine of an amount not exceeding level 4 on the standard scale or to both.

(2) For the purposes of subsection (1) above a person shall not be taken to refuse or neglect to maintain himself or any other person by reason only of anything done or omitted in furtherance of a trade dispute.

(3) [¹Subject to sub-section (4) below,] subsections (6) to (9) of section 78 above shall have effect for the purposes of this Part of this Act as they have effect for the purposes of that section.

[¹(4) For the purposes of this section, in its application to an income-based jobseeker's allowance, a person is liable to maintain another if that other person is his or her spouse.]

AMENDMENT

1. Jobseekers Act 1995, Sched. 2, para. 53 (October 7, 1996).

DERIVATION

1.96 Social Security Act 1986, s.26.

GENERAL NOTE

Subsection (1)

1.97 The criminal offence created by subs. (1) of refusing or neglecting to maintain oneself is at first sight rather extraordinary, but it is only committed if as a consequence income support or income-based JSA is paid. Prosecution is very much a last resort after the ordinary sanctions against voluntary unemployment have been used. In 1984/5 there were none (NACRO, *Enforcement of the Law Relating to Social Security*, para. 8.6). Prosecution of those who refuse or neglect to maintain others is more common.

Liability to maintain

1.98 Under subs. (3), liability to maintain another person for the purposes of Part V is tested, except in relation to income-based JSA, according to s.78(6) to (9). Both men and women are liable to maintain their spouses and children. This liability remains in force despite the enactment of the Child Support Act 1991, with the result that the DSS retains its power to enforce that liability under ss.106 to 108. But although this power remains, in practice the DSS does not enforce the liability to maintain children now that the Child Support Agency has acquired this role. Note also that since April 5, 1993, the courts have not had power to make new orders for maintenance for children (s.8(3) Child Support Act 1991). Under subs. (4) the only liability to maintain which is relevant to s.105 for the purposes of income-based JSA is the liability of one spouse to maintain the other.

The definition of child goes beyond the usual meaning in s.137 of the Contributions and Benefits Act of a person under 16 to include those under 19 who count as a dependant in someone else's income support entitlement (s.78(6)(d)). The effect of the reference in s.78(4) to s.1 of the Family Law Reform Act 1987 is that in determining whether a person is the father or mother of a child it is irrelevant whether the person was married to the other parent at the time of the birth or not. If a married couple divorce, their liability to maintain each other ceases for the purposes of Part V, but the obligation to maintain their children remains. This then is the remnant of the old family means-test that used to extend much wider until the Poor Law was finally "abolished" by the National Assistance Act 1948. For the enforcement of this liability, see ss.106 to 108, and for a criminal offence, subs. (1).

Section 78(6)(c) was new in 1980. In *R. v. W. London SBAT, ex p. Clarke* [1975] 1 W.L.R. 1396, SB7, the court had held that the sponsor of an immigrant was under no obligation to maintain the immigrant for supplementary benefit purposes. This position is now reversed, and s.78(9) provides for conclusive certificates of an undertaking to maintain to be produced. The liability to maintain is enforced under s.106. The SBC policy struck down in *Clarke*'s case had deemed the immigrant to be receiving the support from his sponsor even where it was not forthcoming. This is not now the case. It is only a resource when actually received.

Recovery of expenditure on benefit from person liable for maintenance

106.—(1) Subject to the following provisions of this section, if income support is claimed by or in respect of a person whom another person is liable to maintain or paid to or in respect of such a person, the Secretary of State may make a complaint against the liable person to a magistrates' court for an order under this section.

(2) On the hearing of a complaint under this section the court shall have regard to all the circumstances and, in particular, to the income of the liable person, and may order him to pay such sum, weekly or otherwise, as it may consider appropriate, except that in a case falling within section 78(6)(c) above that sum shall not include any amount which is not attributable to income support (whether paid before or after the making of the order).

(3) In determining whether to order any payments to be made in respect of income support for any period before the complaint was made, or the amount of any such payments, the court shall disregard any amount by which the liable person's income exceeds the income which was his during that period.

(4) Any payments ordered to be made under this section shall be made—
  (a) to the Secretary of State in so far as they are attributable to any income support (whether paid before or after the making of the order);

(b) to the person claiming income support or (if different) the dependant; or

(c) to such other person as appears to the court expedient in the interests of the dependant.

(5) An order under this section shall be enforceable as a magistrates' court maintenance order within the meaning of section 150(1) of the Magistrates' Court Act 1980.

(6) In the application of this section to Scotland, subsection (5) above shall be omitted and for the references to a complaint and to a magistrates' court there shall be substituted respectively references to an application and to the sheriff.

(7) On an application under subsection (1) above a court in Scotland may make a finding as to the parentage of a child for the purpose of establishing whether a person is, for the purposes of section 105 above and this section, liable to maintain him.

DERIVATION

1.100   Social Security Act 1986, s.24.

DEFINITION

"child"—see ss.105(3) and 78(b).

GENERAL NOTE

This section gives the DSS an independent right to enforce the liability to maintain in s.78(6), which now covers both spouses and children, by an order in the magistrates' court, providing that income support has been claimed or paid for the person sought to be maintained.

Children

From April 1993 the Child Support Act 1991 has introduced an entirely new system of determining and enforcing the liability of parents to maintain children, through the Child Support Agency. This book does not deal with that system, for which, see Jacobs and Douglas, *Child Support Legislation*. But the DSS's rights under s.106 remain in force not only between spouses, but also as between parents and children. It is not clear in what circumstances action against a parent may be taken under s.106 rather than through the Child Support Agency. The DSS have said that they do not intend to use the s.106 power in relation to children, and this seems to be implicit in the Income Support Special Circumstances Guide, paras. 6000–6014. The Child Support Agency phased in applications for child support maintenance for income support claimants. It was originally intended that all income support claimants would have been required to apply under s.6 of the Child Support Act 1991 by April 1996; however, there have been some delays in taking on cases. Despite the delays, claimants receiving maintenance under a court order or an arrangement with liable relative officers were given priority by the Child Support Agency and so there should no longer be any cases where maintenance for dependent children is still being dealt with by the Benefits Agency. Benefit may only be reduced for failure to comply with obligations under s.6, not for failure to co-operate in relation to the liability to maintain in s.78(6). Note also that since April 5, 1993, the courts have not had the power to make new orders for maintenance for children (s.8(3) Child Support Act 1991).

Spouses

The usual procedure was last described in detail in Chapter 13 of the *Supplementary Benefits Handbook* (1984 ed.) and will presumably continue to apply, since it was repeated in essence in the DSS *Guide to Income Support*, although there were some administrative changes. The current Income Support Guide does not contain the liable relative procedure. This apparently is now in an internal guide called "Residual Liable Relatives and Proceedings Guide". The most common situation is where a breakdown of marriage leads to separation or divorce and the woman claims income support. The same procedures can apply if it is the man who claims benefit. If there has already been a divorce then there is no liability to maintain between the ex-spouses. If there has merely been a separation then the wife is entitled to benefit as a single person, but there will be an investigation of the circumstances to ensure that the separation is genuine. If the husband is already paying maintenance under a court order or the wife has taken proceedings herself which are reasonably advanced, no approach to the husband will be made by the DSS. Otherwise, the wife will be asked for information about the whereabouts of the liable relative (although producing the information cannot be made a condition of receiving benefit) and he will be contacted as soon as possible. The husband is asked to pay as much as he can, if possible enough to remove the need for income support to be paid to the wife and any children.

In deciding what level of payment is acceptable on a voluntary basis, it is understood that the following formula is used as a starting point. The income support personal allowances and premiums for the man are taken, plus rent, or mortgage payments, council tax and 15 per cent of his net wage. If the man has a new partner, two calculations are done—one as if the man was single and the other using joint incomes. The lower figure is then taken. The excess over this amount is regarded as available to be used as maintenance. But this is only a basis for discussion and payment of a lesser sum may be agreed, particularly if there are other essential expenses. Clearly there is scope for negotiation here. Thus if the man himself is receiving income support he would not be expected to pay anything.

If the husband is unwilling to make a payment voluntarily, although the DSS believe that he has sufficient income, then legal proceedings may be considered. The first step will be to see if the wife will take action. The official policy is that the wife will merely be advised on the advantages of taking proceedings herself (that she may get enough maintenance to lift her off benefit and that an order for maintenance will continue if she ceases to be entitled to income support, as by working full-time). The first advantage is likely to be real in only a small minority of cases and the force of the second has been reduced by the introduction of the procedure in s.107(3) to (14). The choice should be left entirely to the woman. A wife may of course take proceedings herself even though the DSS have accepted voluntary payments from the husband.

The courts have refused to adopt the "liable relative formula" in private proceedings by wives or ex-wives (*Shallow v. Shallow* [1979] Fam. 1) and will only have regard to the man's subsistence level. By this they mean the ordinary scale rates of benefit plus housing costs. A more realistic approach may have been presaged by *Allen v. Allen* [1986] 2 F.L.R. 265, where the Court of Appeal used the long-term scale rate (now disappeared) as a yardstick. In *Delaney v. Delaney* [1990] 2 F.L.R. 457, the Court of Appeal accepted the principle that where the man had insufficient resources after taking account of his reasonable commitments to a new family to maintain his former wife and family properly, a maintenance order should not financially cripple him where the wife is entitled to social security benefits. But no calculation of the man's income support level was made.

If the wife does not take proceedings, then the DSS may. The court is to have regard to all the circumstances, in particular the husband's resources, and may order him to pay whatever sum is appropriate (subs. (2)). Presumably, the same principles will govern the amount of an order as in a private application. There were some new provisions in s.107(1) in cases where the order included amounts for children, but it is not at all clear how these interacted with the general test of appropriateness under subs. (2). Note that since April 5, 1993 the courts have not had the power to make new orders for maintenance for children (s.8(3) Child Support Act 1991). The wife's adultery or desertion or other conduct is only a factor to be taken into account, not a bar to any order. Nor is the existence of a separation agreement under which the wife agrees not to claim maintenance a bar (*National Assistance Board v. Parkes* [1955] 2 Q.B. 506). Although *Hulley v. Thompson* [1981] 1 W.L.R. 159 concerned only the liability to maintain children, because there had been a divorce, it showed that not even a consent order under which the man transferred the matrimonial home to his ex-wife and she agreed to receive no maintenance for herself or the children, barred the statutory liability to maintain the children. However, it seems that the existence of the order could be taken into account in deciding what amount it is appropriate for the man to pay.

Proceedings by the DSS are relatively rare. In 1979 there were only 431 (SBC Annual Report for 1979 (Cmnd. 8033), para. 8.30).

Recovery of expenditure on income support: additional amounts and transfer of orders

1.101

107.—(1) In any case where—
  (a) the claim for income support referred to in section 106(1) above is or was made by the parent of one or more children in respect of both himself and those children; and
  (b) the other parent is liable to maintain those children but, by virtue of not being the claimant's husband or wife, is not liable to maintain the claimant,
the sum which the court may order that other parent to pay under subsection (2) of that section may include an amount, determined in accordance with regulations, in respect of any income support paid to or for the claimant by virtue of such provisions as may be prescribed.

(2) Where the sum which a court orders a person to pay under section 106 above includes by virtue of subsection (1) above an amount (in this section referred to as a "personal allowance element") in respect of income support by virtue of paragraph 1(2) of Schedule 2 to the Income Support (General) Regulations 1987 (personal allowance for lone parent) the order shall separately identify the amount of the personal allowance element.

(3) In any case where—
  (a) there is in force an order under subsection (2) of section 106 above made against a person ("the liable parent") who is the parent of one or more children, in respect of the other parent or the children; and
  (b) payments under the order fall to be made to the Secretary of State by virtue of subsection (4)(a) of that section; and
  (c) that other parent ("the dependent parent") ceases to claim income support,

the Secretary of State may, by giving notice in writing to the court which made the order and to the liable parent and the dependent parent, transfer to the dependent parent the right to receive the payments under the order, exclusive of any personal allowance element, and to exercise the relevant rights in relation to the order, except so far as relating to that element.

(4) Notice under subsection (3) above shall not be given (and if purportedly given, shall be of no effect) at a time when there is in force a maintenance order made against the liable parent—
   (a) in favour of the dependent parent or one or more of the children; or
   (b) in favour of some other person for the benefit of the dependent parent or one or more of the children;
and if such a maintenance order is made at any time after notice under that subsection has been given, the order under section 106(2) above shall cease to have effect.

(5) In any case where—
(a) notice is given to a magistrates' court under subsection (3) above,
(b) payments under the order are required to be made by any method of payment falling within section 59(6) of the Magistrates' Courts Act 1980 (standing order, etc.), and
(c) the clerk to the justices for the petty sessions area for which the court is acting decides that payment by that method is no longer possible,
the clerk shall amend the order to provide that payments under the order shall be made by the liable parent to the clerk.

(6) Except as provided by subsections (8) and (12) below, where the Secretary of State gives notice under subsection (3) above, he shall cease to be entitled—
   (a) to receive any payment under the order in respect of any personal allowance element; or
   (b) to exercise the relevant rights, so far as relating to any such element, notwithstanding that the dependent parent does not become entitled to receive any payment in respect of that element or to exercise the relevant rights so far as so relating.

(7) If, in a case where the Secretary of State gives notice under subsection (3) above, a payment under the order is or has been made to him wholly or partly in respect of the whole or any part of the period beginning with the day on which the transfer takes effect and ending with the day on which the notice under subsection (3) above is given to the liable parent, the Secretary of State shall—
   (a) repay to or for the liable parent so much of the payment as is referable to any personal allowance element in respect of that period or, as the case may be, the part of it in question; and
   (b) pay to or for the dependent parent so much of any remaining balance of the payment as is referable to that period or part;
and a payment under paragraph (b) above shall be taken to discharge, to that extent, the liability of the liable parent to the dependent parent under the order in respect of that period or part.

(8) If, in a case where the Secretary of State has given notice under

subsection (3) above, the dependent parent makes a further claim for income support, then—
  (a) the Secretary of State may, by giving a further notice in writing to the court which made the order and to the liable parent and the dependent parent, transfer back from the dependent parent to himself the right to receive the payments and to exercise the relevant rights; and
  (b) that transfer shall revive the Secretary of State's right to receive payment under the order in respect of any personal allowance element and to exercise the relevant rights so far as relating to any such element.

(9) Subject to subsections (10) and (11) below, in any case where—
  (a) notice is given to a magistrates' court under subsection (8) above, and
  (b) the method of payment under the order which subsists immediately before the day on which the transfer under subsection (8) above takes effect differs from the method of payment which subsisted immediately before the day on which the transfer under subsection (3) above (or, as the case may be, the last such transfer) took effect,
the clerk to the justices for the petty sessions area for which the court is acting shall amend the order by reinstating the method of payment under the order which subsisted immediately before the day on which the transfer under subsection (3) above (or, as the case may be, the last such transfer) took effect.

(10) The clerk shall not amend the order under subsection (9) above if the Secretary of State gives notice in writing to the clerk, on or before the day on which notice under subsection (8) above is given, that the method of payment under the order which subsists immediately before the day on which the transfer under subsection (8) above takes effect is to continue.

(11) In any case where—
  (a) notice is given to a magistrates' court under subsection (8) above,
  (b) the method of payment under the order which subsisted immediately before the day on which the transfer under subsection (3) above (or, if there has been more than one such transfer, the last such transfer) took effect was any method of payment falling within section 59(6) of the Magistrates' Courts Act 1980 (standing order, etc.), and
  (c) the clerk decides that payment by that method is no longer possible,
the clerk shall amend the order to provide that payments under the order shall be made by the liable parent to the clerk.

(12) A transfer under subsection (3) or (8) above does not transfer or otherwise affect the right of any person—
  (a) to receive a payment which fell due to him at a time before the transfer took effect; or
  (b) to exercise the relevant rights in relation to any such payment;
and, where notice is given under subsection (3), subsection (6) above does not deprive the Secretary of State of his right to receive such a

payment in respect of any personal allowance element or to exercise the relevant rights in relation to such a payment.

(13) For the purposes of this section—
(a) a transfer under subsection (3) above takes effect on the day on which the dependent parent ceases to be in receipt of income support in consequence of the cessation referred to in paragraph (c) of that subsection, and
(b) a transfer under subsection (8) above takes effect on—
(i) the first day in respect of which the dependent parent receives income support after the transfer under subsection (3) above took effect, or
(ii) such later day as may be specified for the purpose in the notice under subsection (8).
irrespective of the day on which notice under the subsection in question is given.

(14) Any notice required to be given to the liable parent under subsection (3) or (8) above shall be taken to have been given if it has been sent to his last known address.

(15) In this section—
"child" means a person under the age of 16, notwithstanding section 78(6)(d) above;
"court" shall be construed in accordance with section 106 above;
"maintenance order"—
(a) in England and Wales, means—
(i) any order for the making of periodical payments or for the payment of a lump sum which is, or has at any time been, a maintenance order within the meaning of the Attachment of Earnings Act 1971;
(ii) any order under Part III of the Matrimonial and Family Proceedings Act 1984 (overseas divorce) for the making of periodical payments or for the payment of a lump sum;
(b) in Scotland, has the meaning given by section 106 of the Debtors (Scotland) Act 1987, but disgarding paragraph (h) (alimentary bond or agreement);
"the relevant rights", in relation to an order under section 106(2) above, means the right to bring any proceedings, take any steps or do any other thing under or in relation to the order which the Secretary of State could have brought, taken or done apart from any transfer under this section.

DERIVATION

Social Security Act 1986, s.24A, as amended by the Maintenance Enforcement Act 1991, s.9, with effect from April 1, 1992 (Maintenance Enforcement Act 1991 (Commencement) (No. 2) Order 1992 (S.I. 1992 No. 455)).

1.102

GENERAL NOTE

The predecessors of this section and s.108 formed one of the central strategic objectives of the Social Security Act 1990 (HC *Hansard*, April 3, 1990, Vol. 170, col. 1137 (Tony Newton); HL *Hansard*, April 20, 1990, Vol. 518, col. 234 (Lord Henley)), but were only introduced at the Report stage in the Commons.

They therefore received relatively little Parliamentary discussion due to the operation of the guillotine. The Government carried out a general review of the maintenance system, based on a survey of work in United Kingdom courts and DSS offices and study of overseas systems, and produced radical proposals in *Children Come First* (Cm. 1264), now embodied in the Child Support Act 1991 from April 1993. But action had already been taken to tighten up the assessment of an absent parent's ability to pay maintenance for his family on income support. The new provisions were regarded as desirable in the short term to improve the effectiveness of the present system, pending the more radical reform (HC *Hansard*, March 28, Vol. 170, col. 566). However, ss.107 and 108 remain in force despite the implementation of the Child Support Act.

Section 107 contains two elements. The first relates to the situation where a lone parent is receiving income support, but the absent parent of the child(ren) is not liable to maintain the parent under s.78(6) because the parents are not or are no longer married. Where the DSS seeks its own order against the absent parent, courts are empowered to take into account income support relating to the lone parent in calculating the amount to be paid for the child(ren) and the DSS may of course take this into account in negotiating voluntary agreements. The second is to allow a DSS order to be transferred to the lone parent when that person comes off income support, rather than the lone parent having to obtain a separate private maintenance order. Note that since April 5, 1993, the courts have not had the power to make new orders for maintenance for children (s.8(3) Child Support Act 1991).

Subsections (1) and (2)

1.103 These provisions comprise the first element identified above. They apply when both of conditions (a) and (b) in subs. (1) are satisfied. Under para. (a), s.106 gives the DSS power to obtain an order against a person who is liable to maintain a claimant of income support or a person included in the family for claiming purposes. Section 78(6) defines liability to maintain for this purpose. There is a liability to maintain a spouse and any children. Under s.78(6)(d) "child" includes a person aged 16 to 18 (inclusive) who is still a member of the claimant's family for income support purposes (*e.g.* because still in full-time education). However, s.107(15) provides that for the purposes of s.107 "child" is restricted to a person under the age of 16. Thus, lone parent claimants whose children are all over 15 will fall outside this provision. Under para. (b), the absent parent must not be married to the lone parent, so that the obligation to maintain under s.78(6) is only in respect of the child(ren). If both these conditions are met, a court may include whatever amount the regulations determine in respect of the income support paid for the lone parent. The Income Support (Liable Relatives) Regulations specify in general the children's personal allowances, family premium, lone parent premium (now the higher rate of family premium), disabled child premium and the carer premium in respect of care for a child.

The intention was said to be that the regulation-making power "will be used to specify that once having looked at the allowances and premiums that are paid because there are children, the court should also have regard to the income support personal allowance paid for the mother" (HC *Hansard*, March 28, 1990, Vol. 170, col. 567). The Liable Relatives Regulations provide that if the liable parent has the means to pay in addition to the amounts already specified, a court order may include some or all of the dependent parent's personal allowance.

It was said that in a private maintenance order for children the court could take account of the parent's care costs and that social security law was thus being brought into line with family law. However, there was nothing as specific as s.107 in family law. The existing power of the court on orders sought by the DSS was already wide and it is not clear how much real difference the new powers made. Under s.106(2) the court may order payment of such sum as it may consider appropriate. The assumption seems to be that not only could the personal allowance for a child under 16 be considered under this provision, but also the family premium (paid to all claimants with a child or young person (16–18) in the family) and the additional lone parent premium (now the higher rate of family premium). If such amounts can be considered under the existing law (and they might be considered to reflect the care costs of the lone parent) there seems no reason why the court could not also consider some part of the parent's personal allowance if that was considered "appropriate." However, s.107(1) and the Liable Relatives Regulations make the position clear, which should be an advantage.

It is notable that the court retains a discretion as to what amounts to consider and that the overriding factor under s.106(2) is what is appropriate. Under para. 1 of Sched. 2 to the Income Support (General) Regulations 1987 the personal allowance for a lone parent aged under 18 or over 24 is the same as for a single person with no dependants. There is only a difference (currently £10.50 p.w.) for those aged 18 to 24.

Subs. (2) provides that if the lone parent's personal allowance under Sched. 2 is covered by the order, this element must be separately identified. This has no bearing on subs. (1), but is relevant to the procedure set up by subss. (3) to (14).

Subsections (3) to (15)

These provisions contain the once-important procedure allowing the transfer of a DSS order to the lone parent on coming off income support. The conditions for transfer under subs. (3) are that in such a case (remembering that "child" is defined to cover only those under 16 (subs. (15)) the Secretary of State gives notice to the court which made the order and to both the parents. Then the right to enforce or apply for variation of the order (apart from any personal allowance element identified under subs. (2)) is transferred to the lone parent (known as "the dependent parent"). Thus, the personal allowance element, which is of no net benefit to the lone parent while she is on income support, is removed at the point when its value would actually be felt by the lone parent. The DSS can no longer enforce the personal allowance element of the order (subs. (6)). Under subs. (13)(a) the transfer takes effect on the day on which the dependent parent ceases to receive income support in consequence of ceasing to claim. This is a peculiar way of putting things. If the dependent parent's circumstances change (*e.g.* her capital goes over the cut-off limit or she starts full-time work) her entitlement to income support may be terminated on review by the adjudication officer under s.25. She may well then choose not to claim income support again, as it would be a useless exercise. The dependent parent could with some strain be said to cease to claim income support and so to satisfy subs. (3)(c), but the cessation of receipt of income support is not in consequence of the cessation of claiming but of the review and revision by the adjudication officer.

Subs. (3) is not to apply if a private maintenance order (see subs. (15) for definition) is in existence, and if the dependent parent obtains one after a transfer the right to enforce the DSS order disappears (subs. (4)).

If, after a transfer, the dependent parent makes another claim for income support (presumably only while still having children under 16), the Secretary of State may by giving notice to all parties re-transfer to the DSS the right to enforce the order and revive the personal allowance element on the dependent parent becoming entitled to income support (subss. (8) and (13)(b)). Presum-

1.104

ably, the revival of the personal allowance element depends on the conditions of subss. (1) and (2) being met at the date of revival.

Reduction of expenditure on income support: certain maintenance orders to be enforceable by the Secretary of State

1.105   **108.**—(1) This section applies where—
  (a) a person ("the claimant") who is the parent of one or more children is in receipt of income support either in respect of those children or in respect of both himself and those children; and
  (b) there is in force a maintenance order made against the other parent ("the liable person")—
    (i) in favour of the claimant or one or more of the children, or
    (ii) in favour of some other person for the benefit of the claimant or one or more of the children,
and in this section "the primary recipient" means the person in whose favour that maintenance order was made.

(2) If, in a case where this section applies, the liable person fails to comply with any of the terms of the maintenance order—
  (a) the Secretary of State may bring any proceedings or take any other steps to enforce the order that could have been brought or taken by or on behalf of the primary recipient; and
  (b) any court before which proceedings are brought by the Secretary of State by virtue of paragraph (a) above shall have the same powers in connection with those proceedings as it would have had if they had been brought by the primary recipient.

(3) The Secretary of State's powers under this section are exercisable at his discretion and whether or not the primary recipient or any other person consents to their exercise; but any sums recovered by virtue of this section shall be payable to or for the primary recipient, as if the proceedings or steps in question had been brought or taken by him or on his behalf.

(4) The powers conferred on the Secretary of State by subsection (2)(a) above include power—
  (a) to apply for the registration of the maintenance order under—
    (i) section 17 of the Maintenance Orders Act 1950;
    (ii) section 2 of the Maintenance Orders Act 1958; or
    (iii) the Civil Jurisdiction and Judgments Act 1982; and
  (b) to make an application under section 2 of the Maintenance Orders (Reciprocal Enforcement) Act 1972 (application for enforcement in reciprocating country).

(5) Where this section applies, the prescribed person shall in prescribed circumstances give the Secretary of State notice of any application—
  (a) to alter, vary, suspend, discharge, revoke, revive, or enforce the maintenance order in question; or
  (b) to remit arrears under that maintenance order;
and the Secretary of State shall be entitled to appear and be heard on the application.

(6) Where, by virtue of this section, the Secretary of State commences

any proceedings to enforce a maintenance order, he shall, in relation to those proceedings, be treated for the purposes of any enactment or instrument relating to maintenance orders as if he were a person entitled to payment under the maintenance order in question (but shall not thereby become entitled to any such payment).

(7) Where, in any proceedings under this section in England and Wales, the court makes an order for the whole or any part of the arrears due under the maintenance order in question to be paid as a lump sum, the Secretary of State shall inform the Legal Aid Board of the amount of that lump sum if he knows—
  (a) that the primary recipient either—
    (i) received legal aid under the Legal Aid Act 1974 in connection with the proceedings in which the maintenance order was made, or
    (ii) was an assisted party, within the meaning of the Legal Aid Act 1988, in those proceedings; and
  (b) that a sum remains unpaid on account of the contribution required of the primary recipient—
    (i) under section 9 of the Legal Aid Act 1974 in respect of those proceedings, or
    (ii) under section 16 of the Legal Aid Act 1988 in respect of the costs of his being represented under Part IV of that Act in those proceedings, as the case may be.

(8) In this section "maintenance order" has the same meaning as it has in section 107 above but does not include any such order for the payment of a lump sum.

DERIVATION

Social Security Act 1986, s.24B.

1.106

GENERAL NOTE

Section 108 enables the DSS to enforce certain private maintenance orders in favour of lone parent claimants of income support. Only lone parents are covered by subs. (1)(a), and not mere separated or divorced spouses, but the maintenance order may be in favour either of the parent or the child(ren) or both. The Secretary of State may at his discretion and without the consent of the lone parent take steps (including those specified in subs. (5)) to enforce the order as if he were the person entitled to payment under the order (subss. (2), (3) and (6)). But any sums recovered are payable to the primary recipient under the order (subss. (3) and (6)). Under subs. (5) regulations may specify who has to inform the DSS of applications to vary, suspend etc the private order or to remit arrears. Reg. 3 of the Income Support (Liable Relatives) Regulations specifies various court officials. The Secretary of State is given the right to be heard on any such application, but has no power to make such an application, *e.g.* to increase the amount of an order. This is because subs. (2) only operates when there is a failure to comply with the terms (*i.e.* the existing terms) of the order.

Subs. (7) requires the Secretary of State to inform the Legal Aid Board when a lump sum of arrears is to be paid when the Board might be able to recover a contribution out of the lump sum.

Overall s.108 is a powerful weapon for the DSS to enforce the payment of maintenance orders. If the lone parent has her own order, which is not being paid, income support will make up the shortfall. There is thus no great incentive for the lone parent to go through all the hassle of enforcement, and there may be other circumstances making her reluctant to take action. The DSS will have no such inhibitions.

The Secretary of State predicted that the amount of maintenance recovered by the DSS in respect of lone parents on income support would rise to about £260 million in 1990–91, having gone up from £155 million in 1988–89 to £180 million in 1989–90 (HC *Hansard*, March 28, 1990, Vol. 170, col. 571). The predicted increase was partly based on the provisions now contained in ss.107 and 108 and partly on giving greater priority and resources to such work, with changes in the administrative guidance. These changes are to point up the need to stress to lone parents on benefits the advantages of reflecting the absent parent's proper responsibilities in the maintenance arrangements from the outset and also to indicate that the "normal expectation" should be that a lone parent will co-operate in establishing where responsibility lies. It is, however, recognised that there may be circumstances in which lone parents will not wish to name the father of a child. The White paper, *Children Come First*, proposed reductions in the lone parent's benefit if she declines without good cause to take maintenance proceedings. The Child Support Act 1991 imposes such an obligation only in relation to applications under the Act.

Diversion of arrested earnings to Secretary of State—Scotland

1.107   **109.**—(1) Where in Scotland a creditor who is enforcing a maintenance order or alimentary bond or agreement by a current maintenance arrestment or a conjoined arrestment order is in receipt of income support, the creditor may in writing authorise the Secretary of State to receive any sums payable under the arrestment or order until the creditor ceases to be in receipt of income support or in writing withdraws the authorisation, whichever occurs first.

(2) On the intimation by the Secretary of State—
(a) to the employer operating the current maintenance arrestment; or
(b) to the sheriff clerk operating the conjoined arrestment order;
of an authorisation under subsection (1) above, the employer or sheriff clerk shall, until notified by the Secretary of State that the authorisation has ceased to have effect, pay to the Secretary of State any sums which would otherwise be payable under the arrestment or order to the creditor.

DERIVATION

1.108   Social Security Act 1986, s.25A.

1.109   **Part VI** *Omitted.*

1.110   **121E to 123** *omitted.*

PART VII

INFORMATION

The Registration Service

Provisions relating to age, death and marriage

1.111   **124.**—(1) Regulations made by the Registrar General under section

20 of the Registration Service Act 1953 or section 54 of the Registration of Births, Deaths and Marriages (Scotland) Act 1965 may provide for the furnishing by superintendent registrars and registrars, subject to the payment of such fee as may be prescribed by the regulations, of such information for the purposes—
  (a) of the provisions of the Contributions and Benefits Act to which this section applies;
[¹(aa) of the provisions of Parts I and II of the Jobseekers Act 1995;] and
  (b) the provisions of this Act so far as they have effect in relation to matters arising under those provisions,
including copies or extracts from the registers in their custody, as may be so prescribed.

(2) This section applies to the following provisions of the Contributions and Benefits Act—
  (a) Parts I to VI except section 108;
  (b) Part VII, so far as it relates to income support and family credit;
  (c) Part VIII, so far as it relates to any social fund payment such as is mentioned in section 138(1)(a) or (2);
  (d) Part IX;
  (e) Part XI; and
  (f) Part XII.

(3) Where the age, marriage or death of a person is required to be ascertained or proved for the purposes mentioned in subsection (1) above, any person—
  (a) on presenting to the custodian of the register under the enactments relating to the registration of births, marriages and deaths, in which particulars of the birth, marriage or death (as the case may be) of the first-mentioned person are entered, a duly completed requisition in writing in that behalf; and
  (b) on payment of a fee of £1.50 in England and Wales and £4 in Scotland,
shall be entitled to obtain a copy, certified under the hand of the custodian, of the entry of those particulars.

(4) Requisitions for the purposes of subsection (3) above shall be in such form and contain such particulars as may from time to time be specified by the Registrar General, and suitable forms of requisition shall, on request, be supplied without charge by superintendent registrars and registrars.

(5) In this section—
  (a) as it applies to England and Wales—
  "Registrar General" means the Registrar General for England and Wales; and
  "superintendent registrar" and "registrar" mean a superintendent registrar or, as the case may be, registrar for the purposes of the enactments relating to the registration of births, deaths and marriages; and
  (b) as it applies to Scotland—
  "Registrar General" means the Registrar General of Births, Deaths and Marriages for Scotland;

Social Security Administration Act 1992

"registrar" means a district registrar, senior registrar or assistant registrar for the purposes of the enactment relating to the registration of births, deaths and marriages in Scotland.

AMENDMENT

1. Jobseekers Act 1995, Sched. 2, para. 59 (October 7, 1996).

DERIVATION

1.112   Social Security Act 1975, s.160.

DEFINITIONS

"the Contributions and Benefits Act"—see s.191.
"prescribed"—*ibid.*

Regulations as to notifications of deaths

1.113   **125.**—(1) Regulations [³made with the concurrence of the Inland Revenue] may provide that it shall be the duty of any of the following persons—
(a) the Registrar General for England and Wales;
(b) the Registrar General of Births, Deaths and Marriages for Scotland;
(c) each registrar of births and deaths,
to furnish the Secretary of State, [³or the Inland Revenue, for the purposes of their respective functions] under the Contributions and Benefits Act [¹, the Jobseekers Act 1995] [²the Social Security (Recovery of Benefits) Act 1997] and this Act and the functions of the Northern Ireland Department under any Northern Ireland legislation corresponding to [¹any of those Acts], with the prescribed particulars of such deaths as may be prescribed.

(2) The regulations may make provision as to the manner in which and the times at which the particulars are to be furnished.

AMENDMENTS

1. Jobseekers Act 1995, Sched. 2, para. 60 (October 7, 1996).
2. Social Security (Recovery of Benefits) Act 1997, s.33 and Sched. 3, para. 5 (October 6, 1997).
3. Social Security Contributions (Transfer of Functions, etc.) Act 1999, s.1(1) and Sched. 1, para. 25 (April 1, 1999).

DERIVATION

1.114   Social Security Act 1986, s.60.

DEFINITIONS

"the Contributions and Benefits Act"—see s.191.
"the Northern Ireland Department"—*ibid.*
"prescribed"—*ibid.*

(1992 c.5, s.126)

Personal representatives—income support and supplementary benefit

Personal representatives to give information about the estate of a deceased person who was in receipt of income support or supplementary benefit

126.—(1) The personal representatives of a person who was in receipt of income support [¹, an income-based jobseeker's allowance] or supplementary benefit at any time before his death shall provide the Secretary of State with such information as he may require relating to the assets and liabilities of that person's estate.

(2) If the personal representatives fail to supply any information within 28 days of being required to do so under subsection (1) above, then—
  (a) the appropriate court may, on the application of the Secretary of State, make an order directing them to supply that information within such time as may be specified in the order; and
  (b) any such order may provide that all costs (or, in Scotland, expenses) of and incidental to the application shall be borne personally by any of the personal representatives.

(3) In this section "the appropriate court" means—
  (a) in England and Wales, a county court;
  (b) in Scotland, the sheriff;
and any application to the sheriff under this section shall be made by summary application.

1.115

AMENDMENT

1. Jobseekers Act 1995, Sched. 2, para. 61 (October 7, 1996).

DERIVATION

Social Security Act 1986, s.27A.

1.116

GENERAL NOTE

Under s.71(3) an overpayment which would have been recoverable from a person is recoverable from that person's estate (*Secretary of State for Social Services v. Solly* [1974] 3 All E.R. 922, *CSSB 6/1995*). Section 126 provides a specific obligation for the estate to provide information about the assets in it. However, s.126 only applies to the estates of income support, income-based JSA or supplementary benefit claimants. It does not apply to family credit, FIS, disability working allowance, housing benefit or council tax benefit claimants, all of whom can be overpaid by concealing capital. Nor does it apply to anyone other than a recipient of income support, JSA or supplementary benefit. Sometimes a person other than a recipient may become liable to recovery by making a misrepresentation or failing to disclose a material fact (*R(SB) 21/82* and *R(SB) 28/83*). See the note to s.71(3).

126A. *omitted.*

1.117

127–128A. *Repealed by Sched. 2 to the Social Security Administration (Fraud) Act 1997 (July 1, 1997).*

1.118

Statutory sick pay and other benefits

Disclosure by Secretary of State for purpose of determination of period of entitlement to statutory sick pay

1.119
129. Where the Secretary of State considers that it is reasonable for information held by him to be disclosed to an employer, for the purpose of enabling that employer to determine the duration of a period of entitlement under Part XI of the Contributions and Benefits Act in respect of an employee, or whether such a period exists, he may disclose the information to that employer.

DERIVATION

1.120
SSHBA 1982, s.17(1).

Duties of employers—statutory sick pay and claims for other benefits

1.121
130.—(1) Regulations may make provision requiring an employer, in a case falling within subsection (3) below to furnish information in connection with the making, by a person who is, or has been, an employee of that employer, of a claim for—
(a) [¹ short-term incapacity benefit];
(b) a maternity allowance;
(c) [¹ long-term incapacity benefit];
(d) industrial injuries benefit; or
(e) a severe disablement allowance.
(2) Regulations under this section shall prescribe—
(a) the kind of information to be furnished in accordance with the regulations;
(b) the person to whom information of the prescribed kind is to be furnished; and
(c) the manner in which, and period within which, it is to be furnished.
(3) The cases are—
(a) where, by virtue of paragraph 2 of Schedule 11 to the Contributions and Benefits Act or of regulations made under paragraph 1 of that Schedule, a period of entitlement does not arise in relation to a period of incapacity for work;
(b) where a period of entitlement has come to an end but the period of incapacity for work which was running immediately before the period of entitlement came to an end continues; and
(c) where a period of entitlement has not come to an end but, on the assumption that—
(i) the period of incapacity for work in question continues to run for a prescribed period; and
(ii) there is no material change in circumstances,
the period of entitlement will have ended on or before the end of the prescribed period.

(4) Regulations [² made with the concurrence of the Inland Revenue]—
  (a) may require employers to maintain such records in connection with statutory sick pay as may be prescribed;
  (b) may provide for—
    (i) any person claiming to be entitled to statutory sick pay; or
    (ii) any other person who is a party to proceedings arising under Part XI of the Contributions and Benefits Act,
    to furnish to the Secretary of State [²or the Inland Revenue (as the regulations may require)] within a prescribed period, any information required for the determination of any question arising in connection therewith; and
  (c) may require employers who have made payments of statutory sick pay to furnish to the Secretary of State [²or the Inland Revenue (as the regulations may require)] such documents and information, at such times, as may be prescribed.

AMENDMENTS
  1. Social Security (Incapacity for Work) Act 1994, Sched. 1 (April 13, 1995)
  2. Transfer of Functions Act 1999, Sched. 1 (April 1, 1999).

DERIVATION
SSHBA 1982, ss.9, 17 and 18.

Disclosure by Secretary of State for purpose of determination of period of entitlement to statutory maternity pay

131. Where the Secretary of State considers that it is reasonable for information held by him to be disclosed to a person liable to make payments of statutory maternity pay for the purpose of enabling that person to determine—
  (a) whether a maternity pay period exists in relation to a woman who is or has been an employee of his; and
  (b) if it does, the date of its commencement and the weeks in it in respect of which he may be liable to pay statutory maternity pay,
  he may disclose the information to that person.

DERIVATION
SSA 1986, s.49.

Duties of employers—statutory maternity pay and claims for other benefits

132.—(1) Regulations may make provision requiring an employer in prescribed circumstances to furnish information in connection with the making of a claim by a woman who is or has been his employee for—
  (a) a maternity allowance;
  (b) [¹ short-term incapacity benefit];
  (c) [¹ long-term incapacity benefit under section 30A], 40 and 41 of the Contributions and Benefits Act; or

(d) a severe disablement allowance.
(2) Regulations under this section shall prescribe—
(a) the kind of information to be furnished in accordance with the regulations;
(b) the person to whom information of the prescribed kind is to be furnished; and
(c) the manner in which, and period within which, it is to be furnished.
(3) Regulations [² made with the concurrence of the Inland Revenue]
(a) may require employers to maintain such records in connection with statutory maternity pay as may be prescribed;
(b) may provide for—
  (i) any woman claiming to be entitled to statutory maternity pay; or
  (ii) any other person who is a party to proceedings arising under Part XII of the Contributions and Benefits Act,
 to furnish to the Secretary of State [² or the Inland Revenue (as the regulations may require)], within a prescribed period, any information required for the determination of any question arising in connection therewith; and
(c) may require persons who have made payments of statutory maternity pay to furnish to the Secretary of State [² or the Inland Revenue (as the regulations may require)] such documents and information, at such time, as may be prescribed.

AMENDMENTS

1. Social Security (Incapacity for Work) Act 1994, Sched. 1 (April 13, 1995)
2. Transfer of Functions Act 1999, Sched. 1 (April 1, 1999).

DERIVATION

1.125   SSHBA, 1982, s.49.

Maintenance proceedings

Furnishing of addresses for maintenance proceedings, etc.

1.126   **133.** The Secretary of State may incur expenses for the purpose of furnishing the address at which a man or woman is recorded by him as residing, where the address is required for the purpose of taking or carrying on legal proceedings to obtain or enforce an order for the making by the man or woman of payments—
(a) for the maintenance of the man's wife or former wife, or the woman's husband or former husband; or
(b) for the maintenance or education of any person as being the son or daughter of the man or his wife or former wife, or of the woman or her husband or former husband.

DERIVATION

SSA 1975, s.161.   1.127

134–154 *omitted.*   1.128

PART XI

COMPUTATION OF BENEFITS

Effect of alteration of rates of benefit under Parts II to V of Contributions and Benefits Act

155.—(1) This section has effect where the rate of any benefit to   1.129
which this section applies is altered—
  (a) by an Act subsequent to this Act;
  (b) by an order under section 150 or 152 above; or
  (c) in consequence of any such Act or order altering any maximum rate of benefit;
and in this section "the commencing date" means the date fixed for payment of benefit at an altered rate to commence.

(2) This section applies to benefit under Part II, III, IV or V of the Contributions and Benefits Act.

(3) Subject to such exceptions or conditions as may be prescribed, where—
  (a) the weekly rate of a benefit to which this section applies is altered to a fixed amount higher or lower than the previous amount; and
  (b) before the commencing date an award of that benefit has been made (whether before or after the passing of the relevant Act or the making of the relevant order),
except as respects any period falling before the commencing date, the benefit shall become payable at the altered rate without any claim being made for it in the case of an increase in the rate of benefit or any review of the award in the case of a decrease, and the award shall have effect accordingly.

(4) Where—
  (a) the weekly rate of a benefit to which this section applies is altered; and
  (b) before the commencing date (but after that date is fixed) an award is made of the benefit,
the award either may provide for the benefit to be paid as from the commencing date at the altered rate or may be expressed in terms of the rate appropriate at the date of the award.

(5) Where in consequence of the passing of an Act, or the making of an order, altering the rate of disablement pension, regulations are made varying the scale of disablement gratuities, the regulations may provide that the scale as varied shall apply only in cases where the period taken into account by the assessment of the extent of the disablement in

respect of which the gratuity is awarded begins or began after such day as may be prescribed.

(6) Subject to such exceptions or conditions as may be prescribed, where—
  (a) for any purpose of any Act or regulations the weekly rate at which a person contributes to the cost of providing for a child, or to the maintenance of an adult dependant, is to be calculated for a period beginning on or after the commencing date for an increase in the weekly rate of benefit; but
  (b) account is to be taken of amounts referable to the period before the commencing date,

those amounts shall be treated as increased in proportion to the increase in the weekly rate of benefit.

(7) So long as sections 36 and 37 of the National Insurance Act 1965 (graduated retirement benefit) continue in force by virtue of regulations made under Schedule 3 of the Social Security (Consequential Provisions) Act 1975 or under Schedule 3 to the Consequential Provisions Act, regulation may make provision for applying the provisions of this section—

[¹(a) to the amount of graduate retirement benefit payable for each unit of graduated contributions,
  (b) To increased of such benefit under any provisions made by virtue of section 24(1)(b) of the Social Security Pensions Act 1975 or section 62(1)(a) of the Contributions and Benefits Act, and
  (c) to any addition under section 37(1) of the National Insurance Act 1965 (addition to weekly rate of retirement pension for widows and widowers) to the amount of such benefit].

AMENDMENT

1. Pensions Act 1995, s.131(3) (July 19, 1995).

DERIVATION

1.130   SSA 1986, s.64.

[¹Power to anticipate pensions up-rating order

1.131   **155A.**—(1) This section applies where a statement is made in the House of Commons by or on behalf of the Secretary of State which specifies—
  (a) the amounts by which he proposes, by an order under section 150 above, to increase—
    (i) the weekly sums that are payable by way of retirement pension; or
    (ii) the amount of graduated retirement benefit payable for each unit of graduated contributions; and
  (b) the date of which he proposes to bring the increases into force ("the commencing date").

(2) Where, before the commencing date and after the date on which the statement is made, an award is made of a retirement pension or a graduated retirement benefit, the award wither may provide for the pen-

sion or benefit to be paid as from the commencing date at the increased rate or may be expressed in terms of the rate appropriate at the date of the award.]

AMENDMENT

1. Social Security Act 1998, s.76 (November 16, 1998).

Up-rating under sections 150 above of pensions increased under section 52(3) of the Contributions and benefits Act.

[¹**156.**—(1) This section applies in any case where a person is entitled to a Category A retirement pension with an increase, under section 52(3) of the Contributions and Benefits Act, in the additional pension on account of the contributions of a spouse who had died.

(2) Where in the case of any up-rating order under section 150 above—
  (a) The spouse's final relevant year is the tax year preceding the tax year in which the up-rating order comes into force, but
  (b) The person's final relevant year was an earlier tax year,
then the up-rating order shall not have effect in relation to that part of the additional pension which is attributable to the spouse's contributions.

(3) Where in the case of any up-rating order under section 150 above—
  (a) The person's final relevant year is the tax year preceding the tax year in which the up-rating order comes into force, but
  (b) The spouse's final relevant year was an earlier tax year,
Then the up-rating order shall not have effect in relation to that part of the additional pension which is attributable to the person's contributions.]

1.132

AMENDMENT

1. Pensions Act 1995, s.130(1) (July 19, 1995).

DERIVATION

SSPA 1975, s.23(2A).

1.133

Effect of alteration of rates of child benefit

157.—(1) Subsections (3) and (4) of section 155 above shall have effect where there is an increase in the rate or any of the rates of child benefit as they have effect in relation to the rate of benefit to which that section applies.

(2) Where in connection with child benefit—
  (a) any question arises in respect of a period after the date fixed for the commencement of payment of child benefit at an increased rate—
    (i) as to the weekly rate at which a person is contributing to the cost of providing for a child; or

1.134

Social Security Administration Act 1992

(ii) as to the expenditure that a person is incurring in respect of a child; and

(b) in determining that question account falls to be taken of contributions made or expenditure incurred for a period before that date, the contributions made or expenditure incurred before that date shall be treated as increased in proportion to the increase in the rate of benefit.

DERIVATION

1.135   CBA 1975, s.5(6).

Treatment of excess benefit as paid on account of child benefit

1.136   **158.**—(1) In any case where—
  (a) any benefit as defined in section 122 of the Contributions and Benefits Act or any increase of such benefit ("the relevant benefit or increase") has been paid to a person for a period in respect of a child; and
  (b) subsequently child benefit for that period in respect of the child becomes payable at a rate which is such that, had the relevant benefit or increase been awarded after the child benefit became payable, the rate of the relevant benefit or increase would have been reduced,

then, except in so far as regulations otherwise provide, the excess shall be treated as paid on account of child benefit for that period in respect of the child.

(2) In subsection (1) above "the excess" means so much of the relevant benefit or increase as is equal to the difference between—
  (a) the amount of it which was paid for the period referred to in that subsection; and
  (b) the amount of it which would have been paid for that period if it had been paid at the reduced rate referred to in paragraph (b) of that subsection.

DERIVATION

1.137   SS(MP)A 1977, s.17(4).

GENERAL NOTE

This provision avoids increases of benefits overlapping with, in particular, increase of child benefit. See also paras (4) and (5) of reg. 2 of the Fixing and Adjustment of Rates Regulations.

Effect of alteration in the component rates of income support

1.138   **159.**—(1) Subject to such exceptions and conditions as may be prescribed, where—
  (a) an award of income support is in force in favour of any person ("the recipient"); and
  (b) there is an alteration in any of the relevant amounts, that is to say—
    (i) any of the component rates of income support;

(ii) any of the other sums specified in regulations under Part VII of the Contributions and Benefits Act; or

(iii) the recipient's benefit income; and

(c) the alteration affects the computation of the amount of income support to which the recipient is entitled,

then subsection (2) or (3) below (as the case may be) shall have effect.

(2) Where, in consequence of the alteration in question, the recipient becomes entitled to an increased or reduced amount of income support ("the new amount"), then, as from the commencing date, the amount of income support payable to or for the recipient under the award shall be the new amount, without any further decision of [¹the Secretary of State], and the award shall have effect accordingly.

(3) Where, notwithstanding the alteration in question, the recipient continues on and after the commencing date to be entitled to the same amount of income support as before, the award shall continue in force accordingly.

(4) In any case where—

(a) there is an alteration in any of the relevant amounts; and

(b) before the commencing date (but after that date is fixed) an award of income support is made in favour of a person,

the award either may provide for income support to be paid as from the commencing date, in which case the amount shall be determined by reference to the relevant amounts which will be in force on that date, or may provide for an amount determined by reference to the amounts in force at the date of the award.

(5) In this section—

"alteration" means—

(a) in relation to—

(i) the component rates of income support; or

(ii) any other sums specified in regulations under Part VII of the Contributions and Benefits Act,

their alteration by or under any enactment whether or not contained in that Part; and

(b) in relation to a person's benefit income, the alteration of any of the sums referred to in section 150 above—

(i) by any enactment; or

(ii) by an order under section 150 or 152 above,

to the extent that any such alteration affects the amount of his benefit income;

"benefit income", in relation to any person, means so much of his income as consists of—

(a) benefit under the Contributions and Benefits Act, other than income support; or

(b) a war disablement pension or war widow's pension;

"the commencing date" in relation to an alteration, means the date on which the alteration comes into force in the case of the person in question;

"component rate", in relation to income support, means the amount of—

Social Security Administration Act 1992

(a) the sum referred to in section 126(5)(b)(i) and (ii) of the Contributions and Benefits Act; or
(b) any of the sums specified in regulations under section 135(1) of that Act; and

"relevant amounts" has the meaning given by subsection (1)(b) above.

AMENDMENT

1. S.I. 1999 No. 3178 Sched. 1 (November 29, 1999)

DERIVATION

1.139   Social Security Act 1986, s.64A.

DEFINITIONS

"the Contributions and Benefits Act"—see s.191.
"war disablement pension"—*ibid*.
"war widow's pension"—*ibid*.

GENERAL NOTE

The general rule under s.159 is that if there is an alteration in the prescribed figures for personal allowances, premiums, the relevant sum (*i.e.* assumed "strike pay" in trade dispute cases), or any social security benefits which count as income for income support purposes (subss.(1) and (5)), then any consequent change in the amount of income support which is payable takes effect automatically without the need for a decision by an adjudication officer (subs. (2)). Thus no right of appeal arises against the change in the amount, although the claimant can always request a review of the decision awarding benefit, as altered under s.159.

[¹**Effect of alteration of rates of a jobseeker's allowance**

1.140   **159A.**—(1) This section applies where—
(a) an award of a jobseeker's allowance is in force in favour of any person ("the recipient"); and
(b) an alteration—
  (i) in any component of the allowance, or
  (ii) in the recipient's benefit income,
  affects the amount of the jobseeker's allowance to which he is entitled.

(2) Subsection (3) applies where, as a result of the alteration, the amount of the jobseeker's allowance to which the recipient is entitled is increased or reduced.

(3) As from the commencing date, the amount of the jobseeker's allowance payable to or for the recipient under the award shall be the increased or reduced amount, without any further decision of an adjudication officer; and the award shall have effect accordingly.

(4) In any case where—
(a) there is an alteration of a kind mentioned in subsection (1)(b); and

(b) before the commencing date (but after that date is fixed) an award of a jobseeker's allowance is made in favour of a person,

the award may provide for the jobseeker's allowance to be paid as from the commencing date, in which case the amount of the jobseeker's allowance shall be determined by reference to the components applicable on that date, or may provide for an amount determined by reference to the components applicable at the date of the award.

(5) In this section—

"alteration" means—
  (a) in relation to any component of a jobseeker's allowance, its alteration by or under any enactment; and
  (b) in relation to a person's benefit income, the alteration of any of the sums referred to in section 150 above by any enactment or by an order under section 150 above, to the extent that any such alteration affects the amount of the recipient's benefit income;

"benefit income", in relation to a recipient, means so much of his income as consists of—
  (a) benefit under the Contributions and Benefits Act; or
  (b) a war disablement pension or war widow's pension;

"the commencing date" in relation to an alteration, means the date on which the alteration comes into force in relation to the recipient;

"component", in relation to a jobseeker's allowance, means any of the sums specified in regulations under the Jobseekers Act 1995 which are relevant in calculating the amount payable by way of a jobseeker's allowance.]

AMENDMENT

1. Jobseekers Act 1995, s.24 (October 7, 1996).

DEFINITIONS

"the Contributions and Benefit Act"—see s.191.
"war disablement pension"—*ibid*.
"war widow's pension—*ibid*.

1.141

GENERAL NOTE

This section has the same effect for income-based JSA as s.159 does for income support.

Implementation of increases in income support due to attainment of particular ages

160.—(1) This section applies where—
  (a) an award of income support is in force in favour of a person ("the recipient"); and
  (b) there is a component which becomes applicable, or applicable at a particular rate, in his case if he or some other person attains a particular age.

(2) If, in a case where this section applies, the recipient or other

1.142

Social Security Administration Act 1992

person attains the particular age referred to in paragraph (b) of subsection (1) above and, in consequence—
  (a) the component in question becomes applicable, or applicable at a particular rate, in the recipient's case (whether or not some other component ceases, for the same reason, to be applicable, or applicable at a particular rate, in his case; and
  (b) after taking account of any such cessation, the recipient becomes entitled to an increased amount of income support,

then, except as provided by subsection (3) below, as from the day on which he becomes so entitled, the amount of income support payable to or for him under the award shall be that increased amount, without any further decision of [¹ the Secretary of State], and the award shall have effect accordingly.

(3) Subsection (2) above does not apply in any case where, in consequence of the recipient or other person attaining the age in question, some question arises in relation to the recipient's entitlement to any benefit under the Contributions and Benefits Act, other than—
  (a) the question whether the component concerned, or any other component, becomes or ceases to be applicable, or applicable at a particular rate, in his case; and
  (b) the question whether, in consequence, the amount of his income support falls to be varied.

(4) In this section "component", in relation to a person and his income support, means any of the sums specified in regulations under section 135(1) of the Contributions and Benefits Act.

AMENDMENT

1. S.I. 1999 No 3178, Sched 1. (November 29, 1999)

DERIVATION

1.143 Social Security Act 1986, s.64B.

DEFINITION

"the Contributions and Benefits Act"—see s.191.

GENERAL NOTE

Section 160 extends the process begun by s.159 of taking routine adjustments in the amount of income support out of the ordinary mechanism of review.

[¹ **Implementation of increases in income-based jobseeker's allowance due to attainment of particular ages**

1.144 **160A.**—(1) This section applies where—
  (a) an award of an income-based jobseeker's allowance is in force in favour of a person ("the recipient"); and
  (b) a component has become applicable, or applicable at a particular rate, because he or some other person has reached a particular age ("the qualifying age")

(2) If, as a result of the recipient or other person reaching the qualify-

ing age, the recipient becomes entitled to an income-based jobseeker's allowance of an increased amount, the amount payable to or for him under the award shall, as from the day on which he becomes so entitled, be that increased amount, without any further decision of an adjudication officer; and the award shall have effect accordingly.

(3) Subsection (2) above does not apply where, in consequence of the recipient or other person reaching the qualifying age, a question arises in relation to the recipient's entitlement to—
  (a) a benefit under the Contributions and Benefits Act; or
  (b) a jobseeker's allowance.

(4) Subsection (3)(b) above does not apply to the question—
  (a) whether the component concerned, or any other component, becomes or ceases to be applicable, or applicable at a particular rate, in the recipient's case; and
  (b) whether, in consequence, the amount of his income-based jobseeker's allowance falls to be varied.

(5) In this section "component", in relation to a recipient and his jobseeker's allowance, means any of the amounts determined in accordance with regulations made under section 4(5) of the Jobseekers Act 1995.]

AMENDMENT

1. Jobseekers Act 1995, s.25 (October 7, 1996).

DEFINITION

"the Contributions and Benefits Act"—see s.191.

GENERAL NOTE

See s.160.

PART XII

FINANCE

161–166. *omitted.*

The social fund

167.—(1) The fund known as the social fund shall continue in being by that name.

(2) The social fund shall continue to be maintained under the control and management of the Secretary of State and payments out of it shall be made by him.

(3) The Secretary of State shall make payments into the social fund of such amounts, at such times and in such manner as he may with the approval of the Treasury determine.

(4) Accounts of the social fund shall be prepared in such form, and in such manner and at such times, as the Treasury may direct, and the Comptroller and Auditor General shall examine and certify every such account and shall lay copies of it, together with his report, before Parliament.

(5) The Secretary of State shall prepare an annual report on the social fund.

(6) A copy of every such report shall be laid before each House of Parliament.

DERIVATION

1.148   Subs.(1): Social Security Act 1986, s.32(1).
Subss. (2) to (6): 1986 Act, s.32(5) to (7B).

Allocations from social fund

1.149   **168.**—(1) The Secretary of State shall allocate amounts for payments from the social fund such as are mentioned in section 138(1)(b) of the Contributions and Benefits Act in a financial year.

(2) The Secretary of State may specify the amounts either as sums of money or by reference to money falling into the social fund on repayment or partial repayment of loans, or partly in the former and partly in the latter manner.

(3) Allocations—
   (a) may be for payments by [¹ a particular appropriate officer or group of appropriate fund officers];
   (b) may be for different amounts for different purposes;
   (c) may be made at such time or times as the Secretary of State considers appropriate; and
   (d) may be in addition to any other allocation to the same officer or group of officers or for the same purpose.

(4) The Secretary of State may at any time re-allocate amounts previously allocated, and subsections (2) and (3) above shall have effect in relation to a re-allocation as they have effect in relation to an allocation.

(5) The Secretary of State may give general directions to [¹ appropriate officers] or groups of social fund officers, or to any class of social fund officers, with respect to the control and management by social fund officers or groups of social fund officers of the amounts allocated to them under this section.

[¹(6) In this section "appropriate officer" means an officer of the Secretary of State who, acting under his authority, is exercising functions of the Secretary of State in relation to payments from the social fund such as are mentioned in section 138(1)(b) of the Contributions and Benefits Act.]

AMENDMENT

1. S.I. 1999 No 3178, Sched. 1 (November 29, 1999)

DERIVATION

1.150   Social Security Act 1986, s.32(8A) to (8E).

DEFINITION

"the Contributions and Benefits Act"—see s.191.

Adjustments between social fund and other sources of finance

169.—(1) There shall be made—
(a) out of the social fund into the Consolidated Fund or the National Insurance Fund;
(b) into the social fund out of money provided by Parliament or the National Insurance Fund,
such payments by way of adjustment as the Secretary of State determines (in accordance with any directions of the Treasury) to be appropriate in consequence of any enactment or regulations relating to the repayment or offsetting of a benefit or other payment under the Contributions and Benefits Act.

(2) Where in any other circumstances payments fall to be made by way of adjustment—
(a) out of the social fund into the Consolidated Fund or the National Insurance Fund; or
(b) into the social fund out of money provided by Parliament or the National Insurance Fund,
then, in such cases or classes of cases as may be specified by the Secretary of State by order, the amount of the payments to be made shall be taken to be such, and payments on account of it shall be be made at such times and in such manner, as may be determined by the Secretary of State in accordance with any direction given by the Treasury.

DERIVATION

Social Security Act 1986, s.85(11) and (12).

DEFINITION

"the Contributions and Benefits Act"—see s.191.

170.–176. *omitted.*

PART XIV

SOCIAL SECURITY SYSTEMS OUTSIDE GREAT BRITAIN

Co-ordination

Co-ordination with Northern Ireland

177.—(1) The Secretary of State may with the consent of the Treasury make arrangements with the Northern Ireland Department ("the joint arrangement") for co-ordinating the operation of the legislation to which this section applies with a view to securing that, to the extent

Social Security Administration Act 1992

allowed for in the arrangements, it provides a single system of social security for the United Kingdom.

(2) The Joint Authority consisting of the Secretary of State and the Head of the Northern Ireland Department shall continue in being by that name for the purposes of the enactments mentioned in subsection (5) below; and Schedule 8 to this Act has effect with respect to the Joint Authority.

(3) The responsibility of the Joint Authority shall include that of giving effect to the joint arrangements, with power—
(a) [1 to require the making by the Inland Revenue of] any necessary financial adjustments between the National Insurance Fund and the Northern Ireland National Insurance Fund; and
(b) to discharge such other functions as may be provided under the joint arrangements.

(4) The Secretary of State may make regulations for giving effect to the joint arrangements; and any such regulations may for the purposes of the arrangements provide—
(a) for adapting legislation (including subordinate legislation) for the time being in force in Great Britain so as to secure its reciprocal operation with Northern Ireland;
(b) without prejudice to paragraph (a) above, for securing that acts, omissions and events having any effect for the purposes of the enactments in force in Northern Ireland have a corresponding effect in relation to Great Britain (but not so as to confer any double benefit); and
(c) for determining, in cases where rights accrue both in relation to Great Britain and in relation to Northern Ireland, which of those rights shall be available to the person concerned.

(5) This section applies—
(a) To the Contributions and Benefits Act [1, the Jobseekers Act 1995]2 Chapter II of Part I of the Social Security Act 1998] and this Act; and
(b) To the Northern Ireland contributions and Benefits Act [1, any enactment in Northern Ireland corresponding to the Jobseekers Act 1995] [2 any enactment in Northern Ireland corresponding to Chapter II of Part I of the Social Security Act 1998] and the Northern Ireland Administration act,

except in relation to the following benefits—
    (i) income support;
[3(ia) income-based jobseeker's allowance;]
    (ii) [4 working familes' tax credit];
    (iii) [4 disabled person's tax credit];
    (iv) housing benefit;
    (v) child benefit;
    (vi) Christmas bonus;
    (vii) statutory sick pay;
    (viii) statutory maternity pay.

AMENDMENTS

1. Transfer of Functions Act 1999, Sched. 3 (April 1, 1999)
2. Social Security Act 1998, Sched. 7 (July 5, 1999)

3. Jobseekers Act 1995, Sched. 2 (April 22, 1996)
4. Tax Credits Act 1999, Sched. 1 (October 5, 1999)

DERIVATION

SSA 1975, s.142, as amended. 1.155

Reciprocal arrangements with Northern Ireland—income-related benefits and child benefit

178.—(1) The Secretary of State may with the consent of the Treasury make reciprocal arrangements with the authority administering any scheme in force in Northern Ireland and appearing to him to correspond substantially with a scheme contained in the Contributions and Benefits Act, [¹ the Jobseeker's Act 1995] [² Chapter II of Part I of the Social Security Act 1998] and this Act concerning any of the benefits to which this section applies for co-ordinating the operation of those schemes, and such arrangements may include provision for making any necessary financial adjustments. 1.156

(2) This section applies to the following benefits—
(a) income support;
(aa) [¹ income-based jobseeker's allowance];
(b) [³ working securities' tax credit];
(c) [³ disabled pension's tax credit];
(d) housing benefit; or
(e) child benefit.

(3) Regulations may make provision for giving effect to any such arrangements; and such regulations may in particular provide—
(a) for modifying any provision of this Act, [¹ the Jobseeker's Act 1995] [² Chapter II of Part I of the Social Security Act 1998] or the Contributions and Benefits Act concerning any of the benefits to which this section applies or any regulations made under such a provision;
(b) without prejudice to paragraph (a) above, for securing that acts, omissions and events having any effect for the purposes of the scheme in force in Northern Ireland shall have a corresponding effect for the purposes of this Act, [¹ the Jobseeker's Act 1995] [² Chapter II of Part I of the Social Security Act 1998] and the Contributions and Benefits Act (but not so as to confer any double benefit);
(c) for determining, in cases where rights accrue both under that scheme and under this Act, [¹ the Jobseeker's Act 1995] [² Chapter II of Part I of the Social Security Act 1998] and the Contributions and Benefits Act, which of those rights shall be available to the person concerned.

AMENDMENTS

1. Jobseekers Act 1995, Sched. 2 (April 22, 1996)
2. Social security Act 1998, Sched. 7 (July 5, 1999)
3. Tax credits Act 1999, Sched. 1 (October 5, 1999)

DERIVATION

1.157   SSA 1975, s.14 as amended.

Reciprocal agreements with countries outside the United Kingdom

1.158   179.—(1) For the purpose of giving effect—
  (a) to any agreement with the government of a country outside the United Kingdom providing for reciprocity in matters relating to payments for purposes similar or comparable to the purposes of legislation to which this section applies, or
  (b) to any such agreement as it would be if it were altered in accordance with proposals to alter it which, in consequence of any change in the law of Great Britain, the government of the United Kingdom has made to the other government in question,
Her Majesty may by Order in Council make provision for modifying or adapting such legislation in its application to cases affected by the agreement or proposed alterations.

(2) An Order made by virtue of subsection (1) above may, instead of or in addition to making specific modifications or adaptions, provide generally that legislation to which this section applies shall be modified to such extent as may be required to give effect to the provisions contained in the agreement or, as the case may be, alterations in question.

(3) The modifications which may be made by virtue of subsection (1) above include provisions—
  (a) for securing that acts, omissions and events having any effect for the purposes of the law of the country in respect of which the agreement is made have a corresponding effect for the purposes of this Act, [¹ the Jobseeker's Act 1995], [² Chapter II of Part I of the Social Security Act 1998] [³ Part II of the Social Security Contributions (Transfer of Functions, etc.) Act 1999] and the Contributions and Benefits Act (but not so as to confer a right to double benefit);
  (b) for determining, in cases where rights accrue under such legislation and under the law of that country, which of those rights is to be available to the person concerned;
  (c) for making any necessary financial adjustments.

(4) This section applies—
  (a) to the Contributions and Benefits Act;
  (aa) [¹ to the Jobseeker's Act 1995];
  (ab) [² to Chapter II of Part I of the Social Security Act 1998]
  (ac) [³ to Part II of the Social Security Contributions (Transfers of Functions, etc.) Act 1999]; and
  (b) to this Act,
except in relation to the following benefits—
    (i) community charge benefits;
    (ii) payments out of the social fund;
    (iii) Christmas bonus;
    (iv) statutory sick pay; and
    (v) statutory maternity pay.

(5) The power conferred by subsection (1) above shall also be exercisable in relation to regulations made under the Contributions and Benefits Act or this Act and concerning—
(a) income support;
(aa) [¹ jobseeker's allowance];
(b) [⁴ working securities' tax credit];
(c) [⁴ disabled person's tax credit];
(d) housing benefit; or
(e) child benefit.

AMENDMENTS

1. Jobseekers Act 1995, Sched. 2 (April 22, 1996)
2. Social Security Act 1998, Sched. 7 (July 5, 1999)
3. Transfer of Functions Act 1999, Sched. 7 (April 1, 1999)
4. Tax Credits Act 1999, Sched. 1 (October 5, 1999)

DERIVATION

SSA 1975, s.143 as amended and CBA 1975, s.15 as amended.

GENERAL NOTE

For details of current reciprocal arrangements, see annotations to s.113, of the Contributions and Benefits Act 1992.

PART XV

MISCELLANEOUS

180.–182B. *omitted.*

National insurance numbers

[¹Requirement to apply for national insurance number

182C.—(1) Regulations may make provision requiring a person to apply for a national insurance number to be allocated to him.

[²(1A) Regulations under subsection (1) above may require the application to be made to the Secretary of State or to the Inland Revenue.]

(2) An application required by regulations under subsection (1) above shall be accompanied by information or evidence enabling such a number to be allocated.]

AMENDMENTS

1. Social Security Administration (Fraud) Act 1997, Sched. 1, para. 9 (July 1, 1997).

2. Social Security Contributions (Transfer of Functions, etc.) Act 1999, s.1(1) and Sched. 1, para. 31 (April 1, 1999).

GENERAL NOTE

1.162 See subss. (1A)–(1C) of s.1, inserted by s.19 of the Social Security Administration (Fraud) Act, which make having, or applying for, a national insurance number a condition of entitlement to benefit in most cases.

1.163 183.–185. *omitted.*

Supplementary benefit etc.

Applications of provisions of Act to supplementary benefit etc.

1.164 **186.** Schedule 10 to this Act shall have effect for the purposes of making provision in relation to the benefits there mentioned.

Miscellaneous

Certain benefit to be inalienable

1.165 **187.**—(1) Subject to the provisions of this Act, every assignment of or charge on—
   (a) benefit as defined in section 122 of the Contributions and Benefits Act; [¹(aa) a jobseeker's allowance;]
   (b) any income-related benefit; or
   (c) child benefit,
and every agreement to assign or charge such benefit shall be void; and, on the bankruptcy of a beneficiary, such benefit shall not pass to any trustee or other person acting on behalf of his creditors.
   (2) In the application of subsection (1) above to Scotland—
   (a) the reference to assignment of benefit shall be read as a reference to assignation, "assign" being construed accordingly;
   (b) the reference to a beneficiary's bankruptcy shall be read as a reference to the sequestration of his estate or the appointment on his estate of a judicial factor under section 41 of the Solicitors (Scotland) Act 1980.
   (3) In calculating for the purposes of section 5 of the Debtors Act 1869 or section 4 of the Civil Imprisonment (Scotland) Act 1882 the means of any beneficiary, no account shall be taken of any increase of disablement benefit in respect of a child or of industrial death benefit.

AMENDMENT

1. Jobseekers Act 1995, Sched. 2, para. 72 (October 7, 1996).

DERIVATION

1.166 Social Security Act 1975, s.87.

DEFINITIONS

"the Contributions and Benefits Act"—see s.191.
"income-related benefit"—*ibid.*

GENERAL NOTE

The House of Lords in *Mulvey v. Secretary of State for Social Security* (March 13, 1997) dealt with the part of s.187(1) providing that, on bankruptcy or sequestration of a beneficiary, benefit does not pass to the trustee in bankruptcy. It held that the purpose was "to make clear beyond peradventure that the permanent trustee [the Scottish equivalent of the trustee in bankruptcy] could have no interest in any entitlement of a debtor to receive any of the social security benefits to which it applied" (Lord Jauncey). The Secretary of State's obligation to make payment of benefit is owed to the beneficiary and cannot be owed to the trustee in bankruptcy or permanent trustee. See the notes to s.78(2) for the situation where deductions are being made from benefit for the repayment of social fund loans or the recovery of overpayments.

188. *omitted*

PART XVI

GENERAL

Subordinate legislation

189.—(1) Subject to [...¹] [²any Provision proving for an order or regulations to be made by the Treasury or the Inland Revenue and to] any other express provision of this Act, regulations and orders under this Act shall be made by the Secretary of State.

(2) [...¹]

(3) Powers under this Act to make regulations or orders are exercisable by statutory instrument.

(4) Except in the case of regulations under section [...¹] 175 above and in so far as this Act otherwise provides, any power conferred by this Act to make an Order in Council, regulations or an order may be exercised—
 (a) either in relation to all cases to which the power extends, or in relation to those cases subject to specified exceptions, or in relation to any specified cases or classes of case;
 (b) so as to make, as respects the cases in relation to which it is exercised—
  (i) the full provision to which the power extends or any less provision (whether by way of exception or otherwise);
  (ii) the same provision for all cases in relation to which the power is exercised, or different provision for different cases or different classes of case or different provision as respects the same case or class of case for different purposes of this Act;
  (iii) any such provision either unconditionally or subject to any specified condition;

and where such a power is expressed to be exercisable for alternative purposes it may be exercised in relation to the same case for any or all of those purposes; and powers to make an Order in Council, regulations or an order for the purposes of any one provision of this Act are without prejudice to powers to make regulations or an order for the purposes of any other provision.

(5) Without prejudice to any specific provision in this Act, a power conferred by this Act to make an Order in Council, regulations or an order [...^{1}] includes power to make thereby such incidental, supplementary, consequential or transitional provision as appears to Her Majesty, or the authority making the regulations or order, as the case may be, to be expedient for the purposes of the Order in Council, regulations or order.

(6) Without prejudice to any specific provisions in this Act, a power conferred by any provision of this Act, except section 14, [...^{1}], 130 and 175, to make an Order in Council, regulations or an order includes power to provide for a person to exercise a discretion in dealing with any matter.

(7) Any power conferred by this Act to make orders or regulations relating to housing benefit or [^{3} council tax benefit] shall include power to make different provision for different areas [^{4} or different authorities].

(8) An order under section [^{5} 140B, 140C] 150, 152, [^{6} 165(4)(a)] or 169 above [...^{7}]shall not be made without the consent of the Treasury.

(9) Any powers of the Secretary of State under any provision of this Act, except under sections 80, 154, 175 and 178, to make any regulations or order, where the power is not expressed to be exercisable with the consent of the Treasury, shall if the Treasury so direct be exercisable only in conjunction with them.

(10) [...^{1}].

(11) A power under any of sections 177 to 179 above to make provision by regulations or Order in Council for modifications or adaptations of the Contributions and Benefits Act or this Act shall be exercisable in relation to any enactment passed after this Act which is directed to be construed as one with them, except in so far as any such enactment relates to a benefit in relation to which the power is not exercisable; but this subsection applies only so far as a contrary intention is not expressed in the enactment so passed, and is without prejudice to the generality of any such direction.

(12) Any reference in this section or section 190 below to an Order in Council, or an order or regulations, under this Act includes a reference to an Order in Council, an order or regulations made under any provision of an enactment passed after this Act and directed to be construed as one with this Act; but this subsection applies only so far as a contrary intention is not expressed in the enactment so passed, and without prejudice to the generality of any such direction.

AMENDMENTS

1. Social Security Act 1998, Sched. 7 (September 6, 1999)
2. Transfer of Functions Act 1999, Sched. 3 (April 1, 1999)
3. Local Government Finance Act 1992, Sched. 9 (April 1, 1993)

4. Social Security Administration (Fraud) Act 1997, Sched. 1 (July 1, 1997)
5. Housing Act 1996, Sched. 13 (April 1, 1997)
6. Social Security (Recovery of Benefits) Act 1997, Sched. 3 (October 6, 1997)

GENERAL NOTE

In accordance with s.2(1) of the Tax Credits Act 1999, this section is to be read, in relation to tax credit, as if references to the Secretary of State were references to the Treasury or, as the case may be, the Board.

DERIVATION

SSA 1975, ss.113, 133, 166 and 168 as amended.
Parliamentary control of orders and regulations.

190.—(1) Subject to the provision of this section, a statutory instrument containing (whether alone or with other provisions)—
(a) an order under section 141, 143 [¹] 143A], 145, [. . .²], 150, 152, or 162(7) above; or
(b) regulations under section [. . .³] [⁴122B(1)(b) or] 154 above,
shall not be made unless a draft of the instrument has been laid before Parliament and been approved by a resolution of each House of Parliament.

(2) Subsection (1) above does not apply to a statutory instrument by reason only that it contains regulations under section 154 above which are to be made for the purpose of consolidating regulations to be revoked in the instrument.

(3) A statutory instrument—
(a) which contains (whether alone or with other provisions) orders or regulations made under this Act by the Secretary of State [⁵, the Treasury or the Inland Revenue]; and
(b) which is not subject to any requirement that a draft of the instrument be laid before and approved by a resolution of each House of Parliament,
shall be subject to annulment in pursuance of a resolution of either House of Parliament.

(4) A statutory instrument—
(a) which contains (whether alone or with other provisions) regulations made under this Act by the Lord Chancellor; and
(b) which is not subject to any requirement that a draft of the instrument be laid before and approved by a resolution of each House of Parliament,
shall be subject to annulment in pursuance of a resolution of either House of Parliament.

AMENDMENTS

1. Social Security Act 1998, Sched. 7 (8 September 1998)
2. Social Security Act 1998, Sched. 7 (April 6, 1999)
3. Social Security (Recovery of Benefits) Act 1997, Sched. 3 (October 6, 1997)

4. Social Security Administration (Fraud) Act 1997, Sched. 1 (July 1, 1997)
5. Transfer of Functions Act 1999, Sched. 3 (April 1, 1999).

1.171 GENERAL NOTE

In accordance with s.2(1) of the Tax Credits Act 1999, this section is to be read, in relation to tax credit, as if references to the Secretary of State were references to the Treasury or, as the case may be, the Board.

DERIVATION

SSA 1975, s.167 as amended and CBA 1975, s.22.

Supplementary

Interpretation—general

1.172 191. In this Act, unless the context otherwise requires—
"the 1975 Act" means the Social Security Act 1975;
"the 1986 Act" means the Social Security Act 1986;
"benefit" means benefit under the Contributions and Benefits Act [¹and includes a jobseeker's allowance];
[²"billing authority" has the same meaning as in Part I of the Local Government Finance Act 1992;]
"Christmas bonus" means a payment under Part X of the Contributions and Benefits Act;
"claim" is to be construed in accordance with "claimant";
"claimant" (in relation to contributions under Part I and to benefit under Parts II to IV of the Contributions and Benefits Act) means—
 (a) a person whose right to be excepted from liability to pay, or to have his liability deferred for, or to be credited with, a contribution, is in question;
 (b) a person who has claimed benefit;
and includes, in relation to an award or decision a beneficiary under the award or affected by the decision;
"claimant" (in relation to industrial injuries benefit) means a person who has claimed such a benefit and includes—
 (a) an applicant for a declaration under [³ section 29 of the Social Security Act 1998] that an accident was or was not an industrial accident; and
 (b) in relation to an award or decision, a beneficiary under the award or affected by the decision;
"Commissioner" means the Chief Social Security Commissioner or any other Social Security Commissioner and includes a tribunal of 3 Commissioners constituted under section 57 above;
[. . .⁴]
"the Consequential Provisions Act" means the Social Security (Consequential Provisions) Act 1992;
[⁵"contribution" means a contribution under Part I of the Contributions and Benefit Act;]

["contribution-based jobseeker's allowance" has the same meaning as in the Jobseekers Act 1995;]
"contributions card" has the meaning assigned to it by section 114(6) above;
"the Contributions and Benefits Act" means the Social Security Contributions and Benefits Act 1992;
"disablement benefit" is to be construed in accordance with section 94(2)(a) of the Contributions and Benefits Act;
[7"council tax benefit Scheme" shall be construed in accordance with section 139(1) above;
"the disablement questions" is to be construed in accordance with section 45 above;
"dwelling" means any residential accommodation, whether or not consisting of the whole or part of a building and whether or not comprising separate and self-contained premises;
[9"financial year" has the same meaning as in the Local Government Finance Act 1992;]
"5 year general qualification" is to be construed in accordance with section 71 of the Courts and Legal Services Act 1990;
"housing authority" means a local authority, a new town corporation, Scottish Homes or the Development Board for Rural Wales;
"house benefit scheme" is to be construed in accordance with section 134(1) above;
[1"income-based jobseeker's allowance" has the same meaning as in the Jobseekers Act 1995;]
"income-related benefit" means—
  (a) income support;
  (b) [8 working families tax credit]
  (c) [8 disabled person's tax credit]
  (d) housing benefit; and
[2(e) council tax benefit];
"industrial injuries benefit" means benefit under Part V of the Contributions and Benefits Act, other than under Schedule 8;
[10"Inland Revenue" means the Commissioners of Inland Revenue]
... 10;
... 11;
"local authority" means—
  (a) in relation to England ...12, the council of a district or London borough, the Common Council of the City of London or the Council of the Isles of Scilly;
[11(aa) in relation to Wales, the council of a county or county borough;] and
  (b) in relation to Scotland [12a council constituted under section 2 of the Local Government etc. (Scotland) Act 1994];
"medical examination" includes bacteriological and radiographical tests and similar investigations, and "medically examined" has a corresponding meaning;
"medical practitioner" means—
  (a) a registered medical practitioner; or
  (b) a person outside the United Kingdom who is not a registered

medical practitioner, but has qualifications corresponding (in the Secretary of State's opinion) to those of a registered medical practitioner;

"medical treatment" means medical, surgical or rehabilitative treatment (including any course of diet or other regimen), and references to a person receiving or submitting himself to medical treatment are to be construed accordingly;

[15 "money purchase contracted-out scheme" has the same meaning as in section 8(1)(a)(ii) of the Pensions Act;]

"new town corporation" means—
  (a) in relation to England and Wales, a development corporation established under the New Towns Act 1981 or the Commission for the New Towns; and
  (b) in relation to Scotland, a development corporation established under the New Towns (Scotland) Act 1968;

"the Northern Ireland Department" means the Department of Health and Social Services for Northern Ireland. [16but in section 122 and sections 122B to 122E also includes the Department of the Environment for Northern Ireland;]

"the Northern Ireland Administration Act" means the Social Security (Northern Ireland) Administration Act 1992;

"occupational pension scheme" has the same meaning as in [15section 1] of the Pensions Act;

"the Old Cases Act" means the Industrial Injuries and Diseases (Old Cases) Act 1975;

"Old Cases payments" means payments under Part I of Schedule 8 to the Contributions and Benefits Act;

[17"pensionable age" has the meaning given by the rules in paragraph 1 of Schedule 4 to the Pensions Act 1995];

"the Pensions Act" means the [15Pension Schemes Act 1993];

"personal pension scheme" has the meaning assigned to it by [15section 1 of the Pensions Act] [15and "appropriate", in relation to such a scheme, shall be construed in accordance with section 7(4) of that Act]

"prescribe" means prescribe by regulations;

"President" means the President of social security appeal tribunals; disability appeal tribunals and medical appeal tribunals;

"rate rebate", [...18] and "rent allowance" shall be construed in accordance with section 134 above;

...18

"tax year" means the 12 months beginning with 6th April in any year;

"10 year general qualification" is to be construed in accordance with section 71 of the Courts and Legal Services Act 1990; and

"widows benefit" has the meaning assigned to it by section 20(1)(e) of the Contributions and Benefits Act.

AMENDMENTS

1. Jobseekers Act 1995, Sched. 2 (April 22, 1996)
2. Local Government Finance Act 1992, Sched. 9 (March 6, 1992)
3. Social Security Act 1998, Sched. 7 (July 7, 1999)

(1992 c.5, s.191)

4. Social Security (Recovery of Benefits) Act 1997, Sched. 3 (October 6, 1997)
5. Social Security Administration (Fraud) Act 1997, Sched. 1 (July 1, 1997)
6. Jobseekers Act 1995, Sched. 2 (April 22, 1996)
7. Housing Benefit Act 1996, Sched. 13 (April 1, 1997)
8. Tax Credits Act 1999, Sched. 1 (October 5, 1999)
9. Local Government Finance Act 1992, Sched. 9 (March 6, 1992)
10. Transfer of Functions Act 1999, Sched. 1 (April 1, 1999)
11. Social Security (Incapacity for Work) Act 1994, Sched. 1 (April 13, 1995)
12. Local Government etc. (Scotland) Act 1994, Sched. 14 (April 1, 1996)
13. Local Government (Wales) Act 1994, Sched. 16 (April 1, 1996)
14. Local Government etc. (Scotland) Act 1994, Sched. 13 (April 1, 1996)
15. Pension Schemes Act 1993, Sched. 8 (February 7, 1994)
16. Social Security Administration (Fraud) Act, Sched 1 (July 1, 1997)
17. Pensions Act 1995, Sched. 4 (July 19, 1995)
18. Housing Act 1996, Sched. 13 (April 1, 1997).

DERIVATION

SSA 1975, s.168 and Sched. 20.   1.173

192.—(1) This Act may be cited as the Social Security Administration   1.174
Act 1992

(2) This Act is to be read, where appropriate, with the Contributions and Benefits Act and the Consequential Provisions Act.

(3) The enactments consolidated by this Act are repealed, in consequence of the consolidation, by the Consequential Provisions Act.

(4) Except as provided in Schedule 4 to the Consequential Provisions Act, this Act shall come into force on 1st July 1992.

(5) The following provisions extend to Northern Ireland—
[. . .^{1}];
[^{2}]
section 170 (with Schedule 5);
section 177 (with Schedule 8);
and this section.

(6) Except as provided by this section, this Act does not extend to Northern Ireland.

AMENDMENTS

1. Social Security Act 1998, Sched. 7 (October 5, 1999)
2. Social Security (Recovery of Benefits) Act 1997, Sched. 3 (October 6, 1997)

SCHEDULES

SCHEDULE 1

CLAIMS FOR BENEFIT MADE OR TREATED AS MADE BEFORE 1ST OCTOBER 1990   1.175

Claims made or treated as made on or after 2nd September 1985 and before 1st October 1986

1. Section 1 above shall have effect in relation to a claim made or treated as made on or after 2nd September 1985 and before 1st October 1986 as if the following subsections were substituted for subsections (1) to (3)—

Social Security Administration Act 1992

"(1) Except in such cases as may be prescribed, no person shall be entitled to any benefit unless, in addition to any other conditions relating to that benefit being satisfied—
  (a) he makes a claim for it—
    (i) in the prescribed manner; and
    (ii) subject to subsection (2) below, within the prescribed time; or
  (b) by virtue of a provision of Chapter VI of Part II of the 1975 Act or of regulations made under such a provision he would have been treated as making a claim for it."

"(2) Regulations shall provide for extending, subject to any prescribed conditions, the time within which a claim may be made in cases where it is not made within the prescribed time but good cause is shown for the delay.

(3) Notwithstanding any regulations made under this section, no person shall be entitled to any benefit (except disablement benefit or industrial death benefit) in respect of any period more than 12 months before the date on which the claim is made."

Claims made or treated as made on or after 1st October 1986 and before 6th April 1987

2. Section 1 above shall have effect in relation to a claim made or treated as made on or after 1986 and before 6th April 1987 as if the subsections set out in paragraph 1 above were substituted for subsections (1) to (3) but with the insertion in subsection (3) of the words "reduced earnings allowance" after the words "disablement benefit".

Claims made or treated as made on or after 6th April 1987 and before 21st July 1989

3. Section 1 above shall have effect in relation to a claim made or treated as made on or after 6th April 1987 and before 21st July 1989, as if—
  (a) the following subsection were substituted for subsection (1)—
"(1) Except in such cases as may be prescribed, no person shall be entitled to any benefit unless, in addition to any other conditions relating to that benefit being satisfied—
  (a) he makes a claim for it in the prescribed manner and within the prescribed time; or
  (b) by virtue of regulations made under section 51 of the 1986 Act he would have been treated as making a claim for it."; and
  (b) there were omitted—
    (i) from subsection (2), the words "except as provided by section 3 below"; and
    (ii) subsection (3).

Claims made or treated as made on or after 21st July 1989 and before 13th July 1990

4. Section 1 above shall have effect in relation to a claim made or treated as made on or after 21st July 1989 and before 13th July 1990 as if there were omitted—
  (a) from subsection (1), the words "and subject to the following provisions of this section and to section 3 below";
  (b) from subsection (2), the words "except as provided by section 3 below"; and
  (c) subsection (3).

Claims made or treated as made on or after 13th July 1990 and before 1st October 1990

5. Section 1 above shall have effect in relation to a claim made or treated as made on or after 13th July 1990 and before 1st October 1990 as if there were omitted—
  (a) from subsection (1), the words "the following provisions of this section and to"; and
  (b) subsection (3)

GENERAL NOTE

See annotations to s.1

1.176 **Schedules 2–9.** *Omitted.*

SCHEDULE 10 — Section 186

SUPPLEMENTARY BENEFIT ETC.

Interpretation
1. In this Schedule—   1.177
"the former National Insurance Acts" means the National Insurance Act 1946 and the National Insurance Act 1965; and
"the former Industrial Injuries Acts" means the National Insurance (Industrial Injuries) Act 1946 and the National Insurance (Industrial Injuries) Act 1965.

Claims and payments
2.—(1) Section 5 above shall have effect in relation to the benefits specified in sub-paragraph (2) below as it has effect in relation to the benefits to which it applies by virtue of subsection (2).
(2) The benefits mentioned in sub-paragraph (1) above are benefits under—
 (a) the former National Insurance Acts;
 (b) the former Industrial Injuries Acts;
 (c) the National Assistance Act 1948;
 (d) the Supplementary Benefit Act 1966;
 (e) the Supplementary Benefits Act 1976;
 (f) the Family Income Supplements Act 1970.

Adjudication
3.—(1) Sections 20 to 29, 36 to 43, 51 to 61 and section 124 above shall have effect for the purposes of the benefits specified in paragraph 2(2) above as they have effect for the purposes of benefit within the meaning of section 122 of the Contributions and Benefits Act other than attendance allowance, disability living allowance and disability working allowance.
(2) Procedure regulations made under section 59 above by virtue of sub-paragraph (1) may make different provision in relation to each of the benefits specified in paragraph 2(2) above.

Overpayments etc.
4.—(1) Section 71 above shall have effect for the purposes of the benefits specified in paragraph 2(2) above as it has effect in relation to the benefits to which it applies by virtue of subsection (11).
(2) Section 74 above shall have effect in relation to supplementary benefit as it has effect in relation to income support.
(3) The reference to housing benefit in section 75 above includes a reference to housing benefits under Part II of the Social Security and Housing Benefits Act 1982.

Inspection
5. Section 110 above shall have effect as if it also applied to—
 (a) the Supplementary Benefits Act 1976,
 (b) the Family Income Supplements Act 1970.

Legal proceedings
6. Section 116 above shall have effect as if any reference to that Act in that section included—
 (a) the National Assistance Act 1948;
 (b) the Supplementary Benefit Act 1966;
 (c) the Supplementary Benefits Act 1976;
 (d) the Family Income Supplements Act 1970.

DERIVATION

Social Security Act 1986, Sched. 7.   1.178

DEFINITION

"the Contributions and Benefits Act"—see s.191.

Social Security (Recovery of Benefits) Act 1997

Social Security (Recovery of Benefits) Act 1997

(1997 c. 27)

ARRANGEMENT OF SECTIONS

Introductory

1.179

1. Cases in which this Act applies.
2. Compensation payments to which this Act applies.
3. "The relevant period".

Certificates of recoverable benefits

4. Applications for certificates of recoverable benefits.
5. Information contained in certificates.

Liability of person paying compensation

6. Liability to pay Secretary of State amount of benefits.
7. Recovery of payments due under section 6.

Reduction of compensation payment

8. Reduction of compensation payment.
9. Section 8: supplementary.

Reviews and appeals

10. Review of certificates of recoverable benefits.
11. Appeals against certificates of recoverable benefits.
12. Reference of questions to medical appeal tribunal.
13. Appeal to Social Security Commissioner.
14. Reviews and appeals: supplementary.

Courts

15. Court orders.
16. Payments into court.
17. Benefits irrelevant to assessment of damages.

Reduction of compensation: complex cases

18. Lump sum and periodical payments.
19. Payments by more than one person.

(1997 c.27)

Miscellaneous

20. Amounts overpaid under section 6.
21. Compensation payments to be disregarded.
22. *Omitted*
23. Provision of information.
24. Power to amend Schedule 2.

Provisions relating to Northern Ireland

25.–27. *Omitted*

General

28. The Crown.
29. General interpretation.
30. Regulations and orders.
31. *Omitted*
32. Power to make transitional, consequential etc. provisions.
33. *Omitted*
34. Short title, commencement and extent.

SCHEDULES:

Schedule 1—Compensation payments.
   Part I—Exempted payments.
   Part II—Power to disregard small payments.
Schedule 2—Calculation of compensation payment.
Schedule 3—*Omitted*
Schedule 4—*Omitted*

An Act to re-state, with amendments, Part IV of the Social Security Administration Act 1992. [19th March 1997]

Introductory

Cases in which this Act applies

1.—(1) This Act applies in cases where—   1.180
  (a) a person makes a payment (whether on his own behalf or not) to or in respect of any other person in consequence of any accident, injury or disease suffered by the other, and
  (b) any listed benefits have been, or are likely to be, paid to or for the other during the relevant period in respect of the accident, injury or disease.

(2) The reference above to a payment in consequence of any accident, injury or disease is to a payment made—
  (a) by or on behalf of a person who is, or is alleged to be, liable to any extent in respect of the accident, injury or disease, or

Social Security (Recovery of Benefits) Act 1997

(b) in pursuance of a compensation scheme for motor accidents;
but does not include a payment mentioned in Part I of Schedule 1.

(3) Subsection (1)(a) applies to a payment made—
(a) voluntarily, or in pursuance of a court order or an agreement, or otherwise, and
(b) in the United Kingdom or elsewhere.

(4) In a case where this Act applies—
(a) the "injured person" is the person who suffered the accident, injury or disease,
(b) the "compensation payment" is the payment within subsection (1)(a), and
(c) "recoverable benefit" is listed benefit which has been or is likely to be paid as mentioned in the subsection (1)(b).

GENERAL NOTE

1.181 As the long title says, this Act, which came into force on October 6, 1997 (see s.2 and the note thereto) re-enacts Part IV of the Social Security Administration Act 1992 with amendments. Some of the amendments are significant, albeit fairly technical, but there has also been a lot of simple redrafting to make the legislation clearer.

The broad scheme of the legislation remains as before. A person making a compensation payment (whether voluntarily or pursuant to a court order or agreement or otherwise—see s.1(3)) in respect of an accident, injury or disease must notify the Compensation Recovery Unit of the Department of Social Security at Reyrolle Building, Hebburn, Tyne and Wear NE31 1XB (Tel: 0191-489 2266) who publish a free guide to the procedures. *Before* making the payment, the compensator must apply for a "certificate of recoverable benefits" under s.4. That certificate will specify the amount of relevant benefits (listed in col. 2 of Sched. 2) paid, or expected to be paid, within the "relevant period" (defined in s.3), *in respect of* the accident injury or disease (see the definition of "recoverable benefit" in s.1(4)(c) which refers back to s.1(1)(b) and see also the note to s.5). The compensator must then pay to the Secretary of State a sum equal to the total amount of recoverable benefits (s.6) and pay to the victim a compensation payment which is reduced under s.8 to reflect the benefits the victim has received. By virtue of s.1(2) and Sched. 1, certain payments are exempted. Ss.10 to 14 provide for reviews of, and appeals from, certificates of recoverable benefits.

For the meaning of "benefit", "compensation scheme for motor accidents" and "listed benefit", see s.29.

Compensation payments to which this Act applies

1.182 **2.** This Act applies in relation to compensation payments made on or after the day on which this section comes into force, unless they are made in pursuance of a court order or agreement made before that day.

GENERAL NOTE

1.183 By virtue of the Social Security (Recovery of Benefits) Act 1997 (Commencement Order) 1997, this section came into force on October 6, 1997. Where a court order or agreement was made before that date, the recovery provisions of Part IV of the Social Security Administration Act 1992 will continue to apply, unless the accident or injury occurred before January 1, 1989 (or, in the case of a disease, benefit was claimed before January 1, 1989), in which case benefits will not be recoverable by the Secretary of State at all (see s.81(7) of the 1992 Act). Regulation 12 of the Social Security (Recovery of Benefits) Regulations 1997 makes transitional provision for cases arising under the 1992 Act.

"The relevant period"

3.—(1) In relation to a person ("the claimant") who has suffered any accident, injury or disease, "the relevant period" has the meaning given by the following subsections.

(2) Subject to subsection (4), if it is a case of accident or injury, the relevant period is the period of five years immediately following the day on which the accident or injury in question occurred.

(3) Subject to subsection (4), if it is a case of disease, the relevant period is the period of five years beginning with the date on which the claimant first claims a listed benefit in consequence of the disease.

(4) If at any time before the end of the period referred to in subsection (2) or (3)—
  (a) a person makes a compensation payment in final discharge of any claim made by or in respect of the claimant and arising out of the accident, injury or disease, or
  (b) an agreement is made under which an earlier compensation payment is treated as having been made in final discharge of any such claim,
the relevant period ends at that time.

1.184

GENERAL NOTE

1.185

Subsection (4)
This is intended to encourage the early settlement of claims because the effect of a compensation payment being made quickly is that the standard five-year "relevant period" provided for in subss. (2) and (3) is shortened and so the amount of recoverable benefits is reduced. This has an obvious attraction from the victim's point of view which the compensator can use to encourage settlement. It has been suggested that the provision creates undue pressure to settle cases but the quality of advice available to the victim is probably a more important factor.

Certificates of recoverable benefits

Applications for certificates of recoverable benefits

4.—(1) Before a person ("the compensator") makes a compensation payment he must apply to the Secretary of State for a certificate of recoverable benefits.

(2) Where the compensator applies for a certificate of recoverable benefits, the Secretary of State must—
  (a) send to him a written acknowledgement of receipt of his application, and

1.186

(b) subject to subsection (7), issue the certificate before the end of the following period

(3) The period is—

(a) the prescribed period, or

(b) if there is no prescribed period, the period of four weeks,

which begins with the day following the day on which the application is received.

(4) The certificate is to remain in force until the date specified in it for that purpose.

(5) The compensator may apply for fresh certificates from time to time.

(6) Where a certificate of recoverable benefits ceases to be in force, the Secretary of State may issue a fresh certificate without an application for one being made.

(7) Where the compensator applies for a fresh certificate while a certificate ("the existing certificate") remains in force, the Secretary of State must issue the fresh certificate before the end of the following period.

(8) The period is—

(a) the prescribed period, or

(b) if there is no prescribed period, the period of four weeks,

which begins with the day following the day on which the existing certificate ceases to be in force.

(9) For the purposes of this Act, regulations may provide for the day on which an application for a certificate of recoverable benefits is to be treated as received.

1.187   GENERAL NOTE

No period has yet been prescribed for the purposes of subss. (3)(a) or (8)(a). By virtue of s.21, the consequence of the Secretary of State failing to issue a certificate of recoverable benefits within the specified period is that no benefits are recoverable and the victim is entitled to the full compensation without deduction. However, for s.21 to apply, the application for the certificate of recoverable benefits must have been accurate and it must have been acknowledged. The Compensation Recovery Unit asks compensators to tell them if an acknowledgement has not been received within 10 days.

In practice, potential compensators are asked to notify the Compensation Recovery Unit of any *claim* for compensation by sending form CRU1 within 14 days of the claim being received. This enables the Unit to start collecting the relevant information from the offices responsible for the payment of benefits. The Unit sends to the potential compensator a form CRU4 which serves as an acknowledgement of the notification and is also the form the compensator must use to obtain the certificate of recoverable benefits. Form CRU4 can also be used by a compensator to obtain, for the purposes of negotiation with the victim, an informal indication of the benefits that have been paid, although the Unit stresses that the accuracy of such an indication depends on how much information they have to hand at that time and a formal certificate of recoverable benefits issued later may be based on more up-to-date information. The victim is, of course, entitled to that information as well and can obtain it directly from the office or offices responsible for payment.

Subsection (9)

See regulation 7(2) of the Social Security (Recovery of Benefits) Regulations 1997

Information contained in certificates

5.—(1) A certificate of recoverable benefits must specify, for each recoverable benefit—
  (a) the amount which has been or is likely to have been paid on or before a specified date, and
  (b) if the benefit is paid or likely to be paid after the specified date, the rate and period for which, and the intervals at which, it is or is likely to be paid.

(2) In a case where the relevant period has ended before the day on which the Secretary of State receives the application for the certificate, the date specified in the certificate for the purposes of subsection (1) must be the day on which the relevant period ended.

(3) In any other case, the date specified for those purposes must not be earlier than the day on which the Secretary of State received the application.

(4) The Secretary of State may estimate, in such manner as he thinks fit, any of the amounts, rates or periods specified in the certificate.

(5) Where the Secretary of State issues a certificate of recoverable benefits, he must provide the information contained in the certificate to—
  (a) the person who appears to him to be the injured person, or
  (b) any person who he thinks will receive a compensation payment in respect of the injured person.

(6) A person to whom a certificate of recoverable benefits is issued or who is provided with information under subsection (5) is entitled to particulars of the manner in which any amount, rate or period specified in the certificate has been determined, if he applies to the Secretary of State for those particulars.

GENERAL NOTE

Note that only "recoverable" benefits should be specified on the certificate and, by virtue of section 1(1)(b) and (4)(c), that means benefits listed in column 2 of Schedule 2 that have been, or are likely to be, paid to or for the victim during the relevant period *in respect of* the accident, injury or disease. Thus, not all benefits paid, or to be paid, during the relevant period should be specified in the certificate; only those that are attributable to the accident, injury or disease are recoverable. However, benefit is paid "in respect of" an accident, injury or disease if the accident, injury or disease is *a*, but not necessarily the only, reason for it being paid. In *Hassall and Pether v. Secretary of State for Social Security* [1995] 1 W.L.R. 812 (also reported as *R(CR) 1/95)*, it was held that income support paid to claimants who were unemployed and already in receipt of income support when they were injured was paid "in respect of" their accidents. That approach could be justified in those cases on the basis that the claimants were required to be available for work as a condition of obtaining income support (at a time before jobseeker's allowance was introduced) and might have obtained employment had the accidents not occurred. However, the reasoning of the Court of Appeal goes further. In cases where the claimant is incapable of work both by reason of a relevant accident and by reason of an enirely unrelated condition or due to the combined effects of the accident and the unrelated condition, benefits paid in respect of incapacity for work are to be regarded as paid "in respect of" the accident and are recoverable (*CCR/5336/*

95). The victim can avoid being out of pocket by seeking special damages for the loss of benefits that he would have received but for the recoupment provisions (*Neal v. Bingle* [1998] Q.B. 466). However, if a claimant can show that, although suffering from a disability due to the relevant accident, he would not have been incapable of work but for an unrelated condition which would have rendered him incapable of work even if the relevant accident had not occurred, benefits paid in respect of incapacity for work are not recoverable (*CCR/4/93, CCR/5336/95*). Similarly, in *CCR/2127/99*, the claimant suffered an injury to his neck in the relevant accident. He had also suffered an injury to his neck in an earlier accident. It was held that benefit paid in respect of incapacity for work due to the condition of his neck was recoverable only in respect of the period for which the relevant accident was an effective cause of disablement. From the date when the effects of the relevant accident had disappeared and the only effective cause of continuing disablement was the earlier accident, benefit would cease to be recoverable. It is respectfully suggested that it follows from *Hassall and Pether* that jobseeker's allowance is recoverable from a person who has lost his or her job due to incapacity caused by a relevant accident and has became fit for work again and that the suggestion to the contrary in *R(CR) 1/96* cannot be reconciled with the Court of Appeal's reasoning. On the other hand, where a claimant has lost a job through incapacity caused by a relevant accident but is still in receipt of incapacity benefit due to some unrelated accident or condition, there is no provision allowing the Secretary of State to recover the amount of jobseeker's allowance that would have been payable in respect of the relevant accident but for that unrelated accident or condition (*CCR/5336/95, CCR/2127/99*).

Where benefit has been paid to a victim on the basis that he or she was incapable of work due to disablement arising out of a relevant accident, it appears not to be open to the compensator to argue that the disablement was not in fact incapacitating and that the benefit ought not to have been awarded (*C6/99(CRS)*). It is, however, open to the compensator or the victim to argue that the benefit was not paid "in respect of" all of a number of conditions mentioned on medical certificates submitted in support of the claim and, possibly, that it was not paid in respect of a single condition mentioned in a certificate (*CCR/5336/95*), although it would, in practice, be necessary to demonstrate that there was some other cause of actual incapacity.

For reviews of, and appeals against, certificates of recoverable benefits, see ss.10 to 14.

Liability of person paying compensation

Liability to pay Secretary of State amount of benefits

1.190   **6.**—(1) A person who makes a compensation payment in any case is liable to pay to the Secretary of State an amount equal to the total amount of the recoverable benefits.

(2) The liability referred to in subsection (1) arises immediately before the compensation payment or, if there is more than one, the first of them is made.

(3) No amount becomes payable under this section before the end of the period of 14 days following the day on which the liability arises.

(4) Subject to subsection (3), an amount becomes payable under this section at the end of the period of 14 days beginning with the day on

which a certificate of recoverable benefits is first issued showing that the amount of recoverable benefit to which it relates has been or is likely to have been paid before a specified date.

GENERAL NOTE

The amount payable by the compensator to the Secretary of State may be greater than the amount of the reduction of the compensation payment (see the note to s.8).   1.191

Recovery of payments due under section 6

7.—(1) This section applies where a person has made a compensation payment but—   1.192
   (a) has not applied for a certificate of recoverable benefits, or
   (b) has not made a payment to the Secretary of State under section 6 before the end of the period allowed under that section.
(2) The Secretary of State may—
   (a) issue the person who made the compensation payment with a certificate of recoverable benefits, if none has been issued, or
   (b) issue him with a copy of the certificate of recoverable benefits or (if more than one has been issued) the most recent one,
and (in either case) issue him with a demand that payment of any amount due under section 6 be made immediately.
(3) The Secretary of State may, in accordance with subsections (4) and (5), recover the amount for which a demand for payment is made under subsection (2) from the person who made the compensation payment.
(4) If the person who made the compensation payment resides or carries on business in England and Wales and a county court so orders, any amount recoverable under subsection (3) is recoverable by execution issued from the county court or otherwise as if it were payable under an order of that court.
(5) If the person who made the payment resides or carries on business in Scotland, any amount recoverable under subsection (3) may be enforced in like manner as an extract registered decree arbitral bearing a warrant for execution issued by the sheriff court of any sheriffdom in Scotland.
(6) A document bearing a certificate which—
   (a) is signed by a person authorised to do so by the Secretary of State, and
   (b) states that the document, apart from the certificate, is a record of the amount recoverable under subsection (3),
is conclusive evidence that that amount is so recoverable.
(7) A certificate under subsection (6) purporting to be signed by a person authorised to do so by the Secretary of State is to be treated as so signed unless the contrary is proved.

GENERAL NOTE

This section provides a simple way of recovering not only sums due under s.6 from compensators who have followed the proper procedures but also sums   1.193

Social Security (Recovery of Benefits) Act 1997

due from those who have failed to apply for a certificate of recoverable benefits at all. For reviews of, and appeals against, certificates issued under s.7(2)(a), see ss.10 to 14.

Reduction of compensation payment

Reduction of compensation payment

1.194
8.—(1) This section applies in a case where, in relation to any head of compensation listed in column 1 of Schedule 2—
  (a) any of the compensation payment is attributable to that head, and
  (b) any recoverable benefit is shown against that head in column 2 of the Schedule.

(2) In such a case, any claim of a person to receive the compensation payment is to be treated for all purposes as discharged if—
  (a) he is paid the amount (if any) of the compensation payment calculated in accordance with this section, and
  (b) if the amount of the compensation payment so calculated is nil, he is given a statement saying so by the person who (apart from this section) would have paid the gross amount of the compensation payment.

(3) For each head of compensation listed in column 1 of the Schedule for which paragraphs (a) and (b) of subsection (1) are met, so much of the gross amount of the compensation payment as is attributable to that head is to be reduced (to nil, if necessary) by deducting the amount of the recoverable benefit or, as the case may be, the aggregate amount of the recoverable benefits shown against it.

(4) Subsection (3) is to have effect as if a requirement to reduce a payment by deducting an amount which exceeds that payment were a requirement to reduce that payment to nil.

(5) The amount of the compensation payment calculated in accordance with this section is—
  (a) the gross amount of the compensation payment, and
  (b) the sum of the reductions made under subsection (3),
(and, accordingly, the amount may be nil).

GENERAL NOTE

1.195
Under Part IV of the Social Security Administration Act 1992, the compensation payment was reduced by the amount of benefits paid within the relevant period in respect of the accident, injury or disease, even if the compensation had been awarded solely in respect of pain and suffering (*CSS/36/92*). Under this new provision, the extent to which the compensation payment may be reduced is limited by the extent to which compensation is attributable to a relevant head (*i.e.* compensation for loss of earnings, compensation for the cost of care or compensation for loss of mobility). Nevertheless, the compensator is obliged by s.6 to pay to the Secretary of State the whole of the amount of recoverable benefits. Thus, if an award of compensation were made up of £10,000 special damages for loss of earnings and £8,000 general damages for pain and suffering and the certificate of recoverable benefits listed £6,000 incapacity benefit and £3,000 disability living allowance, the compensator would be

obliged to pay £9,000 to the Secretary of State and £12,000 to the victim. In that example, the apparent discrepancy might be explained because the victim had received, in consequence of the relevant accident, disability living allowance in respect of care but had been unable to sue for the costs of care because it had been provided at no cost and so the compensator might have little cause to grumble. However, if the amount of incapacity benefit listed on the certificate exceeded the amount of special damages agreed or awarded in respect of loss of earnings, the apparent discrepancy might well reflect a difference of opinion between the compensator or the court on the one hand, and the Secretary of State on the other hand, as to the extent to which benefit was payable "in respect of" the accident, injury or disease (see the note to s.5) and the compensator might wish to consider seeking a review of, or appealing against, the certificate of recoverable benefits. A victim concerned about the size of the reduction in the compensation payment might also wish to challenge the certificate of recoverable benefits. Note, however, that, by s.11(3), no appeal may be brought until the claim has been disposed of and the payment made to the Secretary of State. This has the effect that the Secretary of State does not get caught up in the negotiations between the compensator and the victim and that those negotiations must be conducted on the basis that the outcome of any appeal is uncertain and the chances of success must be assessed realistically. The compensator and victim may sometimes have a common interest against the Secretary of State but in general terms a compensator will be interested only in the amount by which the listed benefits can be reduced to a level that is *no higher* than the amount of the relevant head of compensation and the victim will be interested only in the amount by which the listed benefits can be reduced *below* the amount of the relevant head of damages.

Section 8: supplementary

9.—(1) A person who makes a compensation payment calculated in accordance with section 8 must inform the person to whom the payment is made—
   (a) that the payment has been so calculated, and
   (b) of the date for payment by reference to which the calculation has been made.
   (2) If the amount of a compensation payment calculated in accordance with section 8 is nil, a person giving a statement saying so is to be treated for the purposes of this Act as making a payment within section 1(1)(a) on the day on which he gives the statement.
   (3) Where a person—
   (a) makes a compensation payment calculated in accordance with section 8, and
   (b) if the amount of the compensation payment so calculated is nil, gives a statement saying so,
he is to be treated, for the purpose of determining any rights and liabilities in respect of contribution or indemnity, as having paid the gross amount of the compensation payment.
   (4) For the purposes of this Act—
   (a) the gross amount of the compensation payment is the amount of the compensation payment apart from section 8, and
   (b) the amount of any recoverable benefit is the amount determined in accordance with the certificate of recoverable benefits.

Reviews and appeals

Review of certificates of recoverable benefits

1.197   **10.**—[¹(1) Any certificate of recoverable benefits may be reviewed by the Secretary of State
(a) either within the prescribed period or in prescribed circumstances; and
(b) either on an application made for the purpose or on his own initiative.]
(2) On a review under this section the Secretary of State may either—
(a) confirm the certificate, or
(b) (subject to subsection (3)) issue a fresh certificate containing such variations as he considers appropriate[¹ or
(c) revoke the certificate.]
(3) The Secretary of State may not vary the certificate so as to increase the total amount of the recoverable benefits unless it appears to him that the variation is required as a result of the person who applied for the certificate supplying him with incorrect or insufficient information.

AMENDMENT

1. Social Security Act 1998, Sched. 7, para. 149 (March 4, 1999 for the making of regulations, November 25, 1999 for other purposes).

GENERAL NOTE

Subsection (1)

1.198   Note that the Social Security Act 1998 does not abolish the concept of review in this context. No period has been prescribed, so an application for review may be made at any time. The circumstances in which a decision may be reviewed are prescribed by regulation 9 of the Social Security and Child Support (Decisions and Appeals) Regulations 1999 and are very broad. However, there is no right of appeal against a refusal to review a certificate of recoverable benefits so that it may be unwise to apply for a review instead of appealing if that might cause the time for appealing to expire (particularly as regulation 9(d) of the 1999 Regulations allows the Secretary of State to review a decision if satisfied that a ground of appeal has been made out), although pursuing that alternative course of action might be regarded as a reason for admitting a late appeal and subs. (3) provides protection on a review that is lacking on an appeal.

Subsection (3)

1.199   This is an important provision. Once a certificate has been issued, it cannot be varied on review so as to increase the amount of recoverable benefits unless the person who applied for the certificate (the compensator) caused the error. As the Secretary of State has only four weeks in which to issue the certificate (s.4(3)(b) and (8)(b), it may occasionally be impossible to obtain accurate information and resort may be had to estimation (s.5(4)). If lack of information or an inaccurate estimate results in a calculation that turns out to be unfavourable to the Secretary of State, he is nevertheless bound by it until the certificate expires under s.4(4). However, any new certificate issued in respect of a later period may list the benefit omitted from the earlier one. Furthermore, subs. (3) does not prevent the amount of recoverable benefits from being increased on an appeal (*CSCS/1/95*).

Appeals against certificates of recoverable benefits

11.—(1) An appeal against a certificate of recoverable benefits may be made on the ground—
   (a) that any amount, rate or period specified in the certificate is incorrect, or
   (b) that listed benefits which have been, or are likely to be, paid otherwise than in respect of the accident, injury or disease in question have been brought into account [¹ or
   (c) that listed benefits which have not been, and are not likely to be, paid to the injured person during the relevant period have been brought into account, or
   (d) that the payment on the basis of which the certificate was issued is not a payment within section 1(1)(a)].
(2) An appeal under this section may be made by—
   (a) the person who applied for the certificate of recoverable benefits, or
[¹(aa) (in a case where the certificate was issued under section 7(2)(a)) the person to whom it was so issued, or]
   (b) (in a case where the amount of the compensation payment has been calculated under section 8) the injured person or other person to whom the payment is made.
(3) No appeal may be made under this section until—
   (a) the claim giving rise to the compensation payment has been finally disposed of, and
   (b) the liability under section 6 has been discharged.
(4) For the purposes of subsection (3)(a), if an award of damages in respect of a claim has been made under or by virtue of—
   (a) section 32A(2)(a) of the Supreme Court Act 1981,
   (b) section 12(2)(a) of the Administration of Justice Act 1982, or
   (c) section 51(2)(a) of the County Courts Act 1984,
(orders for provisional damages in personal injury cases), the claim is to be treated as having been finally disposed of.
(5) Regulations may make provision—
   (a) as to the manner in which, and the time within which, appeals under this section may be made,
   (b) as to the procedure to be followed where such an appeal is made, and
   (c) for the purpose of enabling any such appeal to be treated as an application for review under section 10.
(6) [¹ . . .]

AMENDMENT

1. Social Security Act 1998, Sched. 7, para. 150 and Sched. 8 (November 29, 1999).

GENERAL NOTE

Subsection (1)
The grounds on which appeals may be brought have been expanded. The insertion of para. (d) and s.12(4)(c) appears to reverse *CSCR/3/95* in which it

was held that no appeal lay, and resort had to be had to judicial review, in a case where it was asserted that the Act did not apply at all. In *CSCR/746/97*, it was held that a tribunal had no jurisdiction to consider the "validity, properly so called" of a certificate. The victim had argued that the certificate was invalid because it had not been signed on behalf of the Secretary of State. The Commissioner held that such a challenge had to be brought by way of an application for judicial review.

Subsection (3)

1.202   An appeal cannot be brought until after the relevant payments have been made. See regulation 31(3) of the Social Security and Child Support (Decisions and Appeals) Regulations 1999 for the time within which an appeal must be brought.

Subsection (5)

1.203   See regulations 29, 31(3) and (4), 32 to 34, 38 to 40, 42 to 51 and 53 to 57 of the Social Security and Child Support (Decisions and Appeals) Regulations 1999. Note that regulation 29(6) has been made under subs. (5)(c). Note also that a tribunal considering an appeal under this section has no express power either to refer the victim for examination or to examine him themselves because the primary legislation contains no power equivalent to s.20 of the Social Security Act 1998 under which regulations 41 and 52 of the 1999 Regulations are made.

Reference of questions to medical appeal tribunal

1.204   **12.**—[¹(1) The Secretary of State must refer an appeal under section 11 to an appeal tribunal.]

(2) [¹...]

(3) In determining [¹ any appeal under section 11], the tribunal must take into account any decision of a court relating to the same, or any similar, issue arising in connection with the accident, injury or disease in question.

(4) On [¹ an appeal under section 11 an appeal tribunal] may either—

(a) confirm the amounts, rates and periods specified in the certificate of recoverable benefits, or

(b) specify any variations which are to be made on the issue of a fresh certificate under subsection (5) [¹ or

(c) declare that the certificate of recoverable benefits is to be revoked.]

(5) When the Secretary of State has received [¹the decision of the tribunal on the appeal under section 11, he must in accordance with that decision] either—

(a) confirm the certificate against which the appeal was brought, or

(b) issue a fresh certificate [¹ or

(c) revoke the certificate.]

(6) [¹ ...]

(7) Regulations [¹ ...] may (among other things) provide for the non-disclosure of medical advice or medical evidence given or submitted following a reference under subsection (1).

(8) [¹ ...]

AMENDMENT

1. Social Security Act 1999, Sched. 7, para. 151 and Sched. 8 (November 29, 1999).

GENERAL NOTE

The reference in the heading to a "medical appeal tribunal" has become an anachronism now that such tribunals have been replaced by the appeal tribunals introduced by the Social Security Act 1998.

Subsection (1)
An appeal under s.11(1)(b) must be heard by a tribunal consisting of a legally qualified panel member and a medically qualified panel member, whereas appeals under section 11(1)(a), (c) or (d) are heard by a legally qualified panel member sitting alone (regulation 36 of the Social Security and Child Support (Decisions and Appeals) Regulations 1999). What happens if an appeal is brought under both paragraph (b) and one of the other paragraphs is unclear. Note that the primary legislation includes no provision equivalent to s.20 of the Social Security Act 1998. Therefore, even when the tribunal includes a medically qualified panel member, the tribunal has no express power to examine the victim, although there is also no express prohibition on such an examination. Presumably the victim could consent to an examination. There is not even any express power to refer a victim for examination but it is difficult to see any objection to there being such a reference, provided the victim were to consent and some arrangement could be made for the payment of an examining doctor.

1.205

Subsection (4)
In *CCR/4/93* and *CSCR/1/95*, Commissioners held that, on appeals, the Secretary of State was entitled to refer to the tribunal questions which related to benefits that were not on the original "certificates of total benefit" (the forerunners of certificates of recoverable benefits). In the first case the Commissioner held that, on an appeal, all matters were at large. In the second case, the Commissioner took a narrower approach and held that a tribunal were strictly confined to the issues referred to them by the Secretary of State but that, in that case, the new benefits were within the scope of the reference. The Commissioner noted the contrast between the position on appeal and the limitation, now contained in s.10(3), with respect to reviews and warned of the perils of appealing.

Under the new legislation as amended, what are before the tribunal by virtue of subs. (1) are the "appeal" under s.11 and all matters that can fairly be said to arise within that appeal—and within the province of the tribunal bearing in mind its constitution (see the note to subs. (1) above)—are before the tribunal. There is no provision in this Act equivalent to s.12(8)(a) of the Social Security Act 1998, but it is suggested that the approach should be the same: the tribunal may deal with issues not expressly raised by the notice of appeal but are not bound to do so, provided they exercise that discretion judicially.

Subsection (7)
See regulation 42 of the Social Security and Child Support (Decisions and Appeals) Regulations 1999.

1.206

Appeal to Social Security Commissioner

13.—(1) An appeal may be made to a Commissioner against any decision of [¹ an appeal tribunal] under section 12 on the ground that the decision was erroneous in point of law.

1.207

(2) An appeal under this section may be made by—
(a) the Secretary of State,
(b) the person who applied for the certificate of recoverable benefits,
[¹(bb) (in a case where that certificate was issued under section 7(2)(a)) the person to whom it was issued, or]

Social Security (Recovery of Benefits) Act 1997

(c) (in a case where the amount of the compensation payment has been calculated in accordance with section 8) the injured person or other person to whom the payment is made.

(3) [¹Subsections (7) to (12) of section 14 of the Social Security Act 1998] apply to appeals under this section as they apply to appeals under that section.

(4) [¹...]

AMENDMENT

1. Social Security Act 1998, Sched 7, para. 152 and Sched. 8 (November 29, 1999).

GENERAL NOTE

Subsection (1)

1.208   For the scope of the phrase "erroneous in point of law", see the note to s.14 of the Social Security Act 1998.

The terms of s.15 of the 1998 Act are wide enough to permit an appeal to an appropriate court against a decision of a Commissioner given under this section.

Subsection (3)

1.209   S.14(10) of the Social Security Act 1998 provides that an appeal may be brought only with the leave of a tribunal chairman or a Commissioner and s.14(11) enables regulations to be made as to the time within which applications for leave must be made. Unfortunately, even though those provisions apply to appeals under this Act (see s.13(3)), regulation 58 of the Social Security and Child Support (Decisions and Appeals) Regulations 1999 makes provision only in respect of applications for leave to appeal against decisions made under sections 12 and 13 of that Act. S.13(3) of this Act does not provide that regulations made under s.14(11) have effect for the purposes of this Act when expressly limited to appeals under that Act. Therefore, there appears to be no prescribed time for applying to a tribunal chairman for leave to appeal against a decision made under section 12 of this Act.

Reviews and appeals: supplementary

1.210   **14.**—(1) This section applies in cases where a fresh certificate of recoverable benefits is issued as a result of a review under section 10 or an appeal under section 11.

(2) If—

(a) a person has made one or more payments to the Secretary of State under section 6, and

(b) in consequence of the review or appeal, it appears that the total amount paid is more than the amount that ought to have been paid,

regulations may provide for the Secretary of State to pay the difference to that person, or to the person to whom the compensation payment is made, or partly to one and partly to the other.

(3) If—

(a) a person has made one or more payments to the Secretary of State under section 6, and

(b) in consequence of the review or appeal, it appears that the total amount paid is less than the amount that ought to have been paid,

regulations may provide for that person to pay the difference to the Secretary of State.

(4) Regulations under this section may provide—
(a) for the re-calculation in accordance with section 8 of the amount of any compensation payment,
(b) for giving credit for amounts already paid, and
(c) for the payment by any person of any balance or the recovery from any person of any excess,

and may provide for any matter by modifying this Act.

GENERAL NOTE

See reg. 11 of the Social Security (Recovery of Benefits) Regulations 1997. 1.211

Courts

Court orders

15.—(1) This section applies where a court makes an order for a compensation payment to be made in any case, unless the order is made with the consent of the injured person and the person by whom the payment is to be made. 1.212

(2) The court must, in the case of each head of compensation listed in column 1 of Schedule 2 to which any of the compensation payment is attributable, specify in the order the amount of the compensation payment which is attributable to that head.

GENERAL NOTE

Subsection (2)

A court hearing a case within five years of a relevant accident must specify the amount of the compensation awarded that was attributable to any particular head in column 1 of Sched. 2 in respect of the whole five year period, because the court cannot know when payment of the sum awarded will actually be made (*Mitchell v. Laing*) (*The Times,* January 28, 1998). Nonetheless, the compensator was to deduct only those benefits that had been paid or were due to be paid up until the date of the payment of the sum awarded by the court. 1.213

The court's view must be taken into account by any tribunal considering an appeal against a certificate of recoverable benefits (see s.12(3)) and, presumably, also by the Secretary of State considering a review (see regulation 9(d) of the Social Security and Child Support (Decisions and Appeals) Regulations 1999). However, the principal purpose of s.15(2) is to enable s.8 to be operated properly.

Payments into court

16.—(1) Regulations may make provision (including provision modifying this Act) for any case in which a payment into court is made. 1.214

(2) The regulations may (among other things) provide—

Social Security (Recovery of Benefits) Act 1997

(a) for the making of a payment into court to be treated in prescribed circumstances as the making of a compensation payment,
(b) for application for, and issue of, certificates of recoverable benefits, and
(c) for the relevant period to be treated as ending on a date determined in accordance with the regulations.

(3) Rules of court may make provision governing practice and procedure in such cases.

(4) This section does not extend to Scotland.

GENERAL NOTE

1.215   In *McCafferey v. Datta* [1997] 1 W.L.R. 870, the defendant had made a payment into court. The plaintiff obtained judgement for a sum in excess of the payment into court but the whole of the sum obtained was recouped by the Secretary of State. The Court of Appeal held that she was nonetheless entitled to her costs. It was suggested that, if a defendant wishes to protect himself as to costs when he considers that the plaintiff will not recover more than the amount payable to the Compensation Recovery Unit, he must offer a specific sum not exceeding the amount certified by the certificate of total benefit, pointing out that if the offer is accepted he will pay that sum to the Compensation Recovery Unit. If the offer is not accepted and the plaintiff recovers judgement for less than the offer, the defendant will be able to rely on the offer on the question of costs.

1.216   *Subss. (1) and (2)* See regulation 8 of the Social Security (Recovery of Benefits) Regulations 1997.

1.217   *Subs. (3)* See C.P.R. rule 36.23 and P.D. 36, para. 10.

Benefits irrelevant to assessment of damages

1.218   **17.** In assessing damages in respect of any accident, injury or disease, the amount of any listed benefits paid or likely to be paid is to be disregarded.

1.219   GENERAL NOTE

Benefits are disregarded not only when assessing damages but also when calculating interest on the damages, so that recoverable benefits are not to be deducted from damages for loss of earnings before calculating the interest due (*Wisely v. John Fulton (Plumbers) Ltd, Wadey v. Surrey County Council* [2000] 1 W.L.R. 820 (HL)).

Reduction of compensation: complex cases

Lump sum and periodical payments

1.220   **18.**—(1) Regulations may make provision (including provision modifying this Act) for any case in which two or more compensation payments in the form of lump sums are made by the same person to or in respect of the injured person in consequence of the same accident, injury or disease.

(2) The regulations may (among other things) provide—

(a) for the re-calculation in accordance with section 8 of the amount of any compensation payment,
(b) for giving credit for amounts already paid, and
(c) for the payment by any person of any balance or the recovery from any person of any excess.

(3) For the purposes of subsection (2), the regulations may provide for the gross amounts of the compensation payments to be aggregated and for—
(a) the aggregate amount to be taken to be the gross amount of the compensation payment for the purposes of section 8,
(b) so much of the aggregate amount as is attributable to a head of compensation listed in column 1 of Schedule 2 to be taken to be the part of the gross amount which is attributable to that head;

and for the amount of any recoverable benefit shown against any head in column 2 of that Schedule to be taken to be the amount determined in accordance with the most recent certificate of recoverable benefits.

(4) Regulations may make provision (including provision modifying this Act) for any case in which, in final settlement of the injured person's claim, an agreement is entered into for the making of—
(a) periodical compensation payments (whether of an income or capital nature), or
(b) periodical compensation payments and lump sum compensation payments.

(5) Regulations made by virtue of subsection (4) may (among other things) provide—
(a) for the relevant period to be treated as ending at a prescribed time,
(b) for the person who is to make the payments under the agreement to be treated for the purposes of this Act as if he had made a single compensation payment on a prescribed date.

(6) A periodical payment may be a compensation payment for the purposes of this section even though it is a small payment (as defined in Part II of Schedule 1).

GENERAL NOTE

Subsections (1) to (3)
See regulation 9 of the Social Security (Recovery of Benefits) Regulations 1997.

1.221

Subsections (4) to (6)
See regulation 10 of the Social Security (Recovery of Benefits) Regulations 1997.

1.222

Payments by more than one person

19.—(1) Regulations may make provision (including provision modifying this Act) for any case in which two or more persons ("the compensators") make compensation payments to or in respect of the

1.223

same injured person in consequence of the same accident, injury or disease.

(2) In such a case, the sum of the liabilities of the compensators under section 6 is not to exceed the total amount of the recoverable benefits, and the regulations may provide for determining the respective liabilities under that section of each of the compensators.

(3) The regulations may (among other things) provide in the case of each compensator—
   (a) for determining or re-determining the part of the recoverable benefits which may be taken into account in his case,
   (b) for calculating or re-calculating in accordance with section 8 the amount of any compensation payment,
   (c) for giving credit for amounts already paid, and
   (d) for the payment by any person of any balance or the recovery from any person of any excess.

GENERAL NOTE

1.224   See regs 9 and 10 of the Social Security (Recovery of Benefits) Regulations 1997.

Miscellaneous

Amounts overpaid under section 6

1.225   **20.**—(1) Regulations may make provision (including provision modifying this Act) for cases where a person has paid to the Secretary of State under section 6 any amount ("the amount of the overpayment") which he was not liable to pay.

(2) The regulations may provide—
   (a) for the Secretary of State to pay the amount of the overpayment to that person, or to the person to whom the compensation payment is made, or partly to one and partly to the other, or
   (b) for the receipt by the Secretary of State of the amount of the overpayment to be treated as the recovery of that amount.

(3) Regulations made by virtue of subsection (2)(b) are to have effect in spite of anything in section 71 of the Social Security Administration Act 1992 (overpayments—general).

(4) The regulations may also (among other things) provide—
   (a) for the re-calculation in accordance with section 8 of the amount of any compensation payment,
   (b) for giving credit for amounts already paid, and
   (c) for the payment by any person of any balance or the recovery from any person of any excess.

(5) This section does not apply in a case where section 14 applies.

GENERAL NOTE

1.226   No regulations have been made under this section.

Compensation payments to be disregarded

21.—(1) If, when a compensation payment is made, the first and second conditions are met, the payment is to be disregarded for the purposes of sections 6 and 8.

(2) The first condition is that the person making the payment—
(a) has made an application for a certificate of recoverable benefits which complies with subsection (3), and
(b) has in his possession a written acknowledgement of the receipt of his application.

(3) An application complies with this subsection if it—
(a) accurately states the prescribed particulars relating to the injured person and the accident, injury or disease in question, and
(b) specifies the name and address of the person to whom the certificate is to be sent.

(4) The second condition is that the Secretary of State has not sent the certificate to the person, at the address, specified in the application, before the end of the period allowed under section 4.

(5) In any case where—
(a) by virtue of subsection (1), a compensation payment is disregarded for the purposes of sections 6 and 8, but
(b) the person who made the compensation payment nevertheless makes a payment to the Secretary of State for which (but for subsection (1)) he would be liable under section 6,

subsection (1) is to cease to apply in relation to the compensation payment.

(6) If, in the opinion of the Secretary of State, circumstances have arisen which adversely affect normal methods of communication—
(a) he may by order provide that subsection (1) is not to apply during a specified period not exceeding three months, and
(b) he may continue any such order in force for further periods not exceeding three months at a time.

GENERAL NOTE

If a certificate of recoverable benefits is not issued within four weeks (subject to subs. (6)) following receipt and acknowledgement of a full and accurate application, the Secretary of State loses his right of recovery. It is clear from subs. (4) that the late issue of a certificate will not do. However, if the compensator makes a payment to the Secretary of State in error – perhaps in reliance on an expired certificate – the Secretary of State is not obliged to pay it back because the dispensation under this section ceases to apply (subs. (5)). For the date on which an application is treated as received, see regulation 7(2) of the Social Security (Recovery of Benefits) Regulations 1997 which is made under s.4(9).

Subsection (3)

For the prescribed particulars, see regulation 7(1) of the Social Security (Recovery of Benefits) Regulations 1997.

Subsection (4)

The period allowed under s.4(3) and (8) is four weeks, but see s.21(6).

Subsection (5)

It is not clear whether the Secretary of State can, by issuing an out of time certificate, insist on obtaining more than the payment made by the compensator or whether he is confined to accepting what has been sent, which is likely to have been based on an earlier certificate.

1.232   **22.** *Omitted.*

Provision of information

1.233   **23.**—(1) Where compensation is sought in respect of any accident, injury or disease suffered by any person ("the injured person"), the following persons must give the Secretary of State the prescribed information about the injured person—
  (a) anyone who is, or is alleged to be, liable in respect of the accident, injury or disease, and
  (b) anyone acting on behalf of such a person.

(2) A person who receives or claims a listed benefit which is or is likely to be paid in respect of an accident, injury or disease suffered by him, must give the Secretary of State the prescribed information about the accident, injury or disease.

(3) Where a person who has received a listed benefit dies, the duty in subsection (2) is imposed on his personal representative.

(4) Any person who makes a payment (whether on his own behalf or not)—
  (a) in consequence of, or
  (b) which is referable to any costs (in Scotland, expenses) incurred by reason of,
any accident, injury or disease, or any damage to property, must, if the Secretary of State requests him in writing to do so, give the Secretary of State such particulars relating to the size and composition of the payment as are specified in the request.

(5) The employer of a person who suffers or has suffered an accident, injury or disease, and anyone who has been the employer of such a person at any time during the relevant period, must give the Secretary of State the prescribed information about the payment of statutory sick pay in respect of that person.

(6) In subsection (5) "employer" has the same meaning as it has in Part XI of the Social Security Contributions and Benefits Act 1992.

(7) A person who is required to give information under this section must do so in the prescribed manner, at the prescribed place and within the prescribed time.

(8) Section 1 does not apply in relation to this section.

GENERAL NOTE

1.234   *Subsection (1)*
See regulation 3 of the Social Security (Recovery of Benefits) Regulations 1997.

1.235   *Subsection (2)*
See regulation 4 of the Social Security (Recovery of Benefits) Regulations 1997.

(1997 c.27, s.23)

Subsection (5)
See regulation 5 of the Social Security (Recovery of Benefits) Regulations 1997.   1.236

Subsection (7)
See regulation 6 of the Social Security (Recovery of Benefits) Regulations 1997.   1.237

Power to amend Schedule 2

24.—(1) The Secretary of State may by regulations amend Schedule 2.   1.238
(2) A statutory instrument which contains such regulations shall not be made unless a draft of the instrument has been laid before and approved by resolution of each House of Parliament.

Provisions relating to Northern Ireland

25.–27. *Omitted.*

General

The Crown

28. This Act applies to the Crown.   1.239

GENERAL NOTE

This is effectively a new provision because s.104 of the Social Security Administration Act 1992 was never brought into force (see Social Security (Consequential Provisions) Act 1992, Sched. 4, para. 3).   1.240

General interpretation

29. In this Act—   1.241
  [¹"appeal tribunal" means an appeal tribunal constituted under Chapter I of Part I of the Social Security Act 1998,]
  "benefit" means any benefit under the Social Security Contributions and Benefits Act 1992, a jobseeker's allowance or mobility allowance,
  [¹"Commissioner" has the same meaning as in Chapter II of Part I of the Social Security Act 1998 (see section 39),]
  "compensation scheme for motor accidents" means any scheme or arrangement under which funds are available for the payment of compensation in respect of motor accidents caused, or alleged to have been caused, by uninsured or unidentified persons,
  "listed benefit" means a benefit listed in column 2 of Schedule 2,
  "payment" means payment in money or money's worth, and related expressions are to be interpreted accordingly,

Social Security (Recovery of Benefits) Act 1997

"prescribed" means prescribed by regulations, and
"regulations" means regulations made by the Secretary of State.

Regulations and orders

1.242   **30.**—(1) Any power under this Act to make regulations or an order is exercisable by statutory instrument.

(2) A statutory instrument containing regulations or an order under this Act (other than regulations under section 24 or an order under section 34) shall be subject to annulment in pursuance of a resolution of either House of Parliament.

(3) Regulations under section 20, under section 24 amending the list of benefits in column 2 of Schedule 2 or under paragraph 9 of Schedule 1 may not be made without the consent of the Treasury.

(4) Subsections (4), (5), (6) and (9) of section 189 of the Social Security Administration Act 1992 (regulations and orders—general) apply for the purposes of this Act as they apply for the purposes of that.

1.243   **31.** *Omitted.*

Power to make transitional, consequential etc. provisions

1.244   **32.**—(1) Regulations may make such transitional and consequential provisions, and such savings, as the Secretary of State considers necessary or expedient in preparation for, in connection with, or in consequence of—
   (a) the coming into force of any provision of this Act, or
   (b) the operation of any enactment repealed or amended by a provision of this Act during any period when the repeal or amendment is not wholly in force.

(2) Regulations under this section may (among other things) provide—
   (a) for compensation payments in relation to which, by virtue of section 2, this Act does not apply to be treated as payments in relation to which this Act applies,
   (b) for compensation payments in relation to which, by virtue of section 2, this Act applies to be treated as payments in relation to which this Act does not apply, and
   (c) for the modification of any enactment contained in this Act or referred to in subsection (1)(b) in its application to any compensation payment.

GENERAL NOTE

1.245   See regulation 12 of the Social Security (Recovery of Benefits) Regulations 1997.

1.246   **33.** *Omitted.*

Short title, commencement and extent

34.—(1) This Act may be cited as the Social Security (Recovery of Benefits) Act 1997.

(2) Sections 1 to 24, 26 to 28 and 33 are to come into force on such day as the Secretary of State may by order appoint, and different days may be appointed for different purposes.

(3) Apart from sections 25 to 27, section 33 so far as it relates to any enactment which extends to Northern Ireland, and this section this Act does not extend to Northern Ireland.

SCHEDULES

SCHEDULE 1

COMPENSATION PAYMENTS

PART I

Exempted payments

1. Any small payment (defined in Part II of this Schedule).
2. Any payment made to or for the injured person under section 35 of the Powers of Criminal Courts Act 1973 or section 249 of the Criminal Procedure (Scotland) Act 1995 (compensation orders against convicted persons).
3. Any payment made in the exercise of a discretion out of property held subject to a trust in a case where no more than 50 per cent. by value of the capital contributed to the trust was directly or indirectly provided by persons who are, or are alleged to be, liable in respect of—
   (a) the accident, injury or disease suffered by the injured person, or
   (b) the same or any connected accident, injury or disease suffered by another.
4. Any payment made out of property held for the purposes of any prescribed trust (whether the payment also falls within paragraph 3 or not).
5. Any payment made to the injured person by an insurance company within the meaning of the Insurance Companies Act 1982 under the terms of any contract of insurance entered into between the injured person and the company before—
   (a) the date on which the injured person first claims a listed benefit in consequence of the disease in question, or
   (b) the occurrence of the accident or injury in question.
6. Any redundancy payment falling to be taken into account in the assessment of damages in respect of an accident, injury or disease.
7. So much of any payment as is referable to costs.
8. Any prescribed payment.

PART II

Power to disregard small payments

9.—(1) Regulations may make provision for compensation payments to be disregarded for the purposes of sections 6 and 8 in prescribed cases where the amount of the compensation payment, or the aggregate amount of two or more connected compensation payments, does not exceed the prescribed sum.

(2) A compensation payment disregarded by virtue of this paragraph is referred to in paragraph 1 as a "small payment".

(3) For the purposes of this paragraph—
   (a) two or more compensation payments are "connected" if each is made to or in respect of the same injured person and in respect of the same accident, injury or disease, and

(b) any reference to a compensation payment is a reference to a payment which would be such a payment apart from paragraph 1.

GENERAL NOTE

1.250   For exempted trusts and payments prescribed for the purposes of paras. 4 and 8, see regulation 2 of the Social Security (Recovery of Benefits) Regulations 1997.

No regulations have been made under para. 9. Under the former legislation, payments not exceeding £2,500 were disregarded. Now general damages for pain and suffering are protected, because benefits can be recovered only from compensation for loss of earnings, care or loss of mobility, and so there is not considered to be a need for a general exemption for small claims. In *Black v. Doncaster Metropolitan Borough Council* (*The Times*, July 14, 1998), the defendant had paid £2,500 into court. The plaintiff claimed a far greater sum and the case was set down for trial in late October 1997, two or three weeks after the 1997 Act came into force. £2,500 would have been an exempt payment under the old legislation but under the 1997 Act the defendant was liable to pay £15,000 to the Secretary of State under s.6 if any payment at all were made to the plaintiff. Three days before trial, the plaintiff issued notice of acceptance of payment into court. The Court of Appeal held that payment out should have been refused.

SCHEDULE 2

1.251   CALCULATION OF COMPENSATION PAYMENT

(1) Head of compensation	(2) Benefit
1. Compensation for earnings lost during the relevant period	Disability working allowance Disablement pension payable under section 103 of the 1992 Act Incapacity benefit Income support Invalidity pension and allowance Jobseeker's allowance Reduced earnings allowance Severe disablement allowance Sickness benefit Statutory sick pay Unemployability supplement Unemployment benefit
2. Compensation for cost of care incurred during the relevant period	Attendance allowance Care component of disability living allowance Disablement pension increase payable under section 104 or 105 of the 1992 Act
3. Compensation for loss of mobility during the relevant period.	Mobility allowance Mobility component of disability living allowance

Notes

1.252   **1.**—(1) References to incapacity benefit, invalidity pension and allowance, severe disablement allowance, sickness benefit and unemployment benefit also include any income support paid with each of those benefits on the same instrument of payment or paid concurrently with each of those benefits by means of an instrument for benefit payment.

(2) For the purpose of this Note, income support includes personal expenses addition, special transitional additions and transitional addition as defined in the Income Support (Transitional) Regulations 1987.

2. Any reference to statutory sick pay—
  (a) includes only 80 per cent. of payments made between 6th April 1991 and 5th April 1994, and
  (b) does not include payments made on or after 6th April 1994.

3. In this Schedule "the 1992 Act" means the Social Security Contributions and Benefits Act 1992.

GENERAL NOTE

It may be thought odd that disablement pension should be regarded as paid in respect of loss of earnings rather than in respect of pain and suffering.

Given the way that ss.6 and 8 operate together, compensation for lost earnings presumably includes compensation for loss of *potential* earnings in the case of a person who was not employed at the time of a relevant accident or who was in temporary employment only. A benefit is recoverable only if it was paid "in respect of" the relevant accident, injury or disease (see the note to s.5).

"Compensation for loss of mobility" in para. 3, column 1 refers only to compensation for patrimonial (*i.e.*, financial) loss, such as the cost of fares for journeys by bus or taxi, and does not refer to any element of solatium (*i.e.*, compensation for pain and suffering or loss of amenity) (*Mitchell v. Laing (The Times*, January 28, 1998)).

1.253

Schedules 3 and 4: Omitted.

Social Security Contributions (Transfer of Functions, etc.) Act 1999

(1999 C.2)

ARRANGEMENT OF SECTIONS

PART I

GENERAL

1. to 7. *Omitted.*

1.254

PART II

DECISIONS AND APPEALS

8. Decisions by officers of Board.
9. to 16. *Omitted.*
17. Arrangement for discharge of decision-making functions.
18. and 19. *Omitted.*

Part III

Miscellaneous and supplemental

20 to 26. *Omitted.*

27. Interpretation.
28. Short title, commencement and extent.

Schedules

Omitted.

An Act to transfer from the Secretary of State to the Commissioners of Inland Revenue or the Treasury certain functions relating to national insurance contributions, the National Insurance Fund, statutory sick pay, statutory maternity pay or person schemes and certain associated functions relating to benefits; to enable functions relating to any of those matters in respect of Northern Ireland to be transferred to the Secretary of State, the Commissioners of Inland Revenue or the Treasury; to make further provision, in connection with the functions transferred, as to the powers of the Commissioners of Inland Revenue, the making of decisions and appeals; to provide that rebates payable in respect of members of money purchase contracted-out pension schemes are to be payable out of the National Insurance Fund; and for connected purposes.

[25th February 1999]

Part I

General

1.255 1.–7. *Omitted.*

Part II

Decisions and Appeals

Decisions by officers of Board

1.256 **8.**—(1) Subject to the provisions of the Part, it shall be for an officer of the Board—
   (a) to decide whether for the purposes of Parts I to V of the Social Security Contributions and Benefits Act 1992 a person is or was an earner and, if so, the category of earners in which he is or was to be included,
   (b) to decide whether a person is or was employed in employed earner's employment for the purposes of Part V of the Social Security Contributions and Benefits Act 1992 (industrial injuries),
   (c) to decide whether a person is or was liable to pay contributions of any particular class and, if so, the amount that he is or was liable to pay,
   (d) to decide whether a person is or was entitled to pay contributions

of any particular class that he is or was not liable to pay and, if so, the amount that he is or was entitled to pay,

(e) to decide whether contributions of a particular class have been paid in respect of any period,

(f) subject to and in accordance with regulations made for the purposes of this paragraph by the Secretary of State with the concurrence of the Board, to decide any issue arising as to, or in connection with, entitlement to statutory sick pay or statutory maternity pay,

(g) to make any other decision that falls to be made under Part XI of the Social Security Contributions and Benefits Act 1992 (statutory sick pay) or Part XII of that Act (statutory maternity pay),

(h) to decide any question as to the issue and content of a notice under subsection (2) of section 121C of the Social Security Administration Act 1992 (liability of directors etc. for company's contributions),

(i) to decide any issue arising under section 27 of the Jobseekers Act 1995 (employment of long-term unemployed; deductions by employers), or under any provision of regulations under that section, as to—

　(i) whether a person is or was an employee or employer of another,

　(ii) whether an employer is or was entitled to make any deduction from his contributions payments in accordance with regulations under section 27 of that Act,

　(iii) whether a payment falls to be made to an employer in accordance with those regulations,

　(iv) the amount that falls to be so deducted or paid, or

　(v) whether two or more employers are, by virtue of regulations under section 27 of that Act, to be treated as one,

(j) to decide whether a person is liable to pay interest under paragraph 7B(2)(e) of Schedule 1 to the Social Security Contributions and Benefits Act 1992,

(k) to decide whether a person is liable to a penalty under—

　(i) paragraph 7A(2) or 7B(2)(h) of Schedule 1 to the Social Security Contributions and Benefits Act 1992, or

　(ii) section 113(1)(a) of the Social Security Administration Act 1992,

(l) to decide the amount of interest or penalty payable under any of the provisions mentioned in paragraphs (j) and (k) above, and

(m) to decide such issues relating to contributions, other than the issues specified in paragraphs (a) to (l) above or in paragraphs 16 and 17 of Schedule 3 to the Social Security Act 1998, as may be prescribed by regulations made by the Board.

(2) *Omitted.*

(3) *Omitted.*

(4) *Omitted.*

1.257 GENERAL NOTE

This section provides for a number of matters previously determined by the Secretary of State for Social Security to be determined by the Board of Inland Revenue (see s.27). They are mainly concerned with contributions and employment status (which is important for entitlement to industrial injuries benefits (see para. (b)), but also include statutory sick pay and statutory maternity pay (see paras. (f) and (g)). Entitlement to statutory sick pay and statutory maternity pay had been determined by adjudication officers, until the Social Security Act 1998 transferred that function to the Secretary of State by provisions that never came fully into force because they were overtaken by this Act. Ss.9 to 14 of this Act make provision for decisions by the Board and appeals to the tax appeal Commissioners which are beyond the scope of this book.

This section is included here only because the matters to which it refers are clearly *not* to be decided by the Secretary of State and do *not* fall within the jurisdiction of appeal tribunals constituted under the 1998 Act.

1.258 9.–16. *Omitted.*

Arrangements for discharge of decision-making functions

1.259 **17.**—(1) The Secretary of State may make arrangements with the Board for any his functions under Chapter II of Part I of the Social Security Act 1998 in relation to—
  (a) a decision whether a person was (within the meaning of regulations) precluded from regular employment by responsibilities at home, or
  (b) a decision whether a person is entitled to be credited with earnings or contributions in accordance with regulations made under section 22(5) of the Social Security Contributions and Benefits Act 1992,
to be discharged by the Board or by officers of the Board.

(2) No such arrangements shall effect the responsibility of the Secretary of State or the application of Chapter II of Part I of the Social Security Act 1998 in relation to any decision.

(3) *Omitted.*

1.260 18.–19. *Omitted.*

PART III

MISCELLANEOUS AND SUPPLEMENTAL

1.261 20.–26. *Omitted.*

Interpretation

1.262 **27.** In this Act, unless a contrary intention appears—
  "the Board" means the Commissioners of Inland Revenue;
  "contributions" means contributions under Part I of the Social Security Contributions and Benefits Act 1992.

Short title, commencement and extent

28.—(1) This Act may be cited as the Social Security Contributions (Transfer of Functions, etc.) Act 1999.

1.263

(2) *Omitted.*

(3) *Omitted.*

(4) *Omitted.*

(5) *Omitted.*

(6) *Omitted.*

(7) *Omitted.*

Schedules 1 to 10 Omitted.

1.264

Social Security Act 1998

(1998 c.14)

ARRANGEMENT OF SECTIONS

PART I

DECISIONS AND APPEALS

CHAPTER I

GENERAL

Decisions

1. Transfer of functions to Secretary of State.
2. Use of computers.
3. Use of information.

1.265

Appeals

4. Unified appeal tribunals.
5. President of appeal tribunals.
6. Panel for appointment to appeal tribunals.
7. Constitution of appeal tribunals.

Social Security Act 1998

CHAPTER II

SOCIAL SECURITY DECISIONS AND APPEALS

Decisions

8. Decisions by Secretary of State.
9. Revision of decisions.
10. Decisons superseding earlier decisions.
10A. Reference of issues by Secretary of State to Inland Revenue.
11. Regulations with respect to decisions.

Appeals

12. Appeal to appeal tribunal.
13. Redetermination etc. of appeals by tribunal.
14. Appeal from tribunal to Commissioner.
15. Appeal from Commissioner on point of law.

Procedure etc.

16. Procedure.
17. Finality of decisions.
18. Matters arising as respects decisions.

Medical examinations

19. Medical examination required by Secretary of State.
20. Medical examination required by appeal tribunal.

Suspension and termination of benefit

21. Suspension in prescribed circumstances.
22. Suspension for failure to furnish information etc.
23. Termination in cases of failure to furnish information.
24. Suspension and termination for failure to submit to medical examination.

Appeals dependent on issues falling to be decided by Inland Revenue

24A. Appeals dependent on issues falling to be decided by Inland Revenue.

Decisions and appeals dependent on other cases

25. Decisions involving issues that arise on appeal in other cases.
26. Appeals involving issues that arise on appeal in other cases.

Cases of error

27. Restrictions on entitlement to benefit in certain cases of error.
28. Correct of errors and setting aside of decisions.

Industrial accidents

29. Decision that accident is an industrial accident.
30. Effect of decision.

Other special cases

31. Incapacity for work.
32. Industrial diseases.
33. Christmas bonus.

Housing benefit and council tax benefit

Paras, 34. and 35. *Omitted.*

Social fund payment

36. Appropriate officers.
37. The Social Fund Commissioner and inspectors.
38. Reviews of determinations.

Supplemental

39. Interpretation etc. of Chapter II.

CHAPTER III

OTHER DECISIONS AND APPEALS

40. to 47. *Omitted.*

PART II

CONTRIBUTIONS

48. to 66. *Omitted.*

Social Security Act 1998

PART III

BENEFITS

67. to 76. *Omitted.*

PART IV

MISCELLANEOUS AND SUPPLEMENTAL

77. Pilot schemes.
78. *Omitted.*
79. Regulations and orders.
80. Parliamentary control of regulations.
81. *Reports by Secretary of State.*
82. *Omitted.*
83. *Omitted.*
84. Interpretation: general.
85. *Omitted.*
86. *Omitted.*
87. Short title, commencement and extent.

SCHEDULES

Schedule 1—Appeal tribunals: supplementary provisions.
Schedule 2—Decisions against which no appeal lies.
Schedule 3—Decisions against which an appeal lies.
   Part I—Benefit decisions.
   Part II—*Omitted.*
Schedule 4—Social Security Commissioners.
Schedule 5—Regulations as to procedure: provision which may be made.
Schedule 6—*Omitted.*
Schedule 7—*Omitted.*
Schedule 8—*Omitted.*

An Act to make provision as to the making of decisions and the determination of appeals under enactments relating to social security, child support, vaccine damage payments and war pensions; to make further provision with respect to social security; and for connected purposes   [21st May 1998]

PART I

DECISIONS AND APPEALS

CHAPTER I

GENERAL

Decisions

Transfer of functions to Secretary of State

1.266   **1.** The following functions are hereby transferred to the Secretary of State, namely—

(a) the functions of adjudication officers appointed under section 38 of the Social Security Administration Act 1992 ("the Administration Act");
(b) the functions of social fund officers appointed under section 64 of that Act; and
(c) the functions of child support officers appointed under section 13 of the Child Support Act 1991 ("the Child Support Act").

GENERAL NOTE

This is a transitional provision, transferring existing cases to the new system brought into effect under Chapter II. For the functions of adjudication officers, see s.20 of the Social Security Administration Act 1992 and s.9(6) of the Jobseekers Act 1995. Essentially, all questions arising on, or in connection with, a claim for benefit, other than those already reserved to the Secretary of State, were referred to adjudication officers. At first sight unifying the roles seems a major simplification but in fact it will not make a great deal of difference. The main practical distinction between adjudication officers' decisions and Secretary of State's decisions were that the former were appealable and the latter were not (except in a few cases). Now all decisions are to be made by the Secretary of State but provision is made for some decisions to be unappealable (Sched. 2 to the Act and Sched. 2 to the Social Security and Child Support (Decisions and Appeals) Regulations 1999) whereas others are appealable (s.12(1) and Sched. 3 to the Act). Those that are unappealable are more or less the same decisions that were made by the Secretary of State under the old legislation; those that are appealable are generally the decisions formerly made by adjudication officers. So far as they relate to working families' tax credit and disabled person's tax credit, the functions are now transferred to an officer of the Inland Revenue from October 5, 1999 (Tax Credits Act 1999, s.2(1)(b) and Sched. 2, para. 5(a)).

1.267

Use of computers

2.—(1) Any decision, determination or assessment falling to be made or certificate falling to be issued by the Secretary of State under or by virtue of a relevant enactment, or in relation to a war pension, may be made or issued not only by an officer of his acting under his authority but also—

(a) by a computer for whose operation such an officer is responsible; and
(b) in the case of a decision, determination or assessment that may be made or a certificate that may be issued by a person providing services to the Secretary of State, by a computer for whose operation such a person is responsible.

(2) In this section "relevant enactment" means any enactment contained in—
(a) Chapter II of this Part;
(b) the Social Security Contributions and Benefits Act 1992 ("the Contributions and Benefits Act");
(c) the Administration Act;
(d) the Child Support Act;
(e) the Social Security (Incapacity for Work) Act 1994;
(f) the Jobseekers Act 1995 ("the Jobseekers Act");

1.268

Social Security Act 1998

(g) the Child Support Act 1995; or
(h) the Social Security (Recovery of Benefits) Act 1997.

(3) In this section and section 3 below "war pension" has the same meaning as in section 25 of the Social Security Act 1989 (establishment and functions of war pensions committees).

Use of information

1.269   **3.**—(1) Subsection (2) below applies to information relating to social security, child support or war pensions which is held—
(a) by the Secretary of State or the Northern Ireland Department; or
(b) by a person providing services to the Secretary of State or the Northern Ireland Department in connection with the provision of those services.
(2) Information to which this subsection applies—
(a) may be used for the purposes of, or for any purposes connected with, the exercise of functions in relation to social security, child support or war pensions; and
(b) may be supplied to, or to a person providing services to, the Secretary of State or the Northern Ireland Department for use for those purposes.
(3) The following sections, namely—
(a) section 122C of the Administration Act (supply of information to authorities administering benefit); and
(b) section 122D of that Act (supply of information by authorities administering benefit),
shall each have effect as if the reference in subsection (1) to social security included references to child support and war pensions.
(4) In this section "the Northern Ireland Department" means the Department of Health and Social Services for Northern Ireland.

Appeals

Unified appeal tribunals

1.270   **4.**—(1) Subject to the provisions of this Act—
(a) the functions of social security appeal tribunals, disability appeal tribunals and medical appeal tribunals constituted under Part II of the Administration Act;
(b) the functions of child support appeal tribunals established under section 21 of the Child Support Act; and
(c) the functions of vaccine damage tribunals established by regulations made under section 4 of the Vaccine Damage Payments Act 1979 ("the Vaccine Damage Payments Act"),
are hereby transferred to appeal tribunals constituted under the following provisions of this Chapter.
(2) Accordingly appeals under—
(a) section 12 below;

(b) section 20 of the Child Support Act, as substituted by section 42 below;
(c) section 4 of the Vaccine Damage Payments Act, as substituted by section 46 below; and
(d) section 11 of the Social Security (Recovery of Benefits) Act 1997,

shall be determined by appeal tribunals so constituted (in the following provisions of this Chapter referred to as "appeal tribunals").

GENERAL NOTE

Like s.1, this is a transitional provision, bringing existing cases into the new system established under Chapter II. As with the changes wrought by s.1, the changes made by this section are not quite as dramatic as they might appear at first sight. Tribunals are unified in name but reg. 36 of the Social Security and Child Support (Decisions and Appeals) Regulations 1999 provides that the composition of the tribunal is determined by the subject matter of the appeal. More importantly, the flexibility that one might hope for under a unified tribunal is somewhat reduced because it is far more difficult than it was before for tribunals to draw together all outstanding issues concerning a claimant and deal with them all at once. Everything must first be the subject of a decision by the Secretary of State and then be the subject of a separate appeal. The Secretary of State has no power to refer outstanding questions to a tribunal dealing with another case concerning the same claimant and tribunals no longer have an express power to deal with matters first arising before them (as there was in s.36 of the Social Security Administration Act 1992). See the note to s.12 for further discussion of the significance of these changes.

1.271

President of appeal tribunals

5.—(1) The Lord Chancellor may, after consultation with the Lord Advocate, appoint a President of appeal tribunals.

1.272

(2) A person is qualified to be appointed President if—
(a) he has a 10 year general qualification (construed in accordance with section 71 of the Courts and Legal Services Act 1990); or
(b) he is an advocate or solicitor in Scotland of at least 10 years' standing.

(3) Schedule 1 to this Act shall have effect for supplementing this section.

GENERAL NOTE

By the Transfer of Functions (Lord Advocate and Secretary of State) Order 1999, S.I. 1999/678, art. 2(1) and Sched., the functions of the Lord Advocate under this section are transferred to the Secretary of State.

1.273

Panel for appointment to appeal tribunals

6.—(1) The Lord Chancellor shall constitute a panel of persons to act as members of appeals tribunals.

1.274

(2) Subject to subsection (3) below, the panel shall be composed of such persons as the Lord Chancellor thinks fit to appoint after consultation, in the case of medical practitioners, with the Chief Medical Officer.

(3) The panel shall include persons possessing such qualifications as

may be prescribed by regulations made with the concurrence of the Lord Chancellor.

(4) The numbers of persons appointed to the panel, and the terms and conditions of their appointments, shall be determined by the Lord Chancellor with the consent of the Secretary of State.

(5) A person may be removed from the panel by the Lord Chancellor on the ground of incapacity or misbehaviour.

(6) In this section "the Chief Medical Officer" means—
  (a) in relation to England, the Chief Medical Officer of the Department of Health;
  (b) in relation to Wales, the Chief Medical Officer of the Welsh Office; and
  (c) in relation to Scotland, the Chief Medical Officer of the [¹ Scottish Administration]

AMENDMENT

1. Scotland Act 1998 (Consequential Modifications) (No. 1) Order 1999 (S.I. 1999 No. 1042), art. 5 and Sched. 3, Pt. I, para. 4.

GENERAL NOTE

Subsection (3).

1.275 By reg. 35 of, and Sched. 3 to, the Social Security and Child Support (Decisions and Appeals) Regulations 1999, panel members must be lawyers, doctors, accountants or people other than doctors who are experienced in dealing with the needs of disabled persons. Other lay people no longer have a part to play in tribunals.

Constitution of appeal tribunals

1.276 7.—(1) Subject to subsection (2) below, an appeal tribunal shall consist of one, two or three members drawn by the President from the panel constituted under section 6 above.

(2) The member, or (as the case may be) at least one member, of an appeal tribunal must—
  (a) have a general qualification (construed in accordance with section 71 of the Courts and Legal Services Act 1990); or
  (b) be an advocate or solicitor in Scotland.

(3) Where an appeal tribunal has more than one member—
  (a) the President shall nominate one of the members as chairman;
  (b) decisions shall be taken by a majority of votes; and
  (c) unless regulations otherwise provide, the chairman shall have any casting vote.

(4) Where it appears to an appeal tribunal that a matter before it involves a question of fact of special difficulty, then, unless regulations otherwise provide, the tribunal may require one or more experts to provide assistance to it in dealing with the question.

(5) In subsection (4) above "expert" means a member of the panel constituted under section 6 above who appears to the appeal tribunal concerned to have knowledge or experience which would be relevant in determining the question of fact of special difficulty.

(6) Regulations shall make provision with respect to—
(a) the composition of appeal tribunals;
(b) the procedure to be followed in allocating cases among differently constituted tribunals; and
(c) the manner in which expert assistance is to be given under subsection (4) above.

(7) Schedule 1 to this Act shall have effect for supplementing this section.

GENERAL NOTE

Subsections (2) and (3)
In *Improving decision making and appeals in Social Security* (Cm 3328), para. 5.5, it was suggested that there was no need for every tribunal to have a lawyer among its members. However, the legislation as enacted does require a lawyer who must be a barrister, solicitor or advocate but who need not be of any particular seniority. There is no requirement that the legally qualified member of a two or three person tribunal should be the chairman although that is the invariable practice at the moment.

1.277

Subsection (6)
See regs 36 and 50 of the Social Security and Child Support (Decisions and Appeals) Regulations 1999.

1.278

CHAPTER II

SOCIAL SECURITY DECISIONS AND APPEALS

Decisions

Decisions by Secretary of State

8.—(1) Subject to the provisions of this Chapter, it shall be for the Secretary of State—
(a) to decide any claim for a relevant benefit;
(b) to decide any claim for a social fund payment mentioned in section 138(1)(b) of the Contributions and Benefits Act; [¹ and]
(c) subject to subsection (5) below, to make any decision that falls to be made under or by virtue of a relevant enactment; [¹ . . .]
(d) [¹ . . .]

(2) Where at any time a claim for a relevant benefit is decided by the Secretary of State—
(a) the claim shall not be regarded as subsisting after that time; and
(b) accordingly, the claimant shall not (without making a further claim) be entitled to the benefit on the basis of circumstances not obtaining at that time.

(3) In this Chapter "relevant benefit" [³ . . .] means any of the following, namely—
(a) benefit under Parts II to V of the Contributions and Benefits Act;

1.279

(b) a jobseeker's allowance;
(c) income support;
(d) [²working families' tax credit];
(e) [²disabled person's tax credit];
(f) a social fund payment mentioned in section 138(1)(a) or (2) of the Contributions and Benefits Act;
(g) child benefit;
(h) such other benefit as may be prescribed.

(4) In this section "relevant enactment" means any enactment contained in this Chapter, the Contributions and Benefits Act, the Administration Act, the Social Security (Consequential Provisions) Act 1992 or the Jobseekers Act, other than one contained in—
(a) Part VII of the Contributions and Benefits Act so far as relating to housing benefit and council tax benefit;
(b) Part VIII of the Administration Act (arrangements for housing benefit and council tax benefit and related subsidies).

(5) [¹ Subsection (1)(c) above does not include any decision which under section 8 of the Social Security Contributions (Transfer of Functions, etc.) Act 1999 falls to be made by an officer of the Inland Revenue.]

AMENDMENTS

1. Social Security Contributions (Transfer of Functions, etc.) Act 1999, Sched. 7, para. 22 (April 1, 1999).
2. Tax Credits Act, 1999, Sched. 1 paras 1 and 6(q) (October 5, 1999).
3. Welfare Reform and Pensions Act 1999, s.88 and Sched. 13 (April 6, 2000).

GENERAL NOTE

1.280   This section makes general provision for initial decisions by the Secretary of State. However, by Tax Credits Act 1999, s.2(1)(b) and Sched. 2, para. 5(b)(i), the functions of making initial decisions in respect of working families' tax credit and disabled person's tax credit are now transferred to officers of the Inland Revenue (see also the 1999 Act, Sched. 2, para. 21).

Subsection (2)

1.281   Para. (b) is not well drafted. The point being made in para. (a) is that a claim is effective only until it is decided *by the Secretary of State* (although benefit may then be awarded indefinitely or for a specified period in the future) and para. (b) is intended to make it clear that the consequence is that a change of circumstances taking place after the date of decision cannot give rise to entitlement under the original claim. This means that if a claimant appeals against the Secretary of State's decision, the tribunal cannot award benefit on the basis of a change of circumstances that has taken place between the Secretary of State's decision and its own decision. If no benefit was awarded on the initial claim, a new claim must, as para. (b) makes clear, be made if the claimant wishes to take advantage of the change of circumstances. However, para. (b) overlooks two other possibilities. One is that the claimant was in fact awarded some benefit on the initial claim and the subsequent change of circumstances entitles the claimant either to more or less benefit. In such a case, what is required is not a further claim but a supersession under s.10. The other possibility arises because a claim may be decided some while after the date of claim and may be made in respect of a period beginning before the date of claim. In some cases a claimant will have been entitled to benefit in respect of the early part of the period for which it is claimed but, by reason of a change of circumstances, will have ceased to be entitled to benefit by the time the Secretary of State gives his decision. Read literally, para. (b) would require the claimant to be refused benefit altogether in such a case because, on the basis of circumstances obtaining at the date of decision, he or she would not qualify. However, it is suggested that the word "accordingly" shows that para. (b) merely makes provision for the natural consequence of para. (a) and should be read to the effect that the claimant shall not be entitled to the benefit on the basis of circumstances not obtaining at or before the date of decision. This approach is consistent with that taken in para. 55 of *CDLA 4734/99* in the context of s.12(8)(b).

Subsection (3)
As family credit and disability working allowance have simply been renamed as working families' tax credit and disabled person's tax credit respectively (see Tax Credits Act 1999, s.1), outstanding claims made under the old names still fall within paras (d) and (e). No further benefit has yet been prescribed under para. (h).

1.282

Revision of decisions

9.—(1) Subject to section 36(3) below, any decision of the Secretary of State under section 8 above or section 10 below may be revised by the Secretary of State—
  (a) either within the prescribed period or in prescribed cases or circumstances; and
  (b) either on an application made for the purpose or on his own initiative;
and regulations may prescribe the procedure by which a decision of the Secretary of State may be so revised.

1.283

(2) In making a decision under subsection (1) above, the Secretary of State need not consider any issue that is not raised by the application or, as the case may be, did not cause him to act on his own initiative.

(3) Subject to subsections (4) and (5) and section 27 below, a revision under this section shall take effect as from the date on which the original decision took (or was to take) effect.

(4) Regulations may provide that, in prescribed cases or circumstances, a revision under this section shall take effect as from such other date as may be prescribed.

(5) Where a decision is revised under this section, for the purpose of any rule as to the time allowed for bringing an appeal, the decision shall be regarded as made on the date on which it is so revised.

(6) Except in prescribed circumstances, an appeal against a decision of the Secretary of State shall lapse if the decision is revised under this section before the appeal is determined.

GENERAL NOTE

Subsection (1)
Under the Social Security Administration Act 1992, provision was made for the "review" of decisions. Such reviews are replaced by "revisions" under s.9 and "supersession" under s.10. Note that only a decision of the Secretary of

1.284

State may be revised whereas a decision of the Secretary of State *or* of a tribunal or a Commissioner may be superseded. Apart from that, there is little that can be gleaned from the primary legislation as to the difference between revision and supersession. The most important distinction between the two concepts probably lies in the date from which the new decision takes effect. Where a decision is revised, the revised decision has effect from the effective date (or what should have been the effective date) of the original decision (see s.9(3)). On a supersession, the new decision takes effect from the date on which it is made and does not affect any past period, subject to limited provision for back-dating in some cases (s.10(5)). A related distinction is that there is no appeal under s.12 against a refusal to revise under s.9. Formally, there is only a right of appeal against the original decision but s.9(5) extends the time for appealing against the original decision if it is revised. By contrast, an appeal may be brought under s.12 against any decision under s.10, including a refusal to supersede (but see the note to s.12(9)). Beyond all that, no indication is given by the primary legislation as to the circumstances in which a revision of a decision is more appropriate than a supersession or *vice versa*. For that information, one must look at regs 3 and 4 of the Social Security and Child Support (Decisions and Appeals) Regulations 1999 relating to revisions and at reg. 6 relating to supersession. There would still be some overlap between the two procedures if it were not for reg. 3(9), which has the effect that supersession is always the appropriate procedure where there has been a change of circumstances since the Secretary of State's decision, and for reg. 6(3), which provides that a decision that may be revised cannot be superseded (save in limited circumstances where the revision could not take into account a further ground of supersession).

Happily, an application for supersession may be treated as an application for revision and *vice versa* (regs 3(10) and 6(5)), so that it is not fatal if claimants or their advisors do not fully understand the difference when making the application. These provisions have the effect that, when the Secretary of State follows the wrong procedure (say, revising instead of superseding), a tribunal considering an appeal will be able to correct the error and decide the case under the correct procedure.

Revision is partly a development of the review "on any ground" under s.30(1) of the Social Security Administration Act 1992, but, even to the extent that this is so, there are significant differences. Revision is possible in respect of all benefits and not just disability benefits. Revision is *not* a compulsory step before an appeal may be brought. Generally, action for a revision "on any ground" must be commenced, or applied for, within one month of the original decision but the time may be extended in limited, but nonetheless welcome, circumstances (see regs 3(1) and 4). However, there is no time limit at all in a number of cases including cases where there is no right of appeal (reg. 3(4) to (8)).

It is somewhat unclear whether or not a decision that has already been revised may be revised again. Section 9(1) provides that "any decision . . . under section 8 above or section 10 below" may be revised. However, in s.12(1) there is reference to "any decision . . . under section 8 or 10 above (whether as originally made or as revised under section 9 above)" and similar words referring to section 9 are to be found in s.10(1)(a). Do those references to s.9 in ss 10 and 12 suggest that references to decisions under ss 8 and 10 normally include decisions that have been revised? Or does the fact that there are references to s.9 in ss 10 and 12 but none in s.9 itself suggest that a decision that has already been revised cannot be revised again? It is tentatively submitted that the latter was probably what was intended, partly because it is unlikely that it was intended that repeated applications under reg. 3(1) should be possible. If this is so, there cannot be a second revision under, say, reg. 3(5)(a) either. If a claimant fails to

(1998 c.14, s.9)

appeal against a revision decision (and there is no appeal in cases specified in Sched. 2 to the Act or Sched. 2 to the Regulations), it seems that any official error in the revision cannot be corrected save on a supersession which may have effect from a much later date than the original decision.

The power to revise decisions in respect of working families' tax credit and disabled person's tax credit has been transferred to officers of the Inland Revenue from October 5, 1999 (see Tax Credits Act 1999, s.2(1)(b) and Sched. 2, para. 5(b)(ii)).

Subsection (2)
Note that the Secretary of State "need not", but nonetheless may, consider additional issues. On appeal, the discretion falls to be exercised by a tribunal and there seems no reason in principle why, in appropriate cases, the tribunal should not have regard to matters that were not drawn to the attention of the Secretary of State at all before he made his decision. On the other hand, it is clear that they are not obliged to do so if they do not consider it to be appropriate. In considering this issue, it is suggested that they ought to have regard (among other things) to the adequacy of any alternative action that the claimant or Secretary of State might take to have those other matters taken into account and, if it is not obvious, ought to draw attention to that alternative action (CDLA/15961/96).

1.285

Subsection (4)
See reg. 5 of the Social Security and Child Support (Decisions and Appeals) Regulations 1999 which provides that the only exception to the general rule is where a ground for the revision is that the original decision was made effective from the wrong date in the first place.

1.286

Subsection (5)
This allows a claimant to appeal against a revised decision. Note, however, that an application for a revision has the effect of automatically extending the time for appealing only where the application is brought under reg. 3(1) or (3) of the Social Security and Child Support (Decisions and Appeals) Regulations 1999 (see reg. 31(2)(a)). In other cases, it will generally be wise for any person asking for a revision to lodge an appeal at the same time so that, if the decision is not revised, the claimant will not have to bring a late appeal. The fact that a claimant was waiting for a decision on an application for revision may be regarded as a compelling reason for admitting an appeal late under reg. 32 of the Social Security and Child Support (Decisions and Appeals) Regulations 1999, but a claimant would be unwise to take that for granted. If, the claimant having lodged both an application for revision and an appeal, the decision is not revised, the appeal will proceed. If the decision is revised, the appeal will lapse under subs. (6) only if the revised decision is more advantageous to the claimant that the original decision. This subsection then applies to such a case, enabling the claimant to appeal against the decision as revised. If the original decision is revised otherwise than to the advantage of the claimant, the appeal will not lapse but the claimant will be given another month to make representations in the light of the revision.

1.287

Subsection (6)
See reg. 30 of the Social Security and Child Support (Decisions and Appeals) Regulations 1999.

1.288

Decisions superseding earlier decisions

10.—(1) Subject to [¹ subsection (3)] and section 36(3) below, the following, namely—

1.289

Social Security Act 1998

(a) any decision of the Secretary of State under section 8 above or this section, whether as originally made or as revised under section 9 above; and

(b) any decision under this Chapter of an appeal tribunal or a Commissioner, may be superseded by a decision made by the Secretary of State, either on an application made for the purpose or on his own initiative.

(2) In making a decision under subsection (1) above, the Secretary of State need not consider any issue that is not raised by the application or, as the case may be, did not cause him to act on his own initiative.

(3) Regulations may prescribe the cases and circumstances in which, and the procedure by which, a decision may be made under this section.

(4) [1 . . .]

(5) Subject to subsection (6) and section 27 below, a decision under this section shall take effect as from the date on which it is made or, where applicable, the date on which the application was made.

(6) Regulations may provide that, in prescribed cases or circumstances, a decision under this section shall take effect as from such other date as may be prescribed.

AMENDMENT

1. Social Security Contributions (Transfer of Functions, etc.) Act 1999, Sched. 7, para. 23 (April 1, 1999).

GENERAL NOTE

1.290   For the distinction between revision and supersession, see the note to s.9(1). Note that an application for supersession may be treated as an application for revision and *vice versa* (regs 3(10) and 6(5) of the Social Security and Child Support (Decisions and Appeals) Regulations 1999). In relation to tax credit, references to a decision of the Secretary of State must be construed as references to a decision of an officer of the Inland Revenue from October 5, 1999 (Tax Credits Act 1999, Sched. 2, para. 21).

Subsection (2)
1.291   See the note to s.9(2).

1.292   *Subsection (3)*
See regs 6 and 8 of the Social Security and Child Support (Decisions and Appeals) Regulations 1999.

1.293   *Subsection (6)*
See reg. 7 of the Social Security and Child Support (Decisions and Appeals) Regulations 1999.

[1 *Reference of Issues by Secretary of State to Inland Revenue*

References of issues by Secretary of State to Inland Revenue

1.294   **10A.**—(1) Regulations may make provision requiring the Secretary of State, where on consideration of any claim or other matter he is of the opinion that there arises any issue which under section 8 of the Social Security Contributions (Transfer of Functions, etc.) Act 1999 fals to be

(1998 c.14, s.10A)

decided by an officer of the Inland Revenue, to refer the issue to the Inland Revenue.

Regulations under this section may—
(a) provide for the Inland Revenue to give the Secretary of State a preliminary opinion on any issue referred to them,
(b) specify the circumstances in which an officer of the Inland Revenue is to make a decision under section 8 of the Social Security Contributions (Transfer of Functions, etc.) Act 1999 on a reference by the Secretary of State,
(c) enable or require the Secretary of State, in specified circumstances to deal with any other issue arising on consideration of the claim or other matter pending the decision of the referred issue, and
(d) require the Secretary of State to decide the claim or other matter in accordance with the decision of an officer of the Inland Revenue on the issue referred to them, or in accordance with any determination of the tax appeal Commissioners made on appeal from their decision.]

AMENDMENT

1. Social Security Contributions (Transfer of Functions, etc.) Act 1999, Sched. 7, para. 24 (July 5, 1999).

GENERAL NOTE

See reg. 11A of the Social Security and Child Support (Decisions and Appeals) Regulations 1999.

Regulations with respect to decisions

11.—(1) Subject to the provisions of this Chapter and the Administration Act, provision may be made by regulations for the making of any decision by the Secretary of State under or in connection with the current legislation, or the former legislation, including a decision on a claim for benefit.

(2) Where it appears to the Secretary of State that a matter before him involves a question of fact requiring special expertise, he may direct that in dealing with that matter he shall have the assistance of one or more experts.

(3) In this section—
"the current legislation" means the Contributions and Benefits Act, the Job-seekers Act and the Social Security (Recovery of Benefits) Act 1997;
"expert" means a person appearing to the Secretary of State to have knowledge or experience which would be relevant in determining the question of fact requiring special expertise;
"the former legislation" means the National Insurance Acts 1965 to 1974, the National Insurance (Industrial Injuries) Acts 1965 to 1974, the Social Security Act 1975 and Part II of the Social Security Act 1986.

GENERAL NOTE

1.297 *Subsection (1)*
See reg. 28 of the Social Security and Child Support (Decisions and Appeals) Regulations 1999. In relation to tax credit, the power to make regulations is transferred to the Commissioners of Inland Revenue (Tax Credits Act 1999, Sched. 2, para. 8(a)).

Subsections (2) and (3)
1.298 In relation to tax credit, the functions of the Secretary of State are transferred to officers of the Inland Revenue from October 5, 1999 (Tax Credits Act 1999, s.2(1)(b) and Sched. 2, para. 5(b)(iii)).

Appeals

Appeal to appeal tribunal

1.299 **12.**—(1) This section applies to any decision of the Secretary of State under section 8 or 10 above (whether as originally made or as revised under section 9 above) which—
  (a) is made on a claim for, or on an award of, a relevant benefit, and does not fall within Schedule 2 to this Act; [¹ or]
  (b) is made otherwise than on such a claim or award, and falls within Schedule 3 to this Act; [¹ . . .]
  (c) [¹ . . .]
[¹ (2) In the case of a decision to which this section applies, the claimant and such other person as may be prescribed shall have a right to appeal to an appeal tribunal, but nothing in this subsection shall confer a right of appeal in relation to a prescribed decision, or a prescribed determination embodied in or necessary to a decision.]
  (3) Regulations under subsection (2) above shall not prescribe any decision or determination that relates to the conditions of entitlement to a relevant benefit for which a claim has been validly made or for which no claim is required.
  (4) Where the Secretary of State has determined that any amount is recoverable under or by virtue of section 71 or 74 of the Administration Act, any person from whom he has determined that it is recoverable shall have the same right of appeal to an appeal tribunal as a claimant.
  (5) In any case where—
  (a) the Secretary of State has made a decision in relation to a claim under Part V of the Contributions and Benefits Act; and
  (b) the entitlement to benefit under that Part of that Act of any person other than the claimant is or may be, under Part VI of Schedule 7 to that Act, affected by that decision,
that other person shall have the same right of appeal to an appeal tribunal as the claimant.
  (6) A person with a right of appeal under this section shall be given such notice of a decision to which this section applies and of that right as may be prescribed.
  (7) Regulations may make provision as to the manner in which, and the time within which, appeals are to be brought.

(8) In deciding an appeal under this section, an appeal tribunal—
(a) need not consider any issue that is not raised by the appeal; and
(b) shall not take into account any circumstances not obtaining at the time when the decision appealed against was made.

(9) The reference in subsection (1) above to a decision under section 10 above is a reference to a decision superseding any such decision as is mentioned in paragraph (a) or (b) of subsection (1) of that section.

AMENDMENT

1. Social Security Contributions (Transfer of Functions, etc.) Act 1999, Sched. 7, para. 25 (April 1, 1999).

GENERAL NOTE

Subsection (1)

Note that this section provides only for appeals from decisions under ss 8 and 10 of this Act. Challenges to decisions made under s.9 are brought by appealing against the original decision rather than the s.9 decision. By contrast, the phrase "decision . . . under section . . . 10" is broad enough to permit an appeal against a refusal to supersede a decision unless subs. (9) is to be construed literally. In relation to tax credit, the reference to a decision of the Secretary of State must be construed as a reference to a decision of an officer of the Inland Revenue (Tax Credits Act 1999, Sched. 2, para. 21) so that an appeal lies to an appeal tribunal against a decision of such an officer. Furthermore, this section also has effect in relation to an appeal against a penalty under s.9(1), (3)(a) or (5)(a) of the Tax Credits Act 1999 (see the 1999 Act, Sched. 4, para. 3(2)). The right of appeal from a decision under the Social Security (Recovery of Benefits) Act 1997 continues to arise under ss 11 and 12 of that Act, as amended by this Act and there is also a separate right of appeal to an appeal tribunal under s.121D of the Social Security Administration Act 1992 in relation to a personal liability notice.

The scope of a tribunal's jurisdiction must depend on the scope of the decision which is the subject of the appeal. Para. (a) provides for an appeal against any decision made *on* a claim or award. Section 20(1)(a) and (b) of the Social Security Administration Act 1992 drew a distinction between a "claim" and a "question" and s.36 expressly enabled a tribunal to deal with any question first arising before them and not previously considered by an adjudication officer. The new legislation does not use the terms "claim" and "question" and there is no provision similar to the old s.36. However, it is suggested that this may not make much difference. Para. (a) of subs. (1) is broad enough to allow an appeal against a decision determining a claim or superseding a decision or an appeal against a decision determining just one issue. The distinction may be important when an appeal is allowed on the issue that was the primary concern of the Secretary of State. If the appeal was brought against a decision that was made only on that issue and did not go on to deal with its consequences (because, perhaps, that was the role of another decision-maker), a tribunal could have no jurisdiction to deal with any other issue arising on the claim or award. If, however, the Secretary of State had in the same decision gone on, say, to refuse a claim, then if the claimant succeeded on the main issue, the tribunal could go on to consider any other issue that was necessary to enable them to determine the claim (although they would not be bound to do so—see subs. (8)(a)). Accurately identifying the scope of the decision under appeal may therefore, in a few cases, be very important. It may be necessary to consider the terms of the form or letter of appeal as well as the notice of decision because, if another

1.300

Social Security Act 1998

decision-maker has dealt with the consequences of the first decision, a claimant may have appealed against both decisions in the same letter of appeal.

Subsection (2)

1.301 See regs 26 and 27 of the Social Security and Child Support (Decisions and Appeals) Regulations 1999.

Subsection (3)

1.302 See the note to Sched. 2 to the Social Security and Child Support (Decisions and Appeals) Regulations 1999 in which it is suggested that either much of that schedule is *ultra vires* or else this subsection is of no practical effect.

Subsection (7)

1.303 See regs 31 to 33 of the Social Security and Child Support (Decisions and Appeals) Regulations 1999.

Subsection (8)

1.304 Presumably the word "appeal" in para. (a) means the form or letter of appeal. Para. (a) confers a discretion. It must, of course, be exercised judically and it is suggested that this provision does not remove the inquisitorial function of tribunals which arises from the fact that tribunals form part of the statutory machinery for investigating claims. It was held in *Regina v. Deputy Industrial Commissioner, ex parte Moore* [1965] 1 Q.B. 456 (C.A.) (also reported as an appendix to *R(I) 4/65*, that neither the insurance officer nor the Minister were parties adverse to a claimant and that a tribunal were at liberty to form their own view of a case even if that did not coincide with the view of either the claimant or the insurance officer or Minister. In *R(IS) 11/99*, it was said that there was a duty upon a tribunal to ensure that all relevant questions have been asked of a claimant and that, if a claimant attends a hearing, they ought to ask those questions that have not previously been asked but which should have been asked. It is suggested that it would be wrong to rely on s.12(8)(a) as a ground for refusing to deal with an issue to which the Secretary of State ought to have, but has not, addressed his mind and to which a claimant could not reasonably have been expected to refer when appealing. It is also suggested that, in considering how the discretion conferred by para. (a) should be exercised, tribunal ought to have regard (among other things) to the adequacy of any alternative action that the claimant or Secretary of State might take to have the new issue taken into account and, if it is not obvious, ought to draw attention to that alternative action (*CDLA/15961/96*). If an entirely new point is being taken at a hearing, it is necessary for the parties to have the opportunity of dealing with it but that does not necessarily mean there must be an adjournment because it ought to be possible for most points to be adequately considered immediately. If a party has deliberately chosen not to attend, the question whether there should be an adjournment so that he or she may consider the new point may be more complicated. There are three options: to refuse to consider the new point, to consider it immediately or to adjourn. A lot will depend on the nature of the issue and whether any advance notice was given of it, as well as the possibility of applying for a revision or supersession on the new ground. A wise appellant who wishes to raise a new point will give both the tribunal and the Secretary of State notice as soon as possible.

By contrast, para. (b) confers no discretion. In the light of reg. 3(9) of the Social Security and Child Support (Decisions and Appeals) Regulations 1999 and s.9(5) of the Act, when a decision has been revised under s.9, "the time when the decision appealed against was made" must refer to the date on which the original decision was made. Para. (b) is therefore consistent with the approach that any change of circumstances requires a new claim or a supersession under s.10 and it reverses the effect of *R(S)2/98*. Note, however, that para.

(b) does not apply where the decision under appeal was made before May 21, 1998 when this Act received the Royal Assent and Sched. 6, para. 3 (which made transitory provision preventing social security appeal tribunals and disability appeal tribunals from taking account of circumstances not obtaining at the date of the decision under appeal) came into force. In such a case, a tribunal must still consider the claimant's entitlement to benefit throughout the period to the date of its decision or down to the date from which another decision is effective (*CIB/213/99*).

Note also that para. (b) does not prevent a tribunal having regard to evidence that was not before the Secretary of State and came into existence after the decision was made or to evidence of events after the decision under appeal was made for the purpose of drawing inferences as to the circumstances obtaining when, or before, the decision was made (*CDLA/2934/99, CDLA/4734/99*). This creates particular difficulties where entitlement to benefit depends on a prognosis. Thus, in *CDLA/4734/99*, the claimant would be entitled to disability living allowance only if she was likely to satisfy the relevant conditions for six months. She was recovering from an operation. The Commissioner held that, in such a case, a tribunal was entitled to take account of the actual rate of recovery, even though the evidence of that arose after the date of the decision under appeal, provided that the fact that the claimant had not recovered as quickly as originally expected merely reflected the natural vagaries of an uncertain recovery process. Untoward circumstances arising after the date of the decision had to be disregarded, whether that operated to the claimant's advantage or to her disadvantage. Thus the fact that a claimant recovering from a heart attack developed pneumonia after the Secretary of State's decision was made would have to be ignored. So too would a dramatic improvement in a claimant's condition due to the use of a new drug. The Commissioner observed that s.12(8)(b) required tribunals to indulge in the sort of artificial exercise that is frowned upon in modern courts where judges are not expected to close their eyes to reality and he referred to *Charles v. Hugh James Jones and Jenkins (a firm)* [2000] 1 All E.R. 289, 299 to 301. S.12(8)(b) is of particular importance in disablement benefit cases where tribunals can usually themselves examine the claimant (see regulation 52 of the Social Security and Child Support (Decisions and Appeals) Regulations 1999) and must be careful to distinguish between those of their findings that are relevant to circumstances obtaining at the time of the decision under appeal and those that are not.

S.12(8)(b) would be unobjectionable if, like s.12(8)(a), it said "need not" instead of "shall not". As it is, it introduces an unwelcome element of technicality into appeals to tribunals that were once supposed to user-friendly. The remedy for a claimant is to make a new claim, or application for supersession, whenever there is an event that might be regarded as a new circumstance. There may be some cases where the wise claimant will make such claims or applications at regular intervals while an appeal is pending. The Secretary of State would then be obliged to make separate decisions on each claim or application (because the power to refer claims or applications to a tribunal so that they can be considered with a pending appeal has been abolished) and there would be a separate right of appeal against each decision. However, experience suggests that claimants do not consider new claims or applications to be necessary while an appeal is pending, even though some of the literature provided to them makes the suggestion, and so the reality may be that claimants will lose benefit that they would undoubtedly have been entitled to but for s.12(8)(b).

Of course, s.12(8)(b) can work in a claimant's favour if there has been a new circumstance since the decision under appeal that would have reduced his or her entitlement to benefit. This possibility raises a number of interesting questions as to what remedy the Secretary of State has. It may well be that the

Secretary of State could not supersede the tribunal's decision (see the note to regulation 6(2)(a) of the Social Security and Child Support (Decisions and Appeals) Regulations 1999). If so, the consequence for the Secretary of State is serious. Giving effect to the tribunal's decision in the claimant's favour might, in some cases, give rise to an overpayment that was recoverable under section 71 of the Social Security Administration Act 1992 on the basis that the change of circumstances should have been disclosed to the Secretary of State so that the decision under appeal could have been superseded before the appeal was heard. However, in a case where the Secretary of State had refused benefit altogether in the decision under appeal and benefit had then been awarded by the tribunal on the basis of their findings as to the circumstances obtaining at the date of the Secretary of State's decision, it seems unlikely that there would have been any duty on the claimant to disclose any changes of circumstances while the appeal was pending. Even if the Secretary of State does have power to supersede a tribunal's decision in the light of a change of circumstances arising before the decision was given, another problem facing the Secretary of State may be continued ignorance of the new circumstance. He does not always send a representative to tribunal hearings and he does not usually ask for a copy of the record of proceedings or a full statement of the tribunal's findings and reasoning. Unless a tribunal refers in the short decision notice, recorded under regulation 53(1) of the Social Security and Child Support (Decisions and Appeals) Regulations 1999, to a change of circumstances mentioned at the hearing, the Secretary of State may remain ignorant of it for ever and, of course, the tribunal will have been obliged by s.12(8)(b) to ignore the change when awarding benefit.

An element of discretion in s.12(8)(b) might make it much easier to do justice.

Subsection (9)

1.305　A first reading of this subsection suggests that it is intended to limit the scope of subs. (1) and carries with it the implication that there is no appeal against a decision *refusing* to supersede such a decision as is mentioned in s.10(1)(a) or (b). The consequence of that construction would be monstrous. A less obvious—but it is suggested, preferable—construction requires there to be read in after "superseding" the words "or refusing to supersede" on the basis that the purpose of the subsection is merely to emphasise that *any* decision under s.10 may be the subject of an appeal and not just the first such decision. It is possible that the subsection was drafted in the expectation that regulations under s.10 would provide that, on an application for supersession, the original decision would always be superseded even if the new decision was to the same effect as the old. That, however, is not how reg. 6 of the Social Security and Child Support (Decisions and Appeals) Regulations 1999 has been structured. The Secretary of State may supersede a decision only if certain grounds are made out. Otherwise, presumably, he must refuse to supersede.

Redetermination etc. of appeals by tribunal

1.306　**13.**—(1) This section applies where an application is made to a person under section 14(10)(a) below for leave to appeal from a decision of an appeal tribunal.

(2) If the person considers that the decision was erroneous in point of law, he may set aside the decision and refer the case either for redetermination by the tribunal or for determination by a differently constituted tribunal.

(3) If each of the principal parties to the case expresses the view that

the decision was erroneous in point of law, the person shall set aside the decision and refer the case for determination by a differently constituted tribunal.

[¹(4) In this section and section 14 below "the principal parties" means—
  (a) the persons mentioned in subsection (3)(a) and (b) of that section, and
  (b) Where applicable, the person mentioned in subsection (3)(d) and such a person as is first mentioned in subsection (4) of that section.]

AMENDMENT

1. Social Security Contributions (Transfer of Functions, etc.) Act 1999, Sched. 7, para. 26 (April 1, 1999).

GENERAL NOTE

Subsections (1) and (2)

1:307

The person considering the application for leave to appeal should be the person who was, or who chaired, the tribunal whose decision is challenged, unless that is impractical or inexpedient (see reg. 58(6) of the Social Security and Child Support (Decisions and Appeals) Regulations 1999). Subs. (2), then, is a useful new provision allowing a decision to be set aside where that person realises, in the light of a challenge or otherwise on reconsideration of the case, that the decision was erroneous in point of law. Although reg. 58(6) permits another person to consider the application in a prescribed case and therefore to exercise the power to set aside under subs.(2), it does not permit regional chairman, or other full-time members of the panel, routinely to sit as a court of appeal from their colleagues' decisions. However, with what appears to be a blatant disregard of the terms of reg. 58(6), The Appeal Service has decided that all applications for leave to appeal should be considered by full-time legally qualified panel members.

Subs. (2) is cast in discretionary terms. In principle, one would expect panel member to obtain the views of both parties before exercising the power to set aside rather than grant or dismiss the application for leave to appeal to a Commissioner. If the respondent agreed that the decision was erroneous in point of law, subs. (3) would be brought into play and the panel member would be bound to set the decision aside. However, it appears that the Secretary of State has waived any right to be consulted on a claimant's application for leave to appeal (because having to respond would create additional work, although it is difficult to see why the amount of work should be great if only cases where the panel member was minded to set aside were referred for comment) and is content for any decision to be set aside if the panel member thinks it right to do so. It is not usual for panel members to ask claimant applicants whether they have any objection to a decision being set aside under this provision instead of leave to appeal being granted. Generally, of course, a claimant applicant would be quite content to have a decision set aside but, in a case where there is more than one possible error of law in a tribunal's decision, a claimant may prefer to have leave to appeal and have a major issue of law resolved by a Commissioner rather than have the decision set aside on some minor point and have to argue the major point before another tribunal with the probability of a later appeal to a Commissioner. The purpose of this section is plainly to avoid unnecessary appeals to Commissioners but panel members need to be careful to avoid setting aside decisions when that will prolong litigation, rather than shorten it. Applications by the Secretary of State create different problems because claimants are less likely to agree to a setting aside. It would be a breach of the rules of natural justice not to seek a claimant's view before setting aside a decision that was in his or her favour. If there is active opposition to a setting aside and there is a serious point of law to be determined, it is suggested that the panel member should grant leave to appeal rather than set aside the decision. To do otherwise, would be to usurp the function of the Commissioner. However, there are cases where there has been an obvious procedural error or a tribunal has obviously overlooked a material statutory provision or important piece of evidence so that the only possible conclusion is that the tribunal's decision is erroneous in point of law. In such cases, it is hard to see what objection there could be to a setting aside under subs. (2), but a panel member needs to be sure the error really is clear. If, despite a claimant's opposition, or simple failure to comment, a decision is set aside, it is suggested that a brief reason should be given (for the benefit of the tribunal who must rehear the case as well as the parties). It seems fairly clear that there is no appeal to a Commissioner against a setting aside under this subsection (see the note to s.14(1)) but a person anxious to rely on the decision set aside could apply for judicial review of the setting aside.

Reg. 57 of the Social Security and Child Support (Decisions and Appeals) Regulations 1999 gives an additional power to set aside a decision where a relevant document has gone astray or a person failed to attend the hearing in circumstances where there may have been an injustice without there actually being an error of law. See also s.28(2) for the possibility of an implied further power to set aside decisions to avoid injustice.

1.308   *Subsection (3)*

This is a bizarre provision. It would be wholly unobjectionable if it provided a *power* to set aside a decision rather than imposing a *duty* to do so, although it might be thought that there are few cases not falling within subs. (2) in which a decision should be set aside merely because the parties consent. It is the mandatory terms of the section (in contrast to section 14(7)) which creates the difficulty. The tribunal will have been, or will have included, a lawyer. It is very rare for either party to be represented by a lawyer before a tribunal. Yet if both parties express the view, no matter how unreasonably, that the tribunal has erred *in law*, their view prevails and the decision of the tribunal *must* be set aside. The readiness of the Secretary of State's representatives to agree with unmeritorious grounds of appeal advanced by claimants on appeals to Commissioners has been criticised (see, for instance, *CSIB/611/99*, *CSDLA/737/99* and *CSDLA/868/99*) and the quality of submissions is unlikely to be much better at tribunal level. It is not even necessary for the parties to agree on the error of law. A tribunal may have steered carefully between two extreme views advanced by the parties, all to no avail. If redetermining tribunals took the same approach and the parties remained stubborn, the litigation could go on for ever unless action were taken to avoid this subsection coming into play. Happily, such action is possible because applications for leave to appeal are generally considered *ex parte*. Claimants must be given notice of applications by the Secretary of State but need not be given an opportunity to make comments on them. There is nothing unfair in this. A respondent can hardly complain if leave to appeal is refused, and a grant of leave does not finally determine any person's rights. Thus, the operation of this subsection can be avoided by the simple expedient of determining the application for leave to appeal without seeking the respondent's views. In fact, at the time of writing this note, the Secretary of State is so concerned at the amount of work that the operation of this subsection would generate for his representatives that The Appeal Service has been asked not to refer cases for comment and so the subsection is not being used. Even if the Secretary of State were always asked for comments, it would be open to his representative to decline to express a view as to whether a decision was erroneous in point of law and so allow a case to proceed to a Commissioner and that would probably be done where there had already been a setting aside of a tribunal's decision. Thus the prospect of eternal litigation may be a fanciful one. There is, however, a serious question as to the regularity with which the Secretary of State should be given the opportunity to express a view as to whether a decision, from which a claimant seeks leave to appeal, is erroneous in point of law. If he were given that opportunity on all applications for leave to appeal, his representatives would have a lot of unnecessary work and there would be a substantial risk of too many cases being set aside under this subsection. If he were given the opportunity on all applications which the panel member was not minded to dismiss, he would effectively be able to control access to the Commissioner by deciding whether or not to express the view that the decision was erroneous in point of law. The most satisfactory approach might be for the Secretary of State to be invited to comment only on those applications on which the panel member was minded to set aside the decision under subs. (2). That would give him the opportunity to object to a setting aside or to express the view that the decision was erroneous in point of law so that subs. (3) would apply rather than subs. (2). It would then be unnecessary for the panel member to identify any error of law or to give any reason for the setting aside other than that both parties had expressed the view that the decision was erroneous in point of law.

If both parties seek leave to appeal at the same time and the panel member has to consider both applications together, this subsection will inevitably be brought into play (unless, perhaps, one party not only does not raise any point of law but also fails positively to assert that there is an error of law in the tribunal's decision). What happens if a cross-application is received *after* an application by the other party has been determined? It is tentatively suggested that the answer is that a person who has been refused or granted leave to appeal cannot be assumed to remain a person who "expresses the view that the decision was erroneous in point of law" unless he or she has applied to a Commissioner for leave to appeal or has lodged an appeal, when it is arguable that the decision of the tribunal can no longer be set aside under s.13 and any question of a summary setting aside must be considered under s.14(7) instead, if the Commissioner grants either party leave to appeal.

Appeal from tribunal to Commissioner

14.—(1) Subject to the provisions of this section, an appeal lies to a Commissioner from any decision of an appeal tribunal under section 12 or 13 above on the ground that the decision of the tribunal was erroneous in point of law.

(2) [^{1} ...]

(3) [^{1} ...] An appeal lies under this section at the instance of any of the following—
  (a) the Secretary of State;
  (b) the claimant and such other person as may be prescribed;
  (c) in any of the cases mentioned in subsection (5) below, a trade union; and
  (d) a person from whom it is determined that any amount is recoverable under or by virtue of section 71 or 74 of the Administration Act.

1.309

(4) In a case relating to industrial injuries benefit an appeal lies under this section at the instance of a person whose entitlement to benefit is, or may be, under Part VI of Schedule 7 to the Contributions and Benefits Act, affected by the decision appealed against, as well as at the instance of any person or body such as is mentioned in subsection (3) above.

(5) The following are the cases in which an appeal lies at the instance of a trade union—
  (a) where the claimant is a member of the union at the time of the appeal and was so immediately before the matter in question arose;
  (b) where that matter in any way relates to a deceased person who was a member of the union at the time of his death;
  (c) where the case relates to industrial injuries benefit and the claimant or, in relation to industrial death benefit, the deceased, was a member of the union at the time of the relevant accident.

(6) Subsections (2), (3) and (5) above, as they apply to a trade union, apply also to any other association which exists to promote the interests and welfare of its members.

(7) If each of the principal parties to the appeal expresses the view that the decision appealed against was erroneous in point of law, the Commissioner may set aside the decision and refer the case to a tribunal with directions for its determination.

(8) Where the Commissioner holds that the decision appealed against was erroneous in point of law, he shall set it aside and—
  (a) he shall have power
    (i) give the decision which he considers the tribunal should have given, if he can do so without making fresh or further findings of fact; or
    (ii) if he considers it expedient, to make such findings and to give such decision as he considers appropriate in the light of them; and
  (b) in any other case he shall refer the case to a tribunal with directions for its determination.

(9) Subject to any direction of the Commissioner, a reference under subsection (7) or (8)(b) above shall be to a differently constituted tribunal.

(10) No appeal lies under this section without the leave—
  (a) of the person who constituted, or was the chairman of, the tribunal when the decision was given or, in a prescribed case, the leave of such other person as may be prescribed; or
  (b) subject to and in accordance with regulations, of a Commissioner.

(11) Regulations may make provision as to the manner in which, and the time within which, appeals are to be brought and applications made for leave to appeal.

(12) Schedule 4 to this Act shall have effect with respect to the appointment, remuneration and tenure of office of Commissioners and other matters relating to them.

(1998 c.14, s.14)

AMENDMENT

1. Social Security Contributions (Transfer of Functions, etc.) Act 1999, Sched. 7, para. 27 (April 1, 1999).

GENERAL NOTE

The section has effect in relation to decisions of appeal tribunals with respect to penalties under s.9(1), (3)(a) or (5)(a) of the Tax Credits Act 1999 (see the 1999 Act, Sched. 4, para. 3(2)). Otherwise it applies only to decisions under sections 12 and 13.

1.310

Subsection (1)

The reference to a decision under s.13 must be to the decision of the tribunal redetermining the case following the setting aside of the earlier decision, rather than the setting aside decision itself. This view is expressed partly because a decision to set aside under s.13 may be made by a chairman, or another panel member, rather than by "an appeal tribunal" and partly because the context of s.13 requires that construction if the obvious purpose of *avoiding* appeals is not to be frustrated. In particular, it would be odd if there were a right of appeal against a decision given under s.13(3), given its mandatory terms. A separate right of appeal to a Commissioner is given by s.13 of the Social Security (Recovery of Benefits) Act 1997. There is no right of appeal to a Commissioner against a decision of an appeal tribunal under the Vaccine Damage Payments Act 1979.

The Commissioners have two offices, at 5th Floor, Newspaper House, 8–16 Great New Street, London EC4A 3NN and at 23 Melville Street, Edinburgh EH3 7PW. Most appeals to Commissioners are dealt with by way of written submissions (see regs. 18–20 and 23(1) of the Social Security Commissioners (Procedure) Regulations 1999) but claimants may ask for oral hearings (regs. 23 and 24). Oral hearings usually take place in London or Edinburgh (cases from the far north of England being heard in Edinburgh when that is more convenient although English law is applied) but the Commissioners also regularly travel to sit at the law courts in Cardiff. If a claimant is disabled and would have great difficulty in travelling to one of those centres, it is possible to ask the Commissioners' office to arrange a hearing in a more local court building.

Commissioners are of the same standing as circuit judges. Nevertheless, they have no power to award costs to successful claimants or to the Secretary of State (see *R(FC) 2/90*). Nor is community legal service funding (legal aid) generally available for proceedings before Commissioners although s.6(8)(b) of the Access to Justice Act 1999 enables the Lord Chancellor to authorise the legal services commission to fund representation either in specified circumstances or in an individual case.

In *R(IS) 11/99*, the Commissioner held that an error of law may be revealed if—
  (a) a tribunal has recorded a false proposition of law in its reasons for decision (which includes relying on an *ultra vires* regulation (*Foster v. Chief Adjudication Officer* [1993] A.C. 754, reported as *R(IS) 9/93*));
  (b) a tribunal has reached a decision that is supported by no evidence;
  (c) a tribunal has found facts such that no person acting judicially and properly instructed as to the relevant law could have come to the determination under appeal;
  (d) a tribunal has taken into account matters that ought not to have been taken into account;

(e) a tribunal has refused or neglected to take into account matters that ought to have been taken into account;
(f) a tribunal has failed or neglected to ask material questions pursuant to the duty to act inquisitorially (see, now, the note to s.12(8)(a));
(g) there has been a breach of the rules of natural justice (which may be summarised as the rule that every party to proceedings should have a proper opportunity to present his or her case and the rule against bias);
(h) there has been a material breach of the other procedural rules, statutory and implied, that must be followed by tribunals, panel members and clerks. Such rules are mostly to be found in the Social Security and Child Support (Decisions and Appeals) Regulations 1999.

Whether a breach of such procedural rules renders a decision erroneous in point of law may depend on whether the context suggests that the legislator intended that to be a consequence of such a breach which may, in turn, depend on whether the breach might have made any difference to the decision of the tribunal or whether a party to the proceedings has lost anything (such as the opportunity of advancing a particular argument on appeal) as a result of the breach, so that a rehearing is the only way of remedying the breach. Thus a failure to keep a record of proceedings will render a decision erroneous in point of law if the lack of the record makes it difficult to determine whether or not the tribunal has provided an adequate statement of reasons for the decision (*CDLA/16902/96*). On the other hand, a failure to provide any summary of reasons in a decision notice will not render the decision erroneous in point of law because the remedy is to apply for a full statement of reasons (*CIB/4497/98*).

The most commonly relied upon breach is a breach of the duty to give reasons for a decision in what purports to be a full statement of reasons. See the note to reg. 53 of the Social Security and Child Support (Decisions and Appeals) Regulations 1999.

Decisions of the Commissioners on matters of legal principle are binding on tribunals and the Secretary of State, as are decisions of the superior courts. Where there are conflicting Commissioners' decisions, a reported decision should generally be followed in preference to an unreported decision (*R(I) 12/75*). Generally, where one decision has been carefully considered in a later decision and not followed, the later decision should be followed (*Colchester Estates (Cardiff) v. Carlton Industries PLC* [1986] Ch. 80) and it has been held in a Northern Ireland case that that applies even if the earlier decision was reported and the later was not (*C2/99(FC)*). Decisions of Northern Ireland Commissioners are not strictly binding in Great Britain and the Court of Appeal in Northern Ireland but are highly persuasive (*R(SB)1/90*). A single Commissioner will usually follow a decision of another single Commissioner and will always follow a decision of a Tribunal of Commissioners appointed under s.16(7) (*R(I) 12/75*). A Tribunal of Commissioners will usually follow the decision of another Tribunal but will not always do so if satisfied that it was wrong (*R(U) 4/88*). A Commissioner is bound by a decision of the High Court given on judicial review of a Commissioner's decision but otherwise is not strictly bound by a decision of the High Court, although he or she will rarely depart from a decision of a single High Court judge and will always follow a decision of a divisional court (*R(IS) 15/99*, disagreeing with *R(S) 1/96*). A Tribunal of Commissioners will, on rare occasions, feel free not to follow a decision of a divisional court (*R(SB) 52/83*). All Commissioners are bound by decisions of the Court of Appeal and the House of Lords.

Subsection (3)

1.311   In relation to tax credit, the right of appeal under para. (a) is transferred, not to an officer of the Inland Revenue, but to the Commissioners of Inland Revenue (Tax Credits Act 1999, s.2(1)(c) and Sched. 2, para. 8(a)). No persons have been prescribed under subs. (3)(b) and so not everyone who has a right of appeal to a tribunal under s.12 of the Act and reg. 25 of the Social Security and Child Support (Decisions and Appeals) Regulations 1999 has a right of appeal to a Commissioner. This seems to be a regrettable oversight.

Subsection (7)

Unlike s.13(3), this subsection confers a discretionary power on a Commissioner. Note that the power arises only after leave to appeal has been granted. Note also that the power can only be exercised when the case is to be referred to another tribunal. There is no provision allowing a decision to be set aside summarily and for the Commissioner then to give a final decision, even if the parties are agreed as to the decision to be given. This is presumably because the Commissioner is expected, in such a case, to satisfy himself or herself that the parties' submissions are correct, following which it is not unduly burdensome to issue a short decision to that effect. The Chief Commissioner issued a practice memorandum in relation to the provisions amended by Sched. 6, para. 4 in terms similar to to s.14(7). 1.312

A setting aside under this subsection does not necessarily imply that the Commissioner is satisfied that the decision under appeal was erroneous in point of law. The point of this provision is to enable a decision to be set aside without the Commissioner having to go into the case in the depth necessary to make that judgement. The Commissioner will therefore wish to be able to rely substantially on the parties' submissions. The Secretary of State's representatives have been criticised for submitting too readily that a decision is erroneous in point of law on the ground that the reasoning is inadequate (*CSIB/596/99, CSIB/611/99, CSDLA/505/99*) and it has been held that the Chief Commissioner's practice memorandum requiring the respondent to give some indication of the error of law relied upon when suggesting the use of this subsection requires a party submitting that a tribunal have failed to give reasons for accepting a piece of evidence to state what contradictory evidence there was and to explain why the lack of reasoning is of significance (*CDLA/4102/99*). It was also suggested in *CDLA/4102/99* that it was not appropriate for a decision to be set aside under this subsection in a case where there was a serious dispute of law between the parties upon which the tribunal rehearing the case ought to be given guidance. The Secretary of State's representative was criticised for ignoring such a dispute and submitting that the tribunal's decision should be set aside under this subsection on a ground that would have been immaterial if the tribunal had not erred in their approach to a more important issue in the case.

Subsection (11)

See reg. 58 of the Social Security and Child Support (Decisions and Appeals) Regulations 1999 and regs 9 to 12 of the Social Security Commissioners (Procedure) Regulations 1999. 1.313

Appeal from Commissioner on point of law

15.—(1) Subject to subsections (2) and (3) below, an appeal on a question of law shall lie to the appropriate court from any decision of a Commissioner. 1.314

(2) No appeal under this section shall lie from a decision except—
(a) with the leave of the Commissioner who gave the decision or, in a prescribed case, with the leave of a Commissioner selected in accordance with regulations; or
(b) if he refuses leave, with the leave of the appropriate court.

(3) An application for leave under this section in respect of a Commissioner's decision may only be made by—
  (a) a person who, before the proceedings before the Commissioner were begun, was entitled to appeal to the Commissioner from the decision to which the Commissioner's decision relates;
  (b) any other person who was a party to the proceedings in which the first decision mentioned in paragraph (a) above was given;
  (c) any other person who is authorised by regulations to apply for leave;
and regulations may make provision with respect to the manner in which and the time within which applications must be made to a Commissioner for leave under this section and with respect to the procedure for dealing with such applications.

(4) On an application to a Commissioner for leave under this section it shall be the duty of the Commissioner to specify as the appropriate court—
  (a) the Court of Appeal if it appears to him that the relevant place is in England or Wales;
  (b) the Court of Session if it appears to him that the relevant place is in Scotland; and
  (c) the Court of Appeal in Northern Ireland if it appears to him that the relevant place is in Northern Ireland,
Except that if it appears to him, having regard to the circumstances of the case and in particular to the convenience of the persons who may be parties to the proposed appeal, that he should specify a different court mentioned in paragraphs (a) to (c) above as the appropriate court, it shall be his duty to specify that court as the appropriate court.

(5) In this section—
  "the appropriate court", except in subsection (4) above, means the court specified in pursuance of that subsection;
  "the relevant place", in relation to an application for leave to appeal from a decision of a Commissioner, means the premises where the person or authority whose decision was the subject of the Commissioner's decision usually exercises his or its functions.

1.315 GENERAL NOTE

This re-enacts ss. 24 and 34(5) of the Social Security Administration Act 1992 but it clearly provides for a right of appeal against *any* decision of a Commissioner and not just a decision given under s.14. It therefore applies to decisions under s.13 of the Social Security (Recovery of Benefits) Act 1997 and under the Forfeiture Act 1982. This is an improvement because it was arguable that the general right of appeal against Commissioners' decisions introduced by s.14 of the Social Security Act 1980 was lost in the 1992 consolidation and that appeals could then be brought only against decisions given under ss 23 and 34 of the 1992 Act, although no-one ever took the point. Nevertheless, para. 3(2) of Sched. 4 to the Tax Credits Act 1999 makes express provision for the section to have effect in relation to decisions with respect to penalties under s.9(1), (3)(a) or (5)(a) of that Act.

For what amounts to a question of law, see the note to s.14(1). A decision of a Commissioner to refuse leave to appeal to a Commissioner is not a "decision" against which an appeal lies under this section. Instead, any challenge must be made by way of an application for judicial review (*Bland v. Chief Supplementary Benefit Officer* [1983] 1 W.L.R. 262, also reported as *R(SB) 12/83*). Although s.56 of the Access to Justice Act 1999 allows the Lord Chancellor to make an order requiring appeals in England and Wales to be heard by a court other than the Court of Appeal, no such order has been made in respect of appeals from Commissioners.

Leave to appeal must be obtained. If the Commissioner refuses leave, it is still necessary for him or her to identify the "appropriate court" so that an application for leave (known as "permission" in the Court of Appeal), may be made to that court. For the procedure for applying to the Commissioner for leave, see reg. 33 of the Social Security Commissioners (Procedure) Regulations 1999. Note that the three-month time limit for making an application to the Commissioner may be extended by the Commissioner, under reg. 5(2)(a), but if he or she refuses to do so, the time cannot be extended by the "appropriate court", although the Commissioner's refusal could be challenged by way of an application for judicial review (*White v. Chief Adjudication Officer* [1986] 2 All E.R. 905, also reported as an appendix to *R(S) 8/85*). For the procedure in the Court of Appeal, see C.P.R. Pt. 52. An application for permission to appeal or an appeal must be brought within six weeks of the Commissioner's refusal or grant of leave being sent to the parties (P.D. 52, para. 21.5), although the court has a general power under (C.P.R. rule 52.6) to extend time limits. For the procedure in the Court of Session, see R.C. 290 and 293B.

In *Smith v. Cosworth Casting Processes Ltd* (Practice Note) [1997] 1 W.L.R. 1538, the Court of Appeal gave guidance as to applications for leave to appeal to the Court. The Court would only refuse leave if satisfied that the applicant had "no real prospect" of succeeding on the appeal. The Court could grant an application even if not so satisfied if, for instance, the issue was one the Court considered should, in the public interest, be examined by the Court of Appeal or if it raised an issue where the law needed clarifying. Where leave was refused, the Court would give short reasons. Where leave was granted, the Court might also identify, for the benefit of the parties and the Court hearing the appeal, a reason for giving leave, but it should not be assumed that the Court did not accept that there were other issues to be decided as well as the one identified. A person applying for a grant of leave to be set aside had a heavy onus and such applications were discouraged. See now C.P.R. rule 52.3.

Where the claimant is the appellant, the respondent will be the Secretary of State for Social Security (*not* the Commissioner). The Solicitor to the Departments of Social Security and Health will accept service on behalf of the Secretary of State at New Court, Carey Street, London WC2A 2LS.

Procedure etc.

Procedure

16.—(1) Regulations ("procedure regulations") may make any such provision as is specified in Schedule 5 to this Act.

(2) Procedure regulations prescribing the procedure to be followed in cases before a Commissioner shall provide that any hearing shall be in public except in so far as the Commissioner for special reasons otherwise directs.

(3) It is hereby declared—
(a) that the power to prescribe procedure includes power to make provision as to the representation of one person, at any hearing

1.316

of a case, by another person whether having professional qualifications or not; and

(b) that the power to provide for the procedure to be followed in connection with the making of decisions by the Secretary of State includes power to make provision with respect to the formulation of the matters to be decided, whether on a reference under section 117 of the Administration Act or otherwise.

(4) *Omitted*

(5) *Omitted*

(6) If it appears to a Commissioner that a matter before him involves a question of fact of special difficulty, he may direct that in dealing with that matter he shall have the assistance of one or more experts.

In this subsection "expert" means a person appearing to the Commissioner to have knowledge or experience which would be relevant in determining the question of fact of special difficulty.

(7) If it appears to the Chief Commissioner (or, in the case of his inability to act, to such other of the Commissioners as he may have nominated to act for the purpose) that—

(a) an application for leave under section 14(10)(b) above; or

(b) an appeal,

falling to be heard by one of the Commissioners involves a question of law of special difficulty, he may direct that the application or appeal be dealt with, not by that Commissioner alone, but by a tribunal consisting of any three or more of the Commissioners.

If the decision of the tribunal is not unanimous, the decision of the majority shall be the decision of the tribunal; and the presiding Commissioner shall have a casting vote if the votes are equally divided.

(8) Where a direction is given under subsection (7)(a) above, section 14(10)(b) above shall have effect as if the reference to a Commissioner were a reference to such a tribunal as is mentioned in subsection (7) above.

(9) Except so far as it may be applied in relation to England and Wales by procedure regulations, Part I of the Arbitration Act 1996 shall not apply to any proceedings under this Chapter.

GENERAL NOTE

Subsections (1) to (3)

1.317   See the Social Security and Child Support (Decisions and Appeals) Regulations 1999 and the Social Security Commissioners (Procedure) Regulations 1999. Regulations in respect of Commissioners are made by the Lord Chancellor after consultation with the Secretary of State (s.79(2)). Regulations in respect of appeal tribunals are made by the Secretary of State (s.79(1)).

Subsections (4) and (5)

1.318   These subsections are to be repealed by the Social Security Contributions (Transfer of Functions, etc.) Act 1999, Sched. 7, para. 28, presumably at the same time as the only provisions that would have given them practical effect and which have never been brought into force.

1.319   *Subsection (6)*

There is no longer any general power to sit with assessors but the possibility of doing so is preserved for Commissioners by this subsection. There is no provision allowing the scope of the assistance given under this subsection to be limited by regulations as there is in s.7(6)(c).

Subsections (7) and (8)

The power to appoint a Tribunal of Commissioners to hear an appeal has been extended to enable a Tribunal to hear an application. It has also been provided that a Tribunal may consist of more than three Commissioners, reflecting the fact that three no longer represent even a sizeable proportion of Commissioners, whereas in 1948 they would have represented a majority. In recent years, the Chief Commissioner has seldom appointed more than one or two Tribunals a year and those have tended to be appointed to hear cases giving rise to issues about which single Commissioners have disagreed. A decision of a Tribunal usually settles the dispute because a decision of a Tribunal of Commissioners will always be followed by single Commissioners (*R(I) 12/75*), although not always by another Tribunal (*R(U) 4/88*).

Finality of decisions

17.—(1) Subject to the provisions of this Chapter, any decision made in accordance with the foregoing provisions of this Chapter shall be final; and subject to the provisions of any regulations under section 11 above, any decision made in accordance with those regulations shall be final.

(2) If and to the extent that regulations so provide, any finding of fact or other determination embodied in or necessary to such a decision, or on which such a decision is based, shall be conclusive for the purposes of—

(a) further such decisions;
(b) decisions made under the Child Support Act; and
(c) decisions made under the Vaccine Damage Payments Act.

GENERAL NOTE

Subsection (1)
This re-enacts s.60(1) of the Social Security Administration Act 1992. Decisions are "final" subject to appeals and reviews. Therefore, it is not possible to sue the Secretary of State in negligence in respect of a decision (*Jones v. Department of Employment* [1989] Q.B. 1) although an action could lie in misfeasance. That does not prevent the Department of Social Security being sued in respect of bad advice. The finality of decisions does not prevent decisions being challenged by way of judicial review (*R. v. Medical Appeal Tribunal, ex p. Gilmore* [1957] 1 Q.B. 574, a decision made before there was a right of appeal from a medical appeal tribunal to a Commissioner) although the reluctance of the High Court to allow such challenges when there is a statutory right of appeal means that they are confined to exceptional cases.

Subsection (2)(a)
See reg. 10 of the Social Security and Child Support (Decisions and Appeals) Regulations 1999. Note that there is no express provision re-enacting s.60(2) of the 1992 Act which provided that, as a general rule, a finding in one decision was *not* conclusive for the purpose of any other decision. However, it is suggested that such an express provision is not necessary and that, in the absence of any rule of evidence to the contrary, a person or body making a decision is entitled to rely on an earlier finding but is not bound to do so. If that were not

Matters arising as respects decisions

1.324 **18.**—(1) Regulations may make provision as respects matters arising—
  (a) pending any decision under this Chapter of the Secretary of State, an appeal tribunal or a Commissioner which relates to—
    (i) any claim for a relevant benefit; [¹ or]
    (ii) any person's entitlement to such a benefit or its receipt; [¹ or]
    (iii) [¹ . . .]
    (iv) [¹ . . .]
  (b) out of the revision under section 9 above or on appeal of any such decision.

(2) Regulations under subsection (1) above as it applies to child benefit may include provision as to the date from which child benefit is to be payable to a person in respect of a child in a case where, before the benefit was awarded to that person, child benefit in respect of the child was awarded to another person.

AMENDMENT

1. Social Security Contributions (Transfer of Functions, etc.) Act 1999, Sched. 7, para. 29 (April 1, 1999).

Medical examinations

Medical examination required by Secretary of State

1.325 **19.**—(1) Before making a decision on a claim for a relevant benefit, or as to a person's entitlement to such a benefit [¹ . . .], the Secretary of State may refer the person—
  (a) in respect of whom the claim is made; or
  (b) whose entitlement is at issue,
to a medical practitioner for such examination and report as appears to the Secretary of State to be necessary for the purpose of providing him with information for use in making the decision.

(2) Subsection (3) below applies where—
  (a) the Secretary of State has exercised the power conferred on him by subsection (1) above; and
  (b) the medical practitioner requests the person referred to him to attend for or submit himself to medical examination.

(3) If the person fails without good cause to comply with the request, the Secretary of State shall make the decision against him.

AMENDMENT

1. Social Security Contributions (Transfer of Functions, etc.) Act 1999, Sched. 7, para. 30 (April 1, 1999).

(1998 c.14, s.19)

GENERAL NOTE

Subsections (1) and (2)
This section must be distinguished from reg. 19 of the Social Security and Child Support (Decisions and Appeals) Regulations 1999. Under this section, the Secretary of State (or, in relation to tax credit, the Commissioners of Inland Revenue—see Tax Credits Act 1999, s.2(1)(c) and Sched. 2, para. 8(a)) refers the claimant for examination and report but it is the *medical practitioner* who requests attendance for, or submission to, a medical examination. The penalty imposed by subs. (3) is imposed for failing to comply with the medical practitioner's request. This section, therefore, appears to be for the purpose of obtaining a report—it being for the medical practitioner to decide whether an examination is necessary. Under reg. 19, it is the Secretary of State (or the Commissioners of Inland Revenue) who requires the claimant to attend the examination and the penalty for failure to do so is different. The Social Security (Incapacity for Work) Regulations 1995 continue to contain yet another similar power and associated penalty for failure to comply. Note also that this section applies only to references by the Secretary of State (or the Commissioners): separate provision is made under s.20 for references required to assist tribunals.

1.326

Subsection (3)
What the decision is, depends on what the question was. It may be a decision to reject a whole claim but it may be a decision to award benefit but on a basis less favourable to the claimant than would otherwise have been the case. The claimant will usually be able to appeal against the decision (and apply for revision under s.9) and will be entitled to argue that he did have good cause for failing to comply with the request. He or she would also be entitled to argue that the decision was less favourable than was required by subs. (3), having regard to what was really in issue. The other remedy open to a claimant is to make a new claim (if benefit was not awarded) or make a new application for a supersession (if there is some continuing entitlement). The consequence will be to raise the question again and the Secretary of State (or an officer of the Inland Revenue) will be obliged to make a new decision, which he will not be able to make under subs. (3) unless the claimant has failed without good cause to comply with a new request to attend for, or submit to, a medical examination.

1.327

Medical examination required by appeal tribunal

20.—(1) This section applies where an appeal has been brought under section 12 above against a decision on a claim for a relevant benefit, or as to a person's entitlement to such a benefit [1 . . .].

1.328

(2) An eligible person may, if prescribed conditions are satisfied, refer the person—

(a) in respect of whom the claim is made; or
(b) whose entitlement is at issue,

to a medical practitioner for such examination and report as appears to the eligible person to be necessary for the purpose of providing an appeal tribunal with information for use in determining the appeal.

In this subsection "eligible person" means a person who is eligible to be appointed as the sole member of an appeal tribunal, or to be nominated as the chairman of such a tribunal.

(3) At a hearing before an appeal tribunal, except in prescribed cases or circumstances, the tribunal—

Social Security Act 1998

(a) may not carry out a physical examination of the person mentioned in subsection (2) above; and
(b) may not require that person to undergo any physical test for the purpose of determining whether he satisfies the condition mentioned in section 73(1)(a) of the Contributions and Benefits Act.

AMENDMENT

1. Social Security Contributions (Transfer of Functions, etc.) Act 1999, Sched. 7, para. 31 (April 1, 1999).

GENERAL NOTE

1.329 *Subsection (2)*
A reference may be made only in circumstances set out in reg. 41 of the Social Security and Child Support (Decisions and Appeals) Regulations 1999. Note that it is not a tribunal who has the power to refer, but an "eligible person" who will in practice be a legally qualified panel member. There is no statutory penalty for failing to attend for, or submit to, a medical examination required by an "eligible person" or requested by a medical practitioner making a report under this section. Such a penalty is unnecessary as it is open to the tribunal to draw such inferences from the failure as appear proper when deciding the medical issues arising before them.

1.330 *Subsection (3)*
See reg. 52 of the Social Security and Child Support (Decisions and Appeals) Regulations 1999. In CDLA/433/99, it was held that carrying out a physical examination in breach of the forerunner of this subsection was not an error of law rendering a decision liable to be set aside but relying on evidence from the examination would have been.

Suspension and termination of benefit

Suspension in prescribed circumstances

1.331 **21.**—(1) Regulations may provide for—
(a) Suspending payments of a relevant benefit, in whole or in part, in prescribed circumstances;
(b) the subsequent making in prescribed circumstances of any or all of the payments so suspended.

(2) Regulations made under subsection (1) above may, in particular, make provision for any case where—
(a) it appears to the Secretary of State that an issue arises whether the conditions for entitlement to a relevant benefit are or were fulfilled;
(b) it appears to the Secretary of State that an issue arises whether a decision as to an award of a relevant benefit should be revised (under section 9 above) or superseded (under section 10 above);
(c) an appeal is pending against a decision of an appeal tribunal, a Commissioner or a court; or
(d) an appeal is pending against the decision given in a different case by a Commissioner or a court, and it appears to the Secretary of State that if the appeal were to be determined in a particular way

an issue would arise whether the award of a relevant benefit (whether the same benefit or not) in the case itself ought to be revised or superseded.

(3) For the purposes of subsection (2) above, an appeal against a decision is pending if—
   (a) an appeal against the decision has been brought but not determined;
   (b) an application for leave to appeal against the decision has been made but not determined; or
   (c) in such circumstances as may be prescribed, an appeal against the decision has not been brought (or, as the case may be, an application for leave to appeal against the decision has not been made) but the time for doing so has not yet expired.

(4) [1 . . .]

AMENDMENT

1. Social Security Contributions (Transfer of Functions, etc.) Act 1999, Sched. 7, para. 32 (April 1, 1999).

GENERAL NOTE

See regs 16 and 20 of the Social Security and Child Support (Decisions and Appeals) Regulations 1999.

1.332

Suspension for failure to furnish information etc.

22.—(1) The powers conferred by this section are exercisable in relation to persons who fail to comply with information requirements.

(2) Regulations may provide for—
   (a) suspending payments of a relevant benefit, in whole or in part;
   (b) the subsequent making in prescribed circumstances of any or all of the payments so suspended.

(3) In this section and section 23 below "information requirement" means a requirement, made in pursuance of regulations under subsection (1)(hh) of section 5 of the Administration Act, to furnish information or evidence needed for a determination whether a decision on an award of benefit to which that section applies should be revised under section 9 or superseded under section 10 above.

1.333

GENERAL NOTE

See reg. 17 of the Social Security and Child Support (Decisions and Appeals) Regulations 1999.

1.334

Termination in cases of failure to furnish information

23. Regulations may provide that, except in prescribed cases or circumstances, a person—
   (a) whose benefit has been suspended in accordance with regulations under section 21 above and who subsequently fails to comply with an information requirement; or
   (b) whose benefit has been suspended in accordance with regulations

1.335

under section 22 above for failing to comply with such a requirement,

shall cease to be entitled to the benefit from a date not earlier than the date on which payments were suspended.

GENERAL NOTE

1.336   See reg. 18 of the Social Security and Child Support (Decisions and Appeals) Regulations 1999.

Suspension and termination for failure to submit to medical examination

1.337   **24.** Regulations may make provision—
(a) enabling the Secretary of State to require a person to whom a relevant benefit has been awarded to submit to medical examination;
(b) for suspending payments of benefit, in whole or in part, in a case of a person who fails to submit himself to a medical examination to which he is required to submit in accordance with regulations under paragraph (a) above;
(c) for the subsequent making in prescribed circumstances of any or all of the payments so suspended;
(d) for entitlement to the benefit to cease, except in prescribed cases or circumstances, from a date not earlier than the date on which payments were suspended.

GENERAL NOTE

1.338   See reg. 19 of the Social Security and Child Support (Decisions and Appeals) Regulations 1999.

[¹ *Appeals dependent on issues falling to be decided by Inland Revenue*

Appeals dependent on issues falling to be decided by Inland Revenue

1.339   **24A.**—(1) Regulations may make provision for an appeal tribunal or Commissioner, where on any appeal there arises any issue which under section 8 of the Social Security Contributions (Transfer of Functions, etc.) Act 1999 falls to be decided by an officer of the Inland Revenue, to require the Secretary of State to refer the issue to the Inland Revenue.
Regulations under this section may—
(a) provide for the appeal to be referred to the Secretary of State pending the decision of the Inland Revenue,
(b) enable or require the Secretary of State, in specified circumstances, to deal with any other issue arising on the appeal pending the decision on the referred issue, and
(c) enable the Secretary of State, on receiving the decision of an officer of the Inland Revenue, or any determination of the tax appeal Commissioners made on appeal from his decision—

(i) to revise his decision,
(ii) to make a decision superseding his decision, or
(iii) to refer the appeal to the appeal tribunal or Commissioner for determination.

AMENDMENT

1. Social Security Contributions (Transfer of Functions, etc.) Act 1999, Sched. 7, para. 33 (July 5, 1999).

GENERAL NOTE

See reg. 38A of the Social Security and Child Support (Decisions and Appeals) Regulations 1999.

Decisions and appeals dependent on other cases

Decisions involving issues that arise on appeal in other cases

25.—(1) This section applies where—
 (a) a decision by the Secretary of State falls to be made under section 8, 9 or 10 above in relation to a particular case; and
 (b) an appeal is pending against the decision given in another case by a Commissioner or a court (whether or not the two cases concern the same benefit).

(2) In a case relating to a relevant benefit, the Secretary of State need not make the decision while the appeal is pending if he considers it possible that the result of the appeal will be such that, if it were already determined, there would be no entitlement to benefit.

(3) If the Secretary of State considers it possible that the result of the appeal will be such that, if it were already determined, it would affect the decision in some other way—
 (a) he need not, except in such cases or circumstances as may be prescribed, make the decision while the appeal is pending;
 (b) he may, in such cases or circumstances as may be prescribed, make the decision on such basis as may be prescribed.

(4) Where the Secretary of State acts in accordance with subsection (3)(b) above, following the determination of the appeal he shall if appropriate revise his decision (under section 9 above) in accordance with that determination.

(5) For the purposes of this section, an appeal against a decision is pending if—
 (a) an appeal against the decision has been brought but not determined;
 (b) an application for leave to appeal against the decision has been made but not determined; or
 (c) in such circumstances as may be prescribed, an appeal against the decision has not been brought (or, as the case may be, an application for leave to appeal against the decision has not been made) but the time for doing so has not yet expired.

(6) In paragraphs (a), (b) and (c) of subsection (5) above, any refer-

ence to an appeal, or an application for leave to appeal, against a decision includes a reference to—
  (a) an application for, or for leave to apply for judicial review of the decision under section 31 of the Supreme Court Act 1981; or
  (b) an application to the supervisory jurisdiction of the Court of Session in respect of the decision.

GENERAL NOTE

1.342 *Subsection (1)*
This section applies only where a decision falls to be made by the Secretary of State (or, in relation to tax credit, an officer of the Inland Revenue—see Tax Credits Act 1999, Sched. 2, para. 21). See s.26 where a decision falls to be made by a tribunal or Commissioner. No appeal lies against a decision under this section (see Social Security and Child Support (Decisions and Appeals) Regulations 1999, Sched. 2, para. 7).

"Court" is not defined for the purposes of this section (compare s.27(7)) but the context in which the word appears limits its scope. There must be an appeal pending against a decision "in another case" of a Commissioner or a court. This includes an application for judicial review of a Commissioner's decision (see subs. (6)) but not an application for judicial review of a decision of the Secretary of State or the Inland Revenue or, in a housing benefit case, a local authority. However, an appeal to the Court of Appeal against a decision of the High Court, or to the Inner House of the Court of Session from a decision of the Outer House, on judicial review of the Secretary of State, the Inland Revenue or a local authority would appear to be caught. A renewed application for leave to apply for judicial review made to the Court of Appeal is probably not caught. A reference to the European Court of Justice by a Commissioner is certainly not caught. The words in parenthesis tend to suggest that the court must be concerned with some sort of social security benefit as does the general context of the provision and the need to have some sort of practical boundary. Otherwise, it might be suggested that, say, an appeal to the House of Lords from a decision of the Court of Appeal dealing with the meaning of the word "misrepresentation" in a marine insurance policy was a relevant appeal (because it might possibly assist with the understanding of that word in s.71 of the Social Security Administration Act 1992).

Subsections (2) and (3)
1.343 The Secretary of State (or, in relation to tax credit, the officer of the Inland Revenue) must consider two separate issues. The first is whether a possible result of the appeal would affect the decision before him. The Secretary of State would be a party to most such appeals and it is to be hoped that he does not indulge in too much wishful thinking. The word "possible" is broad. And what is the meaning of "result of the appeal"? Is it confined to the *ratio decidendi* or is it sufficient that the Secretary of State considers that there might be some useful *obiter dicta*? The second issue the Secretary of State (or the officer of the Inland Revenue) must consider is whether he should not make the decision or should decide it in accordance with subs. (3)(b) or whether he should ignore the fact that there is an appeal pending. He has a broad discretion and much will depend on such circumstances as the number of cases, the amount of money at stake, hardship to the claimants and the degree of probability that the court's decision will provide significant assistance with the determination of the cases before him.

For regulations under subs. (3)(b), see reg. 21(1) to (3) of the Social Security and Child Support (Decisions and Appeals) Regulations 1999.

Subsection (4)
The revision usually has effect from the same date as the original decision (see s.9(3)). 1.344

Subsection (5)
See reg. 21(4) of the Social Security and Child Support (Decisions and Appeals) Regulations 1999. 1.345

Appeals involving issues that arise on appeal in other cases

26.—(1) This section applies where— 1.346
  (a) an appeal ("appeal A") in relation to a decision under section 8, 9 or 10 above is made to an appeal tribunal, or from an appeal tribunal to a Commissioner; and
  (b) an appeal ("appeal B") is pending against a decision given in a different case by a Commissioner or a court (whether or not the two appeals concern the same benefit).

(2) If the Secretary of State considers it possible that the result of appeal B will be such that, if it were already determined, it would affect the determination of appeal a, he may serve notice requiring the tribunal or Commissioner—
  (a) not to determine appeal A but to refer it to him; or
  (b) to deal with the appeal in accordance with subsection (4) below.

(3) Where appeal A is referred to the Secretary of State under subsection (2)(a) above, following the determination of appeal B and in accordance with tat determination, he shall if appropriate—
  (a) in a case where appeal A has not been determined by the tribunal, revise (under section 9 above) his decision which gave rise to that appeal; or
  (b) in a case where appeal A has been determined by the tribunal, make a decision (under section 10 above) superseding the tribunal's decision.

(4) Where appeal A is to be dealt with in accordance with this subsection, the appeal tribunal or Commissioner shall either—
  (a) stay appeal A until appeal B is determined; or
  (b) if the tribunal or Commissioner considers it to be in the interests of the appellant to do so, determine appeal A as if—
    (i) appeal B had already been determined; and
    (ii) the issues arising on appeal B had been decided in the way that was most unfavourable to the appellant.
In this subsection "the appellant" means the person who appealed or, as the case may be, first appealed against the decision mentioned in subsection (1)(a) above.

(5) Where the appeal tribunal or Commissioner acts in accordance with subsection (4)(b) above, following the determination of appeal B the Secretary of State shall, if appropriate, make a decision (under section 10 above) superseding the decision of the tribunal or Commissioner in accordance with that determination.

(6) For the purposes of this section, an appeal against a decision is pending if—
  (a) an appeal against the decision has been brought but not determined;

Social Security Act 1998

(b) an application for leave to appeal against the decision has been made but not determined; or
(c) in such circumstances as may be prescribed, an appeal against the decision has not been brought (or, as the case may be, an application for leave to appeal against the decision has not been made) but the time for doing so has not yet expired.
(7) In this section—
(a) the reference in subsection (1)(a) above to an appeal to a Commissioner includes a reference to an application for leave to appeal to a Commissioner; and
(b) any reference in paragraph (a), (b) or (c) of subsection (6) above to an appeal, or to an application for leave to appeal, against a decision includes a reference to—
  (i) an application for, or for leave to apply for, judicial review of the decision under section 31 of the Supreme Court Act 1981; or
  (ii) an application to the supervisory jurisdiction of the Court of Session in respect of the decision.
(8) Regulations may make provision supplementing that made by this section.

GENERAL NOTE

1.347 *Subsection (1)*
See the note to s.25(1) for the meaning of "court". See also subss. (6) and (7).

Subsection (2)
1.348 It is for the Secretary of State (or in relation to tax credit, the Commissioners of Inland Revenue—see Tax Credits Act 1999, s.2(1)(c) and Sched. 2, para. 8(a)) to identify both appeal B and appeal A although there is no reason why one notice may not be issued in respect of several appeals A (see reg. 21 of the Social Security Commissioners (Procedure) Regulations 1999). As in s.25(2) and (3), the Secretary of State (or the Commissioners of Inland Revenue) must first make a judgment as to the possible effects of the decision in appeal B and must then consider whether to serve notice under this subsection. It will not always be appropriate to do so. If the Secretary of State does decide to issue the notice, he must go on to decide whether the tribunal should be required to refer appeal A to him under para. (a) or to deal with the appeal in accordance with subs. (4) under para. (b). Which option is appropriate will depend on the circumstances of the case. It may be thought to be unobjectionable that there be specific provision as to the way appeals should be handled while the decision in a "test case" is awaited, but to be highly objectionable that the decision as to the appropriate procedure should lie wholly in the hands of the Secretary of State who is a party in appeal A and is usually a party in appeal B. It might be better if the legislation merely allowed the Secretary of State to seek a general direction in respect of a block of similar cases from the President of appeal tribunals (or a senior legally qualified panel member) or a Commissioner. As it is, any challenge to the Secretary of State's judgment must be by way of an application for judicial review.

Subsection (3)
1.349 Presumably para. (b) exists in case appeal A was decided in ignorance of the notice requiring it not to be determined. The decision is not rendered ineffective

(1998 c.14, s.26)

and so operates until it is superseded. It is not clear what happens if either party appeals against it.

Subsection (4)

It is for the tribunal or Commissioner to decide whether para. (a) or para. (b) should apply in any particular case. Para. (b) is unlikely to be used a great deal unless either the claimant asks for it to be used or else the tribunal or Commissioner is fairly sure that the decision on appeal B is unlikely to assist the claimant. A judgment as to what is the most unfavourable way in which the issues arising on appeal B might be decided requires that the tribunal or Commissioner be given considerable information about the appeal, including pleadings, so that it can be established what the issues really are. 1.350

Subsection (6)

See reg. 22 of the Social Security and Child Support (Decisions and Appeals) Regulations 1999. 1.351

Subsection (8)

See reg. 21 of the Social Security Commissioners (Procedure) Regulations 1999. There is no equivalent provision in the Social Security and Child Support (Decisions and Appeals) Regulations 1999. 1.352

Cases of error

Restrictions on entitlement to benefit in certain cases of error

27.—(1) Subject to subsection (2) below, this section applies where— 1.353
   (a) the effect of the determination, whenever made, of an appeal to a Commissioner or the court ("the relevant determination") is that the adjudicating authority's decision out of which the appeal arose was erroneous in point of law; and
   (b) after the date of the relevant determination a decision falls to be made by the Secretary of State in accordance with that determination (or would, apart from this section, fall to be so made)—
      (i) in relation to a claim for benefit;
      (ii) as to whether to revise, under section 9 above, a decision as to a person's entitlement to benefit; or
      (iii) on an application made under section 10 above for a decision as to a person's entitlement to benefit to be superseded.

(2) This section does not apply where the decision of the Secretary of State mentioned in subsection (1)(b) above—
   (a) is one which, but for section 25(2) or (3)(a) above, would have been made before the date of the relevant determination; or
   (b) is one made in pursuance of section 26(3) or (5) above.

(3) In so far as the decision relates to a person's entitlement to a benefit in respect of—
   (a) a period before the date of the relevant determination; or
   (b) in the case of a widow's payment, a death occurring before that date,

it shall be made as if the adjudicating authority's decision had been found by the Commissioner or court not to have been erroneous in point of law.

Social Security Act 1998

(4) In deciding whether a person is entitled to benefit in a case where his entitlement depends on his having been entitled to the same or some other benefit before attaining a particular age, subsection (3) above shall be disregarded for the purpose only of deciding whether he was so entitled before attaining that age.

(5) Subsection (1)(a) above shall be read as including a case where—

(a) the effect of the relevant determination is that part or all of a purported regulation or order is invalid; and

(b) the error of law made by the adjudicating authority was to act on the basis that the purported regulation or order (or the part held to be invalid) was valid.

(6) It is immaterial for the purposes of subsection (1) above—

(a) where such a decision as is mentioned in paragraph (b)(i) falls to be made, whether the claim was made before or after the date of the relevant determination;

(b) where such a decision as is mentioned in paragraph (b)(ii) or (iii) falls to be made on an application under section 9 or (as the case may be) 10 above, whether the application was made before or after that date.

(7) In this section—

"adjudicating authority" means—

(a) the Secretary of State;

(b) any former officer, tribunal or body; or

(c) any officer, tribunal or body in Northern Ireland corresponding to a former officer, tribunal or body;

"benefit" means—

(a) benefit under Parts II to V of the Contributions and Benefits Act, other than Old Cases payments;

(b) benefit under Part II of the Social Security Act 1975 (in respect of a period before July 1, 1992 but not before April 6, 1975);

(c) benefit under the National Insurance Act 1946 or 1965, or the National Insurance (Industrial Injuries) Act 1946 or 1965 (in respect of a period before April 6, 1975);

(d) a jobseeker's allowance;

(e) any benefit corresponding to a benefit mentioned in paragraphs (a) to (d) above; and

(f) any income-related benefit;

"the court" means the High Court, the Court of Appeal, the Court of Session, the High Court or Court of Appeal in Northern Ireland, the House of Lords or the Court of Justice in the European Community;

"former officer, tribunal or body" means any of the following, that is to say—

(a) an adjudication officer or, in the case of a decision given on a reference under section 21(2) or 25(1) of the Administration Act, a social security appeal tribunal, a disability appeal tribunal or a medical appeal tribunal;

(b) an adjudicating medical practitioner appointed under section 49 of that Act or a specially qualified adjudicating medical

practitioner appointed in accordance with regulations under section 62(2) of that Act; or
(c) the National Assistance Board, the Supplementary Benefits Commission, the Attendance Allowance Board, a benefit officer, an insurance officer or a supplement officer.

(8) For the purposes of this section, any reference to entitlement to benefit includes a reference to entitlement—
(a) to any increase in the rate of a benefit; or
(b) to a benefit, or increase of benefit, at a particular rate.

(9) The date of the relevant determination shall, in prescribed cases, be determined for the purposes of this section in accordance with any regulations made for that purpose.

(10) Regulations made under subsection (9) above may include provision—
(a) for a determination of a higher court to be treated as if it had been made on the date of a determination of a lower court or a Commissioner; or
(b) for a determination of a lower court or a Commissioner to be treated as if it had been made on the date of a determination of a higher court.

GENERAL NOTE

This section does not apply in any case where the determination relates to tax credit (Tax Credits Act 1999, Sched. 2, para. 19).

1.354

Subsection (1)

The Secretary of State is an adjudicating authority but an appeal tribunal is not (see subs. (7)). As the question for a Commissioner or court is whether an *appeal tribunal* has erred in law, it may not always be easy to tell whether the effect of the Commissioner's or court's determination is that the Secretary of State's decision was erroneous in point of law. See also subss. (5) and (6).

1.355

Para. (b) is in broad terms but it is suggested that, although s.27 would apply to revision under reg. 3(5)(b) of the Social Security and Child Support (Decisions and Appeals) Regulations 1999 (mistake of fact too favourable to the claimant), it would not apply to the related decisions under s.71 of the Social Security Administration Act 1992 as to the amount of the overpayment or the Secretary of State's entitlement to recover the overpayment. Nor does it apply to decisions under the Social Security (Recovery of Benefits) Act 1997.

Subsection (3)

This subsection has the effect that any decision of a Commissioner or court that is unfavourable to the Secretary of State is only prospective in its effect in other cases. Such a provision is not necessarily unreasonable to the extent that it does not require existing decisions in respect of earlier periods to be reversed but this one takes the principle to extremes by requiring the Secretary of State to continue giving erroneous decisions in respect of the period before the Commissioner's or court's decision after the error has been discovered. This is done so that all claimants are treated equally unfavourably in respect of that period. The perceived need for the provision may arise from the general power to revise at any time a decision arising from an official error (reg. 3(5)(a) of the Social Security and Child Support (Decisions and Appeals) Regulations 1999). The corollary is that any supersession as a result of the Commissioner's or court's determination is effective from the date of that determination (reg. 7(6) which

1.356

Social Security Act 1998

tends to operate to the advantage of claimants although it is not entirely clear when supersession would be appropriate rather than revision on the ground of official error in this context. Most, if not all, of the objections to s.27 would be removed if it operated only in relation to the power to revise decisions on the ground of official error and did not catch other claims and applications where the conventional time limits (much more restrictive than when the forerunner of s.27 was first introduced in 1990) adequately limit the extent to which an unexpected decision could apply retrospectively.

Subsection (5)

1.357   This is logical but may be thought to reinforce the view that subs. (3) is objectionable. Parliament has here not only ratified in advance decisions made, presumably in good faith, in excess of powers; it has also enabled (and required) the Secretary of State to continue making decisions (in respect of past periods) in excess of those powers once he knows the limits of the powers. This is despite the fact that Parliament could not have known the extent to which the powers would be exceeded. Henry VIII could hardly have asked for more.

Subsection (7)

1.358   Note that an appeal tribunal is not an "adjudicating authority". Quite why a social security appeal tribunal giving a decision on a reference should have been included as a "former tribunal" is unclear because there was no reason to suppose that their view of the law would necessarily be consistent with that held by the Department of Social Security. Perhaps the draftsman had a particular case in mind. The inclusion of disability appeal tribunals and medical appeal tribunals is even more obscure as there was no power to refer cases to them under the provisions cited. The inclusion of the Court of Appeal in Northern Ireland in the definition of "court" is interesting as a decision of that court is not, strictly speaking, binding in Great Britain. Such a decision is, however, highly persuasive and should usually be followed. The implication is that, if the Secretary of State does decide to follow a decision of the Court of appeal in Northern Ireland, the decision before him "falls to be made . . . in accordance with" the decision of the court for the purpose of subs. (1).

Subsections (9) and (10)

1.359   No regulations have yet been made under these powers.

Correction of errors and setting aside of decisions

1.360   **28.**—(1) Regulations may make provision with respect to—
   (a) the correction of accidental errors in any decision or record of a decision made under any relevant enactment; and
   (b) the setting aside of any such decision in a case where it appears just to set the decision aside on the ground that—
      (i) a document relating to the proceedings in which the decision was given was not sent to, or was not received at an appropriate time by, a party to the proceedings or a party's representative or was not received at an appropriate time by the body or person who gave the decision; or
      (ii) a party to the proceedings or a party's representative was not present at a hearing related to the proceedings.

[¹ (1A) In subsection (1) "decision" does not include any decision made by an officer of the Inland Revenue, other than a decision under or by virtue of Part III of the Pensions Schemes Act 1993.]

(2) Nothing in subsection (1) above shall be construed as derogating

(1998 c.14, s.28)

from any power to correct errors or set aside decisions which is exercisable apart from regulations made by virtue of that subsection.

(3) In this section "relevant enactment" means any enactment contained in—
  (a) this Chapter;
  (b) the Contributions and Benefits Act;
  (c) the Pension Schemes Act 1993;
  (d) the Jobseekers Act; or
  (e) the Social Security (Recovery of Benefits) Act 1997.

AMENDMENT

1. Social Security Contributions (Transfer of Functions, etc.) Act 1999, Sched. 7, para. 34 (July 5, 1999).

GENERAL NOTE

Subsection (1)
See regs 56 and 57 of the Social Security and Child Support (Decisions and Appeals) Regulations 1999 and regs 30 to 32 of the Social Security Commissioners (Procedure) Regulations 1999.

1.361

Subsection (2)
Other powers include those to be found in s.13 but this subsection (which is derived from s.70(2) of the Social Security Administration Act 1992 which contained no equivalent to s.13 of this Act) may contemplate a more general implied power to correct or set aside decisions where it is necessary to do so in the interests of justice. See further the note to reg. 57 of the Social Security and Child Support (Decisions and Appeals) Regulations 1999.

1.362

Industrial accidents

Decision that accident is an industrial accident

29.—(1) Where, in connection with any claim for industrial injuries benefit, it is decided that the relevant accident was or was not an industrial accident—
  (a) an express declaration of that fact shall be made and recorded; and
  (b) subject to subsection (3) below, a claimant shall be entitled to have the issue whether the relevant accident was an industrial accident decided, notwithstanding that his claim is disallowed on other grounds.

1.363

(2) Subject to subsection (3) and section 30 below, any person suffering personal injury by accident shall be entitled, if he claims the accident was an industrial accident—
  (a) to have that issue decided; and
  (b) to have a declaration made and recorded accordingly,
notwithstanding that no claim for benefit has been made in connection with which the issue arises; and this Chapter shall apply for that purpose as if the issue had arisen in connection with a claim for benefit.

(3) The Secretary of State, an appeal tribunal or a Commissioner (as

the case may be) may refuse to decide the issue whether an accident was an industrial accident, if satisfied that it is unlikely to be necessary to decide the issue for the purposes of any claim for benefit and this Chapter shall apply as if any such refusal were a decision on the issue.

(4) Subject to sections 9 to 15 above, any declaration under this section that an accident was or was not an industrial accident shall be conclusive for the purposes of any claim for industrial injuries benefit in respect of that accident.

(5) Where subsection (4) above applies—
  (a) in relation to a death occurring before April 11, 1988; or
  (b) for the purposes of section 60(2) of the Contributions and Benefits Act,
it shall have effect as if at the end there were added the words "whether or not the claimant is the person at whose instance the declaration was made".

(6) For the purposes of this section (but subject to section 30 below), an accident whereby a person suffers personal injury shall be deemed, in relation to him, to be an industrial accident if—
  (a) it arises out of and in the course of his employment;
  (b) that employment is employed earner's employment for the purposes of Part V of the Contributions and Benefits Act; and
  (c) payment of benefit is not under section 94(5) of that Act precluded because the accident happened while he was outside Great Britain.

(7) A decision under this section shall be final except that sections 9 and 10 above apply to a decision under this section that an accident was or was not an industrial accident as they apply to a decision under section 8 above if, but only if, the Secretary of State is satisfied that the decision under this section was given in consequence of any wilful non-disclosure or misrepresentation of a material fact.

GENERAL NOTE

1.364 This section re-enacts section 44 of the Social Security Administration Act 1992 with only minor changes. It provides for the Secretary of State to make a declaration that a person has suffered an industrial accident, whether or not there has been a claim for benefit and whether or not any claim has any prospects of success on other grounds, although, under subs. (3), the Secretary of State (or a tribunal or Commissioner) may refuse to determine that question if it is unlikely there will ever be a claim for benefit.

A determination that there was or was not an industrial accident is conclusive for the purposes of later claims for benefit. However, it is important to note that this section is expressed to be subject to s.30, so that a decision under this section which implies that a person has suffered personal injury as a result of an accident does not require anyone to find that the claimant has suffered disablement as a result of the injury even though the two decisions may appear, in the circumstances of the case, to contradict one another.

The usual rights of appeal apply to declarations under this section, but the power to revise or supersede such decisions is strictly limited, by subs. (7), to cases of *wilful* non-disclosure or misrepresentation of a material fact.

An appeal tribunal hearing an appeal from a decision given under subs. (2) is constituted by a legally-qualified panel member sitting alone (see the note to reg. 36 of the Social Security and Child Support (Decisions and Appeals) Regulations 1999).

Effect of decision

30.—(1) A decision (given under subsection (2) of section 29 above or otherwise) that an accident was an industrial accident is to be taken as determining only that paragraphs (a), (b) and (c) of subsection (6) of that section are satisfied in relation to the accident.

(2) Subject to subsections (3) and (4) below, no such decision is to be taken as importing a decision as to the origin of any injury or disability suffered by the claimant, whether or not there is an event identifiable as an accident apart from any injury that may have been received.

(3) A decision that, on a particular occasion when there was no event so identifiable, a person had an industrial accident by reason of an injury shall be treated as a decision that, if the injury was suffered by accident on that occasion, the accident was an industrial accident.

(4) A decision that an accident was an industrial accident may be given, and a declaration to that effect be made and recorded in accordance with section 29 above, without its having been found that personal injury resulted from the accident.

(5) Subsection (4) above has effect, subject to the discretion under section 29(3) above, to refuse to decide the issue if it is unlikely to be necessary for the purposes of a claim for benefit.

GENERAL NOTE

This section replaces section 60(3) of the Social Security Administration Act 1992. The drafting of the new provision is a great improvement. The overall effect is the same. A finding that there has been an industrial accident does not prevent it from being found that there has been no loss of faculty resulting from the accident even if the two decisions appear to be inconsistent. This is so even in a case where a person suffers a heart attack and the only "accident" found was the heart attack itself. Another decision-maker is still entitled to hold that the heart attack was not the result of an accident. This provision was first introduced by the National Insurance Act 1972 to reverse the effect of *Jones v. Secretary of State for Social Services* [1972] A.C. 944 (also reported as an appendix to *R(I) 3/69*). It is less important than it used to be now that all material decisions are made by the Secretary of State and there is no longer the old division of jurisdiction between adjudication officers and adjudicating medical authorities. However, it still has significance where a declaration is made under section 29(2) (i.e., otherwise than in the course of determining a claim to benefit) or where different decision-makers deal with the question whether there was an industrial accident and the question whether the claimant suffers a loss of faculty as a result of the accident (e.g., where a tribunal reverses a decision to the effect that there was no industrial accident but does not go on and deal with the other questions arising on the claim). In *CI/105/98*, it was pointed out that, quite apart from cases where the accident is indistinguishable from the injury suffered, there are cases where an indication that an accident was one giving rise to personal injury is a necessary part of a decision-maker's reasoning because it may help to explain why a declaration is made in respect of that alleged cause of the injury rather than another. However, it was also made clear that the effect of the forerunner of this section was that any view as to causation expressed when

Social Security Act 1998

making the decision that an accident was an industrial accident could be only provisional.

Other special cases

Incapacity for work

1.367   **31.**—(1) Regulations may provide that a determination that a person is disqualified for any period in accordance with regulations under section 171E of the Contributions and Benefits Act shall have effect for such purposes as may be prescribed as a determination that he is to be treated as capable of work for that period, and vice versa.

(2) Provision may be made by regulations for matters of such descriptions as may be prescribed to be determined by the Secretary of State, notwithstanding that other matters fall to be determined by another authority.

(3) Nothing in this section shall be taken to prejudice the generality of the power conferred by section 17(2) above.

GENERAL NOTE

1.368   *Subsection (1)*
This subsection replaces section 61A(2) of the Social Security Administration Act 1992. See reg. 10 of the Social Security and Child Support (Decisions and Appeals) Regulations 1999.

Subsection (2)
1.369   See reg. 11 of the Social Security and Child Support (Decisions and Appeals) Regulations 1999.

Industrial diseases

1.370   **32.** Regulations shall provide for applying the provisions of this Chapter, subject to any prescribed additions or modifications, in relation to decisions made or falling to be made under sections 108 to 110 of the Contributions and Benefits Act.

GENERAL NOTE

1.371   See the Social Security (Industrial Injuries) (Prescribed Diseases) Regulations 1985 as amended by Article 4(8) of and Schedule 8 to the Social Security Act 1998 (Commencement No. 8 and Savings and Consequential and Transitional Provisions) Order 1999.

Christmas bonus

1.372   **33.**—(1) A decision by the Secretary of State that a person is entitled or not entitled to payment of a qualifying benefit in respect of a period which includes a day in the relevant week shall be conclusive for the purposes of section 148 of the Contributions and Benefits Act.

(2) In this section, expressions to which a meaning is assigned by section 150 of that Act have that meaning.

GENERAL NOTE

This replaces section 67 of the Social Security Administration Act 1992.

Housing benefit and council tax benefit

34. and 35 *omitted*.

Social fund payments

Appropriate officers

36.—(1) In this section and section 38 below, "appropriate officer" means an officer of the Secretary of State who, acting under his authority, is exercising functions of the Secretary of State in relation to such payments out of the social fund as are mentioned in section 138(1)(b) of the Contributions and Benefits Act.

(2) The Secretary of State may nominate for an area an appropriate officer who shall issue general guidance to other such officers in the area about such matters relating to the social fund as the Secretary of State may specify.

(3) In relation to any decision of an appropriate officer, section 38 below shall apply in substitution for sections 9 and 10 above.

GENERAL NOTE

Subsection (1)
The social fund continues to be administered with internal reviews and no right of appeal (see s.38). "Appropriate officers" replace social fund officers and, because they act under the authority of the Secretary of State, subs. (3) is required to disapply ss 9 and 10. There is no right of appeal to an appeal tribunal against decisions of appropriate officers because s.12 applies only to a decision made on a claim or award of a "relevant benefit" and social fund payments under s.138(1)(b) of the Social Security Contributions and Benefits Act 1992 do not fall within the term "relevant benefit" as defined in s.8(3).

Subsection (2)
This re-enacts s.64(3) of the Social Security Administration Act 1992. See s.38(11) and (12) below for the status of general guidance.

The social fund Commissioner and inspectors

37.—(1) There shall continue to be an officer known as "the social fund Commissioner".

(2) The social fund Commissioner shall be appointed by the Secretary of State.

(3) The social fund Commissioner—
  (a) shall appoint such social fund inspectors; and
  (b) may appoint such officers and staff for himself and for social fund inspectors,

as he thinks fit, but with the consent of the Secretary of State as to numbers.

Social Security Act 1998

(4) Appointments under subsection (3) above shall be made from persons made available to the social fund Commissioner by the Secretary of State.

(5) It shall be the duty of the social fund Commissioner—
   (a) to monitor the quality of decisions of social fund inspectors and give them such advice and assistance as he thinks fit to improve the standard of their decisions;
   (b) to arrange such training of social fund inspectors as he considers appropriate; and
   (c) to carry out such other functions in connection with the work of social fund inspectors as the Secretary of State may direct.

(6) The social fund Commissioner shall report annually in writing to the Secretary of State on the standards of reviews by social fund inspectors, and the Secretary of State shall publish his report.

GENERAL NOTE

1.379   This section re-enacts s.65 of the Social Security Administration Act 1992.

Reviews of determinations

1.380   **38.**—(1) An appropriate officer—
   (a) shall review a social fund determination, if an application for a review is made, within such time and in such form and manner as may be prescribed, by or on behalf of the person who applied for the payment to which the determination relates;
   (b) may review such a determination on the ground that the person who applied for the payment to which the determination relates misrepresented, or failed to disclose, any material fact; and
   (c) may review such a determination in such other circumstances as he thinks fit.

(2) The power to review a social fund determination conferred by subsection (1) above includes power to review a determination made on a previous review.

(3) A social fund determination which has been reviewed under subsection (1) above shall be further reviewed by a social fund inspector if an application is made, within such time and in such form and manner as may be prescribed, by or on behalf of the person who applied for the payment to which the determination relates.

(4) On a review under subsection (3) above a social fund inspector shall have the following powers—
   (a) power to confirm the determination made by the appropriate officer;
   (b) power to make any determination which an appropriate officer could have made;
   (c) power to refer the matter to such an officer for determination.

(5) A social fund inspector may review a determination under subsection (3) above made by himself or some other social fund inspector.

(6) In making a determination on a review an appropriate officer or a social fund inspector need not consider—

(a) in the case of a determination on a review under subsection (1)(a) above, any issue that is not raised by the application;
(b) in the case of a determination on a review under subsection (1)(b) above, any issue that is not raised by the material fact;
(c) in the case of a determination on a review under subsection (1)(c) above, any issue that did not cause him to carry out the review.

(7) In making a determination on a review under subsection (1)(a) or (c) above an appropriate officer or a social fund inspector shall—
(a) subject to paragraphs (b) and (c) below, have regard to whichever of the following are applicable, namely—
   (i) all the circumstances of the case and, in particular, the criteria specified in paragraphs (a) to (e) of subsection (1) of section 140 of the Contributions and Benefits Act;
   (ii) the criteria mentioned in paragraphs (a) and (b) of subsection (1A) of that section; and
   (iii) the criterion specified in directions issued by the Secretary of State under that subsection and the criteria mentioned in paragraph (b) of that subsection;
(b) act in accordance with any general directions issued by the Secretary of State under subsection (2) of that section, and any general directions issued by him with regard to reviews; and
(c) take account of any general guidance issued by the Secretary of State under that subsection or with regard to reviews.

(8) In making a determination on a review under subsection (1)(b) above an appropriate officer or a social fund inspector shall—
(a) act in accordance with any general directions issued by the Secretary of State; and
(b) take account of any general guidance issued by the Secretary of State.

(9) Any reference in subsection (6), (7) or (8) above to a determination on a review under a particular provision of subsection (1) above shall be construed, in relation to a social fund inspector, as a reference to a determination on a further review of a determination which has been reviewed under that provision.

(10) Directions under this section may specify—
(a) the circumstances in which a social fund determination is to be reviewed; and
(b) the manner in which a review is to be conducted.

(11) In making a determination on a review under subsection (1)(a) or (c) above an appropriate officer shall take account (subject to any directions or guidance issued by the Secretary of State under this section) of any guidance issued by the appropriate officer nominated for his area under section 36(2) above.

(12) A social fund inspector reviewing a social fund determination which has been reviewed under subsection (1)(a) or (c) above shall be under the same duties in relation to such guidance as the appropriate officer or social fund inspector who made the determination.

(13) In this section "social fund determination" means a determination made under the Contributions and Benefits Act by an appropriate officer.

Social Security Act 1998

GENERAL NOTE

This section replaces s.66 of the Social Security Administration Act 1992 as modified transitorily by Sched. 6, para. 7 to the Social Security Act 1998.

Subsections (1) and (3)

1.381 See the Social Fund (Applications for Review) Regulations 1998 and *Regina v. Social Fund Officer, ex parte Hewson* (June 22, 1995 (QBD)) to which reference is made in the note to reg. 2 of those Regulations (in vol. II).

Subsections (4)

1.382 See *Regina v. Social Fund Inspector, ex parte Ledicott* (*The Times*, May 24, 1995) to which reference is made in the note to the Directions to Social Fund Inspectors (in vol. II).

Subsections (7) to (12)

1.383 See directions 31 to 42 and 45 of the Secretary of State's Directions to Appropriate Officers and see also the Directions to Social Fund Inspectors (in vol. II).

Supplemental

Interpretation etc. of Chapter II

1.384 **39.**—(1) In this Chapter—

"appeal tribunal" means an appeal tribunal constituted under Chapter I of this Part;

"Commissioner" [¹ (except in the expression "tax appeal Commissioners")] means the Chief Social Security Commissioner or any other Social Security Commissioner, and includes a tribunal of three or more Commissioners constituted under section 16(7) above;

"relevant benefit" has the meaning given by section 8(3) above;

[¹ "tax appeal Commissioners" means the Commissioners for the general purposes of the income tax appointed under section 2 of the Taxes Management Act 1970 or the Commissioners for the special purposes of the Income Tax Acts appointed under section 4 of that Act.]

(2) Expressions used in this Chapter to which a meaning is assigned by section 191 of the Administration Act have that meaning in this Chapter.

(3) Part II of the Administration Act, which is superseded by the foregoing provisions of this Chapter, shall cease to have effect.

AMENDMENT

1. Social Security Contributions (Transfer of Functions, etc.) Act 1999, Sched. 7, para. 35 (April 1, 1999).

CHAPTER III

OTHER DECISIONS AND APPEALS

1.385 **40–47.**—*Omitted.*

Part II

Contributions

48–66.—*Omitted.*

Part III

Benefits

67–76.—*Omitted.*

Part IV

Miscellaneous and Supplemental

Pilot schemes

77.—(1) Any regulations to which this subsection applies may be made so as to have effect for a specified period not exceeding 12 months.

(2) Any regulations which, by virtue of subsection (1) above, are to have effect for a limited period are referred to in this section as "a pilot scheme".

(3) A pilot scheme may provide that its provisions are to apply only in relation to—
  (a) one or more specified areas of localities;
  (b) one or more specified classes of person;
  (c) persons selected—
      (i) by reference to prescribed criteria; or
      (ii) on a sampling basis,

(4) A pilot scheme may make consequential or transitional provision with respect to the cessation of the scheme on the expiry of the specified period.

(5) A pilot scheme ("the previous scheme") may be replaced by a further pilot scheme making the same, or similar, provision (apart from the specified period) to that made by the previous scheme.

(6) In so far as a pilot scheme would, apart from this subsection, have the effect of—
  (a) treating as capable of work any person who would not otherwise be so treated; or
  (b) reducing the total amount of benefit that would otherwise be payable to any person,
it shall not apply in relation to that person.

(7) Subsection (1) above applies to—

(a) regulations made under section 171D of the Contributions and Benefits Act (incapacity for work: persons treated as incapable of work); and
(b) in so far as they are consequential on or supplementary to any such regulations, regulations made under any of the provisions mentioned in subsection (8) below.

(8) The provisions are—
(a) subsection (5)(a) of section 22 of the Contributions and Benefits Act (earnings factors);
(b) section 30C of that Act (incapacity benefit);
(c) sections 68 and 69 of that Act (severe disablement allowance);
(d) subsection (1)(e) of section 124 of that Act (income support) and, so far as relating to income support, subsection (1) of section 135 of that Act (the applicable amount);
(e) Part XIIA of that Act (incapacity for work);
(f) section 61A of the Administration Act and section 31 above (incapacity for work).

(9) A statutory instrument containing (whether alone or with other provisions) a pilot scheme shall not be made unless a draft of the instrument has been laid before Parliament and approved by a resolution of each House of Parliament.

1.389   **78.**—*Omitted.*

Regulations and orders

1.390   **79.**—(1) Subject to subsection (2) below and paragraph 6 of Schedule 4 to this Act, regulations under this Act shall be made by the Secretary of State.

(2) Regulations with respect to proceedings before the Commissioners (whether for the determination of any matter or for leave to appeal to or from the Commissioners) shall be made by the Lord Chancellor; and where the Lord Chancellor proposes to make regulations under this Act it shall be his duty to consult the Lord Advocate with respect to the proposal.

(3) Powers under this Act to make regulations or orders are exercisable by statutory instrument.

(4) Any power conferred by this Act to make regulations or orders may be exercised—
(a) either in relation to all cases to which the power extends, or in relation to those cases subject to specified exceptions, or in relation to any specified cases or classes of case;
(b) so as to make, as respects the cases in relation to which it is exercised—
  (i) the full provision to which the power extends or any less provision (whether by way of exception or otherwise);
  (ii) the same provision for all cases in relation to which the power is exercised, or different provision for different cases or different classes of case or different provision as respects

the same case or class of case for different purposes of this Act;

(iii) any such provision either unconditionally or subject to any specified condition;

and where such a power is expressed to be exercisable for alternative purposes it may be exercised in relation to the same case for any or all of those purposes.

(5) Powers to make regulations for the purposes of any one provision of this Act are without prejudice to powers to make regulations for the purposes of any other provision.

(6) Without prejudice to any specific provision in this Act, a power conferred by this Act to make regulations includes power to make thereby such incidental, supplementary, consequential or transitional provision as appears to the authority making the regulations to be expedient for the purposes of those regulations.

(7) Without prejudice to any specific provisions in this Act, a power conferred by any provision of this Act to make regulations includes power to provide for a person to exercise a discretion in dealing with any matter.

(8) Any power conferred by this Act to make regulations relating to housing benefit or council tax benefit shall include power to make different provision for different areas or different authorities.

(9) In this section "Commissioner" has the same meaning as in Chapter II of Part I.

GENERAL NOTE

Subsection (2)
By the Transfer of Functions (Lord Advocate and Secretary of State) Order 1999, S.I. 1999 No. 678, art. 2(1) and Sched., the function of the Lord Advocate under this subsection is transferred to the Secretary of State.

1.391

Parliamentary control of regulations

80.—(1) Subject to the provisions of this section, a statutory instrument containing (whether alone or with other provisions) regulations under—

(a) section 7, 12(2) or 72 above; or

(b) paragraph 12 of Schedule 1, paragraph 9 of Schedule 2 or paragraph 2 of Schedule 5 to this Act,

shall not be made unless a draft of the instrument has been laid before Parliament and been approved by a resolution of each House of Parliament.

(2) A statutory instrument—

(a) which contains (whether alone or with other provisions) regulations made under this Act by the Secretary of State; and

(b) which is not subject to any requirement that a draft of the instrument be laid before and approved by a resolution of each House of Parliament,

shall be subject to annulment in pursuance of a resolution of either House of Parliament.

1.392

Social Security Act 1998

(3) A statutory instrument—
(a) which contains (whether alone or with other provisions) regulations made under this Act by the Lord Chancellor; and
(b) which is not subject to any requirement that a draft of the instrument be laid before and approved by a resolution of each House of Parliament,

shall be subject to annulment in pursuance of a resolution of either House of Parliament.

Reports by Secretary of State

1.393   **81.**—(1) The Secretary of State shall prepare, either annually or at such times or intervals as may be prescribed, a report on the standards achieved by the Secretary of State in the making of decisions against which an appeal lies to an appeal tribunal constituted under Chapter I of Part I.

(2) A copy of every such report shall be laid before each House of Parliament.

1.394   Paragraph 82. *Omitted.*

1.395   Paragraph 83. *Omitted.*

Interpretation: general

1.396   **84.** In this Act—
"the Administration Act" means the Social Security Administration Act 1992;
"the Child Support Act" means the Child Support Act 1991;
"the Contributions and Benefits Act" means the Social Security Contributions and Benefits Act 1992;
"the Jobseekers Act" means the Jobseekers Act 1995;
"the Vaccine Damage Payments Act" means the Vaccine Damage Payments Act 1979;
"prescribe" means prescribe by regulations.

1.397   Paragraph 85. *Omitted.*

1.398   Paragraph 86. *Omitted.*

Short title, commencement and extent

1.399   **87.**—(1) This Act may be cited as the Social Security Act 1998.
(2) This Act, except—
(a) sections 66, 69, 72 and 77 to 85, this section and Schedule 6 to this Act; and
(b) subsection (1) of section 50 so far as relating to a sum which is chargeable to tax by virtue of section 313 of the Income and Corporation Taxes Act 1988, and subsections (2) to (4) of that section,

shall come into force on such day as may be appointed by order made by the Secretary of State; and different days may be appointed for different provisions and for different purposes.

(3) An order under subsection (2) above may make such savings, or such transitional or consequential provision, as the Secretary of State considers necessary or expedient—
   (a) in preparation for or in connection with the coming into force of any provision of this Act; or
   (b) in connection with the operation of any enactment repealed or amended by a provision of this Act during any period when the repeal or amendment is not wholly in force.

(4) This Act, except—
   (a) section 2 so far as relating to war pensions;
   (b) sections 3, 15, 45 to 47, 59, 78 and 85 and this section; and
   (c) section 86 and Schedules 7 an d8 so far as relating to enactments which extend to Northern Ireland,
does not extend to Northern Ireland.

(5) The following provisions of this Act extend to the Isle of Man, namely—
   (a) in section 4, subsections (1)(c) and (2)(c);
   (b) sections 6 and 7 and Schedule 1 so far as relating to appeals under the Vaccine Damage Payments Act;
   (c) sections 45 to 47 and this section;
   (d) paragraphs 5 to 10 of Schedule 7 and section 86(1) so far as relating to those paragraphs; and
   (e) section 86(2) and Schedule 8 so far as relating to the Vaccine Damage Payments Act.

GENERAL NOTE

Subsections (2) and (3)
The following commencement orders have been made. S.I. 1998 No. 2209, S.I. 1998 No. 2708, S.I. 1999 No. 418, S.I. 1999 No. 526, S.I. 1999 No. 528, S.I. 1999 No. 1055, S.I. 1999 No. 1510, S.I. 1999 No. 1958, S.I. 1999 No. 2422, S.I. 1999 No. 2739, S.I. 1999 No. 2860 and S.I. 1999 No. 3178. The main provisions relating to social security adjudication were brought into effect at different times, depending on the benefit in issue, according to the following timetable:

1.400

Industrial injuries benefit; Guardian's allowance; Child benefit; Pension Schemes Act 1993—July 5, 1999 (see, primarily, S.I. 1999 No. 1958).

Retirement pension; Widow's benefit; Incapacity benefit; Severe disablement allowance; Maternity allowance—September 6, 1999 (see, primarily, S.I. 1999 No. 2422).

Working families' tax credit; Disabled person's tax credit—October 5, 1999 (see, primarily, S.I. 1999 No. 2739).

Attendance allowance; Disability living allowance; Invalid care allowance; Jobseeker's allowance; Credits of contributions or earnings; Home responsibilities protection; Vaccine damage payments—October 18, 1999 (see, primarily, S.I. 1999 No. 2860).

All other purposes (including income support)—November 29, 1999 (see, primarily, S.I. 1999 No. 3178).

Social Security Act 1998

SCHEDULES

SCHEDULE 1

APPEAL TRIBUNALS: SUPPLEMENTARY PROVISIONS

Tenure of office

1.401 **1.**—(1) Subject to the following provisions of this paragraph, the President of appeal tribunals shall hold and vacate office in accordance with the terms of his appointment.

(2) The President shall vacate his office on the day on which he attains the age of 70, but subject to section 26(4) to (6) of the Judicial Pensions and Retirement Act 1993 (power to authorise continuance in office up to the age of 75).

(3) The President may be removed from office by the Lord Chancellor on the ground of incapacity or misbehaviour.

(4) Where the Lord Chancellor proposes to exercise a power conferred on him by sub-paragraph (3) above, it shall be his duty to consult the Lord Advocate with respect to the proposal.

Remuneration etc.

1.402 **2.** The Secretary of State may pay, or make such payments towards the provision of, such remuneration, pensions or allowances to or in respect of the President as he may determine.

3. The Secretary of State may pay, or make such payments towards the provision of, such remuneration, pensions or allowances to or in respect of any person appointed under this Chapter to act as a member of an appeal tribunal, or as an expert to such a tribunal, as he may determine.

4.—(1) The Secretary of State may pay—
  (a) to any person required to attend at any proceedings under section 12 of this Act or section 20 of the Child Support Act; or
  (b) to any person required under this Part (whether for the purposes of this Part or otherwise) to attend for or to submit himself to medical or other examination or treatment,
such travelling and other allowances as he may determine.

(2) In this paragraph references to travelling and other allowances including references to compensation for loss of remunerative time but such compensation shall not be paid to any person in respect of any time during which he is in receipt of remuneration under paragraph 3 above.

5.—(1) Subject to sub-paragraph (2) below, the Secretary of State may pay such other expenses in connection with the work of any person or tribunal appointed or constituted under any provision of this Part as he may determine.

(2) Expenses are not payable under sub-paragraph (1) above in connection with the work of a tribunal presided over by a Social Security Commissioner.

Officers and staff

1.403 **6.** The Secretary of State may appoint such officers and staff as he thinks fit for the President and for appeal tribunals.

Functions of President

1.404 **7.** The President shall ensure that appropriate steps are taken by an appeal tribunal to secure the confidentiality, in such circumstances as may be prescribed, of any prescribed material or any prescribed classes or categories of material.

8.—(1) The President shall, after the requisite consultation, arrange such training for persons appointed to the panel constituted under section 6 above as he considers appropriate.

(2) In sub-paragraph (1) above "the requisite consultation" means—
  (a) except in the case of medical practitioners, consultation with the Secretary of State;
  (b) in the case of such practitioners, consultation with the Chief Medical Officers of the Department of Health, the Welsh Office and the Scottish Office.

9. The President shall supply the Secretary of State with such reports and other information with respect to the carrying out of the functions of appeal tribunals as the Secretary of State may require.

10. Each year the President shall make to the Secretary of State a written report, based on the cases coming before appeal tribunals, on the standards achieved by the Secretary of State in the making of decisions against which an appeal lies to an appeal tribunal; and the Secretary of State shall publish the report.

Clerks to appeal tribunals

11. The Secretary of State may by regulations provide— 1.405
(a) for clerks to be assigned to service appeal tribunals; and
(b) for clerks so assigned to be responsible for summoning members of the panel constituted under section 6 above to serve on such tribunals.

Delegation of certain functions of appeal tribunals

12.—(1) The Secretary of State may by regulations provide— 1.406
(a) for officers authorised by the Secretary of State to make any determinations which fall to be made by an appeal tribunal and which do not involve the determination of any appeal, application for leave to appeal or reference;
(b) for the procedure to be followed by such officers in making such determinations;
(c) for the manner in which such determinations by such officers may be called in question.

(2) A determination which would have the effect of preventing an appeal, application for leave to appeal or reference being determined by an appeal tribunal is not a determination of the appeal, application or reference for the purposes of sub-paragraph (1) above.

Certificates

13. A document bearing a certificate which— 1.407
(a) is signed by a person authorised in that behalf by the Secretary of State; and
(b) states that the document, apart from the certificate, is a record of a decision of an appeal tribunal or of an officer of the Secretary of State,
shall be conclusive evidence of the decision; and a certificate purporting to be so signed shall be deemed to be so signed unless the contrary is proved.

GENERAL NOTE

Paragraph 1
By the Transfer of Functions (Lord Advocate and Secretary of State) Order 1.408
1999, S.I. 1999 No. 678, art. 2(1) and Sched., the function of the Lord Advocate under sub-paragraph (4) is transferred to the Secretary of State.

Paragraph 11
See reg. 37 of the Social Security and Child Support (Decisions and Appeals) 1.409
Regulations 1999.

Paragraph 12
See regs 46 to 48 of the Social Security and Child Support (Decisions and 1.410
Appeals) Regulations 1999.

SCHEDULE 2

DECISIONS AGAINST WHICH NO APPEAL LIES

Jobseeker's allowance for persons under 18

1. In relation to a person who has reached the age of 16 but not the age of 18, a 1.411
decision—

(a) whether section 16 of the Jobseekers Act is to apply to him; or
(b) whether to issue a certificate under section 17(4) of that Act.

Christmas bonus

1.412 **2.** A decision whether a person is entitled to payment under section 148 of the Contributions and Benefits Act.

Priority between persons entitled to invalid care allowance

1.413 **3.** A decision as to the exercise of the discretion under section 70(7) of the Contributions and Benefits Act.

Priority between persons entitled to child benefit

1.414 **4.** A decision as to the exercise of the discretion under paragraph 5 of Schedule 10 to the Contributions and Benefits Act.

Persons treated as if present in Great Britain

1.415 **5.** A decision whether to certify, in accordance with regulations made under section 64(1), 71(6), 113(1) or 119 of the Contributions and Benefits Act, that it is consistent with the proper administration of that Act to treat a person as though he were present in Great Britain.

[1 *Work-focused interviews*

1.416 **5A.** A decision terminating or reducing the amount of a person's benefit made in consequence of any decision made under regulations under section 2A of the Administration Act (work-focused interviews).]

Alteration of rates of benefit

1.417 **6.** A decision as to the amount of benefit to which a person is entitled, where it appears to the Secretary of State that the amount is determined by—
(a) the rate of benefit provided for by law; or
(b) an alteration of a kind referred to in—
(i) section 159(1)(b) of the Administration Act (income support); or
(ii) section 159A(1)(b) of that Act (jobseeker's allowance).

Increases in income support due to attainment of particular ages

1.418 **7.** A decision as to the amount of benefit to which a person is entitled, where it appears to the Secretary of State that the amount is determined by the recipient's entitlement to an increased amount of income support or income-based jobseeker's allowance in the circumstances referred to in section 160(2) or 160A(2) of the Administration Act.

Reduction in accordance with reduced benefit direction

1.419 **8.** A decision to reduce the amount of a person's benefit in accordance with a reduced benefit direction (within the meaning of section 46 of the Child Support Act).

Power to prescribe other decisions

1.420 **9.** Such other decisions as may be prescribed.

GENERAL NOTE

Paragraph 9
1.421 See Sched. 2 to the Social Security and Child Support (Decisions and Appeals) Regulations 1999.

(1998 c.14, Sched. 3)

SCHEDULE 3

DECISIONS AGAINST WHICH AN APPEAL LIES

PART I

BENEFIT DECISIONS

Entitlement to benefit without a claim

1. In such cases or circumstances as may be prescribed, a decision whether a person is entitled to a relevant benefit for which no claim is required.

2. If so, a decision as to the amount to which he is entitled.

Payability of benefit

3. A decision whether a relevant benefit (or a component of a relevant benefit) to which a person is entitled is not payable by reason of—
 (a) any provision of the Contributions and Benefits Act by which the person is disqualified for receiving benefit;
 (b) regulations made under section 72(8) of that Act (disability living allowance);
 (c) regulations made under section 113(2) of that Act (suspension of payment); or
 (d) section 19 of the Jobseekers Act (jobseeker's allowance).

Payments to third parties

4. Except in such cases or circumstances as may be prescribed, a decision whether the whole or part of a benefit to which a person is entitled is, by virtue of regulations, to be paid to a person other than him.

Recovery of benefits

5. A decision whether payment is recoverable under section 71 or 71A of the Administration Act.

6. If so, a decision as to the amount of payment recoverable.

Industrial injuries benefit

7. A decision whether an accident was an industrial accident for the purposes of industrial injuries benefit.

Jobseekers' agreements

8. A decision in relation to a jobseeker's agreement as proposed to be made under section 9 of the Jobseekers Act, or as proposed to be varied under section 10 of that Act.

Power to prescribe other decisions

9. Such other decisions relating to a relevant benefit as may be prescribed.

PART II

CONTRIBUTIONS DECISIONS

Paras *10. to 29. Omitted.*

1.422

1.423

SCHEDULE 4

SOCIAL SECURITY COMMISSIONERS

Appointment

1.—(1) Her Majesty may from time to time appoint, from among persons who have a 10 year general qualification or advocates or solicitors in Scotland of at least 10 years' standing—

1.424

(a) a Chief Social Security Commissioner; and
(b) such number of other Social Security Commissioners as Her Majesty thinks fit.

(2) If the Lord Chancellor considers that, in order to facilitate the disposal of the business of Social Security Commissioners, he should make an appointment in pursuance of this sub-paragraph, he may appoint—
(a) a person who has a 10 year general qualification; or
(b) an advocate or solicitor in Scotland of at least 10 years' standing; or
(c) a member of the bar of Northern Ireland or solicitor of the Supreme Court of Northern Ireland of at least 10 years' standing,

to be a Social Security Commissioner (but to be known as a deputy Commissioner) for such period or on such occasions as the Lord Chancellor thinks fit.

(3) In this paragraph "10 year general qualification" shall be construed in accordance with section 71 of the Courts and Legal Services Act 1990.

Remuneration etc.

1.425   2. The Lord Chancellor shall pay to a Commissioner such salary or other remuneration, and such expenses incurred in connection with the work of a Commissioner or any tribunal presided over by a Commissioner, as he may determine.

3.—(1) The Lord Chancellor or, in Scotland, the Secretary of State may pay to any person who attends any proceedings under section 14 of this Act such travelling and other allowances as he may determine.

(2) In this paragraph the reference to travelling and other allowances includes a reference to compensation for loss of remunerative time.

Tenure of office

1.426   4.—(1) Commissioners shall vacate their offices on the day on which they attain the age of 70, but subject to section 26(4) to (6) of the Judicial Pensions and Retirement Act 1993 (power to authorise continuance in office up to the age of 75).

(2) Nothing in sub-paragraph (1) above or in section 13 or 32 of the Judicial Pensions Act 1981 (which relate to pensions for Commissioners) shall apply to a person by virtue of his appointment in pursuance of paragraph 1(2) above.

5.—(1) A Commissioner may be removed from office by the Lord chancellor on the ground of incapacity or misbehaviour.

(2) Nothing in sub-paragraph (1) above applies to a Commissioner appointed before May 23, 1980.

Delegation of functions

1.427   6. The Lord Chancellor may by regulations provide—
(a) for officers authorised by the Lord Chancellor or, in Scotland, by the Secretary of State to make any determinations which fall to be made by Commissioners;
(b) for the procedure to be followed by such officers in making such determinations;
(c) for the manner in which such determinations by such officers may be called in question.

Certificates

1.428   7. A document bearing a certificate which—
(a) is signed by a person authorised in that behalf by the Secretary of State; and
(b) states that the document, apart from the certificate, is a record of a decision of a Commissioner,

shall be conclusive evidence of the decision; and a certificate purporting to be so signed shall be deemed to be so signed unless the contrary is proved.

Supplemental

1.429   8. Where the Lord Chancellor proposes to exercise a power conferred on him by paragraph 1(2), 5(1) or 6 above, it shall be his duty to consult the Lord Advocate with respect to the proposal.

(1998 c.14, Sched. 4)

GENERAL NOTE

Paragraph 6
See reg. 7 of the Social Security Commissioners (Procedure) Regulations 1999.

1.430

Paragraph 8
By the Transfer of Functions (Lord Advocate and Secretary of State) Order 1999, S.I. 1999 No. 678, art. 2(1) and Sched., the function of the Lord Advocate under this paragraph is transferred to the Secretary of State.

1.431

SCHEDULE 5

REGULATIONS AS TO PROCEDURE: PROVISION WHICH MAY BE MADE

1. Provision prescribing the procedure to be followed in connection with—
   (a) the making of decisions or determinations by the Secretary of State, an appeal tribunal or a Commissioner; and
   (b) the withdrawal of claims, applications, appeals or references falling to be decided or determined by the Secretary of State, an appeal tribunal or a Commissioner.
2. Provision as to the striking out or reinstatement of proceedings.
3. Provision as to the form which is to be used for any document, the evidence which is to be required and the circumstances in which any official record or certificate is to be sufficient or conclusive evidence.
4. Provision as to the time within which, or the manner in which—
   (a) any evidence is to be produced; or
   (b) any application, reference or appeal is to be made.
5. Provision for summoning persons to attend and give evidence or produce documents and for authorising the administration of oaths to witnesses.
6. Provision with respect to the procedure to be followed on appeals to and in other proceedings before appeal tribunals.
7. Provision for authorising an appeal tribunal consisting of two or more members to proceed with any case, with the consent of the claimant, in the absence of any member.
8. Provision for empowering an appeal tribunal to give directions for the disposal of any purported appeal which the tribunal is satisfied that it does not have jurisdiction to entertain.
9. Provision for the non-disclosure to a person of the particulars of any medical advice or medical evidence given or submitted for the purposes of a determination.

1.432

GENERAL NOTE

See the Social Security and Child Support (Decisions and Appeals) Regulations 1999 and the Social Security Commissioners (Procedure) Regulations 1999.

1.433

Schedules 6 to 8

Omitted

1.434

PART II

EUROPEAN COMMUNITY LAW

European Communities Act 1972

(1972 c.28) (*as amended*)

ARRANGEMENT OF SECTIONS REPRODUCED

1. Short title and interpretation
2. General implementation of Treaties
3. Decisions on, and proof of, Treaties and Community instruments, etc

PART I

GENERAL PROVISIONS

Short title and interpretation

1.—(1) This Act may be cited as the European Communities Act 1972.

(2) In this Act [¹ . . .]—

"the Communities" means the European Economic Community, the European Coal and Steel Community and the European Atomic Energy Community;

"the Treaties" or "the Community Treaties" means, subject to subsection (3) below, the pre-accession treaties, that is to say, those described in Part I of Schedule 1 to this Act, taken with—

(a) the treaty relating to the accession of the United Kingdom to the European Economic Community and to the European Atomic Energy Community, signed at Brussels on the 22nd January 1972; and

(b) the decision, of the same date, of the Council of the European Communities relating to the accession of the United Kingdom to the European Coal and Steel Community; [² and

(c) the treaty relating to the accession of the Hellenic Republic to the European Economic Community and to the European Atomic Energy Community, signed at Athens on 28th May 1979; and

(d) the decision, of 24th May 1979, of the Council relating to the accession of the Hellenic Republic to the European Coal and Steel Community;] [³ and

(e) the decisions of the Council of 7th May 1985, 24th June 1988, and 31st October 1994, on the Communities' system of own resources; and]

(f) [³ . . .]; [⁴ and

(g) the treaty relating to the accession of the Kingdom of Spain and the Portuguese Republic to the European Economic Community and to the European Atomic Energy Community, signed at Lisbon and Madrid on 12th June 1985; and

(h) the decision, of 11th June 1985, of the Council relating to the accession of the Kingdom of Spain and the Portuguese Republic to the European Coal and Steel Community;] [and

(i) [¹ ...] [⁵ and
(j) the following provisions of the Single European Act signed at Luxembourg and The Hague on 17th and 28th February 1986, namely Title II (amendment of the treaties establishing the Communities) and, so far as they relate to any of the Communities or any Community institution, the preamble and Titles I (common provisions) and IV (general and final provisions);] [⁶ and
(k) Titles II, III and IV of the Treaty on European Union signed at Maastricht on 7th February 1992, together with the other provisions of the Treaty so far as they relate to those Titles, and the Protocols adopted at Maastricht on that date and annexed to the Treaty establishing the European Community with the exception of the Protocol on Social Policy on page 117 of Cm 1934] [⁷ and
(l) the decision, of 1st February 1993, of the Council amending the Act concerning the election of the representatives of the European Parliament by direct universal suffrage annexed to Council Decision 76/787 Euratom of 20th September 1976] [⁸ and
(m) the Agreement on the European Economic Area signed at Oporto on 2nd May 1992 together with the Protocol adjusting that Agreement signed at Brussels on 17th March 1993] [⁹ and
(n) the treaty concerning the accession of the Kingdom of Norway, the Republic of Austria, the Republic of Finland and the Kingdom of Sweden to the European Union, signed at Corfu on 24th June 1994;] [¹⁰ and
(o) the following provisions of the Treaty signed at Amsterdam on 2nd October 1997 amending the Treaty on European Union, the Treaties establishing the European Communities and certain related Acts
  (i) Articles 2 to 9,
  (ii) Article 12, and
  (iii) the other provisions of the Treaty so far as they relate to those Articles,

and the Protocols adopted on that occasion other than the Protocol on Article J.7 of the Treaty on European Union]
  and any other treaty entered into by any of the Communities, with or without any of the member States, or entered into, as a treaty ancillary to any of the Treaties, by the United Kingdom;
and any expression defined in Schedule 1 to this Act has the meaning there given to it.

(3) If Her Majesty by Order in Council declares that a treaty specified in the Order is to be regarded as one of the Community Treaties as herein defined, the Order shall be conclusive that it is to be so regarded; but a treaty entered into by the United Kingdom after the 22nd January 1972, other than a pre-accession treaty to which the United Kingdom accedes on terms settled on or before that date, shall not be so regarded

(1972 c.28, s.1) (as amended)

unless it is so specified, nor be so specified unless a draft of the Order in Council has been approved by resolution of each House of Parliament.

(4) For purposes of subsections (2) and (3) above, "treaty" includes any international agreement, and any protocol or annex to a treaty or international agreement.

AMENDMENTS

1. Interpretation Act 1978, s.25(1).
2. European Communities (Greek Accession) Act 1979, s.1.
3. European Communities Act 1995, s.1.
4. European Communities (Spanish and Portuguese Accession) Act 1985, s.1.
5. European Communities (Amendment) Act 1986, s.1.
6. European Communities (Amendment) Act 1993, s.1.
7. European Parliamentary Elections Act 1993, s.3.
8. European Economic Area Act 1993, s.1.
9. European Union (Accessions) Act 1994, s.1.
10. European Communities (Amendment) Act 1998, s.1.

GENERAL NOTE

The Member States

The Member States of the European Union are: 2.3

Austria	France	Italy	Spain
Belgium	Germany	Luxembourg	Sweden
Denmark	Greece	Netherlands	United Kingdom
Finland	Ireland	Portugal	

There are three additional countries which with the Member States form the countries of the European Economic Area; they are

Iceland   Liechtenstein   Norway

Community social security law generally applies to nationals of the Member States and of the additional countries of the European Economic Area "EEA", since the social security rules are extended to their nationals by the EEA Treaty. For this reason the term "EEA country" or countries is frequently used to describe those countries whose nationals are beneficiaries of the Community rules on social security.

The treaties

The key treaty for social security purposes is the European Community Treaty ("EC Treaty") formerly the European Economic Community Treaty (or "EEC Treaty"). There is now a European Union governed by the Treaty on European Union (or Maastricht Treaty). This has been amended by the Treaty of Amsterdam and now consists of three pillars: the European Communities, Common Foreign and Security Policy, and Police and Judicial Co-operation in Criminal Matters. 2.4

The EC Treaty began life as the EEC Treaty. The EC Treaty has been amended many times. The Treaty on European Union was signed at Maastricht on February 7 1992, and is often referred to as the Maastricht Treaty.

Renumbering and citation of the treaties

The Treaty of Amsterdam, which entered into force in May 1999 amended both the EC Treaty and the Treaty on European Union (the "TEU"). It renumbered both treaties. This has presented the potential for confusion, since there will be a long transitional period during which two sets of numbering will be encountered in the literature. 2.5

The convention has emerged of citing either the old number in parentheses, or, where more appropriate, the new number is parentheses. So, for example, the general prohibition on discrimination on grounds of nationality was originally in Article 6 of the EC Treaty, but this has been renumbered as Article 13. So it would now be cited Article 13 (ex 6) EC. But if reference to the original version is more appropriate, then it would be cited Article 6 (now 13) EC.

The Treaty on European Union is cited as follows: Article 6 TEU. The conventions which apply to citation of the EC Treaty in its original and renumbered form equally apply to the renumbering of this treaty, but note that this treaty was originally structured around letters and numbers rather than just numbers. For example, Article 6 (ex F) TEU, or Article F (now 6) TEU.

General implementation of Treaties

2.—(1) All such rights, powers, liabilities, obligations and restrictions from time to time created or arising by or under the Treaties, and all such remedies and procedures from time to time provided for by or under the Treaties, as in accordance with the Treaties are without further enactment to be given legal effect or used in the United Kingdom shall be recognised and available in law, and be enforced, allowed and followed accordingly; and the expression "enforceable Community right" and similar expressions shall be read as referring to one to which this subsection applies.

(2) Subject to Schedule 2 to this Act, at any time after its passing Her Majesty may by Order in Council, and any designated Minister or department may by regulations, make provision—
  (a) for the purpose of implementing any Community obligation of the United Kingdom, or enabling any such obligation to be implemented, or of enabling any rights enjoyed or to be enjoyed by the United Kingdom under or by virtue of the Treaties to be exercised; or
  (b) for the purpose of dealing with matters arising out of or related to any such obligation or rights or the coming into force, or the operation from time to time, of subsection (1) above;
and in the exercise of any statutory power or duty, including any power to give directions or to legislate by means of orders, rules, regulations or other subordinate instrument, the person entrusted with the power or duty may have regard to the objects of the Communities and to any such obligation or rights as aforesaid.

In this subsection "designated Minister or department" means such Minister of the Crown or government department as may from time to time be designated by Order in Council in relation to any matter or for any purpose, but subject to such restrictions or conditions (if any) as may be specified by the Order in Council.

(3) There shall be charged on and issued out of the Consolidated Fund or, if so determined by the Treasury, the National Loans Fund the amounts required to meet any Community obligation to make payments to any of the Communities or member States, or any Community obligation in respect of contributions to the capital or reserves of the European Investment Bank or in respect of loans to the Bank, or to redeem any notes or obligations issued or created in respect of any such

Community obligation; and, except as otherwise provided by or under any enactment—
(a) any other expenses incurred under or by virtue of the Treaties or this Act by any Minister of the Crown or government department may be paid out of moneys provided by Parliament; and
(b) any sums received under or by virtue of the Treaties or this Act by any Minister of the Crown or government department, save for such sums as may be required for disbursements permitted by any other enactment, shall be paid into the Consolidated Fund or, if so determined by the Treasury, the National Loans Fund.

(4) The provision that may be made under subsection (2) above includes, subject to Schedule 2 to this Act, any such provision (of any such extent) as might be made by Act of Parliament, and any enactment passed or to be passed, other than one contained in this Part of this Act, shall be construed and have effect subject to the foregoing provisions of this section; but, except as may be provided by any Act passed after this Act, Schedule 2 shall have effect in connection with the powers conferred by this and the following sections of this Act to make Orders in Council and regulations.

(5) [[1] . . .] and the references in that subsection to a Minister of the Crown or government department and to a statutory power or duty shall include a Minister or department of the Government of Northern Ireland and a power or duty arising under or by virtue of an Act of the Parliament of Northern Ireland.

(6) A law passed by the legislature of any of the Channel Islands or of the Isle of Man, or a colonial law (within the meaning of the Colonial Laws Validity Act 1865) passed or made for Gibraltar, if expressed to be passed or made in the implementation of the Treaties and of the obligations of the United Kingdom thereunder, shall not be void or inoperative by reason of any inconsistency with or repugnancy to an Act of Parliament, passed or to be passed, that extends to the Island or Gibraltar or any provision having the force and effect of an Act there (but not including this section), nor by reason of its having some operation outside the Island or Gibraltar; and any such Act or provision that extends to the Island or Gibraltar shall be construed and have effect subject to the provisions of any such law.

AMENDMENTS

1. Northern Ireland Constitution Act 1973, s.41.

GENERAL NOTE

The binding nature of Community law
European Community Law is binding on United Kingdom courts and tribunals by virtue of this section. Any rule of law qualifying as "an enforceable Community right" is to be given legal effect in the law of the United Kingdom. Whenever there is a clash between United Kingdom law and European Community law, the rule of European Community law is to prevail: see s.2(4).

2.7

Community legislation
European Community law takes a variety of forms but the forms most likely to be met in tribunals and before the Commissioners are *regulations* and *direct-*

2.8

ives. Article 249 (ex 189) EC provides that regulations are to have the force of law in all the Member States without further implementation, whereas directives are addressed to Member States and require conversion (if necessary) into national law.

Regulations retain their Community character and are binding in all Member States in exactly the same way as that Member State's primary legislation. Individuals may rely on the provisions of regulations by citing them just as if they were statutory provisions emanating from the United Kingdom Parliament. Indeed, they may be regarded as superior to national legislation since no national legislature can alter the form of a Community regulation.

Directives are a form of legislation which is intended to enable Community law to be enacted in each Member State in the manner which best fits the legal traditions of that Member State. So the obligation is to achieve the result required by the directive, but the choice of form and method is for each Member State to select. There is a requirement that each Member State to whom a directive is addressed must notify the Commission of the national law which implements the requirements of the directive.

Every piece of secondary legislation must find its authority in a provision of the EC Treaty. Legal base is important because the provision of the EC Treaty under which it is made will set out the decision-making procedure to be followed. This has generated disputes between the institutions, where an institution takes the view that the secondary legislation should have been made under a Treaty provision which requires its greater involvement in that procedure than under the provision under which the Council has adopted it.

The two most important doctrines developed in the case law of the Court of Justice of the European Communities (hereafter "Court of Justice") are:

- the supremacy of Community law

- the direct effect of Community law.

Supremacy

2.9   The supremacy of Community law requires that any conflict between a rule of Community law and a rule of national law must be decided in favour of the rule of Community law. See Case C-213/89 *R. v. Secretary of State for Transport, ex parte Factortame*, [1990] E.C.R. I-2433; [1991] 3 C.M.L.R. 589. Note the requirements of the doctrine as re-affirmed in this case, which involved a procedural rule in English law which operated as a barrier to a remedy under Community law; significantly, it involved the non-application of a United Kingdom statute.

Direct effect

2.10   A helpful distinction drawn by some authorities is between direct applicability and direct effect.

Direct applicability refers to the *status* of the source of a rule of Community law, and refers to those sources which are automatically law in the national legal orders of all the Member States. Treaty articles have this character, as do regulations. It is not open to a Member State to interfere with the direct application of a regulation in the national legal order. This preserves the Community nature of the source of obligation throughout all the Member States. If you know that an article of a particular regulation gives you a right in your own national legal order, you can be sure that the same right is provided in all the national legal orders under the same article of the same regulation. The only difference is that it will be in another official language of the Community.

The attribute of direct applicability is a feature of the supremacy of Community law.

Note that in some areas the Member States have transferred sole competence to legislate to the Community; one purpose for such transfers of sovereignty is to ensure the uniform application of law throughout the Community. This is sometimes called the doctrine of *pre-emption*. The effect is that once an area is occupied by Community law, Member States cannot legislate in that area.

Direct effect refers to the *content* of a rule, and describes its capacity to give rise to rights for individuals which they can plead before national courts, and which national courts must recognise.

Just as it is the case that not every provision of national law gives rise to rights for individuals, so too it is the case that not every provision of Community law gives rise to direct effect. It is necessary to consider the scope and wording of any provision in order to determine whether it is capable of giving rise to direct effect.

Where the status of the provision of Community law in issue is one which has the attribute of direct applicability, it is simply a matter of interpretation to determine whether direct effect arises. So, in the case of Treaty articles and regulations, the requirements for direct effect are that the rule in question:

- is sufficiently clear and precise; and

- is unconditional.

The direct effect of directives has given rise to particular problems, since Article 249 (ex 189) EC provides that directives are:

- addressed to the Member States; and

- are binding as to the result to be achieved; but

- leave the choice of form and methods to the national authorities of the Member States.

All directives give Member States a time limit within which to implement the requirements of the directive. They are obliged to inform the Commission of the action taken to implement the directive. Failure to implement a directive by the deadline is likely to result in action being taken by the Commission to bring the Member State before the Court of Justice under Article 226 (ex 169) EC for failing to fulfil its obligations under the EC Treaty.

Proper and complete implementation of a directive results in individuals acquiring rights under the implementing national law.

It is now accepted that, where the deadline for implementation has passed without the directive's being implemented or without its being implemented properly, a directive can give rise to direct effect where it contains an obligation as to the result to be achieved which meets the requirements for direct effect set out above, *provided that* the party against whom the right is asserted is the State or "an emanation of the State". This is called a vertical relationship, and so vertical direct effect of directives is said to be permitted. Note particularly the definition of what constitutes an emanation of the State in Case C-188/89 *Foster v. British Gas*, [1990] E.C.R. I-3313; [1990] 2 C.M.L.R. 833.

However, the Court of Justice has ruled that the direct effect of directives does not arise where the right is being asserted against another private party. This is called a horizontal relationship, and so horizontal direct effect of directives is said not to be possible. There are a number of reasons for this:

1. To do so would impose an insuperable burden on private parties. Whereas it is justifiable to refuse to permit the State and its emanations from being able to plead the State's wrongdoing to avoid its liabilities, it would be wrong to impose a similar burden on a private party.

2. Directives are addressed to Member States. To allow the horizontal direct effect of directives would be to remove the distinction between regulations and directives. It would also provide an incentive for Member States not to implement directives, since they would take effect in any event after the expiry of the time for implementation.

The doctrine of indirect effect

2.11 To mitigate the harshness of a rule relating to the direct effect of directives as between private parties, the Court of Justice has imposed obligations on national authorities and national courts to interpret national law compatibly with the requirements of directives so far as it is possible to do so. This obligation flows from the duty of solidarity to be found in Article 10 (ex 5) EC.

State liability for breaches of Community Law

2.12 The Court of Justice has developed rules which ensure the effective enjoyment of Community rights for individuals. The Court has even fashioned the requirement for a remedy where a Member State has failed either wholly or in part to implement a directive, and the relationship between the parties is a horizontal one. However, the remedy is available wherever there has been a breach of Community law of sufficient seriousness to engage the remedy.

Under the *Francovich* line of cases, courts in the Member States are obliged to compensate individuals who have suffered loss as a result of infringements of Community law by Member States. Three conditions for liability are required:

- the rule of Community law grants rights to individuals and the content of those rights is clearly identifiable;

- the breach by the Member State is sufficiently serious to trigger liability for loss;

- there is a direct causal link between the breach of the rule by the Member State and the loss suffered by the individuals concerned.

This important remedy has been refined in subsequent case law. This is helpfully summarised in the decision of the House of Lords of October 28 1999 in *R. v. Secretary of State for Transport, ex parte Factortame Ltd and others*, HL, [1999] 3 W.L.R. 1062; [1999] 4 All E.R. 906; [1999] 3 C.M.L.R. 597.

At one time it was thought that the Community rules on remedies meant that time limits on the backdating of claims would not apply where a Member State had not fully implemented the requirements of a directive. The issue arose in the context of Ireland's failure fully to implement Directive 79/7. In Case 286/85 *Cotter and McDermott v. Minister for Social Welfare and Attorney General*, [1987] E.C.R. 1453; [1987] 2 C.M.L.R. 607, the Court of Justice ruled that Article 4(1) of Directive 79/7 could be relied on by individuals as from December 23, 1984. In Case 208/90 *Emmott v. Minister for Social Welfare and Attorney General*, [1991] E.C.R. I-4269; [1991] 3 C.M.L.R. 507, the Court of Justice ruled that it was contrary to Community law to preserve the discriminatory effect of earlier legislation in the manner provided for in the Irish legislation. Mrs Emmott sought payment of her disability benefit at the same rate paid to married men. Ultimately she began judicial review proceedings but the national authorities pleaded that her application was time-barred since the time limit was three months from the date when the grounds of the application first arose. This completely defeated her claim. The Court of Justice ruled that where directives had not been properly implemented by a Member State, that State could not rely on national rules on time limits to defeat entirely a claim arising from the Member State failure.

However, national rules which simply limit the period prior to the date of claim for which benefit entitlement may be claimed were found not to be inconsistent with Community law in Case C-338/91 *Steenhorst Neerings*, [1993] E.C.R. I-5475 and Case C-410/92 *Johnson v. Chief Adjudication Officer (Johnson II)*, [1994] E.C.R. I-5483. In such cases the ability to claim back payments of benefit is not entirely removed.

Interim relief

A Commissioner has for the first time had to consider whether Community law principles on effective enjoyment of Community rights requires the grant of interim relief in a case where payments of disability living allowance were stopped when the claimant moved to Spain and where a Commissioner had referred questions to the Court of Justice under Article 234 (ex 177) EC. In *CDLA/913/1994* the Commissioner does not directly answer the question since he proceeds on the assumption that there might be such a power but does not consider that the claimant's case met the necessary threshold of being 'strongly arguable' as distinct from being merely 'arguable'. Despite this conclusion the decision raises many of the difficult issues which would arise if the Commissioners were to have such a power. It could well follow that tribunals enjoyed a similar power. A particular difficulty is that tribunals and the Commissioners are concerned with entitlement, whereas the mechanics of payment are matters for the Secretary of State alone. Such a distinction of role (which has, of course, for many purposes been removed by the Social Security Act 1998 without removing all the possible problems) might not be able to survive an onslaught relying on European authority on remedies before national judicial bodies.

2.13

The appellant in the case sought a judicial review of the Commissioner's decision in *R. v. Social Security Commissioner, ex parte Snares*, Divisional Court of QBD, March 24, 1997, not reported. The Divisional Court concluded that the Commissioner could not be faulted in the way he had exercised any discretion he had in the case. The case does not advance matters beyond what the Commissioner said. The trend of the case law of the Court of Justice is, however, that European Community law requires national judicial authorities to have the power to give legal effect to rights arising under Community law. An example of where this might be problematic is the absence of any power for tribunals or the Commissioners to award interest on late benefit or costs: see *R(FC)2/90*.

Decisions on, and proof of, Treaties and Community instruments, etc

3.—(1) For the purposes of all legal proceedings any question as to the meaning or effect of any of the Treaties, or as to the validity, meaning or effect of any Community instrument, shall be treated as a question of law (and, if not referred to the European Court, be for determination as such in accordance with the principles laid down by and any relevant [¹ decision of the European Court or any court attached thereto)].

2.14

(2) Judicial notice shall be taken of the Treaties, of the Official Journal of the Communities and of any decision of, or expression of opinion by, the European Court [¹ or any court attached thereto] on any such question as aforesaid; and the Official Journal shall be admissible as evidence of any instrument or other act thereby communicated of any of the Communities or of any Community institution.

(3) Evidence of any instrument issued by a Community institution, including any judgment or order of the European Court [¹ or any court attached thereto], or of any document in the custody of a Community

institution, or any entry in or extract from such a document, may be given in any legal proceedings by production of a copy certified as a true copy by an official of that institution; and any document purporting to be such a copy shall be received in evidence without proof of the official position or handwriting of the person signing the certificate.

(4) Evidence of any Community instrument may also be given in any legal proceedings—
 (a) by production of a copy purporting to be printed by the Queen's Printer;
 (b) where the instrument is in the custody of a government department (including a department of the Government of Northern Ireland), by production of a copy certified on behalf of the department to be a true copy by an officer of the department generally or specially authorised so to do;

and any document purporting to be such a copy as is mentioned in paragraph (b) above of an instrument in the custody of a department shall be received in evidence without proof of the official position or handwriting of the person signing the certificate, or of his authority to do so, or of the document being in the custody of the department.

(5) *Omitted.*

AMENDMENT

1. European Communities (Amendment) Act 1986, s.2.

GENERAL NOTE

2.15 Questions as to the meaning and effect of the treaties and of any Community legislation are questions of law. Where such questions are decided by national courts or tribunals, they are to be decided in accordance with principles laid down in any decision of the Court of Justice or Court of First Instance. In deciding such questions, judicial notice is to be taken of the treaties and secondary legislation as well as of decisions of the Community courts.

Extracts from the E.C. Treaty

PART ONE

PRINCIPLES

Article 2 (ex 2) E.C.

2.16 The Community shall have as its task, by establishing a common market and an economic and monetary union and by implementing common policies or activities referred to in Articles 3 and 4, to promote

(Article 2)

throughout the Community a harmonious, balanced and sustainable development of economic activities, a high level of employment and of social protection, equality between men and women, sustainable and non-inflationary growth, a high degree of competitiveness and convergence of economic performance, a high level of protection and improvement of the quality of the environment, the raising of the standard of living and quality of life, and economic and social cohesion and solidarity among Member States.

Article 3 (ex 3) E.C.
Extracts from the E.C. Treaty

1. For the purposes set out in Article 2, the activities of the Community shall include, as provided in this Treaty and in accordance with the timetable set out therein:
  (a) the prohibition, as between Member States, of customs duties and quantitative restrictions on the import and export of goods, and of all other measures having equivalent effect;
  (b) a common commercial policy;
  (c) an internal market characterised by the abolition, as between Member States, of obstacles to the free movement of goods, persons, services and capital;
  (d) measures concerning the entry and movement of persons as provided for in Title IV;
  (e) a common policy in the sphere of agriculture and fisheries;
  (f) a common policy in the sphere of transport;
  (g) a system ensuring that competition in the internal market is not distorted;
  (h) the approximation of the laws of Member States to the extent required for the functioning of the common market;
  (i) the promotion of coordination between employment policies of the Member States with a view to enhancing their effectiveness by developing a coordinated strategy for employment;
  (j) a policy in the social sphere comprising a European Social Fund;
  (k) the strengthening of economic and social cohesion;
  (l) a policy in the sphere of the environment;
  (m) the strengthening of the competitiveness of Community industry;
  (n) the promotion of research and technological development;
  (o) encouragement for the establishment and development of trans-European networks;
  (p) a contribution to the attainment of a high level of health protection;
  (q) a contribution to education and training of quality and to the flowering of the cultures of the Member States;
  (r) a policy in the sphere of development cooperation;
  (s) the association of the overseas countries and territories in order to increase trade and promote jointly economic and social development;

(t) a contribution to the strengthening of consumer protection;
(u) measures in the spheres of energy, civil protection and tourism.

2. In all the activities referred to in this Article, the Community shall aim to eliminate inequalities, and to promote equality, between men and women.

GENERAL NOTE

2.18 The Court has frequently found its inspiration for an interpretation of a particular provision of the Treaty or of secondary legislation by reference to the objectives of the Community as set out in Articles 2 and 3: for example, Case 53/81 *Levin v. Staatssecretaris van Justitie*, [1982] E.C.R. 1035 (para. 15 of the judgment), though the terms of these articles are not sufficiently precise to give rise to direct effect: Case 126/86 *Giménz Zaera v. Instituto Nacional de la Seguridad Social y Tesoreria General de la Seguridad Social*, [1987] E.C.R. 3697 (para. 11 of judgment in relation to Article 2).

Article 5 (ex 3b) E.C.

The Community shall act within the limits of the powers conferred upon it by this Treaty and of the objectives assigned to it therein.

In areas which do not fall within its exclusive competence, the Community shall take action, in accordance with the principle of subsidiarity, only if and insofar as the objectives of the proposed action cannot be sufficiently achieved by the Member States and can therefore, by reason of the scale or effects of the proposed action, be better achieved by the Community.

GENERAL NOTE

2.19 Note that Community law on social security only seeks to co-ordinate the different social security systems of the Member States (plus the three EEA countries). There has been no attempt to date to harmonise social entitlements in the Member States, though there are provisions requiring that there be no discrimination on grounds of sex in the application of the social security rules of the Member States: see Directive 79/7 reproduced below.

Article 10 (ex 5) E.C.

2.20 Member States shall take all appropriate measures, whether general or particular, to ensure fulfilment of the obligations arising out of this Treaty or resulting from action taken by the institutions of the Community. They shall facilitate the achievement of the Community's tasks.

They shall abstain from any measure which could jeopardise the attainment of the objectives of this Treaty.

(Article 10)

GENERAL NOTE

This article is sometimes referred to as establishing the principle of "solidarity" under which Member States undertake a legal obligation to further Community objectives. It has been used as the basis for the obligation to interpret national law compatibly with Community law: see Case 14/83 *Von Colson and Kamann v. Land Nordrhein Westfalen*, [1984] E.C.R. 1891; [1986] 2 C.M.L.R. 430; Case C-106/89 *Marleasing SA*, [1990] E.C.R. I-4135; [1992] 1 C.M.L.R. 305; and Case C-168/95 *Criminal Proceedings against Arcaro*, [1996] E.C.R. I-4705.

2.21

Article 12 (ex 6) E.C.

Within the scope of application of this Treaty, and without prejudice to any special provisions contained therein, any discrimination on grounds of nationality shall be prohibited.

The Council, acting in accordance with the procedure referred to in Article 251, may adopt rules designed to prohibit such discrimination.

2.22

GENERAL NOTE

This is the general statement of non-discrimination on grounds of nationality, which applies wherever the provisions of the treaty apply. In Case C-85/96 *María Martínez Sala v. Freistaat Bayern*, [1998] E.C.R. I-2691, it was held that a person lawfully resident in Germany could rely on the principle of non-discrimination to gain access to social security benefits in Germany notwithstanding that she was not a worker within Article 49 (now 39) EC (see below). A crucial aspect of the case which is not fully explained is what constitutes lawful residence in a Member State.

2.23

Article 13 (ex 6a) E.C.

Without prejudice to the other provisions of this Treaty and within the limits of the powers conferred by it upon the Community, the Council, acting unanimously on a proposal from the Commission and after consulting the European Parliament, may take appropriate action to combat discrimination based on sex, racial or ethnic origin, religion or belief, disability, age or sexual orientation.

2.24

Article 14 (ex 7a) E.C.

1. The Community shall adopt measures with the aim of progressively establishing the internal market over a period expiring on December 31 1992, in accordance with the provisions of this Article and of Articles 15, 26, 47(2), 49, 80, 93 and 95 and without prejudice to the other provisions of this Treaty.

2.25

Extracts from the E.C. Treaty

2. The internal market shall comprise an area without internal frontiers in which the free movement of goods, persons, services and capital is ensured in accordance with the provisions of this Treaty.

3. The Council, acting by a qualified majority on a proposal from the Commission, shall determine the guidelines and conditions necessary to ensure balanced progress in all the sectors concerned.

PART TWO

CITIZENSHIP OF THE UNION

Article 17 (ex 8) E.C.

2.26   **1.** Citizenship of the Union is hereby established. Every person holding the nationality of a Member State shall be a citizen of the Union. Citizenship of the Union shall complement and not replace national citizenship.

2. Citizens of the Union shall enjoy the rights conferred by this Treaty and shall be subject to the duties imposed thereby.

Article 18 (ex 8a) E.C.

2.27   **1.** Every citizen of the Union shall have the right to move and reside freely within the territory of the Member States, subject to the limitations and conditions laid down in this Treaty and by the measures adopted to give it effect.

2. The Council may adopt provisions with a view to facilitating the exercise of the rights referred to in paragraph 1; save as otherwise provided in this Treaty, the Council shall act in accordance with the procedure referred to in Article 251. The Council shall act unanimously throughout this procedure.

Article 19 (ex 8b) E.C.

2.28   **1.** Every citizen of the Union residing in a Member State of which he is not a national shall have the right to vote and to stand as a candidate at municipal elections in the Member State in which he resides, under the same conditions as nationals of that State. This right shall be exercised subject to detailed arrangements adopted by the Council, acting unanimously on a proposal from the Commission and after consulting the European Parliament; these arrangements may provide for derogations where warranted by problems specific to a Member State.

(Article 19)

2. Without prejudice to Article 190(4) and to the provisions adopted for its implementation, every citizen of the Union residing in a Member State of which he is not a national shall have the right to vote and to stand as a candidate in elections to the European Parliament in the Member State in which he resides, under the same conditions as nationals of that State. This right shall be exercised subject to detailed arrangements adopted by the Council, acting unanimously on a proposal from the Commission and after consulting the European Parliament; these arrangements may provide for derogations where warranted by problems specific to a Member State.

Article 20 (ex 8c) E.C.

Every citizen of the Union shall, in the territory of a third country in which the Member State of which he is a national is not represented, be entitled to protection by the diplomatic or consular authorities of any Member State, on the same conditions as the nationals of that State. Member States shall establish the necessary rules among themselves and start the international negotiations required to secure this protection. 2.29

Article 21 (ex 8d) E.C.

Every citizen of the Union shall have the right to petition the European Parliament in accordance with Article 194. 2.30

Every citizen of the Union may apply to the Ombudsman established in accordance with Article 195.

Every citizen of the Union may write to any of the institutions or bodies referred to in this Article or in Article 7 in one of the languages mentioned in Article 314 and have an answer in the same language.

Article 22 (ex 8e) E.C.

The Commission shall report to the European Parliament, to the Council and to the Economic and Social Committee every three years on the application of the provisions of this Part. This report shall take account of the development of the Union. 2.31

On this basis, and without prejudice to the other provisions of this Treaty, the Council, acting unanimously on a proposal from the Commission and after consulting the European Parliament, may adopt provisions to strengthen or to add to the rights laid down in this Part, which it shall recommend to the Member States for adoption in accordance with their respective constitutional requirements.

Extracts from the E.C. Treaty

Title III

Free Movement of Persons, Services and Capital

Chapter I

Workers

2.32

Article 39 (ex 48) E.C.

1. Freedom of movement for workers shall be secured within the Community.

2. Such freedom of movement shall entail the abolition of any discrimination based on nationality between workers of the Member States as regards employment, remuneration and other conditions of work and employment.

3. It shall entail the right, subject to limitations justified on grounds of public policy, public security or public health:
  (a) to accept offers of employment actually made;
  (b) to move freely within the territory of Member States for this purpose;
  (c) to stay in a Member State for the purpose of employment in accordance with the provisions governing the employment of nationals of that State laid down by law, regulation or administrative action;
  (d) to remain in the territory of a Member State after having been employed in that State, subject to conditions which shall be embodied in implementing regulations to be drawn up by the Commission.

4. The provisions of this Article shall not apply to employment in the public service.

General Note

2.33 The activities of the Community include an internal market characterised by the abolition, as between Member States, of obstacles to the free movement of goods, persons, services and capital: Article 3 (ex 3) E.C. Free movement of persons is generally regarded as encompassing workers, establishment, and services under Articles 39 (ex 48) to 55 (ex 66) E.C. Directives grant rights of free movement for students and retired persons, provided they are not a burden on the social assistance schemes of the Member State of residence, and for persons of independent means. Article 18 (ex 8a) EC recognises these rights as incidents of European citizenship.

Beneficiaries of the rules are nationals of the Member States. Companies or firms must meet both a nationality and "residence" test; they must, under Article 48 (ex 58) EC be formed under the law of a Member State and have their

(Article 39)

registered office, central administration or principal place of business within the Community. To claim the rights accorded by Community law, there must generally be some activity which engages the Community rules: Case 175/78 *Saunders* [1979] E.C.R. 216; Case C-41/90 *Höfner v. Macrotron* [1991] E.C.R. I-2010. So-called reverse discrimination is permitted. But the rights deriving from Community law can be pleaded against the State of which the person is a national if there is some connecting factor to the situations contemplated by Community law: Cases C-332/90 and C-132/93 *Volker Steen* [1992] E.C.R. I-341 and [1994] E.C.R. I-2715.

Community law defines a worker as someone obliged to provide services for another, in return for reward, and subject to the direction and control of that other person: Case 66/85 *Lawrie-Blum* [1986] E.C.R. 2121. Workers include those in low-paid, part-time work, provided that their work is effective and genuine and not on such a small scale as to be regarded as purely marginal and ancillary: Case 53/81 *Levin* [1982] E.C.R. 1035, though in applying this test account need only be taken of the pattern of work in the Member State of residence: Case C-357/89 *Raulin* [1992] E.C.R. I-1027.

Work or employment should be distinguished from establishment governed by Articles 43–48 EC) which includes self-employment, the setting up of agencies, branches and subsidiaries, and activities by companies or firms. A modest continuing presence will constitute establishment: Case 205/84 *Commission v. Germany* [1986] E.C.R. 3755. Freedom of movement (governed by Articles 49–55 E.C.) also exists for both providers and recipients of services: Case 186/87 *Cowan* [1989] E.C.R. 195. Services are activities provided for remuneration. Education principally financed by public funds is not a service: Case C-109/92 *Wirth*, [1993] E.C.R. 0000.

Where Community law applies, there is a prohibition on any form of discrimination based on nationality. A breach of Community law could flow from a non-discriminatory provision which has the effect of hindering free movement: Case C-415/93, *Bosman*, [1995] E.C.R. I-4921.

Those within the Community provisions have a right of entry and residence in the Member State, and are entitled to a residence permit under Council Directives 68/360 [1968–69] O.J. Spec. Ed. 485 and 73/148 [1973] O.J. L172/14. There are rights for both the economic actor and members of their families. Non-national spouses are treated as if they were nationals of a Member State: Case 131/85 *Gül* [1986] E.C.R. 1573. Council Regulation 1612/68 [1968–69] O.J. Spec. Ed 475 spells out the rights of workers and their families. There is a right to remain after a period of economic activity in a Member State.

Work seekers enjoy a limited right of entry and residence, but not other social rights accorded to those who have found work: Case 316/85 *Lebon* [1987] E.C.R. 2811.

Failure to recognise qualifications, and regulation of the activity by the host State have generated much case law in relation to establishment and services. Equality of treatment with nationals is required, but where there are harmonising directives, those prevail. Among the most important are the Mutual Recognition Directives 89/48 [1989] O.J. L19/16 and 92/51 [1992] O.J. L209/25. But even in the absence of harmonising directives, the equal treatment provisions of the Treaty give rise to an obligation to consider the equivalence of qualifications and schemes of regulation. In all cases there is an obligation to give reasons for any refusal to recognise qualifications, which must be susceptible of challenge in the Member State to test the compatibility of the decision with the requirements of Community law: Case 226/86 *Heylens* [1987] E.C.R. 4097.

National rules regulating economic activity can only be applied where they can be justified by imperative reasons relating to the public interest, where they apply equally to all persons engaged in that activity in the Member State, where there are no applicable safeguards applied in the home State, where the controls are objectively necessary, and where the measures imposed are the least restrictive to secure the legitimate objective: Case C-106/91 *Ramrath* [1992] E.C.R. I-3351.

The rights are subject to exceptions and limitations. Limitations may be imposed on grounds of public policy, public health and public security under Articles 39(3) (ex 48(3)), 46(1) (ex 56(1)) and 55 (ex 66) EC, spelled out in Council Directive 64/221 [1963–64] O.J. Spec. Ed. 117. The public policy ground requires the presence of a genuine and sufficiently serious threat to the requirements of public policy affecting one of the fundamental interests of society: Case 30/77 *Bouchereau* [1977] E.C.R. 1999. The genuineness of the limitation is tested by looking at the regulation of the objectionable conduct within the State: Joined Cases 115 & 116/81 *Adoui and Cornuaille* [1982] E.C.R. 1665.

Article 39(4) (ex 48(4)) EC excludes employment in the public service. A functional test has been adopted for identifying such employment: it must involve the exercise of powers conferred by public law, and responsibility for safeguarding the interests of either central and local government: Case 149/79 *Commission v. Belgium* [1980] E.C.R. 3881 and [1982] E.C.R. 1845. Articles 45 (ex 55) and 55 (ex 66) E.C. exclude from the rights of establishment and services activities connected with the exercise of official authority. Again a functional approach is adopted: Case 2/74 *Reyners* [1974] E.C.R. 631.

Whenever adverse decisions are taken in respect of entry and residence, there are due process guarantees in Article 5 to 9 of Council Directive 64/221 [1963–64], O.J. Spec. Ed. 117).

Article 40 (ex 49) EC

2.34 The Council shall, acting in accordance with the procedure referred to in Article 251 and after consulting the Economic and Social Committee, issue directives or make regulations setting out the measures required to bring about freedom of movement for workers, as defined in Article 39, in particular:

(a) by ensuring close cooperation between national employment services;

(b) by abolishing those administrative procedures and practices and those qualifying periods in respect of eligibility for available employment, whether resulting from national legislation or from agreements previously concluded between Member States, the maintenance of which would form an obstacle to liberalisation of the movement of workers;

(c) by abolishing all such qualifying periods and other restrictions provided for either under national legislation or under agreements previously concluded between Member States as imposed on workers of other Member States conditions regarding the free choice of employment other than those imposed on workers of the State concerned;

(d) by setting up appropriate machinery to bring offers of employment into touch with applications for employment and to facilitate the achievement of a balance between supply and demand in the employment market in such a way as to avoid serious threats

(Article 40)

to the standard of living and level of employment in the various regions and industries.

Article 41 (ex 50) EC

Member States shall, within the framework of a joint programme, encourage the exchange of young workers.

2.35

Article 42 (ex 51) EC

The Council shall, acting in accordance with the procedure referred to in Article 251, adopt such measures in the field of social security as are necessary to provide freedom of movement for workers; to this end, it shall make arrangements to secure for migrant workers and their dependants:

2.36

(a) aggregation, for the purpose of acquiring and retaining the right to benefit and of calculating the amount of benefit, of all periods taken into account under the laws of the several countries;

(b) payment of benefits to persons resident in the territories of Member States.

The Council shall act unanimously throughout the procedure referred to in Article 251.

GENERAL NOTE

Article 42 EC provides for the co-ordination of social security rules in the Member States (extended to the EEA countries by the EEA Agreement) in order to minimise a potential barrier to the free movement of workers. Co-ordination requires co-operation between the Member States to provide interchange between different national social security systems. The Court of Justice has frequently drawn attention to the distinction between harmonisation and co-ordination and noted that the substantive and procedural differences between the social security systems of the Member States remain unaffected by Article 42 and its secondary legislation: Case 41/84 *Pinna*, [1986] E.C.R. 1, at 24–5. But it has also been established that those exercising the right of freedom of movement should not lose advantages in the field of social security; this has come to be known as the *Petroni* principle: Case 24/75 *Petroni*, [1975] E.C.R. 1149, para. 13 of judgment.

2.37

Three general principles emerge from the complex rules of co-ordination which can be found in Regulation 1408/71 and the case law:

1. A national of a Member State (or EEA country) is not to be disqualified from entitlement to benefits on the grounds of nationality or on a change of country or residence within the European Union (or EEA).

2. A national of a Member State (or EEA country) may become entitled to a benefit by having contributions or qualifying periods of employment in one Member State (or EEA country) aggregated with those arising in another Member State (or EEA country).

3. A national of a Member State (of EEA country) should not be better off in relation to entitlement to benefits by reason of his or her exercise of rights to move freely between Member States (or EEA countries).

Extracts from the E.C. Treaty

SECTION 4

THE COURT OF JUSTICE

Article 234 (ex 177) E.C.

2.38 The Court of Justice shall have jurisdiction to give preliminary rulings concerning:
(a) the interpretation of this Treaty;
(b) the validity and interpretation of acts of the institutions of the Community and of the ECB;
(c) the interpretation of the statutes of bodies established by an act of the Council, where those statutes so provide.
Where such a question is raised before any court or tribunal of a Member State, that court or tribunal may, if it considers that a decision on the question is necessary to enable it to give judgment, request the Court of Justice to give a ruling thereon.
Where any such question is raised in a case pending before a court or tribunal of a Member State against whose decisions there is no judicial remedy under national law, that court or tribunal shall bring the matter before the Court of Justice.

GENERAL NOTE

2.39 Any national court or tribunal can refer questions on the interpretation of the EC Treaty, and on the validity and interpretation of Community legislation to the Court of Justice under Article 234 (ex 177) E.C. The objective of the procedure is a partnership between national courts and tribunals and the Court of Justice to ensure the uniform application in all Member States of Community law.

Courts other than final appeal courts have a *discretion* to make a reference, whereas final appeal courts have a *duty* to refer questions for consideration by the Court of Justice where answers to those questions are necessary to enable the national court to determine the question before it.

The effect of a court or tribunal seeking a ruling is that the national proceedings stand adjourned pending the receipt of the ruling of the Court of Justice. The case is then relisted for determination before the national court or tribunal in the light of the ruling of the Court of Justice on the point of Community law. The Court of Justice is careful not to determine the point arising under national law.

It is an error of law for a tribunal to fail to address a point of European Community law raised in the course of an appeal: *R(SB)6/91*, para. 5, and *R(S)2/93*.

Care should be taken whenever a tribunal is called upon to decide an issue involving a national of an EEA country. If a case involves a national of an EEA country, inquiry should be made to determine whether the provisions of European Community law apply to that person and assist in qualifying them for benefit. Failure to do so is an error of law: *CIS/771/1997*.

The Court of Justice has stressed in Case 166/73 *Rheinmühlen*, [1974] E.C.R. 33, at 38, that the objective of the preliminary ruling procedure is a

(Article 234)

partnership between national courts and tribunals and the Court of Justice with a view to ensuring the uniform application of Community law in all the Member States.

Under the procedure, the Court of Justice advises on the meaning of Community law put to it by a national court or tribunal. The discretion as to whether a reference is made is a wide one, and may be exercised by the court or tribunal of its own notion or on application for the court or tribunal to consider doing so by the parties. The leading case of the Court of Justice on the exercise of the discretion to refer is Joined Cases 36 & 71/80 *Irish Creamery Milk Supplies Association v. Ireland*, [1981] E.C.R. 735. The principles laid down in this case have been approved in Case 72/83 *Campus Oil v. Minister for Industry and Energy*, [1984] E.C.R. 2727; and Case 14/86 *Pretore di Salo v. Persons Unknown*, [1987] E.C.R. 2545. The following points emerge from this line of cases:

1. It is for the national court or tribunal to decide at what stage of proceedings it is appropriate for a preliminary ruling to be requested.

2. In order to assist the Court of Justice, it is essential for the national court or tribunal to define the legal context in which the reference is made.

3. This suggests that in some cases it might well be appropriate for the facts in the case to be established and for questions of purely national law to be settled at the time of the reference.

4. Attempts to fetter or limit the discretion of the national court or tribunal are inconsistent with Community law.

5. The discretion to refer is that of the national court or tribunal and not that of the parties.

Practice in English courts and tribunals has been influenced by the guidelines expressed by Lord Denning in *Bulmer v. Bollinger*, [1974] Ch 401, but these are not binding on any court or tribunal and aspects of them are inconsistent with statements of the Court of Justice. Distilling a considerable body of case law and adding points specific to the social security jurisdictions, the following factors are relevant in the determination by a tribunal or Commissioner of the exercise of the discretion to refer questions to the Court of Justice, namely whether:

1. a serious point of Community law arises in the case which has been fully argued by the parties;

2. the relevant facts have been found or are substantially agreed;

3. the point of law will be substantially determinative of the case;

4. there is any Community authority precisely or closely in point;

5. there is any Commissioners' authority addressing the point of Community law; and

6. it seems certain that at some stage in the life of the case, it will have to be referred to the Court of Justice.

The expense and delay caused by an inappropriate reference will be issues every tribunal and Commissioner will consider. The factors set out above are consistent with Community law on the exercise of the discretion to refer. The absence of full argument on the Community point—from both the claimant and the Secretary of State—(and full argument is likely to be rare in tribunals) suggests that caution should be the order of the day before the tribunals. On the other hand, tribunals should not be inhibited from making a reference if the relevant facts have been found, if the point has been fully argued, if the tribunal concludes that the appeal turns on the proper interpretation of a point of Community law, if there is no relevant authority which suggests that the question of interpretation is free from doubt, and if it seems certain that at some stage a reference will need to be made to resolve the question. It is probably fair to say that such circumstances will not be common place in the tribunals.

The Court of Justice has itself issued guidance for national courts and tribunals on the making of references and this is reproduced at the end of the annotations to this Article.

Although there are prescribed forms of order for references from the High Court, the Court of Justice does not make any formal requirements as to form. The tribunal (or Commissioner) is responsible for drafting the questions it wishes to refer. The question should be couched in terms which pose a general question of law rather than the specific issues raised in the case. The questions should be self-contained and self-explanatory, since they will be notified to the Commission, Council and the Member States under Article 20 of the Statute of the Court. These may choose within two months of the notification to submit written observations on the questions raised. Though the only requirement is the formulation of questions for the Court of Justice, it will be helpful to the Court to provide the following further information:

1. the facts of the case;

2. the relevant provisions of United Kingdom law;

3. the relevant provisions of Community law;

4. a summary of the contentions of the parties on the question or questions referred;

5. if necessary, the reasons why the answers to the questions referred are considered necessary to decide the case.

A ruling given by the Court of Justice is binding on the national court or tribunal as to the interpretation of the Community law in question. It will also bind future courts or tribunal determining similar questions: see s.3(1), European Communities Act 1972.

In *CIS/501/1993* the Commissioner had to consider whether he had jurisdiction to consider the validity of a reference to the Court of Justice made by a tribunal. The Commissioner, of course, only has jurisdiction when there is a "final" decision of a tribunal. The question was whether a reference could be regarded as a final decision. The Commissioner relied on RSC Ord.114, r.6 and *R. v. International Stock Exchange of the United Kingdom and the Republic of Ireland Ltd, ex parte Else (1982) Ltd*, [1993] Q.B. 534 in holding that an order referring questions to the Court of Justice is to be treated as a final decision against which appeal will lie. He then set aside the decision to refer since the answer to the question posed was clearly not "necessary" to enable the tribunal to resolve the issue before it. The Commissioner also makes reference to the guidelines set down by the Court of Appeal in *Bulmer*. Those guidelines are, as noted above, not wholly consistent with statements made by the Court of Justice and care should be taken in relying exclusively upon them without referring to the relevant decisions of the Court of Justice and subsequent decisions of the

(Article 234)

United Kingdom courts: see generally A. Arnull, "References to the European Court" (1990) 15 E.L.Rev. 375.

The Court of Justice guidance is as follows:

Court of Justice of the European Communities

NOTE FOR GUIDANCE ON REFERENCES BY NATIONAL COURTS FOR PRELIMINARY RULINGS

The development of the Community legal order is largely the result of co-operation between the Court of Justice of the European Communities and national courts and tribunals through the preliminary ruling procedure under Article 177 of the EC Treaty and the corresponding provisions of the ECSC and Euratom Treaties.[1]

2.40

In order to make this co-operation more effective, and so enable the Court of Justice better to meet the requirements of national courts by providing helpful answers to preliminary questions, this Note for Guidance is addressed to all interested parties, in particular to all national courts and tribunals.

It must be emphasised that the Note is for guidance only and has no binding or interpretative effect in relation to the provisions governing the preliminary ruling procedure. It merely contains practical information which, in the light of experience in applying the preliminary ruling procedure, may help to prevent the kind of difficulties which the Court has sometimes encountered.

1. Any court or tribunal of a Member State may ask the Court of Justice to interpret a rule of Community law, whether contained in the Treaties or in acts of secondary law, if it considers that this is necessary for it to give judgement in a case pending before it.

    Courts or tribunals against whose decisions there is no judicial remedy under national law must refer questions of interpretation arising before them to the Court of Justice, unless the Court has already ruled on the point or unless the correct application of the rule of Community law is obvious.[2]

2. The Court of Justice has jurisdiction to rule on the validity of acts of the Community institutions. National courts or tribunals may reject a plea challenging the validity of such an act. But where a national court (even one whose decision is still subject to appeal) intends to question the validity of a Community act, it must refer that question to the Court of Justice.[3]

    Where, however, a national court or tribunal has serious doubts about the validity of a Community act on which a national measure is based, it may, in exceptional cases, temporarily suspend application of the latter measure or grant other interim relief with respect to it. It must then refer the question of validity to the Court of Justice, stating the reasons for which it considers that the Community act is not valid.[4]

3. Questions referred for a preliminary ruling must be limited to the interpretation of a provision of Community law, since the Court of Justice does not have jurisdiction to interpret national law or assess its validity. It is for the referring court or tribunal to apply the relevant rule of Community law in the specific case pending before it.

4. The order of the national court or tribunal referring a question to the Court of Justice for a preliminary ruling may be in any form allowed by

national procedural law. Reference of a question or questions to the Court of Justice generally involves a stay of the national proceedings until the Court has given its ruling, but the decision to stay proceedings is one which is for the national court alone to take in accordance with its own national law.

5. The order for reference containing the question or questions referred to the Court will have to be translated by the Court's translators into the other official languages of the Community. Questions concerning the interpretation or validity of Community law are frequently of general interest and the Member States and Community institutions are entitled to submit observations. It is therefore desirable that the reference should be drafted as clearly and precisely as possible.

6. The order for reference should contain a statement of reasons which is succinct but sufficiently complete to give the Court, and those to whom it must be notified (the Member States, the Commission and in certain cases the Council and the European Parliament), a clear understanding of the factual and legal context of the main proceedings.[5]

In particular, it should include:
- a statement of the facts which are essential to a full understanding of the legal significance of the main proceedings;
- an exposition of the national law which may be applicable;
- a statement of the reasons which have prompted the national court to refer the question or questions to the Court of Justice; and
- where appropriate, a summary of the arguments of the parties.

The aim should be to put the Court of Justice in a position to give the national court an answer which will be of assistance to it. The order for reference should also be accompanied by copies of any documents needed for a proper understanding of the case, especially the text of the applicable national provisions. However, as the case-file or documents annexed to the order for reference are not always translated in full into the other official languages of the Community, the national court should ensure that the order for reference itself includes all the relevant information.

7. A national court or tribunal may refer a question to the Court of Justice as soon as it find that a ruling on the point or points of interpretation or validity is necessary to enable it to give judgment. It must be stressed, however, that it is not for the Court of Justice to decide issues of fact or to resolve disputes as to the interpretation or application of rules of national law. It is therefore desirable that a decision to refer should not be taken until the national proceedings have reached a stage where the national court is able to define, if only as a working hypothesis, the factual and legal context of the question; on any view, the administration of justice is likely to be best served if the reference is not made until both sides have been heard.[6]

8. The order for reference and the relevant documents should be sent by the national court directly to the Court of Justice, by registered post, addressed to: The Registry, Court of Justice of the European Communities, L-2925. Telephone (352) 43031. The Court Registry will remain in contact with the national court until judgment is given, and will send copies of the various documents (written observations, Report for the Hearing, Opinion of the Advocate General). The Court will also send its judgment to the national court. The Court would appreciate being informed about the application of its judgment in the national proceedings and being sent a copy of the national court's final decision.

9. Proceedings for a preliminary ruling before the Court of Justice are free of charge. The Court does not rule on costs.

(Article 234)

FOOTNOTES

1. A preliminary ruling is also provided for by protocols to several conventions concluded by the Member States, in particular the Brussels Convention on Jurisdiction and the Enforcement of Judgments in Civil and Commercial Matters.
2. Judgment in Case 283/81 *CILFIT* v. *Ministry of Health*, [1982] E.C.R. 3415.
3. Judgment in Case 314/85 *Foto-Frost* v. *Hauptzollamt Lübeck-Ost*, [1987] E.C.R. 4199.
4. Judgments in Joined Cases C-143/88 and C-92/89 *Zuckerfabrik Südertitmarschen and Zuckerfabrik Soest*, [1991] E.C.R. I-415 and in Case C-465/93 *Atlanta Fruchthendelsgesellschaft*, [1995] E.C.R. I-2761.
5. Judgment in Joined cases C-320/90, C-321/90 and C-322/90 *Telemarsicabruzzo*, [1993] E.C.R. I-393.
6. Judgments in Case 70/77 *Simmenthal* v. *Amministrazione delle Finanze dello Stato*, [1978] E.C.R. 1453.

PART SIX

GENERAL AND FINAL PROVISIONS

Article 308 (ex 235) E.C.

If action by the Community should prove necessary to attain, in the course of the operation of the common market, one of the objectives of the Community and this Treaty has not provided the necessary powers, the Council shall, acting unanimously on a proposal from the Commission and after consulting the European Parliament, take the appropriate measures.

2.42

GENERAL NOTE

This provision is sometimes referred to as the "reserve power", since it give the Community a power to take action in the absence of a specific authority to do so in the Treaty where action is necessary to attain one of the objectives of the Community. The power has been used in relation to certain social security measures, for example, Directive 79/7 (see below).

2.43

Council Regulation (EEC) No. 1408/71 on the application of social security schemes to employed persons, to self-employed persons and to members of their families moving within the Community

TEXT AS AMENDED BY COUNCIL REGULATION (EC) 118/97 OF DECEMBER 2 1996

[1997] O.J. L28/4 (AS FURTHER AMENDED)

ARRANGEMENT OF REGULATIONS

TITLE I: GENERAL PROVISIONS (ARTICLES 1 TO 12)

2.44

Council Regulations (EEC) No. 1408/71

Title II: Determination of the Legislation Applicable
(Articles 13 to 17a)

Title III: Special Provisions Relating to the Various Categories of Benefits

Chapter 1: Sickness and maternity

Section 1: Common provisions (Article 18)
Section 2: Employed or self-employed persons and members of their families (Articles 19 to 24)
Section 3: Unemployed persons and members of their families (Article 25)
Section 4: Pension claimants and members of their families (Article 26)
Section 5: Pensioners and members of their families (Articles 27 to 34)
Section 6: Miscellaneous provisions (Article 35)
Section 7: Reimbursement between institutions (Article 36)

Chapter 2: Invalidity

Section 1: Employed or self-employed persons subject only to legislations under which the amount of invalidity benefits is independent of the duration of periods of insurance (Articles 37 to 39)
Section 2: Employed or self-employed persons subject either only to legislations under which the amount of invalidity benefit depends on the duration of periods of insurance or residence or to legislations of this type and of the type referred to in Section 1 (Article 40)
Section 3: Aggravation of invalidity (Article 41)
Section 4: Resumption of provision of benefits after suspension or withdrawal—Conversion of invalidity benefits into old-age benefits. Recalculation of benefits granted under Article 39 (Articles 42 and 43)

Chapter 3: Old age and death (pensions) (Articles 44 to 51)

Chapter 4: Accidents at work and occupational disease

Section 1: Right to benefits (Articles 52 to 59)
Section 2: Aggravation of an occupational disease for which the benefit has been awarded (Article 60)
Section 3: Miscellaneous provisions (Articles 61 and 62)
Section 4: Reimbursements between institutions (Article 63)

Chapter 5: Death grants (Articles 64 to 66)

Chapter 6: Unemployment benefits

Section 1: Common provisions (Articles 67 and 68)
Section 2: Unemployed persons going to a Member State other than the competent State (Articles 69 and 70)
Section 3: Unemployed persons who, during their last employment, were residing in a Member State other than the competent State (Article 71)

(Article 1)

Chapter 7: *Family benefits (Articles 72 to 76)*

Chapter 8: *Benefits for dependent children of pensioners and for orphans (Articles 77 to 79)*

TITLE IV: ADMINISTRATIVE COMMISSION ON SOCIAL SECURITY FOR MIGRANT WORKERS (ARTICLES 80 AND 81)

TITLE V: ADVISORY COMMITTEE ON SOCIAL SECURITY FOR MIGRANT WORKERS (ARTICLES 82 AND 83)

TITLE VI: MISCELLANEOUS PROVISIONS (ARTICLES 84 TO 93)

TITLE VII: TRANSITIONAL AND FINAL PROVISIONS (ARTICLES 94 TO 98).

GENERAL NOTE

A consolidated version of Regulation 1408/71 was passed in December 1996. The version of the regulation printed here is based on that text. Amendments made prior to December 1996 are not noted, but the text has been updated to take account of subsequent amendments of the Regulation and annotated to show the source of those amendments in the same manner as for United Kingdom statutory material.

TITLE I

GENERAL PROVISIONS

Article 1

Definitions

For the purpose of this Regulation: 2.45
  (a) employed person and self-employed person mean respectively:
    (i) [^{1}any person who is insured, compulsorily or on an optional continued basis, for one or more of the contingencies covered by the branches of a social security scheme for employed or self-employed persons or by a special scheme for civil servants];
    (ii) any person who is compulsorily insured for one or more of the contingencies covered by the branches of social security dealt with in this Regulation, under a social security dealt with in this Regulation, under a social security scheme for all residents or for the whole working population, if such person:
      — can be identified as an employed or self-employed person by virtue of the manner in which such scheme is administered or financed, or,
      — failing such criteria, is insured for some other contin-

gency specified in Annex I under a scheme for employed or self-employed persons, or under a scheme referred to in (iii), either compulsorily or on an optional continued basis, or, where no such scheme exists in the Member State concerned, complies with the definition given in Annex I;

(iii) any person who is compulsorily insured for several of the contingencies covered by the branches dealt with in this Regulation, under a standard social security scheme for the whole rural population in accordance with the criteria laid down in Annex I;

(iv) any person who is voluntarily insured for one or more of the contingencies covered by the branches dealt with in this Regulation, under a social security scheme of a Member State for employed or self-employed persons or for all residents or for certain categories of residents:
— if such person carries out an activity as an employed or self-employed person, or
— if such person has previously been compulsorily insured for the same contingency under a scheme for employed or self-employed persons for the same Member State;

(b) *frontier worker* means any employed or self-employed person who pursues his occupation in the territory of a Member State and resides in the territory of another Member State to which he returns as a rule daily or at least once a week; however, a frontier worker who is posted elsewhere in the territory of the same or another Member State by the undertaking to which he is normally attached, or who engages in the provision of services elsewhere in the territory of the same or another Member State, shall retain the status of frontier worker for a period not exceeding four month, even if he is prevented, during that period, from returning daily or at least once a week to the place where he resides;

(c) *seasonal worker* means any employed person who goes to the territory of a Member State other than the one in which he is resident to do work there of a seasonal nature for an undertaking or an employer of that State for a period which may on no account exceed eight month, and who stays in the territory of the said State for the duration of this work; work of a seasonal nature shall be taken to mean work which, being dependent on the succession of the seasons, automatically recurs each year;

[²(ca) *student* means any person other than an employed or self-employed person or a member of his family or survivor within the meaning of this Regulation who studies or receives vocational training leading to a qualification officially recognised by the authorities of a Member State, and is insured under a general social security scheme or a special social security scheme applicable to students].

(d) *refugee* shall have the meaning assigned to it in Article 1 of the

(Article 1)

Convention of the Status of Refugees, signed at Geneva on 28 July 1951;
(e) *stateless person* shall have the meaning assigned to it in Article 1 of the Convention on the Status of Stateless Persons, signed in New York on 28 September 195
(f) [³(i) Where the legislation of a Member State does not enable members of the family to be distinguished from the other persons to whom it applies, the term "member of the family shall have the meaning given in Annex I];
    (ii) where, however, the benefits concerned are benefits for disabled persons granted under the legislation of a Member State to all nationals of that State who fulfil the prescribed conditions, the term "member of the family" means at least the spouse of an employed or self-employed person [²or student] and the children of such person who are either minors or dependent upon such person;
(g) *survivor* means any person defined or recognized as such by the legislation under which the benefits are granted; where, however, the said legislation regards as a survivor only a person who was living under the same roof as the deceased, this condition shall be considered satisfied if such person was mainly dependent on the deceased;
(h) *residence* means habitual residence;
(i) *stay* means temporary residence;
(j) *legislation* means in respect of each Member State statutes, regulations and other provisions and all other implementing measures, present or future, relating to the branches and schemes of social security covered by Article 4 (1) and (2) or those special non-contributory benefits covered by Article 4 (2a).

The term excludes provisions of existing or future industrial agreements, whether or not they have been the subject of a decision by the authorities rendering them compulsory or extending their scope. However, in so far as such provisions:
    (i) serve to put into effect compulsory insurance imposed by the laws and regulations referred to in the preceding subparagraph; or
    (ii) set up a scheme administered by the same institution as that which administers the schemes set up by the laws and regulations referred to in the preceding subparagraph,
the limitation on the term may at any time be lifted by a declaration of the Member State concerned specifying the schemes of such a kind to which this Regulation applies. Such a declaration shall be notified and published in accordance with the provisions of Article 97.

The provisions of the preceding subparagraph shall not have the effect of exempting from the application of this Regulation the schemes to which Regulation No 3 applied.

The term "legislation" also excludes provisions governing special schemes for self-employed persons the creation of which is left to the initiatives of those concerned or which apply only to a part of the territory of the Member State concerned, irrespective of whether or not the authorities decided to make them compulsory or extend their scope. The special schemes in question are specified in Annex II;

[¹(ja) *special scheme of civil servants* means any social security scheme which is different from the general social security scheme applicable to employed persons in the Member States concerned and to which all, or certain categories of, civil servants or persons treated as such are directly subject];

(k) *social security convention* means any bilateral or multilateral instrument which binds or will bind two or more Member States exclusively, and any other multilateral instrument which binds or will bind at least two Member States and one or more other States in the field of social security, for all or part of the branches and schemes set out in Article 4 (1) and (2), together with agreements, of whatever kind, concluded pursuant to the said instruments;

(l) *competent authority* means, in respect of each Member State, the Minister, Ministers or other equivalent authority responsible for social security schemes throughout or in any part of the territory of the State in question;

(m) *Administrative Commission* means the commission referred to in Article 80;

(n) *institution* means, in respect of each Member State, the body or authority responsible for administering all or part of the legislation;

(o) *competent institution* means:

  (i) the institution with which the person concerned is insured at the time of the application for benefit;

or

  (ii) the institution from which the person concerned is entitled or would be entitled to benefits if he or a member or members of his family were resident in the territory of the Member State in which the institution is situated; or

  (iii) the institution designated by the competent authority of the member State concerned; or

  (iv) in the case of a scheme relating to an employer's liability in respect of the benefits set out in Article 4 (1), either the employer or the insurer involved or, in default thereof, a body or authority designated by the competent authority of the Member State concerned;

(p) *institution of the place of residence* and *institution of the place of stay*' means respectively the institution which is competent to provide benefits in the place where the person concerned resides and the institution which is competent to provide benefits in the place where the person concerned is staying, under the legislation administered by that institution or, where no such institution exists, the institution designated by the competent authority of the Member State in question;

(Article 1)

(q) *competent State* means the Member State in whose territory the competent institution is situated;

(r) *periods of insurance* means periods of contribution or period of employment or self-employment as defined or recognized as periods of insurance by the legislation under which they were completed or considered as completed, and all periods treated as such, where they are regarded by the said legislation as equivalent to periods of insurance; [¹ periods completed under a special scheme for civil servants are also considered as periods of insurance];

(s) *periods of employment* and *periods of self-employment* means periods so defined or recognized by the legislation under which they were completed, and all periods treated as such, where they are regarded by the said legislation as equivalent to periods of employment or of self-employment; [¹ periods completed under a special scheme for civil servants are also considered as periods of insurance];

(sa) *periods of residence* means periods as defined or recognized as such by the legislation under which they were completed or considered as completed;

(t) *benefits and pensions* mean all benefits and pensions, including all elements thereof payable out of public funds, revalorization increases and supplementary allowances, subject to the provisions of Title III, as also lump-sum benefits which may be paid in lieu of pensions, and payments made by way of reimbursement of contributions;

(u)
  (i) the term *family benefits* means all benefits in kind or in cash intended to meet family expenses under the legislation provided for in Article 4 (1) (h), excluding the special childbirth or adoption allowances referred to in Annex II;
  (ii) *family allowances* means periodical cash benefits granted exclusively by reference to the number and, where appropriate, the age of members of the family;

(v) *death grants* means any once-for-all payment in the event of death exclusive of the lump-sum benefits referred to in subparagraph (t).

AMENDMENTS

1. Regulation 1606/98 [1998] O.J. L209/1 (October 28, 1998)
2. Regulation 307/99 [1999] O.J. L307/99 (May 1, 1999)
3. Regulation 1290/97 [1997] O.J. L176/1 (October 4, 1997)

GENERAL NOTE

Article 1 contains crucial definitions in the application of the co-ordinating rules it contains. These are autonomous concepts under Community law and are to be applied from a Community perspective.
Note that the definition of "habitual residence" in this regulation is not the same as the requirement of habitual residence as a condition of entitlement

2.46

[¹Article 2

Persons covered

2.47   1. This Regulation shall apply to employed and self-employed persons and to students who are or have been subject to the legislation of one or more Member States and who are nationals of one of the Member States or who are stateless persons or refugees residing within the territory of one of the Member States, as well as to members of their families and their survivors.

2. This Regulation shall apply to the survivors of employed or self-employed persons and of students who have been subject to the legislation of one or more Member States, irrespective of the nationality of such persons, where their survivors are nationals of one of the Member States, or stateless persons or refugees residing within the territory of one of the Member States.]

AMENDMENTS

1. Regulation 307/99, [1999] O.J. L307/99

GENERAL NOTE

2.48   The latest amendment brings students into the framework of the Regulation. Note that the regulation applies to both employed and self-employed persons. It also covers their families who have rights as such and not simply derivative rights flowing from the work of another member of their family: Case C-308/93 *Cabanis-Issarte*, [1996] E.C.R.I-2097. In order to be a beneficiary of the rules in the Regulation, a person must be a national of an EEA country.

Article 3

Equality of treatment

2.49   1. Subject to the special provisions of this Regulation, persons resident in the territory of one of the Member States to whom this Regulation applies shall be subject to the same obligations and enjoy the same benefits under the legislation of any Member State as the nationals of the State.

2. The provisions of paragraph 1 shall apply to the right to elect members of the organs of social security institutions or to participate in their nomination, but shall not affect the legislative provisions of any Member State relating to eligibility or methods of nomination of persons concerned to those organs.

3. Save as provided in Annex III, the provisions of social security conventions which remain in force pursuant to Article 7 2. (c) and the

(Article 3)

provisions of conventions concluded pursuant to Article 8 (1), shall apply to all persons to whom this Regulation applies.

GENERAL NOTE

The obligation in this article is central to the system of co-ordination established by the regulation. Equality of treatment is a foundational principle of the Community which is set out in Article 12 (ex 6) EC. The prohibition is restated in Article 39(2) (ex 48(2) E.C. on the free movement of workers; the co-ordination of social security is part of the chapter on the free movement of workers. The requirement of equal treatment has been given a broad interpretation by the Court of Justice, which has consistently stated that it covers not only overt forms of discrimination but also covert forms of discrimination under which certain requirements and conditions which are not on their face based on nationality in effect operate to discriminate between nationals of the EEA countries: see Case 237/78 *Toia*, [1979] E.C.R. 2645.

2.50

Article 4

Matters covered

1. This Regulation shall apply to all legislation concerning the following branches of social security:
(a) sickness and maternity benefits;
(b) invalidity benefits, including those intended for the maintenance or improvement of earning capacity;
(c) old-age benefits;
(d) survivors' benefits;
(e) benefits in respect of accidents at work and occupational diseases;
(f) death grants;
(g) unemployment benefits;
(h) family benefits.
2. This Regulation shall apply to all general and special social security schemes, whether contributory or non-contributory, and to schemes concerning the liability of an employer or shipowner in respect of the benefits referred to in paragraph 1.
2a. This Regulation shall also apply to special non-contributory benefits which are provided under legislation or schemes other than those referred to in paragraph 1 or excluded by virtue of paragraph 4, where such benefits are intended:
(a) either to provide supplementary, substitute or ancillary cover against the risks covered by the branches of social security referred to in paragraph 1 (a) to (h);
or
(b) solely as specific protection for the disabled.
2b. This Regulation shall not apply to the provisions in the legislation of a Member State concerning special non-contributory benefits, referred to in Annex II, Section III, the validity of which is confined to part of its territory.
3. The provisions of Title III of this Regulation shall not, however,

2.51

affect the legislative provisions of any Member State concerning a shipowner's liability.

4. This Regulation shall not apply to social and medical assistance, to benefit schemes for victims of war or its consequences, [¹ . . .].

AMENDMENT

1. Regulation 1606/98, [1998] O.J. L209/1 (October 25, 1998).

GENERAL NOTE

2.52   The regulation applies to all legislation governing benefits protecting against the eight named risks. These social risks are those identified in ILO Convention 102. It does not matter whether the specified benefits are provided under contributory or non-contributory schemes. Special non-contributory benefits are also covered where they provide supplementary, substitute or ancillary cover against the social risk set out in the article, or are specific protection for disabled people.

Social assistance is excluded from the scope of the regulation together with medical assistance, and schemes for war victims.

The distinction between social insurance and social assistance used to be more clear cut than it is today. Social insurance as originally conceived related to insurance-based schemes in respect of certain risk against which workers or their employers would insure; it also included provision for what might be regarded as the certainties of life: birth, old age and death. By contrast social assistance is support provided by the State at its discretion on the basis of need. There is also a third group of benefits which are provided on the basis of need, but are a matter of legal entitlement and not discretion. Considerable debate still surrounds the true nature of benefits like income support in the United Kingdom which are means-tested but are paid as a matter of legal right to those who meet closely specified conditions of entitlement and at a rate also set out in regulations.

In *Perry v. Chief Adjudication Officer*, [1999] 2 C.M.L.R. 439, the Court of Appeal held that income support was not a special non-contributory benefit (see Article 10a below) within the meaning of the regulation, but this decision must now be read in the light of Case C-90/97 *Swaddling v. Adjudication Officer*, [1999] E.C.R. nyr; [1999] 2 C.M.L.R. 679 in which the Court of Justice ruled that income support is a special non-contributory benefit within the meaning of the regulation.

Article 5

Declarations by the Member States on the scope of this Regulation

2.53   The Member States shall specify the legislation and schemes referred to in Article 4 (1) and (2), the special non-contributory benefits referred to in Article 4 (2a), the minimum benefits referred to in Article 50 and the benefits referred to in Articles 77 and 78 in declarations to be notified and published in accordance with Article 97.

GENERAL NOTE

Little assistance is provided by reference to declarations made by Member States, since they are not always kept up to date. The United Kingdom declaration is certainly out of date.

2.54   ARTICLES 6–9 OMITTED

(Article 10)

Article 10

Waiving of residence clauses—Effect of compulsory insurance on reimbursement of contributions

1. Save as otherwise provided in this Regulation invalidity, old-age or survivors' cash benefits, pension for accidents at work or occupational diseases and death grants acquired under the legislation of one or more Member States shall not be subject to any reduction, modification, suspension, withdrawal or confiscation by reason of the fact that the recipient resides in the territory of a Member State other than that in which the institution responsible for payment is situated. The first subparagraph shall also apply to lump-sum benefits granted in cases of remarriage of a surviving spouse who was entitled to a survivors' pension.

2. Where under the legislation of a Member State reimbursement of contributions is conditional upon the person concerned having ceased to be subject to compulsory insurance, this condition shall not be considered satisfied as long as the person concerned is subject to compulsory insurance [¹ . . .]

2.55

AMENDMENTS

1. Regulation 307/99, [1999] O.J. L307/99 (May 1, 1999)

GENERAL NOTE

This article and Article 10a deal with the exportability of benefits. They set out the general rules on which a benefit acquired in one EEA country may continue in payment where the beneficiary moves to another EEA country. Though issues remain as to the classification of certain benefits, those rules seem fairly clear. Member States tend to argue that benefits are social assistance and are not capable of exportation. So in Case 139/82 *Piscitello*, [1983] E.C.R. 1427, the Italian government argued that the *pensione sociale* was social assistance, but the Court concluded that it was a benefit analogous to an old age pension and so Paolo Piscitello could take it with her when she moved from Italy to Belgium to join members of her family living there.

2.56

The exportability of sickness and maternity, and unemployment benefits applies only to a very limited extent, since the Member States are extremely cautious about losing the ability to monitor the genuineness of the claim or the claimant's continuing job search activities. The putting together of sickness and maternity benefits is unfortunate in this regard.

The concern of the Member States that certain individuals would tour the Member States collecting the most favourable benefit entitlements and exporting them to where they wanted to live led to a new regime being introduced for what are called special non-contributory benefits. Such benefits are under Article 10a payable only in the territory of the Member State to those resident there. Special non-contributory benefits must be listed in Annex IIa of the Regulation. Though payability is linked to residence, the process of acquisition is not tied to a single Member State.

Article 10a

Special non-contributory benefits

2.57   **1.** Nothwithstanding the provisions of Article 10 and Title III, persons to whom this Regulation applies shall be granted the special non-contributory cash benefits referred to in Article 4 (2a) exclusively in the territory of the Member State in which they reside, in accordance with the legislation of that State, provided that such benefits are listed in Annex IIa. Such benefits shall be granted by and at the expense of the institution of the place of residence.

2. The institution of a Member State under whose legislation entitlement to benefits covered by paragraph 1 is subject to the completion of periods of employment, self-employment or residence shall regard, to the extent necessary, periods of employment, self-employment or residence completed in the territory of any other Member State as periods completed in the territory of the first Member State.

3. Where entitlement to a benefit covered by paragraph 1 but granted in the form of a supplement is subject, under the legislation of a Member State, to receipt of a benefit covered by Article 4 (1) (a) to (h), and no such benefit is due under that legislation, any corresponding benefit granted under the legislation of any other Member State shall be treated as a benefit granted under the legislation of the first Member State for the purposes of entitlement to the supplement.

4. Where the granting of a disability or invalidity benefit covered by paragraph 1 is subject, under the legislation of a Member State, to the condition that the disability or invalidity should be diagnosed for the first time in the territory of that Member State, this condition shall be deemed to be fulfilled where such diagnosis is made for the first time in the territory of another Member State.

GENERAL NOTE

2.58   See notes to Article 10.

The nature of disability living allowance was considered in Case C-20/96 *Snares v. The Adjudication Officer*, [1997] E.C.R. I-6057, and of attendance allowance in Case C-297/96 *Partridge v. The Adjudication Officer*, [1998] E.C.R. I-J467. The Court of Justice took the view that the listing of the benefit in Annex IIa must be accepted as establishing the nature of the benefit; the absence of a revised declaration under Article 5 did not prejudice this position. The result was the same in *Partridge*.

2.59   *Article 11 omitted*

Article 12

Prevention of overlapping of benefits

2.60   **1.** This Regulation can neither confer nor maintain the right to several benefits of the same kind for one and the same period of compulsory insurance. However, this provision shall not apply to benefits in respect

(Article 12)

of invalidity, old age, death (pensions) or occupational disease which are awarded by the institutions of two or more Member States, in accordance with the provisions of Articles 41, 43 2. and (3), 46, 50 and 51 or Article 60 (1) (b).

2. Save as otherwise provided in this Regulation, the provisions of the legislations of a Member State governing the reduction, suspension or withdrawal of benefits in cases of overlapping with other social security benefits or any other form of income may be invoked even where such benefits were acquired under the legislation of another Member State or where such income was acquired in the territory of another Member State.

3. The provisions of the legislation of a Member State for reduction, suspension or withdrawal of benefit in the case of a person in receipt of invalidity benefits or anticipatory old-age benefits pursuing a professional or trade activity may be invoked against such person even though he is pursuing his activity in the territory of another Member State.

4. An invalidity pension payable under Netherlands legislation shall, in case where the Netherlands institution is bound under the provisions of Article 57 (5) or 60 (29) (b) to contribute also to the cost of benefits for occupational disease granted under the legislation of another Member State, be reduced by the amount payable to the institution of the other Member State which is responsible for granting the benefits for occupational disease.

GENERAL NOTE

Article 12 contains the Community rules on overlapping benefits, which provide the authority for national systems to adjust national benefit by reason of entitlement to a benefit in another EEA country which is awarded by reason of the application of the Community co-ordination rules. Article 12 lays down a number principles relating to overlapping of benefits: 2.61

1. Regulation 1408/71 can neither confer nor maintain the right to several benefits *of the same kind* for one and the same period of compulsory insurance.

2. The rules apply only to short-term benefits since the rules on aggregation and apportionment which apply to long-term benefits achieve the same effect without the need for rules relating to the overlapping of benefits.

3. The rules only apply where acquisition of a benefit arises through the application of the Community rules.

See also Articles 7–10a of Regulation 574/72 reproduced below.

TITLE II

DETERMINATION OF THE LEGISLATION APPLICABLE

Article 13

General rules

1. [¹Subject to Articles 14c and 14f, persons to whom this Regulation 2.62

applies shall be subject to the legislation of a single Member State only. That legislation shall be determined in accordance with the provisions of this Title.]

2. Subject to Articles 14 to 17:
   (a) a person employed in the territory of one Member State shall be subject to the legislation of that State even if he resides in the territory of another Member State or if the registered office or place of business of the undertaking or individual employing him is situated in the territory of another Member State;
   (b) a person who is self-employed in the territory of one Member State shall be subjected to the legislation of that State even if he resides in the territory of another Member State;
   (c) a person employed on board a vessel flying the flag of a Member State shall be subject to the legislation of the State;
   (d) civil servants and persons treated as such shall be subject to the legislation of the Member State to which the administration employing them is subject;
   (e) a person called up or recalled for service in the armed forces, or for civilian service, of a Member State shall be subject to the legislation of that State. If entitlement under that legislation is subject to the completion of periods of insurance before entry into or after release from such military or civilian service, periods of insurance completed under the legislation of any other Member State shall be taken into account, to the extent necessary, as if they were periods of insurance completed under the legislation of the first State. The employed or self-employed person called up or recalled for service in the armed forces or for civilian service shall retain the status of employed or self-employed person;
   (f) a person to whom the legislation of a Member State ceases to be applicable, without the legislation of another Member State becoming applicable to him in accordance with one of the rules laid down in the aforegoing subparagraphs or in accordance with one of the exceptions or special provisions laid down in Articles 14 to 17 shall be subject to the legislation of the Member State in whose territory he resides in accordance with the provisions of that legislation alone.

AMENDMENTS

1. Regulation 1606/98, [1998] O.J. L209/1 (October 25, 1998).

GENERAL NOTE

2.63   Title II of Regulation 1408/71 provides a complete system of the conflict of laws for answering questions concerning both jurisdiction and the choice of law to apply to any situation involving an international element between EEA countries. The basic proposition is that persons to whom the regulation applies are at any given time subject to the legislation of a single EEA country only, which will normally apply its own social security laws to the matter subject to the co-ordinating rules in the regulation. The starting point to which there are

(Article 13)

exceptions is that priority is given to the place of employment. There are, however, very many special situations where this rule is displaced.

Article 14

Special rules applicable to persons, other than mariners, engaged in paid employment

Article 13 (2) (a) shall apply subject to the following exceptions and circumstances: 2.64

1. (a) A person employed in the territory of a Member State by an undertaking to which he is normally attached who is posted by that undertaking to the territory of another Member State to perform work there for that undertaking shall continue to be subject to the legislation of the first Member State, provided that the anticipated duration of that work does not exceed 12 months and that he is not sent to replace another person who has completed his term of posting.
   (b) if the duration of the work to be done extends beyond the duration originally anticipated, owing to unforeseeable circumstances, and exceeds 12 months, the legislation of the first Member State shall continue to apply until the completion of such work, provided that the competent authority of the Member State in whose territory the person concerned is posted or the body designated by that authority gives its consent; such consent must be requested before the end of the initial 12-month period. Such consent cannot, however, be given for a period exceeding 12 months.
2. A person normally employed in the territory of two or more Member States shall be subject to the legislation determined as follows:
   (a) A person who is a member of the travelling or flying personnel of an undertaking which, for hire or reward or on its own account, operates international transport services for passengers or goods by rail, road, air or inland waterway and has its registered office or place of business in the territory of a Member State shall be subject to the legislation of the latter State, with the following restrictions:
     (i) where the said undertaking has a branch or permanent representation in the territory of a Member State other than that in which it has its registered office or place of business, a person employed by such branch or permanent representation shall be subject to the legislation of the Member State in whose territory such branch or permanent representation is situated;
     (ii) where a person is employed principally in the territory of the Member State in which he resides, he shall be subject to the legislation of that State, even if the undertaking which

employs him has no registered office or place of business or branch or permanent representation in that territory.
(b) A person other than that referred to in (a) shall be subject:
   (i) to the legislation of the Member State in whose territory he resides, if he pursues his activity partly in that territory or if he is attached to several undertakings or several employers who have their registered offices or places of business in the territory of different Member States;
   (ii) to the legislation of the Member State in whose territory is situated the registered office or place of business of the undertaking or individual employing him, if he does not reside in the territory of any of the Member States where he is pursuing his activity.
3. A person who is employed in the territory of one Member State by an undertaking which has its registered office or place of business in the territory of another Member State and which straddles the common frontier of these States shall be subject to the legislation of the Member State in whose territory the undertaking has its registered office or place of business.

Article 14a

Special rules applicable to persons, other than mariners, who are self-employed

2.65   Article 13 (2) (b) shall apply subject to the following exceptions and circumstances:
1. (a) A person normally self-employed in the territory of a Member State and who performs work in the territory of another Member State shall continue to be subject to the legislation of the first Member State, provided that the anticipated duration of the work does not exceed 12 months.
   (b) If the duration of the work to be done extends beyond the duration originally anticipated, owing to unforeseeable circumstances, and exceeds 12 months, the legislation of the first Member State shall continue to apply until the completion of such work, provided that the competent authority of the Member State in whose territory the person concerned has entered to perform the work in question or the body appointed by that authority gives its consent; such consent must be requested before the end of the initial 12-month period, Such consent cannot, however, be given for a period exceeding 12 months.
2. A person normally self-employed in the territory of two or more Member States shall be subject to the legislation of the Member State in whose territory he resides if he pursues any part of his activity in the territory of that Member State. If he does not

(Article 14a)

pursue any activity in the territory of the Member State in which he resides, he shall be subject to the legislation of the Member State in whose territory he pursue his main activity. The criteria used to determine the principal activity are laid down in the Regulation referred to in Article 98.

3. A person who is self-employed in an undertaking which has its registered office or place of business in the territory of one Member State and which straddles the common frontier of two Member States shall be subject to the legislation of the Member State in whose territory the undertaking has its registered office or place of business.

4. If the legislation to which a person should be subject in accordance with paragraph 2 or 3 does not enable that person, even on a voluntary basis, to join a pension scheme, the person concerned shall be subject to the legislation of the other Member State which would apply apart from these particular provisions, or should the legislations of two or more Member States apply in this way, he shall be subject to the legislation decided on by common agreement amongst the Member States concerned or their competent authorities.

Article 14b omitted

Article 14c

Special rules applicable to persons who are simultaneously employed in the territory of one Member State and self-employed in the territory of another Member State

A person who is simultaneously employed in the territory of one Member State and self-employed in the territory of another Member State shall be subject:
 (a) save as otherwise provided in subparagraph (b) to the legislation of the Member State in the territory of which he is engaged in paid employment or, where he pursues such an activity in the territory of two or more Member States, to the legislation determined in accordance with Article 14 (2) or (3);
 (b) in the cases mentioned in Annex VII:
  — to the legislation of the Member State in the territory of which he is engaged in paid employment, that legislation having been determined in accordance with the provisions of Article 14 (2) or (3), where he pursues such an activity in the territory of two or more Member States,

and
  — to the legislation of the Member State in the territory of which he is self-employed, that legislation having been determined in accordance with article 14a (2), (3) or (4), where he pursues such an activity in the territory of two or more Member States.

Article 14d (5)

Miscellaneous provisions

2.68
1. [¹The person referred to in Article 14(2) and (3), Article 14a(2), (3) and (4), Article 14c(a) and Article 14e shall be treated, for the purposes of application of the legislation laid down in accordance with these provisions, as if he pursued all his professional activity or activities in the territory of the Member State concerned.]

2. The person referred to in Article 14c (b) shall be treated, for the purposes of determining the rates of contributions to be charged to self-employed workers under the legislation of the Member State in whose territory he is self-employed, as if he pursued his paid employment in the territory of the Member State concerned.

3. The provisions of the legislation of a Member State under which a pensioner who is pursuing a professional or trade activity is not subject to compulsory insurance in respect of such activity shall also apply to a pensioner whose pension was acquired under the legislation of another Member State, unless the person concerned expressly asks to be so subject by applying to the institution designated by the competent authority of the first Member State and named in Annex 10 to the Regulation referred to in Article 98.

AMENDMENTS

1. Regulation 1606/98, [1998] O.J. L209/1 (October 25, 1998)

2.69 *Articles 14e–16 omitted*

Article 17

Exceptions to Articles 13 to 16

2.70
Two or more Member States, the competent authorities of these States or the bodies designated by these authorities may by common agreement provide for exceptions to the provisions of Articles 13 to 16 in the interest of certain categories of persons or of certain persons.

GENERAL NOTE

2.71
This provision was used in Case 101/83 *Brusse* [1984] E.C.R. 2223 to "rescue" a claimant from a long gap in his contribution record in the United Kingdom. The terms of the agreement covered a period before the United Kingdom was a Member State of the European Community but was expressly made under Article 17 in relation to the period from January 1, 1973 (when the United Kingdom acceded). The Court of Justice ruled that agreements under Article 17 could be retrospective; the test was whether the agreement was in the interests of the worker concerned. This approach was confirmed in Case C-454/93 *van Gestel* [1995] E.C.R. I-1707. The scope of agreements under Article 17 is accordingly very wide.

(Article 17a)

Article 17a

Special rules concerning recipients of pensions due under the legislation of one or more Member State

The recipient of a pension due under the legislation of a Member State or of pensions due under the legislation of several Member States who resides in the territory of another Member State may at his request be exempted from the legislation of the latter State provided that he is not subject to that legislation because of the pursuit of an occupation.

2.72

TITLE III

SPECIAL PROVISIONS RELATING TO THE VARIOUS CATEGORIES OF BENEFITS

CHAPTER 1

SICKNESS AND MATERNITY

SECTION 1

COMMON PROVISIONS

Article 18

Aggregation of periods of insurance, employment or residence

1. The competent institution of a Member State whose legislation makes the acquisition, retention or recovery of the right to benefits conditional upon the completion of periods of insurance, employment or residence shall, to the extent necessary, take account of periods of insurance, employment or residence completed under the legislation of any other Member State as if they were periods completed under the legislation which it administers.

2. The provisions of paragraph 1 shall apply to seasonal workers, even in respect of periods prior to any break in insurance exceeding the period allowed by the legislation of the competent State, provided, however, that the person concerned has not ceased to be insured for a period exceeding four months.

2.73

SECTION 2

EMPLOYED OR SELF-EMPLOYED PERSONS AND MEMBERS OF THEIR FAMILIES

Article 19

Residence in a Member State other than the competent State—General rules

1. An employed or self-employed person residing in the territory of a

2.74

Member State other than the competent State, who satisfies the conditions of the legislation of the competent State for entitlement to benefits, taking account where appropriate of the provisions of Article 18, shall receive in the State in which he is resident:
  (a) benefits in kind provided on behalf of the competent institution by the institution of the place of residence in accordance with the provisions of the legislation administered by that institution as though he were insured with it;
  (b) cash benefits provided by the competent institution in accordance with the legislation which it administers. However, by agreement between the competent institution and the institution of the place of residence, such benefits may be provided by the latter institution on behalf of the former, in accordance with the legislation of the competent State.

2. The provisions of paragraph 1 shall apply by analogy to members of the family who reside in the territory of a Member State other than the competent State in so far as they are not entitled to such benefits under the legislation of the State in whose territory they reside.

Where the members of the family reside in the territory of a Member State under whose legislation the right to receive benefits in kind is not subject to condition of insurance or employment, benefits in kind which they receive shall be considered as being on behalf of the institution with which the employed or self-employed person is insured, unless the spouse or the person looking after the children pursues a professional or trade activity in the territory of the said Member State.

2.75   *Article 20 omitted.*

Article 21

Stay in or transfer of residence to the competent State

2.76   **1.** The employed or self-employed person referred to in Article 19 (1) who is staying in the territory of the competent State shall receive benefits in accordance with the provisions of the legislation of that State as though he were resident there, even if he has already received benefits for the same case of sickness or maternity before his stay.

2. Paragraph 1 shall apply by analogy to the members of the family referred to in Article 19 (2).

However, where the latter reside in the territory of a Member State other than the one in whose territory the employed or self-employed person resides, benefits in kind shall be provided by the institution of the place of stay on behalf of the institution of the place of residence of the persons concerned.

3. Paragraphs 1 and 2 shall not apply to frontier workers and the members of their families.

4. An employed or self-employed person and members of his family referred to in Article 19 who transfer their residence to the territory of the competent State shall receive benefits in accordance with the provi-

(Article 21)

sions of the legislation of that State even if they have already received benefits for the same case of sickness or maternity before transferring their residence.

Article 22

Stay outside the competent State—Return to or transfer of residence to another Member State during sickness or maternity—Need to go to another Member State in order to receive appropriate treatment

1. An employed or self-employed person who satisfies the conditions of the legislation of the competent State for entitlement to benefits, taking account where appropriate of the provisions of Article 18, and:
   (a) whose condition necessitates immediate benefits during a stay in the territory of another Member State;
or
   (b) who, having become entitled to benefits chargeable to the competent institution, is authorized by that institution to return to the territory of the Member State where he resides, or to transfer his residence to the territory of another Member State;
or
   (c) who is authorized by the competent institution to go to the territory of another Member State to receive there the treatment appropriate to his condition,
shall be entitled:
   (i) to benefits in kind provided on behalf of the competent institution by the institution of the place of stay or residence in accordance with the provisions of the legislation which it administers, as though he were insured with it; the length of the period during which benefits are provided shall be governed, however, by the legislation of the competent State;
   (ii) to cash benefits provided by the competent institution in accordance with the provisions of the legislation which it administers. However, by agreement between the competent institution and the institution of the place of stay or residence, such benefits may be provided by the latter institution on behalf of the former, in accordance with the provisions of the legislation of the competent State.

2. The authorization required under paragraph 1 (b) may be refused only if it is established that movement of the person concerned would be prejudicial to his state of health or the receipt of medical treatment.

The authorization required under paragraph 1 (c) may not be refused where the treatment in question is among the benefits provided for by the legislation of the Member State on whose territory the person concerned resided and where he cannot be given such treatment within the time normally necessary for obtaining the treatment in question in the

Member State of residence taking account of his current state of health and the probable course of the disease.

3. The provisions of paragraphs 1 and 2 shall apply by analogy to members of the family of an employed or self-employed person.

However, for the purpose of applying paragraph 1 (a) and (c) (i) to the members of the family referred to in Article 19 (2) who reside in the territory of a Member State other than the one in whose territory the employed or self-employed person resides:
(a) benefits in kind shall be provided on behalf of the institution of the Member State in whose territory the members of the family are residing by the institution of the place of stay in accordance with the provisions of the legislation which it administers as if the employed or self-employed person were insured there. The period during which benefits are provided shall, however, be that laid down under the legislation of the Member State in whose territory the members of the family are residing;
(b) the authorization required under paragraph 1 (c) shall be issued by the institution of the Member State in whose territory the members of the family are residing.

4. The fact that the provisions of paragraph 1 apply to an employed or self-employed person shall not affect the right to benefit of members of his family.

GENERAL NOTE

2.78   Article 22 seeks to strike a balance between the desirability of cross-border health care provision and control of budgets by paying States. A blanket provision permitting free choice of the place of treatment could bypass national rules on the availability of treatment and who should receive it at the public expense.

Where entitlement to benefits in kind (that is, treatment or medication and the like) is in issue, such benefits are to be awarded on behalf of the competent institution by the institution of the place of stay or residence (as defined in Article 1) in accordance with its own legislation, but the length of the period during which they are provided is governed by the legislation of the competent State.

Where cash benefits are in issue, they are to be awarded by the competent institution in the competent State in accordance with its own legislation, subject to any agreement for them to be paid in the State of stay or residence on behalf of the institution of the competent State.

This distinction is logical, wince benefits in kind are likely to be needed immediately in the territory in which the insured person or a member of his or her family is staying at the time. I would be inappropriate to require a social security institution to apply the legislation of another EEA country in such circumstances.

The application of the rules in the EC Treaty on the free movement of goods and services may require a rethink of the rules on certain benefits in kind. Two cases concerning the purchase of spectacles and the provision of orthodontic treatment established that social security rules are not insulated from the Treaty rules on the free movement of goods and services in the particular circumstances presented by these cases: C-120/95 *Decker*, [1998] E.C.R. I-1831 (spectacles) and C-158/96 *Kohll*, [1998] E.C.R. I-1831 (dental treatment).

2.79   *Articles 22a and 22b omitted.*

(Article 23)

Article 23

Calculation of cash benefits

1. The competent institution of a Member State whose legislation provides that the calculation of cash benefits shall be based on average earnings or on average contributions, shall determine such average earnings or contributions exclusively by reference to earnings or contributions completed under the said legislation.

2. The competent institution of a Member State whose legislation provides that the calculation of cash benefits shall be based on standard earnings, shall take account exclusively of the standard earnings or, where appropriate, of the average of standard earnings for the periods completed under the said legislation.

3. The competent institution of a Member State under whose legislation the amount of cash benefits varies with the number of members of the family, shall also take into account the members of the family of the person concerned who are resident in the territory of another Member State as if they were resident in the territory of the competent State.

Article 24

Substantial benefits in kind

1. Where the right of an employed or self-employed person or a member of his family to a prosthesis, a major appliance or other substantial benefits in kind has been recognized by the institution of a Member State before he becomes insured with the institution of another Member State, the said employed of self-employed person shall receive such benefits at the expense of the first institution, even if they are granted after he becomes insured with the second institution.

2. The Administrative Commission shall draw up the list of benefits to which the provisions of paragraph 1 apply.

Articles 25–66a omitted

CHAPTER 6

UNEMPLOYMENT BENEFITS

SECTION 1

COMMON PROVISIONS

Article 67

Aggregation of periods of insurance or employment

1. The competent institution of a Member State whose legislation makes the acquisition, retention or recovery of the right to benefits subject to the completion of periods of insurance shall take into account,

to the extent necessary, periods of insurance or employment completed as an employed person under the legislation of any other Member State, as though they were periods of insurance completed under the legislation which it administers, provided, however, that the periods of employment would have been counted as periods of insurance had they been completed under that legislation.

2. The competent institution of a Member State whose legislation makes the acquisition, retention or recovery of the right to benefits subject to the completion of periods of employment shall take into account, to the extent necessary, periods of insurance or employment completed as an employed person under the legislation of any other Member State, as though they were periods of employment completed under the legislation which it administers.

3. Except in the cases referred to in Article 71 (1)(a)(ii) and (b)(ii), application of the provisions of paragraphs 1 and 2 shall be subject to the condition that the person concerned should have completed lastly:

— in the case of paragraph 1, periods of insurance,
— in the case of paragraph 2, periods of employment,

in accordance with the provisions of the legislation under which the benefits are claimed.

4. Where the length of the period during which benefits may be granted depends on the length of periods of insurance or employment, the provisions of paragraph 1 or 2 shall apply, as appropriate.

General Note

2.84   The provisions of Regulation 1408/71 dealing specifically with unemployment benefit demonstrate an overly cautious view by the Member States of the motives of unemployed persons moving between the Member States. Provision is made in Article 67 for periods of employment or insurance to be aggregated in order to determine entitlement to unemployment benefits. But there is a sting in the tail of the provision. Aggregation is only possible under the legislation of the country in which the person claiming "lastly" completed periods of insurance or employment. The result is, for example, that a British national living and working in Germany who becomes unemployed cannot return to the United Kingdom and claim jobseeker's allowance on the basis of contributions to the German scheme, because he or she will not have lastly completed a period of insurance in the United Kingdom unless they could bring themselves within the scope of Article 71: see below. This territorial limitation on aggregation seems unnecessarily restrictive, and has been the subject of criticism: See, for example, Wikeley, N., "Migrant Workers and Unemployment Benefit in the European Community" [1988] J.S.W.L. 300.

The severity of the rule is illustrated in Case C-62/91 *Gordon Sinclair Gray* v. *Adjudication Officer*, [1992] E.C.R. I-2737. Gray, a British national, had lived and worked in Spain running a restaurant from 1971 to 1990. He returned to the United Kingdom after selling the business without having registered as unemployed in Spain. He claimed unemployment benefit in the United Kingdom, and appealed the refusal to award him the benefit to the Bognor Regis social security appeal tribunal. It was argued by the adjudication officer that there was no entitlement in the United Kingdom because the claimant was last insured in Spain. Furthermore since he had not registered as unemployed in Spain, no question could arise as to any entitlement under Article 69. The tribunal also concluded that the

(Article 67)

claimant had been habitually resident in Spain and so could not take the benefit of the rules in Article 71. The lay members of the tribunal (the lawyer chairman of the tribunal considered that the provisions were consistent with the Treaty rules) clearly saw an injustice and felt that certain provisions of Articles 67 and 69 militated against the Treaty rules on free movement of persons. They clearly insisted (as they were entitled to) that a reference be made concerning the validity of the provisions in question. The Court, however, concluded that there was no factor of such a kind as to affect the validity of the provisions in issue. Both conferred on workers rights which they would not otherwise enjoy.

Article 68
Calculation of benefits

1. The competent institution of a Member State whose legislation provides that the calculation of benefits should be based on the amount of the previous wage or salary shall take into account exclusively the wage or salary received by the person concerned in respect of his last employment in the territory of that State.

However, if the person concerned had been in his last employment in that territory for less than four weeks, the benefits shall be calculated on the basis of the normal wage or salary corresponding, in the place where the unemployed person is residing or staying, to an equivalent or similar employment to his last employment in the territory of another Member State.

2. The competent institution of a Member State whose legislation provides that the amount of benefits varies with the number of members of the family, shall take into account also members of the family of the person concerned who are residing in the territory of another Member State, as though they were residing in the territory of the competent State. This provision shall not apply if, in the country of residence of the members of the family, another person is entitled to unemployment benefits for the calculation of which the members of the family are taken into consideration.

2.85

GENERAL NOTE

Article 68(1) provides that where unemployment benefit is linked to a previous wage or salary, the salary or wages to be taken into account are those in respect of the last employment in that State: Case 67/79 *Waldemar Fellinger v. Bundesanstalt für Arbeit, Nuremberg*, [1980] E.C.R. 535. However, where the amount of benefit varies with the number of members of the family, members of the family residing in another EEA country are to be treated as residing in the competent State.

2.86

SECTION 2

UNEMPLOYED PERSONS GOING TO A MEMBER STATE OTHER THAN THE COMPETENT STATE

Article 69

Conditions and limits for the retention of the right to benefits

1. An employed or self-employed person who is wholly unemployed

2.87

and who satisfies the conditions of the legislation of a Member State for entitlement to benefits and who goes to one or more other Member States in order to seek employment there shall retain his entitlement to such benefits under the following conditions and within the following limits:

(a) Before his departure, he must have been registered as a person seeking work and have remained available to the employment services of the competent State for at least four weeks after becoming unemployed, However, the competent services or institutions may authorise his departure before such time has expired.

(b) He must register as a person seeking work with the employment services of each of the Member States to which he goes and be subject to the control procedure organised therein. This condition shall be considered satisfied for the period before registration if the person concerned registered within seven days of the date when he ceased to be available to the employment services of the State he left. In exceptional cases, this period may be extended by the competent services or institutions.

(c) Entitlement to benefits shall continue for a maximum period of three months from the date when the person concerned ceased to be available to the employment services of the State which he left, provided that the total duration of the benefits does not exceed the duration of the period of benefits he was entitled to under the legislation of that State. In the case of a seasonal worker such duration shall, moreover, be limited to the period remaining until the end of the season for which he was engaged.

2. If the person concerned returns to the competent State before the expiry of the period during which he is entitled to benefits under the provisions of paragraph 1 (c), he shall continue to be entitled to benefits under the legislation of that State; he shall lose all entitlement to benefits under the legislation of the competent State if he does not return there before the expiry of that period. In exceptional cases, this time limit may be extended by the competent services or institutions.

3. The provisions of paragraph 1 may be invoked only once between two periods of employment.

4. Where the competent State is Belgium, an unemployed person who returns there after the expiry of the three month period laid down in paragraph 1 (c), shall not requalify for benefits in that country until he has been employed there for at least three months.

GENERAL NOTE

2.88   Article 69 provides a limited right to export unemployment benefit for up to three months where the person goes to another EEA country for the purpose of seeking work. Strict conditions surround the right to export the benefit, and failure to return to the competent State within the three month period normally results in the loss of all entitlement to benefits under the legislation of the competent State. The right to export unemployment benefit can only be exercised once in any period of unemployment. Under Article 70 benefits are paid by the unemployment benefit institution in the place to which the person goes but are to be reimbursed by the competent State.

(Article 69)

Because of the limitation on aggregation, the rules in Article 71 take on extra significance and have been the subject of many references to the Court of Justice. They provide exceptions to the rule that the competent State is that in which the claimant lastly worked, and permit claims in the EEA country in which persons are habitually resident where that country is different from that in which they worked. There are separate rules for frontier workers and others.

In Joined Cases 41, 121 and 796/79 *Vittorio Testa, Salvino Maggio and Carmine Vitale v. Bundesanstalt für Arbeit*, [1980] E.C.R. 1979, the validity of Article 69(2) of Regulation 1408/71 was questioned in circumstances where each of three Italian nationals lost the residual entitlement to unemployment benefit in Germany when they did not return within three months to Germany from an authorised stay in Italy in order to look for work there. In two of the cases, the later return was explained by an intervening illness. The Court had little difficulty in concluding that there was nothing to impugn the validity of the provisions of Article 69(2) which provided that all entitlement to unemployment benefit would cease if the beneficiary did not return to the competent State before the expiry of the authorised period of absence. There was, according to the Court, a clear advantage to the person in that they were, during their period of absence abroad, exempt from the controls applicable in the competent State (even though they would be subject to the controls in the country to which they went).

The only glimmer of hope related to the Court's advice on how the discretion to extend the period in exceptional cases should be applied: see also Case 139/78 *Giovanni Coccioli v. Bundesanstalt für Arbeit*, [1979] E.C.R. 991. Firstly, retrospective applications for extensions of the period are admissible. Secondly, the competent institution in exercising its discretion must take account of the principle of proportionality in Community law. In each case, the institution must consider the extent to which the three month period has been exceeded, the reasons for the delay in returning, and the seriousness of the legal consequences arising from the delay. This would, presumably, include consideration of the residual amount of benefit which might be forfeit if all entitlement were to cease.

The Commission's Proposal for a Council Regulation amending, for the benefit of unemployed workers, Regulation 1408/71 on the application of social security schemes to employed persons and their families moving within the Community, 18 June 1980, [1980] O.J. C169/22, contained amendments which would not deprive workers of entitlement to any residual period of entitlement in the territory of the Member State they left. The proposals have not been implemented.

Article 70

Provision of benefits and reimbursements

1. In the cases referred to in Article 69 (1), benefits shall be provided by the institution of each of the States to which an unemployed person goes to seek employment.

The competent institution of the Member State to whose legislation an employed or self-employed person was subject at the time of his last employment shall he obliged to reimburse the amount of such benefits.

2. The reimbursements referred to in paragraph 1 shall be determined and made in accordance with the procedure laid down by the imple-

2.89

menting Regulation referred to in Article 98, on proof of actual expenditure, or by lump sum payments.

3. Two or more Member States, or the competent authorities of those States, may provide for other methods of reimbursement or payment, or may waive all reimbursement between the institutions coming under their jurisdiction.

SECTION 3

UNEMPLOYED PERSONS WHO, DURING THEIR LAST EMPLOYMENT, WERE RESIDING IN A MEMBER STATE OTHER THAN THE COMPETENT STATE

Article 71

2.90 **1.** An unemployed person who was formerly employed and who, during his last employment, was residing in the territory of a Member State other than the competent State shall receive benefits in accordance with the following provisions:

(a)(i) A frontier worker who is partially or intermittently unemployed in the undertaking which employs him, shall receive benefits in accordance with the provisions of the legislation of the competent State as if he were residing in the territory of that State; these benefits shall be provided by the competent institution.

(ii) A frontier worker who is wholly unemployed shall receive benefits in accordance with the provisions of the legislation of the Member State in whose territory he resides as though he had been subject to that legislation while last employed; these benefits shall be provided by the institution of the place of residence at its own expense.

(b)(i) An employed person, other than a frontier worker, who is partially, intermittently or wholly unemployed and who remains available to his employer or to the employment services in the territory of the competent State shall receive benefits in accordance with the provisions of the legislation of that State as though he were residing in its territory; these benefits shall be provided by the competent institution.

(ii) An employed person, other than a frontier worker, who is wholly unemployed and who makes himself available for work to the employment services in the territory of the Member State in which he resides, or who returns to that territory, shall receive benefits in accordance with the legislation of that State as if he had last been employed there; the institution of the place of residence shall provide such benefits at its own expense. However, if such an employed person has become entitled to benefits at the expense of the competent institution of the Member State to whose legislation he was last subject, he shall receive benefits

(Article 71)

under the provisions of Article 69. Receipt of benefits under the legislation of the State in which he resides shall be suspended for any period during which the unemployed person may, under the provisions of Article 69, make a claim for benefits under the legislation to which he was last subject.

2. An unemployed person may not claim benefits under the legislation of the Member State in whose territory he resides while he is entitled to benefits under the provisions of paragraph 1 (a) (i) or (b) (i).

GENERAL NOTE

Some of the rigours of the limited aggregation and exportability rules is moderated by the provisions of Article 71, which concern situations in which the claimant was residing, during their last period of work, in a country other than the competent State. Since the provisions of Article 71 are exceptions to the rules in Articles 67 and 69, the Court of Justice has said that they must be strictly interpreted: Case 73/76 *Silvani di Paolo* v. *Office de l'Emploi*, [1977] E.C.R. 315, paras 12 and 13 of the judgment.

The rules in Article 71(1)(a) concern frontier workers, who are defined by Article 1(b) as persons who work in one Member State and reside in a different Member State to which they return "as a rule daily or at least once a week." Note that there is specific provision made in Article 1(b) for posted frontier workers enabling them to retain the status of frontier worker for four months even where the posting prevents them from returning home at least once a week.

Under Article 71(1)(a)(i), frontier workers who are "partially or intermittently unemployed" receive unemployment benefits in accordance with the legislation of the competent State as though they were residing there. Under Article 71(1)(a)(ii), frontier workers who are "wholly unemployed" receive unemployment benefits in accordance with the legislation of the country in which they reside as though they had been subject to that legislation while working.

Article 71(1)(b) deals with workers other than frontier workers, and is rather more complex, since it permits a wholly unemployed worker to choose whether unemployment benefits are paid in the country of last employment or in the country of residence. Article 71(1)(b)(i) provides that workers who are "partially, intermittently or wholly unemployed" and who remain available for work in the territory of the competent State receive unemployment benefits in accordance with the provisions of the legislation of the competent State as though they resided there. Article 71(1)(b)(ii) provides that wholly unemployed workers may make themselves available to the employment office in the country of residence and receive unemployment benefits there as though they had been last employed there.

The references to residence in Article 71 refer to the concept of "habitual residence" which has a specific meaning in Community law. Workers, other than frontier workers, will only be able to take advantage of the more favourable rules on entitlement to unemployment benefit if they can show that they were habitually resident in a country other than that in which they worked. For a decision of a Social Security Commissioner holding that a determination by the Inland Revenue that a person is "ordinarily resident" in the United Kingdom for tax purposes "has no relevant whatsoever" in assessing whether a person is habitually resident here, see *R(U)4/86*. It may be putting it too strongly to say that it has no relevance whatsoever, but it is clearly not determinative of the question.

2.91

It is not difficult to imagine the complexity of the circumstances presented in many cases, where, for example, the employment is of comparatively short duration, or where a family is split with certain family members remaining in one country while others live with the worker in the place of work. For a useful survey of the case-law on Article 71(1)(b)(ii), see the Advocate General's Opinion in Case 388/87 *Bestuur van de Nieuwe Algemene Bedrijfsvereniging v. W.F.J.M. Warmerdam-Steggerda*, [1989] E.C.R. 1203. Article 71(2) contains anti-overlapping provisions precluding the payment of unemployment benefits in the country of residence alongside payment of benefits under the legislation of the country of last employment.

The Court in *Di Paolo* had indicated that the special rules in Article 71 were justified for certain categories of workers who retain close ties, in particular of a personal and vocational nature, with the country where they have settled and are habitually resident. There is in such cases the best possibility of finding new employment in that country. It is consistent with this principle to permit a person to change their habitual residence from the country of work to another country during the course of their employment.

In Case 236/87 *Anna Bergemann v. Bundesanstalt für Arbeit*, [1988] E.C.R. 5125 Anna Bergemann, a Dutch national living and working in the Netherlands, married and during a period of leave moved to Germany with her husband. She remained on leave from her employment until it ended and did not return to the Netherlands. The question arose as to whether Article 71(1)(b)(ii) applied to someone in her situation. Having regard to the justification set out above, the Court concluded that her move during a period of leave and the fact that she had not returned to work in the Netherlands did not preclude her being regarded as within the terms of the article.

Similarly, the Court had little difficulty in regarding a university employee who had undertaken a fixed term two year exchange with a university in another Member State and who returned home in the vacations as falling within the ambit of the provision: Case C-216/89 *Beate Reibold v. Bundesanstalt für Arbeit*, [1990] E.C.R. I-4163.

In such cases account should be taken of the duration and continuity of the residence of the persons concerned before they moved, of the length and purpose of their absence, of the nature of the work in the other EEA country, and of their intentions as ascertained from all the surrounding circumstances.

The circumstances presented in Case C-102/91 *Doris Knoch v. Bundesanstalt für Arbeit*, [1991] E.C.R. I-4341, were a little more complex. Doris Knoch was employed at the University of Bath as a language assistant for two years. At the end of her contract she claimed and was awarded unemployment benefit in England for the best part of July and August. She subsequently returned to Germany where she claimed unemployment benefit in December. The question arose as to whether she could claim in Germany after having claimed in England, and, if so, how the German authorities should deal with any unemployment benefit paid in England. The Court rules that, provided that Knoch was habitually resident in Germany during her employment in England, she was entitled to the benefit of the rules in Article 71. There was nothing in those rules which precluded a person first claiming under the legislation of the country where they were employed and subsequently in the country in which they were habitually resident. However, the benefits received would almost certainly overlap under the provisions of Article 12 of Regulation 1408/71. It followed that in determining entitlement under the legislation of the country of residence, a deduction should be made of the benefit received in respect of the days for which unemployment benefit had been paid in the country of employment. Entitlement to unemployment benefit would, of course, be suspended for any

(Article 71)

period in which such a person exported their unemployment benefit entitlement in accordance with the rules in Article 69.

Articles 71a omitted.

CHAPTER 7

FAMILY BENEFITS

Article 72

Aggregation of periods of insurance, employment or self-employment

Where the legislation of a Member State makes acquisition of the right to benefits conditional upon completion of periods of insurance, employment or self-employment, the competent institution of that State shall take into account for this purpose, to the extent necessary, periods of insurance, employment or self-employment completed in any other Member State, as if they were periods completed under the legislation which it administers.

Article 72a

Employed persons who have become fully unemployed

An employed person who has become fully unemployed and to whom Article 71 (1) (a) (ii) or (b) (ii), first sentence, apply shall, for the members of his family residing in the territory of the same Member State as he, receive family benefits in accordance with the legislation of the State, as if he had been subject to that legislation during his last employment, taking account, where appropriate, of the provisions of Article 72. These benefits shall be provided by, and at the expense of, the institution of the place of residence.

Where that institution applies legislation providing for deduction of contributions payable by unemployed persons to cover family benefits, it shall be authorized to make such deductions in accordance with the provisions of its legislation.

Article 73

Employed or self-employed persons the members of whose families reside in a Member State other than the competent State

An employed or self-employed person subject to the legislation of a Member State shall be entitled, in respect of the members of his family who are residing in another Member State, to the family benefits provided for by the legislation of the former State, as if they were residing in that State, subject to the provisions of Annex VI.

Article 74

Unemployed persons the members of whose families reside in a Member State other than the competent State

2.96 An unemployed person who was formerly employed or self-employed and who draws unemployment benefits under the legislation of a Member State shall be entitled, in respect of the members of his family residing in another Member State, to the family benefits provided for by the legislation of the former State, as if they were residing in that State, subject to the provisions of Annex VI.

Article 75

Provisions of benefits

2.97 1. Family benefits shall be provided, in the cases referred to in Article 73, by the competent institution of the State to the legislation of which the employed or self-employed person is subject and, in the cases referred to in Article 74, by the competent institution of the State under the legislation of which an unemployed person who was formerly employed or self-employed receives unemployment benefits. They shall be provided in accordance with the provisions administered by such institutions, whether or not the natural or legal person to whom such benefits are payable is residing or staying in the territory of the competent State or in that of another Member State.

2. However, if the family benefits are not used by the person to whom they should be provided for the maintenance of the members of the family, the competent institution shall discharge its legal obligations by providing the said benefits to the natural or legal person actually maintaining the members of the family, at the request of, and through the agency of, the institution of their place of residence or of the designated institution or body appointed for this purpose by the competent authority of the country of their residence.

3. Two or more Member States may agree, in accordance with the provisions of Article 8, that the competent institution shall provide the family benefits due under the legislation of those States or of one of those States to the natural or legal person actually maintaining the members of the family, either directly or through the agency of the institution of their place of residence.

(Article 76)

Article 76

Rules or priority in cases of overlapping entitlement to family benefits under the legislation of the competent State and under the legislation of the Member State of residence of the members of the family

1. Where, during the same period, for the same family member and by reason of carrying on an occupation, family benefits are provided for by the legislation of the Member State in whose territory the members of the family are residing, entitlement to the family benefits due in accordance with the legislation of another Member State, if appropriate under Article 73 or 74, shall be suspended up to the amount provided for in the legislation of the first Member State.

2. If an application for benefits is not made in the Member States in whose territory the members of the family are residing, the competent institution of the other Member State may apply the provisions of paragraph 1 as if benefits were granted in the first Member State.

2.98

[¹Article 76a

Students

The provisions of Article 72 shall apply by analogy to students.]

2.99

AMENDMENTS

1. Regulation 307/99, [1999] O.J. L307/99 (May 1, 1999)

Articles 77–85 omitted.

2.100

Article 86

Claims, declarations or appeals submitted to an authority, institution or tribunal of a Member State other than the competent State

1. Any claim, declaration or appeal which should have been submitted, in order to comply with the legislation of one Member State, within a specified period to an authority, institution or tribunal of that State shall be admissible if it is submitted within the same period to a corresponding authority, institution or tribunal of another Member State. In such a case the authority, institution, or tribunal receiving the claim, declaration or appeal shall forward it without delay to the competent authority, institution or tribunal of the former State either directly or through the competent authorities of the Member State concerned. The date on which such claims, declarations or appeals were submitted to the authority, institution or tribunal of the Second State shall be considered as the date of their submission to the competent authority, institution or tribunal.

2.101

Council Regulations (EEC) No. 1408/71

2. Where a person entitled to do so under the legislation of a Member State has submitted to that State a claim for family benefits even though that State is not competent by priority right, the date on which that first application was made shall be considered as the date on which it was submitted to the competent authority, institution or tribunal, provided that a new application is submitted in the Member State which is competent by priority right by a person entitled to do so under the legislation of that State. The second application must be submitted within a period of one year after notification of the rejection of the first application or the cessation of payment of benefits in the first Member State.

Article 87

Medical examinations

2.102 1. Medical examinations provided for by the legislation of one Member State may be carried out at the request of the competent institution, in the territory of another Member State, by the institution of the place of stay or residence of the person entitled to benefits, under conditions laid down in the implementing Regulation referred to in Article 98 or, failing these, under conditions agreed upon between the competent authorities of the Member States concerned.

2. Medical examinations carried out under the conditions laid down in paragraph I shall be considered as having been carried out in the territory of the competent State.

2.103 *Articles 88–98 omitted*

2.104 *Annexes I-II omitted*

Annex IIa

Special Non-Contributory Benefits

2.105 *(Article 10a of the Regulation)*

...

O. UNITED KINGDOM
    (a) ...
    (b) Invalid care allowance (Social Security Act 1975 of March 20 1975, Section 37, and Social Security (Northern Ireland) Act 1975 of March 20 1975, Section 37).
    (c) Family credit (Social Security Act 1986, of July 25 1986, Sections 20 to 22, and Social Security (Northern Ireland) Order 1986 of November 5 1986, Articles 21 to 23).

(Annex IIA)

(d) Attendance allowance (Social Security Act 1975 of March 20 1975, Section 35, and Social Security (Northern Ireland) Act 1975 of March 20 1975, Section 35).
(e) Income support (Social Security Act 1986 of July 25 1986, Section 20 to 22 and Section 23, Social Security (Northern Ireland) Order 1986 of November 5 1986, Articles 21 to 24).
(f) Disability living allowance (Disability Living Allowance and Disability Working Allowance Act 1991 of June 27 1991, Section 1 and Disability Living Allowance and Disability Working Allowance (Northern Ireland) Order 1991 of July 24 1991, Article 3).
(g) Disability working allowance (Disability Living Allowance and Disability Working Allowance Act 1991 of June 27 1991, Section 6, and Disability Living Allowance and Disability Working Allowance (Northern Ireland) Order 1991 of July 24 1991, Article 8).
(h) Income-based allowances for jobseekers (Jobseekers Act 1995, 28 June 1995, Sections I (2) (d) (ii) and 3, and Jobseekers (Northern Ireland) Order 1995, 18 October 1995, Articles 3 (2) (d) (ii) and 5).

Annexes III-VIII omitted.

Council Regulation (EEC) No 574/72 of March 21 1972 laying down the procedure for implementing Regulation (EEC) No 1408/71 on the application of social security schemes to employed persons, to self employed persons, to self-employed persons and to their families moving within the Community

[1994] O.J. L244/72

CONTENTS

TITLE I: GENERAL PROVISIONS (ARTICLES 1 TO 4).

TITLE II: IMPLEMENTATION OF THE GENERAL PROVISIONS OF THE REGULATION (ARTICLES 5 TO 10A)

TITLE III: IMPLEMENTATION OF THE PROVISIONS OF THE REGULATION FOR DETERMINING THE LEGISLATION APPLICABLE (ARTICLES 10B TO 14).

TITLE IV: IMPLEMENTATION OF THE SPECIAL PROVISIONS OF THE REGULATION RELATING TO THE VARIOUS CATEGORIES OF BENEFITS

Chapter 1: General rules for the aggregation of periods (Article 15)
Chapter 2: Sickness and maternity (Articles 16 to 34)
Chapter 3: Invalidity, old-age and death (pensions) (Articles 35 to 59)
Chapter 4: Accidents at work and occupational diseases (Articles 60 to 77)
Chapter 5: Death grants (Articles 78, 79)
Chapter 6: Unemployment benefits (Articles 80 to 84)

Chapter 7: Family benefits (Articles 85 to 88)
Chapter 8: Benefits for dependent children of pensioners and for orphans (Articles 90 to 92)

TITLE V: FINANCIAL PROVISIONS (ARTICLES 93 TO 107)

TITLE VI: MISCELLANEOUS PROVISIONS (ARTICLES 108 TO 117)

TITLE VII: TRANSITIONAL AND FINAL PROVISIONS (ARTICLES 118 TO 122)
ANNEXES
Annex 1: Competent authorities
Annex 2: Competent institutions
Annex 3: Institutions of the place of residence and institutions of the place of stay
Annex 4: Liaison bodies
Annex 5: Implementing provisions of bilateral conventions which remain in force
Annex 6: Procedure for the payment of benefits
Annex 7: Banks
Annex 8: Grant of family benefits
Annex 9: Calculation of the average annual cost of benefits in kind
Annex 10: Institutions and bodies designated by the competent authorities
Annex 11: Schemes referred to in Articles 35 (2) of the Regulation
Appendix: Article 95

2.108 *Articles 1–6 omitted*

IMPLEMENTATION OF ARTICLE 12 OF THE REGULATION

Article 7

General rules on the application of the provisions designed to prevent overlapping

2.109   **1.** Where the benefits due under the legislation of two or more Member States are conditional upon mutual reductions, suspensions or withdrawals, the amounts which would not be paid in strict application of the provisions concerning reduction, suspension or withdrawal provided for by the legislation of the Member States concerned shall be divided by the number of benefits subject to reduction, suspension or withdrawal.

    2. In order to implement Article 12 (2), (3) and (4), Article 46a, Article 46b and Article 46c of the Regulation, the competent institutions concerned shall provide each other, at their own request, with all appropriate information.

(Article 8)

Article 8

Rules applicable in the case of overlapping of rights to sickness or maternity benefits under the legislation of several Member States

1. If an employed or self-employed person or a member of his family is entitled to claim maternity benefits under the legislations of two or more Member States, those benefits shall be granted exclusively under the legislation of the Member State in whose territory the confinement took place or, if the confinement did not take place in the territory of one of these Member States, exclusively under the legislation of the Member State to which the employed or self-employed person was last subject.

2. If an employed or self-employed person is entitled to claim sickness benefits under the legislation of Ireland and the United Kingdom for the same period of incapacity for work, those benefits shall be granted exclusively under the legislation of the Member State to which the person concerned was last subject.

3. [1 In the cases referred to in Article 14c(b) and 14f of the Regulation, where the person in question or a member of his family is entitled to claim benefits in kind in respect of sickness or maternity under the two legislations in question, the following rules shall be applicable:]

   (a) Where at least one of those legislations stipulates that the benefits shall be awarded in the form of a reimbursement to the person entitled to benefit, this shall be the exclusive responsibility of the institution of the Member State in whose territory they have been awarded.

   (b) If the benefits have been awarded in the territory of a Member State other than the two Member States in question, they shall be the exclusive responsibility of the institution of the Member State to whose legislation the person in question is subject by virtue of his paid employment.

AMENDMENT

1. Regulation 1606/98, [1998] O.J. L209/1 (October 25, 1998)

Article 8a

Rules applicable in the case of overlapping of rights to sickness benefits, benefits with respect to accidents at work or occupational disease under Greek legislation and the legislation of one or more other Member States

If during the same period an employed or self-employed person or member of his family is entitled to claim sickness benefits, benefits with respect to accidents at work or occupational disease under Greek legislation and under the legislation of one or more Member States, these benefits shall be granted exclusively under the legislation to which the person concerned was last subject.

Council Regulations (EEC) No. 574/72

2.112   Article 9 omitted

Article 9a

Rules applicable in the case of overlapping of rights to unemployment benefits

2.113   If an employed or self-employed person, entitled to unemployment benefits under the legislation of a Member State to which he was subject during his last employment or self-employment pursuant to Article 69 of the Regulation, goes to Greece where he is also entitled to unemployment benefits by virtue of a period of insurance, employment or self-employment previously completed under Greek legislation, the right to benefits under Greek legislation shall be suspended for the period laid down in Article 69(1)(c) of the Regulation.

Article 10

Rules applicable in the case of overlapping of rights to family benefits or family allowances for employed or self-employed persons

2.114   1.(a) Entitlement to benefits or family allowances due under the legislation of a Member State, according to which acquisition of the right to those benefits or allowances is not subject to conditions of insurance, employment or self-employment, shall be suspended when, during the same period and for the same member of the family, benefits are due only in pursuance of the national legislation of another Member State or in application of Articles 73, 74, 77 or 78 of the Regulation, up to the sum of those benefits.
   (b) However, where a professional or trade activity is carried out in the territory of the first member State:
      (i) in the case of benefits due either only under national legislation of another Member State or under Articles 73 or 74 of the Regulation to the person entitled to family benefits or to the person to whom they are to be paid, the right to family benefits due either only under national legislation of that other Member State or under theses Articles shall be suspended up to the sum of family benefits provided for by the legislation of the Member State in whose territory the member of the family is residing. The cost of the benefits paid by the Member State in whose territory the member of the family is residing shall be borne by that Member State;
      (ii) in the case of benefits due either only under national legislation of another Member State or under articles 77 or 78 of the Regulation, to the person entitled to these benefits or to the person to whom they are payable, the right to these family benefits or family allowances due either only under

(Article 10)

the national legislation of that other Member State or in application of those Articles shall be suspended; where this is the case, the person concerned shall be entitled to the family benefits or family allowances of the Member State in whose territory the children reside, the cost to be borne by that Member State, and, where appropriate, to benefits other than the family allowances referred to in Article 77 or Article 78 of the Regulation, the cost to be borne by the competent State as defined by those Articles.

2. If an employed person subject to the legislation of a Member State is entitled to family allowances by virtue of periods of insurance or employment previously completed under Greek legislation, this right shall be suspended where, during the same period and for the same member of the family, family benefits or allowance are due under the legislation of the first Member State pursuant to Articles 73 and 74 of the Regulation, up to the sum of those benefits.

3. Where family benefits are due, over the same period and for the same member of the family, from two Member States pursuant to Articles 73 and/or 74 of the Regulation, the competent institution of the Member State with legislation providing for the highest levels of benefit shall pay the full amount of such benefit and be reimbursed half this sum by the competent institution of the other Member State up to the limit of the amount provided for in the legislation of the latter Member State.

Article 10a

Rules applicable where an employed or self-employed person is subject successively to the legislation of several Member States during the same period or part of a period

Where an employed or self-employed person has been subject successively to the legislation of two Member States during the period separating two dates for the payment of family benefits as provided for by the legislation of one or both of the Member States concerned, the following rules shall apply:
(a) The family benefits which the person concerned may claim by virtue of being subject to the legislation of each one of these States shall correspond to the number of daily benefits due under the relevant legislation. Where such legislation does not provide for daily benefits, the family benefits shall be granted in proportion to the length of time during which the person concerned has been subject to the legislation of each one of the Member States in relation to the period fixed by the legislation concerned.
(b) Where the family benefits have been provided by an institution during a period when they should have been provided by another institution, there shall be an adjustment of accounts between the said institutions.
(c) For the purposes of subparagraphs (a) and (b), where periods of

employment or self-employment completed under the legislation of one Member State are expressed in units different from those which are used for the calculation of family benefits under the legislation of another Member State to which the person concerned has also been subject during the same period, the conversion shall be carried out in accordance with the provisions of Article 15 (3) of the implementing Regulation.

(d) Notwithstanding the provisions of subparagraph (a) in respect of dealings between the Member States listed in Annex 8 to the implementing regulation, the institution bearing the costs of the family benefits by reason of the first employment or self-employment during the period concerned shall bear such costs throughout the entire current period.

2.116 ARTICLES 10B–122 OMITTED
2.117 ANNEXES I–II AND APPENDIX OMITTED.

Council Directive 79/7/EEC of December 19 1978 on the progressive implementation of the principle of equal treatment for men and women in matters of social security

[1979] O.J. L6/24

THE COUNCIL OF THE EUROPEAN COMMUNITIES,

2.118 *Having regard* to the Treaty establishing the European Economic Community, and in particular Article 235 thereof,

Having regard to the proposal from the Commission,[1]

Having regard to the opinion of the European Parliament,[2]

Having regard to the opinion of the Economic and Social Committee,[3] whereas Article 1 (2) of Council Directive 76/207 of February 9 1976 on the implementation of the principle of equal treatment for men and women as regards access to employment, vocational training and promotion, and working conditions[4] provides that, with a view to ensuring the progressive implementation of the principle of equal treatment in matters of social security, the Council, acting on a proposal from the Commission, will adopt provisions defining its substance its scope and the arrangements for its application;

whereas the Treaty does not confer the specific powers required for this purpose;

whereas the principle of equal treatment in matters of social security should be implemented in the first place in the statutory schemes which

(Article 1)

provide protection against the risks of sickness, invalidity, old age, accidents at work, occupational diseases and unemployment, and in social assistance in so far as it is intended to supplement or replace the above-mentioned schemes;

whereas the implementation of the principle of equal treatment in matters of social security does not prejudice the provisions relating to the protection of women on the ground of maternity;

whereas, in this respect, Member States may adopt specific provisions for women to remove existing instances of unequal treatment,

HAS ADOPTED THIS DIRECTIVE:

FOOTNOTES

1. [1977] O.J. C34/3
2. [1977] O.J. C299/13
3. [1977] O.J. C180/36
4. [1976] O.J. L39/40

GENERAL NOTE

The Community institutions recognised that moves to secure the principle of equal treatment for men and women would be incomplete without the inclusion of provisions dealing with social security. Directive 79/7 was made under Article 235 EC, and was part of the programme of legislation flowing from the commitment to equal pay for equal work to be found in Article 141 (ex 119) EC, rather than part of the programme for securing the free movement of workers.

Unfortunately a number of concepts in the directive have been interpreted slightly differently from what might be regarded as corresponding provisions of Regulation 1408/71. Furthermore, the coverage of Directive 79/7 is not the same as that of Regulation 1408/71 in terms of the benefits covered.

The Directive was required to be implemented in all the Member States from and including December 23, 1984.

Article 1

2.119 The purpose of this Directive is the progressive implementation, in the field of social security and other elements of social protection provided for in Article 3, of the principle of equal treatment for men and women in matters of social security, hereinafter referred to as "the principle of equal treatment".

Article 2

2.120 This Directive shall apply to the working population—including self-employed persons, workers and self-employed persons whose activity is interrupted by illness, accident or involuntary unemployment and persons seeking employment – and to retired or invalided workers and self-employed persons.

GENERAL NOTE

2.121   Those within the personal scope of this Directive are not the same as those who are within the personal scope of Regulation 1408/71. The Directive applies to the "working population". There is a link with employment (which includes self-employment) related social security benefits in the Directive which makes it more limited than the concept of insured persons under Regulation 1408/71.

The Court of Justice has given a very wide meaning to the term "working population", holding that it covers any worker, including those who are seeking work: Case C-280/94 *Van Damme*, [1996] E.C.R. I-179. It extends to include someone who gives up work to care for a sick relative: Case 150/85 *Drake v. Chief Adjudication Officer*, [1986] E.C.R. 1995. But it does not include those who have never worked in a paid capacity: Joined Cases 48/88, 106/88 and 107/88 *Achterberg te Riele*, [1989] E.C.R. 1963. Nor does it cover someone who gives up work to look after healthy children, since this is not one of the risks covered in Article 3: Case C-31/90 *Johnson v. Chief Adjudication Officer (Johnson I)*, [1991] E.C.R. 3723.

In *CG/5425/1995* the Commissioner held that the Directive did not apply to a woman who had last worked in 1949, and who claimed invalid care allowance to look after her mother in 1989. It is clear that there must be a causal link between giving up work and the incidence of one of the risks covered by Article 3.

In *CJSA/4840/1998* the Commissioner held that income-based Jobseeker's Allowance is not within the scope of Directive 79/7.

Article 3

2.122   1. This Directive shall apply to:
(a) statutory schemes which provide protection against the following risks:
— sickness,
— invalidity,
— old age,
— accidents at work and occupational diseases,
— unemployment;
(b) social assistance, in so far as it is intended to supplement or replace the schemes referred to in (a).

2. This Directive shall not apply to the provisions concerning survivors' benefits nor to those concerning family benefits, except in the case of family benefits granted by way of increases of benefits due in respect of the risks referred to in paragraph 1(a).

3. With a view to ensuring implementation of the principle of equal treatment in occupational schemes, the Council, acting on a proposal from the Commission, will adopt provisions defining its substance, its scope and the arrangements for its application.

(Article 3)

GENERAL NOTE

In Case 150/85 *Drake v. Chief Adjudication Officer*, [1986] E.C.R. 1995, the Court of Justice said that:

2.123

"Article 3(1) must be interpreted as including any benefit which in a broad sense forms part of one of the statutory schemes referred to or a social assistance provision intended to supplement or replace such a scheme." (para. 21)

In case C-243/90 *R. v. Secretary of State for Social Security, ex p. Smithson*, [1992] E.C.R. I-467, the Court explained,

"In order to fall within the scope of the Directive, the benefit must be directly and effectively linked to the protection against one of the risks specified in Article 3(1)." (para.14)

R(A)2/94 holds that attendance allowance is an "invalidity benefit" within the meaning of Article 10 of Regulation 1408/71. It follows that it also falls within the scope of this directive, as will disability living allowance. The position is not changed by the categorisation of those benefits as special non-contributory benefits which are not exportable under Regulation 1408/71.

The Court of Justice has ruled that income support constitutes social assistance: Joined Cases C-63/91 and C-64/91 *Jackson and Cresswell v. Chief Adjudication Officer*, [1992] E.C.R. I-4737 (printed as appendix to *R(IS)10/91*). But discriminatory treatment may fall foul of Council Directive 76/207 on the implementation of the principle of equal treatment for men and women as regards access to employment, vocational training and promotion and working conditions, [1976] O.J. L39/40. A similar view has been taken in relation to family credit (now working families' tax credit), see Case C-116/94 *Meyers v. Chief Adjudication Officer*, [1995] E.C.R. I-2131.

The classification of family credit (now working families' tax credit) remains somewhat problematic. It has been classified as a family benefit for the purposes of Regulation 1408/71: Case C-78/91 *Hughes v. Chief Adjudication Officer*, [1992] E.C.R. I-4839. However, it could arguably be regarded as providing protection against the risk of unemployment through its role in topping up low pay.

In Case C-137/94 *R. v. Secretary of State for Health, ex parte Richardson*, [1995] E.C.R. I-3407, the Court ruled that free prescription charges fell within the material scope of the directive; it did not matter that these were regarded as a health benefit in the United Kingdom. In Case C-382/98 *R. v. Secretary of State for Social security, ex parte Taylor*, Judgment of December 16, 1999, [1999] E.C.R. nyr, the Court ruled that winter fuel payments under the social fund were also within the material scope of the directive.

Article 4

1. The principle of equal treatment means that there shall be no discrimination whatsoever on ground of sex either directly, or indirectly by reference in particular to marital or family status, in particular as concerns:

2.124

— the scope of the schemes and the conditions of access thereto,
— the obligation to contribute and the calculation of contributions,
— the calculation of benefits including increases due in respect of a spouse and for dependants and the conditions governing the duration and retention of entitlement to benefits.

2. The principle of equal treatment shall be without prejudice to the provisions relating to the protection of women on the grounds of maternity.

GENERAL NOTE

2.125   The Court of Justice has ruled that Article 4 outlaws both direct and indirect forms of discrimination: Case 30/85 *Teuling*, [1987] E.C.R. 2497, and Case C-226/91 *Molenbroek*, [1992] E.C.R. I-5943.

The test to be applied was laid down in Case C-229/89 *Commission v. Belgium*, [1991] E.C.R. I-2205:

> "Article 4(1) of Directive 79/7 precludes less favourable treatment from being accorded to a social group when it is shown to be made up of a much greater number of person or one or other sex, unless the provision ins question is 'based on objectively justified factors unrelated to any discrimination on grounds of sex'." (para. 13)

Article 5

2.126   Member States shall take the measures necessary to ensure that any laws, regulations and administrative provisions contrary to the principle of equal treatment are abolished.

Article 6

2.127   Member States shall introduce into their national legal systems such measures as art necessary to enable all persons who consider themselves wronged by failure to apply the principle of equal treatment to pursue their claims by judicial process, possibly after recourse to other competent authorities.

GENERAL NOTE

2.128   In Case C-66/95 *R. v. Secretary of State for Social Security, ex parte Sutton*, [1997] E.C.R. I-2163, the Court of Justice ruled that Article 6 required a judicial process which would ensure that those who had been wronged by discrimination prohibited by the directive could get the benefit to which they were entitled, but went on to rule that "the payment of interest on arrears of benefits cannot be regarded as an essential component of the right as so defined." (para. 25). Contrast certain decisions under the European Convention on Human Rights which seem to assume that just satisfaction under the Convention will require the payment of interest: see annotations to Article 41 E.C.H.R.

Article 7

2.129   1. This Directive shall be without prejudice to the right of Member States to exclude from its scope:
    (a) the determination of personable age for the purposes of granting

(Article 7)

old-age and retirement pensions and the possible consequences thereof for other benefits;
(b) advantages in respect of old-age pension schemes granted to persons who have brought up children; the acquisition of benefit entitlements following periods of interruption of employment due to the bringing up of children;
(c) the granting of old-age or invalidity benefit entitlements by virtue of the derived entitlements of a wife;
(d) the granting of increases of long-term invalidity, old-age, accidents at work and occupational disease benefits for a dependent wife;
(e) the consequences of the exercise, before the adoption of this Directive, of a right of option not to acquire rights or incur obligations under a statutory scheme.

2. Member States shall periodically examine matters excluded under paragraph 1 in order to ascertain, in the light of social developments in the matter concerned, whether there is justification for maintaining the exclusions concerned.

GENERAL NOTE

Cases involving the directive frequently raise issues of the scope of the derogations to be found in this article. The Court of Justice always takes the view that exceptions should be strictly construed, whereas freedoms are to be liberally construed.

Article 7(1)(a)
In Case C-9/91 *R. v. Secretary of State for Social Security, ex parte Equal Opportunities Commission*, [1992] E.C.R. I-4297, the Court of Justice ruled that Article 7(1)(a) permitted a Member State which retained differential pensionable ages for men and women and in which pensions were funded from contributions to retain a system under which men continued to be contribute for five years longer than women in order to be entitled to the same basic pension and by requiring men who work until the age of 65 to pay contributions whereas a woman who chooses to work beyond the age of 60 is not required to continue to pay contributions. The difference in treatment must, however, be necessarily linked to the difference in the statutory pensionable age.

In Case C-328/91 *Thomas v. Secretary of State for Social Security*, [1993] E.C.R. I-1247, the Court of Justice was called upon to rule on the nature of non-contributory invalidity benefits having regard to whether the different entitlement of men and women were such as to have "possible consequences . . ." for the purposes of prescribing different pensionable ages within the meaning of Article 7(1)(a). The Court ruled that the situations envisaged by the words "possible consequences thereof for other benefits" were limited to the forms of discrimination which are necessarily and objectively linked to the difference in retirement age.

In Case C-92/94 *Secretary of State for Social security v. Graham and others*, [1995] E.R.C.R. I-2521, concerned entitlement to invalidity benefit and the differential requirements applied to men and women. Rose Graham was 58 when she ceased work after several years in self-employment. As a person within five years of pensionable age who was not entitled to the invalidity allowance component of invalidity benefit; when she reached the age of 60 her entitlement to an invalidity pension was limited to the amount of her retirement pension (a condition which does not apply to a man until the age of 65), and her retirement was taxable whereas invalidity pension was tax-free. The claimant argued that

2.130

the differential treatment was neither necessarily nor objectively linked to the difference in retirement age. The Court is somewhat unsatisfactory reasoning holds that the differential treatment is within the exception having regard to the coherence of the social security system. It is estimated that there were almost 40,000 look-alike cases affected by the decision. Where there are appeals on the grounds of links between invalidity benefit or unemployment benefit (by analogy), they seem certain to fail.

By contrast in Case C-137/94 *R. v. Secretary of State for Health, ex parte Richardson*, [1995] E.C.R. I-3407, it was held that the discriminatory treatment of men and women in relation to the restriction of entitlement to free prescriptions to those over retirement age unlawfully discriminated against men, since there was no necessary or objective link to pensionable age in the case of this social benefit. See also Case C-382/98 *R. v. Secretary of State for Social security, ex parte Taylor*, Judgment of December 16, 1999, [1999] E.C.R. nyr, in which the Court ruled that the different conditions of entitlement for man and women to winter fuel payments under the social fund could be be justified under the derogations in this article.

In *CIB/13368/1996* (starred as 31/99) the Commissioner ruled that the claimant (and all women whose entitlement to incapacity benefit derives from industrial injury or prescribed disease) are entitled to continue to receive the benefit after the age of 60 and before reaching the age of 65 since there is a breach of the principle of equal treatment in the United Kingdom regulations which does not fall within the exemption in Article 7(1)(a).

Article 7(1)(c)

2.131   In *R(P) 1/96* the Commissioner held that the question of whether United Kingdom contribution requirements breached the prohibition of discrimination in Directive 79/7 is a question of law and so was not be determined by the Secretary of State. The claimant, who had been married more than once, was arguing that the failure to take into account her first husband's contributions in determining her entitlement to a retirement pension constituted indirect discrimination against women. The Commissioner considered that such discrimination as there might bewas permitted by Article 7(1)(c).

Article 7(1)(d)

2.132   In case C-420/92 *Bramhill* v *Chief Adjudication Officer*, [1994] E.C.R. 3191, the Court of Justice ruled that,

> "Article 7(1)(d) of Council Directive 79/7 ... does not preclude a Member State which provided for increases in long-term old-age benefits in respect of a dependent spouse to be granted only to me from abolishing that discrimination solely with regard to women who fulfil certain conditions."

Article 7/(2)

2.133   This would appear to be insufficiently precise to give rise to direct effect, since the term "periodically" is so open-ended. It is also difficult to see what right an individual could claim as a result of any such review.

Article 8

2.134   **1.** Member States shall bring into force the laws, regulations and administrative provisions necessary to comply with this Directive within six years of its notification. They shall immediately inform the Commission thereof.

2. Member States shall communicate to the Commission the text of

(Article 8)

laws, regulations and administrative provisions which they adopt in the field covered by this Directive, including measures adopted pursuant to Article 7(2).

They shall inform the Commission of their reasons for maintaining any existing provisions on the matters referred to in Article 7(1) and of the possibilities for reviewing them at a later date.

GENERAL NOTE

The Directive was required to be implemented from and including December 23, 1984. Those of its provisions that meet the requirements for direct effect have so operated since that date. 2.135

Article 9

Within seven years of notification of this Directive, Member States shall forward all information necessary to the Commission to enable it to draw up a report on the application of this Directive for submission to the Council and to propose such further measures as may be required for the implementation of the principle of equal treatment. 2.136

Article 10

This Directive is addressed to the Member States. 2.137

A select bibliography on European social security law

Cox, S and others, *Migration and Social Security Handbook* (2nd ed., CPAG, London, 1997)

European Commission, *Compendium of Community Provisions on Social Security 1995* 4th, Office for Official Publications of the European Communities Luxembourg, ed., 1995)

European Commission, *Judgments of the Court of Justice of the European Communities related to Social Security for Migrant Workers* Office for Official Publications of the European Communities, Luxembourg 1995)

European Commission, *Your Social Security Rights when Moving within the European Union. A Practical Guide* Office for Official Publications of the European Communities, Luxembourg 1997)

Hervey, T, "Social Security" in T Hervey, *European Social Law and Policy* (Longman, London, 1998), ch. 5

Luckhaus, L, "European Social Security Law" in A Ogus and N

Wikeley, *The Law of Social Security*, (4th ed., Butterworths, London, 1995), ch. 18

Pennings, F, *Introduction to European Social Security Law*, (2nd ed., Kluwer Law International, The Hague 1998)

White, R, *EC Social Security Law*, (Longman, London, 1999).

PART III

HUMAN RIGHTS LAW

Human Rights Act 1998

(1998 c.42)

ARRANGEMENT OF SECTIONS

Introduction 3.1

1. The Convention Rights
2. Interpretation of Convention Rights

Legislation

3. Interpretation of legislation
4. Declaration of incompatibility
5. Right of Crown to intervene

Public authorities

6. Act of public authorities
7. Proceedings
8. Judicial remedies
9. Judicial acts

Remedial action

10. Power to take remedial action

Other proceedings and rights

11. Safeguard for existing human rights
12. Freedom of expression
13. Freedom of thought, conscience and religion

Derogations and reservations

14. Derogations
15. Reservations
16. Period for which designated derogations have effect
17. Periodic review of designated reservations

Human Rights Act 1998

Judges of the European Court of Human Rights

18. Appointment to the European Court of Human Rights (*Omitted*)

Parliamentary procedure

19. Statements of compatibility

Supplemental

20. Orders etc. under this Act
21. Interpretation, etc.
22. Short title, commencement, application and extent

SCHEDULES

Schedule 1—The Articles
   Part I—The Convention
   Part II—The First Protocol
   Part III—The Sixth Protocol
Schedule 2—Remedial Orders
Schedule 3—Derogation and Reservation
   Part I—Derogation
   Part II—Reservation
Schedule 4—Judicial Pensions (*Omitted*)

GENERAL NOTE

This Act has been described as "the first historic step . . . towards a constitutional Bill of Rights" (Lester, A and Pannick, D (ed.) *Human Rights Law and Practice*, (Butterworths, London, 1999, at para. 1.44). It followed a Labour consultation paper of December 1996 entitled *Bringing Rights Home*, a manifesto commitment by the Labour Party, and on its election in May 1997, and an October 1997 White Paper entitled *Rights Brought Home: The Human Rights Bill*, Cm.3782.

The Act is to enter into force on October 2, 2000: The Human Rights Act 1998 (Commencement No. 2) Order 2000 (S.I. 2000 No. 1851). The commencement of each section is noted in the annotation to each section.

The United Kingdom has been a party to the European Convention on Human Rights since September 23, 1953 and has recognised the right of individual petition under the Convention continuously since January 14, 1966. Until this Act comes into force, rights accruing for individuals under the Convention cannot be invoked directly to determine whether they have been victims of a violation of the rights protected by the Convention. Individuals within the jurisdiction can only use the "ordinary" law of the land to secure their rights. If they believe that these have been denied them by the State or a part of the State, and they have sought redress under the national legal order (exhausted domestic remedies in the language of the Convention), they have been able to make an application to the Commission of Human Rights (prior to November 1, 1998) and direct to the Court of Human Rights (from November 1, 1998) claiming to be victims of a violation of one of the rights protected. If the application is admitted, then the Court of Human Rights may adjudicate on the issue. The Convention organs, which are

IMPORTANT NOTICE

Thank you for purchasing Social Security: Legislation 2000, (Volume III: Administration, Adjudication and the European Dimension).

Receiving Your Supplements – Set Up a Standing Order

We recognise that practitioners wish to be kept up to date between editions of major works. As a result we publish reasonably priced paperback supplements to the main work. **Please note** that important updating **supplementation** will not automatically be sent to you for **Sweet & Maxwell** titles unless you send us your instruction to set up a standing order by signing and returning this form to the address overleaf, or your usual supplier.

I would like to receive updating supplements upon publication for the following **Sweet & Maxwell** titles:

Either

☐ Social Security: Legislation 2000 (Volume III: Administration, Adjudication and the European Dimension)

Or

☐ All supplemented Sweet & Maxwell titles that I have purchased

Name

Organisation

Address

Signature

We cannot send your supplements without your signature

I understand I can return the supplement within 28 days if it does not meet my requirements, and that I can cancel this agreement at any time.

NO STAMP REQUIRED WITHIN THE U.K.

STANDING ORDER DEPARTMENT

SWEET & MAXWELL LTD

FREEPOST LON 12091

LONDON

NW3 4YS

UNITED KINGDOM

part of the Council of Europe, are located in Strasbourg; they should not be confused with the institutions of the European Union. The Court of Justice of the European Communities is located in Luxembourg.

Introduction

The Convention Rights

1.—(1) In this Act "the Convention rights" means the rights and fundamental freedoms set out in—
  (a) Articles 2 to 12 and 14 of the Convention,
  (b) Articles 1 to 3 of the First Protocol, and
  (c) Articles 1 and 2 of the Sixth Protocol,
as read with Articles 16 to 18 of the Convention.

(2) Those Articles are to have effect for the purposes of this Act subject to any designated derogation or reservation (as to which see sections 14 and 15).

(3) The Articles are set out in Schedule 1.

(4) The Secretary of State may by order make such amendments to this Act as he considers appropriate to reflect the effect, in relation to the United Kingdom, of a protocol.

(5) In subsection (4) "protocol" means a protocol to the Convention—
  (a) which the United Kingdom has ratified; or
  (b) which the United Kingdom has signed with a view to ratification.

(6) No amendment may be made by an order under subsection (4) so as to come into force before the protocol concerned is in force in relation to the United Kingdom.

COMMENCEMENT

October 2, 2000: The Human Rights Act 1998 (Commencement No. 2) Order 2000 (S.I. 2000 No. 1851).

GENERAL NOTE

The Preamble to the Act describes its objective as to give "further effect" to the rights and freedoms guaranteed by the European Convention on Human Rights. The further effect given to the rights encompassed by the Act is their effect within the national legal order, so that they can be invoked directly in proceedings before United Kingdom courts. This is the scheme of incorporation adopted for the United Kingdom. The late former President of the Court has expressed the advantages of incorporation as follows,

> "It has in fact two advantages: it provides the national court with the possibility of taking account of the Convention and the Strasbourg case-law to resolve the dispute before it, and at the same time it gives the European organs an opportunity to discover the views of the national courts regarding the interpretation of the Convention and its application to a specific set of circumstances. The dialogue which thus develops between those who are called upon to apply the Convention on the domestic level and those who must do so on the European level is crucial for an effective protection of the rights guaran-

teed under the Convention.' (Rolv Ryssdal, Speech at the ceremony for the 40th anniversary of the European Convention on Human Rights at Trieste, 18 Dec. 1990, Council of Europe document Cour (90) 318, 2.

Convention rights are defined in subs. (1) as Articles 2–12 and 14 of the Convention itself, together with certain articles of the First and Sixth Protocols as read with Articles 16 to 18 of the Convention. These articles are set out in Schedule 1. Their effect is subject to the terms of any derogation under Article 15 of the Convention or any reservation filed by the United Kingdom Government. Derogations are governed in more detail by s.14, and reservations by s.15; the current derogations and reservation are set out in Schedule 3. The Secretary of State is given power to amend the Act to give effect to rights contained in protocols to the Convention which have not yet been ratified by the United Kingdom. For example, the United Kingdom Government has indicated that consideration is being given to ratification of certain provisions of the Seventh Protocol, but not of the Fourth Protocol.

Convention rights as defined in s.1 do not include either Article 1 which provides that parties to the Convention 'shall secure to everyone within their jurisdiction the rights and freedoms' set out in Articles 2–18 of the Convention. Nor do they include Article 13 which gives a right to an effective remedy in the following terms:

> Everyone whose rights and freedoms as set forth in this Convention are violated shall have an effective remedy before a national authority notwithstanding that the violation has been committed by persons acting in an official capacity.

The incorporation of Article 1 among Convention rights named by the Act is probably not necessary since the purpose of the Act is to give effect to Convention rights within the national legal order. However, it should be noted that the rights given by the Convention are not linked in any way to the nationality of an individual; they are guaranteed to all within the United Kingdom's jurisdiction. This differs from many rights given by European Union law where the beneficiaries are nationals of the Member States of the European Union.

The failure to include Article 13 among the Convention rights may be more problematic, though the Lord Chancellor stoutly argued that its inclusion was not necessary because the Act gives effect 'to Article 13 by establishing a scheme under which Convention rights can be raised before out domestic courts': HL Vol. 583 col. 475 (November 18, 1997). In the Commons, the Home Secretary made a similar point. There is apparently some concern that inclusion of the article might lead all manner of courts and tribunals to 'invent' new remedies for violation of Convention rights. The Act is cautious on the issue of remedies where a violation is found: see commentary to s.8. However, both the Lord Chancellor and the Home Secretary conceded that in considering any question of remedies, courts or tribunals may have regard to the terms of Article 13 under s.2 of the Act. However, situations may arise where the scheme of the Act arguably does not offer an effective remedy for the violation, though it should be noted that the nature and scope of the effectiveness of the remedy required under Article 13 has hardly been touched on in the Strasbourg case law.

An example might help to illustrate the possible lacuna. Suppose a claimant before an appeal tribunal succeeds in persuading the tribunal that there has been an excessive delay in giving judgment on an appeal; This would constitute a violation of Article 6(1) E.C.H.R. In this type of case, the Court of Human Rights has often awarded some compensation for the delay, but an appeal tribunal has no power to award compensation, or interest on late benefit. This would leave the individual without a remedy unless the mere statement that there was a violation was considered sufficient in the circumstances of the case. Any claim for compensation would have to be the subject of separate (and wholly novel) proceedings in a different forum. It is at least arguable that making a person in this position go to two judicial bodies for a remedy for the same violation is a failure to provide an effective remedy.

Interpretation of Convention rights

2.—(1) A court or tribunal determining a question which has arisen in connection with a Convention right must take into account any—
  (a) judgment, decision, declaration or advisory opinion of the European Court of Human Rights,
  (b) opinion of the Commission given in a report adopted under Article 31 of the Convention,
  (c) decision of the Commission in connection with Article 26 or 27(2) of the Convention, or
  (d) decision of the Committee of Ministers taken under Article 46 of the Convention,
whenever made or given, so far as, in the opinion of the court or tribunal, it is relevant to the proceedings in which that question has arisen.

(2) Evidence of any judgment, decision, declaration or opinion of which account may have to be taken under this section is to be given in proceedings before any court or tribunal in such manner as may be provided by rules.

(3) In this section "rules" means rules of court or, in the case of proceedings before a tribunal, rules made for the purposes of this section—
  (a) by the Lord Chancellor or the Secretary of State, in relation to any proceedings outside Scotland;
  (b) by the Secretary of State, in relation to proceedings in Scotland; or
  (c) by a Northern Ireland department, in relation to proceedings before a tribunal in Northern Ireland—
    (i) which deals with transferred matters; and
    (ii) for which no rules made under paragraph (a) are in force.

COMMENCEMENT

October 2, 2000: The Human Rights Act 1998 (Commencement No. 2) Order 2000 (S.I. 2000 No. 1851).

GENERAL NOTE

Introduction
This section requires courts and tribunals to have regard to the Strasbourg case law, past, present and future, in deciding any question relating to a Convention right. Note that the Strasbourg case law is not binding. There are two reasons for this. First, it will not always be easy to transplant directly the point being made by the Strasbourg organ where the case involves the complexities of other legal systems. Secondly, the Convention sets a minimum standard; one possibly dramatic effect of incorporation is that the United Kingdom authorities will set a higher standard than the common European standard which is set by the Strasbourg organs.

The section refers to dispositions of three Strasbourg organs: the Commission, the Court and the Committee of Ministers. In order to understand the reasons for this, both the old and the new Strasbourg systems must be understood.

The "old" system of protection

3.7 The Convention, in its original form, created two organs "to ensure the observance of the engagements undertaken by the High Contracting Parties": the European Commission of Human Rights and the European Court of Human Rights. The main function of these two organs, sometimes collectively referred to as the Strasbourg organs, (together with the Committee of Ministers discussed later) was to deal with applications made by States and by individuals alleging violations of the Convention. Under old Article 24, any State party to the Convention could refer to the Commission any alleged breach of the provisions of the Convention by another State party. Under old Article 25, the Commission could receive applications from any person, non-governmental organization, or group of individuals claiming to be the victim of a violation by one of the Member States of the rights set forth in the Convention and any relevant Protocols. The procedure differed depending on whether the application is made under Article 24 or 25; what follows describes the process in relation to individual applications under Article 25.

Once an application was registered, the Commission first considered, and issued a *decision* on, whether the application met the admissibility requirements. If it did not, that was an end of the matter. If the application was declared admissible, the Commission went on to conduct an investigation into the merits of the complaint and to consider whether there had been a violation of the Convention. The result was a *report* from the Commission expressing an *opinion* (which is not legally binding) as to whether or not there has been a violation. The report was communicated on a confidential basis to the applicant and to the State concerned and was delivered to the Committee of Ministers, the political organ of the Council of Europe. Throughout this time, attempts would have been made to secure a friendly settlement "on the basis of respect for human rights".

Final decisions on cases on which the Commission had reported and which had not resulted in a friendly settlement were made by the Committee of Ministers, or the Court of Human Rights. Recognition of the jurisdiction of the Court was technically voluntary under old Article 46 of the Convention. Within three months of the transmission of the Commission report to the Committee of Ministers, the application could be referred to the Court for determination by the Commission, the defendant State, or the State whose national was alleged to be the victim. The applicant had no standing to refer the application to the Court, unless the defendant State was a party to Protocol 9. Where this was so, the applicant could refer the matter to the Court, but (unless it was also referred to the Court by the Commission or a State) it first had to be submitted to a panel of three judges, who could decide unanimously that the application should not be considered by the Court because it did not raise a serious question affecting the interpretation or application of the Convention.

If the case was referred to the Court and heard by it, there was a full judicial procedure, and even where Protocol 9 had not been ratified, some accommodations were made which allowed limited participation by the applicant. The Courts at in plenary session or in Chambers of nine. Decisions were made by a majority of the judges present and voting, with the President enjoying a casting vote if this was necessary. Separate opinions could be attached to the judgment of the majority.

Those cases which were not referred to the Court within three months of transmission of the Commission's report to the Committee of Ministers were automatically referred to the Committee of Ministers for final decision. The practice of the Committee of Ministers in recent years was simply to endorse the Commission report without any further investigation of the merits of the case.

The use of a political organ was a compromise to ensure that all applications resulted in a final determination. In the early years, there were States which had not recognised the competence of the Court, and there have always been cases which no one has referred to the Court.

The "new" system of protection

Protocol 11 has amended the Convention to make provision for a new wholly judicial system of determination of applications. The Commission and the Court have been replaced from November 1, 1998 by a new permanent Court, which handles both the admissibility and merits phases of application. The Court is also charged with seeking to secure friendly settlement of matters before it.

3.8

Individual applications are made to the Court under Article 34 and individuals have full standing before the Court. Complaints are initially considered by a three-judge committee which will consider whether the application meets the Convention's admissibility criteria, but it can only rule an application to be inadmissible if it is unanimous. These criteria have not changed and flow from the terms of Articles 34 and 35 and involve the consideration of nine questions:

1. Can the applicant claim to be a victim?
2. Is the defendant State a party to the Convention?
3. Have domestic remedies been exhausted?
4. Is the application filed within the six-month time-limit?
5. Is the application signed?
6. Has the application been brought before?
7. Is the application compatible with the Convention?
8. Is the application manifestly ill-founded?
9. Is there an abuse of the right of petition?

In recent years somewhere around one in four to one in seven applications has been declared admissible, though over the life of the Convention fewer than one in ten applications has progressed beyond the admissibility phase.

Those cases which are not ruled inadmissible by the three judge committee are put before a seven judge chamber of the Court, which will include the judge sitting in respect of the defendant State. The chamber will consider the written arguments of the parties, investigate the material facts if these are in contention, and hear oral argument. This stage of the proceedings concludes with a decision whether the complaint is admissible and whether a friendly settlement is possible. There follows a consideration of the merits. In some cases, no doubt the admissibility and merits phases will be joined.

Certain cases of special difficulty can be referred by a chamber to a Grand Chamber of seventeen judges.

The Court has an advisory jurisdiction, but the procedure has not been used to date. Its limited focus means than it is unlikely ever to be used.

Which authorities are the most important?

Though the section requires courts and tribunals to have regard to authorities from all three Strasbourg organs, but there can be little doubt that the most important are the judgments of the Court of Human Rights.

3.8.1

Too great a reliance should not be placed on decisions on admissibility of any antiquity, since these have not always been fully reasoned and where the decision is to declare an application inadmissible are, by definition, not based on any comprehensive consideration of the merits. Furthermore the volume of such decisions has been such that the quality of the reasoning in admissibility decisions can be opaque. How much can be learned from a decision which outlines some facts as asserted in the application and then decides that the application is "manifestly ill-founded"? In many cases no observations had been sought from the respondent government.

Authorities on the interpretation of the concept of a "victim" of a violation of the Convention may be particularly persuasive, because of the drafting of s.7(7): see commentary to that section. The same view is taken of the concept of "just satisfaction" in s.8(3): see commentary to that section.

Legislation

Interpretation of legislation

3.9
3.—(1) So far as it is possible to do so, primary legislation and subordinate legislation must be read and given effect in a way which is compatible with the Convention rights.
(2) This section—
(a) applies to primary legislation and subordinate legislation whenever enacted;
(b) does not affect the validity, continuing operation or enforcement of any incompatible primary legislation; and
(c) does not affect the validity, continuing operation or enforcement of any incompatible subordinate legislation if (disregarding any possibility of revocation) primary legislation prevents removal of the incompatibility.

COMMENCEMENT

3.10
October 2, 2000: The Human Rights Act 1998 (Commencement No. 2) Order 2000 (S.I. 2000 No. 1851).

GENERAL NOTE

There is a powerful new principle of statutory interpretation here: so far as it is *possible* to do so, primary and secondary legislation whenever enacted *must* be read in a way which is compatible with Convention rights whenever a question of Convention rights is in issue. The requirement applies to all users of the legislation; it does not apply solely to courts and tribunals, nor does it require that a public authority (see s.6) is a party to the issue raised.

The principle is clearly mandatory and strongly so. A judge writing in a journal has said that the section creates a rebuttable presumption in favour of an interpretation consistent with Convention rights: Lord Steyn, "Incorporation and Devolution—A Few Reflections on the Changing Scene" [1998] E.H.R.L.R. 153, at 155.

however, where primary legislation cannot be read compatibly with Convention rights, then a court or tribunal does not have the power to strike down or ignore the incompatible primary legislation. Certain courts may, however, declare the legislation incompatible with Convention rights. This preserves the sovereignty of Parliament and is one of the clever features of the Act that have enabled it to fit into the constitutional traditions of the United Kingdom.

Where secondary legislation cannot be read compatibly with Convention rights, two possibilities will arise. First, if the incompatibility of the secondary legislation is required by the primary legislation under which it is made, then the status of the secondary legislation is the same as that of incompatible primary legislation. Its validity, continuing operation and enforcement are unaffected. But if the incompatibility is not required by the primary legislation, then it cannot be said to be within the powers of the primary legislation under which it is enacted, and any court or tribunal (and seemingly anyone called on to interpret that legislation) can disregard it: its validity, continuing operation and enforcement will be affected.

To some extent, this obligation to force an interpretation from a statutory provision is not entirely new, since European Community law requires legislation implementing the requirements of Community law to be read, so far as it is possible to do so, in a manner which achieves the objectives of the E.C. Treaty: see the view taken in the House of Lords in *Webb v. EMO Air Cargo (UK) Ltd*, [1992] 2 All E.R. 929.

Declaration of incompatibility

4.—(1) Subsection (2) applies in any proceedings in which a court determines whether a provision of primary legislation is compatible with a Convention right.

(2) If the court is satisfied that the provision is incompatible with a Convention right, it may make a declaration of that incompatibility.

(3) Subsection (4) applies in any proceedings in which a court determines whether a provision of subordinate legislation, made in the exercise of a power conferred by primary legislation, is compatible with a Convention right.

(4) If the court is satisfied—
  (a) that the provision is incompatible with a Convention right, and
  (b) that (disregarding any possibility of revocation) the primary legislation concerned prevents removal of the incompatibility,
it may make a declaration of that incompatibility.

(5) In this section "court" means—
  (a) the House of Lords;
  (b) the Judicial Committee of the Privy Council;
  (c) the Courts-Martial Appeal Court;
  (d) in Scotland, the High Court of Justiciary sitting otherwise than as a trial court or the Court of Session;
  (e) in England and Wales or Northern Ireland, the High Court or the Court of Appeal.

(6) A declaration under this section ("a declaration of incompatibility")—
  (a) does not affect the validity, continuing operation or enforcement of the provision in respect of which it is given; and
  (b) is not binding on the parties to the proceedings in which it is made.

COMMENCEMENT

October 2, 2000: The Human Rights Act 1998 (Commencement No. 2) Order 2000 (S.I. 2000 No. 1851).

GENERAL NOTE

This section gives certain courts power to make declarations of incompatibility where primary or secondary legislation cannot be read compatibly with Con-

Human Rights Act 1998

vention rights. It is a discretionary power available to the higher courts only. It arises in any proceedings; there is again no requirement that one of the parties is a public authority. Neither appeal tribunals nor Commissioners have the power to make declarations of incompatibility.

It is perhaps unfortunate that the only routes to declarations of incompatibility in the social security jurisdiction are appeal from a Commissioner to the Court of Appeal, or taking judicial review proceedings in the High Court against a tribunal or a Commissioner.

The effect of a declaration of incompatibility is not to declare the legislation invalid, inoperative or unenforceable. The impeached provision will continue in full force and effect pending any amendment. The effect of a declaration of incompatibility is to put the Government on notice of the incompatibility. The Government may then choose to take the remedial action provided for in s.10 and Schedule 2 of the Act.

Right of Crown to intervene

3.13　**5.**—(1) Where a court is considering whether to make a declaration of incompatibility, the Crown is entitled to notice in accordance with rules of court.

(2) In any case to which subsection (1) applies—
 (a) a Minister of the Crown (or a person nominated by him),
 (b) a member of the Scottish Executive,
 (c) a Northern Ireland Minister,
 (d) a Northern Ireland department,
is entitled, on giving notice in accordance with rules of court, to be joined as a party to the proceedings.

(3) Notice under subsection (2) may be given at any time during the proceedings.

(4) A person who has been made a party to criminal proceedings (other than in Scotland) as the result of a notice under subsection (2) may, with leave, appeal to the House of Lords against any declaration of incompatibility made in the proceedings.

(5) In subsection (4)—
 "criminal proceedings" includes all proceedings before the Courts-Martial Appeal Court; and
 "leave" means leave granted by the court making the declaration of incompatibility or by the House of Lords.

Commencement

3.14　October 2, 2000: The Human Rights Act 1998 (Commencement No. 2) Order 2000 (S.I. 2000 No. 1851).

Public authorities

Acts of public authorities

3.15　**6.**—(1) It is unlawful for a public authority to act in a way which is incompatible with a Convention right.

(2) Subsection (1) does not apply to an act if—

(a) as the result of one or more provisions of primary legislation, the authority could not have acted differently; or

(b) in the case of one or more provisions of, or made under, primary legislation which cannot be read or given effect in a way which is compatible with the Convention rights, the authority was acting so as to give effect to or enforce those provisions.

(3) In this section "public authority" includes—

(a) a court or tribunal, and

(b) any person certain of whose functions are functions of a public nature,

but does not include either House of Parliament or a person exercising functions in connection with proceedings in Parliament.

(4) In subsection (3) "Parliament" does not include the House of Lords in its judicial capacity.

(5) In relation to a particular act, a person is not a public authority by virtue only of subsection (3)(b) if the nature of the act is private.

(6) "An act" includes a failure to act but does not include a failure to—

(a) introduce in, or lay before, Parliament a proposal for legislation; or

(b) make any primary legislation or remedial order.

COMMENCEMENT

October 2, 2000: The Human Rights Act 1998 (Commencement No. 2) Order 2000 (S.I. 2000 No. 1851).

3.16

GENERAL NOTE

The obligation in s.6(1) is at the heart of the scheme of incorporation in the Act. It could be said that all the other provision flow from the requirement that public authorities of any kind act compatibly with Convention rights. Note that there is a "defence" in s.6(2) where there was a statutory requirement to act in a particular manner. Here there will, of course, be an incompatibility between the statutory provision and Convention rights.

The key concept in the section is that of a public authority. This includes courts and tribunals, but not either House of Parliament, and is extended to "any person certain of whose functions are functions of a public nature" The difficult two words become very difficult twelve words. Only "certain" of the authority's functions need be of a public nature, and there is no liability in respect of the exercise of their functions of a private nature.

The question of what constitutes a public authority is reminiscent of the definitional problem of determining what are "emanations of the State" for the purposes of the horizontal application of E.C. Directives. The test is certainly not the same, but the same difficulties will arise in determining those institutions at the margins of State power which constitute public authorities. The definition will require judicial interpretation, but it is clearly a functional test.

There is, however, no doubt that the Benefits Agency and all its constituent parts constitute public authorities, as, of course, do the tribunals and other judicial bodies. All must act compatibly with Convention rights. This means that they must take up obvious Convention points even if they are not raised by the parties, since otherwise they would be acting unlawfully by acting in a manner which is not compatible with Convention rights.

Proceedings

3.17   7.—(1) A person who claims that a public authority has acted (or proposes to act) in a way which is made unlawful by section 6(1) may—
   (a) bring proceedings against the authority under this Act in the appropriate court or tribunal, or
   (b) rely on the Convention right or rights concerned in any legal proceedings,

but only if he is (or would be) a victim of the unlawful act.

(2) In subsection (1)(a) "appropriate court or tribunal" means such court or tribunal as may be determined in accordance with rules; and proceedings against an authority include a counterclaim or similar proceeding.

(3) If the proceedings are brought on an application for judicial review, the applicant is to be taken to have a sufficient interest in relation to the unlawful act only if he is, or would be, a victim of that act.

(4) If the proceedings are made by way of a petition for judicial review in Scotland, the applicant shall be taken to have title and interest to sue in relation to the unlawful act only if he is, or would be, a victim of that act.

(5) Proceedings under subsection (1)(a) must be brought before the end of—
   (a) the period of one year beginning with the date on which the act complained of took place; or
   (b) such longer period as the court or tribunal considers equitable having regard to all the circumstances,

but that is subject to any rule imposing a stricter time limit in relation to the procedure in question.

(6) In subsection (1)(b) "legal proceedings" includes—
   (a) proceedings brought by or at the instigation of a public authority; and
   (b) an appeal against the decision of a court or tribunal.

(7) For the purposes of this section, a person is a victim of an unlawful act only if he would be a victim for the purposes of Article 34 of the Convention if proceedings were brought in the European Court of Human Rights in respect of that act.

(8) Nothing in this Act creates a criminal offence.

(9) In this section "rules" means—
   (a) in relation to proceedings before a court or tribunal outside Scotland, rules made by the Lord Chancellor or the Secretary of State for the purposes of this section or rules of court,
   (b) in relation to proceedings before a court or tribunal in Scotland, rules made by the Secretary of State for those purposes,
   (c) in relation to proceedings before a tribunal in Northern Ireland—
      (i) which deals with transferred matters; and
      (ii) for which no rules made under paragraph (a) are in force, rules made by a Northern Ireland department for those purposes,

and includes provision made by order under section 1 of the Courts and Legal Services Act 1990.

(10) In making rules, regard must be had to section 9.

(11) The Minister who has power to make rules in relation to a particular tribunal may, to the extent he considers it necessary to ensure that the tribunal can provide an appropriate remedy in relation to an act (or proposed act) of a public authority which is (or would be) unlawful as a result of section 6(1), by order add to—
  (a) the relief or remedies which the tribunal may grant; or
  (b) the grounds on which it may grant any of them.

(12) An order made under subsection (11) may contain such incidental, supplemental, consequential or transitional provision as the Minister making it considers appropriate.

(13) "The Minister" includes the Northern Ireland department concerned.

COMMENCEMENT

October 2, 2000: The Human Rights Act 1998 (Commencement No. 2) Order 2000 (S.I. 2000 No. 1851).

3.18

GENERAL NOTE

Introduction

This section is full of difficulty. A person who believes that a public authority has acted unlawfully by not acting in a manner compatible with Convention rights may bring proceedings under s.7. Such a person must under subs (7) show that they would be a victim for the purposes of Article 34 of the Convention if proceedings were brought before the Court of Human Rights in respect of the allegedly unlawful act.

3.19

The section refers to at least three different types of proceedings: (1) the so-called new "constitutional tort" under subs (1)(a); (2) judicial review under subs. (3); and (3) "any legal proceedings" in subs.(1)(b).

Changes to the Civil Procedures Rules to accommodate these proceedings left a number of questions unanswered.

Standing to raise the complaint: the victim requirement

Under subs. (7) which applies to the whole section, only a person who can show that they would fall within the victim requirement under Article 34 of the Convention has standing to complain of the unlawful act by the public authority. The concept of "victim" is a particular concept under Convention case law, and for this reason the interpretative requirement to have regard to Convention case law must be particularly strong since otherwise the specific reference to Article 34 in subs. (7) would be otiose. Article 34 has replaced Article 25 in the original version of the Convention prior to its amendment by Protocol 11.

3.20

Fortunately, the Strasbourg authorities—and here admissibility decisions of the Commission under the "old" system of protection (see commentary to s.2) will be particularly useful—have been generous in the matter of standing to make an application under the Convention.

The term "person" under the Convention (*personne physique* in the French text) clearly refers only to natural persons, but the Commission has accepted applications from corporate and unincorporated bodies whose rights under the Convention have been violated. So complaints have been accepted from companies, partnerships, trades unions, churches, political parties, and numerous other types of institution. It would seem that only public bodies themselves are excluded from the possibility of making an individual petition. Furthermore there are no restrictions on grounds of nationality, residence or any other status.

Standing has been extended to representative complaints, for example, by parents on behalf of children where that is appropriate, though there is no age limit for making an application: App. 10929/84 *Nielsen v. Denmark*, (1986) 46 DR 55 and App. 22920/93 *MB v. United Kingdom*, (1994) 77-A DR 42. Equally, there is no bar to application by persons under a disability: App. 1572/62 *X v. Austria*, (1962) 5 Yearbook 238.

Associations have no standing to bring actions in a representative capacity: App. 10581/83 *Norris and National Gay Federation v. Ireland*, (1984) 44 D.R. 132, though if they provide evidence that they are acting on behalf of specified individuals, the application may be accepted: App. 10983/84 *Confédération des Syndicats médicaux français et Fédération nationale des Infirmiers v. France*, (1986) 47 D.R. 225.

In some cases potential victims may make an application, such as in cases where covert surveillance might take place without any notification of the possibility to the individual: *Klass v. Germany*, Judgment of September 6, 1978, Series A No 28; (1979–80) 2 E.H.R.R. 214.

The Commission and the Court will not, however, countenance an application in the abstract as a means of testing the compatibility of provisions of a national legal order: App. 9297/81 *X Association v. Sweden*, (1982) 28 D.R. 204. Drawing the distinction between potential victims and claims in the abstract is not always easy: see App. 10039/82 *Leigh and others v. United Kingdom*, (1984) 38 D.R. 74.

Subs. (1)(a): the new constitutional tort

3.21 A person who can show that they meet the victim test may bring proceedings against the authority "in the appropriate court or tribunal". This is to be determined in accordance with rules to be made, outside Scotland, by the Lord Chancellor or the Secretary of State. The Civil Procedure Rules simply map this action onto the existing division of responsibilities between the county courts and the High Court.

The time limits for such an action are, however, specified in subs. (5). The action is to be brought within one year of the date on which the act complained of took place or such longer period as the court or tribunal considers equitable having regard to all the circumstances. There is a proviso that both the one year time limit and any extension of it is to be without prejudice to any rule imposing a stricter time limit "in relation to the procedure in question." An example would be judicial review where the normal time limit is three months unless this is extended by the court. However, where an action is brought under a procedure with a longer limitation period, it would seem that the longer limitation period will apply; such proceedings would not, however, arise under subs (1)(a) but presumably under subs (1)(b).

Under s.9(1), where the unlawful act of which the applicant complains is a judicial act, it is stated that proceedings under s.7(1)(a) may be brought only by exercising a right of appeal, seeking judicial review against those bodies susceptible to judicial review, or "in such other forum as may be prescribed by rules."

Judicial review: subs (3) and (4)

3.22 Where the proceedings are by way of judicial review on the grounds that a public authority has acted unlawfully, the normal sufficient interest test of standing (which would permit action by a representative body or a pressure group) is replaced by a test that the applicant must satisfy the victim test in subs. (7).

Raising Convention rights in any legal proceedings: subs. (1)(b)

3.23 Convention rights may be raised in any legal proceedings, provided that the person can show that they would be a victim under Article 34 of the Convention. So a person bringing proceedings on a well-established cause of action can raise his or her Convention rights at any time. Indeed, the court or tribunal is under a duty by virtue of s.6(1) to take obvious Convention points since they are under a duty to act in a manner compatible with the Convention.

Apart from judicial review claims (which may be important if a person is seeking the possibility of a money remedy), Convention rights are most likely to be raised in the course of appeals to the appeal tribunals and before the Commissioners. The commentary to the Convention rights set out in Schedule 1 give some indication of the sorts of issues which might be raised under them.

In *CSIB/973/1999* a Scottish Commissioner warns of the need for responsible resort to the taking of human rights points. He complains of a point which was "in the nature of a wrap up omnibus ground of appeal placed before the Commissioners no doubt in the hope that there was something in the point." The Commissioner regrets the absence of rules setting out the manner in which human rights points are to be taken before the Commissioners. He goes on to indicate the content of those rules; this might assist those contemplating raising human rights points before both tribunals and Commissioners. The provision of the Convention which it is argued has been breached should be identified, together with the remedy sought in respect of the breach. The legal principles and authorities relied on and any error of law by the tribunal which it is asserted were made consequent on the breach should also be identified. Such points should be taken on proper notice so that both parties can research them and focus on them in their arguments to the adjudicating body. That is, no doubt, good advice, but the duty in s.6(1) on public authorities to act compatibly with Convention rights means that adjudicating bodies must themselves consider obvious points arising under the Convention even if they are not raised by the parties.

Judicial remedies

8.—(1) In relation to any act (or proposed act) of a public authority which the court finds is (or would be) unlawful, it may grant such relief or remedy, or make such order, within its powers as it considers just and appropriate.

(2) But damages may be awarded only by a court which has power to award damages, or to order the payment of compensation, in civil proceedings.

(3) No award of damages is to be made unless, taking account of all the circumstances of the case, including—
   (a) any other relief or remedy granted, or order made, in relation to the act in question (by that or any other court), and
   (b) the consequences of any decision (of that or any other court) in respect of that act,
the court is satisfied that the award is necessary to afford just satisfaction to the person in whose favour it is made.

(4) In determining—
   (a) whether to award damages, or
   (b) the amount of an award,
the court must take into account the principles applied by the European Court of Human Rights in relation to the award of compensation under Article 41 of the Convention.

(5) A public authority against which damages are awarded is to be treated—

3.24

(a) in Scotland, for the purposes of section 3 of the Law Reform (Miscellaneous Provisions) (Scotland) Act 1940 as if the award were made in an action of damages in which the authority has been found liable in respect of loss or damage to the person to whom the award is made;

(b) for the purposes of the Civil Liability (Contribution) Act 1978 as liable in respect of damage suffered by the person to whom the award is made.

(6) In this section—

"court" includes a tribunal;

"damages" means damages for an unlawful act of a public authority; and

"unlawful" means unlawful under section 6(1).

COMMENCEMENT

3.25 October 2, 2000: The Human Rights Act 1998 (Commencement No. 2) Order 2000 (S.I. 2000 No. 1851).

GENERAL NOTE

3.26 Section 8(1) grants a broad competence, but the nature of the remedies available will vary according to the forum. The relief, remedy or order open to the court or tribunal must be one already within its powers. So the Act gives no new competence to decision-making bodies to provide a remedy for a violation of a Convention right. The decision not to extend the powers of all courts and tribunals to include new remedies for violations of Convention rights was apparently motivated by a concern that there would be an explosion of damages awards in this area across a wide range of decision-making bodies. This was the same concern which led to the exclusion of Article 13 of the Convention from the incorporated rights. There is, accordingly, a wide but not unlimited range of remedies available for breaches of Convention rights.

The drafting of section 8 reveals a concern that damages for violations of Convention rights should be contained. Section 8(2) provides that damages for an unlawful act of a public authority under the Act may be awarded only by a court (or tribunal) which has power to award damages, or to order the payment of compensation, in civil proceedings. Furthermore, damages, though not the remedy of last resort, are circumscribed since they are not to be made unless the court is satisfied that the award is necessary to afford just satisfaction to the person in whose favour the award is made, having regard to all the circumstances of the case, and in particular any other remedy or relief granted and the consequences of any decision in respect of the breach of Convention rights: subs. (3). As noted above, decisions about the award of damages and the amount of damages are to be informed by reference to the case law of the Court of Human Right in awarding just satisfaction.

A number of observations need to be made about the structure of section 8. It assumes that the range of remedies currently available to United Kingdom courts will be adequate to remedy breaches of Convention rights. It seeks to discourage an explosion of damages awards. The Lord Chancellor indicated that the intent was to match the awards victims would get if they received just satisfaction under Article 41: HL Vol 582 col 1232, November 3, 1997. It establishes a system in which the luck of the forum will determine whether duplication of litigation will be needed to secure a money remedy. A good example would be an appeal heard by an appeal tribunal, which has no power to award damages, and it has been established that it has no power award interest on the late payment of benefit; This undoubtedly follows from the reasoning of the Social Security Commissioner in *R(FC)2/90*; see also the decision of the Court of Justice in *R. v. Secretary of State for Social Security, ex parte Sutton*, [1997] E.C.R. I-2163; [1997] 2 C.M.L.R. 382. Nor it seems would any other court. Yet the Court of Human Rights has awarded interest on the late payment of benefit: *Schuler-Zgraggen v. Switzerland*, Judgment of June 24, 1993, Series A, No. 263; (1993) 16 E.H.R.R. 405. In the early days of Community law, an action for a declaration was one means of securing a judicial statement of an entitlement under Community law. This would seem to be the only route open within the national legal order to a victim who had only received social security benefit to which he or she was entitled some years late and who wished to raise the claim for interest on the late payment. Otherwise, such a person would have to raise the complaint that no interest was available before the Court in Strasbourg.

Perhaps the most pertinent point to make is that the deference to the provisions of the Convention on just satisfaction in the national legislation is misplaced. The provisions in Article 41 of the Convention on affording just satisfaction are a safety net where the national legal order does not offer full compensation for the breach of the Convention.

The starting point is that the national legal order should determine what remedies are appropriate for breaches of the Convention. Such an obligation flows from Article 13 of the Convention. Indeed, it could be argued that the effect of section 8 replicates the failures of earlier years to recognise what was demanded by the Convention. It assumes that the current panoply of remedies available in the national legal order meets the requirements of the Convention. It also reveals a deep anxiety about damages as a remedy for breach of a Convention right.

The potential gap in remedies available can, however, be cured under the rule-making power in s.7(11) and (12) which enables additional powers to be given to tribunals to add to the remedies open to them, and to define the grounds on which any additional remedies may be granted.

Where the act complained of is a judicial act, damages as a remedy is limited to compensation for unlawful detention awarded in accordance with Article 5(5): s.9(3)

Judicial acts

9.—(1) Proceedings under section 7(1)(a) in respect of a judicial act may be brought only

(a) by exercising a right of appeal;

(b) on an application (in Scotland a petition) for judicial review; or

(c) in such other forum as may be prescribed by rules.

(2) That does not affect any rule of law which prevents a court from being the subject of judicial review.

(3) In proceedings under this Act in respect of a judicial act done in good faith, damages may not be awarded otherwise than to compensate a person to the extent required by Article 5(5) of the Convention.

(4) An award of damages permitted by subsection (3) is to be made against the Crown; but no award may be made unless the appropriate person, if not a party to the proceedings, is joined.

(5) In this section—

"appropriate person" means the Minister responsible for the court concerned, or a person or government department nominated by him;

3.27

Human Rights Act 1998

"court" includes a tribunal;
"judge" includes a member of a tribunal, a justice of the peace and a clerk or other officer entitled to exercise the jurisdiction of a court;
"judicial act" means a judicial act of a court and includes an act done on the instructions, or on behalf, of a judge; and
"rules" has the same meaning as in section 7(9).

COMMENCEMENT

3.28   October 2, 2000: The Human Rights Act 1998 (Commencement No. 2) Order 2000 (S.I. 2000 No. 1851).

Remedial action

Power to take remedial action

3.29   **10.**—(1) This section applies if—
  (a) a provision of legislation has been declared under section 4 to be incompatible with a Convention right and, if an appeal lies—
    (i) all persons who may appeal have stated in writing that they do not intend to do so;
    (ii) the time for bringing an appeal has expired and no appeal has been brought within that time; or
    (iii) an appeal brought within that time has been determined or abandoned; or
  (b) it appears to a Minister of the Crown or Her Majesty in Council that, having regard to a finding of the European Court of Human Rights made after the coming into force of this section in proceedings against the United Kingdom, a provision of legislation is incompatible with an obligation of the United Kingdom arising from the Convention.

(2) If a Minister of the Crown considers that there are compelling reasons for proceeding under this section, he may by order make such amendments to the legislation as he considers necessary to remove the incompatibility.

(3) If, in the case of subordinate legislation, a Minister of the Crown considers—
  (a) that it is necessary to amend the primary legislation under which the subordinate legislation in question was made, in order to enable the incompatibility to be removed, and
  (b) that there are compelling reasons for proceeding under this section,
he may by order make such amendments to the primary legislation as he considers necessary.

(4) This section also applies where the provision in question is in subordinate legislation and has been quashed, or declared invalid, by reason of incompatibility with a Convention right and the Minister proposes to proceed under paragraph 2(b) of Schedule 2.

(5) If the legislation is an Order in Council, the power conferred by subsection (2) or (3) is exercisable by Her Majesty in Council.

(6) In this section "legislation" does not include a Measure of the Church Assembly or of the General Synod of the Church of England.

(7) Schedule 2 makes further provision about remedial orders.

COMMENCEMENT

October 2, 2000: The Human Rights Act 1998 (Commencement No. 2) Order 2000 (S.I. 2000 No. 1851).

3.30

GENERAL NOTE

This section and Schedule 2 make provision for a fast track Parliamentary procedure to respond to a declaration of incompatibility by a court.

Other rights and proceedings

Safeguard for existing human rights

11.—A person's reliance on a Convention right does not restrict—
(a) any other right or freedom conferred on him by or under any law having effect in any part of the United Kingdom; or
(b) his right to make any claim or bring any proceedings which he could make or bring apart from sections 7 to 9.

3.31

COMMENCEMENT

October 2, 2000: The Human Rights Act 1998 (Commencement No. 2) Order 2000 (S.I. 2000 No. 1851).

3.32

GENERAL NOTE

The rights given to persons under s.7 to complain of unlawful acts by public authorities in acting in a manner incompatible with the Convention does not limit in any way existing rights under United Kingdom law. The new rights are additional to existing rights and not in substitution for them.

Freedom of expression

12.—(1) This section applies if a court is considering whether to grant any relief which, if granted, might affect the exercise of the Convention right to freedom of expression.

3.33

(2) If the person against whom the application for relief is made ("the respondent") is neither present nor represented, no such relief is to be granted unless the court is satisfied—
(a) that the applicant has taken all practicable steps to notify the respondent; or
(b) that there are compelling reasons why the respondent should not be notified.

(3) No such relief is to be granted so as to restrain publication before trial unless the court is satisfied that the applicant is likely to establish that publication should not be allowed.

(4) The court must have particular regard to the importance of the Convention right to freedom of expression and, where the proceedings

relate to material which the respondent claims, or which appears to the court, to be journalistic, literary or artistic material (or to conduct connected with such material), to—
  (a) the extent to which—
    (i) the material has, or is about to, become available to the public; or
    (ii) it is, or would be, in the public interest for the material to be published;
  (b) any relevant privacy code.
(5) In this section—
"court" includes a tribunal; and
"relief" includes any remedy or order (other than in criminal proceedings).

COMMENCEMENT

3.34   October 2, 2000: The Human Rights Act 1998 (Commencement No. 2) Order 2000 (S.I. 2000 No. 1851).

GENERAL NOTE

This section is a response to concerns expressed by media interests that the Act would limit freedom of expression by giving priority to the development of privacy under Article 8 of the Convention. The section is not needed, since the Strasbourg case law makes it clear that a balance has to be struck between the privacy of the individual and the freedom of the press.

Freedom of thought, conscience and religion

3.35   **13.**—(1) If a court's determination of any question arising under this Act might affect the exercise by a religious organisation (itself or its members collectively) of the Convention right to freedom of thought, conscience and religion, it must have particular regard to the importance of that right.
(2) In this section "court" includes a tribunal.

COMMENCEMENT

3.36   October 2, 2000: The Human Rights Act 1998 (Commencement No. 2) Order 2000 (S.I. 2000 No. 1851).

GENERAL NOTE

This section was included in response to concerns expressed on behalf of religious groups that priority would be given to other provisions of the Convention than the provision on freedom of religion in Article 9 and that churches would find themselves being required in the name of human rights to do things contrary to their tenets. Like s.12, this section is not needed, since the Strasbourg case law makes it clear that a balance has to be struck between the pluralism of a modern democratic societies and respect for religious and personal beliefs.

(1998 c.42, s.14)

Derogations and reservations

Derogations

14.—(1) In this Act "designated derogation" means—   3.37
  (a) the United Kingdom's derogation from Article 5(3) of the Convention; and
  (b) any derogation by the United Kingdom from an Article of the Convention, or of any protocol to the Convention, which is designated for the purposes of this Act in an order made by the Secretary of State.

(2) The derogation referred to in subsection (1)(a) is set out in Part I of Schedule 3.

(3) If a designated derogation is amended or replaced it ceases to be a designated derogation.

(4) But subsection (3) does not prevent the Secretary of State from exercising his power under subsection (1)(b) to make a fresh designation order in respect of the Article concerned.

(5) The Secretary of State must by order make such amendments to Schedule 3 as he considers appropriate to reflect—
  (a) any designation order; or
  (b) the effect of subsection (3).

(6) A designation order may be made in anticipation of the making by the United Kingdom of a proposed derogation.

COMMENCEMENT

October 2, 2000: The Human Rights Act 1998 (Commencement No. 2)   3.38
Order 2000 (S.I. 2000 No. 1851).

Reservations

15.—(1) In this Act "designated reservation" means—   3.39
  (a) the United Kingdom's reservation to Article 2 of the First Protocol to the Convention; and
  (b) any other reservation by the United Kingdom to an Article of the Convention, or of any protocol to the Convention, which is designated for the purposes of this Act in an order made by the Secretary of State.

(2) The text of the reservation referred to in subsection (1)(a) is set out in Part II of Schedule 3.

(3) If a designated reservation is withdrawn wholly or in part it ceases to be a designated reservation.

(4) But subsection (3) does not prevent the Secretary of State from exercising his power under subsection (1)(b) to make a fresh designation order in respect of the Article concerned.

(5) The Secretary of State must by order make such amendments to this Act as he considers appropriate to reflect—
  (a) any designation order; or
  (b) the effect of subsection (3).

COMMENCEMENT

3.40   October 2, 2000: The Human Rights Act 1998 (Commencement No. 2) Order 2000 (S.I. 2000 No. 1851).

Period for which designated derogations have effect

3.41   16.—(1) If it has not already been withdrawn by the United Kingdom, a designated derogation ceases to have effect for the purposes of this Act—
   (a) in the case of the derogation referred to in section 14(1)(a), at the end of the period of five years beginning with the date on which section 1(2) came into force;
   (b) in the case of any other derogation, at the end of the period of five years beginning with the date on which the order designating it was made.
(2) At any time before the period—
   (a) fixed by subsection (1)(a) or (b), or
   (b) extended by an order under this subsection,
comes to an end, the Secretary of State may by order extend it by a further period of five years.
(3) An order under section 14(1)(b) ceases to have effect at the end of the period for consideration, unless a resolution has been passed by each House approving the order.
(4) Subsection (3) does not affect—
   (a) anything done in reliance on the order; or
   (b) the power to make a fresh order under section 14(1)(b).
(5) In subsection (3) "period for consideration" means the period of forty days beginning with the day on which the order was made.
(6) In calculating the period for consideration, no account is to be taken of any time during which—
   (a) Parliament is dissolved or prorogued; or
   (b) both Houses are adjourned for more than four days.
(7) If a designated derogation is withdrawn by the United Kingdom, the Secretary of State must by order make such amendments to this Act as he considers are required to reflect that withdrawal.

COMMENCEMENT

3.42   October 2, 2000: The Human Rights Act 1998 (Commencement No. 2) Order 2000 (S.I. 2000 No. 1851).

Periodic review of designated reservations

3.43   17.—(1) The appropriate Minister must review the designated reservation referred to in section 15(1)(a)—
   (a) before the end of the period of five years beginning with the date on which section 1(2) came into force; and
   (b) if that designation is still in force, before the end of the period of five years beginning with the date on which the last report relating to it was laid under subsection (3).

(2) The appropriate Minister must review each of the other designated reservations (if any)—
   (a) before the end of the period of five years beginning with the date on which the order designating the reservation first came into force; and
   (b) if the designation is still in force, before the end of the period of five years beginning with the date on which the last report relating to it was laid under subsection (3).

(3) The Minister conducting a review under this section must prepare a report on the result of the review and lay a copy of it before each House of Parliament.

COMMENCEMENT

October 2, 2000: The Human Rights Act 1998 (Commencement No. 2) Order 2000 (S.I. 2000 No. 1851).   3.44

Judges of the European Court of Human Rights

Section 18 omitted   3.45

Parliamentary procedure

Statements of compatibility

19.—(1) A Minister of the Crown in charge of a Bill in either House of Parliament must, before Second Reading of the Bill—   3.46
   (a) make a statement to the effect that in his view the provisions of the Bill are compatible with the Convention rights ("a statement of compatibility"); or
   (b) make a statement to the effect that although he is unable to make a statement of compatibility the government nevertheless wishes the House to proceed with the Bill.

(2) The statement must be in writing and be published in such manner as the Minister making it considers appropriate.

COMMENCEMENT

Section 19 entered into force on November 24, 1998: (S.I. 1998 No 2882).   3.47

GENERAL NOTE

Part of the scheme of the Act is to require improved pre-legislative scrutiny of legislation to ensure its compliance with Convention rights. The use of the section to date has been disappointing, since no reasoning is publicly available to elaborate a simple Ministerial statement that the provisions of a Bill are compatible with Convention rights.

Supplemental

3.48 *Section 20 omitted*

Interpretation, etc.

3.49 **21.**—(1) In this Act—
"amend" includes repeal and apply (with or without modifications);
"the appropriate Minister" means the Minister of the Crown having charge of the appropriate authorised government department (within the meaning of the Crown Proceedings Act 1947);
"the Commission" means the European Commission of Human Rights;
"the Convention" means the Convention for the Protection of Human Rights and Fundamental Freedoms, agreed by the Council of Europe at Rome on 4th November 1950 as it has effect for the time being in relation to the United Kingdom;
"declaration of incompatibility" means a declaration under section 4;
"Minister of the Crown" has the same meaning as in the Ministers of the Crown Act 1975;
"Northern Ireland Minister" includes the First Minister and the deputy First Minister in Northern Ireland;
"primary legislation" means any—
  (a) public general Act;
  (b) local and personal Act;
  (c) private Act;
  (d) Measure of the Church Assembly;
  (e) Measure of the General Synod of the Church of England;
  (f) Order in Council—
     (i) made in exercise of Her Majesty's Royal Prerogative;
     (ii) made under section 38(1)(a) of the Northern Ireland Constitution Act 1973 or the corresponding provision of the Northern Ireland Act 1998; or
     (iii) amending an Act of a kind mentioned in paragraph (a), (b) or (c);
  and includes an order or other instrument made under primary legislation (otherwise than by the National Assembly for Wales, a member of the Scottish Executive, a Northern Ireland Minister or a Northern Ireland department) to the extent to which it operates to bring one or more provisions of that legislation into force or amends any primary legislation;
"the First Protocol" means the protocol to the Convention agreed at Paris on March 20 1952;
"the Sixth Protocol" means the protocol to the Convention agreed at Strasbourg on April 28 1983;
"the Eleventh Protocol" means the protocol to the Convention (restructuring the control machinery established by the Convention) agreed at Strasbourg on May 11 1994;
"subordinate legislation" means any—
  (a) Order in Council other than one—

(i) made in exercise of Her Majesty's Royal Prerogative;
(ii) made under section 38(1)(a) of the Northern Ireland Constitution Act 1973 or the corresponding provision of the Northern Ireland Act 1998; or
(iii) amending an Act of a kind mentioned in the definition of primary legislation;
(b) Act of the Scottish Parliament;
(c) Act of the Parliament of Northern Ireland;
(d) Measure of the Assembly established under section 1 of the Northern Ireland Assembly Act 1973;
(e) Act of the Northern Ireland Assembly;
(f) order, rules, regulations, scheme, warrant, byelaw or other instrument made under primary legislation (except to the extent to which it operates to bring one or more provisions of that legislation into force or amends any primary legislation);
(g) order, rules, regulations, scheme, warrant, byelaw or other instrument made under legislation mentioned in paragraph (b), (c), (d) or (e) or made under an Order in Council applying only to Northern Ireland;
(h) order, rules, regulations, scheme, warrant, byelaw or other instrument made by a member of the Scottish Executive, a Northern Ireland Minister or a Northern Ireland department in exercise of prerogative or other executive functions of Her Majesty which are exercisable by such a person on behalf of Her Majesty;

"transferred matters" has the same meaning as in the Northern Ireland Act 1998; and

"tribunal" means any tribunal in which legal proceedings may be brought.

(2) The references in paragraphs (b) and (c) of section 2(1) to Articles are to Articles of the Convention as they had effect immediately before the coming into force of the Eleventh Protocol.

(3) The reference in paragraph (d) of section 2(1) to Article 46 includes a reference to Articles 32 and 54 of the Convention as they had effect immediately before the coming into force of the Eleventh Protocol.

(4) The references in section 2(1) to a report or decision of the Commission or a decision of the Committee of Ministers include references to a report or decision made as provided by paragraphs 3, 4 and 6 of Article 5 of the Eleventh Protocol (transitional provisions).

(5) Any liability under the Army Act 1955, the Air Force Act 1955 or the Naval Discipline Act 1957 to suffer death for an offence is replaced by a liability to imprisonment for life or any less punishment authorised by those Acts; and those Acts shall accordingly have effect with the necessary modifications.

COMMENCEMENT

Section 21(5) entered into force on November 9, 1998. The remainder of the section entered into force on October 2, 2000: The Human Rights Act 1998 (Commencement No. 2) Order 2000 (S.I. 2000 No. 1851).

Short title, commencement, application and extent

3.50   **22.**—(1) This Act may be cited as the Human Rights Act 1998.

(2) Sections 18, 20 and 21(5) and this section come into force on the passing of this Act.

(3) The other provisions of this Act come into force on such day as the Secretary of State may by order appoint; and different days may be appointed for different purposes.

(4) Paragraph (b) of subsection (1) of section 7 applies to proceedings brought by or at the instigation of a public authority whenever the act in question took place; but otherwise that subsection does not apply to an act taking place before the coming into force of that section.

(5) This Act binds the Crown.

(6) This Act extends to Northern Ireland.

(7) Section 21(5), so far as it relates to any provision contained in the Army Act 1955, the Air Force Act 1955 or the Naval Discipline Act 1957, extends to any place to which that provision extends.

GENERAL NOTE

3.51   This section entered into force on November 9, 1998.

Subs. (4), which entered into force on November 9, 1998, provides that the lawfulness of an act of a public authority may be called into question in proceedings under s.7(1)(b) (any legal proceedings in which Convention rights are raised) whenever that act took place if those proceedings are begun by a public authority. In other words, it has a retrospective effect in this regard, but if the proceedings are brought other than by a public authority, no complaint can be made about an act of a public authority prior to the entry into force of s.7(1)(b).

SCHEDULES

SCHEDULE 1

THE ARTICLES

PART I

THE CONVENTION

RIGHTS AND FREEDOMS

Article 2—Right to life

3.52   1. Everyone's right to life shall be protected by law. No one shall be deprived of his life intentionally save in the execution of a sentence of a court following his conviction of a crime for which this penalty is provided by law.

2. Deprivation of life shall not be regarded as inflicted in contravention of this Article when it results from the use of force which is no more than absolutely necessary:
   (a) in defence of any person from unlawful violence;
   (b) in order to effect a lawful arrest or to prevent the escape of a person lawfully detained;
   (c) in action lawfully taken for the purpose of quelling a riot or insurrection.

General Note

This article is unlikely to have much relevance in the social security jurisdiction. It is not a vehicle for arguing for a particular allocation of resources by the State. So arguments that without the payment of benefit, a person's life will be at risk and so the State cannot be said to be protecting by law everyone's right to life are destined to fail. This would appear to follow from those cases where the relatives of murder victims have sought to argue that the police failed to protect the victim: App. 9837/82 *M.v. United Kingdom and Ireland*, (1986) 47 D.R. 27.

3.53

Article 3—Prohibition of torture

No one shall be subjected to torture or to inhuman or degrading treatment or punishment.

3.54

General Note

This article is concerned with conduct which attains at least a minimum level of severity. It is not concerned with anything which a person might find degrading. See *Ireland v. United Kingdom*, Judgment of January 18, 1978, Series A No 25; (1979–80) 2 E.H.R.R. 25, para. 162 of judgment, and *Tyrer v. United Kingdom*, Judgment of April 25, 1978, Series A No 26; (1979–80) 2 E.H.R.R. 1, para. 30 of the judgment. The effect of setting a high threshold is that trivial complaints and even activity which is considered undesirable or illegal, will not fall within the scope of the article unless they cause sufficiently serious suffering or humiliation to the victim. The assessment of seriousness is relative. In its judgment in *Ireland v. United Kingdom*, the Court suggested that the following factors are relevant in determining the existence of inhuman treatment: the duration of the treatment, its physical and mental effects, and the sex, age, and state of health of the victim. But it should also be remembered that the Convention is a "living instrument" whose standards are not set in stone; it receives a living interpretation and must be considered in the light of present day circumstances.

3.55

It follows that arguments, for example, that a medical examination in connection with a benefit claim was felt to be degrading or inhuman by the claimant will fall well below the threshold required to engage this article even where the doctor behaves improperly.

Article 4—Prohibition of slavery and forced labour

1. No one shall be held in slavery or servitude.
2. No one shall be required to perform forced or compulsory labour.
3. For the purpose of this Article the term "forced or compulsory labour" shall not include:
    (a) any work required to be done in the ordinary course of detention imposed according to the provisions of Article 5 of this Convention or during conditional release from such detention;
    (b) any service of a military character or, in case of conscientious objectors in countries where they are recognised, service exacted instead of compulsory military service;
    (c) any service exacted in case of an emergency or calamity threatening the life or well-being of the community;
    (d) any work or service which forms part of normal civic obligations.

3.56

General Note

Being required to be available for work as a condition of entitlement to benefit will not constitute forced or compulsory labour.

3.57

Human Rights Act 1998

Article 5—Right to liberty and security

3.58
1. Everyone has the right to liberty and security of person. No one shall be deprived of his liberty save in the following cases and in accordance with a procedure prescribed by law:
   (a) the lawful detention of a person after conviction by a competent court;
   (b) the lawful arrest or detention of a person for non-compliance with the lawful order of a court or in order to secure the fulfilment of any obligation prescribed by law;
   (c) the lawful arrest or detention of a person effected for the purpose of bringing him before the competent legal authority on reasonable suspicion of having committed an offence or when it is reasonably considered necessary to prevent his committing an offence or fleeing after having done so;
   (d) the detention of a minor by lawful order for the purpose of educational supervision or his lawful detention for the purpose of bringing him before the competent legal authority;
   (e) the lawful detention of persons for the prevention of the spreading of infectious diseases, of persons of unsound mind, alcoholics or drug addicts or vagrants;
   (f) the lawful arrest or detention of a person to prevent his effecting an unauthorised entry into the country or of a person against whom action is being taken with a view to deportation or extradition.

2. Everyone who is arrested shall be informed promptly, in a language which he understands, of the reasons for his arrest and of any charge against him.

3. Everyone arrested or detained in accordance with the provisions of paragraph 1 (c) of this Article shall be brought promptly before a judge or other officer authorised by law to exercise judicial power and shall be entitled to trial within a reasonable time or to release pending trial. Release may be conditioned by guarantees to appear for trial.

4. Everyone who is deprived of his liberty by arrest or detention shall be entitled to take proceedings by which the lawfulness of his detention shall be decided speedily by a court and his release ordered if the detention is not lawful.

5. Everyone who has been the victim of arrest or detention in contravention of the provisions of this Article shall have an enforceable right to compensation.

GENERAL NOTE

3.59
There are two parts to the protections afforded by Article 5. First, it prohibits detention save in the exhaustive list of circumstances listed in paragraph (1). Secondly, it offers a set of procedural guarantees for those detained. Though the article refers to liberty and security of the person, the Strasbourg organs have not treated liberty and security as different concepts; there is no authority for arguing that security of the person refers to physical integrity independent of liberty. The article has little application in the field of social security.

Article 6—Right to a fair trial

3.60
1. In the determination of his civil rights and obligations or of any criminal charge against him, everyone is entitled to a fair and public hearing within a reasonable time by an independent and impartial tribunal established by law. Judgment shall be pronounced publicly but the press and public may be excluded from all or part of the trial in the interest of morals, public order or national security in a democratic society, where the interests of juveniles or the protection of the private life of the parties so require, or to the extent strictly necessary in the opinion of the court in special circumstances where publicity would prejudice the interests of justice.

2. Everyone charged with a criminal offence shall be presumed innocent until proved guilty according to law.

3. Everyone charged with a criminal offence has the following minimum rights:
   (a) to be informed promptly, in a language which he understands and in detail, of the nature and cause of the accusation against him;
   (b) to have adequate time and facilities for the preparation of his defence;
   (c) to defend himself in person or through legal assistance of his own choosing or, if he has not sufficient means to pay for legal assistance, to be given it free when the interests of justice so require;

(d) to examine or have examined witnesses against him and to obtain the attendance and examination of witnesses on his behalf under the same conditions as witnesses against him;
(e) to have the free assistance of an interpreter if he cannot understand or speak the language used in court.

GENERAL NOTE

Article 6 is central to the scheme of protection in the Convention, and has generated the largest number of applications and judgments. Article 6 is an omnibus provision which contains a blueprint for what constitutes a fair trial. Accordingly, it warrants extensive treatment.

Does the resolution of social security disputes involve the determination of civil rights and obligations?

The first question which must be addressed is whether decision-making in social security constitutes 'the determination of . . . civil rights and obligations'. Answering this question requires detailed discussion of a line of Convention cases. The formulation in Article 6 would seem to exclude the initial decisions by decision-makers since the article contemplates a situation in which there is a dispute. This is clearer from the French text, which refers to *contestations*. It cannot be said that there is a dispute when what is at issue is an initial determination of entitlement to benefit (see *Feldbrugge* v. *The Netherlands*, Judgment of May 29, 1986, Series A, No. 99; (1986) 8 E.H.R.R. 425, para. 25 of the Judgment); the vast majority of such decisions are not the subject of appeal to a tribunal. But what of the tribunals? Are they determining civil rights and obligations? The essential question is whether Article 6 covers only private law rights to the exclusion of public law matters: a distinction which is much more formal in continental systems of law than in the United Kingdom's common law system.

It was not long before the issue came before the Court of Human Rights in the *Ringeisen* case (*Ringeisen* v. *Austria*, Judgment of July 16, 1971, Series A, No. 13; (1979–80) 1 EHRR 455) after the majority of the Commission had concluded that Article 6 should be construed restrictively as including only those proceedings which are typical of relations between private individuals and as excluding those proceedings in which the citizen is confronted by those who exercise public authority. The Court took a different view. Article 6 covers all proceedings the result of which is decisive for the private rights and obligations of individuals, and neither the character of the legislation (whether, for example civil, commercial or administrative) nor that of the authority with jurisdiction over the dispute (whether, for example, court, tribunal or administrative body) are of great consequence. Since the decision in this case, the Court has adopted a liberal interpretation of the concept of civil rights and obligations.

Several cases have considered whether social security disputes involve the determination of civil rights and obligations.

The *Feldbrugge* case (*Feldbrugge* v. *The Netherlands*, Judgment of May 29, 1986, Series A, No. 99; (1986) 8 E.H.R.R. 425) concerned a dispute over entitlement to a sickness allowance in The Netherlands. Mrs Feldbrugge had been registered as unemployed, but then ceased to register because she had become ill and did not consider herself fit for work. The Occupational Association (the body responsible for administering sickness allowance in The Netherlands) arranged for her to be medically examined by their consulting doctor, who concluded that she was fit for work. The sickness allowance was stopped. The claimant appealed to the Appeals Board and the President of the Appeals Board arranged for her to be seen by a gynaecologist who was one of the permanent medical experts attached to the Appeals Board. That doctor examined her and

3.61

3.62

gave her an opportunity to comment. The doctor consulted another gynaecologist and two general practitioners (one of whom was the claimant's GP). They all agreed with the decision that the claimant was fit for work, but the permanent medical expert considered that an orthopaedic specialist should also be consulted. An orthopaedic surgeon examined the claimant who was again given an opportunity to comment. The three practitioners consulted by the gynaecologist were also consulted following this examination. The orthopaedic surgeon concluded in the light of all the medical findings that the claimant was fit for work in accordance with the initial contested decision. The President of the Appeals Board then ruled against the claimant, who filed an objection which raised the matter before the Appeals Board itself, which found the objection lacking in substance. An appeal to the Central Appeals Board was unsuccessful. Mrs Feldbrugge complained that she had not had a fair trial before the President of the Appeals Board in violation of Article 6(1). The Court had to face squarely the issue of whether the adjudication of the claimant's dispute was a matter concerning her civil rights and obligations. The Court weighed the features of the case which suggested that the matter was one of public law against the features which suggested that it was one of private law. The public law nature of the legislation on sickness allowances, the compulsory nature of insurance against illness, and the assumption by the State of responsibility for social protection had to be weighed against the personal and economic nature of the asserted right, its connection with the contract of employment, and affinities with insurance under the ordinary law. After weighing these interests, the Court ruled by a majority of ten votes to seven, that, taken together, the private law aspects of the sickness allowance scheme were "predominant" and the adjudication of Mrs Feldbrugge's claim was therefore covered by Article 6(1).

The *Deumeland* case (*Deumeland v. Germany*, Judgment of May 29, 1986, Series A, No. 100; (1986) 8 E.H.R.R. 448), decided on the same day as the *Feldbrugge* case, concerned industrial injury pensions in Germany. The proceedings in Germany were extraordinarily protracted, and this was the substance of the applicant's complaint. Gerhard Deumeland had in January 1970 slipped on a snow covered pavement as he was coming home from an appointment with an ear-nose-and-throat specialist whom he had consulted on leaving his workplace. He died in March 1970, and his widow claimed a widow's supplementary pension on the basis that the death of Gerhard had been the consequence of an industrial accident. The first set of proceedings before the Berlin Social Security Court of Appeal lasted from June 1970 to December 1972. The outcome of these proceedings was a decision that the accident in question was neither an industrial accident nor an accident on the way to or from work. There was accordingly no entitlement to a widow's supplementary pension. Mrs Deumeland appealed to the Berlin Social Security Court of Appeal, where the first set of proceedings lasted from November 1972 to September 1973. These were unsuccessful. An appeal on a point of law was pursued before the Bundessozialgericht (Federal Social Security Court) which lasted from October 1973 to May 1975. In the course of these proceedings, the claimant challenged a judge for bias accusing him of delaying the proceedings. That challenge was not successful and the appeal decision was taken by a panel which included the unsuccessfully challenged judge. The decision of the Bundessozialgericht was to set aside the decision of the Berlin Social Security Court of Appeal and to remit the case for a fresh hearing.

The second set of proceedings before the Berlin Social Security Court of Appeal lasted from May 1975 to March 1979. In December 1976 during the course of these proceedings, Mrs Deumeland died and her son, Klaus, was allowed to continue the proceedings. The outcome was a decision that the claim to the widow's pension was unfounded. Klaus Deumeland sought to appeal to the Bundessozialgericht. Leave to appeal was eventually refused. Leave for a further appeal to the Bundesverfassungsgericht (Federal Constitutional Court) was refused by that Court, and a subsequent application to the Berlin Social Security Court of Appeal by Klaus Deumeland to have the proceedings re-opened was not only unsuccessful but also resulted in his being fined DM800 for bringing vexatious proceedings. For reasons which are very similar to those in the Feldbrugge case, the Court, by a majority of 9 votes to 8, concluded that the proceedings of which the applicant complained had been concerned with the determination of civil rights and obligations.

The *Feldbrugge* and *Deumeland* cases had involved benefits which flowed from an insurance principle, and this feature might be seen as critical in drawing a distinction between social insurance and social assistance. The latter term refers to those benefits which fall outside the sphere of social insurance and involve the State stepping in to provide benefits for those who have no entitlement to insurance-based benefits, or whose entitlement is such that their income is below subsistence level. The distinction came before the Court in the *Salesi* case (*Salesi v. Italy*, Judgment of February 26, 1993, Series A, No. 257-E). Enrica Salesi had claimed a monthly disability allowance in the Lazio social security department, which had been refused. In February 1986, she brought proceedings against the Minister of the Interior before the pretore del lavoro (magistrates' court exercising their labour jurisdiction) in Rome seeking payment of the benefit. The Minister appealed against the decision of the pretore awarding the benefit, and the Rome District Court dismissed the appeal in May 1989. A subsequent appeal to the Court of Cassation was also dismissed. Even though the claimant was ultimately the winning party, she complained to the Commission alleging a violation of Article 6(1) by reason of the length of the proceedings.

The Court re-affirmed its decisions in *Feldbrugge* and *Deumeland* noting,

". . . the development in the law that was initiated by those judgments and the principle of equality of treatment warrant taking the view that today the general rule is that Article 6(1) does apply in the field of social insurance."

The Court went on,

"In the present case, however, the question arises in connection with welfare assistance and not . . . social insurance. Certainly there are differences between the two, but they cannot be regarded as fundamental at the present stage of development of social security law. This justifies following, in relation to the entitlement to welfare allowances, the opinion which emerges from [the judgments in *Feldbrugge* and *Deumeland*] as regards the classification of the right to social insurance benefits, namely that State intervention is not sufficient to establish that Article 6(1) is inapplicable." (para. 19 of the Judgment).

The Court concluded that there were no convincing reasons for distinguishing welfare benefits from the rights to social insurance benefits asserted in the earlier cases. The decision of the Court may be criticised for its poverty of reasoning, but nevertheless remains an authority for the extension of Article 6(1) to all disputes concerning social security benefits.

The *Schuler-Zgraggen* case (*Schuler-Zgraggen* v. *Switzerland*, Judgment of June 24, 1993, Series A, No. 263; (1993) 16 E.H.R.R. 405) concerned a claim to an invalidity pension. The claimant had been employed and paid contributions into the federal invalidity insurance scheme. She contracted open pulmonary tuberculosis and applied for an invalidity pension. The Compensation Office awarded a half pension, which was subsequently increased to a full pension. In 1984 the applicant gave birth to a son. In 1985 she was required to undergo a medical examination by doctors appointed by the Invalidity Insurance Board. This resulted in a decision to terminate the award of the invalidity pension. The claimant appealed to the relevant Appeals Board. In the course of these proceedings she was refused a sight of her medical file which had been seen by the Appeals Board. The Board subsequently dismissed her appeal. The claimant lodged an appeal against this decision with the Federal Insurance Court, whose decision was to remit the case to the Compensation Office, whose reconsideration did not result in the award of a pension. The Court followed its earlier decisions in concluding that the proceedings in issue were concerned with the determination of civil rights and obligations. The Court also followed the decision in *Salesi* in virtually identical language,

> "... the development in the law that was initiated by those judgments [in *Feldbrugge* and *Deumeland*] and the principle of equality of treatment warrant taking the view that today the general rule is that Article 6(1) does apply in the field of social insurance, including even welfare assistance." (para. 46 of the Judgment).

The *Schouten and Meldrum* case (*Schouten and Meldrum v. The Netherlands*, Judgment of December 9, 1994, Series A, No. 304; (1994) 19 E.H.R.R. 432) concerned the liability of persons in similar positions to employers to pay contributions to an occupational association in respect of physiotherapists who worked for them. This was the first case in which the Court had been called upon to determine an issue involving the payment of contributions under a social security scheme as distinct from disputes concerning entitlement to benefits. The Court took the view that the approach adopted in *Feldbrugge* and *Deumeland* was appropriate in the case of liability to pay contributions. The public law and private law aspects of the arrangements should be weighed to see whether one or the other were predominant. Using exactly the same factors as had been in issue in *Feldbrugge*, the Court concluded that the private law aspects were predominant and that Article 6(1) applied.

A challenge to the system of recovering State benefits from personal injury awards has also failed at the admissibility stage (App. 2877/95, *Graeme Knightley v. United Kingdom*, Decision of September 4, 1997). See also *Stevens and Knight v. United Kingdom*, Decision of September 9, 1998, in which the Commission simply ignored arguments that the determination of claims to sickness benefit, statutory sick pay and invalidity benefit did not constitute the determination of civil rights and obligations.

These cases establish beyond a peradventure that adjudication of social security disputes involves the determination of civil rights and obligations to which the procedural guarantees of Article 6(1) apply: see also *CDLA/5413/1999* starred as 07/00. They have been followed even in cases where the pensions of those employed in the public service were involved (*Lombardo v. Italy*, Judgment of November 26, 1992, Series A, No 249-B, (1996) 21 E.H.R.R. 188; and *Massa v. Italy*, Judgment of August 24, 1993, Series A, No 265-B, (1994) 18 E.H.R.R. (266). It follows that the rules on what constitutes a fair trial apply to the proceedings of tribunals, the Commissioners and the courts when dealing with social security questions.

What is a fair trial under Article 6(1)?

3.64 The Strasbourg organs have indicated that Article 6(1) demands not only an overall requirement of a fair hearing but also the presence of specific features in order for there to be a fair trial. The overall requirement has been summarised as follows,

> "The effect of Article 6(1) is, *inter alia*, to place the 'tribunal' under a duty to conduct a proper examination of the submissions, arguments and evidence

adduced by the parties, without prejudice to its assessment of whether they are relevant to its decision." (*Kraska v. Switzerland*, Judgment of 19 Apr. 1993, Series A, No. 254-B; (1994) 18 E.H.R.R. 188, para. 30 of the Judgment).

It is important that the general requirements for a fair trial are appreciated, since they continue to be developed in specific circumstances by the Strasbourg organs. Certain of the requirements are of a general nature, whereas others are more specifically stated in Article 6.

Four features *inherent* in the concept of a fair trial appear to have flowed from this general notion of a fair trial.

The first and perhaps most important is the concept of *égalité des armes*, which translates inelegantly into English as "equality of arms". In English law, it is an aspect of the requirement of natural justice. It requires that each party has a broadly equal opportunity to present a case in circumstances which do not place one of the parties as a substantial disadvantage as regards the opposing party (see *Dombo Beheer BV v. The Netherlands*, Judgment of October 27, 1993, Series A, No. 274-A; (1994) 18 E.H.R.R. 213, para. 33 of the Judgment). In *CDLA/ 5413/1999*, starred as 07/00, the Commissioner expresses concern that the principle of equality of arms may be breached by the provisions of the Adjudication Regulations on notice, which provide that notice required to be given or sent by the Department are, if sent by post, deemed to be given on the day of posting, whereas notice required to be given by a claimant is only treated as given when it reaches the Department.

Secondly, there must be a judicial process, which requires each side to have the opportunity to have knowledge of and comment on the observations filed or evidence adduced by the opposing party (*Ruiz-Mateos v. Spain*, Judgment of June 23, 1993, Series A, No. 262; (1993) 16 E.H.R.R. 505, para. 63 of the Judgment). Non-disclosure of material by one side to the other is likely to give rise to violations of this feature of a fair trial, as might issues of the circumstances in which evidence was acquired. In the *Feldbrugge* case, the applicant complained that she had not had a proper opportunity to present her case. The Court found that the proceedings before the President of the Appeals Board "were not attended to a sufficient degree, by one of the principal guarantees of a judicial procedure" (para. 44 of the Judgment) in that, although the applicant had been afforded the opportunity to comment on her condition during the medical examinations, she was neither able to present oral argument nor to file written pleadings before the President of the Appeals Board; nor was she able to consult the two reports of the consultants and to formulate objections to them.

Thirdly, there is a requirement for a reasoned decision, which is regarded as implicit in the notion of a fair trial. The level of reasoning need not be detailed. If a court gives reasons, then the requirement for a reasoned decision is *prima facie* met, but a decision which on its face shows that it was made on a basis not open to the judge cannot be said to be a reasoned decision (see *De Moor v. Belgium*, Judgment of June 23, 1994, Series A, No. 292-A; (1994) 18 E.H.R.R. 372). The introduction of short-form decisions in tribunals is unlikely to fall foul of this provision, since a party is entitled to a full statement of reasons on application within one month of the day on which the decision notice was notified to the parties. Decisions of the Commissioners are always given in full, except a decision made with the consent of the parties to set aside a tribunal decision and remit the case for a rehearing by the tribunal.

The final issue is whether a trial can be fair if there is no right of appearance in person. The law here remains in a state of development and the Court has yet to pronounce in detail on this in civil cases, but the Commission has held that in some cases a fair trial is only possible in the presence of the parties. An example would be a case where the personal character and manner of life of a party are directly relevant to the formation of the court's opinion on the point at issue. Custody disputes over children might be such cases (See App. 434/58, *X v. Sweden,* June 30 1959, 2 Y.B. 354, 370). Presence may need to be distinguished from participation. In the *Schuler-Zgraggen* case, the applicant had not availed herself of the opportunity to request a hearing, but nevertheless complained that the proceedings were unfair because the Federal Insurance Court had not ordered a hearing of its own motion. The Court accepted the arguments of the Government that purely written proceedings did not in the circumstances of this case prejudice the interests of the litigant. It was accepted that a written procedure would offer advantages of efficiency and speed which might be jeopardised if oral hearings became the rule. The Court concluded,

"The Court reiterates that the public character of court hearings constitutes a fundamental principle enshrined in Article 6(1). Admittedly, neither the letter nor the spirit of this provision prevents a person from waiving of his own free will, either expressly or tacitly, the entitlement to have his case heard in public, but any such waiver must be made in an unequivocal manner and must not run counter to any important public interest." (para 58 of the Judgment).

These comments have relevance both for paper hearings before appeal tribunals and for procedure before the Commissioners (see below).

There are four *specific features* of a fair trial to be found on the face of Article 6:

Firstly, trial must be before "an independent and impartial tribunal established by law." This requirement includes a subjective and an objective element. The subjective test involves an enquiry into whether the particular judge in the case was actually biased, or lacking in independence or impartiality. Propriety will be presumed in the absence of specific evidence of bias. The objective test involves determination of whether the court or tribunal offers guarantees sufficient to exclude any legitimate doubt about its impartiality or independence. This can include both specific difficulties caused by certain persons being involved in particular decisions, as well as what might be called structural problems with the forum for the resolution of the dispute. A good example of structural problems can be found in the English courts-martial cases, which have determined that the role (at the time) of the convening officer in the management of the prosecution case conflicted with his role as convenor of the courtmartial, in particular his appointment of its members (who were subordinate in rank to himself and fell within his chain of command) (see *Findlay v. United Kingdom,* Judgment of February 25, 1997; (1997) 24 E.H.R.R. 221; and *Coyne v. United Kingdom,* Judgment of September 24, 1997).

Secondly, publicity is seen as one of the guarantees of the fairness of a trial, but the requirement for hearings to be in public is surrounded by a substantial list of circumstances in which the presumption of public hearings is displaced. It is now also clear that interlocutory matters do not have to be in public. So the Commission has rejected a complaint that interlocutory proceedings before a High Court Master in Chambers without elaborating its reasons violated Article 6 App. 3860/68, *X v. United Kingdom,* (1970) 30 C.D. 70). A similar view would almost certainly be taken of proceedings for leave to appeal. As already noted, a written procedure may suffice provided that there are proper opportunities for requesting or ordering an oral hearing.

Thirdly, Article 6(1), on its face, requires that judgment is pronounced publicly, and this requirement is not expressed to be subject to the list of limitations which apply to a public trial. The leading case is *Pretto* (*Pretto and others v. Italy,* Judgment of December 8, 1983, Series A, No. 71; (1984) 6 E.H.R.R. (182).

The Court seems to have been very accommodating to a wide range of practice in this regard among the Contracting States, indicating that the form of publicity to be given to a judgment is to be assessed in the light of special features of particular proceedings. It certainly appears to be the case that nothing more than the formal disposition need be announced publicly, and it seems that the public availability of the outcome is as important as the matter being read out in open court. So in the *Pretto* case, the availability of the disposition in the court registry was considered to meet the requirements for public pronouncement of the judgment.

Lastly, under Article 6(1), litigants are entitled to judgment in a reasonable time. Complaints of violations of this requirements have been the single most numerous sort of alleged violation of the Convention. Such cases have rarely involved the United Kingdom (but see *Robins v. United Kingdom*, Judgment of September 23, 1997; (1997) 26 E.H.R.R. 527). Though the case law is voluminous, the principles can be stated quite simply. The first task is to determine the period or periods in issue, before moving on to consider the reasonableness of the length of the proceedings. The period in issue will include any appellate proceedings. In forming judgments on the reasonableness of the length of the proceedings, the following factors are relevant: the complexity of the case, the behaviour of the applicant, the conduct of the judicial authorities, and what is at stake for the applicant. However, backlogs of judicial business are not a defence to unreasonable delays. In *Deumeland*, the period in issue was ten years, seven months and three weeks from the application to the Berlin Social Security Court to the rejection of the application to the Bundesverfassungsgericht. The claim to benefit involved a straightforward factual issue involving no great legal complexity, but the behaviour of Klaus Deumeland had protracted the proceedings. Detailed examination of the progress of the case through the various courts showed that the case had lain dormant before the Berlin Social Security Court for significant periods, and the period taken to resolve the second set of proceedings before the appellate body was excessive. There was a violation of the right to judgment within a reasonable time, but it is significant that the Court also finds that the mere declaration of a violation was in the circumstances of the case considered to be adequate just satisfaction under what is now Article 41 of the Convention. A delay of a little over six years in the *Salesi* case was also found to constitute a violation of Article 6(1). The reasonableness of the time taken to give judgment must be determined in each case in the light of its own particular circumstances.

The application of Article 6(1) to appeal proceedings

Article 6 does not require Contracting States to have a system of appeals from decisions at first instance in civil cases (*De Cubber v. Belgium*, Judgment of October 26, 1984 Series A, No. 86; (1985) 7 E.H.R.R. 236, para. 32 of the Judgment), but if the State does provide a system of appeals, it too must comply with the guarantees to be found in Article 6(1) (*Fedje v. Sweden*, Judgment of September 26, 1991, Series A, No. 212-C; (1994) 17 E.H.R.R. 14, para. 32 of the Judgment). It follows that a defect at first instance might be corrected at the appellate stage of the proceedings. Where there is an appeal, the requirement to exhaust domestic remedies before a complaint can be made under the Convention means that it must be used, and it will then be the totality of the domestic proceedings which is considered by the Commission and Court. It will always be necessary to look at the character of the appellate proceedings to determine the extent to which they are able to remedy any deficiency at first instance. For example, the shortcoming identified in the *Feldbrugge* case could not be remedied on appeal, because the nature of the appeal was restricted to four very narrow grounds, none of which offered the opportunity for the applic-

3.65

ant to participate to the extent required by Article 6 in the proceedings which determined her dispute.

A fair appeal is unlikely to be able to correct a defect arising from a structural problem in the first instance court or tribunal which results in its not being an independent and impartial tribunal (*De Cubber v. Belgium*, Judgment of October 26, 1984, Series A, No. 86; (1985) 7 E.H.R.R. 236, para. 33 of the Judgment). There is a suggestion that the quashing by an appeal court on the specific ground that the first instance court or tribunal was not independent and impartial might have cured the defect, but this could amount to recognition that there was no right to a court in the particular instance. This is a right which the Court has read in to Article 6.

The right to a court

3.66 The Court has recognised that Article 6 must contain a right of access to a court for the determination of a particular issue. So the prohibition (at the time) in English Prison Rules on bringing a defamation action against a prison officer, who was alleged to have accused the prisoner wrongly of having assaulted him, violated this right (*Golder v. United Kingdom*, Judgment of February 21, 1975, Series A, No. 18; (1979–80) 1 E.H.R.R. 524). A similar conclusion was reached in a case originating from Ireland where there was no procedure by which a father could challenge a decision of the authorities placing his daughter for adoption (*Keegan v. Ireland*, Judgment of May 26, 1994, Series A, No. 290; (1994) 18 E.H.R.R. 342). The right might even include a right to some sort of representation in order to make the right effective. In the *Airey* case (*Airey v. Ireland*, Judgment of October 9, 1979, Series A, No. 32; (1979–80) 2 E.H.R.R. 305), the applicant had been unable to find a lawyer to act for her because of her financial position and the absence of legal aid. She needed a separation order to protect her from her husband who was prone to violence towards her. The procedure was complex and not such as could be managed effectively by a litigant in person. The Court concluded that, in such circumstances, Article 6 requires the provision of legal assistance where "such assistance proves indispensable for an effective access to court." (para. 26 of the Judgment). The case is sometimes wrongly read too sweepingly as imposing an obligation on State to have a legal aid scheme, at least for complex litigation. The judgment is rather more limited; it will be necessary to look at the nature of the right being protected by the litigation, what is at stake for the applicant, and the complexity of the procedure before the particular decision-making body in making a judgment as to whether Article 6 requires a State to provide legal assistance.

Application to social security procedure

3.67 As noted above, initial decision-making on claims to benefit does not fall within Article 6, though appeals to the appeal tribunals and onward appeals to the Social Security Commissioners do attract the due process guarantees of Article 6.

Procedure before the tribunals is unlikely to raise any difficulties under Article 6. It is just possible that an issue could arise from the introduction of paper hearings. However, paper hearings will only arise where the claimant does not ask for an oral hearing. There might be an arguable violation of Article 6 where a paper hearing proceeds in a case which is for particular reasons more appropriate for an oral hearing. Regulation 39(5) of the Decisions and Appeals Regulations provides a power for the chairman of an appeal tribunal of his or her own motion to direct an oral hearing of an appeal. A good example of an appeal which might not be appropriate for a paper hearing might be a case involving a substantial overpayment of benefit where the claimant maintained that disclosure had taken place. Here issues of credibility are raised which can best be resolved by seeing and hearing the claimant.

In *CDLA/5413/1999*, starred as 07/00, the Commissioner concluded that the claimant had been denied a fair hearing when she had asked for an oral hearing and an appeal proceeded in her absence because the deemed notice of the hearing had never reached her. The Commissioner says,

> "49. Rehearsing again the salient features of this case in the light of the above analysis [of the requirements of Article 6 ECHR], it is one where the claimant asked, in accordance with regulations, for an oral hearing. The hearing was to be before the only tribunal or court competent to give her case a full hearing as to issues of fact. It was a case in which her presence and evidence were clearly relevant to the issue before the tribunal. She was unrepresented. She was not present at the hearing. The Secretary of State was not represented. There was no clerk present. The tribunal heard the case, and in doing so both assumed it had the capacity to do so and that it did not need to adjourn. It did that because the claimant was assumed to know about the hearing because of the deemed notice provision. But the claimant did not know about the hearing through no fault of her own.
>
> 50. The question for me on those facts is whether there was a fair hearing of this case before the decision of the tribunal was made, in the judicial sense of 'fair hearing'. In my view there was not. This is because the claimant asked for an oral hearing and did not receive it. This was through no fault of her own but because of the operation, against her interests, of a rule of procedure that was not a 'fair balance' as between her and the other party to the appeal, the Secretary of State.
>
> 51. It does not matter whether that unfairness was the result of the decision of the tribunal itself to continue with the case or whether it was the result of some failure in the method by which the claimant was supposed to be given notice and for which the tribunal itself had no direct responsibility. The essential matter is that the decision under appeal was reached without the tribunal hearing the claimant and without if having any of the permissible grounds for not hearing her."

It will also be important to ensure that the requirements implicit in "égalité des armes" are always met; this will mean that the claimant always has the opportunity to respond to the case put forward on behalf of the Secretary of State, and that new evidence is not put before the tribunal at such a late stage that the claimant has no opportunity to comment upon it.

It is possible that a claimant might take issue with the composition of a tribunal in which there is no guarantee that, for example, a medically qualified panel member is not also a member of the panel of examining medical practitioners used by the Benefits Agency. There would clearly be a breach of natural justice (and a violation of Article 6(1)) if a doctor who had examined a claimant sat on the tribunal which heard the appeal, but it is clear that this would be obvious from the papers and that the normal expectation is that the doctor would not sit. The requirement that an applicant must exhaust all domestic remedies before complaining of a breach of the Convention would mean that an applicant would need to pursue an appeal to the Social Security Commissioner, who would, in the face of the circumstances described, have no hesitation in setting the tribunal decision aside for breach of natural justice and remitting the case for an oral hearing before a properly constituted tribunal. In this way, a remedy would be provided for the breach of Article 6 in the domestic courts. However, where the objection related to the *possibility* of inclusion of a doctor on the tribunal who also conducted examinations for the Benefits Agency, it is difficult to see how a remedy could be provided by the tribunal. A claimant might find little sympathy given to the argument that he or she has no complaint about the impartiality of the specific member of the tribunal, but objects that a medical member might also be an examining medical practitioner for the Benefits Agency. There is something slightly odd about a tribunal holding in the abstract that it is not an independent and impartial tribunal. For this reason, it may well be that judicial review would be the proper route to raise such a challenge, although to be a victim for the purposes of the Convention, the claimant would of necessity also have an appeal to the tribunal.

The tribunals are structured in such a way that claimants can appear in person. It is unlikely that the significant evidence that represented claimants do better than unrepresented ones (Genn, H. and Genn, Y., *The Effectiveness of Representation at Tribunals*, (London: Lord Chancellor's Department, 1989)) would persuade the Court of Human Rights that proceedings before the tribunals were such that the State was obliged to provide legal assistance.

Perhaps the tribunals are most at risk of complaints that judgment has not been given in a reasonable time, particularly where an appeal to the Commissioner has resulted in the setting aside of the decision and the remission of the case for a fresh hearing. Current delays both before the tribunals and the Commissioners can result in four or more years passing before a final decision is made. This could in a simple case be regarded as excessive under Article 6, particularly if the case had lain dormant for some time either in the Commissioner's office after the papers were ready for determination, or within the appeals service awaiting listing for the rehearing. The existence of backlogs and excessive workloads on the judiciary are not accepted as justifications for unreasonable delays. The Court has consistently stated that the Contracting States must organise their judicial systems in such a way that their tribunals can meet the requirement to give judgment within a reasonable time (see, for example, *Massa v. Italy*, Judgment of August 24, 1993, Series A, No 265-B, (1994) 18 E.H.R.R. 266, para 28 of the Judgment).

Two particular aspects of procedure before the Commissioner might be problematic. The first relates to entitlement to an oral hearing. The Social Security Commissioners Procedure Regulations 1999 provide that, where a request is made for a hearing, the Commissioner "shall grant the request unless he is satisfied that the application or appeal can properly be determined without a hearing" (reg. 23(2)). Most appeals to the Commissioner are determined without a hearing, but many applications for a hearing are refused. The standard reasons simply repeat the words of the regulation. Many appeals are pursued before the Commissioner without the benefit of expert advice and assistance. Since the appeal to the Commissioner lies only on a point of law, the underlying argument is that an unrepresented appellant is unlikely to be able in oral argument to advice the position established by the exchange of written arguments between adjudication officer and appellant. There is a provision that a Commissioner can of his or her own motion direct an oral hearing (reg. 23(4)). It would be conceivable that an appellant might try to argue that the presumption in the regulation has effectively been reversed in practice, and that an oral hearing will only be granted if the appellant can show reasons why there should be one.

A second exposure under Article 6 of the Convention could result from argument that legal assistance is necessary to enable a person to pursue an appeal effectively before the Commissioner. The arguments that would be advanced by the appellant would be that the jurisdiction of the Social Security Commissioners is described by themselves as broadly equivalent to an appeal to the High Court and is available only on points of law. Furthermore social security law is of great complexity and specialist assistance is needed to construct and argue legal points involved in appeals. The countervailing arguments would, no doubt, be that the Commissioners adopt an inquisitorial approach to the file, and considerable preparatory work is undertaken by legal officers to ensure that the file is complete before it is placed before a Commissioner for determination of the appeal. There is force in both arguments. Which would prevail if the matter came before the Court of Human Rights is hard to predict.

The Social Security Act 1998

A number of aspects of the Social Security Act 1998 would appear to leave open the possibility of challenge for compatibility with Convention rights.

3.68

One of the great achievements of the Office of the President of Social Security Appeal Tribunals (OPSSAT) and its successor, the Independent Tribunal Service (ITS), has been to emphasise the independence of the tribunals hearing appeals by claimants against decisions of adjudication officers in the Department of Social Security. That success has dramatically increased respect for the tribunals. Certain provisions of the Social Security Act 1998 at best undermine that independence, and at worst may leave the structure exposed to challenges under the Convention as not constituting independent and impartial tribunals. New "unified appeal tribunals" have replaced the tribunals which formed part of the ITS, which is itself abolished. Appointment to the panels is happily not a matter for the Secretary of State for Social Security, but for the Lord Chancellor (or Lord Advocate in Scotland), though section 6 provides that the number of appointments and their terms and conditions are subject to the consent of the Secretary of State. Appeal tribunals may consist of one, two or three members and the requirements for a lawyer chairman of the tribunals goes.

The authority of the new tribunals is, however, undermined by the provision that the Secretary of State may supersede any decision of a tribunal or of a Social Security Commissioner (s 11(1)). That power is subject to provisions of the Decisions and Appeals Regulations, which broadly limit the exercise of the power to situations where there is a change of circumstances or new evidence comes to light. Formerly such limitations appeared in the primary legislation (s 35, Social Security Administration Act 1992), and it is disturbing to see that this practice has been discontinued.

Section 13(3) contains a bizarre provision (see commentary on it in this volume), which raises interesting questions about the relationship between the parties and the tribunal, but, for the reasons set out in the commentary to the provision, it is unlikely to have real significance.

Section 26 would appear to be objectionable in that it enables the Secretary of State who is one of the parties to the dispute to direct the tribunal on the determination of the appeal. Such a provision must result in the tribunal not being independent and impartial, since it is a characteristic of an independent and impartial tribunal that it is not susceptible to instructions concerning the exercise of its judicial function (*Ettl v. Austria*, Judgment of April 23, 1987, Series A, No. 117; (1988) 10 E.H.R.R. 255, para. 38 of the Judgment).

The Council on Tribunals has suggested that the proposed new structure for the tribunals could resemble the unsatisfactory system which was abandoned many years ago, and has suggested that the new arrangements are a cause for concern (*Annual Report of the Council on Tribunals for 1996/97*, (1997–98) H.C. 376). There may, accordingly, be challenges to the compatibility of the new structure with the requirement that tribunals are independent and impartial. The Secretary of State, who is a party to proceedings before the tribunals is also the paymaster and, in certain circumstances, is able to overrule their decisions. Their independence certainly appears less clear cut than that of their predecessors, which may well also be relevant were the matter to be considered by the Court of Human Rights.

Criminal charges

3.69 A question arises as to whether determinations of the Commissioners under the Forfeiture Act of 1982, of proceedings for penalty additions to overpayments under the Social Security Administration (Fraud) Act 1997, and of possible penalty proceedings under the Tax Credits Act 1999 constitute the determination of criminal charges under Article 6 and so attract the additional protections for such matters in the article. Though these matters are largely outside the ambit of these volumes, it may be helpful to express a view on this question.

The concept of a criminal charge is an autonomous one under the Convention, and so it is not the classification of the matter under national law which is determinative of the issue. National classification is not, however, wholly irrelevant since the Strasbourg organs have always regarded as a criminal charge something so considered by national law.

In other cases the following factors have been taken into account in making the determination: the nature of the "offence", the severity of the sanction imposed having regard in particular to any loss of liberty since this is a principal characteristic of criminal liability: see *Engel and others v. The Netherlands*, Judgment of June 8, 1976; Series A, No 22; (1979–80) 1 E.H.R.R. 647. Having regard to this case and to the judgment of the Court in *Ravnsborg v. Sweden*, (Judgment of March 23, 1994, Series A, No 283-B; (1994) 18 E.H.R.R. 38), it is argued that such proceedings would not constitute the determination of a criminal charge. The essence of the penalty provision is civil rather than criminal in nature.

Article 7—No punishment without law

3.70 **1.** No one shall be held guilty of any criminal offence on account of any act or omission which did not constitute a criminal offence under national or international law at the time when it was committed. Nor shall a heavier penalty be imposed than the one that was applicable at the time the criminal offence was committed.

2. This Article shall not prejudice the trial and punishment of any person for any act or omission which, at the time when it was committed, was criminal according to the general principles of law recognised by civilised nations.

Article 8—Right to respect for private and family life

3.71 **1.** Everyone has the right to respect for his private and family life, his home and his correspondence.

2. There shall be no interference by a public authority with the exercise of this right except such as is in accordance with the law and is necessary in a democratic society in the interests of national security, public safety or the economic well-being of the country, for the prevention of disorder or crime, for the protection of health or morals, or for the protection of the rights and freedoms of others.

GENERAL NOTE

Introduction

3.72 Article 8 is one of the most open-ended provisions of the Convention and is not yet fully developed in its scope. The concept of private life is very wide and not easily contained within a single comprehensive definition. The article has encompassed such diverse matters as the interception of communications, various forms of surveillance, the collection and retention of personal data, the protection of the physical integrity of the individual, the preservation of family ties, harassment and nuisance affecting the home, and environmental protection. Like the series of articles which follows, the rights given in paragraph (1) are limited by the exceptions listed in paragraph (2). If there is an interference with one of the rights protected in the first paragraph, then it will be necessary to see whether this is justified under the limitations in the second paragraph. Here the Strasbourg organs have consistently required the interference to be (1) for one of the specified reasons; (2) in accordance with law; (3) necessary in a democratic society; and (4) proportionate in the sense that there is no other way of protecting the recognised interest which constitutes a lesser interference with the right.

Benefit and family life

Article 8 of the Convention guarantees respect, among other things, for family life, subject to the limitation contained in the article. Family life encompasses ties between near relatives, which certainly extends to children, parents and grandparents, though it is unclear how far it includes relationships between siblings, aunts and uncles. In general the Strasbourg organs have preferred relationships in the vertical line to those in the horizontal line. 3.73

In the *Gaygusuz* case (the judgment is discussed in detail below), the applicant had complained that the refusal to award him the emergency assistance requested violated respect for his family life (presumably on the grounds that refusal of the assistance threatened the break up of, or hardship to, his family); the admissibility decision is not specific on the basis for declaring this part of his complaint admissible (see (1994) 18 E.H.R.R. CD51). Neither the Commission nor the Court found it necessary to consider this aspect of the complaint since they concluded that there was a violation of Article 14 read in conjunction with Article 1 of Protocol 1. Nevertheless, it remains open for the limits of the protection under Article 8 to be explored in the context of entitlements to social security. But it would be fair to say that there are few indications that the Strasbourg organs regard the Convention right here as including an obligation on the State to make payments to families for their support.

The Commission has held that there was no hindrance to family life where a wife was obliged to pay insurance contributions for her husband who was a househusband, even though husbands did not have to pay contributions in respect of housewives. Since the matter could not be brought within Article 8, the question of discrimination under Article 14 (see below) could not be considered.

The Social Security Administration (Fraud) Act 1997

Section 14 of the Social Security Administration (Fraud) Act 1997 adds a s.122(1A) to the Social Security Administration Act 1992 making it an offence for a person, without reasonable excuse, to fail to notify a change of circumstances, or, knowingly, to cause or allow another person to fail to notify a change of circumstances which is required to be notified to the Benefits Agency, where the person knows that the other person is required to notify the change. The effect of this provision is that a welfare rights adviser might commit an offence if a client provides information which would have an effect on the award of a benefit and indicates that this information has not been disclosed to the Benefits Agency. If the adviser gave clear advice that there was a duty to disclose the information to the Benefits Agency, that would probably constitute reasonable excuse for not then themselves notifying the information. The provision is designed to catch those likely to benefit from the failure to disclose, such as fraudulent landlords receiving housing benefit. 3.74

The conflict faced by the adviser is clear. It is between confidentiality and the proper administration of the social security benefits schemes. It is not difficult to imagine claimants complaining that disclosure of the confidential information by the adviser was a breach of their private life. They could argue by analogy with the surveillance cases under the Convention that there was an interference with private life under Article 8 which would then need to be tested against the permitted limitations in paragraph (2) of the Article. It would follow that if the claimant is to be protected, so too should the adviser who is exposed to possible prosecution, though the adviser would probably avoid the commission of the offence by advising that disclosure should be made by the claimant. This would, it is argued, result in the adviser having reasonable excuse for not making the disclosure.

The 1997 Act also contains (as does s.3 of the Social Security Act 1998) provisions on the exchange of information by Government departments which might be open to challenge for similar reasons. But such challenges would be highly speculative and would require development of the law protecting private life beyond that which is currently recognised in the case-law of the Court.

Article 9—Freedom of thought, conscience and religion

3.75
1. Everyone has the right to freedom of thought, conscience and religion; this right includes freedom to change his religion or belief and freedom, either alone or in community with others and in public or private, to manifest his religion or belief, in worship, teaching, practice and observance.

2. Freedom to manifest one's religion or beliefs shall be subject only to such limitations as are prescribed by law and are necessary in a democratic society in the interests of public safety, for the protection of public order, health or morals, or for the protection of the rights and freedoms of others.

GENERAL NOTE

3.76
Reliance on this article to avoid the normal requirements, for example, to pay national insurance contributions are most unlikely to succeed. The Commission has held that a Dutch system of old-age pension insurance, alleged to interfere with the religious duty of caring for old people, did not violate the article: App. 1497/62 *Reformed Church of X v The Netherlands*, (1962) 5 Y.B. 286; and App. 2065/63 X v *The Netherlands*, (1965) 8 Y.B. 266.

Article 10—Freedom of expression

3.77
1. Everyone has the right to freedom of expression. This right shall include freedom to hold opinions and to receive and impart information and ideas without interference by public authority and regardless of frontiers. This Article shall not prevent States from requiring the licensing of broadcasting, television or cinema enterprises.

2. The exercise of these freedoms, since it carries with it duties and responsibilities, may be subject to such formalities, conditions, restrictions or penalties as are prescribed by law and are necessary in a democratic society, in the interests of national security, territorial integrity or public safety, for the prevention of disorder or crime, for the protection

Article 11—Freedom of assembly and association

1. Everyone has the right to freedom of peaceful assembly and to freedom of association with others, including the right to form and to join trade unions for the protection of his interests.

2. No restrictions shall be placed on the exercise of these rights other than such as are prescribed by law and are necessary in a democratic society in the interests of national security or public safety, for the prevention of disorder or crime, for the protection of health or morals or for the protection of the rights and freedoms of others. This Article shall not prevent the imposition of lawful restrictions on the exercise of these rights by members of the armed forces, of the police or of the administration of the State.

3.78

Article 12—Right to marry

Men and women of marriageable age have the right to marry and to found a family, according to the national laws governing the exercise of this right.

3.79

Article 14—Prohibition of discrimination

The enjoyment of the rights and freedoms set forth in this Convention shall be secured without discrimination on any ground such as sex, race, colour, language, religion, political or other opinion, national or social origin, association with a national minority, property, birth or other status.

3.80

GENERAL NOTE

Article 14 prohibits discrimination on the grounds of sex, race, colour, language, religion, political or other opinion, national or social origin, association with a national minority, property, birth or other status. However, the protection is only applicable to the enjoyment of the rights and freedoms set forth in the Convention. It is the linking of Article 14 with another article of the Convention which gives it substance. In order to have effect, it does not have to be shown that there is a violation of the substantive article, merely that the alleged discrimination operates in a field which is covered by the protections afforded by those provisions. Indeed the practice of the Court has been to decline to consider Article 14 in conjunction with another article if they find a violation of the article on its face. The article is likely to be a fruitful source of complaint in social security cases.

3.81

Where Article 14 is considered, the Court asks itself whether there is a difference of treatment between two groups which may properly be compared on one of the grounds mentioned (and the list is not closed by reason of the last two words referring to "other status"). The question in then asked whether that difference of treatment pursues a legitimate aim. Finally, the Court considers whether the means employed are proportionate to the legitimate aim pursued. In making this judgment, due regard will be had to the State's margin of appreciation, which will vary depending on the circumstances of each case. Where the discrimination is based on sex, there is little room for a margin of appreciation, but where broader policy issues are under consideration (such as housing allocation policies to ensure a supply of housing for poorer people), the margin of appreciation will be wider (see *Gillow v. United Kingdom*, Judgment of November 24, 1986, Series A, No. 109; (1989) 11 E.H.R.R. 335, para. 66 of the Judgment).

The importance of the prohibition of discrimination in the enjoyment of the rights protected by the Convention has already been mentioned. Furthermore the *Gaygusuz* case (discussed in detail in the commentary to Article 1 of Protocol 1) provides a clear example of the application of the provision in a social security context.

The coupling of Article 14 and Article 1 of Protocol 1 opens up the possibility for considerable case-law development of the principle of equality in social security entitlement. The adjudicating authorities have already had to wrestle with issues of discrimination flowing from Community law under the equal treatment directives, but that has focused on discrimination between men and women. Community rights are also linked in some cases to worker status under Community law. By contrast, there are no such limitations in relation to equal treatment under Article 14. In the *Van Breedam* case App. 11577, *Van Breedam v. Belgium*, (1989) 62 D.R. 109) the Commission ruled inadmissible an application concerning liability to pay supplementary social security contributions where the discrimination alleged was between painters and sculptors on the one hand and writers and musicians on the other in relation to the treatment of royalties as a basis for levying contributions. Although the application was ruled inadmissible, the Commission does not appear to question the legitimacy of the comparative groups put forward by the applicant, since the grounds of their decision are that there was a legitimate reason for the difference of treatment.

In the *Krafft and Rougeot* case (App. 11543/85, *Krafft and Rougeot v. France*, (1990) 65 D.R. 51) the calculation of judicial pensions in France was in issue, and again the Commission did not appear to question the legitimacy of comparing the treatment of those appointed to judicial office from private practice and those appointed from within the court service. Again the difference of treatment was found to have a legitimate basis.

It is not difficult to imagine the sort of comparisons which might be raised challenging aspects of the United Kingdom social security system. The whole system is replete with differences. Examples are differences between single and married people, between same sex couples and married people, between students and non-students, between those who are habitually resident and those who are not. It may even be possible to re-open some of the challenges on grounds of alleged sex discrimination which have been made and lost under Community rules. Such cases are bound to be very complex and time-consuming, involving as they do issues of the legitimacy of the comparators chosen and whether there is objective and reasonable justification of any difference of treatment between those groups.

Benefits for widowers

A series of cases before the Court of Human Rights show the potential application of Article 14 in conjunction with Article 8 and Article 1 of Protocol

(1998 c.42, Sched. 1)

1 for changing the shape of social security provision. In *App. 365789/97, Cornwell v. United Kingdom* and *App. 38890/97, Leary v. United Kingdom,* two widowers complained that they were not entitled to benefits which would have been available to them had they been widows. The U.K. Government did not contest the admissibility of either case (save in relation to one of the periods in respect of which Cornwell complained): see admissibility decisions of May 11, 1999 in both cases. The cases have been struck out of the Court's list on a friendly settlement being reached. The Government indicated that it would pay the applicants, on an extra-statutory basis, the amounts to which they would have been entitled had they been widows. The Government also drew attention to provisions in what are now ss 54 to 56 of the Welfare Reform and Pensions Act 1999 making provision for bereavement payments, allowances for bereaved spouses, and certain new pension arrangements, which avoid the discrimination which previously existed as between widows and widowers.

A third case, *App. 36042/97, Willis v. United Kingdom,* a similar application has been made where a man would receive, if he were a widow, a widow's payment, widowed mother's allowance, and a widow's pension. Again the British Government has not contested the admissibility of the claim, but it is understood that no friendly settlement similar to that offered in the other cases has been forthcoming (see *Welfare Rights Bulletin 156,* June 2000 at 15). A key issue appears to be that the new bereavement provisions in the Welfare Reform and Pensions Act 1999 (expected to be paid from April 2001) do not make provision for widow's benefits at the same level as at present, but those currently entitled to a widow's pension will have their entitlement protected. Similar protection is not afforded to widowers who would have been entitled to a "protected" widow's pension if they were a woman. Willis is arguing that he should be put in the same position for the future as a widow with protected benefits but is deprived of this possibility by the current discrimination between widows and widowers.

The substantial period before the effects of discrimination which it appears to be conceded is in breach of Convention rights is likely to generate a fair number of claims which from October 2, 2000 tribunals and Commissioners will have to deal with, though it should be noted that the current absence of widower's benefits arises from rules in primary legislation. Neither tribunals nor Commissioners can make declarations of incompatibility.

Article 16—Restrictions on political activity of aliens

Nothing in Articles 10, 11 and 14 shall be regarded as preventing the High Contracting Parties from imposing restrictions on the political activity of aliens. 3.82

Article 17—Prohibition of abuse of rights

Nothing in this Convention may be interpreted as implying for any State, group or person any right to engage in any activity or perform any act aimed at the destruction of any of the rights and freedoms set forth herein or at their limitation to a greater extent than is provided for in the Convention. 3.83

Human Rights Act 1998

Article 18—Limitation on use of restrictions on rights

3.84   The restrictions permitted under this Convention to the said rights and freedoms shall not be applied for any purpose other than those for which they have been prescribed.

PART II

THE FIRST PROTOCOL

Article 1—Protection of property

3.85   Every natural or legal person is entitled to the peaceful enjoyment of his possessions. No one shall be deprived of his possessions except in the public interest and subject to the conditions provided for by law and by the general principles of international law. The preceding provisions shall not, however, in any way impair the right of a State to enforce such laws as it deems necessary to control the use of property in accordance with the general interest or to secure the payment of taxes or other contributions or penalties.

GENERAL NOTE

Introduction

3.85   Article 1 of Protocol 1, as explained in the *Sporrong and Lönnroth* case (*Sporrong and Lönnroth v. Sweden*, (A/52): (1983) 5 E.H.R.R. 35), comprises three distinct rules. First, there is a right to peaceful enjoyment of possessions. Secondly, persons can only be deprived of their possessions subject to certain conditions; and, thirdly, States are entitled to control the use of property in accordance with the general interest.

The notion of a "possession" under the article has an autonomous meaning under the Convention. Certain rights and interests which constitute assets can be regarded as possessions. The law in this area is not entirely settled. It now seems clear that contributions to a pension fund (see below) may create a property right in an undefined part of the total fund. But where social security systems are involved, there is no entitlement to a specific sum by way of pension: see App. 4288/69 *X v United Kingdom*, (1970) 13 Y.B. 892.

It is unclear whether a legal claim can be a pecuniary right. One case concerning enforcement of an arbitration award suggested that an enforceable debt is a pecuniary right: *Stran Greek Refineries and Stratis Andreadis v. Greece*, (A/301–B) (1995) 19 E.H.R.R. 293. In another case a legitimate expectation that a claim would be dealt with in accordance with normal tort principles was treated as a pecuniary right: *Pressos Compania Naviera SA and others v. Belgium*, (1996) 21 E.H.R.R. 301, and contrast *National and Provincial Building Social and others v United Kingdom*, J (1998) 25 E.H.R.R. 127.

Property rights and social security

3.86 The Commission considered in 1975 (*Müller v. Austria*, (1975) 3 D.R. 25) the nature of any property rights in pension entitlements. The applicant had been a member of a compulsory contributory pension scheme in Austria and had become a frontier worker moving into Liechtenstein for work. He was permitted for a while to continue to contribute to the Austrian scheme on a voluntary basis, but this was treated as a supplementary pension arrangement. The result was that, on his retirement, the applicant considered that he received a lesser pension than if he had continued to pay the same contributions into the compulsory scheme. His attempts to seek redress before the Austrian courts left him aggrieved and he complained to the Commission. The Commission was willing to consider that Article 1 of Protocol 1 was applicable, but that article only gave the applicant a right as a beneficiary of a compulsory social insurance scheme to any payments made by the fund; it did not give him any entitlement to a specific sum. The applicant's second line of argument was that his position as a frontier worker was different from that of resident workers, and that, in the enjoyment of his property rights, he was the victim of discrimination in violation of Article 14. The Commission disagreed. There was a difference of treatment (and it was legitimate to compare resident and frontier workers) but this was justified because frontier workers would gain an entitlement to two pensions: one in Austria under the voluntary arrangements, and one under the Liechtenstein scheme. There was furthermore no difference of treatment of Liechtenstein frontier workers and frontier workers working in other neighbouring states. The Commission's opinion that there was no violation of the Convention was confirmed by the Committee of Ministers.

Similar issues came before the Court in the *Gaygusuz* case (*Gaygusuz v. Austria*, (1997) 23 E.H.R.R. 364). The key issue in the case proved to be a simple one. Gaygusuz was a Turkish national who had worked in Austria. He had paid contributions under the Austrian social security scheme, but had experienced periods of unemployment and periods when he was unfit for work. He applied for an advance on his retirement pension as a form of emergency assistance, but was refused because he was not an Austrian national. His attempts to redress his grievance using domestic procedures were unsuccessful and he complained to the Commission that there had been a violation of a number of articles of the Convention. Among his complaints was a complaint of a violation of Article 14 taken in conjunction with Article 1 of Protocol 1. The first question was whether the substance of the claim was a matter covered by the protection of property in Article 1 of Protocol 1, since otherwise Article 14 could have no application. Both the Commission and the Court concluded that Article 1 of Protocol 1 was relevant, but for somewhat different reasons. The Commission concluded that the article was brought into play because the obligation to pay "taxes or other contributions" falls within its field of application, and so the ensuing benefits are also within its field of application (para. 47 of Commission Opinion). The Court, however, concludes:

> "The Court considers that the right to emergency assistance—in so far as provided for in the applicable legislation—is a pecuniary right for the purposes of Article 1 of Protocol 1. That provision is therefore applicable without it being necessary to rely solely on the link between entitlement to emergency assistance and the obligation to pay 'taxes or other contributions'." (para. 41 of the Judgment).

This was enough to engage Article 14. The discrimination here was blatant. Nationals had an entitlement, and non-nationals did not. It is difficult to see how such discrimination might be justified. The Austrian government argued that there was a special responsibility on a State to care for its own nationals, and there were certain exceptions to the nationality condition (which had not assisted *Gaygusuz*). Neither the Court nor the Commission was persuaded by these arguments. There had been a violation because there was discrimination within Article 14 which was not capable of objective and reasonable justification.

Attempts have been made to argue that the suspension of retirement pension for those serving terms of imprisonment breached the property rights in Article 1 of Protocol 1, but the applications were declared inadmissible (Apps. 27004/95, *Josef Szrabjer v. United Kingdom*, and 27011/95, *Walther Clarke v. United Kingdom*, Decision of October 23, 1997) and invalidity benefit (App. 27537/95, *George Carlin v. United Kingdom*, Decision of December 3, 1997). The public interest was served by avoiding a situation in which prisoners enjoyed the advantage of accumulating a lump sum by receiving a State benefit without any outgoing living expenses. Arguments based on discrimination between prisoners and non-prisoners were dismissed as a comparison of two different factual situations. Other comparisons were also found to be without merit. See also discussion of benefits for widowers in the commentary on Article 14 above.

Article 2—Right to education

3.87 No person shall be denied the right to education. In the exercise of any functions which it assumes in relation to education and to teaching, the State shall respect the right of parents to ensure such education and teaching in conformity with their own religious and philosophical convictions.

GENERAL NOTE

3.88 The full scope of this right is yet to be determined. The existing case law is mainly concerned with primary education, but the Commission has not ruled out the application of the provision to higher education (see, for example, *Sulak v. Turkey*, (1996) 84 D.R. 101). The confused state of the exclusion of students in full-time higher education from entitlement to most social security benefits might well leave the United Kingdom exposed to challenge under this provision. On the assumption that the provision applies to higher education, it could be argued that students are currently required to abandon their courses completely in order to become eligible for certain social security benefits with the result that they lose entitlement to the balance of finance to support their studies if they wish to return to their courses later on. This could be argued to operate to deny them the right to an education.

Article 3—Right to free elections

3.89 The High Contracting Parties undertake to hold free elections at reasonable intervals by secret ballot, under conditions which will ensure the free expression of the opinion of the people in the choice of the legislature.

(1998 c.42, Sched. 3)

PART III

THE SIXTH PROTOCOL

Omitted (concerns the abolition of the death penalty).

Schedule 2 omitted 3.90

SCHEDULE 3

DEROGATION AND RESERVATION

PART I

DEROGATION

The 1988 notification

The United Kingdom Permanent Representative to the Council of Europe presents his compliments to the Secretary General of the Council, and has the honour to convey the following information in order to ensure compliance with the obligations of Her Majesty's Government in the United Kingdom under Article 15(3) of the Convention for the Protection of Human Rights and Fundamental Freedoms signed at Rome on 4 November 1950. 3.91

There have been in the United Kingdom in recent years campaigns of organised terrorism connected with the affairs of Northern Ireland which have manifested themselves in activities which have included repeated murder, attempted murder, maiming, intimidation and violent civil disturbance and in bombing and fire raising which have resulted in death, injury and widespread destruction of property. As a result, a public emergency within the meaning of Article 15(1) of the Convention exists in the United Kingdom.

The Government found it necessary in 1974 to introduce and since then, in cases concerning persons reasonably suspected of involvement in terrorism connected with the affairs of Northern Ireland, or of certain offences under the legislation, who have been detained for 48 hours, to exercise powers enabling further detention without charge, for periods of up to five days, on the authority of the Secretary of State. These powers are at present to be found in Section 12 of the Prevention of Terrorism (Temporary Provisions) Act 1984, Article 9 of the Prevention Terrorism (Supplemental Temporary Provisions) Order 1984 and Article 10 of the Prevention of Terrorism (Supplemental Temporary Provisions) (Northern Ireland) Order 1984.

Section 12 of the Prevention of Terrorism (Temporary Provisions) Act 1984 provides for a person whom a constable has arrested on reasonable grounds of suspecting him to be guilty of an offence under Section 1, 9 or 10 of the Act, or to be or to have been involved in terrorism connected with the affairs of Northern Ireland, to be detained in right of the arrest for up to 48 hours and thereafter, where the Secretary of State extends the detention period, for up to a further five days. Section 12 substantially re-enacted Section 12 of the Prevention of Terrorism (Temporary Provisions) Act 1976 which, in turn, substantially re-enacted Section 7 of the Prevention of Terrorism (Temporary Provisions) Act 1974.

Article 10 of the Prevention of Terrorism (Supplemental Temporary Provisions) (Northern Ireland) Order 1984 (S.I. 1984 No. 417) and Article 9 of the Prevention of Terrorism (Supplemental Temporary Provisions) Order 1984 (S.I. 1984 No. 418) were both made under Sections 13 and 14 of and Schedule 3 to the 1984 Act and substantially re-enacted powers of detention in Orders made under the 1974 and 1976 Acts. A person who is being examined under Article 4 of either Order on his arrival in, or on seeking to leave, Northern Ireland or Great Britain for the purpose of determining whether he is or has been involved in terrorism connected with the affairs of Northern Ireland, or whether there are grounds for suspecting that he has committed an offence under Section 9 of the 1984 Act, may be detained under Article 9 or 10, as appropriate, pending the conclusion of his examination. The period of this examination may exceed 12 hours if an examining officer has reasonable grounds for suspecting him to be or to have been involved in acts of terrorism connected with the affairs of Northern Ireland.

Where such a person is detained under the said Article 9 or 10 he may be detained for up to 48 hours on the authority of an examining officer and thereafter, where the Secretary of State extends the detention period, for up to a further five days.

In its judgment of November 29 1988 in the Case of Brogan and Others, the European Court of Human Rights held that there had been a violation of Article 5(3) in respect of each of the applicants, all of whom had been detained under Section 12 of the 1984 Act. The Court held that even the shortest of the four periods of detention concerned, namely four days and six hours, fell outside the constraints as to time permitted by the first part of Article 5(3). In addition, the Court held that there had been a violation of Article 5(5) in the case of each applicant.

Following this judgment, the Secretary of State for the Home Department informed Parliament on December 6 1988 that, against the background of the terrorist campaign, and the over-riding need to bring terrorists to justice, the Government did not believe that the maximum period of detention should be reduced. He informed Parliament that the Government were examining the matter with a view to responding to the judgment. On 1988, the Secretary of State further informed Par-

(1998 c.42, Sched. 3)

liament that it remained the Government's wish, if it could be achieved, to find a judicial process under which extended detention might be reviewed and where appropriate authorised by a judge or other judicial officer. But a further period of reflection and consultation was necessary before the Government could bring forward a firm and final view.

Since the judgment of November 29 1988 as well as previously, the Government have found it necessary to continue to exercise, in relation to terrorism connected with the affairs of Northern Ireland, the powers described above enabling further detention without charge for periods of up to five days, on the authority of the Secretary of State, to the extent strictly required by the exigencies of the situation to enable necessary enquiries and investigations properly to be completed in order to decide whether criminal proceedings should be instituted. To the extent that the exercise of these powers may be inconsistent with the obligations imposed by the Convention the Government has availed itself of the right of derogation conferred by Article 15(1) of the Convention and will continue to do so until further notice.

Dated 23 December 1988.

The 1989 notification

The United Kingdom Permanent Representative to the Council of Europe presents his compliments to the Secretary General of the Council, and has the honour to convey the following information. 3.92

In his communication to the Secretary General of 23 December 1988, reference was made to the introduction and exercise of certain powers under section 12 of the Prevention of Terrorism (Temporary Provisions) Act 1984, Article 9 of the Prevention of Terrorism (Supplemental Temporary Provisions) Order 1984 and Article 10 of the Prevention of Terrorism (Supplemental Temporary Provisions) (Northern Ireland) Order 1984.

These provisions have been replaced by section 14 of and paragraph 6 of Schedule 5 to the Prevention of Terrorism (Temporary Provisions) Act 1989, which make comparable provision. They came into force on March 22 1989. A copy of these provisions is enclosed.

The United Kingdom Permanent Representative avails himself of this opportunity to renew to the Secretary General the assurance of his opportunity to renew to the Secretary General the assurance of his highest consideration.

March 23 1989.

PART II

RESERVATION

At the time of signing the present (First) Protocol, I declare that, in view of certain provisions of the Education Acts in the United Kingdom, the principle affirmed in the second sentence of Article 2 is accepted by the United Kingdom only so far as it is compatible with the provision 3.93

of efficient instruction and training, and the avoidance of unreasonable public expenditure.

Dated March 20 1952. Made by the United Kingdom Permanent Representative to the Council of Europe.

3.94   Schedule 4 omitted

A Select Bibliography on Human Rights Law

The following material may be found to be helpful on the Human Rights Act 1998:

Baker, C. (ed.), *Human Rights Act 1998: A Practitioner's Guide* (Sweet & Maxwell, London. 1998): see particularly ch. 12 entitled "Social Security".

Grosz, S., Beatson, J. and Duffy, P., *Human Rights. The 1998 Act and the European Convention*, (Sweet & Maxwell, London, 2000)

Lester, A. and Pannick, D. (ed.) *Human Rights Law and Practice*, (Butterworths, London, 1999)

Starmer, K., *European Human Rights Law/The Human Rights Act 1998 and the European Convention on Human Rights*, (Legal Action Group, London, 1999)

Wadham, J. and Mountfield, H., *Blackstone's Guide to the Human Rights Act 1998*, (Blackstone Press, London, 1999).

Three useful texts on the European Convention on Human Rights are:

Harris, D, O'Boyle, M and Warbrick, C, *Law of the European Convention on Human Rights*, (London: Butterworths, 1995)

Jacobs, F and White, R, *The European Convention on Human Rights*, (Oxford: Oxford University Press, 2nd ed., 1996)

Reid, K, *A Practitioner's Guide to the European Convention on Human Rights*, (London: Sweet & Maxwell, 1998).

PART IV

REGULATIONS

REGULATIONS

REFERENCES TO THE SOCIAL SECURITY ADMINISTRATION ACT 1992 AND THE SOCIAL SECURITY CONTRIBUTIONS AND BENEFITS ACT 1992 IN REGULATIONS

The regulations governing the detailed administration of the benefits system have not yet been consolidated and the existing regulations are deemed to contain references to the provisions of the new legislation which replace the old legislation.

In order to be as helpful as possible to users of this volume, the authors have, wherever practicable, inserted in square brackets reference to the relevant provisions of the 1992 legislation.

The regulations—particularly the older regulations—contain many references to legislation which has either been repealed or is only of significance to those able to retain an entitlement to a defunct benefit. In these cases, reference has generally been left to the earlier legislation. Equally, in some regulations, it was considered that it might mislead if the interpretation regulation was amended.

Readers should therefore note that the material appearing in square brackets is the authors' amendment to include reference to the 1992 legislation. Such amendments have no official standing. All other references to legislation are as they appear in the current version of the regulations printed in this volume.

An important note on a new provision affecting a number of sets of regulations in this volume

Article 2 of the Employment Action (Miscellaneous Provisions) Order 1991, effective October 1, 1991, provides that for the purposes of certain social security regulations, a person using facilities under an Employment Action Programme (set up under section 2 of the Employment and Training Act 1973) "shall be treated as not being employed but as participating in an arrangement for training under section 2 of the 1973 Act and, accordingly, any payment made to such person in connection with his use of those facilities shall be treated in the same manner as a payment made in respect of such training." The regulations affected in the main volume are the Claims and Payments Regulations 1987, the Overlapping Benefits Regulations, the Overpayments Regulations and the USI Regulations. To the same effect see: the Training for Work (Scottish Enterprise and Highlands and Islands Enterprise Programmes) October 1993 (S.I. 1993 No. 498), effective March 29, 1993; and the Training for Work (Miscellaneous Provisions) Order 1993 (S.I. 1993 No. 348).

The Social Security (Claims and Payments) Regulations

The Social Security (Claims and Payments) Regulations 1979

(S.I. 1979 No. 628) (*as amended*)

ARRANGEMENT OF REGULATIONS

PART I

GENERAL

1. Citation, commencement and interpretation
2.—23. Interpretation
3. *Revoked*

PART IV

SPECIAL PROVISIONS RELATING TO INDUSTRIAL INJURIES BENEFIT ONLY

24. Notice of accidents
25. Obligations of employers
26. Obligations of claimants for, and beneficiaries in receipt of, disablement benefit
27—32. *Revoked*

SCHEDULE 4. Particulars to be given of accidents

PART I

GENERAL

Citation and commencement

1. These regulations may be cited as the Social Security (Claims and Payments) Regulations 1979 and shall come into operation on 9th July 1979.

Interpretation

2.—(1) In these regulations, unless the context otherwise requires—
"the Act" means the Social Security Act 1975;
"approved place" means a place approved by the Secretary of State for the purpose of obtaining payment of benefit;
"benefit order" means an order for the payment of a weekly sum on account of benefit to which regulation 16 applies or of a weekly instalment of a gratuity;
"claim for benefit" includes an application for a declaration that an accident was an industrial accident and an application for the review of an award or a decision for the purpose of obtaining any increase of benefit mentioned in Schedule 1 to these regulations but does not include any other application for the review of an

award or a decision and the expression "claim benefit" and every reference to a claim shall be construed accordingly;

[¹. . .]

"instrument of payment" means a serial order, benefit order, or any other instrument whatsoever which is intended to enable a person to obtain payment of benefit;

"serial order" means one of a series of orders, including benefit orders, for the payment of a sum on account of benefit which is or has been contained in a book of such orders;

"unemployment benefit office" means any office or place appointed by the Secretary of State for the purpose of claiming unemployment benefit;

and other expressions have the same meaning as in the Act.

[²(1A) The provision in paragraph (1) for the interpretation of the words "claim for benefit" shall not be taken to preclude the application of the regulations to a claim for attendance allowance expressed as an application for review of an earlier determination but which discloses no grounds on which such a determination could be reviewed.]

(2) Unless the context otherwise requires, any reference in these regulations to—

(a) a numbered section is a reference to the section of the Social Security Act 1975 bearing that number;

(b) a numbered regulation is a reference to the regulation bearing that number in these regulations and any reference in a regulation to a numbered paragraph is a reference to the paragraph of that regulation bearing that number;

(c) any provision made by or contained in an enactment or instrument shall be construed as a reference to that provision as amended or extended by any enactment or instrument and as including a reference to any provision which it re-enacts or replaces, or which may re-enact or replace it, with or without modification.

(3) For the purposes of the provisions of these regulations relating to the making of claims every increase of benefit mentioned in Schedule 1 to these regulations shall be treated as a separate benefit.

(4) The provisions of Schedule 1 and 2 to these regulations shall have effect; and the following provisions of these regulations shall, in relation to any particular benefit, have effect subject to any provisions in those Schedules affecting that benefit.

AMENDMENTS

1. The Social Security Act 1998 (Commencement No. 8, and Savings and Consequential and Transitional Provisions) Order 1999 (S.I. 1999 No. 1958), Sched. 4, para. 1 (July 4, 1999).

2. The Social Security (Attendance Allowance) Amendment Regulations 1980 (S.I. 1980 No. 1136), reg. 6(1) (August 25, 1980).

GENERAL NOTE

Most of the rules relating to claims and payments can now be found in the Claims and Payments Regulations 1987. The only surviving part of these regula-

(S.I. 1979 No. 628, reg. 2) (as amended)

tions relate to specific aspects of claims and payments in industrial injuries cases.

Regulations 3 to 23 revoked.

PART IV

SPECIAL PROVISIONS RELATING TO INDUSTRIAL INJURIES BENEFIT ONLY

Notice of accidents

24.—(1) Every employed earner who suffers personal injury by accident in respect of which benefit may be payable shall give notice of such accident either in writing or orally as soon as is practicable after the happening thereof.

Provided that any such notice required to be given by an employed earner may be given by some other person acting on his behalf.

(2) Every such notice shall be given to the employer, or (if there is more than one employer) to one of such employers, or to any foreman or other official under whose supervision the employed earner is employed at the time of the accident, or to any person designated for the purpose by the employer, and shall give the appropriate particulars.

(3) Any entry of the appropriate particulars of an accident made in a book kept for that purpose in accordance with the provisions of regulation 25 shall, if made as soon as practicable after the happening of an accident by the employed earner or by some other person acting on his behalf, be sufficient notice of the accident for the purposes of this regulation.

(4) In this regulation—

"employer" means, in relation to any person, the employer of that person at the time of the accident and "employers" shall be construed accordingly; and

"employed earner" means a person who is or is treated as an employed earner for the purposes of industrial injuries benefit.

(5) In this regulation and regulation 25, "appropriate particulars" mean the particulars indicated in Schedule 4 to these regulations.

Obligations of employers

25.—(1) Every employer shall take reasonable steps to investigate the circumstances of every accident of which notice is given to him or to his servant or agent in accordance with the provisions of regulation 24 and, if there appear to him to be any discrepancies between the circumstances found by him as a result of his investigation and the circumstances appearing from the notice so given, he shall record the circumstances so found.

(2) Every employer who is required to do so by the Secretary of State shall furnish to an officer of the Department within such reasonable period as may be required, such information and particulars as shall be required—

(a) of any accident or alleged accident in respect of which benefit may be payable to, or in respect of the death of, a person employed by him at the time of the accident or alleged accident; or

(b) of the nature of and other relevant circumstances relating to any occupation prescribed for the purposes of Chapter V of Part II of the Act in which any person to whom or in respect of whose death benefit may be payable under that Chapter was or is alleged to have been employed by him.

(3) Every owner or occupier (being an employer) of any mine or quarry or of any premises to which any of the provisions of the Factories Act 1961 applies and every employer by whom 10 or more persons are normally employed at the same time on or about the same premises in connection with a trade or business carried on by the employer shall, subject to the following provisions of this paragraph—

(a) [¹ keep readily accessible a means (whether in a book or books or by electronic means), in a form approved by the Secretary of State, by which a person employed by the employer or some other person acting on his behalf may record the appropriate particulars (as defined in regulation 24) of any accident causing personal injury to that person; and

(b) preserve every such record for the period of at least 3 years from the date of its entry.]

AMENDMENT

1. The Social Security (Claims and Payments) Amendment (No. 3) Regulations 1993 (S.I. 1993 No. 2113), reg. 2 (September 27, 1993)

Obligations of claimants for, and beneficiaries in receipt of [¹. . .] disablement benefit

26.—(1) Subject to the following provisions of this regulation, every claimant for, and every beneficiary in receipt of [¹. . .] disablement benefit shall comply with every notice given to him by the Secretary of State which requires him either—

(a) to submit himself to a medical examination by a medical [² practitioner who has experience in the issues specified in regulation 12(1) of the Social Security and Child Support (Decisions and Appeals) Regulations 1999] for the purpose of determining the effects of the relevant accident or the treatment appropriate to the relevant injury or loss of faculty; or

(b) to submit himself to such medical treatment for the said injury or loss of faculty as is considered appropriate in his case by the medical practitioner in charge of the case [³ . . .]

(2) Every notice given to a claimant or beneficiary requiring him to submit himself to medical examination shall be given in writing and shall specify the time and place for examination and shall not require the claimant or beneficiary to submit himself [⁴ to examination before the expiration of the period to 6 days beginning with the date of the notice or such shorter period as may be reasonable in the circumstances]

(S.I. 1979 No. 628, reg. 26) (as amended)

(3) Every claimant and every beneficiary who, in accordance with the foregoing provisions of this regulation, is required to submit himself to a medical examination or to medical treatment—
  (a) shall attend at every such place and at every such time as may be required; and
  (b) may, in the discretion of the Secretary of State, be paid such travelling and other allowances (including compensation for loss of remunerative time) as the Secretary of State may with the consent of the Minister for the Civil Service determine.

(4) [⁵ . . .]

AMENDMENTS

1. The Social Security (Abolition of Injury Benefit) (Consequential) Regulations 1983 (S.I. 1983 No. 186), reg. 11 (April 6, 1983)
2. The Social Security Act 1998 (Commencement No. 8, and Savings and Consequential and Transitional Provisions) Order 1999 (S.I. 1999 No. 1958), Sched. 4, para. 2(a)(i) (July 4, 1999)
3. The Social Security Act 1998 (Commencement No. 8, and Savings and Consequential and Transitional Provisions) Order 1999 (S.I. 1999 No. 1958), Sched. 4, para. 2(a)(ii) (July 4, 1999)
4. The Social Security Act 1998 (Commencement No. 8, and Savings and Consequential and Transitional Provisions) Order 1999 (S.I. 1999 No. 1958), Sched. 4, para. 2(b) (July 4, 1999)
5. The Social Security Act 1998 (Commencement No. 8, and Savings and Consequential and Transitional Provisions) Order 1999 (S.I. 1999 No. 1958), Sched. 4, para. 2(c) (July 4, 1999)

Regulations 27 to 32 revoked.   **4.9**

Schedules 1–3 revoked   **4.10**

SCHEDULE 4   **Regulations 24 and 25**

PARTICULARS TO BE GIVEN OF ACCIDENTS   **4.11**

(1) Full name, address and occupation of injured person;
(2) Date and time of accident;
(3) Place where accident happened;
(4) Cause and nature of injury;
(5) Name, address and occupation of person giving the notice, if other than the injured person.

Schedule 5 revoked.   **4.12**

The Social Security (Claims and Payments) Regulations 1987

The Social Security (Claims and Payments) Regulations 1987

(S.I. 1987 No. 1968) (*as amended*)

ARRANGEMENTS OF REGULATIONS

PART I

General

4.13
1. Citation and commencement
2. Interpretation

PART II

Claims

3. Claims not required for entitlement to benefit in certain cases
4. Making a claim for benefit
5. Amendment and withdrawal of claim
6. Date of claim
7. Evidence and information
8. Attendance in person
9. Interchange with claims for other benefits
10. Claim for incapacity benefit or severe disablement allowance where no entitlement to statutory sick pay or statutory maternity pay
11. Special provisions where it is certified that a woman is expected to be confined or where she has been confined
12. Self-certified claims for first 7 days of a spell of incapacity for work (*revoked*)
13. Advance claims and awards
13A. Advance award of disability living allowance
13B. Advance claim for and award of disability working allowance
13C. Further claim for and award of disability living allowance
14. Advance claim for and award of maternity allowance
15. Advance notice of retirement and claim for and award of pension
15A. Cold weather payments (*revoked*)
16. Date of entitlement under an award for the purpose of payability of benefit and effective date of change of rate
17. Duration of awards
18. Duration of disallowance (*revoked*)
19. Time for claiming benefit

PART III

Payments

20. Time and manner of payment: general provision
20A. Payment a presentation of an involvement for payment benefit
21. Direct credit transfer
22. Long term benefits

(S.I. 1987 No. 1968) (as amended)

23. Child benefit
24. Unemployment benefit, incapacity benefit, maternity allowance and severe disablement allowance
25. Payment of attendance allowance and constant attendance allowance at a daily rate
26. Income support
26A. Jobseeker's allowance
27. Family credit and disability working allowance
28. Fractional amounts of benefit
29. Payments to persons under age 18
30. Payments on death
31. Time and manner of payments of industrial injuries gratuities
32. Information to be given when obtaining payment of benefit

PART IV

Third Parties

33. Persons unable to act
34. Payment to another person on the beneficiary's behalf
34A. Deductions of mortgage interest which shall be made from benefit and paid to qualifying lenders
35. Deductions which may be made from benefit and paid to third parties
35A. Transitional provisions for persons in hostels or certain residential accommodation
36. Payment to a partner as alternative payee

PART V

Suspension and Extinguishment

37. Suspension in individual cases (*revoked*)
37A. Suspension in identical cases (*revoked*)
37AA. Withholding of benefit in prescribed circumstances (*revoked*)
37AB. Payment of withheld benefit (*revoked*)
37B. Withholding payment of arrears of benefit (*revoked*)
38. Extinguishment of right to payment of sums by way of benefit where payment is not obtained within the prescribed period.

PART VI

Mobility Component of Disability Living Allowance and Disability Living Allowance for Children

42. Cases where allowance not to be payable
43. Children
44. Payment of disability living allowance on behalf of a beneficiary
45. Power for the Secretary of State to terminate an arrangement
46. Restriction on duration of arrangements by the Secretary of State

The Social Security (Claims and Payments) Regulations 1987

PART VII

Miscellaneous

47. Instruments of payment
48. Revocations

SCHEDULES

1. PART I—Benefit claims and other benefit which may be treated as if claimed in addition or in the alternative
   PART II—Interchange of claims for child benefit with claims for other benefits
2. Special provisions relating to claims for unemployment benefit during period connected with public holidays
3. Duration of disallowance (*revoked*)
4. Prescribed times for claiming benefit
5. Miscellaneous provisions which vary the prescribed times under Schedule 4 (*revoked*)
6. Days for payment of long term benefits
7. Manner and time of payment, effective date of change of circumstances and commencement of entitlement in income support cases
8. Election to have child benefit paid weekly
9. Deductions from benefit and direct payment to third parties
9A. Deductions of mortgage interest from benefit and payment to qualifying lenders
10. Revocation (not reproduced)

PART I

GENERAL

Citation and commencement

4.14   **1.** These Regulations may be cited as the Social Security (Claims and Payments) Regulations 1987 and shall come into operation on 11th April 1988.

Interpretation

4.15   **2.**—(1) In these Regulations, unless the context otherwise requires—
[[13]"adjudicating authority" means any person or body with responsibility for making decisions about claims for benefit or related matters;]
"appropriate office" means an office of the [[2]Department of Social Security] or [[10]the Department for Education and Employment]
[[13]"the Board" means the Commissioners of the Inland Revenue; and references to "the Board" in these Regulations have effect only with respect to working families' tax credit and disabled person's tax credit;]

(S.I. 1987 No. 1968, reg. 2) (as amended)

[¹¹"claim for asylum" has the same meaning as in the Asylum and Immigration Appeals Act 1993;]
"claim for benefit" includes—
(a) an application for a declaration that an accident was an industrial accident;
(b) [³...]
(c) an application for [¹⁴a revision under section 9 of the Social Security Act 1998 or a supersession under section 10 of that Act] a decision for the purpose of obtaining any increase of benefit [⁶in respect of a child or adult dependant under the Social Security Act 1975 or an increase in disablement benefit under section 60 (special hardship), 61 (constant attendance), 62 (hospital treatment allowance) or 63 (exceptionally severe disablement) of the Social Security Act 1975], but does not include any other application for [¹⁴a revision under section 9 of the Social Security Act 1998 or a supersession under section 10 of that Act] a decision;
[¹³"'disabled person's tax credit' and 'working families' tax credit" shall be construed in accordance with section 1(1) of the Tax Credits Act 1999]
[⁸"instrument for benefit payment" means an instrument issued by the Secretary of State [¹³or the Board] under regulation 20A on the presentation of which benefit due to a beneficiary shall be paid in accordance with the arrangements set out in that regulation;]
[¹⁰"the Jobseekers Act" means the Jobseekers Act 1995;
"jobseeker's allowance" means an allowance payable under Part I of the Jobseekers Act;
"the Jobseeker's Allowance Regulations" means the Jobseeker's Allowance Regulations 1996;]
"long-term benefits" means any retirement pension, a widowed mother's allowance, a widow's pension, attendance allowance, [⁵disability living allowance], invalid care allowance, [¹²...], any pension or allowance for industrial injury or disease and any increase in any such benefit;
"married couple" means a man and a woman who are married to each other and are members of the same household;
"partner" means one of a married or unmarried couple; [⁴...]
[⁹"pension fund holder" means with respect to a personal pension scheme or retirement annuity contract, the trustees, managers or scheme administrators, as the case may be, of the scheme or contract concerned;]
[⁹"personal pension scheme" has the same meaning as in section 1 of the Pension Schemes Act 1993 in respect of employed earners and in the case of self-employed earners, includes a scheme approved by the Board of Inland Revenue under Chapter IV of Part XIV of the Income and Corporation Taxes Act 1988;]
[¹¹"refugee" means a person recorded by the Secretary of State as a refugee within the definition in Article 1 of the Convention relating to the Status of Refugees done at Geneva on 28th July 1951 as extended by Article 1(2) of the Protocol relating to the Status of Refugees done at New York on 31st January 1967;]

The Social Security (Claims and Payments) Regulations 1987

[⁹"retirement annuity contract" means a contract or trust scheme approved under Chapter III of Part XIV of the Income and Corporation Taxes Act 1988;]

"unmarried couple" means a man and a woman who are not married to each other but are living together as husband and wife otherwise than in prescribed circumstances; and

"week" means a period of 7 days beginning with midnight between Saturday and Sunday.

(2) Unless the context otherwise requires, any reference in these Regulations to—

(a) a numbered regulation, Part or Schedule is a reference to the regulation, Part or Schedule bearing that number in these Regulations and any reference in a regulation to a numbered paragraph is a reference to the paragraph of that regulation having that number;

(b) a benefit includes any benefit under the Social Security Act 1975 [SSCBA], child benefit under Part I of the Child Benefit Act 1975, income support [⁷, family credit and disability working allowance under the Social Security Act 1986 [SSCBA] and any social fund payments such as are mentioned in section 32(2)(a) [¹and section 32(2A)] of that Act [SSCBA, s.138(1)(a) and (2)] [¹⁰and a jobseeker's allowance under Part I of the Jobseekers Act].

[¹⁰(2A) References in regulations 20, 21 (except paragraphs (3) and (3A)), 29, 30, 32 to 34, 37 (except paragraph (1A)), 37A, 37AA (except paragraph (3)), 37AB, 37B, 38 and 47 to "benefit", "income support" or "a jobseeker's allowance", include a reference to a back to work bonus which, by virtue of regulation 25 of the Social Security (Back to Work Bonus) Regulations 1996, is to be treated as payable as income support or, as the case may be, as a jobseeker's allowance.]

(3) For the purposes of the provisions of these Regulations relating to the making of claims every increase of benefit under the Social Security Act 1975 [SSCBA] shall be treated as a separate benefit [¹². . .].

AMENDMENTS

1. The Social Security (Common Provisions) Miscellaneous Amendments Regulations 1988 (S.I. 1988 No. 1725), reg. 3 (November 7, 1988).

2. Transfer of Functions (Health and Social Security) Order 1988 (S.I. 1988 No. 1843), art. 3(4) (November 28, 1988).

3. The Social Security (Medical Evidence, Claims and Payments) Amendment Regulations 1989 (S.I. 1989 No. 1686), reg. 3 (October 9, 1989).

4. The Social Security (Miscellaneous Provisions) Amendment Regulations 1991 (S.I. 1991 No. 2284), reg. 5 (November 1, 1991).

5. The Social Security (Claims and Payments) Amendment Regulations 1991 (S.I. 1991 No. 2741), reg. 2(a) (February 3, 1992).

6. The Social Security (Miscellaneous Provisions) Amendment Regulations 1992 (S.I. 1992 No. 247), reg. 9 (March 9, 1992).

7. The Social Security (Claims and Payments) Amendment Regulations 1991 (S.I. 1991 No. 2741), reg. 2(b) (March 10, 1992).

8. The Social Security (Claims and Payments) Amendment (No. 4) Regulations 1994 (S.I. 1994 No. 3196), reg. 2 (January 10, 1995).

9. Income-related benefit Schemes and Social Security (Claims and

Payments) (Miscellaneous Amendments) Regulations 1995 (S.I. 1995 No. 2303), reg. 10(2) (October 2, 1995).

10. The Social Security (Claims and Payments) (Jobseeker's Allowance Consequential Amendments) Regulations 1996 (S.I. 1996 No. 1460), reg. 2(2) (October 7, 1996).

11. The Income Support and Social Security (Claims and Payments) (Miscellaneous Amendments) Regulations 1996 (S.I. 1996 No. 2431), reg. 7(a) (October 15, 1996).

12. The Social Security (Claims and Payments) Amendment Regulations 1999 (S.I. 1999 No. 2358), reg. 2 (September 20, 1999) and The Child Benefit, Child Support and Social Security (Miscellaneous Amendments) Regulations 1996 (S.I. 1996 No. 1803), reg. 18 (April 7, 1997).

13. The Tax Credits (Claims and Payments) (Amendment) Regulations 1999 (S.I. 1999 No. 2572), reg. 3 (October 5, 1999)

14. The Social Security Act 1998 (Commencement No. 9 and Savings and Consequential and Transitional Provisions) Order 1999 (S.I. 1999 No. 2422), Sched 7 (September 6, 1999).

GENERAL NOTE

Claim for benefit
Under sub-para. (c) a claim includes, for the purposes of these Regulations, an application for review for the purpose of securing any increase of benefit. The March 1992 amendment restricts the scope of this provision to applications for review to obtain increases for spouses or dependants or the listed industrial injury "benefits" which are (or were, since special hardship allowance and hospital treatment allowance have ceased to exist) technically not separate benefits, but increases of disablement benefit. In *CIS 515/1990*, the Commissioner took the view that the pre-amendment form of the definition applied to any application for review which requested an increase in the amount of any benefit. The subsequent amendment cannot affect the authority of this decision before the date of the amendment, but para. (3) makes it dubious.

See the notes to s.137(1) of the Contributions and Benefits Act for "married couple" and "unmarried couple."

PART II

CLAIMS

Claims not required for entitlement to benefit in certain cases

3. It shall not be a condition of entitlement to benefit that a claim be made for it in the following cases—

(a) In the case of a Category C retirement pension where the beneficiary is in receipt of—
  (i) another retirement pension under the Social Security Act 1975; or
  (ii) widow's benefit under Chapter 1 of Part II of that Act; r
  (iii) benefit by virtue of section 39(4) of that Act corresponding to a widow's pension or a widowed mother's allowance;
(b) in the case of a Category D retirement pension where the beneficiary—

4.16

(i) was ordinarily resident in great Britain on the day on which he attained 80 years of age; and
(ii) is in receipt of another retirement pension under the Social Security Act 1975;
(c) age addition in any case;
(d) in the case of a Category A or B retirement pension—
  (i) where the beneficiary is a woman over the age of 65 and entitled to a widowed mother's allowance, on her ceasing to be so entitled; or
  (ii) where the beneficiary is a woman under the age of 65 and in receipt of widow's pension, on her attaining that age
(e) [¹in the case of retirement allowance]
(f) [²...]
(g) [³ in the case of a jobseeker's allowance where—
  (i) that allowance has previously been claimed and an award made;
  (ii) the Secretary of State has directed under regulation [⁴ 16(2) of the Social Security and Child Support (Decisions and Appeals) Regulations 1999] that payment under that award be suspended for a definite or indefinite period on the ground that a question arises whether the conditions for entitlement to that allowance are or were fulfilled or the award ought to be revised under [⁴ section 9 of the Social Security Act 1998 or superseded under section 10 of that Act]
  (iii) subsequently that suspension expires or is cancelled in respect of a part only of the period for which it has been in force;
  (iv) it is then determined that the award should be revised [⁴ or superseded] to the effect that there was no entitlement to the allowance in respect of all or any part of the period between the start of the period over which the award has been suspended and the date when the suspension expires or is cancelled; and
  (v) there are no other circumstances which cast doubt on the claimant's entitlement.]
(h) [⁵ in the case of income support where the beneficiary—
  (i) is a person to whom regulation 6(2) of the Income Support (General) Regulations 1987 (persons not treated as engaged in remunerative work) applies;
  (ii) was in receipt of an income-based jobseeker's allowance on the day before the day on which he was first engaged in the work referred to in sub-paragraph (a) of that paragraph; and
  (iii) would satisfy the conditions of entitlement to income support (apart from the condition of making a claim would apply in the absence of this paragraph) only by virtue of regulation 6(3) of those regulations.]

AMENDMENTS

1. The Social Security (Claims and Payments on account, Overpayments and Recovery) Amendment Regulations 1989 (S.I. 1989 No. 136), reg. 3 (April 10, 1989)

(S.I. 1987 No. 1968, reg. 3) (as amended)

2. The Social Security (Claims and Payments) Amendment (No. 2) Regulations 1994 (S.I. 1994 No. 2943), reg. 2 (April 13, 1995)

3. The Social Security (Claims and Payments) (Jobseeker's Allowance Consequential Amendments) Regulations 1996 (S.I. 1996 No. 1460), reg. 2(3) (October 7, 1996)

4. The Social Security Act 1998 (Commencement No. 11 and Transitional Provisions) Order 1989 (S.I. 1999 No. 2860), Sched. 3 (October 18, 1999)

5. The Social Security (Miscellaneous Amendments) (No. 2) Regulations 1999 (S.I. 1999 No. 2556), reg.7, (October 4, 1999)

GENERAL NOTE

On the meaning of "ordinarily resident" see annotation to reg. 5 of the Persons Abroad Regulations.

The Training for Work (Scottish Enterprise and Highlands and Islands Enterprise Programmes) Order 1993 (S.I. 1993 No. 498) provides that for the purpose of these regulations, a person using facilities under the training programmes to which the Order refers are treated as participating in arrangments for training under s.2(3) of the Enterprise and New Towns (Scotland) Act 1990 and payments made to persons on those programmes are treated as payments in respect of training. See also, to the same effect, the Training for Work (Miscellaneous Provisions) October 1993 (S.I. 1993 No. 348.)

4.17

Making a claim for benefit

4.—(1) Every claim for benefit [⁷other than a claim for income support or jobseeker's allowance] shall be made in writing on a form approved by the Secretary of State [³for the purpose of the benefit for which the claim is made], or in such other manner, being in writing, as the Secretary of State [⁸ or the Board] may accept as sufficient in the circumstances of any particular case.

[⁷ (1A) In the case of a claim for income support or jobseeker's allowance, the claim shall—
 (a) be made in writing on a form approved by the Secretary of State for the purpose of the benefit for which the claim is made;
 (b) unless any of the reasons specified in paragraph (1B) applies, be made in accordance with the instructions on the form; and
 (c) unless any of the reasons specified in paragraph (1B) applies, include such information and evidence as the form may require in connection with the claim.

(1B) The reasons referred to in paragraph (1A) are—
 (a) (i) the person making the claim is unable to complete the form in accordance with the instructions or to obtain the information or evidence it requires because he has a physical, learning, mental or communication difficulty; and
  (ii) it is not reasonably practicable for the claimant to obtain assistance from another person to complete the form or obtain the information or evidence;
or
 (b) the information or evidence required by the form does not exist;
or
 (c) the information or evidence required by the form can only be

4.18

347

The Social Security (Claims and Payments) Regulations 1987

obtained at serious risk of physical or mental harm to the claimant, and it is not reasonably practicable for the claimant to obtain the information or evidence by other means;

or

(d) the information or evidence required by the form can only be obtained from a third party, and it is not reasonably practicable for the claimant to obtain such information or evidence from such third party;

or

(e) the Secretary of State is of the opinion that the person making the claim has provided sufficient information or evidence to show that he is not entitled to the benefit for which the claim is made, and that it would be inappropriate to require the form to be completed or further information or evidence to be supplied.

(1C) If a person making a claim is unable to complete the claim form or supply the evidence or information it requires because one of the reasons specified in sub-paragraphs (a) to (d) of paragraph (1B) applies, he may so notify an appropriate office by whatever means.]

[⁸In the case of a claim for working families' tax credit, where a married or unmarried couple is included in the family, the claim shall be made by whichever partner they agree should so claim.

(2A) Where, in a case to which paragraph (2) applies, the partners are unable to agree which of them should make the claim, the Board may in their discretion determine that the claim shall be made by the partner who, on the information available to the Board at the time of their determination, is in their opinion mainly caring for the children.]

(3) [⁵Subject to paragraph (3C),] in the case of a married or unmarried couple, a claim for income support shall be made by whichever partner they agree should so claim or, in default of agreement, by such one of them as the Secretary of State shall in his discretion determine.

[²(3A) In the case of a married or unmarried couple where both partners satisfy the conditions set out in [⁸ section 129(1) of the Social Security Contributions and Benefits Act 1992], a claim for [⁸ disabled persons tax credit] shall be made by whichever partner they agree should so claim, or in default of agreement, by such one of them as the Secretary of State [⁸ or the Board] shall determine.]

[⁴(3B) For the purposes of income-based jobseeker's allowance—

(a) in the case of a married or unmarried couple, a claim shall be made by whichever partner they agree should so claim or, in default of agreement, by such one of them as the Secretary of State shall in his discretion determine;

(b) where there is no entitlement to contribution-based jobseeker's allowance on a claim made by one partner and the other partner wishes to claim income-based jobseeker's allowance, the claim made by that other partner shall be treated as having been made on the date on which the first partner made his claim; and

(c) where entitlement to income-based jobseeker's allowance arises on the expiry of entitlement to contribution-based jobseeker's allowance consequent on a claim made by one partner and the other partner then makes a claim—

(S.I. 1987 No. 1968, reg. 4) (as amended)

    (i) the claim of the first partner shall be terminated; and
    (ii) the claim of the second partner shall be treated as having been made on the day after the entitlement to contribution-based jobseeker's allowance expired.]

[⁵(3C) In the case of a claim for income support for a period to which [⁹ regulation 21ZB(2)] of the Income Support (General) Regulations 1987 (treatment of refugees) refers, the claim shall be made by the refugee or in the case of a married or unmarried couple both of whom are refugees, by either of them.]

(4) Where one of a married or unmarried couple is entitled to income support under an award and, with his agreement, his partner claims income support that entitlement shall terminate on the day before that claim is made or treated as made.

[⁶(5) Where a person who wishes to make a claim for benefit and who has not been supplied with an approved form of claim notifies an appropriate office (by whatever means) of his intention to make a claim, he shall be supplied, without charge, with such form of claim by such person as the Secretary of State [⁸ or the Board] may appoint or authorise for that purpose.]

[⁴(6) A person wishing to make a claim for benefit shall—
  (a) if it is a claim for a jobseeker's allowance, unless the Secretary of State otherwise directs, attend in person at an appropriate office or such other place, and at such time, as the Secretary of State may specify in his case in a notice under regulation 23 of the Jobseeker's Allowance Regulations;
  (b) if it is a claim for any other benefit, deliver or send the claim to an appropriate office.]

(7) If a claim [⁷ other than a claim for income support or jobseeker's allowance,] is defective at the date when it is received or has been made in writing but not on the form approved for the time being, the Secretary of State [⁸ or the Board] may refer the claim to the person making it or, as the case may be, supply him with the approved form, and if the form is received properly completed within one month, or such longer period as the Secretary of State [⁸ or the Board] may consider reasonable, from the date on which it is so referred or supplied, the Secretary of State shall treat the claim as if it has been duly made in the first instance.

[⁷ 7(A) In the case of a claim for income support or jobseeker's allowance, if a defective claim is received, the Secretary of State shall advise the person making the claim of the defect and of the relevant provisions of regulation 6(1A) or 6(4A) relating to the date of claim.

(8) A claim, other than a claim for income support or jobseeker's allowance, which is made on the form approved for the time being is, for the purposes of these Regulations, properly completed if completed in accordance with the instructions on the form and defective if not so completed.

[⁸(8A) Where—
  (a) the Board determine under paragraph (2A) that a claim for working families' tax credit shall be made by the partner who in their opinion is mainly caring for the children,

The Social Security (Claims and Payments) Regulations 1987

(b) a claim for working families' tax credit is made by that partner on the form approved for the time being, and

(c) the claim is not completed in accordance with the instructions on the form by reason only that, in consequence of the other partner not agreeing which of them should make the claim, it has not been signed by the other partner

the Board may in their discretion treat that claim as completed in accordance with the instructions on the form for the purposes of paragraph (8), notwithstanding that it has not been signed by the other partner in accordance with those instructions.]

(9) In the case of a claim for income support or jobseeker's allowance, a properly completed claim is a claim which meets the requirements of paragraph (1A) and a defective claim is a claim which does not meet those requirements.]

AMENDMENTS

1. The Social Security (Miscellaneous Provisions) Amendment Regulations 1990 (S.I. 1990 No. 2208), reg. 8 (December 5, 1990).

2. The Social Security (Claims and Payments) Amendment Regulations 1991 (S.I. 1991 No. 2741), reg. 3 (February 3, 1992).

3. The Social Security (Miscellaneous Provisions) Amendment Regulations 1992 (S.I. 1992 No. 247), reg. 10 (March 9, 1992).

4. The Social Security (Claims and Payments) (Jobseeker's Allowance Consequential Amendments) Regulations 1996 (S.I. 1996 No. 1460), reg. 2(4) (October 7, 1996).

5. The Income Support and Social Security (Claims and Payments) (Miscellaneous Amendments) Regulations 1996 (S.I. 1996 No. 2431), reg. 7(b) (October 15, 1996).

6. The Social Security (Miscellaneous Amendments) (No. 2) Regulations 1997 (S.I. 1997 No. 793), reg. 2(4) (April 7, 1997).

7. The Social Security (Miscellaneous Amendments) (No. 2) Regulations 1997 (S.I. 1997 No. 793), reg. 2 (October 6, 1997).

8. The Tax Credits (Claims and Payments) (Amendment) Regulations 1999 (S.I. 1999 No. 2572), reg. 4 (October 5, 1999)

9. The Social Security (Immigration and Asylum) Consequential Amendments Regulations 2000 (S.I. 2000 No. 636), (April 3, 2000)

4.19 DEFINITIONS

"appropriate office"—see reg. 2(1).
"benefit"—see reg. 2(2).
"claim for benefit"—see reg. 2(1).
"jobseeker's allowance"—*ibid.*
"married couple"—*ibid.*
"partner"—*ibid.*
"refugee"—*ibid.*
"unmarried couple"—*ibid.*

GENERAL NOTE

Introduction

Section 1 of the Administration Act requires a claim to be submitted for any benefit except where regulations otherwise prescribe (see reg. 3), as a condition of entitlement to benefit. This largely removes the effect of the decision of the

(S.I. 1987 No. 1968, reg. 4) (as amended)

House of Lords in *Insurance Officer v. McCaffrey* [1984] 1 W.L.R. 1353, though some doubt remained in relation to entitlement prior to September 2, 1985, when the first version of s. I was implemented. This is now resolved by s.2.

Claims are required to be in writing on the appropriate prescribed form which must be duly completed.

A fine line used to be drawn between the responsibilities of the Secretary of State and the adjudicating authorities under this regulation. It has been consistently held that it is for the Secretary of State to say whether a document (not in the prescribed form) is acceptable as "sufficient in the circumstances of the particular case," but the duty lies on the adjudicating authorities to decide whether such a document is a claim for benefit: *R(U)9/60* and *R(S)1/63*. It may be significant that in both these cases the Commissioner concluded that a document accepted by the Secretary of State did not constitute a claim for benefit. It is sometimes argued that the Secretary of State's authority under para. (1) extends to determining the date of the claim. This is not so. The sole issue reserved for the Secretary of State under para. (1) is whether the *form* of the claim (if not on a prescribed form) is acceptable as a claim. It is left for adjudication officers and tribunals to determine the date of the claim and what has been claimed once the Secretary of State has determined that it is in acceptable form: *R(SB)5/89* confirmed in *CU/94/1994*. This distinction now largely disappears with the abolition of adjudication officers.

Once a claim has been made, it may only be withdrawn before it has been adjudicated upon by an adjudication officer: *R(U)2/79* and *R(U)7/83* and see reg. 5(2).

Paragraph (1)

Note that from October 6, 1997, para. (1) no longer applies to claims for income support and JSA, for which see paras. (1A) to (1C).

4.20

For other benefits, para. (1) provides that claims must be made in writing, normally on an official form, although the Secretary of State may accept some other kind of written claim. In such a case, under para. (7), the Secretary of State may require the claimant to fill in the proper form. If this is done in the proper time the claim is treated as duly made in the first instance. It no longer seems possible for an oral claim to be accepted. However, see reg. 6(1)(aa) for the position when a claimant contacts an office with a view to making a claim. Note also reg. 19(6), under which the Secretary of State still has the power to extend the time for claiming by up to a month if it is considered that to do so would be consistent with the proper administration of benefit. But the discretion is no longer open-ended and one of the circumstances in reg. 19(7) must apply. If the claim is properly made within the month, it is treated under reg. 6(3) as made at the beginning of the period specified by the Secretary of State under reg. 19(6) (which normally will be equal to the time taken to return the claim form). The procedure provided for in reg. 19(6) and (7) also applies to income support and JSA, whereas reg. 6(1)(aa) does not apply to claims for those benefits where the first notification of an intention to claim was received after October 5, 1997. But for income support and JSA claims after that date, see reg. 6(1A) and (4A)–(4AB).

Note also *R(SB) 9/84* where a Tribunal of Commissioners holds that where a claim has been determined, the Secretary of State must be deemed, in the absence of any challenge at the time, to have accepted that the claim was made in sufficient manner. See the notes to reg. 33. See also *CDLA/1596/1996* in which the Commissioner set aside the tribunal's decision because they had failed to consider whether they should refer to the Secretary of State the question whether the claimant's application for review should be treated as a claim under para. (1).

The Social Security (Claims and Payments) Regulations 1987

Paragraphs (1A) to (1C)

4.21   These new provisions, together with the new reg. 6(1A) and (4A) to (4AB), introduce the so-called "onus of proof" changes for claims for income support and JSA from October 6, 1997. The aim is to place more responsibility on claimants for these benefits to provide information and evidence to support their claim (see the DSS's Memorandum to the Social Security Advisory Committee (SSAC) annexed to the Committee's report (Cm. 3586) on the proposals). SSAC supported this principle but considered that it was "premature to introduce penalties for failure to provide information when it is more likely that the current problems lie more with the forms and procedures than with dilatory or obstructive claimants". As the Committee pointed out, the current claim forms are lengthy, complex and difficult for many people to understand, and moreover in the past told claimants not to delay sending in the claim form even if they had not got all the required information. Furthermore, since income support and income-based JSA are basic subsistence benefits, claimants have every incentive to cooperate in providing all the information needed to get an early payment. Thus SSAC's main recommendation was that the claim forms and guidance to claimants should first be revised and tested "before introducing new penalties, which together with the proposed changes to backdating rules [see reg. 19], will only serve to complicate the social security system and penalise the most disadvantaged claimants". But this recommendation was rejected by the Government, although the final form of the regulations did take limited account of some of SSAC's other recommendations.

Under the new rules, in order for a claim for income support or JSA to be validly made, it must be in writing on a properly completed approved form (there is no longer any provision for the Secretary of State to accept any other kind of written claim) and all the information and evidence required by the form must have been provided (para. (1A)). However, the requirement to complete the form fully or to provide the required evidence does not apply in the circumstances set out in para. (1B). The list in para. (1B) is exhaustive and there is no category of analogous circumstances. If any of sub-paras. (a) to (d) of para. (1B) do apply, the person can inform an appropriate office (defined in reg. 2(1)) "by whatever means" (*e.g.* verbally or through a third party) (para. (1C)). Note that the obligation to provide information and evidence only relates to that required by the claim form; if a claim is accepted as validly made it will still be open to the Benefits Agency to seek further information if this is required in order to decide the claim, but this will not alter the date of claim.

See reg. 6(1A) for the date of claim for an income support claim and reg. 6(4A)–(4AB) for the date of claim for JSA claims (and note the differences).

Thus the major effect of these new rules is that there is now a requirement to produce the specified information and evidence *before* a claim is treated as having been made (although see reg. 6(1A) and (4A)–(4AB) for the date of claim). Whether the necessary evidence has been produced or whether a claimant is exempt under para. (1B) will therefore be a decision for the Secretary of State, *i.e.* there will be no right of appeal to a tribunal in cases of dispute. SSAC's proposal that the decision as to whether a person is exempt from the claiming requirements should be for an AO was not accepted by the Government. But note *R(SB) 9/84(T)* which holds that where a claim has been determined, the Secretary of State must be deemed, in the absence of any challenge at the time, to have accepted that the claim was made in sufficient manner. See the notes to reg. 33.

Note also s.1(1A) of the Administration Act, under which claimants will not be entitled to benefit unless they satisfy requirements relating to the provision of national insurance numbers.

(S.I. 1987 No. 1968, reg. 4) (as amended)

Paragraph (2) and (2A)
In working granted tax credit cases, if a couple is involved, the claim may be made by either partner.

4.22

Paragraph (3)
In income support cases, where a couple is involved, either partner can be the claimant, except in the case of a refugee under para. (3C). The exceptionally complex rules of reg. 1A of the Supplementary Benefit (Aggregation) Regulations, incorporating the "nominated breadwinner" scheme, were abandoned. There is now free choice. If the couple cannot jointly agree who should claim, the Secretary of State is to break the tie. There are still some differences in entitlement according to which partner is the claimant, particularly since only the claimant is required to be available for work. In addition, head (b) of para. 12(1) of Sched. 2 to the Income Support Regulations (disability and higher pensioner premium) can only be satisfied by the claimant. But there is now no long-term rate and the full-time employment of either partner excludes entitlement to income support. See reg. 7(2). Under the Income Support (Transitional) Regulations transitional protection is lost if the claimant for the couple changes. *CIS 8/1990* and *CIS 375/1990* challenged this rule on the grounds that it was indirectly discriminatory against women (since in 98 per cent. of couples (at that time) the man was the claimant). Following the European Court of Judicer's decision in the *Cresswell* case that income support is not covered by E.C. Directive 79/7 on equal treatment for men and women in social security (see the notes to reg. 36 of the Income Support Regulations), the claimants could not rely on European law. The Commissioner also rejects a submission that the Sex Discrimination Act 1975 prevented the discriminatory effect of regs. 2 and 10 of the Transitional Regulations. Para. (4) below deals with changes of partner.

4.23

Paragraph (3A)
Normally a claim for disability working allowance must be made by the person who is disabled and in remunerative work. Under para. (3A), if both partners in a couple satisfy the conditions of entitlement, they may choose which one of them is to claim. If they cannot choose, the Secretary of State makes the decision.

4.24

Paragraph (3B)
Sub-para. (a) applies the normal income support rule for couples to income-based JSA. Sub-paras. (b) and (c) make provision about the deemed date of the claim for income-based JSA by one partner when a claim for contribution-based JSA by the other partner fails or entitlement comes to an end.

4.25

Paragraph (3C)
Where one of a couple is a refugee, the claim for income support must be made by that partner. If both are refugees, there is a free choice.

4.26

Paragraph (4)
If there is a change of claimant within a couple in the middle of a continuing income support claim, the claims are not to overlap. The change is a matter of a new claim for benefit, not review as it was for supplementary benefit (*R(SB) 1/93*). In *CSIS 66/1992* the Commissioner rejects the argument that para. (4) combined with s.20(9) of the Social Security Act 1986 (SSCBA s.134(2)) meant that a change of claimant could not be backdated. If the claimant could show good cause for her delay in claiming, regs. 19(2) and 6(3) enabled her claim to be backdated to the date from which she had good cause (subject to the then 12-month limit in reg. 19(4)). Duplication of payment could be avoided by the AO reviewing the claimant's husband's entitlement for any past period in

4.27

The Social Security (Claims and Payments) Regulations 1987

respect of which the claimant was held to be entitled to benefit and applying reg. 5(1) and (2), Case 1, of the Payments Regulations. By becoming the claimant the wife qualified for a disability premium. There is a specific provision in para. 19 of Sched. 7 to the Income Support Regulations for arrears of a disability premium in these circumstances.

Paragraph (6)

4.28   The claim, except in the case of JSA, must be delivered or sent to the appropriate office. In *CS 175/1988* the claimant took a claim form to the local office. The counter-clerk told him to get his employer to correct a mistake and he took it away. The Commissioner holds that a claim was not made on that date, because it was not lodged, but merely shown to the clerk for advice. This distinction is unrealistic.

In *CSIS 48/1992* the Commissioner considered the effect of para. (6) in the light of s.7 and s.23 of the Interpretation Act 1978. He concludes that the effect of these provisions is that a claim for a social security benefit is a document authorised by an Act to be served by post, which is presumed to have been delivered in the ordinary course of post unless this is proved not to have been the case. The SSAT should therefore have considered whether it accepted that the claim had been posted, and, if so, whether the presumption of delivery had been rebutted by the AO. *CSIS 48/1992* has been followed in *CIS 759/1992*.

For JSA, a claimant wishing to make an initial claim must normally go in person to the nearest Job Centre to obtain a claim pack from the new jobseeker receptionist. An appointment will then be made for the claimant to return, usually within five days, for a new jobseeker interview. This is all part of the concept of "active signing". The claim will be treated as made on the date of the first attendance, if it is received properly completed within a month (reg. 6(1)(aa) and (4A)).

Paragraphs (7) and (8)

4.29   Para. (7), which does not apply to claims for income support or JSA (for which see para. (7A)), deals with written claims not made on the proper form (for which, see para. (1)), and situations where the proper form is not completed according to the instructions (see para. 8)). The Secretary of State may simply treat this as an ineffective attempt to claim, but also has power to refer the form back to the claimant. Then there is one month (extendable by the Secretary of State) to complete the form properly, in which case the claim is treated as made on the date of the original attempt to claim (see reg. 6(1)(b)). Note also *R(SB) 9/84*; see the note to para. (1).

Paragraphs (7A) and (9)

4.30   If a claim for income support or JSA is defective (on which see para. (9)), the Secretary of State will simply advise the claimant of the defect and of the rules in reg. 6(1A) (for income support claims) or reg. 6(4A) (for JSA claims) as appropriate. It will then be up to the claimant to comply with those provisions if he is in a position to do so.

[1 Further provisions as to claims

4.31   **4A.**—(1) Where a claimant resides in both—
  (a) the area of a local authority specified in Part I or II of Schedule 1 to the Social Security (Claims and Information) Regulations 1999; and
  (b) a postcode district identified in Part I or II of Schedule 2 to the Social Security (Claims and Information) Regulations 1999,
any claim for a benefit to which paragraph (2) applies may be made to

(S.I. 1987 No. 1968, reg. 4A) (as amended)

any office displaying the ONE logo(a) (whether or not that office is situated within the area of the local authority in which the claimant resides).

(2) The benefits to which this paragraph applies are—
(a) a jobseeker's allowance;
(b) income support;
(c) incapacity benefit;
(d) invalid care allowance;
(e) severe disablement allowance;
(f) widow's benefit;
(g) bereavement benefits;
(h) disability living allowance.

(3) A claim made in accordance with paragraph (1), other than a claim for income support or a jobseeker's allowance, shall be made in writing on a form approved by the Secretary of State for the purpose of the benefit to which the claim is made, or in such other manner, being in writing, as the person to whom the claim is made may accept as sufficient in the circumstances of the particular case.

(4) In the case of a claim for income support or a jobseeker's allowance, the provisions of regulation 4(1A) to (1C) shall apply.

(5) In its application to the area of any authority specified in Part I or II of Schedule 1 to the Social Security (Claims and Information) Regulations 1999, the "appropriate office" in these Regulations includes also an office of an authority or person to whom claims may be made in accordance with paragraph (1).

(6) In these Regulations, a "participating authority" means any local authority or person to whom claims may be made in accordance with paragraph (1).

AMENDMENT

1. This regulation inserted by The Social Security (Claims and Information) Regulations 1999 (S.I. 1999 No. 3108), reg, 5 (November 29, 1999)

Forwarding claims and information

4B.—(1) A participating authority may—
(a) record information or evidence relating to any social security matter supplied by or obtained from a person at an office displaying the ONE logo, whether or not the information or evidence is supplied or obtained in connection with the making of a claim for benefit;
(b) give information or advice with respect to any social security matter to persons who are making, or have made, claims for any benefit to which regulation 4A(2) applies.

(2) A participating authority shall forward to the Secretary of State—
(a) any claim for benefit, other than a claim for housing benefit or council tax benefit, together with any information or evidence supplied to the authority in connection with that claim; and
(b) any information or evidence relating to any other social security matter, except where the information or evidence relates solely to

housing benefit or council tax benefit given to the authority by a person making a claim for, or who has claimed, a benefit to which regulation 4A(2) applies.]

AMENDMENT

1. This regulation inserted by The Social Security (Claims and Information) Regulations 1999 (S.I. 1999 No. 3108), reg, 5 (November 29, 1999)

Amendment and withdrawal of claim

5.—(1) A person who has made a claim may amendit at any time by notice in writing received in an appropriate office before a determination has been made on the claim, and any claim so amended may be treated as if it had been so amended in the first instance.

(2) A person who has made a claim may withdraw it at any time before a determination has been made on it, by notice to an appropriate office, and any such notice of withdrawal shall have effect when it is received.

DEFINITION

"appropriate office"—see reg. 2(1).

Date of claim

6.—(1) [³Subject to the following provisions of this regulation] the date on which a claim is made shall be—
  (a) in the case of a claim which meets the requirements of regulation 4(1), the date on which it is received in an appropriate office;
[¹²(aa) in the case of a claim for—
  [¹⁴working families' tax credit];
  [¹⁴disabled persons tax credit];
  jobseeker's allowance if first notification is received before 6th October 1997; or
  income support if first notification is received before 6th October 1997;
which meets the requirements of regulation 4(1) and which is received in an appropriate office within one month of first notification in accordance with regulation 4(5), whichever is the later of—
    (i) the date on which that notification is received; and
    (ii) the first date on which that claim could have been made in accordance with these Regulations;]
  (b) in the case of a claim which does not meet the requirements of regulation 4(1) but which is treated, under regulation 4(7) as having been duly made, the date on which the claim was received in an appropriate office in the first instance.
[¹³ (1A) In the case of a claim for income support—
  (a) subject to the following sub-paragraphs, the date on which a claim is made shall be the date on which a properly completed

(S.I. 1987 No. 1968, reg. 6) (as amended)

claim is received in an appropriate office or the first day in respect of which the claim is made if later;
  (b) where a properly completed claim is received in an appropriate office within one month of first notification of intention to make that claim, the date of claim shall be the date on which that notification is deemed to be made or the first day in respect of which the claim is made if later;
  (c) a notification of intention to make a claim will be deemed to be made on the date when an appropriate office receives—
    (i) a notification in accordance with regulation 4(5); or
    (ii) a defective claim.]
(2) [^{1}...]
[^{1}(3) In the case of a claim for income support, [^{14} working families' tax credit, disabled person's tax credit] [^{12}or jobseeker's allowance][^{5}...], where the time for claiming is extended under regulation 19 the claim shall be treated as made on the first day of the period in respect of which the claim is, by reason of the operation of that regulation, timeously made.
(4) Paragraph (3) shall not apply when the time for claiming income support [^{14} working families' tax credit, disabled person's tax credit] or jobseeker's allowance]] has been extended under regulation 19 and the failure to claim within the prescribed time for the purposes of that regulation is for the reason only that the claim has been sent by post.]
[^{13}(4A) Where a person notifies the Secretary of State (by whatever means) that he wishes to claim a jobseeker's allowance—
  (a) if he is required to attend under regulation 4(6)(a)—
    (i) if he subsequently attends for the purpose of making a claim for that benefit at the time and place specified by the Secretary of State and complies with the requirements of paragraph (4AA), the claim shall be treated as made on whichever is the later of first notification of intention to make that claim and the first day in respect of which the claim is made;
    (ii) if, without good cause, he fails to attend for the purpose of making a claim for that benefit at either the time or place so specified, or does not comply with the requirements of paragraph (4AA), the claim shall be treated as made on the first day on which he does attend at that place and does provide a properly completed claim;
  (b) if under regulation 4(6)(a) the Secretary of State directs that he is not required to attend—
    (i) subject to the following sub-paragraph, the date on which the claim is made shall be the date on which a properly completed claim is received in an appropriate office or the first day in respect of which the claim is made if later;
    (ii) where a properly completed claim is received in an appropriate office within one month of first notification of intention to make that claim, the date of claim shall be the date of that notification.
(4AA) Unless the Secretary of State otherwise directs, a properly completed claim shall be provided at or before the time when the person

making the claim for a jobseeker's allowance is required to attend for the purpose of making a claim.

(4AB) The Secretary of State may direct that the time for providing a properly completed claim may be extended to a date no later than the date one month after the date of first notification of intention to make that claim.]

(4B) Where a person's entitlement to a jobseeker's allowance has ceased in any of the circumstances specified in regulation 25(1)(a), (b) or (c) of the Jobseeker's Allowance Regulations (entitlement ceasing on a failure to comply) and—
  (a) where he had normally been required to attend in person, he shows that the failure to comply which caused the cessation of his previous entitlement was due to any of the circumstances mentioned in regulation 30(c) or (d) of those Regulations, and no later than the day immediately following the date when those circumstances cease to apply he makes a further claim for jobseeker's allowance; or
  (b) where he had not normally been required to attend in person, he shows that he did not receive the notice to attend and he immediately makes a further claim for jobseeker's allowance,
that further claim shall be treated as having been made on the day following that cessation of entitlement.

(4C) Where a person's entitlement to a jobseeker's allowance ceases in the circumstances specified in regulation 25(1)(b) of the Jobseeker's Allowance Regulations (failure to attend at time specified) and that person makes a further claim for that allowance on the day on which he failed to attend at the time specified, that claim shall be treated as having been made on the following day.]

[¹¹(4D) In the case of a claim for income support to which regulation 4(3C) (claim by refugee) refers, the claim shall be treated as made [¹⁵ on the date on which his claim for asylum was recorded by the Secretary of State as having been made.]

[²(5) Where a person submits a claim for attendance allowance [⁶or disability living allowance or a request under paragraph (8)] by post and the arrival of that [⁶claim or request] at an appropriate office is delayed by postal disruption caused by industrial action, whether within the postal service or elsewhere, the [⁶claim or request] shall be treated as received on the day on which it would have been received if it had been delivered in the ordinary course of post.]

[³(6) Where—
  (a) on or after 9th April 1990 a person satisfies the capital condition in section 22(6) of the Social Security Act 1986 [SSCBA, s.134(1)] for income support and he would not have satisfied that condition had the amount prescribed under regulation 45 of the Income Support (General) Regulation 1987 been £6,000; and
  (b) a claim for that benefit is received from him in an appropriate office not later than 27th May 1990;
the claim shall be treated as made on the date [⁴not later than 5th December 1990] determined in accordance with paragraph (7).

(7) For the purpose of paragraph (6), where—

(S.I. 1987 No. 1968, reg. 6) (as amended)

(a) the claimant satisfies the other conditions of entitlement to income support on the date on which he satisfies the capital condition, the date shall be the date on which he satisfies that condition;

(b) the claimant does not satisfy the other conditions of entitlement to income support on the date on which he satisfies the capital condition, the date shall be the date on which he satisfies the conditions of entitlement to that benefit.]

[⁶(8) [⁸Subject to paragraph (8A),] where—
(a) a request is received in an appropriate office for a claim form for disability living allowance or attendance allowance; and
(b) in response to the request a claim form for disability living allowance or attendance is issued from an appropriate office; and
(c) within the time specified the claim form properly completed is received in an appropriate office,

the date on which the claim is made shall be the date which the request was received in the appropriate office.

[⁸(8A) Where, in a case which would otherwise fall within paragraph (8), it is not possible to determine the date when the request for a claim form was received in an appropriate office because of a failure to record that date, the claim shall be treated as having been made on the date 6 weeks before the date on which the properly completed claim form is received in an appropriate office.]

(9) [⁹In paragraph (8) and (8A)]—
"a claim form" means a form approved by the Secretary of State under regulation 4(1); "properly completed" has the meaning assigned by regulation 4(8);
"the time specified" means 6 weeks from the date on which the request was received or such longer period as the Secretary of State may consider reasonable.]

[⁷(10) Where a person starts a job on a Monday or Tuesday in any week and he makes a claim for [¹⁴ disabled person's tax credit] in that week the claim shall be treated as made on the Tuesday of that week.

(11) [¹⁴ . . .]

[¹² (12) [¹⁴ . . .] Where a person has claimed [¹⁴ disabled person's tax credit] and that claim ("the original claim") has been refused, and a further claim is made in the circumstances specified in paragraph (13), that further claim shall be treated as made—
(a) on the date of the original claim; or
(b) on the first date in respect of which the qualifying benefit was payable, whichever is the later.

(13) The circumstances referred to in paragraph (12) are that—
(a) the original claim was refused on the ground that the claimant did not qualify under section 129(2) of the Contributions and Benefits Act;
(b) at the date of the original claim the claimant had made a claim for a qualifying benefit and that claim had not been determined;
(c) after the original claim had been determined, the claim for the qualifying benefit was determined in the claimant's favour; and
(d) the further claim for [¹⁴ disabled person's tax credit] was made

within three months of the date that the claim for the qualifying benefit was determined.

(14) [¹⁴ . . .]

(15) In paragraphs (12) and (13) "qualifying benefit" means any of the benefits referred to in section 129(2) of the Contributions and Benefits Act.

(16) Where a person has claimed severe disablement allowance and that claim ("the original claim") has been refused, and a further claim is made in the circumstances specified in paragraph (17), that further claim shall be treated as made—
  (a) on the date of the original claim; or
  (b) on the first date in respect of which the highest rate of the care component of disability living allowance was payable,
whichever is the later.

(17) The circumstances referred to in paragraph (16) are that—
  (a) the original claim eas refused on the ground that the claimant's disablement was less than 80 per cent.;
  (b) at the date of the original claim the claimant had made a claim for disability living allowance, and that claim had not been determined;
  (c) after the original claim had been determined, the claimant was awarded the highest rate of the care component of disability living allowance; and
  (d) the further claim for severe disablement allowance was made within three months of the date that the claim for disability living allowance was determined.

(18) Where a person has ceased to be entitled to incapacity benefit, and a further claim for incapacity benefit is made in the circumstances specified in paragraph (19), that further claim shall be treated as made—
  (a) on the date that entitlement to incapacity benefit ceased; or
  (b) on the first date in respect of which the qualifying benefit was payable;
whichever is the later.

(19) The circumstances referred to in paragraph (18) are that—
  (a) entitlement to incapacity benefit ceased on the ground that the claimant was not incapable of work;
  (b) at the date that entitlement to incapacity benefit ceased the claimant had made a claim for a qualifying benefit and that claim had not been determined;
  (c) after entitlement to incapacity benefit had ceased, the claim for the qualifying benefit was determined in the claimant's favour; and
  (d) the further claim for incapacity benefit was made within three months of the date that the claim for the qualifying benefit was determined.

(20) In paragraphs (18) and (19) "qualifying benefit" means of the payments referred to in regulation 10(2)(a) of the Social Security (Incapacity for Work) (General) Regulations 1995.

(21) Where a person has claimed invalid care allowance and that claim ("the original claim" has been refused, and a further claim is

made in the circumstances specified in paragraph (22), that further claim shall be treated as made—
   (a) on the date of the original claim; or
   (b) on the first date in respect of which the qualifying benefit was payable in respect of the disabled person,
whichever is the later.
   (22) The circumstances referred to in paragraph (21) are that—
   (a) the original claim was refused on the ground that the disabled person was not a severely disabled person within the meaning of section 70(2) of the Contributions and Benefits Act;
   (b) at the date of the original claim the disabled person had made a claim for a qualifying benefit, and that claim had not been determined;
   (c) after the original claim had been determined, the claim for the qualifying benefit was determined in the disabled person's favour; and
   (d) the further claim for invalid care allowance was made within three months of the date that the claim for the qualifying benefit was determined.
   (23) In paragraphs (21) and (22)—
   (a) "the disabled person" means the person for whom the invalid care allowance claimant is caring in accordance with section 70(1)(a) of the Contributions and Benefits Act; and
   (b) "qualifying benefit" means any benefit or payment referred to in section 70(2) of the Contributions and Benefits Act.
   (24) Where a person has claimed a social fund payment in respect of maternity or funeral expenses and that claim ("the original claim") has been refused, and a further claim is made in the circumstances specified in paragraph (25), that further claim shall be treated as made—
   (a) on the date of the original claim; or
   (b) on the first date in respect of which the qualifying benefit was awarded,
whichever is the later.
   (25) The circumstances referred to in paragraph (24) are that—
   (a) the original claim was refused on the ground that the claimant had not been awarded a qualifying benefit;
   (b) at the date of the original claim the claimant had made a claim for a qualifying benefit and that claim had not been determined;
   (c) after the original claim had been determined, the claim for the qualifying benefit was determined in the claimant's favour; and
   (d) the further claim for a social fund payment was made within three months of the date that the claim for the qualifying benefit was determined.
   (26) In paragraphs (24) and (25) "qualifying benefit" means—
   (a) in the case of a claim for a social fund payment in respect of maternity expenses, any benefit referred to in regulation 5(1)(a) of the Social Fund Maternity and Funeral Expenses (General) Regulations 1987;
   (b) in the case of a claim for a social fund payment in respect of

The Social Security (Claims and Payments) Regulations 1987

funeral expenses, any benefit referred to in regulation 7(1)(a) of those Regulations.

(27) Where a claim is made for [¹⁴ working families' tax credit or disabled person's tax credit], and—
  (a) the claimant had previously made a claim for income support or jobseeker's allowance ("the original claim");
  (b) the original claim was refused on the ground that the claimant or his partner was in remunerative work; and
  (c) the claim for [¹⁴ working families' tax credit or disabled person's tax credit] was made within 14 days of the date that the original claim was determined,
that claim shall be treated as made on the date of the original claim, or, if the claimant so requests, on a later date specified by the claimant.

(28) Where a claim is made for income support or jobseeker's allowance, and—
  (a) the claimant had previously made a claim for [¹⁴ working families' tax credit or disabled person's tax credit] ("the original claim");
  (b) the original claim was refused on the ground that the claimant or his partner was not in remunerative work; and
  (c) the claim for income support or jobseeker's allowance was made within 14 days of the date that the original claim was determined,
that claim shall be treated as made on the date of the original claim, or, if the claimant so requests, on a later date specified by the claimant.]

AMENDMENTS

1. The Social Security (Claims and Payments) Amendment Regulations 1988 (S.I. 1988 No. 522), reg. 2 (April 11, 1988).

2. The Social Security (Medical Evidence, Claims and Payments) Amendment Regulations 1989 (S.I. 1989 No. 1686), S.I. 1989 No. 1686, reg. 4 (October 9, 1989).

3. The Social Security (Claims and Payments) Amendment Regulations 1990 (S.I. 1990 No. 725), reg. 2 (April 9, 1990).

4. The Social Security (Miscellaneous Provisions) Amendment Regulations 1990 (S.I. 1990 No. 2208), reg. 9 (December 5, 1990).

5. The Social Security (Miscellaneous Provisions) Amendment Regulations 1991 (S.I. 1991 No. 2284), reg. 6 (November 1, 1991).

6. The Social Security (Claims and Payments) Amendment Regulations 1991 (S.I. 1991 No. 2741), reg. 4 (February 3, 1992).

7. The Social Security (Claims and Payments) Amendment Regulations 1991 (S.I. 1991 No. 2741), reg. 4 (March 10, 1992).

8. The Social Security (Claims and Payments) Amendment (No. 3) Regulations 1993 (S.I. 1993 No. 2113), reg. 3 (September 27, 1993).

9. The Social Security (Claims and Payments) Amendment Regulations 1994 (S.I. 1994 No. 2319), reg. 2 (October 3, 1994).

10. The Social Security (Claims and Payments) (Jobseeker's Allowance Consequential Amendments) Regulations 1996 (S.I. 1996 No. 1460), reg. 2(5) (October 7, 1996).

11. The Income Support and Social Security (Claims and Payments) (Miscellaneous Amendments) Regulations 1996 (S.I. 1996 No. 2431), reg. 7(c) (October 15, 1996).

12. The Social Security (Miscellaneous Amendments) (No. 2) Regulations 1997 (S.I. 1997 No. 793), reg. 3 (April 7, 1997).

(S.I. 1987 No. 1968, reg. 6) (as amended)

13. The Social Security (Miscellaneous Amendments) (No. 2) Regulations 1997 (S.I. 1997 No. 793), reg. 3(3) and (5) (October 6, 1997).

14. The Tax Credits (Claims and Payments) (Amendment) Regulations 1999 (S.I. 1999 No. 2572), reg. 5 (October 5, 1999)

15. The Social Security (Immigration and Asylum) Consequential Amendments Regulations 2000 (S.I. 2000 No. 636), reg. 5 (April 3, 2000)

DEFINITIONS   4.36
"appropriate office"—see reg. 2(1).
"claim for asylum"—*ibid*.
"claim for benefit"—*ibid*.
"jobseeker's allowance"—*ibid*.

GENERAL NOTE

Introduction
Claims are not made until received in any appropriate office.
R(SB)8/89 concerns the date of a claim for a single payment of supplementary benefit, but, since the date of claims for most non-means tested benefits is also the date of receipt in the office of the Department, the decision is directly in point in relation to these benefits. The Commissioner's comments are worth quoting at length since the determination of the date of claim is often an issue arising on appeals:

"In order for the claim to be made it is not alone necessary for the claimant to despatch the form but it is also necessary for the office of the Department to receive it. In my judgment if the office of the Department puts it out of its power to receive the claim by closing its offices and also arranging with the Post Office not to deliver mail on the days upon which the office is closed, then it put it out of its power to receive the claim. It may be that the claim can be received by the office of the Department whether such office is open or closed, but it cannot be received in circumstances where the Department arranges that mail should not be delivered. In her submission to me the adjudication officer now concerned refers to no deliveries being made by the Post Office on days upon which the office of the Department are [sic] closed. It will be a question of fact for the new tribunal to find whether such is by arrangement between the Department and Post Office and then to consider whether the Department has put it out of its power to receive claims on a Saturday. If they come to the conclusion that it did and find that in the normal course of delivery on that day then such is the date of claim." (para. 7).

Where claim packs are sent out for disability living allowance and attendance allowance, it is not the practice of the Benefits Agency (in contrast to the position where enquiries are made about other benefits) to follow the matter up if no completed claim is returned. The Claims and Payments Regulations clearly do not require such action, but it is understood that a number of welfare rights units are concerned that the variation in practice may operate to the disadvantage of claimants. It is, of course, the receipt of a completed claim (or at least some document which can be regarded as a claim under reg. 4) which constitutes a claim under the regulations.

Paragraph (1)
A properly completed claim on the proper form is made on the date that it is   4.37
received in a benefit office. See *CS/175/1988*, discussed in the notes to reg. 4(6). If a claim is treated as properly made under reg. 4(7), it is made on the date when the original attempt to claim was received.

The Social Security (Claims and Payments) Regulations 1987

There are now many complications around this basic rule in sub-paras (a) and (b), following the introduction of JSA and the severe restriction on the backdating of claims under reg. 19 from April 1997. These appear in sub-para. (aa) and the later provisions in reg. 6.

The main addition is under sub-para. (aa). In claims for family credit or disability working allowance or, up to October 5, 1997, income support or JSA, providing that the claimant is supplied with a claim form on notifying an office of the intention to claim, there is automatically a period of a month for the properly completed claim form to be returned. The claim is then treated as having been made on the earliest appropriate date back to the date of notificaton. For income support and JSA claims after October 5, 1997, see para. (1A) and (4A)–(4AB) respectively.

R(SB) 8/89 holds that if the DSS puts it out of its power to receive a claim, as by closing its office and arranging with the Post Office not to deliver mail, *e.g.* on a Saturday, then if that day is the day on which the claim would have been delivered, it is the date of claim. It can be said that by making the arrangement with the Post Office the DSS constitute the Post Office bailees of the mail (see *Hodgson v. Armstrong* [1967] Q.B. 299 and *Lang v. Devon General Limited* [1987] I.C.R. 4). The Commissioner does not deal expressly with the situation where the office is closed, but there is no arrangement about the mail, *e.g.* if an office is closed on a Saturday and the Saturday and Monday mail is all stamped with the Monday date in the office. Here, principle would suggest that if it can be shown that in the normal course of the post delivery would have been on the Saturday, then the Saturday is the date of receipt and the date of claim. If a claimant proves a delivery by hand when the office is closed, the date of delivery is the date of receipt.

See *CSIS 48/1992* in the notes to reg. 4(6) on the presumption of delivery for claims sent by post.

4.38 *Paragraph (1A)*

This provides that the date of claim for an income support claim will be the date a properly completed claim (*i.e.* one that complies with reg. 4(1A) (reg. 4(9)) is received (or the first day claimed for, if later). But if such a claim is received within one month of the date that the person first contacted the Benefits Agency with a view to making a claim, or a previous defective claim (*i.e.* one that does not comply with reg. 4(1A)), the date of claim will be the date of that initial contact or defective claim (or the first day claimed for, if later). Thus if more than a month elapses before the claimant complies with the requirements of reg. 4(1A), the date of claim will be the date of that compliance (unless the rules on backdating apply: see reg. 19(4) to (7)). See further the note to reg. 4(1A) to (1C).

4.39 *Paragraph (3)*

For these benefits, if the time for claiming is extended under reg. 19, the claim is treated as made at the beginning of the period for which the claim is deemed to be in time. Initial claims for family credit and disability working allowance and claims for income support and JSA have to be made on the first day of the period claimed for (Sched. 4, paras. 6, 7 and 11).

4.40 *Paragraph (4)*

The interaction of this provision with others is far from clear (at least to me). It does not look as though it can apply directly in a case where the Secretary of State has extended the time for claiming by up to a month under reg. 19(6). If the claim is not actually made (*i.e.* received: para. (1)) within the extended period, the claim is not timeously made and para. (3) above does not apply anyway. Postal delay is not a circumstance listed in reg. 19(5) (replacing the

(S.I. 1987 No. 1968, reg. 6) (as amended)

old good cause rule), but may be relevant to the reasonableness of the delay in claiming. See also reg. 19(7).

Paragraphs (4A) to (4AB) 4.41
In the case of JSA, if the person attends the JobCentre for the purpose of making a claim when required to do so and provides a properly completed claim (*i.e.* with all the necessary information: see reg. 4(1A) and (9)), the date of claim will be the date the person first contacted the JobCentre (or the first day claimed for, if later) (para. (4)(a)(i) and (4AA)). Note the *discretion* to extend the time for delivery of a properly completed claim form under para. (4AB); unlike income support (and JSA postal signers) the month's allowance to return the fully completed claim form is not automatic. Note also para. (4A)(a)(ii) which provides that if the person fails to comply with these requirements without good cause the date of claim will be the date that he does comply. Thus if the person does have good cause for not so complying, presumably para. (4A)(a)(i) will apply when he does attend and does provide a fully completed claim form (and note the discretion in relation to the claim form under para. (4AB)). For claimants who are not required to attend the JobCentre in person (*i.e.* who are allowed to apply by post), their claim will be treated as made on the day they first contacted the JobCentre with a view to making a claim (or on the first day claimed for, if later) if a properly completed claim is received within one month, or the date the properly completed claim is received if more than one month has elapsed (para. (4A)(b)). See further the note to reg. 4(1A) to (1C)).

Paragraphs (4B) and (4C) 4.42
These paragraphs deal with certain cases where entitlement to JSA has ceased because of a failure to attend the Job Centre or to provide a signed declaration of availability and active search for employment, so that a new claim is necessary.

Paragraph (4D) 4.43
These are special rules for claims by refugees.

Paragraphs (6) and (7) 4.44
These provisions create a special rule on the increase of the capital limit for income support to £8,000. Where, from April 9, 1990, a claimant has capital of more than £6,000 but not more than £8,000, a claim made before May 28, 1990, can be back-dated to the date on which all the conditions of entitlement are satisfied.

Paragraph (10) 4.45
Where a claimant starts work on a Monday or Tuesday and makes a claim for disability working allowance at any time in that week (*i.e.* Sunday to Saturday), the claim is treated as made on the Tuesday.

Paragraphs (12) to (15) 4.46
Where a claim for disability working allowance is disallowed on the ground that a qualifying benefit is not payable, although a claim for that benefit has been made, and later the qualifying benefit is awarded, a fresh claim for disability working allowance made within three months of the award of the qualifying benefit is to be treated as made on the date of the original claim (or the date from which the qualifying benefit is awarded, if later). This rule is made necessary by the restrictions from April 1997 on the backdating of claims under reg. 19 and on the effect of reviews.

Paragraphs (24) to (26) 4.47
These provisions apply a similar rule to that in paras (12) to (15) to claims for maternity or funeral payments under the social fund.

The Social Security (Claims and Payments) Regulations 1987

Paragraphs (27) and (28)

4.48 These paragraphs apply where a claim for income support or JSA is disallowed on the ground that the claimant or any partner is in remunerative work (para. (27)) or a claim for family credit or disability working allowance is disallowed on the ground that the claimant and any partner is *not* in remunerative work (para. (28)). Providing that a claim for the right benefit is made within 14 days of the disallowance, it is treated as made on the date of the original claim.

Claims by persons subject to work-focused interviews

4.49 [¹6A.—(1) This regulation applies to any person who is required to take part in a work-focused interview in accordance with regulation 4 of the Social Security (Work-focused Interviews) Regulations 2000 ("the Work-focused Interviews Regulations").

(2) Subject to the following provisions of this regulation, where a person takes part in a work-focused interview, the date on which the claim is made shall be—
  (a) in a case where—
    (i) the claim made by the claimant meets the requirements of regulation 4(1), or
    (ii) the claim made by the claimant is for income support and meets the requirements of regulation 4(1A),
  the date on which the calm is received in the appropriate office.
  (b) in a case where a claim does not meet the requirements of regulation 4(aO but is treated, under regulation 4(7), as having been duly made, the date on which the claim was treated as received in the appropriate office in the first instance;
  (c) in a case where—
    (i) first notification of intention to claim income support is made to an appropriate office, or
    (ii) a claim for income support is received in an appropriate office which does not meet the requirements of regulation 4(1A),
the date of notification of, as the case may be, the date the claim is first received where the properly complete claim form is received within 1 month of notification or the date the claim is first received, or the day on which a properly completed claim form is received where these requirements are not met.

(3) In a case where a decision is made that a person is regarded as not having made a claim for any benefit because he failed to take part in a work-focused interview but subsequently claims such a benefit, in applying paragraph (2) to that claim no regard shall be had to any claim regarded as not having been made in consequence of that decision.

(4) Paragraph (2) shall not apply in any case where a decision has been made that the claimant has failed to take part in a work-focused interview.

(5) In regulation 4 and this regulation, "work-focused interview" has the meaning it has in regulation 3 of the Work-focused Interviews Regulations and in this regulation "designated authority" has the meaning it has in regulation 2(1) of the Work-focused Interviews regulations.]

(S.I. 1987 No. 1968, reg. 6A) (as amended)

AMENDMENT
1. Regulation inserted by The Social Security (Work-focused Interviews) Regulations 2000 (S.I. 2000 No. 897) (April 3, 2000)

Evidence and information

7.—(1) [³Subject to paragraph (7),] every person who makes a claim for benefit shall furnish such certificates, documents, information and evidence in connection with the claim, or any question arising out of it, as may be required by the Secretary of State [⁴ or the Board] and shall do so within one month of being required to do so or such longer period as the Secretary of State [⁵Board] may consider reasonable.

(2) [³Subject to paragraph (7),] where a benefit may be claimed by either of two partners or where entitlement to or the amount of any benefit is or may be affected by the circumstances of a partner, the Secretary of State may require the partner other than the [⁵claimant to do either or both of the following, within one month of being required to do so or such longer period as the Board may consider reasonable—
  (a) to certify in writing whether he agrees to the claimant making or, as the case may be, that he confirms the information given about his circumstances;
  (b) to furnish such certificates, documents, information and evidence in connection with the claim, or any question arising out of it, as the Board may require.]
claimant to certify in writing whether he agrees to the claimant making the claim or, as the case may be, that he confirms the information given about his circumstances.

(3) In the case of a claim for the claimant or, as the case may be, of the partner shall [⁴ working families tax credit in disabled persons tax credit] furnish such certificates, documents, information and evidence in connection with the claim or any question arising out of it as may be required by the Secretary of State [⁵within one month of being required to do so or such longer period as the Board may consider reasonable].

[²(4) In the case of a person who is claiming [⁵Board], [³, income support or jobseeker's allowance], where that person or any partner is aged not less than 60 and is a member of, or a person deriving entitlement to a pension under, a personal pension scheme, or is a party to, or a person deriving entitlement to a pension under, a retirement annuity contract, he shall where [⁴ disabled persons tax credit, working families tax credit] the Secretary of State so requires furnish the following information—[⁵Board so require, within one month of being required to do so or such longer period as the Board may consider reasonable]
  (a) the name and address of the pension fund holder;
  (b) such other information including any reference or policy number as is needed to enable the personal pension scheme or retirement annuity contract to be identified.

(5) Where the pension fund holder receives from the Secretary of State [⁵Board] a request for details concerning the personal pension scheme or retirement annuity contract relating to a person or any partner to whom paragraph (4) refers, the pension fund holder shall [⁵,

within one month of the request or such longer period as the Board may consider reasonable] provide the Secretary of State [⁵Board] with any information to which paragraph (6) refers.

(6) The information to which this paragraph refers is—
(a) where the purchase of an annuity under a personal pension scheme has been deferred, the amount of any income which is being withdrawn from the personal pension scheme;
(b) in the case of—
  (i) a personal pension scheme where income withdrawal is available, the maximum amount of income which may be withdrawn from the scheme; or
  (ii) a personal pension scheme where income withdrawal is not available, or a retirement annuity contract, the maximum amount of income which might be withdrawn from the fund if the fund were held under a personal pension scheme where income withdrawal was available,

calculated by or on behalf of the pension fund holder by means of tables prepared from time to time by the Government Actuary which are appropriate for this purpose.]

[³(7) Paragraphs (1) and (2) do not apply in the case of jobseeker's allowance.]

[⁴(8) Every person providing childcare in respect of which a claimant to whom regulation 46A of the Family Credit (General) Regulations 1987 applies is incurring relevant childcare charges, including a person providing childcare on behalf of a school, local authority, childcare scheme or establishment within paragraph (2)(b), (c) or (d) of that regulation, shall furnish such certificates, documents, information and evidence in connection with the claim made by the claimant, or any question arising out of it, as may required by the Board, and shall do so within one month of being required to do so or such longer period as the Board may consider reasonable.

(9) In paragraph (8) "relevant childcare charges" has the meaning given vy regulation 46A(2) of the Family Credit (General) Regulations 1987.]

AMENDMENTS

1. The Social Security (Claims and Payments) Amendment Regulations 1991 (S.I. 1991 No. 2741), reg. 5 (March 10, 1992).
2. Income-related benefit Schemes and Social Security (Claims and Payments) (Miscellaneous Amendments) Regulations 1995 (S.I. 1995 No. 2303), reg. 10(3) (October 2, 1995).
3. The Social Security (Claims and Payments) (Jobseeker's Allowance Consequential Amendments) Regulations 1996 (S.I. 1996 No. 1460), reg. 2(6) (October 7, 1996).
4. The Tax Credits (Claims and Payments) (Amendment) Regulations 1999 (S.I. 1999 No. 2572), reg. 6 (October 5, 1999).
5. For tax credits purposes only: The Tax Credits (Claims and Payments) (Amendment) Regulations 1999 (S.I. 1999 No. 2572), reg. 6 (October 5, 1999)

DEFINITIONS

"benefit"—see reg. 2(2).
"claim for benefit"—see reg. 2(1).

(S.I. 1987 No. 1968, reg. 7) (as amended)

"jobseeker's allowance"—*ibid.*
"partner"—*ibid.*
"pension fund holder"—*ibid.*
"personal pension scheme"—*ibid.*
"retirement annuity contract"—*ibid.*

GENERAL NOTE

From time to time, adjudication officers suggest that a person is not entitled to benefit because they have failed to furnish the Secretary of State with information within the one month referred to in reg. 7(1). *R(IS)4/93* was just such a case. The adjudication officer decided that the claimant was not entitled to income support because the claimant had failed—*inter alia* to provide sufficient evidence as to the amount of capital held. The tribunal confirmed the adjudication officer's decision and the claimant appealed to the Commissioner.

Deputy Commissioner Mesher (as he then was) concluded that both the adjudication officer and the tribunal had misunderstood the operation of reg. 7(1). Drawing on the reasoning of the Court of Appeal in *R. v. Secretary of State for Social services, ex p Child Poverty Action Group* [1990] 2 Q.B. 540, the Deputy Commissioner explains that reg. 7(1) is concerned with the responsibilities of the Secretary of State to collect information so that the Secretary of State can submit a claim to an adjudication officer for determination:

"Once such a submission is made, it is simply irrelevant whether or not the claimant has satisfied the Secretary of State under reg. 7(1) of the Claims and Payments Regulations or whether or not the claimant has furnished sufficient information for the Secretary of State to refer the claim to the adjudication officer. Those matters are entirely for the Secretary of State [see para. 11 of *R(SB)29/83*]. Once the claim is submitted to him under section 98(1) [now s.20(1) of the Administration Act], the adjudication officer's duty is to take it into consideration and, so far as practicable, dispose of it within 14 days of its submission (Social Security Act 1975, s.99(1)) [now s.21(1) of the Administration Act]. As decided by the Court of Appeal in the passage quoted above, the adjudication officer has the power to make further investigations or call for further evidence before determining the claim. Or he may determine the claim on the evidence currently available, especially if he considers that the claimant has already had a reasonable opportunity of producing the required information or evidence." (para. 13).

The Deputy Commissioner goes on to advise that adjudication officers and tribunals when presented with a claim for determination (whether initially or on appeal) must focus on the "essential elements of entitlement directly" in the light of the evidence available. Since claimants generally have the burden of showing on the balance of probabilities that they meet the conditions of entitlement, the absence of information from the claimant will often result in a finding against them.

The Deputy Commissioner does not spell out how tribunals should proceed if the absence of information means that the tribunal cannot make any findings of fact. There will be cases where there is insufficient information to find positively some fact which results in there being no entitlement. In these rare cases where a claimant's reluctance to participate defeats the inquisitorial jurisdiction of tribunals, it is open to the tribunal to decide the matter purely on the burden of proof. In such cases the proper approach is for the tribunal:

— to record no findings of fact, or perhaps only those that are proved, *avoiding* the inclusion of reference to those issues on which facts cannot be found

— to record in the decision that the claimant is not entitled to the benefit on the claim made on such and such a day because they have not proved on the balance of probabilities that they meet the conditions of entitlement for the benefit

— to explain fully in the reasons for the decision what the relevant conditions of entitlement are and why the tribunal is unable to make findings of fact on all the material issues.

Attendance in person

4.52   8—(1)[¹. . .]
(2) Every person who makes a claim for benefit [¹(other than a jobseeker's allowance)] shall attend at such office or place and on such days and at such times as the Secretary of State[²or the Board] may direct, for the purpose of furnishing certificates, documents, information and evidence under regulation 7, if reasonably so required by the Secretary of State[²or the Board]

AMENDMENT

1. The Social Security (Claims and Payments) (Jobseeker's Allowance Consequential Amendments) Regulations 1996 (S.I. 1996 No. 1460), reg. 2(7) (October 7, 1996).
2. The Tax Credits (Claims and Payments) (Amendment) Regulations 1999 (S.I. 1999 No. 2572), reg. 20 (October 5, 1999)

DEFINITIONS

4.53   "benefit"—see reg. 2(2).
"claim for benefit"—see reg. 2(1).

GENERAL NOTE

There seems now to be no direct sanction for a failure to comply with reg. 8(2) in relation to benefits other than JSA. For JSA obligations, see reg. 23 of the Jobseeker's Allowance Regulations

Interchange with claims for other benefits

4.54   **9.**—(1) Where it appears that a person who has made a claim for benefit specified in column (1) of Part I of Schedule 1 may be entitled to the benefit specified opposite to it in column (2) of that Part, any such claim may be treated by the Secretary of State [¹or the Board] as a claim alternatively, or in addition, to the benefit specified opposite to it in that column.

(2) Where it appears that a person who has claimed any benefit specified in Part II of Schedule 1 in respect of a child may be entitled to child benefit in respect of the same child, the Secretary of State may treat the claim alternatively, or in addition, for the benefit in question as a claim by that person for child benefit.

(3) Where it appears that a person who has claimed child benefit in respect of a child may be entitled to any benefit specified in Part II of Schedule 1 [². . .] in respect of the same child, the Secretary of State may

(S.I. 1987 No. 1968, reg. 9) (as amended)

treat the claim for child benefit as a claim alternatively, or in addition, by that person for the benefit in question specified in that Part.

(4) Where it appears that a person who has made a claim for benefit other than child benefit is not entitled to it, but that some other person may be entitled to an increase of benefit in respect of him, the Secretary of State may treat the claim as if it were a claim by such other person for an increase of benefit in respect of the claimant.

(5) Where it appears that a person who has made a claim for an increase of benefit other than child benefit in respect of a child or adult dependant is not entitled to it but that some other person may be entitled to such an increase of benefit in respect of that child or adult dependant, the Secretary of State may treat the claim as if it were a claim by that other person for such an increase.

(6) Where it appears that a person who has made a claim for a guardian's allowance in respect of any child is not entitled to it, but that the claimant or the wife or husband of the claimant, may be entitled to an increase of benefit for that child, the Secretary of State may treat the claim as if it were a claim by the claimant or the wife or husband of the claimant for an increase of benefit for that child.

[³ (7) In determining whether he [¹or they] should treat a claim alternatively or in addition to another claim (the original claim) under this regulation the Secretary of State shall treat the alternative or additional claim, whenever made, as having been made at the same time as the original claim.]

AMENDMENTS

1. The Tax Credits (Claims and Payments) (Amendment) Regulations 1999 (S.I. 1999 No. 2572), regs. 20 and 22, (October 5, 1999)
2. The Child Benefit, Child Support and Social Security (Miscellaneous Amendments) Regulations 1996 (S.I. 1996 No. 1803), reg. 19 (April 7, 1997)
3. The Social Security (Miscellaneous Provisions) Amendment Regulatins 1992 (S.I. 1992 No. 247), reg. 12 (March 9, 1992).

GENERAL NOTE

This invaluable provision removes some of the rigour of ensuring that a claimant chooses the right benefit to claim and is not prejudiced by making a mistaken choice. The regulation now also covers interchange of claims for child benefit with claims for other benefits. There was originally some doubt over whether a decision to treat a claim as one in the alternative was for the adjudicating authorities or the Secretary of State. Note that, with the introduction of incapacity benefit, the arrangement whereby claims for unemployment benefit may be treated as claims for one of the sickness benefits has been ended.

In *R. v. Secretary of State for Social Security, ex parte Cullen* and *Secretary of State for Social Security v. Nelson* (*The Times*, May 16, 1997), the Court of Appeal confirmed the decision of Harrison J. in *Cullen* (November 16, 1996) and reversed the decision of the Commissioner in *Nelson* (*CA 171/1993*). In both cases, unsuccessful claims for supplementary benefit had been made prior to April 11, 1988. At that time, the 1979 Claims and Payments regulations allowed the Secretary of State to treat a claim for supplementary benefit as in the alternative a claim for attendance allowance. The 1987 Claims and Payments Regulations, which came into effect on April 11, 1988, contained no such

4.55

power. In 1991 (Cullen) and 1993 (Nelson) claims for attendance allowance were made and it was sought to have the supplementary benefit claims treated as claims for attendance allowance. The Court of Appeal held that the Secretary of State had no power to do so, so that the Commissioner in *CA 171/1993* was wrong to refer the question to the Secretary of State for determination. Once the 1979 Regulations were revoked, the Secretary of State could no longer exercise a power which no longer existed. As the Secretary of State had only had a discretion under the 1979 Regulations whether or not to treat a supplementary benefit claim as in the alternative a claim for attendance allowance, the claimants had no accrued rights which were preserved on the revocation of the 1979 Regulations under s.16 of the Interpretation Act 1978.

[¹Claim for incapacity benefit or severe disablement allowance where no entitlement to statutory sick pay or statutory maternity pay]

4.56   10—(1) Paragraph (2) applies to a claim for incapacity benefit or severe] disablement allowance for a period of incapacity for work of which the claimant gave his employer a notice of incapacity under regulation 7 of the Statutory Sick Pay (General) Regulations 1982, and for which he has been informed in writing by his employer that there is no entitlement to statutory sick pay.

(2) A claim to which this paragraph applies shall be treated as made on the date accepted by the claimant's employer as the first day of incapacity, provided that he makes the claim—
 (a) within the appropriate time specified in paragraph 2 of Schedule 4 beginning with the day on which he is informed in writing that he was not entitled to statutory sick pay; or
 (b) [² . . .]

(3) Paragraph (4) applies to a claim for maternity allowance for a pregnancy or confinement by reason of which the claimant gave her employer notice of absence from work under [section 164(4) of the Social Security Contributions and Benefits Act 1992] and regulation 23 of the Statutory Maternity Pay (General) Regulations 1986 and in respect of which she has been informed in writing by her employer that there is no entitlement to statutory maternity pay.

(4) A claim to which this paragraph applies shall be treated as made on the date when the claimant gave her employer notice of absence from work or at the beginning of the 14th week before the expected week of confinement, whichever is later, provided that she makes the claim—
 (a) within three months of being informed in writing that she was not entitled to statutory maternity pay; or
 (b) [² . . .]

AMENDMENTS

1. The Social Security (Claims and Payments) Amendment (No. 2) Regulations 1994 (S.I. 1994 No. 2943), reg. 3 (April 13, 1995)

2. The Social Security (Miscellaneous Amendments) (No. 2) Regulations 1997 (S.I. 1997 No. 793), reg. 4 (April 7, 1997)

(S.I. 1987 No. 1968, reg. 11) (as amended)

Special provisions where it is certified that a woman is expected to be confined or where she has been confined

11.—(1) Where in a certificate issued or having effect as issued under the Social Security (Medical Evidence) Regulations 1976 it has been certified that it is to be expected that a woman will be confined, and she makes a claim for maternity allowance in expectation of that confinement any such claim may, unless the Secretary of State otherwise directs, be treated as a claim for [¹ incapacity city benefit] or severe disablement allowance made in respect of any days in the period beginning with either—
   (a) the beginning of the 6th week before the expected week of confinement; or
   (b) the actual date of confinement, whichever is the earlier, and ending in either case on the 14th day after the actual date of confinement.

(2) Where, in a certificate issued under the Social Security (Medical Evidence) Regulations 1976 it has been certified that a woman has been confined and she claims maternity allowance within [² three months] of that date, her claim may be treated in the alternative or in addition as a claim for incapacity benefit or severe disablement allowance for the period beginning with the date of her confinement and ending 14 days after that date.

AMENDMENTS

1. The Social Security (Claims and Payments) Amendment (No. 2) Regulations 1994 (S.I. 1994 No. 2943), reg. 4 (April 13, 1995).
2. The Social Security (Miscellaneous Amendments) (No. 2) Regulations 1997 (S.I. 1997 No. 793), reg. 5 (April 7, 1997).

GENERAL NOTE

In *R(S)1/74* the Commissioner held that a similarly worded predecessor to this regulation which made similar, though not identical, provision neither confers title to sickness benefit nor restricts the right to it. The regulation does no more than define the period for which, having made an unsuccessful claim to maternity allowance, a woman may be treated as having made a claim to incapacity benefit. There is nothing to prevent her seeking to prove incapacity for some period or periods additional to that to which her claim is taken to relate.

Regulation 12 revoked by The Social Security (Claims and Payments on account, Overpayments and Recovery) Amendment Regulations 1989 (S.I. 1989 No. 136) (February 27, 1989)

Advance claims and awards

13.—(1) Where, although a person does not satisfy the requirements for entitlement to a benefit on the date on which the claim is made, the [⁶ Secretary of State] is of the opinion that unless there is a change of circumstances he will satisfy those requirements for a period beginning on a day ("the relevant day") not more than 3 months after the date on which the claim is made, then [⁶ Secretary of State] may—

The Social Security (Claims and Payments) Regulations 1987

(a) treat the claim as if made for a period beginning with the relevant day; and

(b) award benefit accordingly, subject to the condition that the person satisfies the requirements for entitlement when benefit becomes payable under the award.

(2) [6 A decision pursuant to paragraph (1)(b) to award benefit may be revised under section 9 of the Social Security Act 1998] if the requirements for entitlement are found not to have been satisfied on the relevant day.

(3) [5 Subject to paragraph (4), paragraphs (1) and (2) do not apply] to any claim for maternity allowance [2 attendance allowance [2 disability living allowance], retirement pension or increase, [7 working families' tax credit, disabled person's tax credit], or any claim within regulation 11(1)(a) or (b).

[1(4) Paragraphs (1) and (2) of this regulation shall apply to a claim for [7 working families' tax credit] made—

(a) on or after 10th March 1992 and before 7th April 1992;

(b) in respect of a period beginning on or after 7th April 1992; and

(c) by a person who, if he is a member of a married or unmarried couple, he or the other member of the couple, is engaged and normally engaged in remunerative work for not less than 16 but less than 24 hours a week on the date the claim is made.

(5) In paragraph (4)(c) "remunerative work" and "engaged and normally engaged in remunerative work" shall be construed in accordance with regulations 4 and 5 respectively of the Family Credit (General) Regulations 1987 [3save that in their application to paragraph 4(c) those regulations shall be read as though for the words "not less than 24 hours" there were substituted the words "not less than 16 hours but less than 24 hours"].]

[5(6) Where a person claims [7 working families' tax credit or disabled person's tax credit] but does not satisfy the requirements for entitlement to that benefit on the date on which the claim is made, and the adjudicating authority is of the opinion that he will satisfy those requirements for a period beginning on a day not more than 3 days after the date on which the claim is made, the adjudicating authority may treat the claim as if made for a period beginning with that day, and award benefit accordingly.]

[7 Where on or after 7th September 1999 but before 5th October 1999 a person claims family credit or disability working allowance but does not satisfy the requirements for entitlement to that benefit on the date on which the claim is made, and the adjudicating authority is of the opinion that he will satisfy the requirements for working families' tax credit or disabled person's tax credit for a period beginning on 5th October 1999, the claim shall be treated by the adjudicating authority as a claim made on 5th October for a period starting on that date.

(8) Where on or after 20th September 1999 but before 2nd October 1999 a person claims working families' tax credit or disabled person's tax credit, the claim shall be treated by the adjudicating authority as a claim made on 5th October 1999 for a period starting on that date or on such later date as is specified in the claim.]

(S.I. 1987 No. 1968, reg. 13) (as amended)

AMENDMENTS

1. The Social Security (Miscellaneous Provisions) Amendment Regulations 1991 (S.I. 1991 No. 2284), reg. 7 (November 1, 1991).
2. The Social Security (Claims and Payments) Amendment Regulations 1991 (S.I. 1991 No. 2741), S.I. 1991 No. 2741, reg. 6(a) (February 3, 1992).
3. The Social Security (Miscellaneous Provisions) Amendment Regulations 1992 (S.I. 1992 No. 247), reg. 13 (March 9, 1992).
4. The Social Security (Claims and Payments) Amendment Regulations 1991 (S.I. 1991 No. 2741), reg. 6(b) (March 10, 1992).
5. The Social Security (Claims and Payments) Amendment Regulations 1994 (S.I. 1994 No. 2319), reg. 3 (October 3, 1994).
6. The Social Security Act 1998 (Commencement No. 9, and Savings and Consequential and Transitional Provisions) Order 1999 (S.I. 1999 No 2422), Sched 7 (September 6 1999).
7. The Tax Credits (Claims and Payments) (Amendment) Regulations 1999 (S.I. 1999 No. 2572), reg. 7 (October 5, 1999)

DEFINITIONS

"adjudicating authority"—see reg. 2(1). 4.61
"benefit"—see reg. 2(2).
"married couple"—see reg. 2(1).
"unmarried couple"—*ibid.*

GENERAL NOTE

Paras. (1) and (2) contain a useful power in income support and social fund maternity and funeral expenses cases, to make awards in advance, subject to review if circumstances change. Para. (1) gives a wide discretion (*CIS/459/1994*).

The general rule in para. (3) is that the power in paras. (1) and (2) does not apply to family credit, but para. (4) allowed advance claims immediately in advance of the change in the number of qualifying hours from 24 to 16 in April 1992. See also para. (6).

The power in paras. (1) and (2) does not apply to disability working allowance (para. (3)), but see reg. 13B for claims in advance of the start of the scheme, and para. (6).

From October 1994, para. (6) allows family credit and disability working allowance claims to be made up to three days in advance.

Advance award of disability living allowance

[¹ **13A.**—(1) Where, although a person does not satisfy the requirement for entitlement to disability living allowance on the date on which the claim is made, the [² Secretary of State] is of the opinion that unless there is a change of circumstances he will satisfy those requirements for a period beginning on a day ("the relevant day" not more than 3 months after the date on which the claim is made, then [² the Secretary of State] may award disability living allowance from the relevant day subject to the condition that the person satisfies the requirements for entitlement on the relevant day. 4.62

(2) Where a person makes a claim for disability living allowance on or after 3rd February 1992 and before 6th April 1992 the adjudicating authority may award benefit for a period beginning on or after 5th April

1992 being a day not more than three months after the date on which the claim was made, subject to the condition that the person satisfies the requirements for entitlement when disability living allowance becomes payable under the award.

(3) [² A decision pursuant to paragraph (1) or (2) to award benefit may be revised under section 9 of the Social Security Act 1998] if the requirements for entitlement are found not to have been satisfied when disability living allowance becomes payable under the award.]

AMENDMENTS

1. The Social Security (Claims and Payments) Amendment Regulations 1991 (S.I. 1991 No. 2741), reg. 7 (February 3, 1992).
2. The Social Security Act 1998 (Commencement No. 11 and Transitional Provisions) Order 1999 (S.I. 1999 No. 2860), Sched 3 (October 18, 1999)

[¹ **Advance claim for and award of disability working allowance**

13B.—(1) Where a person makes a claim for disability working allowance on or after 10th March 1992 and before 7th April 1992 the adjudicating authority may—
   (a) treat the claim as if it were made for a period beginning on 7th April 1992; and
   (b) An award benefit accordingly, subject to the condition that the person satisfies the requirements for entitlement on 7th April 1992.

(2) An award under paragraph (1)(b) shall be reviewed by the adjudicating authority if the requirements for entitlement are found not to have been satisfied on 7th April 1992.]

AMENDMENT

The Social Security (Claims and Payments) Amendment Regulations 1991 (S.I. 1991 No. 2741), reg. 7(2) (March 10, 1992).

DEFINITION

"adjudicating authority"—see reg. 2(1).

GENERAL NOTE

This allowed an advance claim in the few weeks immediately before the start of the scheme on April 7, 1992.

[¹**Further claim for and award of disability living allowance**

13C.—(1) A person entitled to an award of disability living allowance may make a further claim for disability living allowance during the period of six months immediately before the existing award expires.

(2) Where a person makes a claim in accordance with paragraph (1) the [² Secretary of State] may—
   (a) treat the claim as if made on the first day after the expiry of the existing award ("the renewal date"); and
   (b) award benefit accordingly, subject to the condition that the

(S.I. 1987 No. 1968, reg. 13C) (as amended)

person satisfies the requirements for entitlement on the renewal date.

(3) [³ A decision pursuant to paragraph (2)(b) to award benefit may be revised under section 9 of the Social Security Act 1998] if the requirements for entitlement are found not to have been satisfied on the renewal date.]

AMENDMENTS

1. This whole regulation was inserted by The Social Security (Claims and Payments) Amendment Regulations 1991 (S.I. 1991 No 2741), reg. 8 (March 10, 1992).
2. The Social Security Act 1998 (Commencement No. 11 and Transitional Provisions) Order 1999 (S.I. 1999 No 2860), Sched. 3 (October 18, 1999)
3. The Social Security Act 1998 (Commencement No. 12 and Consequential and Transitional Provisions) Order 1999 (S.I. 1999 No. 3178), Sched. 6 (November 29, 1999)

GENERAL NOTE

This permits a continuation claim for disability living allowance to be made during the last six months of an existing award.

In *CDLA/14895/96*, it was held that reg. 13C(2) should not be applied until it has been considered whether, if the claim were treated as an application for review under s.30(13) of the Social Security Administration Act 1992, there would be grounds for review. If there are grounds for review, the existing award should be reviewed. Otherwise, the claim should be treated as a renewal claim, effective only from the end of the existing award.

4.65

Advance claim for and award of maternity allowance

14.—(1) Subject to the following provisions of this regulation, a claim for maternity allowance in expectation of confinement, or for an increase in such an allowance in respect of an adult dependent, and an award on such a claim, may be made not earlier than 14 weeks before the beginning of the expected week of confinement.

(2) A claim for an increase of maternity allowance in respect of an adult dependant may not be made in advance unless, on the date when made, the circumstances relating to the adult dependant concerned are such as would qualify the claimant for such an increase if they occurred in a period for which she was entitled to a maternity allowance.

4.66

Advance notice of retirement and claim for and award of pension

15.—(1) A claim for a retirement pension of any category, and for any increase in any such pension, and an award on such a claim, may be made at any time not more than 4 months before the date on which the claimant will, subject to the fulfilment of the necessary conditions, become entitled to such a pension.

(2) [¹. . .]
(3) [¹. . .]
(4) [¹. . .]
[² (5) Where a person claims a Category A or Category B retirement

4.67

377

pension and is, or but for that claim would be, in receipt of [³ incapacity benefit] [⁴. . .] for a period which includes the first day to which the claim relates, then if that day is not the appropriate day for the payment of retirement pension in his case, the claim shall be treated as if the first day of the claim was instead the next following such pay day.

(6) Where the spouse of such a person as is mentioned in paragraph (5) above claims a Category A or Category B retirement pension and the first day of that claim is the same as the first day of the claim made by that person, the provisions of that paragraph shall apply also to the claim made by the spouse.]

(7) For the purposes of facilitating the determination of a subsequent claim for a Category A, B or C retirement pension, a person may at any time not more than 4 months before the date on which he will attain pensionable age, and notwithstanding that he [⁵ intends to defer his entitlement to a Category A or Category B retirement pension] at that date, submit particulars in writing to the Secretary of State in a form approved by him for that purpose with a view to the determination (in advance of the claim) of any question under the Act relating to that person's title to such a retirement pension [⁵. . .] and subject to the necessary modifications, the provisions of these regulations shall apply to any such particulars.

AMENDMENTS

1. Social Security Act 1986 (October 1, 1989)
2. The Social Security (Abolition of Earnings Rule) (Consequential) Regulations 1989 (S.I. 1989 No. 1642), reg. 2(2) (October 1, 1989)
3. The Social Security (Claims and Payments) Amendment (No. 2) Regulations 1994 (S.I. 1994 No. 2943), reg. 5 (April 13, 1995)
4. The Social Security (Claims and Payments) (Jobseeker's Allowance Consequential Amendments) Regulations 1996 (S.I. 1996 No. 1460), reg. 2 (October 7, 1996)
5. The Social Security (Abolition of Earnings Rule) (Consequential) Regulations 1989 (S.I. 1989 No. 1642), reg. 2(3) (October 1, 1989)

GENERAL NOTE

4.68   In *CP/1074/1997* a Commissioner had to consider the proper approach to be taken to the determination of a date of birth in relation to a claim for retirement pension. The claimant had been born in the Punjab, and his year of birth had been consistently stated on a number of documents as 1931, but there was no clear evidence of the day he was born in that year. On September 13, 1995 he made a claim for retirement pension, but the adjudication officer treated his date of birth as December 31, 1931 and concluded that the claim made on September 13, 1995 could not be accepted. This would have required the claimant to have been born no later than January 13, 1931 in order to be within the four months provided for in reg. 15(1). The claimant adduced evidence that he had been born on December 18, 1930, but his was not accepted by the tribunal. In dealing with the appeal the Commissioner addresses a number of arguments put forward on behalf of the claimant. The Commissioner accepted that the claimant did not need to prove a particular date of birth, merely that he had reached retirement age by a particular date. He did not, however, accept a second argument which was based on the application of a mathematical approach to the evidential test of the balance of probabilities. The claimant argued that as each day passed in the year in which it was accepted that a person was born, it became more probable that the person had been born by that day in the year. By the beginning of July it could therefore be said that it was more probable than not that the claimant had been born by that date. In such circumstances, the practice of the adjudication officer in using the last day of the year as the date of birth was an error of law. The Commissioner rejects this argument, citing *Re JS (a minor)* [1980] 1 All E.R. 1061, for the proposition that the concept of evidential probability is not the same as the mathematical concept. The Commissioner approves the proposition in that case that the civil burden of proof requires the party on whom the burden falls to "satisfy the court that it is reasonably safe in all the circumstances of the case to act on the evidence before the court, bearing in mind the consequences which will follow". The Commissioner finally notes that this may not, in every case where a date of birth in the year is not known, result in the choice of the last day in the year. Regard must be had to all the evidence available at the time the decision is made in determining which date in the year is to be selected as the date by which the person was born.

Cold weather payments

15A. [^{1}...] 4.69

AMENDMENT

1. Social Security (Miscellaneous Provisions) Amendment Regulations 1991 (S.I. 1991 No. 2284), reg. 8 (November 1, 1991).

GENERAL NOTE

Claims for cold weather payments are no longer necessary or possible. 4.70

Date of entitlement under an award for the purpose of payability of benefit and effective date of change of rate

16.—(1) For the purpose only of determining the day from which benefit is to become payable, where a benefit other than one of those specified in paragraph (4) is awarded for a period of a week, or weeks, and the earliest date on which entitlement would otherwise commence is not the first day of a benefit week entitlement shall begin on the first day of the benefit week next following. 4.71

[^{1}(1A) Where a claim for [^{6} working families' tax credit] is made in accordance with paragraph 7(a) [^{2} or (aa)] of Schedule 4 for a period following the expiration of an existing award of family credit [^{6} or disabled person's tax credit], entitlement shall begin on the day after the expiration of that award.

(1B) Where a claim for [^{6} working families' tax credit or disabled person's tax credit] is made on or after the date when an up-rating order is made under [^{6} section 150 of the Social Security Administration Act 1992], but before the date when that order comes into force, and—
  (a) an award cannot be made on that claim as at the date it is made but could have been made if that order were then in force, and
  (b) the period beginning with the date of claim and ending immedi-

The Social Security (Claims and Payments) Regulations 1987

ately before the date when the order came into force does not exceed 28 days,
entitlement shall begin from the date the up-rating order comes into force.]

[²(1C) Where a claim for [⁶ disabled person's tax credit] is made in accordance with paragraph 11(a) or (b) of Schedule 4 for a period following the expiration of an existing award of [⁶ disabled person's tax credit or working families' tax credit], entitlement shall begin on the day after the expiration of that award.]

(2) Where there is a change in the rate of any benefit to which paragraph (1) applies the change, if it would otherwise take effect on a day which is not the appropriate pay day for that benefit, shall take effect from the appropriate pay day next following.

[¹(3) For the purposes of this regulation the first day of the benefit week—

(a) in the case of child benefit [⁵ and guardian's allowance] is Monday,

(b) in the case of [⁶ disabled person's tax credit or working families' tax credit] is Tuesday, and

(c) in any other case is the day of the week on which the benefit is payable in accordance with regulation 22 (long-term benefits).]

(4) The benefits specified for exclusion from the scope of paragraph (1) are [⁴jobseeker's allowance], [³incapacity benefit], maternity allowance, [¹. . .], severe disablement allowance, income support [¹. . .] and any increase of those benefits.

Amendments

1. The Social Security (Claims and Payments) Amendment Regulations 1988 (S.I. 1988 No. 522), reg. 3 (April 11, 1988).

2. The Social Security (Claims and Payments) Amendment Regulations 1991 (S.I. 1991 No. 2741), reg. 9 (March 10, 1992).

3. The Social Security (Claims and Payments) Amendment (No. 2) Regulations 1994 (S.I. 1994 No. 2943), reg. 6 (April 13, 1995).

4. The Social Security (Claims and Payments) (Jobseeker's Allowance Consequential Amendments) Regulations 1996 (S.I. 1996 No. 1460), reg. 2(9) (October 7, 1996).

5. The Social Security (Claims and Payments) Amendment Regulations 1999 (S.I. 1999, No. 2358), reg. 2 (September 20, 1999)

Definitions

"benefit"—see reg. 2(2).
"jobseeker's allowance"—see reg. 2(1).
"week"—*ibid.*

General Note

This regulation restates in part the rules formerly contained in reg. 16(10) of the Claims and Payments Regulations 1979. In *R(P)2/73* it was held that the effect of a similarly worded predecessor to reg. 16(10) was not just to make benefit payable from the next pay day but to make it begin on that day. The Commissioner made clear, though, that the regulation was concerned with "payability not title". The new wording does not appear wholly to resolve the

(S.I. 1987 No. 1968, reg. 16) (as amended)

difficulty, since para. (1) is prefaced by the intention only to concern itself with payability, though later the word "entitlement" is used. Presumably that means "entitlement to payment of benefit" and not title to the benefit itself. There are occasions where title to the benefit arising on an earlier date than the first date of payment has significant consequences.

Duration of awards

17.—(1) Subject to the provisions of this regulation and of section [¹37ZA(3) of the Social Security Act 1975 (disability living allowance) and section] 20(6) [²and (6F)] of the Social Security Act 1986 [⁴ working families' tax credit and disabled person's tax credit] [SSCBA, ss.71(3), 128(3) and 129(6)] a claim for benefit shall be treated as made for an indefinite period and any award of benefit on that claim shall be made for an indefinite period.

[³(1A) Where an award of income support or an income-based jobseeker's allowance is made in respect of a married or unmarried couple and one member of the couple is, at the date of claim, a person to whom section 126 of the Contributions and Benefits Act or, as the case may be, section 14 of the Jobseekers Act applies, the award of benefit shall cease when the person to whom section 126 or, as the case may be, section 14 applies returns to work with the same employer.]

(2) [³. . .]

(3) If [³. . .] it would be inappropriate to treat a claim as made and to make an award for an indefinite period (for example where a relevant change of circumstances is reasonably to be expected in the near future) the claim shall be treated as made and the award shall be for a definite period which is appropriate in the circumstances.

(4) In any case where benefit is awarded in respect of days subsequent to the date of claim the award shall be subject to the condition that the claimant satisfies the requirements for entitlement [⁵. . .].

(5) The provisions of Schedule 2 shall have effect in relation to claims for [³jobseeker's allowance] made during periods connected with public holidays.

4.73

AMENDMENTS

1. The Social Security (Claims and Payments) Amendment Regulations 1991 (S.I. 1991 No. 2741), reg. 10 (February 3, 1992).
2. The Social Security (Claims and Payments) Amendment Regulations 1991 (S.I. 1991 No. 2741), reg. 10 (March 10, 1992).
3. The Social Security (Claims and Payments) (Jobseeker's Allowance Consequential Amendments) Regulations 1996 (S.I. 1996 No. 1460), reg. 2(10) (October 7, 1996).
4. The Tax Credits (Claims and Payments) (Amendment) Regulations 1999 (S.I. 1999 No. 2572), reg. 24 & 25 (October 5, 1999).
5. The Social Security Act 1998 (Commencement No. 12 and Consequential and Transitional Provisions) Order 1999 (S.I. 1999 No. 3178), Sched 6, (November 29, 1999)

DEFINITIONS

4.74

"benefit"—see reg. 2(2).
"claim for benefit"—see reg. 2(1).

"jobseeker's allowance"—*ibid*.
"the Jobseekers Act"—*ibid*.

GENERAL NOTE

Introduction

4.75   In general awards are to be made for an indefinite period (para. (1)) subject to review where the claimant ceases to meet the conditions of entitlement (para. (4)). Para. (3) deals with short-term situations and allows the award for a definite period.

The effect of reg. 17(1) is that awards of most benefits are now made for an indefinite period. Entitlement only ceases where there has been a review under reg. 17(4) which establishes that the conditions of entitlement are no longer met. There was a tendency for adjudication officers to argue that a claimant must prove continuing entitlement in such cases. The effect of the regulation is, however, that the adjudication officer (now decision maker) must show that there is some ground to review entitlement and that it is right to end the entitlement to the benefit. So the onus will be on the claimant to show the conditions of entitlement on a new award, but once an award has been made, it will generally be for an indefinite period and on review it will be for the decision maker to demonstrate that the claimant has ceased to qualify for the benefit. This interpretation is confirmed by the Commissioner in *R(S)3/90*.

In *CIS/620/1990*, the Commissioner stressed that the requirements of reg. 17 are not a mere technicality. An indefinite award of benefit can only be terminated on review if it is shown that the conditions of entitlement cases to be met. In any other circumstances the original award continues and any subsequent award cannot overlap with it. There is no jurisdiction to make such an award since the matter is *res judicata*: see paras 8 and 11 of the decision.

The implications of the interpretation of reg. 17(4) accepted in *R(S)3/90* are further considered in *R(S)1/92* where the commissioner notes that *R(S)4/86* is concerned with a different provision of the social security legislation (what was then s.104 of the Social Security Act 1975). The requirement of reg. 17(4) is for a review terminating entitlement to the benefit. The Commissioner also considers whether the power to make an award for a definite period in reg. 17(3) is in any way circumscribed. He notes that the regulation requires it to be "inappropriate" to make an open ended award, and confirms that the regulation is wide enough to contemplate a situation in which "the yardstick by which the claimant's capacity for work should be judged" is the basis for a fixed term award. It is not limited to situations in which there is a realistic prospect that the claimant's condition will alter for the better in the foreseeable future.

The cumulative effect of these decisions is that it will be important to determine whether the original award was for a definite or an indefinite period and why. Experience in tribunals is that answers to these questions have not always been available from the papers or a presenting adjudication officer.

In *CIS/254/1989* the Commissioner confirms that tribunals should determine whether an award is for an indefinite period or for a fixed period, and should make specific findings as to the days subsequent to the date of claim in respect of which there has been an award. He goes on to remind tribunals that, where the award is an indefinite one, the onus of proving that the requirements for entitlement are not satisfied, and the date form which this is so, rests on the adjudication officer and not on the claimant. The point is repeated in *CIS/620/1990*.

In *CS/062/1992* it was argued that reg. 17(4) was *ultra vires*, but the Commissioner found no basis for this argument. He goes on to note that adjudication officers are at liberty to look at awards of invalidity benefit (and presumably

(S.I. 1987 No. 1968, reg. 17) (as amended)

now any benefit awarded for an open-ended period) if they *believe* that claimants are no longer entitled but that they have authority to *revise* the decision only if they can *prove* that claimant do not meet the conditions of entitlement (para. (9). While it might be preferable to have the terms of the original award before them, tribunals are entitled, unless the facts obviously suggest otherwise, to proceed on the basis that an initial award is based on the conclusion that the claimant is unfit for *usual work* and that there will in due course be a review to determine whether the claimant is unfit for *all work*.

Application to income support

In income support cases, the question of the scope and effect of reg. 17(4) has arisen where an adjudication officer has decided that a claimant is no longer entitled to income support on the ground of incapacity for work. The Commissioners in *R(IS)2/98* set out how a tribunal should approach disputed review decisions in such cases. An adjudication officer's decision should not be held invalid solely on the basis that the only reference is to para (4), without considering whether grounds for review have in fact arisen. If a review had not been properly carried out, the tribunal should decide whether they have sufficient information to carry out the review themselves. They should also, as far as possible, conduct any later review that may be needed down to the date of their decision. But note that, under the Social Security Act 1998, that is no longer possible for appeals made on or after May 21, 1998 when the tribunal is limited to considering matters as at the date of the award. 4.76

The Tribunal in *R(IS)2/98* also confirmed that a decision that a person was not incapable of work did not itself trigger the operation of para. (4) because incapacity was not at that time a condition of entitlement to income support (see *CSIS/99/1994* and *CIS/783/1994*). However, if entitlement to the disability premium was involved, para. (4) required a review as soon as the conditions for this ceased to be met.

The effect of *R(IS)2/98* is thus that an adjudication officer will have to establish grounds for review. A different medical opinion is not a change of circumstances, although it may be evidence of an underlying change if there is other evidence of this, for example, if the person has resumed work or has recovered (*R(S)6/78* and *R(S)4/86*). This is confirmed in *R(IS)2/98*. The Commissioners approved the approach in *CIS/856/1994* that, although not a relevant change in itself, an up-to-date medical report may nevertheless disclose new facts that would constitute a change of circumstances. Another relevant change could be if the time has come to apply a different test to ascertain the claimant's capacity for work (see *CIS/251/1993*). However, grounds for review will not be shown on a second or subsequent application of the all work test by the adjudication officer simply scoring the claimant at less than 15 points: *CIS/3899/1997*. The Commissioner states that a comparison with the evidence which led to the previous decision was necessary and therefore adjudication officers and tribunals would need to have available and to take into consideration the evidence relating to the previous application of the all work test to see whether grounds for review had been made out. The Commissioner in *CIS/3899/1997* also confirms that where there had been an adjudication officer's decision that the claimant satisfies the all work test, a subsequent decision that the claimant was not incapable of work could only take effect if there had been a review of the earlier decision.

The scope of the review in paragraph (4)

The scope of reg 17(4) has been considered by a Tribunal of Commissioners in *CSIS/137/1994* heard together with *CSIS/134/1994* and *CSS/035/1995* and detailed guidance is given in the common appendix on the application of the provision both to income-related and to non-means tested benefits. *R(S)5/89* which had held that reg. 17(4) contained an independent basis of review from 4.77

The Social Security (Claims and Payments) Regulations 1987

that contained in the Administration Act is considered to have been wrong decided and should no longer be followed. The guidance in the appendix to the new decision is as follows.

Regulation 17(4) imposes a requirement for review whenever, during the currency of an award, it becomes apparent that the requirements for entitlement are not or are no longer satisfied (para. 17).

Regulation 17(4) contains no independent basis for review separate from that in sections 25, 30 and 31 of the Administration Act but makes review under the normal powers mandatory once it appears that the requirements for entitlement are not or are no longer met (para. 18).

Without a review, the payment of benefit must continue. Actual payment of benefit does not cease automatically when the conditions of entitlement cease to be satisfied (para. 20 and 21).

While it is well established law that a different medical *opinion* does not constitute a "relevant change of circumstances" for the purposes of a review, a later medical examination and report can be good evidence of an *actual* change of circumstances warranting a review and revision of an award (para. 29).

It will be preferable for adjudication officers to refer to the underlying basis of any review rather than simply to a review under regulation 17(4) but provided that the underlying basis for the review is present, a reference to a review under regulation 17(4) without reference to the underlying basis will not render the decision to review and revise invalid (paras 31 and 32).

Regulation 17(4) contains no special rule allowing retrospective reviews. The determination of the date from which any review arising as a result of the application of reg. 17(4) depends on the reasons for the review and the facts of the case (paras 33 and 34).

The distinction between review and revision is stressed, but there is nothing wrong in review and revision taking place as part of the same decision, nor in there being two decisions: one to review and one to revise. In the latter case both decisions should be notified to the claimant and either or both aspects can be appealed (paras 35–38).

The Commissioners define "the requirements for entitlement" as follows:

> "In this context, 'the requirements for entitlement' must in our view mean, and mean only, the totality of the requirements attaching to the individual claimant's entitlement under the award as currently in force. If that totality ceases to exist, even though only one element in it cease to apply to the claimant, then the basis of which he or she has been given an indefinite right to payment of benefit at the rate awarded has materially changed. A review is needed to see what effect this has on the entitlement, and to adjust or terminate it to reflect that change." (para. 40).

4.78   *Regulation 18 revoked by The Social Security (Claims and Payments) (Jobseeker's Allowance Consequential Amendments) Regulations 1996 (S.I. 1996 No. 1460) (October 7, 1996).*

[¹Time for claiming benefit

4.79   **19.**—(1) Subject to the following provisions of this regulation, the prescribed time for claiming any benefit specified in column (1) of Schedule 4 is the appropriate time specified opposite that benefit in column (2) of that Schedule.

(2) The prescribed time for claiming the benefits specified in paragraph (3) is three months beginning with any day on which, apart from

(S.I. 1987 No. 1968, reg. 19) (as amended)

satisfying the condition of making a claim, the claimant is entitled to the benefit concerned.

(3) The benefits to which paragraph (2) applies are—
(a) child benefit;
(b) guardian's allowance;
(c) graduated retirement benefit;
(d) invalid care allowance;
(e) maternity allowance;
(f) retirement pension of any category;
(g) widow's benefit;
(h) except in a case to which section 3(3) of the Social Security Administration Act 1992 applies (late claims for widowhood benefits where death is difficult to establish), any increase in any benefit (other than income support or jobseeker's allowance) in respect of a child or adult dependant.

(4) Subject to paragraph (8), in the case of a claim for income support, jobseeker's allowance, [³ working families' tax credit or disabled persons' tax credit], where the claim is not made within the time specified for that benefit in Schedule 4, the prescribed time for claiming the benefit shall be extended, subject to a maximum extension of three months, to the date on which the claim is made, where—
(a) any of the circumstances specified in paragraph (5) applies or has applied to the claimant; and
(b) as a result of that circumstance or those circumstances the claimant could not reasonably have been expected to make the claim earlier.

(5) The circumstances referred to in paragraph (4) are—
(a) the claimant has difficulty communicating because—
   (i) he has learning, language or literacy difficulties; or
   (ii) he is deaf or blind,
   and it was not reasonably practicable for the claimant to obtain assistance from another person to make his claim;
(b) except in the case of a claim for jobseeker's allowance, the claimant was ill or disabled, and it was not reasonably practicable for the claimant to obtain assistance from another person to make his claim;
(c) the claimant was caring for a person who is ill or disabled, and it was not reasonably practicable for the claimant to obtain assistance from another person to make his claim;
(d) the claimant was given information by an officer of the Department of Social Security or of the Department for Education and Employment[³ or the Board] which led the claimant to believe that a claim for benefit would not succeed;
(e) the claimant was given written advice by a solicitor or other professional adviser, a medical practitioner, a local authority, or a person working in a Citizens Advice Bureau or a similar advice agency, which led the claimant to believe that a claim for benefit would not succeed;
(f) the claimant or his partner was given written information about his income or capital by his employer or former employer, or by

The Social Security (Claims and Payments) Regulations 1987

a bank or building society, which led the claimant to believe that a claim for benefit would not succeed;
   (g) the claimant was required to deal with a domestic emergency affecting him and it was not reasonably practicable for him to obtain assistance from another person to make his claim; or
   (h) the claimant was prevented by adverse weather conditions from attending the appropriate office.
(6) In the case of a claim for income support jobseeker's allowance, [3 working families' tax credit or disabled person's tax credit] where—
   (a) the claim is not made within the time specified for that benefit in Schedule 4, but is made within one month of the expiry of that time; and
   (b) the Secretary of State considers [3 or they consider] that to do so would be consistent with the proper administration of benefit,
the Secretary of State may direct that the prescribed time for claiming shall be extended by such period as he considers appropriate, subject to a maximum of one month, where any of the circumstances specified in paragraph (7) applies.
   (7) The circumstances referred to in paragraph (6) are—
   (a) the appropriate office where the claimant would be expected to make a claim was closed and alternative arrangements were not available;
   (b) the claimant was unable to attend the appropriate office due to difficulties with his normal mode of transport and there was no reasonable alternative available;
   (c) there were adverse postal conditions;
   (d) the claimant was previously in receipt of another benefit, and notification of expiry of entitlement to that benefit was not sent to the claimant before the date that his entitlement expired;
   (e) in the case of a claim for family credit, the claimant had previously been entitled to income support or jobseeker's allowance ("the previous benefit"), and the claim for family credit was made within one month of expiry of entitlement to the previous benefit;
   (f) except in the case of a claim for family credit or disability working allowance, the claimant had ceased to be a member of a married or unmarried couple within the period of one month before the claim was made; [2 . . .]
   (g) during the period of one month before the claim was made a close relative of the claimant had died, and for this purpose "close relative" means partner, parent, son, daughter, brother or [2 sister; or]
[2(h) in the case of a claim for disability working allowance, the claimant had previously been entitled to income support, jobseeker's allowance, incapacity benefit or severe disablement allowance ("the previous benefit"), and the claim for disability working allowance was made within one month of expiry of entitlement to the previous benefit.]
(8) This regulation shall not have effect with respect to a claim to which [4 regulation 21ZB(2)] of the Income Support (General) Regulations 1987 (treatment of refugees) applies.]

(S.I. 1987 No. 1968, reg. 19) (as amended)

AMENDMENTS

1. The Social Security (Miscellaenous Amendments) (No. 2) Regulations 1997 (S.I. 1997 No. 793), reg. 6 (April 7, 1997).
2. The Social Security (Claims and Payments and Adjudication) Amendment (No. 2) Regulations 1997 (S.I. 1997 No. 2290), reg. 6 (October 13, 1997).
3. The Tax Credits (Claims and Payments) (Amendment) Regulations 1999 (S.I. 1999 No. 2572), regs 24 & 25 (October 5, 1999)
4. The Social Security (Immigration and Asylum) Consequential Amendments Regulations 2000 (S.I. 2000 No. 636), reg 5 (April 3, 2000)

DEFINITIONS

"appropriate office"—see reg. 2(1). 4.80
"jobseeker's allowance"—*ibid.*
"married couple"—*ibid.*
"partner"—*ibid.*
"unmarried couple"—*ibid.*

GENERAL NOTE

Introduction
Regulation 19 is completely re-drafted to remove references to good cause, 4.81
and with it decades of case law. Administrative complexity in dealing with backdated claims is said to justify the entirely new approach.

There are now broadly two groups of benefits, those which must be claimed on the day in respect of which the situation giving rise to the claim first occurs and those where three months is allowed for claiming.

For the first group, which are income-related benefits (including jobseeker's allowance whether income-related or contribution-based), there is a possibility of an extension of the time limit for claiming to up to one month by decision of the Secretary of State where any of the circumstances set out in the regulation can be proved, and of backdating for up to a maximum of three months, where special reasons as defined in the regulation can be proved.

Paragraph (1)
If a claimant signs an ordinary income support claim form, which contains 4.82
no question asking from what date benefit is claimed, the claim will be interpreted as a claim for an indefinite period from the date on which the claim is made. If the claimant wishes to claim for a past period, that must be stated expressly *(R(SB) 9/84)*. Note *CIS/2057/1998* in which the Commissioner accepted that by putting the words "disabled—aged 16" on her claim form the claimant had indicated an intention to claim income support from her sixteenth birthday. If, before a decision is made on an ordinary claim, the claimant indicates a wish to claim for a past period, that can operate as an amendment of the original claim taking effect on the original date. But if, after there has been a decision on the claim, the claimant indicates such a wish (as often happens when the original claim has been successful), it is generally assumed that that can only be treated as a fresh claim on the date on which it was made and that any question of backdating under reg. 19(4) has to be assessed according to that date of claim.

Paragraphs (2) and (3)
The prescribed time for claiming the benefits listed in para. (3) is three 4.83
months beginning with any day of potential entitlement. The contrast between this formulation of normal backdating and the technique adopted for income-related benefits may be important.

The Social Security (Claims and Payments) Regulations 1987

Paragraphs (4) and (5)

4.84 From April 1997 the time-honoured test of good cause for backdating claims, for most, but not all, benefits subject to a 12-month limit under s.1(2) of the Administration Act, has been abolished. The new test for income related benefit is by comparison, severely limited in two ways. First, the limit of backdating is fixed at three months rather than 12. Secondly, the flexibility of the good cause test has been replaced by a limited list of circumstances which must exist before a claim can be backdated. In the Memorandum to the Social Security Advisory Committee (SSAC) on the amending regulations (in Cm. 3586) it is estimated that the change in the rules will result in a saving of £22 million in 1997/98 and similar savings in future years.

The thinking behind the change is set out in the Government's response to the SSAC's recommendation that the backdating rules, subject to the good cause test, should remain as they stand:

"The Government does not accept this proposal or the Committee's view that the backdating rules are already substantially aligned. As the Department's memorandum to the Committee states, there are now ten different rules for backdating claims and six for backdating reviews. The Government believes that this degree of complexity stands in the way of more efficient administration and can be confusing for both the Department's staff and customers. The current provisions on whether a claimant has good cause for making a late claim are particularly complex and time consuming to apply since they require consideration of a substantial body of caselaw when deciding whether to award backdating. The objective of the changes to the backdating rules is to improve administrative efficiency. The Committee's recommendation would not support this objective."

"Administrative efficiency" includes assisting in the aim of "developing a single, streamlined computer system" (para. 3 of the Memorandum to the SSAC).

Although it is common to speak of the backdating of claims, it is vital to appreciate that the technique of para. (4) is to extend the time for claiming for a past period forward from the first day of that period. There is an immediate problem in the working of the three-month limit. If on May 31, 1997 a claim is made for income support for the period from February 1, 1997 to May 30 1997, it appears that the time for claiming for the whole period cannot be extended under para. (4) because that would go beyond the three-month limit. It does not matter that one of the listed circumstances has made it reasonable for the claim not to be made earlier. The claim could be amended before it is adjudicated on, so as to make it a claim from March 1, 1997. Then there could be an extension. It would therefore be good practice for decision-makers if dealing with a claim which inevitably breaks the three-month limit, not to decide the claim, but to invite the claimant to amend the period claimed for. It remains to be seen if that practice will be adopted. An alternative approach could be for an decision-maker to treat a claim for an extension that exceeds three months as being for the maximum period that is permitted, *i.e.*, three months. It seems likely that most claimants, if asked, would say that they would prefer this approach, if the alternative was the total rejection of their claim for an extension.

In *CJSA/3994/1998* the Deputy Commissioner held that a claimant who had asked for his claim to be "backdated" for nearly a year should be treated as asking for the time for his making his claim to be extended to the maximum permitted by the regulations.

Although reg. 5(1) only expressly provides for a claim to be amended before a determination on it has been made, it does not explicitly state that a claim may not be amended after a determination has been made. Thus if such an amendment is made before, or at, the appeal hearing, it is suggested that a

(S.I. 1987 No. 1968, reg. 19) (as amended)

tribunal would be able to deal with the claim for an extension, as amended. Since the tribunal is conducting a complete rehearing of all the issues under appeal, it may also wish to consider whether to treat the claim as simply being a claim for the maximum period allowed for an extension, whatever period was initially requested by the claimant. It certainly does seem doubtful that the intention was that only claims made for extensions of three months or less could be considered under para. (4).

There are two questions to be answered before there can be an extension under para. (4). The first is that one of the circumstances listed in para. (5) has applied to the claimant. There is no condition that the circumstance must have applied throughout the period claimed for or continues to apply at the date of claim. Such consideration may come in under the second question, which is whether as a result of the circumstance or a combination of them, the claimant could not reasonably have been expected to make the claim earlier. Thus, if a claimant who has been affected by a listed circumstance, such as illness, delays unreasonably after the circumstance ceases to exist, the claim for extension of time will fail on the second question. Such a claim could also fail if there has been unreasonable delay at some earlier stage, before one of the listed circumstances intervenes.

Under the first question, in para. (4)(a), at least one of the circumstances listed in para. (5) must at some time have applied or currently apply to the claimant. The list in para. (5) is exhaustive and there is no category of analogous circumstances to deal with meritorious cases which were not foreseen by the draftsman.

At this point, no detailed analysis is attempted of the eight sub-paragraphs of para. (5), as no doubt authority on them will soon arise (see below for the first Commissioners' decisions that are now emerging). Adjudicating authorities must consider the actual words of para. (5). A few points may be noted. Ignorance of one's rights or of the procedure for claiming, whether reasonable or otherwise, does not feature in para. (5). Several sub-paragraphs refer to the question of whether it is reasonably practicable for the claimant to obtain assistance from some other person. While practicability might point one to physical feasibility, the addition of reasonableness requires a judgment to be made about the individual circumstances. If one person is physically available to assist the claimant and that person is reasonably ignorant of the claimant's rights or the need to make any inquiry, is that relevant? Is there a difference between the giving of information (see sub-para. (d) on official information) and giving advice (see sub-para. (e) on advice from advisers)? If a claimant genuinely believes as a result of information received from an officer of the DSS that a claim for benefit would not succeed, but that belief is unreasonably drawn from the information given, is the case nonetheless within sub-para. (d)? Is the information in a leaflet given by an officer of the DSS? Enough has been said to show that the new test will be a fertile source of misunderstanding, dispute and troublesome administration.

See the notes to reg. 25 of the JSA Regulations where the claimant is appealing against a decision not to backdate a fresh claim for JSA made after a previous claim has been "closed" on the grounds that the claimant has failed to sign on.

Interpretation of para. (5)

In *CJSA/3121/1998* the Deputy Commissioner held that paras (5)(e) and (f) indicate a specific set of circumstances which must exist before time limits can be extended. There is no scope for a tribunal to extend the requirements to situations which might be regarded as analogous to those set out in the regulation. The provisions of reg. 19(5) are exhaustive and not merely illustrative of the circumstances where time limits may be extended. There is no scope in the

4.85

wording of the regulation which allows a more generalised test of reasonable conduct justifying the backdating of a claim to be applied.

A very common problem is the gap in benefit that often occurs when a claimant transfers from JSA to income support because he has become incapable of work. It was thus perhaps predictable that the first Commissioners' decisions on the new rules for the backdating of income support claims would stem from this issue. In *CIS/610/1998* the claimant, who had been claiming JSA, took a Med 3 issued by his G.P. to the Benefits Agency. There was a queue so he approached the security guard. The guard advised him that he did not have to fill in any forms, took his medical certificate and wrote his N.I. number in a logging-in book. A week later he received an incapacity benefit claim form in the post, which he filled in and took to the Benefits Agency. While in the queue he was advised by another claimant that he should complete an income support claim form as well. He checked this advice when he reached the counter and then submitted an income support claim form with his incapacity benefit claim form. The adjudication officer refused to backdate his claim for income support. The Commissioner considered both para. (5)(b) and (d). On sub-para. (d), he holds that on the facts of this case the security guard constituted an "officer of the Department", and that because of what he was told by the guard the claimant may have been under the impression that he did not need to make another claim in connection with his transfer from JSA to income support and that in that sense any new claim would not succeed ("claim" in sub-para. (d) referred to the new claim(s) that the person was being advised about). On sub-para. (b), the Commissioner states that the tribunal should have investigated the nature of the claimant's illness and whether this prevented him from queuing. The Commissioner also drew attention to the powers of the Secretary of State to treat the claim as validly made under regs. 4(1) and (7) and 19(6).

See also *CIS/1721/1998* in which the claimant was given an incapacity benefit claim form when she went to the Job Centre with a medical certificate after fracturing her wrist. Two weeks later her claim for incapacity benefit was refused and she was advised to claim income support. The AO refused to backdate her income support claim. The Commissioner accepts that the implication of the advice to claim incapacity benefit was that the claimant would be entitled to that benefit and not income support. He considered that this was a reasonable belief on her part (incapacity benefit, if payable, would have exceeded her income support applicable amount). The Commissioner also took account of reg. 4(5). The official to whom she produced her medical certificate should have supplied her with an income support claim form. A failure to supply such a form would also have led to a belief that there was no entitlement to income support. *CIS/3749/1998* expands on this point. The Commissioner states that in his view claimants were entitled by reason of reg. 4(5) to assume that they had been given the right forms for the benefits they requested, and if they were not, sub-para. (d) clearly should be considered. The claimant in that case had been receiving income-based JSA, so there was at least a reasonable possibility that a claim for incapacity benefit would fail for lack of contributions. The Commissioner also drew attention to the fact that a failure to provide the right form brought reg. 4(7A) into effect, which would give the Secretary of State a discretion to accept a late claim.

On "not reasonably practicable for the claimant to obtain assistance from another person to make his claim" (see para. (5)(a), (b), (c) and (g)), note *CIS/2057/1998*. The Commissioner points out that the question is whether it is reasonably practicable for the claimant to seek assistance from another person to make the claim, not whether it is reasonably practicable for another person to take the initiative in offering assistance. The claimant in that case had learning difficulties. She made a claim for income support which was awarded. Later her

(S.I. 1987 No. 1968, reg. 19) (as amended)

mother requested on her behalf that benefit be backdated to her sixteenth birthday (no-one had been appointed to act on behalf of the claimant). The tribunal took the view that the claimant had a supportive family who should have taken the initiative in finding out about her benefit entitlement. However, the Commissioner considered that she came within para. (5)(a)(i).

In *C12/98(IS)* (starred as 27/99) the Chief Commissioner in Northern Ireland reminds tribunals that paragraphs (4) and (5) contain a twofold test for the claimant to satisfy before backdating a claim is permitted. First, (in an illness or disability case) the claimant must show that he or she was ill *and* that it was not reasonably practicable for him to have obtained assistance from another person to make his claim (para. (4)(a) and (5)(b). Secondly, as a consequence, the claimant could not reasonably have been expected to make the claim earlier (para. (4)(b). The Chief Commissioner goes on:

"'Reasonably practicable for him to obtain assistance' accordingly must mean something other than 'can reasonably have been expected to make the claim earlier', otherwise there would be no need for the two sub-paragraphs to consist of different terminology in qualifying reasonableness" (para. 11)

The Chief Commissioner adds:

". . . I accept that [the adjudication officer] is correct in submitting that regulation 19(5)(b) places an obligation on a sick or disabled person to seek assistance with his or her claim unless it is not practicable for him to obtain it; but while it might be more likely that someone who suffers from a mental health problem could satisfy the provisions of regulation 19(4) and (5), it is necessary for the Adjudicating Authorities to look at the circumstances of each case and they are not entitled to make an assumption that a person suffering from a mental health problem would automatically be unable to seek assistance from another person to make a claim." (para. 13).

In *CIS/3994/1998* the claimant had received advice that he was not entitled to income support on making two enquiries of the Department. That advice seemed to be correct in the light of the evidence of what the claimant had told the Department when he telephoned. The tribunal had ruled that this was not enough to bring the claimant within sub-paragraph (5)(d) in that the information he had received was reasonable. The Deputy Commissioner could find no such qualification in the sub-paragraph; the claimant had made an enquiry and had received information which caused him not to make a claim for income support sooner than he did. He was entitled to have the time limit for claiming extended to three months.

CJSA/1136/1998 considers the requirement in sub-para. (e) that the advice must be in writing. The claimant had been dismissed and was advised by his trade union official not to claim any benefit until the reasons for his dismissal had been investigated through his employers' appeal procedure. This advice was confirmed in writing in a letter produced for the tribunal hearing in January 1998. The Commissioner states that the reason sub-para. (e) required the advice to be in writing was to avoid any doubt or argument as to the contents of that advice. If before the decision made by the AO or tribunal, the advice was confirmed in writing, these difficulties were avoided and the advice then amounted to written advice for the purposes of sub-para. (e). But note effect of s.22(8) Administration Act for appeals lodged on or after May 21, 1998.

Paragraphs (6) and (7)
For income-related benefit claims, the Secretary of State retains the existing power to extend the time for claiming by up to a month if it is considered that to do so would be consistent with the proper administration of benefit. The

4.86

The Social Security (Claims and Payments) Regulations 1987

difference is that the discretion is no longer an open-ended one. One of the circumstances set out in para. (7) must apply. Once again, the list is exhaustive and has no category of analogous circumstances. It by no means covers the circumstances in which the Secretary of State would formerly use the discretion, but see reg. 6(1)(aa) and (1A) for the automatic allowance of a month to return claim forms; note, however, that in the case of JSA the month's extension is discretionary (see reg. 6(4AB)), unless the claimant is a postal signer when it is automatic if a properly completed claim is received within a month (see reg. 6(4A)(b)(ii)). No doubt the principle of *CSIS/61/1992* still applies, that in every case where a claim is made outside the limit specified in Sched. 4, the Secretary of State should consider the use of the discretion under para. (6) before the claim is referred to an decision-maker for decision.

PART III

PAYMENTS

Time and manner of payment: general provision

4.87   20. Subject to the provisions of [¹regulations 20A to 27], benefit shall be paid in accordance with an award as soon as is reasonably practicable after the award has been made, by means of an instrument of payment or by such other means as appears to the Secretary of State to be appropriate in the circumstances of any particular case.

AMENDMENT

1. The Social Security (Claims and Payments) Amendment (No. 4) Regulations 1994 (S.I. 1994 No. 3196), reg. 3 (January 10, 1995).

DEFINITION

4.88   "benefit"—see reg. 2(2).

[¹Payment on presentation of an instrument for benefit payment

4.89   20A.—(1) Where it appears to the Secretary of State [³or the Board] to be appropriate in any class of case, benefit due to a beneficiary falling within such a class shall be paid on presentation of an instrument for benefit payment in accordance with the arrangements set out in this regulation.

[²(2) Where a beneficiary falls within a class mentioned in paragraph (1) the Secretary of State [³or the Board] shall issue an instrument for benefit payment to whichever one or more of the following persons seems to him [³or then] to be appropriate in the circumstances of the case—
   (a) that beneficiary;
   (b) in England and Wales, the receiver appointed by the Court of Protection with power to receive benefit on behalf of that claimant;
   (c) in Scotland, the tutor, curator or other guardian acting or

(S.I. 1987 No. 1968, reg. 20A) (as amended)

appointed in terms of law to administer the estate of that beneficiary;
- (d) the person appointed by the Secretary of State under regulation 33 to act on behalf of that beneficiary;
- (e) subject to paragraph (4A), the person authorised by that beneficiary to act on his behalf;
- (f) the person to whom benefit is to be paid on that beneficiary's behalf further to a direction by the Secretary of State under regulation 34; and
- (g) the alternative payee under regulation 36.]

(3) Instruments for benefit payment shall be in such form as the Secretary of State may from time to time approve.

(4) Benefit shall not be paid under this regulation other than to—
- (a) a person to whom an instrument for benefit payment has been issued in accordance with paragraph (2); or
- (b) [²Subject to paragraph (4A),] a person not falling within sub-paragraph (a) who has been authorised by a beneficiary to whom an instrument for benefit payment has been issued to act on his behalf.

[²(4A) A person authorised by the beneficiary to act on his behalf under paragraph (2)(e) must be so authorised in respect of all benefits, payment of which may be obtained by means of that instrument for benefit payment.]

(5) The Secretary of State shall provide the paying agent with information as to the amount of benefit, if any, due to the beneficiary where the paying agent uses the instrument for benefit payment to request that information.

[²(5A) When an instrument for benefit payment is presented for payment the Secretary of State may require the person presenting that instrument to accept payment—
- (a) if the instrument is presented—
  - (i) for the purpose of obtaining payment of any benefit to which the person presenting it is entitled in his own right; or
  - (ii) by a person such as is mentioned in paragraph (2)(b), (c), (d), (e) or (f) for the purpose of obtaining payment of any benefit to which the person in respect of whom the appointment, authorisation or, as the case may be, direction mentioned in those provisions relate is so entitled,

of all monies then due in respect of such benefits; or
- (b) if the instrument is presented for the purpose of obtaining payment of any benefit which that person is entitled to receive by virtue of regulation 36 (payment to a partner as alternative payee), of all monies then due in respect of such benefits,

payment of which may be obtained by means of that instrument.]

(6) Where a paying agent pays benefit in accordance with this regulation, the person receiving it shall sign a receipt in a form approved by the Secretary of State [³or the Board] and such signature shall be sufficient discharge to the Secretary of State [³or the Board] for any sum so paid.

(7) In this regulation, "paying agent" means a person authorised by the Secretary of State [³or the Board] to make payments of benefit in

The Social Security (Claims and Payments) Regulations 1987

accordance with the arrangements for payment set out in this regulation.]

AMENDMENTS

1. The Social Security (Claims and Payments) Amendment (No. 4) Regulations 1994 (S.I. 1994 No. 3196), reg. 4 (January 10, 1995).
2. The Social Security (Claims and Payments, etc.) Amendment Regulations 1996 (S.I. 1996 No. 672), reg. 2(2) (April 4, 1996).
3. The Tax Credits (Claims and Payments) (Amendment) Regulations 1999 (S.I. 1999 No. 2572), regs 20 & 23 (October 5, 1999)

DEFINITIONS

4.90 "instrument for benefit payment"—see reg. 2(1).
"benefit"—see reg. 2(2).

GENERAL NOTE

This regulation and the amendments to regs. 27 and 47 have been introduced as a consequence of the Government's plans eventually to replace benefit order books by social security payment cards.

Direct credit transfer

4.91 **21.**—(1) Subject to the provisions of this regulation, [¹benefit [⁵. . .]] may, on the application of the person claiming, or entitled to it, and with the consent of the Secretary of State [⁷or the Board], be paid by way of automated [¹. . .] credit transfer into a bank or other account—
  (a) in the name of the person entitled to benefit, or his spouse [³or partner], or a person acting on his behalf, or
  (b) in the joint names of the person entitled to benefit and his spouse [³or partner], or the person entitled to benefit and a person acting on his behalf.
(2) An application for benefit to be paid in accordance with paragraph (1)—
  (a) shall be in writing on a form approved for the purpose by the Secretary of State [⁷or the Board] or in such other manner, being in writing, as he [⁷or they] may accept as sufficient in the circumstances, and
  (b) shall contain a statement or be accompanied by a written statement made by the applicant declaring that he has read and understood the conditions applicable to payment of benefit in accordance with this regulation
(3) [²Subject to paragraph (3A)] benefit shall be paid in accordance with paragraph (1) within seven days of the last day of each successive period of entitlement as may be provided in the application [⁷or, so far as concerns working familiar tax credit, within such time as the Board may direct]
[²(3A) Income Support shall be paid in accordance with paragraph (1) within 7 days of the time determined for the payment of income support in accordance with Schedule 7.]
[⁶(3B) Where child benefit is payable in accordance with paragraph

(S.I. 1987 No. 1968, reg. 21) (as amended)

(1), any application to which paragraph (2) refers shall also have effect for any guardian's allowance to which the claimant is entitled and that allowance shall be paid in the same manner as the child benefit due in his case.

(3C) Where guardian's allowance is payable in accordance with paragraph (1), any application to which paragraph (2) refers shall also have effect for the child benefit to which the claimant is entitled and that child benefit shall be paid in the same manner as the guardian's allowance which is due in his case.]

(4) In respect of benefit which is the subject of an arrangement for payment under this regulation, the Secretary of State [⁷or the Board] may make a particular payment by credit transfer otherwise than is provided by paragraph (3) [²or (3A)] if it appears to him [⁷or them] appropriate to do so for the purpose of—
  (a) paying any arrears of benefit, or
  (b) making a payment in respect of a terminal period of an award or for any similar purpose.

(5) The arrangement for benefit to be payable in accordance with this regulation may be terminated—
  (a) by the person entitled to benefit or a person acting on his behalf by notice in writing delivered or sent to an appropriate office or
  (b) by the Secretary of State [⁷or the Board] if the arrangement seems to him [⁷or them] to be no longer appropriate to the circumstances of the particular case.

(6) [⁵...]

AMENDMENTS

1. The Social Security (Miscellaneous Provisions) Amendment Regulations 1992 (S.I. 1992 No. 247), reg. 15 (March 9, 1992).
2. The Social Security (Claims and Payments) Amendment (No. 2) Regulations 1993 (S.I. 1993 No. 1113), reg. 2 (May 12, 1993).
3. The Social Security (Claims and Payments) Amendment Regulations 1994 (S.I. 1994 No. 2319), reg. 4 (October 3, 1994).
4. The Social Security (Claims and Payments) Amendment Regulations 1994 (S.I. 1994 No. 2319), reg. 8 (April 13, 1995).
5. The Social Security (Claims and Payments) Amendment Regulations 1996 (S.I. 1996 No. 672), reg. 2(3) (April 4, 1996).
6. The Social Security (Claims and Payments) Amendment Regulations 1999 (S.I. 1999 No. 2358), reg. 2 (September 20, 1999).
7. The Tax Credits (Claims and Payments) (Amendment) Regulations 1999 (S.I. 1999 No. 2572), regs 20, 23 & 24 (October 5, 1999)

DEFINITION

"appropriate office"—see reg. 2(1).
"partner"—*ibid.*.

GENERAL NOTE

Until May 12, 1993, it was not possible for income support to be paid by direct credit transfer.

4.92

The Social Security (Claims and Payments) Regulations 1987

Long term benefits

4.93 22.—(1) Subject to the provisions of this regulation and of [¹regulation 21 and 25(1)], long term benefits shall be paid at intervals of four weeks in the case of [²disability living allowance] but otherwise weekly in advance, by means of benefit orders [³or on presentation of an instrument for benefit payment] at such place as the Secretary of State, after inquiry of the beneficiary, may from time to time specify, unless in any particular case the Secretary of State arranges otherwise.

(2) Where the amount of long-term benefit payable is less than⁴£5.00] a week the Secretary of State may direct that it shall be paid (whether in advance or in arrears) at such intervals as may be specified not exceeding 12 months.

(3) Schedule 6 specifies the days of the week on which the various long term benefits are payable.

AMENDMENTS

1. The Social Security (Claims and Payments) Amendment Regulations 1991 (S.I. 1991 No. 2741), reg. 12(a) (February 3, 1992)
2. The Social Security (Claims and Payments) Amendment Regulations 1991 (S.I. 1991 No. 2741), reg. 12(b) (February 3, 1992)
3. The Social Security (Claims and Payments) Amendment (No. 4) Regulations 1994 (S.I. 1994 No. 3196), reg. 5 (January 10, 1995)
4. The Social Security (Claims and Payments and Adjudication) Amendment Regulations 1996 (S.I. 1996 No. 2306), reg. 22(2) (October 7, 1996)

[¹Child benefit and guardian's allowance.]

4.94 23.—(1) Subject to the provisions of this regulation and of regulation 21 (direct credit transfer), child benefit shall be payable as follows:—
  (a) in a case where a person entitled to child benefit elects to receive payment weekly in accordance with the provisions of Schedule 8, child benefit shall be payable weekly from the first convenient date after the election has been made;
  (b) in any other case child benefit shall be payable in the last week of each successive period of four weeks of the period of entitlement.

(2) Subject to paragraph (3) and regulation 21, child benefit payable weekly or four-weekly shall be payable on Mondays or Tuesdays (as the Secretary of State may in any case determine) [²by means of serial orders or on presentation of an instrument for benefit payment]

(3) In such cases as the Secretary of State may determine, child benefit shall be payable otherwise than—
  (a) by means of serial order [²or on presentation of an instrument for benefit payment,]
  (b) on Mondays or Tuesdays, or
  (c) at weekly or four-weekly intervals,
and where child benefit is paid at four-weekly intervals in accordance with paragraph (1)(b) the Secretary of State shall arrange for it to be paid weekly if satisfied that payment at intervals of four weeks is causing hardship.

[¹(3A) Where a claimant for child benefit is also entitled to guardian's allowance, that allowance shall be payable in the same manner and at the same intervals as the claimant's child benefit under this regulation.]

(4) The Secretary of State shall take steps to notify persons to whom child benefit is payable of the arrangements he has made for payment so far as those arrangements affect such persons.

AMENDMENTS

1. The Social Security (Claims and Payments) Amendment Regulations 1999 (S.I. 1999 No 2358), reg. 2(5) (September 20, 1999)
2. The Social Security (Claims and Payments) Amendment (No. 4) Regulations 1994 (S.I. 1994 No 3196), reg. 6 (January 10, 1995)

[¹**Incapacity benefit, maternity allowance and severe disablement allowance**

24.—(1) Subject to regulation 21 and paragraphs (2) and (3), incapacity benefit and severe disablement allowance shall be paid fortnightly in arrears unless, in any particular case, the Secretary of State arranges otherwise.

(2) Subject to regulation 21 and paragraph (3), incapacity benefit and severe disablement allowance shall be paid weekly in arrears where—
 (a) immediately before 13th April 1995 a person was entitled to sickness benefit, invalidity benefit or severe disablement allowance and—
  (i) in the case of severe disablement allowance, there has been no break in the entitlement to that benefit on or after that date;
  (ii) in the case of sickness benefit and invalidity benefit, there has been no break in the entitlement to incapacity benefit on or after that date;
 (b) a claim for incapacity benefit or severe disablement allowance is made on or after 13th April 1995 and immediately before the date of the claim income support on the grounds of incapacity for work was being paid weekly.

(3) If the weekly amount of incapacity benefit or severe disablement allowance is less than £1.00 it may be paid in arrears at intervals of 4 weeks.

(4) Maternity allowance shall be paid on Friday in the week for which it is payable unless in any particular case the Secretary of State arranges otherwise.]

4.95

AMENDMENTS

1. Reg. 24 substituted by The Social Security (Claims and Payments) Amendment (No. 2) Regulations 1994 (S.I. 1994 No. 2943), reg. 9 (April 13, 1995); words in heading to and certain words in regulation deleted by The Social Security (Claims and Payments) (Jobseeker's Allowance Consequential Amendments) Regulations 1996 (S.I. 1996 No. 1460), reg. 2(13) (October 7, 1996).

Payment of attendance allowance and constant attendance allowance at a daily rate

4.96   **25.**—(1) Attendance allowance [¹or disability living allowance] [²...] shall be paid in respect of any person, for any day falling within a period to which paragraph (2) applies, at the daily rate (which shall be equal to ⅐th of the weekly rate) and attendance allowance [¹or disability living allowance] [²...] payable in pursuance of this regulation shall be paid weekly or as the Secretary of State may direct in any case.

(2) This paragraph applies to any period which—
  (a) begins on the day immediately following the last day of the period during which a person was living in [³a hospital specified in or other accommodation provided as specified in regulations made under [section 72(8) of the Social Security Contributions and Benefits Act 1992] ("specified hospital or other accommodation")]; and
  (b) ends—
    (i) if the first day of the period was a day of payment, at midnight on the day preceding the [³4th] following day of payment, or
    (ii) if that day was not a day of payment, at midnight on the day preceding the [³5th] following day of payment, or
    (iii) if earlier, on the day immediately preceding the day on which [³he next lives in specified hospital or other accommodation],
if on the first day of the period it is expected that, before the expiry of the period of [³28 days] beginning with that day, he will return to [³specified hospital or other accommodation].

(3) An increase of disablement pension under [section 104 of the Social Security Contributions and Benefits Act 1992] where constant attendance is needed ("constant attendance allowance") shall be paid at a daily rate of 1/7th of the weekly rate in any case where it becomes payable for a period of less than a week which is immediately preceded and immediately succeeded by periods during which the constant attendance allowance was not payable because regulation 21(1) of the Social Security (General Benefit) Regulations 1982 applied.

AMENDMENTS

1. The Social Security (Claims and Payments) Amendment Regulations 1991 (S.I. 1991 No. 2741), reg. 13(a) (April 6, 1992)
2. The Social Security (Disability Living Allowance and Claims and Payments) Amendment Regulations 1996 (S.I. 1996 No. 1436), reg. 3 (July 31, 1996)
3. The Social Security (Claims and Payments) Amendment Regulations 1991 (S.I. 1991 No. 2741), reg 13(b)-(f) (April 6, 1992)

Income support

4.97   **26.**—(1) [³Subject to regulation 21 (direct credit transfer), Schedule 7] shall have effect for determining the manner in and time at which income support is to be paid, [⁴the date for which a superseding decision

(S.I. 1987 No. 1968, reg. 26) (as amended)

on the ground of a relevant change of circumstances has] effect and the day when entitlement to income support is to begin.

(2) Where income support paid by means of a book of serial orders is increased [²or reduced] [⁴. . .] by an amount which, with any previous such increase [²or reduction], is less than 50 pence per week, the Secretary of State may defer payment of that increase [²or disregard the reduction] until not later than either—
  (a) the termination of entitlement; or
  (b) the expiration of the period of one week from the date specified for payment in the last order in that book of serial orders,
whichever is the earlier.

[²(3) Where income support is payable to a beneficiary by means of a book of serial orders and a payment to a third party under Schedule 9 is increased so that the amount of income support payable to the beneficiary is reduced by an amount which with any previous reduction is less than 50 pence per week, the Secretary of State may make the payment to the third party and disregard the reduction in respect of the beneficiary for the period to which the book relates.]

(4) Where the entitlement to income support is less than 10 pence or, in the case of a beneficiary to whom [¹section 23(a)] of the Social Security Act 1986 [SSCBA, s.126] applies, £5, that amount shall not be payable unless the claimant is also entitled to payment of any other benefit with which income support [²may be paid] under arrangements made by the Secretary of State.

AMENDMENTS

1. The Social Security (Claims and Payments) Amendment Regulations 1988 (S.I. 1988 No. 522), reg. 6 (April 11, 1988).
2. The Social Security (Claims and Payments and Payments on account, Overpayments and Recovery) Amendment Regulations 1989 (S.I. 1989 No. 136), reg. 2 (February 27, 1989).
3. The Social Security (Claims and Payments) Amendment (No. 2) Regulations 1993 (S.I. 1993 No. 1113), reg. 3 (May 12, 1993).
4. The Social Security Act 1998 (Commencment No. 12 and Consequential and Transitional Provisions) Order 1999 (S.I. 1999 No. 3178), Sched. 6, (November 29, 1999).

[¹**Jobseeker's allowance**

26A.—(1) Subject to the following provisions of this regulation, jobseeker's allowance shall be paid fortnightly in arrears unless in any particular case or class of case the Secretary of State arranges otherwise.

4.98

(2) The provisions of paragraph 2A of Schedule 7 (payment of income support at times of office closure) shall apply for the purposes of payment of a jobseeker's allowance as they apply for the purposes of payment of income support, except that in sub-paragraph (1)(b) of that paragraph the reference to an office of the Department of Social Security or associated office shall be read as a reference to an office of the Department for Education and Employment.

(3) Where the amount of a jobseeker's allowance is less than £1.00 a week the Secretary of State may direct that it shall be paid at such

intervals, not exceeding 13 weeks, as may be specified in the direction.

(4) Subject to paragraphs (5) to (8), where [³a decision in respect of a claim for jobseeker's allowance is superseded] on the ground that there has been, or there is expected to be, a relevant change of circumstances, the [³supersession] shall have effect from the first day of the benefit week (as defined in regulation 1(3) of the Jobseeker's Allowance Regulations) in which that relevant change of circumstances ocurred or is expected to occur.

(5) Where the relevant change of circumstances giving rise to the [³supersession] is that—
   (a) entitlement to jobseeker's allowance ends, or is expected to end, for a reason other than that the claimant no longer satisfies the provisions of section 3(1)(a) of the Jobseekers Act; or
   (b) a child or young person who is normally in the care of a local authority or who is detained in custody lives, or is expected to live, with the claimant for a part only of a benefit week; or
   (c) the claimant or his partner enters, or is expected to enter, a nursing home or residential care home for a period of no more than 8 weeks; or
   (d) the partner of the claimant or a member of his family ceases, or is expected to cease, to be a hospital in-patient for a period of less than a week,

the [³supersession] shall have effect on the date that the relevant change of circumstances occurs or is expected to occur.

(6) Where the relevant change of circumstances giving rise to a [³supersession] is any of those specified in paragraph (5), and, in consequence of those circumstances ceasing to apply, [³a further superseding decision is made, that further superseding decision] shall have effect on the date that those circumstances ceased to apply.

(7) Where, under the provisions of regulation 96 [²or 102C(3)] of the Jobseeker's Allowance Regulations, income is treated as paid on a certain date and that payment gives rise, or is expected to give rise, to a relevant change of circumstances resulting in a [³supersession], that revised award shall have effect on that date.

(8) Where a relevant change of circumstances occurs which results, or is expected to result, in a reduced award of jobseeker's allowance then, if the Secretary of State is of the opinion that it shall have effect on the first day of the benefit week following that in which the relevant change of circumstances occurs.]

AMENDMENTS

1. The Social Security (Claims and Payments) (Jobseeker's Allowance Consequential Amendments) Regulations 1996 (S.I. 1996 No. 1460), reg. 2(14) (October 7, 1996).

2. The Social Security (Miscellaneous Amendments) (No. 4) Regulations 1998 (S.I. 1998 No. 1174), reg. 8(3)(a) (June 1, 1998).

3. The Social Security Act 1998 (Commencement No. 12 and Consequential and Transitional Provisions) Order 1999 (S.I. 1999 No. 3178), Sched. 6 (November 29, 1999).

(S.I. 1987 No. 1968, reg. 26A) (as amended)

DEFINITIONS

"jobseeker's allowance"—see reg. 2(1).
"the Jobseeker's Allowance Regulations"—*ibid.*
"partner"—*ibid.*
"week"—*ibid.*

4.99

[¹[²Working families' tax credit and disabled persons' tax credit]

27.—(1) Subject to regulation 21 [³and paragraph (1A)] [²working families' tax credit] and [²disabled persons' tax credit] shall be payable in respect of any benefit week on the Tuesday next following the end of that week by means of a book of serial orders [³or on presentation of an instrument for benefit payment] unless in any case the Secretary of State arranges [⁴Board arrange] otherwise.

[⁵(1A) Subject to paragraph (2), where an amount of [²working families' tax credit] and [²disabled persons' tax credit] becomes payable which is at a weekly rate of note more than £4.00, that amount shall, if the Secretary of State so directs [⁴Board so direct], be payable as soon as practicable by means of a single payment; except that if that amount represents an increase in the amount of either of those benefits which has previously been paid in respect of the same period, this paragraph shall apply only if that previous payment was made by means of a single payment.]

(2) Where the entitlement to [²working families' tax credit] and [²disabled persons' tax credit] is less than 50 pence a week that amount shall not be payable.]

4.100

AMENDMENTS

1. Reg. 27 substituted by The Social Security (Claims and Payments) Amendment Regulations 1991 (S.I. 1991 No. 2741), reg. 14 (April 6, 1992)
2. The Tax Credits (Claims and Payments) (Amendment) Regulations 1999 (S.I. 1999 No. 2752), regs 24 and 25 (October 5, 1999)
3. The Social Security (Claims and Payments) Amendment (No. 3) Regulations 1993 (S.I. 1993 No. 2113), reg. 3(4) (October 25, 1993)
4. For tax credits purposes only, these words are substitue for the words "Secretary of State arranges": The Tax Credits (Claims and Payments) (Amendment) Regulations 1999 (S.I. 1999 No. 2572), reg. 12(a) (October 5, 1999)
5. The Social Security (Claims and Payments) Amendment (No. 3) Regulations 1993 (S.I. 1993 No. 2113), reg. 3(4) (October 25, 1993).

Fractional amounts of benefit

28. Where the amount of any benefit payable would, but for this regulation, include a fraction of a penny, that fraction shall be disregarded if it is less than half a penny and shall otherwise be treated as a penny.

4.101

DEFINITION

"benefit"—see reg. 2(2).

4.102

[¹Payments to persons under age 18

4.103 **29.** Where benefit is paid to a person under the age of 18 (whether on his own behalf or on behalf of another) the receipt of that person shall be a sufficient discharge to the Secretary of State [³or the Board].]

AMENDMENT

1. The Social Security (Claims and Payments etc.) Amendment Regulations 1996 (S.I. 1996 No. 672), reg. 2(4) (April 4, 1996).
2. The Tax Credits (Claims and Payments) (Amendment) Regulations 1999 (S.I. 1999 No 2572), reg. 30 (October 5, 1999)

DEFINITION

4.104 "benefit"—see reg. 2(2).

Payments on death

4.105 **30.**—(1) On the death of a person who has made a claim for benefit, the Secretary of State [¹or the Board] may appoint such person as he [¹or they] may think fit to proceed with the claim.

(2) Subject to paragraph (4), any sum payable by way of benefit which is payable under an award on a claim proceeded with under paragraph (1) may be paid or distributed by the Secretary of State to or amongst persons over the age of 16 claiming as personal representatives, legatees, next of kin, or creditors of the deceased (or, where the deceased was illegitimate, to or amongst other persons over the age of 16), and the provisions of regulation 38 (extinguishment of right) shall apply to any such payment or distribution; and—
  (a) the receipt of any such person shall be a good discharge to the Secretary of State [¹or the Board] for any sum so paid; and
  (b) where the Secretary of State is satisfied [¹or the Board an satisfies] that any such sum or part thereof is needed for the benefit of any person under the age of 16, he [¹or they] may obtain a good discharge therefor by paying the sum or part thereof to a person over that age who satisfies the Secretary of State [¹or the Board] that he will apply the sum so paid for the benefit of the person under the age of 16.

(3) Subject to paragraph (2), any sum payable by way of benefit to the deceased, payment of which he had not obtained at the date of his death, may, unless the right thereto was already extinguished at that date, be paid or distributed to or amongst such persons as are mentioned in paragraph (2), and regulation 38 shall apply to any such payment or distribution, except that, for the purpose of that regulation, the period of 12 months shall be calculated from the date on which the right to payment of any sum is treated as having arisen in relation to any such person and not from the date on which that right is treated as having arisen in relation to the deceased.

(4) Paragraphs (2) and (3) shall not apply in any case unless written application for the payment of any such sum is made to the Secretary of State [¹or the Board] within 12 months from the date of the de-

ceased's death or within such longer period as the Secretary of State [¹or the Board] may allow in any particular case.

(5) Where the conditions specified in paragraph (6) are satisfied, a claim may be made on behalf of the deceased to any benefit other than [²jobseeker's allowance,] income support, [³working families' tax credit or disabled person's tax credit] or a social fund payment such as is mentioned in section 32(2)(a) [⁴and section 32(2A)] of the Social security Act 1986 [⁵, or reduced earnings allowance or disablement benefit], to ehich he would have been entitled if he had claimed it in the prescribed manner and within the prescribed time.

(6) [⁶Subject to the following provisions of this regulation,] the following conditions are specified for the purposes of paragraph (5)—
  (a) Within six months of the death an application must have been made in writing to the Secretary of State for a person, whom the Secretary of State thinks fit to be appointed to make the claim, to be so appointed;
  (b) a person must have been appointed by the Secretary of State to make the claim;
  (c) there must have been no longer period than six months between the appointment and the making of the claim.

[⁷(6A) Where the conditions specified in paragraph (6B) are satisfied, a person may make a claim for reduced earnings or disablement benefit, including any increase under [section 104 or 105 of the Social Security Contributions and Benefits Act 1992], in the name of a person who had died.

(6B) [⁸Subject to the following provisions of this regulation,] the conditions specified for the purposes of paragraph (6A) are—
  (a) that the person who had died would have been entitled to the benefit claimed if he had made a claim for it in the prescribed manner and within the prescribed time;
  (b) that within 6 months of a death certificate being issued in respect of the person who has died, the person making the claim has applied to the Secretary of State to be made an appointee of the person who has died

[⁹(ba) that person has been appointed by the Secretary of State to make the claim]
  (c) the claim is made within six months of the appointment.]

[¹⁰(6C) Subject to paragraph (6D), where the Secretary of State certifies that to do so would be consistent with the proper administration of the Social Security Contributions and Benefits Act 1992 the period specified in paragraphs (6)(a) and (c) and (6B)(b) and (c) shall be extended to such period, not exceeding 6 months, as may be specified in the certificate.

(6D)(a) Where a certificate is given under paragraph (6C) extending the period specified in paragraph (6)(a) or (6B)(b), the period specified in paragraph (6)(c) or (6B)(c) shall be shortened by a period corresponding to the period specified in the certificate;
  (b) no certificate shall be given under paragraph (6C) which would enable a claim to be made more than 12 months after the date of death (in a case falling within paragraph (6)) or the date of a

death certificate being issued in respect of the person who has died (in a case falling within paragraph (6B)); and

(c) in the application of sub-paragraph (b) any period between the date when an application for a person to be appointed to make a claim is made and the date when that appointment is made shall be disregarded.]

(7) A claim made in accordance with paragraph (5) [[11]or paragraph (6A)] shall be treated, for the purposes of these regulations, as if made by the deceased on the date of his death.

(8) The Secretary of State [[1]or the Board] may dispense with strict proof of the title of any person claiming in accordance with the provisions of this regulation.

(9) In paragraph (2) "next of kin" means—

(a) in England and Wales, the persons who would take beneficially on an intestacy; and

(b) in Scotland, the persons entitled to the moveable estate of the deceased on intestacy.

AMENDMENTS

1. The Tax Credits (Claims and Payments) (Amendment) Regulations 1999 (S.I. 1999 No. 2572), regs 13, 20 and 22 (October 5, 1999).

2. The Social Security (Claims and Payments) (Jobseeker's Allowance Consequential Amendments) Regulations 1996 (S.I. 1996 No. 1460), reg. 2(15) (October 7, 1996).

3. The Tax Credits (Claims and Payments) (Amendments) Regulations 1999 (S.I. 1999 No. 2572), regs 24 and 25 (October 5, 1999).

4. The Social Security (Claims and Payments) Amendment Regulations 1991 (S.I. 1991 No. 2741), reg. 15 (March 10, 1992).

5. The Social Security (Common Provisions) Miscellaneous Amendments Regulations 1988 (S.I. 1988 No. 1725), reg. 3(6) (November 7, 1988).

6. The Social Security (Claims and Payments) Amendment (No. 3) Regulations 1993 (S.I. 1993 No. 2113), reg. 3(5)(a) (September 27, 1993).

7. Paras (6A) and (6B) inserted by The Social Security (Miscellaneous Provisions) Amendment Regulations 1990 (S.I. 1990 No. 2208), reg. 11(3) (December 5, 1990).

8. The Social Security (Claims and Payments) Amendment (No. 3) Regulations 1993 (S.I. 1993 No. 2113), reg. 3(5)(a) (September 29, 1993).

9. The Social Security (Claims and Payments) Amendment Regulations 1994 (S.I. 1994 No. 2319), reg. 5 (October 3, 1994).

10. Paras (6C) and (6D) inserted by The Social Security (Claims and Payments) Amendment (No. 3) Regulations 1993 (S.I. 1993 No. 2113), reg. 3(5)(b) (September 27, 1993).

11. The Social Security (Miscellaneous Provisions) Amendment Regulations 1990 (S.I. 1990 No. 2208), reg. 11(4) (December 5, 1990)

GENERAL NOTE

4.106   Note the decisions referred to in the annotations to reg. 33.

It would seem that the power of appointment in reg. 30(1) on the death of the claimant is a separate appointment from that under reg. 33. It would follow that where a claimant has an appointee under reg. 33 and dies, there should at least be confirmation of continuation of the appointment under reg. 33 to enable the appointee to act under reg. 30. The better course, since there are specific

(S.I. 1987 No. 1968, reg. 30) (as amended)

requirements in the regulation, would be for a separate appointment to be made.

Note that paras (4)–(7) contain a special power of appointment to enable *a claim* to be made after a person's death.

Death of claimant pending appeal to the Commissioner

It sometimes happens that the claimant dies while the appeal is pending before the Commissioner. In such cases the surviving partner may not wish to take on an appointment enabling the matter to continue, and there may be no personal representatives because there is no estate. The result is that, where there is a claimant's appeal, there is no one who can withdraw the appeal. In such circumstances, the practice of the Commissioners is to treat the appeal as abated: see *R(S)7/56, R(1)2/83* and *R(SB)25/84*. For all practical purposes the matter is then closed, though the possibility remains that the matter could be revived on application. This could happen if, for example, the Secretary of State chose to appoint someone to act for the deceased claimant. The most likely appointee would be the Official Solicitor, but is difficult to imagine circumstances in which it would be appropriate to take such action. In overpayment cases, care should be taken to ensure that the Benefits Agency has given an assurance that it will not seek recovery from the estate before treating an appeal as abated, since abatement of a claimant's appeal without such an assurance would not preclude recovery against the estate.

The use of the abatement procedure is not appropriate where the appellant is the adjudication officer. In such cases, the proper course of action is for the adjudication officer to withdraw the appeal: *R(1)2/83*, para. 6.

Time and manner of payments of industrial injuries gratuities

31.—(1) This regulation applies to any gratuity payable under [Part V of the Social Security Contributions and Benefits Act 1992].

(2) Subject to the following provisions of this regulation, every gratuity shall be payable in one sum.

(3) A gratuity may be payable by instalments of such amounts and at such times as appear reasonable in the circumstances of the case to the adjudicating authority awarding the gratuity if—
  (a) the beneficiary to whom the gratuity has been awarded is, at the date of the award, under the age of 18 years, or
  (b) in any other case, the amount of the gratuity so awarded (not being a gratuity payable to the widow of a deceased person on her remarriage) exceeds £52 and the beneficiary requests that payments should be made by instalments.

(4) An appeal shall not be brought against any decision that a gratuity should be payable by instalments or as to the amounts of any such instalments or the time of payment.

(5) Subject to the provisions of regulation 37 (suspension), a gratuity shall—
  (a) if it is payable by equal weekly instalments, be paid in accordance with the provisions of regulation 22 insofar as they are applicable; or

4.107

(b) in any case, be paid by such means as may appear to the Secretary of State to be appropriate in the circumstances.

AMENDMENT

1. The Social Security Act 1998 (Commencement No. 12 and Consequential and Transitional Provisions) Order 1999 (S.I. 1999 No 3178), Sched. 6 (November 29, 1999).

Information to be given when obtaining payment of benefit

4.108   32.—(1) [³Except in the case of a jobseeker's allowance,] every beneficiary and every person by whom or on whose behalf sums payable by way of benefit are receivable shall furnish in such manner and at such times as the Secretary of State [⁴or the Board] may determine such certificates and other documents and such information or facts affecting the right to benefit or to its receipt as the Secretary of State [⁴or the Board] may require (either as a condition on which any sum or sums shall be receivable or otherwise), and in particular shall notify the Secretary of State [⁴or the Board] of any change of circumstances which he might reasonably be expected to know might affect the right to benefit, or to its receipt, as soon as reasonably practicable after its occurrence, by giving notice in writing [¹(unless the Secretary of State [⁴or the Board] determines in any particular case to accept notice given otherwise than in writing)] of any such change to the appropriate office.

(2) Where any sum is receivable on account of an increase of benefit in respect of an adult dependant, the Secretary of State may require the beneficiary to furnish a declaration signed by such dependant confirming the particulars respecting him, which have been given by the claimant.

[²(3) In the case of a person who is claiming income support [³or a jobseeker's allowance], where that person or any partner is aged not less than 60 and is a member of, or a person deriving entitlement to a pension under, a personal pension scheme, or is a party to, or a person deriving entitlement to a pension under, a retirement annuity contract, he shall where the Secretary of State so requires furnish the following information—
  (a) the name and address of the pension fund holder;
  (b) such other information including any reference or policy number as is needed to enable the personal pension scheme or retirement annuity contract to be identified.

(4) Where the pension fund holder receives from the Secretary of State a request for details concerning a personal pension scheme or retirement annuity contract relating to a person or any partner to whom paragraph (3) refers, the pension fund holder shall provide the Secretary of State with any information to which paragraph (5) refers.

(5) The information to which this paragraph refers is—
  (a) where the purchase of an annuity under a personal pension scheme has been deferred, the amount of any income which is being withdrawn from the personal pension scheme;
  (b) in the case of—

(S.I. 1987 No. 1968, reg. 32) (as amended)

    (i) a personal pension scheme where income withdrawal is available, the maximum amount of income which may be withdrawn from the scheme; or

    (ii) a personal pension scheme where income withdrawal is not available, or a retirement annuity contract, the maximum amount of income which might be withdrawn from the fund if the fund were held under a personal pension scheme where income withdrawal was available,

calculated by or on behalf of the pension fund holder by means of tables prepared from time to time by the Government Actuary which are appropriate for this purpose.]

AMENDMENTS

1. The Social Security (Miscellaneous Provisions) Amendment (No. 2) Regulations 1992 (S.I. 1992 No. 2595), reg. 4 (November 16, 1992).
2. Income-related benefit Schemes and Social Security (Claims and Payments) (Miscellaneous Amendments) Regulations 1995 (S.I. 1995 No. 2303), reg. 10(4) (October 2, 1995).
3. The Social Security (Claims and Payments) (Jobseeker's Allowance Consequential Amendments) Regulations 1996 (S.I. 1996 No. 1460), reg. 2(16) (October 7, 1996).
4. The Tax Credits (Claims and Payments) (Amendment) Regulations 1999 (S.I. 1999 No 2572), reg. 14, (October 5, 1999).

DEFINITIONS

    "appropriate office"—see reg. 2(1).   4.109
    "beneficiary"—see Social Security Act 1975, Sched. 20.
    "benefit"—see reg. 2(2).
    "jobseeker's allowance—see reg. 2(1).
    "pension fund holder"—*ibid.*
    "personal pension scheme"—*ibid.*
    "retirement annuity contract"—*ibid.*

GENERAL NOTE

Paragraph (1)

Notes in order books and on notices of determination require claimants to   4.110
inform the DSS of various changes of circumstances, and there is also a general duty to report changes of circumstances which the claimant might reasonably be expected to know might affect entitlement. This obligation can be relevant to the recoverability of an overpayment under s.71 of the Administration Act. Although reg. 32 requires notice generally to be given in writing, the Secretary of State can now accept notification otherwise than in writing. Oral disclosures have always counted as disclosure under s.71 *(R(SB) 40/84)*. See reg. 24 of the Jobseeker's Allowance Regulations, in particular para. (7), for the obligations in JSA cases.

See reg. 37AA(1) for the withholding of benefit if para. (1) is not complied with and reg. 37AB for payment of benefit that has been withheld.

Paragraphs (3) to (5)

See reg. 42(2A)–(2C) of the Income Support Regulations and the note to   4.111
those paragraphs and reg. 105(3) to (5) of the Jobseeker's Allowance Regulations.

The Social Security (Claims and Payments) Regulations 1987

Part IV

Third Parties

Persons unable to act

4.112 33.—(1) Where—
(a) a person is, or is alleged to be, entitled to benefit, whether or not a claim for benefit has been made by him or on his behalf; and
(b) that person is unable for the time being to act; and either
(c) no receiver has been appointed by the Court of Protection with power to claim, or as the case may be, receive benefit on his behalf; or
(d) in Scotland, his estate is not being administered by any tutor, curator or other guardian acting or appointed in terms of law,

the Secretary of State [² or the Board] may, upon written application made to him by a person who, if a natural person, is over the age of 18, appoint that person to exercise, on behalf of the person who is unable to act, any right to which that person may be entitled and to receive and deal on his behalf with any sums payable to him.

(2) Where the Secretary of State has made [² or the Board have made] an appointment under paragraph (1)—
(a) he [² or they] may at any time revoke it;
(b) the person appointed may resign his office after having given one month's notice in writing to the Secretary of State [² or the Board] of his intention to do so;
(c) any such appointment shall terminate when the Secretary of State is notified [² or the Board are notified] that a receiver or other person to whom paragraph (1)(c) or (d) applies has been appointed.

(3) Anything required by these regulations to be done by or to any person who is for the time being unable to act may be done by or to the receiver, tutor, curator or other guardian, if any, or by or to the person appointed under this regulation or regulation 43 [¹(disability living allowance for a child)] and the receipt of any person so appointed shall be a good discharge to the Secretary of State [² or the Board] for any sum paid.

Amendments

1. The Social Security (Claims and Payments) Amendment Regulations 1991 (S.I. 1991 No. 2741), reg. 16 (February 3, 1992).
2. The Tax Credits (Claims and Payments) (Amendment) Regulations 1999 (S.I. 1999 No 2572), regs 15, 20, 22 & 23 (October 5, 1999).

Definitions

4.113 "benefit"—see reg. 2(2).
"claim for benefit"—see reg. 2(1).

(S.I. 1987 No. 1968, reg. 33) (as amended)

GENERAL NOTE

Even if no appointment has been made, a claim made by a person unable to act, or by an "unauthorised person" on their behalf, is still valid (*CIS/812/1992*, applying para. 8 of *R(SB) 9/84* where a Tribunal of Commissioners holds that in the absence of any challenge at the time the Secretary of State must be deemed to have accepted that the claim was made in sufficient manner). In *Walsh v. CAO* (Consent Order, January 19, 1995) the Court of Appeal also applied *R(SB) 9/84* when setting aside *CIS/638/1991* in which the Commissioner had held that a claim made on behalf of a person unable to act by a person who had not been formally appointed was a nullity.

Note that any subsequent appointment has retrospective effect *(R(SB) 5/90)*.

In *CIS/642/1994* the claimant's husband was her appointee under reg. 33. She died before the tribunal hearing. The Commissioner holds that the tribunal decision was a nullity because there had been no appointment under reg. 30 (deceased persons). Appointments under reg. 30 were a distinct and different form of appointment from reg. 33 appointments. He dissents from para. 8 of *R(SB) 9/84* and repeats his view (see *CIS/638/1991*) that it is open to adjudication officers and tribunals (and Commissioners) to determine that a claim is a nullity in cases where a person is unable to act and there has been no valid appointment. This is out of step with the current weight of authority.

CIS/812/1992 also confirms that, in relation to the pre-April 1997 form of the rules for backdating claims, if there has been no appointment it is only necessary to decide whether the claimant has good cause for a late claim; it is not necessary to consider the reasonableness of the failure to claim of a person who has been acting informally on his behalf. The Commissioner declines to follow paras. 12 and 13 of *R(IS) 5/91* since this could not be reconciled with paras. 9 and 10 of *R(SB) 9/84* (which was a Tribunal of Commissioners' decision). See also *CSB/168/1993* which takes a similar view and contains a useful summary of the authorities on this issue.

Under the current form of reg. 19(5) the test is also of the claimant's personal circumstances, if there is no appointee, but those circumstances sometimes expressly include whether there is anyone who could help the claimant.

The Secretary of State's normal practice in making appointments is not to make an appointment generally but to limit it to a specific benefit: see *R(IS)5/91*. *R(IS)5/91* concerned the effect of an appointment for supplementary benefit purposes on a subsequent income support claim following the 1988 changes. There is some doubt whether such a limited appointment has survived the changes brought about then. There is now a single regulation governing appointments, and some argue that, at a consequence appointments are for all benefits. Tribunals do, however, continue to see appointments limited to certain benefits. The message is that the scope of the appointment needs to be considered in every case where it is relevant, though in the absence of any limiting conditions, there is a strong case for considering that it applies to all benefits.

Where a claimant has died, the Secretary of State may appoint a person to act: *R(SB)8/88*. Unless the Secretary of State does so, the tribunal has no jurisdiction to proceed in the absence of action by a personal representative under a grant of probate or letters of administration.

In starred Commissioner's Decision *R(SB)5/90*, Commissioner Goodman clarifies the decision in *R(SB)8/88* in holding that the appointment of a person to act by the Secretary of State operates retrospectively. Thus, so far as tribunals are concerned, an appointment after the date of the appeal but before the date of the hearing will be sufficient to ground jurisdiction. The power of appointment is to be found in reg. 30(1).

Note that the power of appointment under this regulation is a separate power

The Social Security (Claims and Payments) Regulations 1987

of appointment from that under reg. 30 which arises on the death of the claimant, or where a claim is made after death, a potential claimant.

On the liability of appointees in respect of overpayments of benefit, see the discussion in the notes to s.71 of the Administration Act.

The practice of the Secretary of State in making appointments under reg. 33 appears to vary. Since April 1988 there has been a single regulation governing appointments and the regulation is drafted in sufficiently wide terms to encompass a single appointment to cover all social security benefits; it covers "any sums payable to him". Previously there were separate sets of regulations covering means-tested and non-means-tested benefits, and it was the interaction of the sets of regulations which was primarily in issue in *R(IS)5/91*. The experience of tribunals appears to be that in some cases the appointment is for all benefits, and in other cases it is limited to particular benefits. Indeed, in some cases it is not clear what the scope of the appointment is, as when a claimant asks for an appointment in relation to a particular benefit and the appointment is made in general terms. The nature of the appointment seldom seems to be an issue upon which the appeal turns.

See also annotation to reg. 30.

Payment to another person on the beneficiary's behalf

4.114   **34.** The Secretary of State [² or the Board] may direct that benefit shall be paid, wholly or in part, to [¹another natural person] on the beneficiary's behalf if such a direction as to payment appears to the Secretary of State [² or the Board] to be necessary for protecting the interests of the beneficiary, or any child or dependant in respect of whom benefit is payable.

AMENDMENTS

1. The Social Security (Miscellaneous Provisions) Amendment (No. 2) Regulations 1992 (S.I. 1992 No. 2595), reg. 5 (January 4, 1993).
2. The Tax Credits (Claims and Payments) (Amendment) Regulations 1999 (S.I. 1999 No 2572), reg 20 (October 5, 1999).

DEFINITIONS

4.115   "beneficiary"—see Social Security Act 1975, Sched. 20.
"benefit"—see reg. 2(2).
"child"—see 1986 Act, s.20(11).

[¹Deductions of mortgage interest which shall be made from benefit and paid to qualifying lenders

4.116   **34A.**—(1) In relation to cases to which section 51C(1) of the Social Security Act 1986 [SSAA, s.15A(1)] (payment out of benefit of sums in respect of mortgage interest etc.) applies and in the circumstances specified in Schedule 9A, such part of any relevant benefits to which a relevant beneficiary is entitled as may be specified in that Schedule shall be paid by the Secretary of State directly to the qualifying lender and shall be applied by that lender towards the discharge of the liability in respect of that mortgage interest.

(2) The provisions of Schedule 9A shall have effect in relation to mortgage interest payments.]

(S.I. 1987 No. 1968, reg. 34A) (as amended)

AMENDMENT

1. The Social Security (Claims and Payments) Amendment Regulations 1992 (S.I. 1992 No. 1026), reg. 3 (May 25, 1992).

DEFINITIONS

"qualifying lender"—see Administration Act, s.15A(3).
"relevant beneficiary"—see Administration Act, s.15A(1).
"relevant benefits"—see Administration Act, s.15A(4).

4.117

[¹[³**Deductions which may be made from benefit and paid to third parties**

35.—(1) Except as provided for in regulation 34A and Schedule 9A, deductions] may be made from benefit and direct payments may be made to third parties on behalf of a beneficiary in accordance with the provisions of Schedule 9.

(2) Where a social fund payment for maternity or funeral expenses [²or expenses for heating which appear to the Secretary of State to have been or to be likely to be incurred in cold weather] is made, wholly or in part, in respect of a debt which is, or will be, due to a third person, the instrument of payment may be, and in the case of funeral expenses shall be, made payable to that person and it may, in any case, be delivered or sent to that person as a direct payment.]

4.118

AMENDMENTS

1. The Social Security (Claims and Payments) Amendment Regulations 1988 (S.I. 1988 No. 522), reg. 7 (April 11, 1988).
2. The Social Security (Common Provisions) Miscellaneous Amendments Regulations 1988 (S.I. 1988 No. 1725), reg. 3, (November 7, 1988).
3. The Social Security (Claims and Payments) Amendment Regulations 1992 (S.I. 1992 No. 1026), reg. 4 (May 25, 1992).

DEFINITIONS

"beneficiary"—see Social Security Act 1975, Sched. 20.
"benefit"—see reg. 2(2).

4.119

[¹ **Transitional provisions for persons in hostels or certain residential accommodation**

35A.—(1) In this regulation—
"benefit week" has the same meaning as it has in Schedule 7, paragraph 4; "specified benefit" has the same meaning as it has in Schedule 9, paragraph 1; and
"Schedule 3B" means Schedule 3B to the Income Support (General) Regulations 1987.
(2) Expressions used in this regulation and in Schedule 3B have, unless the context otherwise requires, the same meanings in this regulation as they have in that Schedule.
(3) Where—
(a) immediately before the coming into force of Schedule 3B a bene-

4.120

ficiary was in, or temporarily absent from, a hostel and a payment in respect of his accommodation charges was, or would but for that absence have been, made for the first week to a third party under—
  (i) Schedule 9, paragraph 4 (miscellaneous accommodation costs), or
  (ii) regulation 34 (payment to another person on the beneficiary's behalf); and
(b) the beneficiary is entitled to eligible housing benefit for the period mentioned in sub-paragraph (b) of the expression "eligible housing benefit"; and
(c) the beneficiary continues to reside in the same hostel.
the adjudicating authority shall in a case to which paragraph (6) applies determine that an amount of specified benefit shall, subject to paragraphs (8) and (9), be paid to that third party.

(4) Where a beneficiary is in, or is temporarily absent from, accommodation which—
(a) was a hostel before the March benefit week; and
(b) in the second week is residential accommodation within the meaning of regulation 21 of the Income Support (General) Regulations 1987,
paragraph (3) shall apply as if sub-paragraph (b) was omitted and as if the reference to paragraph (6) was a reference to paragraph (7).

(5) An amount of specified benefit shall not be paid to a third party under paragraph (3), as applied by paragraph (4), where the beneficiary—
(a) is in residential accommodation in the benefit week which commences in the period of 7 consecutive days beginning on 9th October 1989, but
(b) is a person to whom a protected sum is not applicable in accordance with paragraph 3(3) of Schedule 3B.

(6) This paragraph applies in a case where—
(a) the amount of the eligible housing benefit referred to in paragraph (3)(b) is less than
(b) the amount of the direct payment or the payment under regulation 34 in respect of the first week or the amount which would have been payable but for the temporary absence of the beneficiary in the first week;
and where this paragraph applies the amount of the specified benefit determined in accordance with paragraph (3) shall be the difference between the amounts specified in sub-paragraphs (a) and (b).

(7) This paragraph applies where the applicable amount which was appropriate to the beneficiary by way of personal expenses in the first week is less than the total applicable amount appropriate to the beneficiary in the second week; and where this paragraph applies the amount of the specified benefit determined in accordance with paragraph (3) as applied by paragraph (4) shall be the difference between those two amounts.

(8) Where immediately before the coming into force of Schedule 3B a beneficiary was temporarily absent from a hostel and the charge levied

(S.I. 1987 No. 1968, reg. 35A) (as amended)

on him during that period of absence was less than the full charge for the accommodation, an amount of specified benefit shall not be paid to the third party in respect of the period for which less than the full charge was levied but shall be paid when the full charge is levied.

(9) Specified benefit shall not be paid to a third party in accordance with this regulation unless the amount of the beneficiary's award of the specified benefit is not less than the total of the amount otherwise authorised to be so paid under this regulation plus 10 pence.

(10) For the purposes of paragraph (3(c) residence shall be regarded as continuous where the only absences occurred during the permitted period and for this purpose "permitted period" has the same meaning as it has in regulation 3A of the Income Support (General) Regulations 1987.

(11) This regulation shall cease to apply, where a beneficiary's benefit week in the week commencing 2nd April 1990—
> (i) begins on that day, on the day immediately following 8th April 1990;
> (ii) begins on a day other than that day, on the day immediately following the last day in his benefit week.]

AMENDMENT

1. The Social Security (Medical Evidence, Claims and Payments) Amendment Regulations 1989 (S.I. 1989 No. 1686), reg. 6 (October 9, 1989).

DEFINITIONS

"adjudicating authority"—see reg. 2(1). 4.121
"beneficiary"—see Social Security Act 1975, Sched. 20.
"eligible housing benefit"—see Income Support (General) Regulations, Sched. 3B, para. 1(1).
"first week"—*ibid.*
"hostel"—*ibid.*
"March benefit week"—*ibid.*
"second week"—*ibid.*

Payment to a partner as alternative payee

36. [¹ Except where a wife has elected in accordance with regulation 6A of the Social Security (Guardian's Allowances) Regulation 1975 (prescribed manner of making an election under section 77(9) of the Social Security Contributions and Benefits Act 1992) that guardian's allowance is not to be paid to her husband,] where one of a married or unmarried couple residing together is entitled to child benefit [² working families' tax credit, disabled person's tax credit] [¹ or guardian's allowance] the Secretary of State [² or the Board] may make arrangements whereby that benefit as well as being payable to the person entitled to it, may, in the laternative, be paid to that person's partner on behalf of the person entitled. 4.122

The Social Security (Claims and Payments) Regulations 1987

AMENDMENTS

1. The Social Security (Claims and Payments) Amendment Regulations 1999 (S.I. 1999 No 2358), reg. 2(6) (September 20, 1999)
2. The Tax Credits (Claims and Payments) (Amendment) Regulations 1999 (S.I. 1999 No 2752), regs 20, 24 and 25 (October 5, 1999)

4.123 Regulation 36A revoked by The Social Security (Claims and Payments) Amendment Regulations 1991 (S.I. 1991 No 2741), reg. 18 (April 6, 1992)

PART V

[¹ . . .] Extinguishment

AMENDMENT

1. Words in heading omitted by The Social Security Act 1998 (Commencement No. 8, and Savings and Consequential and Transitional Provisions) Order 1999 (S.I. 1999 No 1958), Sched. 9 (July 5, 1999)

4.124 Regulations 37 to 37B revoked by The Social Security Act 1998 (Commencement No. 8, and Savings and Consequential and Transitional Provisions) Order 1999 (S.I. 1999 No 1958), Sched. 9 (July 5, 1999)

Extinguishment of right to payment of sums by way of benefit where payment is not obtained within the prescribed period

4.125 **38.**—(1) [¹Subject to paragraph (2A), the right to payment of any sum by way of benefit shall be extinguished] where payment of that sum is not obtained within the period of 12 months from the date on which the right is to be treated as having arisen; and for the purposes of this regulation the right shall be treated as having arisen—
  (a) in relation to any such sum contained in an instrument of payment which has been given or sent to the person to whom it is payable, or to a place approved by the Secretary of State [⁴ or the Board] for collection by him (whether or not received or collected as the case may be)—
    (i) on the date of the said instrument of payment, or
    (ii) if a further instrument of payment has been so given or sent as a replacement, on the date of the last such instrument of payment;
  [³(aa) in relation to any such sum which is payable by means of an instrument for benefit payment, on the first date when payment of that benefit could be obtained by that means;]
  (b) in relation to any such sum to which sub-paragraph (a) does not apply, where notice is given (whether orally or in writing) or is sent that the sum contained in the notice is ready for collection

(S.I. 1987 No. 1968, reg. 38) (as amended)

on the date of the notice or, if more than one such notice is given or sent, the date of the first such notice;

(c) in relation to any such sum to which [³none of (a), (aa) or (b) apply], on such date as the Secretary of State determines [⁴ or the Board determine].

(2) The giving or sending of an instrument of payment under paragraph (1)(a), or of a notice under paragraph (1)(b), shall be effective for the purposes of that paragraph, even where the sum contained in that instrument, or notice, is more or less than the sum which the person concerned has the right to receive.

[¹(2A) Where a question arises whether the right to payment of any sum by way of benefit has been extinguished by the operation of this regulation and the [⁵ Secretary of State] is satisfied that—

(a) [⁵ he] first received [⁴ or the Board first received] written notice requesting payment of that sum after the expiration of 12 months; and

(b) from a day within that period of 12 months and continuing until the day the written notice was given, there was good cause for not giving the notice; and

[²(c) [⁵. . .] either—

 (i) [⁵. . .] no instrument of payment has been given or sent to the person to whom it is payable and [⁵. . .] no payment has been made under the provisions of regulation 21 (automated credit transfer); or

 (ii) that such instrument has been produced to [⁵ the Secretary of State] and [⁵. . .] no further instrument has been issued as a replacement,]

the period of 12 months shall be extended to the date on which the [⁵ Secretary of State] decides that question, and this regulation shall accordingly apply as though the right to payment had arisen on that date.]

(3) For the purposes of paragraph (1) the date of an instrument of payment is the date of issue of that instrument or, if the instrument specifies a date which is the earliest date on which payment can be obtained on the instrument and which is later than the date of issue, that date.

(4) This regulation shall apply to a person authorised or appointed to act on behalf of a beneficiary as it applies to a beneficiary.

(5) This regulation shall not apply to the right to a single payment of any industrial injuries gratuity or in satisfaction of a person's right to graduated retirement benefit.

AMENDMENTS

1. The Social Security (Medical Evidence, Claims and Payments) Amendment Regulations 1989 (S.I. 1989 No. 1686), reg. 7 (October 9, 1989).

2. Social Security (Claims and Payments) Amendment (No. 3) Regulations 1993 (S.I. 1993 No. 2113). reg. 3(8) (September 27, 1993).

3. Social Security (Claims and Payments Etc.) Amendment Regulations 1996 (S.I. 1996 No. 672), reg. 2(5) (April 4, 1996).

The Social Security (Claims and Payments) Regulations 1987

4. The Tax Credits (Claims and Payments) (Amendment) Regulations 1999 (S.I. 1999 No 2572), reg. 20 (October 5, 1999).

5. The Social Security Act 1998 (Commencement No. 9, and Savings and Consequential and Transitional Provisions) Order 1999 (S.I. 1999 No 2422), Sched. 7 (September 6, 1999).

DEFINITIONS

4.126 "beneficiary"—see Social Security Act 1975, Sched. 20.
"benefit"—see reg. 2(2).
"instrument for benefit payment"—see reg. 2(1).

GENERAL NOTE

4.127 It is a common feature of social security benefit that the right to payment of benefit does not survive a delay of more than twelve months in obtaining payment of it. The determination of the date on which the right to payment is treated as arising may be crucial and is a matter for the Secretary of State (or Board of the Inland Revenue as appropriate). Three possibilities arise under this regulation. The right to payment may be treated as arising:

(1) on the date of the instrument of payment, or of its replacement for any reason, where any sum is contained in an instrument of payment and has been either:

 (a) given or sent to the beneficiary; or
 (b) given or sent to a place approved by the Secretary of State for collection by the beneficiary (for example, a post office); or

(2) if (1) does not apply, on the date a notice (whether written or oral and if more than one relating to the same sum, the first such notice) is given or sent to the beneficiary; or

(3) if neither (1) nor (2) applies, on such date as the Secretary of State may determine.

Paragraph (2A) deals with a particular set of circumstances which are likely to arise only rarely, but when they do, the concept of good cause must be explored with care. The paragraph deals only with a case where a person has been sent an instrument of payment, delays the cashing of the instrument beyond the twelve month period and then makes a written request for the payment of the sum and can prove good cause for not giving the notice requesting payment of the benefit, and the Secretary of State has not issued any duplicate instrument.

The test of good cause is the test which formerly existed under the replaced regulation 19 of the Claims and Payments Regulations. Reference to the 1996 edition of *Non-Means Tested Benefits: The Legislation* contains a detailed account of the case law, but the classic definition of good cause is that found in *R(S)2/63:*

"In Decision CS 371/49 the Commissioner said '"Good cause"' means, in my opinion, some fact which, having regard to all the circumstances (including the claimant's state of health and the information which he had received and that which he might have obtained) would probably have cuased a reasonable person of his age and experience to act (or fail to act) as the claimant did." This description of good cause has been quoted in countless cases. It has stood the test of time. In our judgment it is correct. The word "fact" of course includes a combination of events happening either simultaneously or in succession."

Although the determination of the date on which the right to payment of benefit

(S.I. 1987 No. 1968, reg. 38) (as amended)

arises is a matter for the adjudicating authorities, generally questions concerning the payment of benefit do not attract any right of appeal. In *CSU/13/1992* the Commissioner said,

> "the question whether any award has been implemented is not concerned with the question whether it is payable but on the contrary relates to the Secretary of State's obligation to give effect to decision of the statutory adjudication authorities." (para. 5)

Only where reg. 38(2A) applies does any issue for the adjudicating authorities arise. Then it is only whether the right to payment has been extinguished, but it will still be for the Secretary of State to determine "whether there should be a replacement instrument." (para. 7).

Cases in which the claimant says that no giro was received are governed by *R(IS) 7/91* under which questions of payment were held not to be questions relating to the award of benefit.

Unravelling those matters which are for the adjudicating authorities and those matters which do not attract a right of appeal will become more complicated under the new system under which there adjudication officers have been abolished and all decisions are taken by the Secretary of State with some attracting a right of appeal and others not.

Note that *R(P)3/93* was concerned with the version of this regulation in force until September 27, 1993, and has no application to the present version of the regulation.

Part VI

[¹Mobility Component of Disability Living Allowance and Disability Living Allowance for Children]

Amendment

1. The Social Security (Claims and Payments) Amendment Regulations 1991 (S.I. 1991 No 2741), reg. 19(a) (February 3, 1992)

Regulations 39 to 41 revoked by The Social Security (Claims and Payments) Amendment Regulations 1991 (S.I. 1991 No. 2741), reg. 19(b) (February 3, 1992)

4.128

Cases where allowance not to be payable

42.—(1) Subject to the provisions of this regulation, [¹disability living allowance by virtue of entitlement to the mobility component] shall not be payable to any person who would otherwise be entitled to it in respect of any period—

    (a) during which that person has the use of an invalid carriage or other vehicle provided by the Secretary of State under section 5(2) of and Schedule 2 to the National Health Service Act 1977 or section 46 of the National Health Service (Scotland) Act 1978 which is a vehicle propelled by petrol engine or by electric power supplied for use on the road and to be controlled by the occupant; or

4.129

(b) in respect of which that person has received, or is receiving, any payment—
    (i) by way of grant under the said section 5(2) and Schedule 2 or section 46 towards the costs of running a private car, or
    (ii) of mobility supplement under the Naval, Military and Air Forces etc., (Disablement and Death) Service Pensions Order 1983 or the Personal Injuries (Civilians) Scheme 1983 or under the said Order by virtue of the War Pensions (Naval Auxiliary Personnel) Scheme 1964, the Pensions (Polish Forces) Scheme 1964, the War Pensions (Mercantile Marine) Scheme 1964 or an Order of Her Majesty in relation to the Home Guard dated 21st December, 1964 or 22nd December, 1964 or in relation to the Ulster Defence Regiment dated 4th January, 1971,

or any payment out of public funds which the Secretary of State is satisfied is analogous thereto.

(2) A person who has notified the Secretary of State that he no longer wishes to use such an invalid carriage or other vehicle as if referred to in paragraph (1)(a) and has signed an undertaking that he will not use it while it remains in his possession awaiting collection, shall be treated, for the purposes of this regulation, as not having the use of that invalid carriage or other vehicle.

(3) Where a person in respect of whom [¹disability living allowance] is claimed for any period has received any such payment as referred to in paragraph (1)(b) for a period which, in whole or in part, covers the period for which the allowance is claimed, such payment shall be treated as an aggregate of equal weekly amounts in respect of each week in the period for which it is made and, where in respect of any such week a person is treated as having a weekly amount so calculated which is less than the weekly rate of [¹mobility component of disability living allowance to which, apart from paragraph (1), he would be entitled], any allowance to which that person may be entitled for that week shall be payable at a weekly rate reduced by the weekly amount so calculated.

(4) In a case where the Secretary of State has issued a certificate to the effect that he is satisfied—
  (a) that the person in question either—
      (i) has purchased or taken on hire or hire-purchase; or
      (ii) intends to purchase or take on hire or hire-purchase a private car or similar vehicle ("the car") for a consideration which is more than nominal, on or about a date (not being earlier than 13th January, 1982) specified in the certificate ("the said date");
  (b) that that person intends to retain possession of the car at least during, and to learn to drive it within, the period of 6 months or greater or lesser length of time as may be specified in the certificate ("the said period") beginning on the said date; and
  (c) that the person will use [¹disability living allowance by virtue of entitlement to the mobility component] in whole or in part during the said period towards meeting the expense of acquiring the car, paragraph (1)(a) shall not apply, and shall be treated as having

(S.I. 1987 No. 1968, reg. 42) (as amended)

never applied, during a period beginning on the said date and ending at the end of the said period or (if earlier) the date on which the Secretary of State cancels the certificate because that person has parted with possession of the car or for any other reason.

AMENDMENT

1. The Social Security (Claims and Payments) Amendment Regulations 1991 (S.I. 1991 No 2741), reg. 20 (February 3, 1992)

Children

43.—(1) In any case where a claim for [¹disability living allowance] for a child is received by the Secretary of State, he shall, in accordance with the following provisions of this regulation, appoint a person to exercise, on behalf of the child, any right to which he may be entitled under the [Social Security Contributions and Benefits Act 1992] in connection with [¹disability living allowance] and to receive and deal on his behalf with any sums payable by way of [¹that allowance].

(2) Subject to the following provisions of this regulation, a person appointed by the Secretary of State under this regulation to act on behalf of the child shall—
(a) be a person with whom the child is living; and
(b) be over the age of 18; and
(c) be either the father or mother of the child, or, if the child is not living with either parent, be such other person as the Secretary of State may determine; and
(d) have given such undertaking as may be required by the Secretary of State as to the use, for the child's benefit, of any allowance paid.

(3) For the purpose of paragraph (2)(a), a person with whom a child has been living shall, subject to paragraph (4) and to the power of the Secretary of State to determine in any case that the provisions of this paragraph should not apply, be treated as continuing to live with that child during any period—
(a) during which that person and the child are separated but such separation has not lasted for a continuous period exceeding [¹12 week]; or
(b) during which the child is absent by reason only of the fact that he is receiving full-time education at a school; or
(c) during which the child is absent and undergoing medical or other treatment as an in-patient in a hospital or similar institution; or
(d) during such other period as the Secretary of State may in any particular case determine:

Provided that where the absence of the child under (b) has lasted for a continuous period of 26 weeks or the child is absent under (c), that person shall only be treated as continuing to live with that child if he satisfies the Secretary of State that he has incurred, or has undertaken to incur, expenditure for the benefit of the child of an amount not less than the allowance payable in respect of such period of absence.

4.130

(4) Where a child in respect of whom an allowance is payable, is, by virtue of any provision of an Act of Parliament—
  (a) committed to, or received into the care of, a local authority; or
  (b) subject to a supervision requirement and residing in a residential establishment under arrangements made by a local authority in Scotland;
any appointment made under the foregoing provisions of this regulation shall terminate forthwith:

Provided that, when a child is committed to, or received into, care or is made subject to a supervision requirement for a period which is, and when it began was, not intended to last for more than [¹12 weeks] the appointment shall not terminate by virtue of this paragraph until such period has lasted for 8 weeks.

(5) In any case where an appointment on behalf of any child in the care of, or subject to a supervision requirement under arrangements made by, a local authority is terminated in accordance with paragraph (4), the Secretary of State may, upon application made to him by that local authority or by an officer of such authority nominated for the purpose by that authority, appoint the local authority or nominated officer thereof or appoint such other person as he may, after consultation with the local authority, determine, to exercise on behalf of the child any right to which that child may be entitled under the Act in connection with the allowance and to receive and deal on his behalf with any sums payable to him by way of [¹disability living allowance] for any period during which he is in the care of, or, as the case may be, subject to a supervision requirement under arrangements made by, that authority.

(6) Where a child is undergoing medical or other treatment as an inpatient in a hospital or similar institution and there is no other person to whom [¹disability living allowance] may be payable by virtue of an appointment under this regulation, the Secretary of State may, upon application made to him by the district health authority [¹ National Health Service Trust] or, as the case may be, social services authority, controlling the hospital or similar institution in which the child is an in-patient, or by an officer of that authority [¹ or Trust] nominated for the purpose by the authority, appoint that authority [¹ or Trust] or the nominated officer thereof or such other person as the Secretary of State may, after consultation with that authority [¹ or Trust], determine, to exercise on behalf of the child any right to which that child may be entitled in connection with the allowance and to receive and deal on his behalf with any sums payable to him by way of [¹ disability living allowance] for any period during which he is an in-patient in a hospital or similar institution under the control of that authority [¹ or Trust].

(7) For the purpose of this regulation—
"district health authority" means, in relation to England and Wales a District Health Authority within the meaning of the National Health Service Act 1977 and, in relation to Scotland, a Health Board within the meaning of the National Health Services (Scotland) Act 1978;
"child's father" and "child's mother" include a person who is a

(S.I. 1987 No. 1968, reg. 43) (as amended)

child's father or mother by adoption or would be such a relative if an illegitimate child had been borne legitimate;

"hospital or similar institution" means any premises for the reception of and treatment of person suffering from any illness, including any mental disorder, or of persons suffering from physical disability and any premises used for providing treatment during convalescence or for medical rehabilitation;

"local authority" means, in relation to England and Wales, a local authority as defined in the Local Government Act 1972 and, in relation to Scotland, a local authority as defined in the Local Government (Scotland) Act 1973;

"social services authority" means—
(a) in relation to England and Wales, the social services committee established by a local authority under section 2 of the Local Authority Social Services Act 1970; and
(b) in relation to Scotland, the social work committee established by a local authority under section 2 of the Social Work (Scotland) Act 1968.

AMENDMENTS

1. The Social Security (Claims and Payments) Amendment Regulations 1991 (S.I. 1991 No 2741), reg. 21 (February 3, 1992)

Payment of [1 disability living allowance] on behalf of a beneficiary

44.—(1) Where, under arrangements made or negotiated by Motability, an agreement has been entered into by or on behalf of a beneficiary in respect of whom [1 disability living allowance is payable by virtue of entitlement to the mobility component at the higher rate] for the hire or hire-purchase of a vehicle, the Secretary of State may arrange that any [1 disability living allowance by virtue of entitlement to the mobility component at the higher rate payable] to the beneficiary shall be paid in whole or in part on behalf of the beneficiary in settlement of liability for payments due under that agreement.

(2) Subject to regulations 45 and 46 an arrangement made by the Secretary of State under paragraph (1) shall terminate at the end of whichever is the relevant period specified in paragraph (3), in the case of hire, or paragraph (4), in the case of a hire-purchase agreement.

(3) In the case of hire the relevant period shall be—
(a) where the vehicle is returned to the owner at or before the expiration of the original term of hire, the period of the original term; or
(b) where the vehicle is retained by or on behalf of the beneficiary with the owner's consent after the expiration of the original term of hire, the period of the original term; or
(c) where the vehicle is retained by or on behalf of the beneficiary otherwise than with the owner's consent after the expiration of the original term of hire or its earlier termination, whichever is the longer of the following periods.

4.131

The Social Security (Claims and Payments) Regulations 1987

(i) the period ending with the return of the vehicle to the owner; or
(ii) the period of the original term of hire.

(4) In the case of a hire-purchase agreement, the relevant period shall be—
  (a) the period ending with the purchase of the vehicle; or
  (b) where the vehicle is returned to the owner or is repossessed by the owner under the terms of the agreement before the completion of the purchase, the original period of the agreement.

[²(5) In this regulation "Motability" means the company, set up under that name as a charity and originally incorporated under the Companies Act 1985 and subsequently incorporated by Royal Charter].

AMENDMENTS

1. The Social Security (Claims and Payments) Amendment Regulations 1991 (S.I. 1991 No 2741), reg. 22 (February 3, 1992)
2. The Social Security (Miscellaneous Provisions) Amendment Regulations 1990 (S.I. 1990 No 2208), reg. 13 (December 5, 1990)

Power for the Secretary of State to terminate an arrangement

4.132   **45.** The Secretary of State may terminate an arrangement for the payment of [¹disability living allowance by virtue of entitlement to the mobility component at the higher rate] on behalf of a beneficiary under regulation 44 on such date as he shall decide—
  (a) if requested to do so by the owner of the vehicle to which the arrangement relates, or
  (b) where it appears to him that the arrangement is causing undue hardship to the beneficiary and that it should be terminated before the end of any of the periods specified in regulation 44(3) or 44(4).

AMENDMENT

1. The Social Security (Claims and Payments) Amendment Regulations 1991 (S.I. 1991 No 2741), reg. 23 (February 3, 1992)

Restriction on duration of arrangements by the Secretary of State

4.133   **46.** The Secretary of State shall end an arrangement for the payment of [¹ disability living allowance by virtue of entitlement to the mobility component at the higher rate] on behalf of a beneficiary made under regulation 44, where he is satisfied that the vehicle to which the arrangement relates has been returned to the owner, and that the expenses of the owner arising out of the hire or hire-purchase agreement have been recovered following the return of the vehicle.

(S.I. 1987 No. 1968, reg. 46) (as amended)

PART VII

MISCELLANEOUS

[¹**Instruments of payment, etc and instruments for benefit payment**

47.—(1) Instruments of payment, books of serial orders and instruments for benefit payment issued by the Secretary of State [¹or the Board] shall remain his [¹or their] property.

(2) Any person having an instrument of payment or book of serial orders shall, on ceasing to be entitled to the benefit to which such instrument or book relates, or when so required by the Secretary of State [¹or the Board] deliver it to the Secretary of State [¹or the Board] or such other person as he [¹or they] may direct.

(3) Any person having an instrument for benefit payment shall, when so required by the Secretary of State [¹or the Board], deliver it to the Secretary of State [¹or the Board] or such other person as he [¹ or they] may direct.]

AMENDMENTS

1. The Social Security (Claims and Payments) Amendment (No. 4) Regulations 1994 (S.I. 1994 No. 3196), reg. 8 (January 10, 1995).
2. The Tax Credits (Claims and Payments) (Amendment) Regulations 1999 (S.I. 1999 No. 2572), regs 19, 20 & 22 (October 5, 1999).

DEFINITIONS

"instrument for benefit payment"—see reg. 2(1).
"benefit"—see reg. 2(2).

Revocations

48. The regulations specified in column (1) of Schedule 10 to these regulations are hereby revoked to the extent mentioned in column (2) of that Schedule, in exercise of the powers specified in column (3).

Savings

49. [¹. . .]

AMENDMENT

1. The Social Security (Miscellaneous Provisions) Amendment (No. 2) Regulations 1992 (S.I. 1992 No. 2595), reg. 6 (November 16, 1992).

GENERAL NOTE

Reg. 49 maintained in force regulations about claims and reviews relating to supplementary benefit and family income support. See *CIS/465/1991*. Because its terms led to the mistaken impression that the substantive terms of the schemes survived the repeal of the Supplementary Benefits Act 1976 and the Family Income Supplements Act 1970 by the Social Security Act 1986, reg. 49

has been revoked from November 16, 1992. See *R(SB) 1/94*. It is not immediately apparent that reg. 49 was necessary in order to allow claims to be made for supplementary benefit for periods prior to April 11, 1988, and reviews of entitlement for such periods to be carried out. Therefore its revocation may have no effect on such matters. See Sched. 10 to the Administration Act. However, *CSB 168/1993* is to the contrary.

In *CIS/12016/1996* a Commissioner, after a detailed review of the legal issues, concluded that from November 16, 1992, it has been impossible for an effective claim to be made for supplementary benefit. This was in spite of the powerful argument that an underlying entitlement to supplementary benefit for a period before April 11, 1988, and the right to pursue a remedy in respect of that entitlement could be preserved by s.16(1) of the Interpretation Act 1978 on the revocation of the supplementary benefit legislation. The reason was that any remedy protected would be under reg. 3(1) of the Supplementary Benefit (Claims and Payments) Regulations 1981, which required a claim for weekly supplementary benefit to be made in writing on a form approved by the Secretary of State or in such other manner as the Secretary of State accepted as sufficient. In *CIS/12016/1996* the claim was made in a letter in July 1993. By that date, the Secretary of State had no power to accept the manner of claim as sufficient, because the 1981 Regulations no longer existed. Since the Secretary of State's power was discretionary, the claimant had no accrued right which could be preserved by s.16(1). It had been held in *R. v. Secretary of State for Social Security, ex parte Cullen* (November 21, 1996), now confirmed by the Court of Appeal (*The Times*, May 16, 1997, and see the notes to reg. 9) that the hope of having a discretion to treat a claim for supplementary benefit as in the alternative a claim for attendance allowance was not preserved by s.16(1) as an accrued right. The same had to apply to the power to accept claims as made in sufficient manner.

Note also *CIS/7009/1995* which confirms that it was not possible to make a late claim for National Assistance after the start of the supplementary benefit scheme on November 24, 1966. There were no savings provisions to enable claims for National Assistance to succeed after that date (see *CSB 61/1995*).

SCHEDULE 1

PART I

BENEFIT CLAIMED AND OTHER BENEFIT WHICH MAY BE TREATED AS IF CLAIMED IN ADDITION OR IN THE ALTERNATIVE

4.139

Benefit claimed (1)	Alternative benefit (2)
[¹ Incapacity benefit]	[¹ Severe disablement allowance]
[² ...]	[² ...]
Severe disablement allowance	[¹ Incapacity benefit]
[² ...]	[² ...]
[¹ Incapacity benefit for a woman]	[¹ Maternity allowance]
Severe disablement allowance for a woman	Maternity allowance
Maternity allowance	[¹ Incapacity benefit or severe disablement allowance]

(S.I. 1987 No. 1968, Sched. 1) (as amended)

A retirement pension of any category	Widow's benefit
A retirement pension of any category	A retirement pension of any other category [³ or graduated retirement benefit]
[¹ An increase of incapacity benefit]	An increase of severe disablement allowance
Attendance allowance	An increase of disablement pension where constant attendance is needed
An increase of disablement pension where constant attendance is needed	Attendance allowance [⁴ or disability living allowance]
An increase of severe disablement allowance	[¹ An increase of incapacity benefit]
Income support	[⁵ . . .] [⁴ . . .] or an invalid care allowance
[⁶ Widow's benefit]	[⁶ A retirement pension of any category or graduated retirement benefit]
[⁴ Disability living allowance]	[⁴ Attendance allowance or an increase of disablement pension where constant attendance is needed]
[⁴ Attendance allowance or an increase of disablement pension where constant attendance is needed]	[⁴ Disability living allowance]
[⁷ Disabled person's tax credit]	[⁷ Working families' tax credit]
[⁷ Working families' tax credit]	[⁷ Disabled person's tax credit]

In this part of this Schedule—
(a) Reference to an increase of any benefit (other than an increase of disablement pension where constant attendance is needed) are to an increase of that benefit in respect of a child or adult dependant;
(b) "widow's benefit" means widow's benefit under [Part II of the Social Security Contributions and Benefits Act 1992] and benefit by virtue of section [78(9)] of that Act corresponding to a widow's pension or a widowed mother's allowance.

Part II

Interchange of Claims for Child Benefit with Claims for Other Benefits

[⁸ . . .]   4.140
Guardian's allowance
Maternity allowance claimed after confinement
Increase of child dependant by virtue of [sections 80 and 90 of the Social Security Contributions and Benefits Act 1992], or regulations made under [section 78(9)] of that Act.

The Social Security (Claims and Payments) Regulations 1987

AMENDMENTS

1. The Social Security (Claims and Payments) Amendment (No. 2) Regulations 1994 (S.I. 1994 No 2943), reg. 10 (April 13, 1995).
2. The Social Security (Claims and Payments) (Jobseeker's Allowance Consequential Amendments) Regulations 1996 (S.I. 1996 No 1460), reg. 2 (October 7, 1996).
3. The Social Security (Claims anb Payments) Amendment Regulations 1988 (S.I. 1988 No 522), reg. 8 (April 11, 1988).
4. The Social Security (Claims and Payments) Amendment Regulations 1991 (S.I. 1991 No 2741), reg. 25 (February 3, 1992).
5. The Social Security (Miscellaneous Provisions) Amendment (No. 2) Regulations 1992 (S.I. 1992 No 2595), reg. 7 (November 16, 1992).
6. The Social Security (Miscellaneous Provisions) Amendment Regulations 1990 (S.I. 1990 No 2208), reg. 14 (December 5, 1990).
7. The Tax Credits (Claims and Payments) (Amendment) Regulations 1999 (S.I. 1999 No 2572), regs. 24 and 25 (October 5, 1999).
8. The Child Benefit, Child Support and Social Security (Miscellaneous Amendments) Regulations 1996 (S.I. 1996 No 1803), reg. 20 (April 7, 1997).

SCHEDULE 2   Regulation 17(5)

SPECIAL PROVISIONS RELATING TO CLAIMS FOR [¹JOBSEEKER'S ALLOWANCE] DURING PERIODS CONNECTED WITH PUBLIC HOLIDAYS

4.141

1.—(1) In this Schedule—
  (a) "public holiday" means, as the case may be, Christmas Day, Good Friday or a Bank Holiday under the Banking and Financial Dealings Act 1971 or in Scotland local holidays; and "Christmas and New Year holidays" and "Good Friday and Easter Monday" shall be construed accordingly and shall in each case be treated as one period;
  (b) "office closure" means a period during which an [¹ office of the Department for Education an Employment] or associated office is closed in connection with a public holiday;
  (c) in computing any period of time Sundays shall not be disregarded.
(2) Where any claim for [¹a jobseeker's allowance] is made during one of the periods set out in paragraph (3), the following provisions shall apply—
  (a) a claim for [¹a jobseeker's allowance] may be treated by [² the Secretary of State as a claim for that benefit for period, to be specified in his decision, not exceeding 35 days after the date of the claim where that claim is made during the period specified in sub-paragraph (a) of paragraph (3), or 21 days after the date of claim where the claim is made during the period specified in either sub-paragraph (b) or (c) of paragraph (3);
  (b) on any claim so treated, benefit may be awarded as if the provisions of paragraph (4) of regulation 17 applied.
(3) For the purposes of paragraph (2) the periods are—
  (a) in the case of Christmas and New Year holidays, a period beginning with the start of the 35th day before the first day of office closure and ending at midnight between the last day of office closure and the following day;
  (b) in the case of Good Friday and Easter Monday, a period beginning with the start of the 16th day before the first day of the office closure and ending at midnight between the last day of office closure and the following day;
  (c) in the case of any public holiday, a period beginning with the start of the 14th day before the first day of office closure and ending at midnight between the last day of office closure and the following day.

(S.I. 1987 No. 1968, Sched. 2) (as amended)

AMENDMENTS

1. The Social Security (Claims and Payments) (Jobseeker's Allowance Consequential Amendments) Regulations 1996 (S.I. 1996 NO 1460), reg. 2 (October 7, 1996)
2. The Social Security Act 1998 (Commencement No. 11 and Transitional Provisions) Order 1999 (S.I. 1999 No 2860), Sched. 3 (October 18, 1999)

Schedule 3 revoked by The Social Security (Claims and Payments) (Jobseeker's Allowance Consequential Amendments) Regulations 1996 (S.I. 1996 No 1460), reg. 2 (October 7, 1996)

4.142

SCHEDULE 4

PRESCRIBED TIME FOR CLAIMING BENEFIT

4.143

Description of benefit (1)	Prescribed time for claiming benefit (2)
1. [¹ Jobseeker's allowance]	[¹ The first day of the period in respect of which the claim is made]
[² 2. Incapacity benefit or severe disablement allowance]	[² The day in respect of which the claim is made and period of [³ 3 months] immediately following it.]
3. Disablement benefit (not being an increase of benefit)	As regards any day on which, apart from satisfying the condition of making a claim, the claimant is entitled to benefit, that day and the period of 3 months immediately following it.
4. Increase of disablement benefit under section 61 (constant attendance), or 63 (exceptionally severe disablement) of the Social Security Act 1975.	As regards any day which apart form satisfying the conditions that there is a current award of disablement benefit and the making of a claim, the claimant is entitled to benefit, that day and the period of 3 months immediately following it.
5. Reduced earnings allowance	As regards any day on which apart from satisfying the conditions that there is an assessment of disablement of not less than one percent. and the making of a claim, the claim is entitled to the allowance, that day and the period of 3 months immediately following it.
6. Income support	The first day of the period in respect of which the claim is made.
7. [⁴ Working families' tax credit]	(a) Where [⁴ working families' tax credit] has previously been claimed and awarded the period beginning 28 days before and ending 14 days after the last day of that award; [⁵ (aa) where [⁴ disabled person's tax credit] has previously been claimed and awarded the period beginning

4.144

	42 days before and ending 14 days after the last day of that award of [⁴ disabled person's tax credit]]
	(b) Subject to [⁵ (a) and (aa)], the first day of the period in respect of which the claim is made;
	(c) where a claim for [⁴ working families' tax credit] is treated as if made for a period beginning with the relevant day by virtue of regulation 13 of these Regulations, the period beginning on 10ᵗʰ March 1992 and ending on 6ᵗʰ April 1992]
8. Social fund payment in respect of maternity expenses	[⁷ The period beginning 11 weeks before the first day of the expected week of confinement and ending three months after—
	(a) the actual date of confinement; or
	(b) in the case of an adopted child, the date of the adoption order; or
	(c) in the case of a child in respect of whom an order has been granted pursuant to section 30 of the Human Fertilisation and Embryology Act, the date of that Order.]
9. Social fund payment in respect of funeral expenses	[⁸ The period beginning with the date of death and ending 3 months after the date of the funeral.]
9A. [⁹ . . .]	
10. Increase of disablement benefit under [¹⁰ section 60 of the Social Security Act 1975 on grounds of special hardship or] section 62 of the Social Security Act1975 on the grounds of receipt of hospital treatment.	A regards any day on which, apart form satisfying the conditions that there is a current award of disablement benefit and the making of a claim, the claimant is entitled to benefit, that day and the period 3 months immediately following it.
[¹¹ 11.[¹² Disabled person's tax credit]	(a) Where [¹² disabled person's tax credit] has previously been claimed and awarded the period beginning 42 days before and ending 14 days after the last day of that award;
	(b) where [¹² working families' tax credit] has previously been claimed and awarded the period beginning 28 days before and ending 14 days after the last day of that award of [¹² working families' tax credit];
	(c) subject to (a) and (b), the first day of the period in respect of which the claim is made;
	(d) where a claim for [¹² disabled

4.145

(S.I. 1987 No. 1968, Sched. 4) (as amended)

person's tax credit] is made by virtue of regulation 13B(1), the period beginning on 10th March 1992 and ending on 6th April 1992.]

For the purposes of this Schedule—

"actual date of confinement" means the date of the issue of the child or, if the woman is confined of twins or a greater number of children, the date of the issue of the last of them; and

"confinement" means labour resulting in the issue of a living child, or labour after 28 weeks of pregnancy resulting in the issue of a child whether alive or dead.

AMENDMENTS

1. The Social Security (Claims and Payments) (Jobseeker's Allowance Consequential Amendments) Regulations 1996 (S.I. 1996 No 1460), reg. 2 (October 7, 1996)
2. The Social Security (Claims and Payments) Amendment (No. 2) Regulations 1994 (S.I. 1994 No 2943), reg. 12 (April 13, 1995)
3. The Social Security (Miscellaneous Provisions) (No. 2) Regulations 1997 (S.I. 1997 No 793), reg. 7 (April 7, 1997)
4. The Tax Credits (Claims and Payments) (Amendment) Regulations 1999 (S.I. 1999 No 2572), regs 24 and 25 (October 5, 1999)
5. The Social Security (Claims and Payments) Amendment Regulations 1991 (S.I. 1991 No 2741), reg. 26 (March 10, 1992
6. The Social Security (Miscellaneous Provisions) Amendment Regulations 1991 (S.I. 1991 No 2284), reg. 10 (November 1, 1991)
7. The Social Security (Social Fund and Claims and Payments) (Miscellaneous Amendments) Regulations 1997 (S.I. 1997 No 792), reg. 8 (April 7, 1997)
8. The Social Security (Claims and Payments and Adjudication) Amendment Regulations 1996 (S.I. 1996 No 2306), reg. 6 (October 7, 1996)
9. The Social Security (Miscellaneous Provisions) Amendment Regulations 1991 (S.I. 1991 No 2284), reg. 11 (November 1, 1991)
10. The Social Security (Claims and Payments) Amendment Regulations 1988 (S.I. 1988 No 522), reg. 9 (April 11, 1988)
11. The Social Security (Claims and Payments) Amendment Regulations 1991 (S.I. 1991 No 2741), reg 26(b) (March 10, 1992)
12. The Tax Credits (Claims and Payments) (Amendment) Regulations 1999 (S.I. 1999 No 2572), regs 24 and 25 (October 5, 1999)

Schedule 5 revoked by The Social Security (Claims and Payments and Adjudication) Amendment Regulations 1996 (S.I. 1996 No 2306), reg. 7 (October 7, 1996).

4.146

SCHEDULE 6   Regulation 22(3)

DAYS FOR PAYMENT OF LONG TERM BENEFITS

4.147

[¹ **Attendance allowance and disability living allowance**

1. Subject to the provisions of regulation 25 (payment of attendance allowance, constant attendance allowance and the care component of a disability living allowance at a daily rate) attendance allowance shall be payable on Wednesdays, except that the Secretary of State may in a particular case arrange for either allowance to be payable on any other day of the week and where it is in payment to any person and the day on which it is payable

The Social Security (Claims and Payments) Regulations 1987

is changed, it shall be paid at a daily rate of 1/7th of the weekly rate in respect of any of the days for which payment would have been made but for that change.]

2.[^{2}...]

Industrial injuries benefit

3. Any pension or allowance under [Part V of the Social Security Contributions and Benefits Act 1992], including any increase, shall be payable on Wednesdays.

Invalid care allowance

4. Invalid care allowance shall be payable on Mondays, except that where a person is entitled to that allowance in respect of a severely disabled person by virtue of regulation 3 of the Social Security (Invalid Care Allowance) Regulations 1976 the invalid care allowance shall be payable on Wednesdays.

Retirement pension

5. Retirement pension shall be payable on Mondays, except that—
   (a) where a person became entitled to a retirement pension before September 28, 1984, that pension shall be payable on Thursdays;
   (b) where a woman was entitled to a widow's benefit immediately before becoming entitled to a retirement pension, that pension shall be payable on Tuesdays;
   (c) where a woman becomes entitled to a retirement pension immediately following the payment to her husband of an increase of retirement pension in respect of her, the retirement pension to which she becomes entitled shall be payable on the same days as those upon which the retirement pension of the husband is payable;
   (d) the Secretary of State may, notwithstanding anything contained in the foregoing provisions of this paragraph, arrange for retirement pension to be payable on such other day of the week as he may in any particular case determine;
   (e) where, in relation to any person, any particular day of the week has become the appropriate day of the week for the payment of retirement pension, that day shall thereafter remain the appropriate day in his case for such payment.

Widowed mother's allowance and widow's pension

6. Widowed mother's allowance and widow's pension shall be payable on Tuesdays.

7. [^{1}...]

AMENDMENTS

1. The Social Security (Claims and Payments) Amendment Regulations 1991 (S.I. 1991 No 2741), reg. 27 (April 6, 1992)

2. The Social Security (Claims and Payments) Amendment Regulations 1999 (S.I. 1999 No 2358), reg. 2 (September 20, 1999)

SCHEDULE 7   Regulation 26

Manner and Time of Payment, Effective Date of [^{11} superseding decision] and Commencement of Entitlement in Income Support Cases

Manner of payment

4.148

1. Except as otherwise provided in these Regulations income support shall be paid in arrears in accordance with the award by means of an instrument of payment [^{8}or an instrument for benefit payment].

Time of payment

4.149

2. Income support shall be paid in advance where the claimant is—
   (a) in receipt of retirement pension; or
   (b) over pensionable age and not in receipt of [^{9}...] [^{7}incapacity benefit or severe disablement allowance and is not a person to whom section 126 of the Social Security Contributions and Benefits Act 1992 (trade disputes) applies] unless he was in receipt of income support immediately before the trade dispute began; or
   (c) in receipt of widow's benefit and is not registering or required to register as available for work or providing or required to provide medical evidence of incapacity for work; or

(S.I. 1987 No. 1968, Sched. 7) (as amended)

(d) a person to whom [¹section 23(a)] of the Social Security Act 1986 [SSCBA, s.127] applies, but only for the period of 15 days mentioned in that subsection.

[²**2A.**—(1) For the purposes of this paragraph— 4.150
(a) "public holiday" means, as the case may be, Christmas Day, Good Friday or a Bank Holiday under the Banking and Financial Dealings Act 1971 or in Scotland local holidays, and
(b) "office closure" means a period during which an office of the Department of Social Security or associated office is closed in connection with a public holiday.

(2) Where income support is normally paid in arrears and the day on which the benefit is payable by reason of paragraph 3 is affected by office closure it may for that benefit week be paid wholly in advance or partly in advance and partly in arrears and on such a day as the Secretary of State may direct.

(3) Where under this paragraph income support is paid either in advance or partly in advance and partly in arrears it shall for any other purposes be treated as if it was paid in arrears.]

[³**3.** (1) Subject to [⁷sub-paragraph (1A) and to] any direction given by the Secretary of 4.151
State in accordance with sub-paragraph (2), income support in respect of any benefit week shall, if the beneficiary is entitled to a relevant social security benefit or would be so entitled but for failure to satisfy the contribution conditions or had not exhausted his entitlement, be paid on the day and at the intervals appropriate to payment of that benefit.

[⁷(1A) Subject to sub-paragraph (2), where income support is paid to a person on the grounds of incapacity for work, that entitlement commenced on or after 13th April 1995, and no relevant social security benefit is paid to that person, the income support shall be paid fortnightly in arrears.]

(2) The Secretary of State may direct that income support in respect of any benefit week shall be paid at such intervals and on such days as he may in any particular case or class of case determine.

3A.—(1) Income support for any part-week shall be paid in accordance with an award 4.152
on such day as the Secretary of State may in any particular case direct.

(2) In this paragraph, "part-week" has the same meaning as it has in Part VII of the Income Support (General) Regulations 1987.]

4. [¹In this Schedule]— 4.153

"benefit week" means, if the beneficiary is entitled to a relevant social security benefit or would be so entitled but for failure to satisfy the contribution conditions or had not exhausted his entitlement, the week corresponding to the week in respect of which that benefit is paid, and in any other case a period of 7 days beginning or ending with such day as the Secretary of State may direct;

[¹"Income Support Regulations" means the Income Support (General) Regulations 1987;] and

"relevant social security benefit" means [⁹. . .] [⁷incapacity benefit], severe disablement allowance, retirement pension or widow's benefit.

Payment of small amounts of income support

5. Where the amount of income support is less than £1.00 a week the Secretary of State 4.154
may direct that it shall be paid at such intervals as may be specified not exceeding 13 weeks.

Commencement of entitlement to income support

6.—(1) Subject to sub-paragraphs (3) and (4), in a case where income support is pay- 4.155
able in arrears entitlement shall commence on the date of claim.

(2) [¹Subject to sub-paragraphs (2A) and (3)], in a case where, under paragraph 2, income support is payable in advance entitlement shall commence on the date of claim if that day is a day for payment of income support as determined under paragraph 3 but otherwise on the first such day after the date of claim.

[¹(2A) Where income support is awarded under regulation 17(3) for a definite period which is not a benefit week or a multiple of such a week entitlement shall commence on the date of claim.

(3) In a case where regulation 13 applies, entitlement shall commence on the day which is the relevant day for the purposes of that regulation [⁵except where income support is paid in advance, when entitlement shall commence on the relevant day, if that day is a day for payment as determined under paragraph 3 but otherwise on the first day for payment after the relevant day].]

The Social Security (Claims and Payments) Regulations 1987

(4) [¹...]

[⁹(5) If a claim is made by a claimant within 3 days of the date on which he became resident in a resettlement place provided pursuant to section 30 of the Jobseekers Act or at a centre providing facilities for the rehabilitation of alcoholics or drug addicts, and the claimant is so resident for the purposes of that rehabilitation, then the claim shall be treated as having been made on the day the claimant became so resident.]

(6) Where, in consequence of a further claim for income support such as is mentioned in sub-paragraph 4(7) of Schedule 3 to the Income Support (General) Regulations 1987, a claimant is treated as occupying a dwelling as his home for a period before moving in, that further claim shall be treated as having been made on the date from which he is treated as so occupying the dwelling or the date of the claim made before he moved in to the dwelling and referred to in that subparagraph, whichever is the later.

4.156

7.—(1) Subject to the following sub-paragraphs, where the amount of income support payable under an award is [¹¹changed by a superseding decision made on guard of a change of circumstances that superseding decision] shall have effect—

(i) where income support is paid in arrears, from the first day of the benefit week in which the change occurs or is expected to occur; or

(ii) where income support is paid in advance, from the date of the relevant change of circumstances, or the day on which the relevant change of circumstances is expected to occur, if either of those days is the first day of the benefit week and otherwise from the next following such day, and

for the purposes of this paragraph any period of residence in temporary accommodation pursuant to arrangements for training under section 2 of the Employment and Training Act 1973 [⁵or section 2 of the Enterprise and New Towns (Scotland) Act 1990] for a period which is expected to last for seven days or less shall not be regarded as a change of circumstances.]

(2) In the cases set out in sub-paragraph (3) [¹¹the superseding decision] shall have effect on the day on which the relevant change of circumstances occurs or is expected to occur.

(3) The cases referred in sub-paragraph (2) are where—

(a) income support is paid in arrears and entitlement ends, or is expected to end, for a reason other than that the claimant no longer satisfies the provisions of section 20(3)(b) of the Social Security Act 1986 [SSCBA, s.124(1)(b)];

(b) a child or young person referred to in regulation 16(6) of the Income Support Regulations (child in care of a local authority or detained in custody) lives, or is expected to live, with the claimant for part only of the benefit week;

(c) a claimant or his partner (as defined in regulation 2(1) of the Income Support Regulations) enters, or is expected to enter, a nursing home or a residential care home (as defined in regulation 19(3) of those Regulations) or residential accommodation (as defined in regulation 21(3)(a) to (d) of those Regulations) for a period of not more than 8 weeks;

(d) a person referred to in paragraphs 1, 2, 3 or 18 of Schedule 7 to the Income Support Regulations either—

(i) ceases, or is expected to cease, to be a patient, or

(ii) a member of his family ceases, or is expected to cease, to be a patient, in either case for a period of less than a week;

[⁶(dd) a person referred to in paragraph 8 of Schedule 7 to the Income Support Regulations either—

(i) ceases to be a prisoner, or.

(ii) becomes a prisoner;]

(e) a person to whom section 23 of the Social Security Act 1986 [SSCBA, s.126] (trade disputes) applies either—

(i) becomes incapable of work by reason of disease or bodily or mental disablement, or

(ii) enters the maternity period (as defined in section 23(2) of that Act) or the day is known on which that person is expected to enter the maternity period;

(f) during the currency of a claim the claimant makes a claim for a relevant social security benefit—

(i) the result of which is that his benefit week changes; or

(ii) under regulation 13 and an award of that benefit on the relevant day for the purposes of that regulation means that his benefit week is expected to change.

(S.I. 1987 No. 1968, Sched. 7) (as amended)

[¹¹ (4) A superseding decision made in consequence of a payment of income being treated as paid on a particular day under regulation 31(1)(b) or 39C(3) of the Income Support Regulations (date on which income is treated as paid) shall have effect on the day on which that payment is treated as paid.

(5) Where—
  (a) it is decided upon supersession on the ground of a relevant change of circumstances that the amount of income support is, or is to be, reduced; and
  (b) the Secretary of State certifies that it is impracticable for a superseding decision to have effect from the day prescribed in the preceding sub-paragraphs (other than where sub-paragraph (3)(f) or (4) applies),
that superseding decision shall have effect—
    (i) where the relevant change has occurred, from the first day of the benefit week following that in which that superseding decision is made; or
    (ii) where the relevant change is expected to occur, from the first day of the benefit week following that in which that change of circumstances is expected to occur.

(6) Where—
  (a) a superseding decision ("the former supersession") was made on the ground of a relevant change of circumstances in the cases set out in subparagraph (3)(b) to (f); and
  (b) that superseding decision is itself superseded by a subsequent decision because the circumstances which gave rise to the former supersession cease to apply ("the second change"),
that subsequent decision shall have effect from the date of the second change.

AMENDMENTS

1. The Social Security (Claims and Payments) Amendment Regulations 1988 (S.I. 1988 No. 522), reg. 10 (April 11, 1988).
2. Transfer of Functions (Health and Social Security) Order 1988 (S.I. 1988 No. 1843); The Social Security (Claims and Payments and Payments on account, Overpayments and Recovery) Amendment Regulations 1989 (S.I. 1989 No. 136), reg. 2(b) (February 27, 1989).
3. The Social Security (Medical Evidence, Claims and Payments) Amendment Regulations 1989 (S.I. 1989 No. 1686), reg. 8 (October 9, 1989).
4. The Social Security (Miscellaneous Provisions) Amendment Regulations 1990 (S.I. 1990 No. 2208), reg. 15 (December 5, 1990).
5. The Enterprise (Scotland) Consequential Amendments Order 1991 (S.I. 1991 No. 387), art. 2 and Sched. (April 1, 1991).
6. The Social Security (Miscellaneous Provisions) Amendment Regulations 1992 (S.I. 1992 No. 247), reg. 17 (March 9, 1992).
7. The Social Security (Claims and Payments) Amendment (No. 2) Regulations 1994 (S.I. 1994 No. 2943), reg. 14 (April 13, 1995).
8. The Social Security (Claims and Payments etc.) Amendment Regulations 1996 (S.I. 1996 No. 672), reg. 2(6) (April 4, 1996).
9. The Social Security (Claims and Payments) (Jobseeker's Allowance Consequential Amendments) Regulations 1996 (S.I. 1996 No. 1460), reg. 2(24) (October 7, 1996).
10. The Social Security (Miscellaneous) Amendment (No. 4) Regulations 1998 (S.I. 1998 No. 1174), reg. 8(3)(b) (June 1, 1998).
11. The Social Security Act 1998 (Commencement No. 12 and Consequential and Transitional Provisions) Order 1999 (S.I. 1999 No. 3178), Sched 6 (November 29, 1999)

GENERAL NOTE

Paragraph 1
One of the most significant changes from supplementary benefit is encapsulated in this provision. The general rule is that income support is paid in arrears,

4.157

rather than in advance. This is perhaps a further step in the integration of means-tested benefits (where the approach in the past has been to make the benefit available at the time of need) with other kinds of benefit. Exceptions to the general rule are in paras. 2 and 2A. The day of payment is dealt with in paras. 3 to 4.

If a claimant is without resources until the first payment of income support at the end of the first benefit week then there may be eligibility for a crisis loan under the social fund. Any resources actually available or which could be obtained in time to meet the need must be considered. A crisis loan may be made for living expenses (see Social Fund Directions 18–20).

On the changeover to income support from April 11, 1988, a special transitional payment of income support was to be paid after that date to bridge the gap from supplementary benefit paid in advance to income support paid in arrears (Income Support (Transitional) Regulations, reg. 7).

Paragraph 2

4.158   These categories of claimant are paid income support in advance. Apart from pensioners and most widows, those returning to work after a trade dispute are covered.

Paragraphs 3 and 4

4.159   Where a claimant meets the conditions of entitlement for one of the benefits listed as a "relevant social security benefit," the income support benefit week, pay-day and interval of payment is the same as for that benefit. Thus, those incapable of work are paid fortnightly in arrears (reg. 24(1)), although under reg. 24 the Secretary of State can arrange payment of incapacity benefit at other intervals (*e.g.* weekly), in which case income support follows suit. Otherwise the benefit week is to be defined by the Secretary of State. Income support paid for a definite period under reg. 17(3) need not be in terms of benefit weeks. Para. 3A provides that payments for part-weeks may be made as the Secretary of State directs.

Paragraph 6

4.160   The general rule for income support paid in arrears is that entitlement begins on the date of claim. The first payment on the pay day at the end of the first benefit week (or the second benefit week in the case of the unemployed) can thus be precisely calculated to include the right number of days. Payments can then continue on a weekly basis.

If income support is paid in advance, then, as for supplementary benefit, entitlement begins on the next pay day following the claim or coinciding with the date of claim.

Where the award is for a definite period under reg. 17(3) entitlement begins with the date of claim (sub-para. (2A)). Sub-para. (3) deals with the special case of advance awards. Sub-paras. (5) and (6) cover other special cases.

Paragraph 7

4.161   This provision deals with the date on which a review on the ground of a change of circumstances (Administration Act, s.25(1)(b); 1975 Act, s.104(1)(b)) or an anticipated change of circumstances (Administration Act, s.25(1)(c); 1975 Act, s.104(1)(bb)) takes effect. The review legislation does not specify the date on which a revised decision on review is to take effect.

Although sub-para. (1) refers to the amount of income support payable being changed, it is apparent from the rest of para. 7 that changes which result in entitlement to income support being entirely removed are equally covered. Sub-para. (1) establishes two general rules, which are subject to exceptions in sub-paras. (2) to (6).

The general rule where benefit is paid in arrears is that the change of circumstances is to take effect from the first day of the benefit week (defined in para. 4) in which it occurs, or is expected to occur (sub-para. (1)(i)). Where benefit is paid in advance the change takes effect from the first day of the benefit week which starts on the date of the change or in the next six days (sub-para. (1)(ii)). Sub-para. (3) lists cases in which the change of circumstances takes effect on the date of the change. The most important is (a), which covers the ending of entitlement (other than on capital grounds) where benefit is being paid in arrears. Sub-para. (4) deals with changes in most payments of income. Sub-para. (5) provides a general exception allowing the effect of a change to be deferred to the next benefit week following the normal day, if the Secretary of State certifies that it would be impracticable to follow the normal rule.

SCHEDULE 8   Regulation 23(1)(a)

ELECTION TO HAVE CHILD BENEFIT PAID WEEKLY

1. A person to whom benefit is payable for an uninterrupted period beginning before and ending after March 15, 1982 may make an election, in accordance with paragraph 3, that benefit be payable weekly after that date, if either—   4.162
   (a) he makes the election before the end of the 26th week from the day on which benefit was payable for the first four weeks in respect of which the Secretary of State made arrangements for four-weekly payment to the person entitled in accordance with regulation 21 or regulation 23(1)(b); or
   (b) he was absent from Great Britain on the March 15, 1982 for one of the reasons specified in paragraph 4 and he makes the election before the end of the 26th week of the period beginning with the first week in respect of which benefit became payable to him in Great Britain on his return.

2. Subject to paragraph 5, a person entitled to benefit may make an election, in accordance with paragraph 3, that benefit be paid weekly if he satisfies either of the following conditions:
   (a) he is a lone parent within the meaning set out in regulation 2(2) of the Child Benefit and Social Security (Fixing and Adjustment of Rates) Regulations 1976, or]
   (b) he, or his spouse residing with him or the person with whom he is living as husband and wife, is receiving income support, [²an incomed-based jobseeker's allowance], [³ or payment in accordance with an award of family credit or disability working allowance which was awarded with effect for a date falling before 5th October 1999.]

3. An election for benefit to be payable weekly under paragraphs 1 or 2 shall be effected by giving notice in writing to the Secretary of State delivered or sent to the appropriate office and shall be made when it is received.

4. An election may not be made under paragraph 1(b) unless the person's absence abroad on the March 15, 1982 was by reason of his being—
   (a) a serving member of the forces, as defined by regulation 1(2) of the Social Security (Contributions) Regulations 1979, or
   (b) the spouse of such a member, or
   (c) a person living with such a member as husband and wife.

5. Every person making an election for benefit to be paid weekly under paragraph 2 shall furnish such certificates, documents and such other information of facts as the Secretary of State may, in his discretion, require, affecting his right to receive payment of benefit weekly and in particular shall notify the Secretary of State in writing of any change of circumstances which he might reasonably be expected to know might affect the right to receive payment of benefit weekly, as soon as reasonably practicable after the occurrence thereof.

6. Where a person makes an election, in accordance with this regulation, for benefit to be paid weekly, it shall continue to be so payable—
   (a) in the case of an election under paragraph 1, so long as that person remains continually entitled to benefit, or
   (b) in the case of an election under paragraph 2, so long as that person remains continu-

The Social Security (Claims and Payments) Regulations 1987

ally entitled to benefit and the conditions specified in that paragraph continue to be satisfied.

7. A person who has made an election that benefit be payable weekly may cancel it at any time by a notice in writing delivered or sent to the appropriate office; and effect shall be given to such a notice as soon as is convenient.

AMENDMENTS

1. The Child Benefit, Child Support and Social Security (Miscellaneous Amendments) Regulations 1996 (S.I. 1996 No 1803), reg. 21 (April 7, 1997)

2. The Social Security (Claims and Payments) (Jobseeker's Allowance Consequential Amendments) Regulations 1996 (S.I. 1996 No 1460), reg. 2 (October 7, 1996)

3. The Social Security and Child Support (Tax credits) Consequential Amendments Regulations 1999 (S.I. 1999 No 2566), Sched. 8 (September 5, 1999).

SCHEDULE 9   **Regulation 35**

DEDUCTIONS FROM BENEFIT AND DIRECT PAYMENT TO THIRD PARTIES

Interpretation

1. [[20]—(1)] In this Schedule—

[[11]"the Community Charges Regulations" means the Community Charges (Deductions from Income Support (No. 2) Regulations 1990;
"the Community Charges (Scotland) Regulations" means the Community Charges (Deductions from Income Support) (Scotland) Regulations 1989;]
[[21]"contribution-based jobseeker's allowance" means any contribution-based jobseeker's allowance which does not fall within the definition of "specified benefit";]
"family" in the case of a claimant who is not a member of a family means that claimant;
[[11]"the Fines Regulations" means the Fines (Deductions from Income Support) Regulations 1992;]
[[6]"5 per cent of the personal allowance for the single claimant aged not less than 25" means where the percentage is not a multiple of 5 pence the sum obtained by rounding that 5 per cent to the next higher such multiple;
"hostel" means a building other than a residential care home or nursing home within the meaning of regulation 19(3) of the Income Support Regulations or residential accommodation within the meaning of regulation 21(3) of those Regulations—
   (a) in which there is provided for persons generally, or for a class of persons. accommodation, otherwise than in separate and self-contained premises, and either board or facilities of a kind set out in paragraph 4A(1)(d) below adequate to the needs of those persons and—
   (b) which is—
      (i) managed by or owned by a housing association registered with the Housing Corporation established by the Housing Act 1964; or
      (ii) managed or owned by a housing association registered with Scottish Homes established by the Housing (Scotland) Act 1988; or
      (iii) operated other than on a commercial basis and in respect of which funds are provided wholly or in part by a government department or a local authority; or
      (iv) managed by a voluntary organisation or charity and provides care, support or supervision with a view to assisting those persons to be rehabilitated or resettled within the community.
   (c) In sub-paragraph (iv) above, "voluntary organisation" shall mean a body the activities of which are carried out otherwise than for profit, but shall not include any public or local authority;
"housing authority" means a local authority, a new town corporation, Scottish Homes or the Rural Development Board for Rural Wales;]

(S.I. 1987 No. 1968, Sched. 9) (as amended)

"the Housing Benefit Regulations" means the Housing Benefit (General) Regulations 1987;

[20"housing costs" means any housing costs met under—
- (a) Schedule 3 to the Income Support Regulations but—
  - (i) excludes costs under paragraph 17(1)(f) of that Schedule (tents and tent sites); and
  - (ii) includes costs under paragraphs 17(1)(a) (ground rent and feu duty) and 17(1)(c) (rentcharges) of that Schedule but only when they are paid with costs under paragraph 17(1)(b) of that Schedule (service charges); or
- (b) Schedule 2 to the Jobseeker's Allowance Regulations but—
  - (i) excludes costs under paragraph 16(1)(f) of that Schedule (tents and tent sites); and
  - (ii) includes costs under paragraphs 16(1)(a) (ground rent and feu duty) and 16(1)(c) (rentcharges) of that Schedule but only when they are paid with costs under paragraph 16(1)(b) of that Schedule (service charges);]

[2"income support" means income support under Part II of the Social Security Act 1986 [SSCBA, Part VII] and includes transitional addition, personal expenses addition and special transitional addition as defined in the Income Support (Transitional) Regulations 1987;]

"the Income Support Regulations" means the Income Support (General) Regulations 1987;

"miscellaneous accommodation costs" has the meaning assigned by paragraph 4(1);

[20"mortgage payment" means the aggregate of any payments which fall to be met under—
- (a) Schedule 3 to the Income Support Regulations in accordance with paragraphs 6 to 10 of that Schedule (housing costs to be met in income support) on a loan which qualifies under paragraph 15 or 16 of that Schedule, but less any amount deducted under paragraph 18 of that Schedule (non-dependant deductions); or
- (b) Schedule 2 to the Jobseeker's Allowance Regulations in accordance with paragraphs 6 to 9 of that Schedule (housing costs to be met in jobseeker's allowance) on a loan which qualifies under paragraph 14 or 15 of that Schedule, but less any amount deducted under paragraph 17 of that Schedule (non-dependant deductions),

as the case may be.]

"personal allowance for a single claimant aged not less than 25 years" means the amount specified in [6paragraph 1(1)(e)] of column 2 of Schedule 2 to the Income Support Regulations [20or, as the case may be, paragraph 1(1)(e) of Schedule 1 to the Jobseeker's Allowance Regulations];

[2. . .]

"rent" has the meaning assigned to it in the Housing Benefit Regulations and, for the purposes of this Schedule
- (a) includes any water charges which are paid with or as part of the rent;
- (b) where in any particular case a claimant's rent includes elements which would not otherwise fall to be treated as rent, references to rent shall include those elements; and
- (c) references to "rent" include references to part only of the rent; and

[17"specified benefit" means—
- (a) in respect of any period during which benefit is paid by means of an instrument of payment, income support either alone or together with any [20. . .] incapacity benefit, retirement pension or severe disablement allowance which is paid by means of the same instrument of payment; and
- (b) in respect of any period during which benefit is paid by means of an instrument for benefit payment, income support and, where paid concurrently with income support, [20. . .], incapacity benefit, retirement pension or severe disablement allowance; [20 and
- (c) subject to sub-paragraph (2), jobseeker's allowance;]

[23but does not include any sum payable by way of child maintenance bonus in accordance with section 10 of the Child Support Act 1995) and the [24Social Security (Child Maintenance Bonus)] Regulations 1996;]]

[8"water charges" means charges for water or sewerage under Chapter I of Part V of the Water Industry Act 1991;]

437

The Social Security (Claims and Payments) Regulations 1987

[⁶"water undertaker" means a company which has been appointed under section 11(1) of the Water Act 1989 to be the water or sewerage undertaker for any area in England and Wales.]

[²⁰(2) For the purposes of the definition of "specified benefit" in sub-paragraph (1), "jobseeker's allowance" means—
  (a) income-based jobseeker's allowance; and
  (b) in a case where, if there was no entitlement to contribution-based jobseeker's allowance, there would be entitlement to income-based jobseeker's allowance at the same rate, contribution-based jobseeker's allowance.]

General

4.164 **2.**—(1) The specified benefit may be paid direct to a third party in accordance with the following provisions of this Schedule in discharge of a liability of the beneficiary or his partner to that third party in respect of—
  (a) housing costs;
  (b) miscellaneous accommodation costs;
[⁶(bb) hostel payments;]
  (c) service charges for fuel, and rent not falling within head (a) above;
  (d) fuel costs; [¹⁰. . .]
  (e) water charges; [¹⁰ and
  (f) payments in place of payments of child support maintenance under section 43(1) of the Child Support Act 1991 and regulation 28 of the Child Support (Maintenance Assessments and Special Cases) Regulations 1992.]

(2) No payment to a third party may be made under this Schedule under the amount of the beneficiary's award of the specified benefit is not less than the total of the amount otherwise authorised to be so paid under this Schedule plus 10 pence.

(3) A payment to be made to a third party under this Schedule shall be made, at such intervals as the Secretary of State may direct, on behalf of and in discharge (in whole or in part) of the obligation of the beneficiary or, as the case may be, of his partner, in respect of which the payment is made.

Housing costs

4.165 **3.**—(1) Subject to [⁷sub-paragraphs (4) to (6)] and paragraph 8, where a beneficiary who has been awarded the specified benefit or his partner is in debt for any item of housing costs which continues to be applicable to the beneficiary in the determination of his applicable amount, the [²⁵Secretary of State] may, if in [²⁷his] opinion it would be in the interests of the family to do so, determine that the amount of the award of the specified benefit ("the amount deductible") calculated in accordance with the following sub-paragraphs shall be paid in accordance with sub-paragraph 2(3).

(2) [⁷Subject to sub-paragraphs (2A) and (3)], the amount deductible shall be such weekly aggregate of the following as is appropriate:—
  (a) in respect of any debt to which sub-paragraph (1) applies, or where the debt owed is in respect of an amount which includes more than one item of housing costs, a weekly amount equal to 5 per cent. of the personal allowance for a single claimant aged not less than 25 [¹. . .] for such period as it is necessary to discharge the debt, so however that in aggregate the weekly amount calculated under this sub-paragraph shall not exceed 3 times that 5 per cent;
  (b) for each such debt—
    (i) in respect of mortgage payments, the weekly amount of the mortgage payment in that case; and
    (ii) for any other housing item, the actual weekly cost necessary in respect of continuing needs for the relevant items,
and the [²⁵Secretary State] may direct that, when the debt is discharged, the amount determined under sub-paragraph (b) shall be the amount deductible.

[⁷(2A) Where a payment falls to be made to a third party in accordance with this Schedule, and—
  (a) more than one item of housing costs falls to be taken into account in determining the beneficiary's applicable amount; and
  (b) in accordance with [¹⁶paragraph 4(8) or (11) or] [¹⁵paragraph 18] of Schedule 3 to the Income Support Regulations [²⁰or, as the case may be, paragraph 4(8) or (11) or paragraph 17 of Schedule 2 to the Jobseeker's Allowance Regulations] an amount

(S.I. 1987 No. 1968, Sched. 9) (as amended)

is not allowed or a deduction falls to be made from the amount to be met by way of housing costs,
then in calculating the amount deductible, the weekly aggregate amount ascertained in accordance with sub-paragraph (2) shall be reduced by an amount determined by applying the formula—

$$C \times \frac{B}{A}$$

where—
- A = housing costs;
- B = the item of housing costs which falls to be paid to a third party under this Schedule;
- C = the sum which is not allowed or falls to be deducted in accordance with [[15]paragraph 4(8) or (11) or paragraph 18] of Schedule 3 to the Income Support Regulations. [[20]or, as the case may be, paragraph 4(8) or (11) or paragraph 17 of Schedule 2 to the Jobseeker's Allowance Regulations]]

(3) Where the aggregate amount calculated under sub-paragraph (2) is such that paragraph 2(2) would operate to prevent any payment under this paragraph being made that aggregate amount shall be adjusted so that 10 pence of the award is payable to the beneficiary.

(4) Sub-paragraph (1) shall not apply to any debt which is either—
(a) in respect of mortgage payments and the beneficiary or his partner has in the preceding 12 weeks paid sums equal to [[8]or greater than] 8 week's mortgage payments due in that period; or
(b) for any other item of housing costs and is less than half the annual amount due to be paid by the beneficiary or his partner in respect of that item,
unless, in either case, in the opinion of the adjudicating authority it is in the overriding interests of the family that paragraph (1) should apply.

[[7](5) No amount shall be paid pursuant to this paragraph in respect of mortgage interest in any case where a specified part of relevant benefits—
(a) is required to be paid directly to a qualifying lender under regulation 34A and Schedule 9A; or
(b) would have been required to be paid to a body which, or a person who, would otherwise have been a qualifying lender but for an election given under paragraph 9 of Schedule 9A not to be regarded as such.

(6) In sub-paragraph (5), "specified part" and "relevant benefits" have the meanings given to them in paragraph 1 of Schedule 9A.]

Miscellaneous accommodation costs

[[9]4.—(1) Where an award of income support [[20]or jobseeker's allowance]—
(a) is made to a person in a residential care home or nursing home as defined in regulation 19(3) of the Income Support Regulations [[20]or, as the case may be, regulation 1(3) of the Jobseeker's Allowance Regulations], or
(b) includes an amount under Schedule 4 (persons in residential care and nursing homes) or paragraph 13 (residential accommodation) or 13A (Polish resettlement) of Schedule 7 to the Income Support Regulations [[20]or, as the case may be, Schedule 4 (applicable amounts of persons in residential care and nursing homes) or paragraph 15 of Schedule 5 (persons in residential accommodation) to the Jobseeker's Allowance Regulations],
(hereafter in this paragraph referred to as "miscellaneous accommodation costs")]
the [[25]Secretary of State] may determine that an amount of the specified benefit shall be paid direct to the person or body to whom the charges in respect of that accommodation are payable, but, except in a case to which paragraph [[6]13A] [[4]. . .] of Schedule 7 to the Income Support Regulations apply or where the accommodation is [[2]run by a voluntary organisation either for purposes similar to the purposes for which resettlement units are provided] or which provides facilities for alcoholics or drug addicts, only if the adjudicating authority is satisfied that the beneficiary has failed to budget for the charges and that it is in the interests of the family.

(2) [[2]Subject to sub-paragraph (3), in relation to miscellaneous accommodation costs the amount] of any payment of income support [[20]or jobseeker's allowance] to a third party determined [[2]under sub-paragraph (1)] shall be—
(a) the amount of the award under paragraph 1(1)(a) of Schedule 4 to the Income

4.166

Support Regulations excluding any increase under paragraph 2(2) of that Schedule [²⁰or, as the case may be, the amount of the award under paragraph 1(1)(a) of Schedule 4 to the Jobseeker's Allowance Regulations excluding any increase under paragraph 2(2) of that Schedule]; or

[⁹(aa) an amount equal to the amount of any payment the beneficiary is liable to make to the local authority under section 22 of the National Assistance Act 1948;]

[¹²(ab) in a case where the beneficiary does not have a preserved right within the meaning of regulation 19 of the Income Support Regulations and is not liable to make a payment to a local authority under section 22 of the National Assistance Act 1948 an amount equal to the amount of the award of income support [²⁰or jobseeker's allowance] payable to the claimant but excluding an amount, if any, which when added to any other income of the beneficiary (as determined in accordance with regulation 28 of the Income Support Regulations [²⁰or, as the case may be, regulation 93 of the Jobseeker's Allowance Regulations]) will equal the aggregate of the amount—

  (i) prescribed by paragraph 13 of Schedule 4 to the Income Support Regulations [²⁰or, as the case may be, paragraph 11 of Schedule 4 to the Jobseeker's Allowance Regulations]; and

  (ii) where the charge for the accommodation does not include the provision of all meals, an amount calculated under paragraph 2(2)(b) of [²⁰whichever of those Schedules is applicable].]

(b) [⁴. . .]

(c) the amount of the award [²under paragraph 13(1)(a), (b), (c), or (e)], [⁴or, as the case may be, 14] of Schedule 7 to [²⁰the Income Support Regulations or, as the case may be, under paragraph 15(1)(a), (b), (c) or (e) of Schedule 5 to the Jobseeker's Allowance Regulations] excluding the amount allowed by those paragraphs in respect of personal expenses,

as the case may be.

[²[²⁰(3) In relation to miscellaneous accommodation costs—

(a) where an award of income support is calculated in accordance with Part VII of the Income Support Regulations (calculation of income support for part-weeks) the amount of any payment of income support to a third party determined under sub-paragraph (1) shall be—

  (i) where the amount is calculated under regulation 73(1) of the Income Support Regulations, an amount calculated in accordance with sub-paragraph (2)(a) or, as the case may be, (c) above, divided by 7 and multiplied by the number of days in the part-week; or

  (ii) where the amount is calculated under regulation 73(2) of those Regulations, an amount calculated in accordance with regulation 73(4)(a)(i) or (b)(i) as the case may be; or

(b) where an award of jobseeker's allowance is calculated in accordance with Part XI of the Jobseeker's Allowance Regulations (part-weeks) the amount of any payment of jobseeker's allowance to a third party determined under sub-paragraph (1) shall be—

  (i) where the amount is calculated under regulation 150(1) of the Jobseeker's Allowance Regulations, an amount calculated in accordance with sub-paragraph (2)(a) or, as the case may be, (c) above, divided by 7 and multiplied by the number of days in the part-week; or

  (ii) where the amount is calculated under regulation 151(1) of those Regulations, an amount calculated in accordance with regulation 151(2)(a)(i) or (b)(i) as the case may be,

and no payment shall be made to a third party under this sub-paragraph where the Secretary of State certifies it would be impracticable to do so in that particular case.]

(4) Where the amount calculated under sub-paragraph (2) or (3) is such that paragraph 2(2) would operate to prevent any payment under this paragraph being made the amount shall be adjusted so that 10 pence of the award is payable to the beneficiary.]

[⁶**Hostel payments**

4A.—(1) This paragraph applies to a beneficiary if—

(a) he has been awarded specified benefit; and

(S.I. 1987 No. 1968, Sched. 9) (as amended)

(b) he or his partner has claimed housing benefit in the form of a rent rebate or rent allowance; and
(c) he or his partner is resident in a hostel; and
(d) the charge for that hostel includes a payment, whether direct or indirect, for one or more of the following services—
  (i) water;
  (ii) a service charge for fuel;
  (iii) meals;
  (iv) laundry;
  (v) cleaning (other than communal areas).

(2) Subject to sub-paragraph (3) below, where a beneficiary [8 . . .] has been awarded specified benefit the [25 Secretary of State] may determine that an amount of specified benefit shall be paid to the person or body to whom the charges referred to in sub-paragraph (1)(d) above are or would be payable.

(3) The amount of any payment to a third party under this paragraph shall be either—
(a) the aggregate of the amounts determined by a housing authority in accordance with the provisions specified in sub-paragraph (4); or
(b) if no amount has been determined under paragraph (a) of this sub-paragraph, an amount which the adjudicating authority estimates to be the amount which is likely to be so determined.

(4) The provisions referred to in sub-paragraph (3)(a) above are regulation 10(6) of, and paragraphs 1(a)(ii) and (iv), [81A, 2, 3 and either 5(1)(b) or 5(2) or 5(2A)] of Schedule 1 to, the Housing Benefit Regulations.

(5) Sub-paragraph (2) above shall not apply to a deduction in respect of a service charge for fuel if that charge is one such as is mentioned in paragraph 5(5) of Schedule 1 to the Housing Benefit Regulations (variable service charges for fuel) unless the [25 Secretary of State] is satisfied on the evidence available at the date of the determination that the amount of the charge does not normally alter more than twice in any one year.

[20(6) Where—
(a) an award of income support is calculated in accordance with regulation 73(1) of the Income Support Regulations (calculation of income support for part-weeks); or
(b) an award of jobseeker's allowance is calculated in accordance with regulation 150(1) of the Jobseeker's Allowance Regulations (amount of a jobseeker's allowance payable),
the amount of any payment of income support or, as the case may be, jobseeker's allowance payable to a third party determined under sub-paragraph (2) above shall be an amount calculated in accordance with sub-paragraph (3)(a) or (b) above divided by 7 and multiplied by the number of days in the part-week, and no payment shall be made to a third party under this sub-paragraph where the Secretary of State certifies that it would be impracticable to do so in that particular case.]]

Service charges for fuel, and rent not falling within paragraph 2(1)(a)

5.—(1) Subject to paragraph 8, this paragraph applies to a beneficiary if—
(a) he has been awarded the specified benefit; and
(b) he or his partner is entitled to housing benefit in the form of a rent rebate or rent allowance; and
(c) he or his partner has arrears of rent which equal or exceed four times the full weekly rent payable and—
  (i) there are arrears of rent in respect of at least 8 weeks and the landlord has requested the Secretary of State to make payments in accordance with this paragraph; or
  (ii) there are arrears of rent in respect of less than 8 weeks and in the opinion of the [25 Secretary of State] it is in the overriding interests of the family that payments shall be made in accordance with this paragraph.

(2) For the purposes of sub-paragraph (1) arrears of rent do not include—
(a) the 20 per cent of eligible rates excluded from a rent allowance under regulation 61 of the Housing Benefit Regulations (maximum housing benefit); or
(b) any amount falls to be deducted when assessing a person's rent rebate or rent allowance under regulation 63 of those Regulations (non-dependants).

(3) Subject to sub-paragraph (4), the adjudicating authority shall determine that a weekly amount of the specified benefit awarded to the beneficiary shall be paid to his or his partner's landlord if—

4.168

(a) he or his partner is entitled to housing benefit and in calculating that benefit a deduction is made under regulation 10(3) of the Housing Benefit Regulations in respect of either or both of water charges or service charges for fuel; and
(b) the amount of the beneficiary's award is not less than the amount of the deduction, and the amount to be paid shall be equal to the amount of the deduction.

(4) Sub-paragraph (3) shall not apply to a deduction in respect of a service charge for fuel if that charge is one such as is mentioned in paragraph 5(5) of Schedule 1 to the Housing Benefit Regulations (variable service charges for fuel) unless the adjudicating authority is satisfied on the evidence available at the date of the determination that the amount of the charge does not normally alter more than twice in any one year.

[20(5) A determination under this paragraph shall not be made without the consent of the beneficiary if the aggregate amount calculated in accordance with sub-paragraphs (3) and (6) exceeds a sum equal to 25 per cent of the applicable amount for the family as is awarded under—
(a) in the case of income support, sub-paragraphs (a) to (d) of regulation 17(1) (applicable amounts) or sub-paragraphs (a) to (e) of regulation 18(1) (polygamous marriages) of the Income Support Regulations; or
(b) in the case of jobseeker's allowance, paragraphs (a) to (e) of regulation 83 (applicable amounts) or sub-paragraphs (a) to (f) of regulation 84(1) (polygamous marriages) of the Jobseeker's Allowance Regulations.]

(6) In a case to which sub-paragraph (1) applies the adjudicating authority may determine that a weekly amount of the specified benefit awarded to that beneficiary equal to 5 per cent. of the personal allowance for a single claimant aged not less than 25 [6 . . .] shall be paid to his landlord until the debt is discharged.

[8(7) Immediately after the discharge of any arrears of rent to which sub-paragraph (1) applies and in respect of which a determination has been made under sub-paragraph (6) the adjudicating authority may, if satisfied that it would be in the interests of the family to do so, direct that an amount, equal to the amount by which the eligible rent is to be reduced by virtue of regulation 10(3) of the Housing Benefit Regulations in respect of charges for water or service charges for fuel or both, shall be deductible.]

Fuel costs

4.169 6.—(1) Subject to sub-paragraph (6) and paragraph 8, where a beneficiary who has been awarded the specified benefit or his partner is in debt for any item of mains gas or mains electricity [13including any charges for the reconnection of gas or disconnection or reconnection of electricity] ("fuel item") to an amount not less than the rate of personal allowance for a single claimant aged not less than 25 and continues to require that fuel, the [5 Secretary of State], if in its opinion it would be in the interests of the family to do so, may determine that the amount of the award of the specified benefit ("the amount deductible") calculated in accordance with the following paragraphs shall be paid to the person or body to whom payment is due in accordance with paragraph 2(3).

(2) The amount deductible shall, in respect of any fuel item, be such weekly aggregate of the following as is appropriate:—
[6(a) in respect of each debt to which sub-paragraph (1) applies ("the original debt"), a weekly amount equal to 5 per cent of the personal allowance for a person aged not less than 25 for such period as is necessary to discharge the original debt, but the aggregate of the amounts, calculated under this paragraph shall not exceed twice 5 per cent of the personal allowance for a single claimant aged not less than 25;]
(b) except where current consumption is paid for by other means (for example prepayment meter), an amount equal to the estimated average weekly cost necessary to meet the continuing needs for that fuel item, varied, where appropriate, in accordance with sub-paragraph (4)(a).

(3) [6 . . .]

(4) Where an amount is being paid direct to a person or body on behalf of the beneficiary or his partner in accordance with a determination under sub-paragraph (1) and [27 a decision which enbodies that determination falls to be reviewed]—
(a) where since the date of that determination the average weekly cost estimated for the purpose of sub-paragraph (2)(b) has either exceeded or proved insufficient to meet the actual cost of continuing consumption so that in respect of the continuing needs for that fuel item the beneficiary or his partner is in credit or, as the case may be, a further debt has accrued, the adjudicating authority may determine that

(S.I. 1987 No. 1968, Sched. 9) (as amended)

the weekly amount calculated under that paragraph shall, for a period of 26 weeks [⁸or such longer period as may be reasonable in the circumstances of the case], be adjusted so as to take account of that credit or further debt;
   (b) where an original debt in respect of any fuel item has been discharged the adjudicating authority may determine that the amount deductible in respect of that fuel item shall be the amount determined under sub-paragraph (2)(b).
(5) [⁶ . . .]
[²⁰(6) Subject to paragraph 8, a determination under this paragraph shall not be made without the consent of the beneficiary if the aggregate amount calculated in accordance with sub-paragraph (2) exceeds a sum equal to 25 per cent of the applicable amount for the family as is awarded under—
   (a) in the case of income support, sub-paragraphs (a) to (d) of regulation 17(1) (applicable amounts) or sub-paragraphs (a) to (e) of regulation 18(1) (polygamous marriages) of the Income Support Regulations; or
   (b) in the case of a jobseeker's allowance, paragraphs (a) to (e) of regulation 83 (applicable amounts) or sub-paragraphs (a) to (f) of regulation 84(1) (polygamous marriages) of the Jobseeker's Allowance Regulations.]
(7) [⁶ . . .]

[⁶**Water charges**
7.—(1) This paragraph does not apply where water charges are paid with rent; and in this paragraph "original debt" means the debt to which sub-paragraph (2) applies, [¹³including any disconnection or reconnection charges and any other costs (including legal costs) arising out of that debt].
   (2) Where a beneficiary or his partner is liable, whether directly or indirectly, for water charges and is in debt for those charges, the [²⁵ Secretary of State] may determine, subject to paragraph 8, that a weekly amount of the specified benefit shall be paid either to a water undertaker to whom that debt is owed, or to the person or body authorised to collect water charges for that undertaker, [⁸but only if [²⁷ the Secretary of State] is satisfied that the beneficiary or his partner has failed to budget for those charges, and that it would be in the interests of the family to make the determination.]
   (3) Where water charges are determined by means of a water meter, the weekly amount to be paid under sub-paragraph (2) shall be the aggregate of—
   (a) in respect of the original debt, an amount equal to 5 per cent of the personal allowance for a single claimant aged not less than 25 years; and
   (b) the amount which the [²⁵ Secretary of State] estimates to be the average weekly cost necessary to meet the continuing need for water consumption.
   (4) Where the sum estimated in accordance with sub-paragraph (3)(b) proves to be greater or less than the average weekly cost necessary to meet continuing need for water consumption so that a beneficiary or his partner accrues a credit, or as the case may be a further debt, the adjudicating authority may determine that the sum so estimated shall be adjusted for a period of 26 weeks [⁸or such longer period as may be reasonable in the circumstances of the case] to take account of that credit or further debt.
   (5) Where water charges are determined other than by means of a water meter the weekly amount to be paid under sub-paragraph (2) shall be the aggregate of—
   (a) the amount referred to in sub-paragraph (3)(a); and
   (b) an amount equal to the weekly cost necessary to meet the continuing need for water consumption.
   (6) Where the original debt in respect of water charges is discharged, the [²⁵ Secretary of State] may direct that the amount deductible shall be—
   (a) where water charges are determined by means of a water meter, the amount determined under sub-paragraph (3)(b) taking into account any adjustment that may have been made in accordance with sub-paragraph (4); an
   (b) in any other case, the amount determined under sub-paragraph (5)(b).
   (7) Where the beneficiary or his partner is in debt to two water undertakers—
   (a) only one weekly amount under sub-paragraph (3)(a) or (5)(a) shall be deducted; and
   (b) a deduction in respect of an original debt for sewerage shall only be made after the whole debt in respect of an original debt for water has been paid; and
   (c) deductions in respect of continuing charges for both water and for sewerage may be made at the same time.

The Social Security (Claims and Payments) Regulations 1987

[²⁰(8) Subject to paragraph 8 (maximum amount of payments to third parties), a determination under this paragraph shall not be made without the consent of the beneficiary if the aggregate amount calculated in accordance with sub-paragraphs (3), (4), (5) and (6) exceeds a sum equal to 25 per cent of the applicable amount for the family as is awarded under—

(a) in the case of income support, sub-paragraphs (a) to (d) of regulation 17(1) (applicable amounts) or sub-paragraphs (a) to (e) of regulation 18(1) (polygamous marriages) of the Income Support Regulations; or

(b) in the case of jobseeker's allowance, paragraphs (a) to (e) of regulation 83 (applicable amounts) or sub-paragraphs (a) to (f) of regulation 84(1) (polygamous marriages) of the Jobseeker's Allowance Regulations.]]

[¹⁰ **Payments in place of payments of child support maintenance**

4.171   7A—[¹²(1) Subject to paragraph (2), where [²⁶ the Secretary of State] (within the meaning of section 13 of the Child Support Act 1991) has determined that section 43 of that Act and regulation 28 of the Child Support (Maintenance Assessments and Special Cases) Regulations 1992 (contribution to maintenance by deduction from benefit) apply in relation to a beneficiary or his partner, the [²⁵ Secretary of State] shall (subject to paragraph 8), if it is satisfied that there is sufficient specified benefit in payment, determine that a weekly amount of that benefit shall be deducted by the Secretary of State for transmission to the person or persons entitled to it.]

(2) Not more than one deduction shall be made under [¹²sub-paragraph (1)] in any one benefit week as defined in paragraph 4 of Schedule 7.

(3) [¹⁸Subject to sub-paragraph (4),] the amount of specified benefit to be paid under this paragraph shall be the amount prescribed by regulation 28(2) of the Child Support (Maintenance Assessments and Special Cases) Regulations 1992 for the purposes of section 43(2)(a) of the Child Support Act 1991 [¹⁸ . . .].]

[¹⁸(4) Where, apart from the provisions of this sub-paragraph, the provisions of paragraphs 8(1) and 9 would result in the maximum aggregate amount payable equalling 2 times 5 per cent of the personal allowance for a single claimant aged not less than 25 years, the amount of specified benefit to be paid under this paragraph shall be one half of the amount specified in sub-paragraph (3).]

[²¹**Arrears of child support maintenance**

4.172   **7B.**—(1) Where a beneficiary is entitled to contribution-based jobseeker's allowance and an arrears notice has been served on the beneficiary, the Secretary of State may request in writing that an amount in respect of arrears of child support maintenance be deducted from the beneficiary's jobseeker's allowance.

(2) Where a request is made in accordance with sub-paragraph (1), the [²⁵ Secretary of State] shall determine that an amount in respect of the arrears of child support maintenance shall be deducted from the beneficiary's jobseeker's allowance for transmission to the person entitled to it.

(3) Subject to sub-paragraphs (4) and (5), the amount to be deducted under sub-paragraph (2) shall be the weekly amount requested by the Secretary of State, subject to a maximum of one-third of the age-related amount applicable to the beneficiary under section 4(1)(a) of the Jobseekers Act.

(4) No deduction shall be made under this paragraph where a deduction is being made from the beneficiary's contribution-based jobseeker's allowance under the Community Charges Regulations, the Community Charges (Scotland) Regulations, the Fines Regulations or the Council Tax Regulations.

(5) Where the sum that would otherwise fall to be deducted under this paragraph includes a fraction of a penny, the sum to be deducted shall be rounded down to the next whole penny.

(6) In this paragraph—

"arrears notice" means a notice served in accordance with regulation 2(2) of the Child Support (Arrears, Interest and Adjustment of Maintenance Assessments) Regulations 1992; and

"child support maintenance" means such periodical payments as are referred to in section 3(6) of the Child Support Act 1991.]

Maximum amount of payments to third parties

4.173   **8.**—(1) The maximum aggregate amount payable under [¹⁹paragraphs] 3(2)(a), 5(6), 6(2)(a)[⁶, 7(3)(a)[¹¹, 7(5)(a) and 7A]] [²² . . .] [¹¹, and [¹³regulation 7 of the Council Tax

(S.I. 1987 No. 1968, Sched. 9) (as amended)

Regulations] and regulation 6 of the Fines Regulations] shall not exceed an amount equal to 3 times 5 per cent. of the personal allowance for a single claimant aged not less than 25 years.

(2) The maximum [⁵aggregate] amount payable under [⁶paragraphs 3(2)(a), 5, 6 and 7] shall not without the consent of the beneficiary, exceed a sum equal to 25 per cent. of so much of the applicable amount for the family as is awarded under—

[²⁰(a) in the case of income support, sub-paragraphs (a) to (d) of regulation 17(1) (applicable amounts) or sub-paragraphs (a) to (e) of regulation 18(1) (polygamous marriages) of the Income Support Regulations; or

(b) in the case of a jobseeker's allowance, paragraphs (a) to (e) of regulation 83 (applicable amounts) or sub-paragraphs (a) to (f) of regulation 84(1) (polygamous marriages) of the Jobseeker's Allowance Regulations.]

(3) [²²...]

Priority as between certain debts

[¹¹9.—(1)(A) Where in any one week—   4.174

(a) more than one of the paragraphs 3 to 7A are applicable to the beneficiary; or
(b) one or more of those paragraphs are applicable to the beneficiary and one or more of the following provisions, namely, [²²...] regulation 2 of the Community Charges Regulations, regulation 2 of the Community Charges (Scotland) Regulations, regulation 6 of the Fines Regulations and regulation 7 of the Council Tax Regulations also applies; and
(c) the amount of the specified benefit which may be made to third parties is insufficient to meet the whole of the liabilities for which provision is made;

the order of priorities specified in sub-paragraph (1)(B) shall apply.

(1)(B) The order of priorities which shall apply in sub-paragraph (1)(A) is—

(za) [²²...]
(a) any liability mentioned in paragraph 3 (housing costs);
(b) any liability mentioned in paragraph 5 (service charges for fuel and rent not falling within paragraph 2(1)(a));
(c) any liability mentioned in paragraph 6 (fuel costs);
(d) any liability mentioned in paragraph 7 (water charges);
(e) any liability mentioned in regulation 2 of the Community Charges Regulations (deductions from income support), regulation 2 of the Community Charges (Scotland) Regulations (deductions from income support) or any liability mentioned in regulation 7 of the Council Tax Regulations (deductions from debtor's income support);
(f) any liability mentioned in regulation 6 of the Fines Regulations (deductions from offenders income support);
(g) any liability mentioned in paragraph 7A (payments in place of payments of child support maintenance).]

(2) As between liability for items of housing costs liabilities in respect of mortgage payments shall have priority over all other items.

(3) As between liabilities for items of gas or electricity the [²⁵ Secretary of State] shall give priority to whichever liability it considers it would, having regard to the circumstances and to any requests of the beneficiary, be appropriate to discharge.

(4) [⁶...]

AMENDMENTS

1. The Social Security (Claims and Payments) Amendment Regulations 1988 (S.I. 1988 No. 522), reg. 11 (April 11, 1988).

2. The Social Security (Claims and Payments and Payments on account, Overpayments and Recovery) Amendment Regulations 1989 (S.I. 1989 No. 136), reg. 2(7) (February 27, 1989).

3. The Social Security (Claims and Payments and Payments on account, Overpayments and Recovery) Amendment Regulations 1989 (S.I. 1989 No. 136), reg. 2(7) (April 10, 1989).

4. The Social Security (Medical Evidence, Claims and Payments) Amendment Regulations 1989 (S.I. 1989 No. 1686), reg. 9 (October 9, 1989).

The Social Security (Claims and Payments) Regulations 1987

5. The Social Security (Miscellaneous Provisions) Amendment Regulations 1990 (S.I. 1990 No. 2208), reg. 16 (December 5, 1990).
6. The Social Security (Miscellaneous Provisions) Amendment Regulations 1991 (S.I. 1991 No. 2284), regs. 12 to 20 (November 1, 1991).
7. The Social Security (Claims and Payments) Amendment Regulations 1992 (S.I. 1992 No. 1026), reg. 5 (May 25, 1992).
8. The Social Security (Miscellaneous Provisions) Amendment (No. 2) Regulations 1992 (S.I. 1992 No. 2595), reg. 8 (November 16, 1992).
9. The Social Security (Miscellaneous Provisions) Amendment (No. 2) Regulations 1992 (S.I. 1992 No. 2595), Sched. 1, para. 8 (April 1, 1993).
10. The Social Security (Claims and Payments) Amendment Regulations 1993 (S.I. 1993 No. 478), reg. 2 (April 1, 1993).
11. The Deductions from Income Support (Miscellaneous Amendments) Regulations 1993 (S.I. 1993 No. 495), reg. 2 (April 1, 1993).
12. The Social Security (Claims and Payments) Amendment (No. 3) Regulations 1993 (S.I. 1993 No. 2113), reg. 3 (September 27, 1993).
13. The Social Security (Claims and Payments) Amendment Regulations 1994 (S.I. 1994 No. 2319), reg. 7 (October 3, 1994).
14. The Social Security (Claims and Payments) Amendment (No. 2) Regulations 1994 (S.I. 1994 No. 2943), reg. 15 (April 13, 1995).
15. The Social Security (Income Support and Claims and Payments) Amendment Regulations 1995 (S.I. 1995 No. 1613), reg. 3 and Sched. 2 (October 2, 1995).
16. The Social Security (Income Support, Claims and Payments and Adjudication) Amendment Regulations 1995 (S.I. 1995 No. 2927), reg. 3 (December 12, 1995).
17. The Social Security (Claims and Payments etc.) Amendment Regulations 1996 (S.I. 1996 No. 672), reg. 2(7) (April 4, 1996).
18. The Child Support (Maintenance Assessments and Special Cases) and Social Security (Claims and Payments) Amendment Regulations 1996 (S.I. 1996 No. 481), reg. 5 (April 8, 1996).
19. The Child Support (Maintenance Assessments and Special Cases) and Social Security (Claims and Payments) Amendment Regulations 1996 (S.I. 1996 No. 481), reg. 6 (April 8, 1996).
20. The Social Security (Claims and Payments) (Jobseeker's Allowance Consequential Amendments) Regulations 1996 (S.I. 1996 No. 1460), reg. 2(26) (October 7, 1996).
21. The Social Security (Jobseeker's Allowance Consequential Amendments) (Deductions) Regulations 1996 (S.I. 1996 No. 2344), reg. 25 (October 7, 1996).
22. The Social Security and Child Support (Miscellaneous Amendments) Regulations 1997 (S.I. 1997 No. 827), reg. 7(2) (April 7, 1997).
23. The Social Security (Child Maintenance Bonus) Regulations 1996 (S.I. 1996 No. 3195), reg. 16(2) (April 7, 1997).
24. The Social Security (Miscellaneous Amendments) Regulations 1997 (S.I. 1997 No. 454), reg. 8(10) (April 6, 1997).
25. The Social Security Act 1998 (Commencement No. 11 and Transitional Provisions) Order 1999 (S.I. 1999 No. 2860), Sched. 3 (October 18, 1999).
26. The Social Security Act 1998 (Commencement No. 7 and Consequential and Transitional Provisions) Order 1999 (S.I. 1999 No. 1510), Sched. 4 (June 1, 1999).
27. The Social Security Act 1998 (Commencement No. 12 and Consequential and Transitional Provisions) Order 1999 (S.I. 1999 No. 3178), Sched. 6 (November 29, 1999).

(S.I. 1987 No. 1968, Sched. 9) (as amended)

DEFINITIONS

"adjudicating authority"—see reg. 2(1).
"beneficiary"—see Social Security Act 1975, Sched. 20.
"family"—see 1986 Act, s.20(11) (SSCBA, s.137(1)).
"instrument for benefit payment"—see reg. 2(1).
"jobseeker's allowance"—*ibid.*
"partner"—*ibid.*
"qualifying lender"—see Administration Act, s.15A(3).
Note that these references are only to phrases defined outside Sched. 9 itself. See para. 1 for definitions special to Sched. 9.

4.175

GENERAL NOTE

The provisions for part of weekly benefit to be diverted direct to a third party are of great importance in determining the actual weekly incomes of claimants. There have been changes in the provisions on fuel and water charges and Sched. 9A now deals specifically with payments of mortgage interest.
On deductions in respect of rent arrears under para. 5(6), *R(IS) 14/95* holds that the arrears must be proved, at least where these are disputed. In addition, the existence of an arguable counterclaim in possession proceedings is a matter that an adjudicating authority might properly take into account in deciding whether to exercise the discretionary power to make deductions under para. 5(6).

[¹SCHEDULE 9A

DEDUCTIONS OF MORTGAGE INTEREST FROM BENEFIT AND PAYMENT TO QUALIFYING LENDERS

Interpretation
1. In this Schedule—
[⁹...]

4.176

"Income Support Regulations" means the Income Support (General) Regulations 1987;
[⁷"relevant benefits" means—
  (a) in respect of any period during which benefit is paid by means of an instrument of payment, income support either alone or together with any [⁸...] incapacity benefit, retirement pension or severe disablement allowance which is paid by means of the same instrument of payment; and
  (b) in respect of any period during which benefit is paid by means of an instrument for benefit payment, income support and, where paid concurrently with income support, [⁸...] incapacity benefit, retirement pension or severe disablement allowance; [⁸and
  (c) income-based jobseeker's allowance;]
[¹⁰but does not include any sum payable by way of child maintenance bonus in accordance with section 10 of the Child Support Act 1995 and the [¹¹Social Security (Child Maintenance Bonus)] Regulations 1996;]]
"specified part" shall be construed in accordance with paragraph 3.

Specified circumstances
[⁵2. The circumstances referred to in regulation 34A are that—
[⁸(a) the amount to be met under Schedule 3 to the Income Support Regulations or, as the case may be, Schedule 2 to the Jobseeker's Allowance Regulations is determined by reference to the standard rate (whether at the full rate or a lesser rate) and, in the case of income support, to any amount payable in accordance with paragraph 7 of Schedule 3 to the Income Support Regulations;] and
  (b) the relevant benefits to which a relevant beneficiary is entitled are payable in respect of a period of 7 days or a multiple of such a period.]

4.177

447

The Social Security (Claims and Payments) Regulations 1987

SPECIFIED PART OF RELEVANT BENEFIT

4.178 3. [⁵(1) Subject to the following provisions of this paragraph, the part of any relevant benefits which, as determined by the [¹⁴ Secretary of State in accordance with regulation 34A, shall be paid] directly to the qualifying lender ("the specified part") is[⁸, in the case of income support,] a sum equal to the amount of mortgage interest to be met in accordance with paragraphs 6 and 8 to 10 of Schedule 3 to the Income Support Regulations (housing costs) together with an amount (if any) determined under paragraph 7 of that Schedule (transitional protection) [⁸or, in the case of jobseeker's allowance, a sum equal to the amount of mortgage interest to be met in accordance with paragraphs 6 to 9 of Schedule 2 to the Jobseeker's Allowance Regulations].]

(2) [⁵. . .]

(3) Where, in determining a relevant beneficiary's applicable amount for the purposes of income support [⁸or income-based jobseeker's allowance]—

(a) a sum in respect of housing costs is brought into account in addition to a sum in respect of mortgage interest; and

(b) in accordance with [⁵paragraph 4(8) or (11) or paragraph 18] of Schedule 3 to the Income Support Regulations [⁸or, as the case may be, paragraph 4(8) or (11) or paragraph 17 of Schedule 2 to the Jobseeker's Allowance Regulations] an amount is not allowed or a deduction falls to be made from the amount to be met under [⁸either of those Schedules],

then the specified part referred to in sub-paragraph (1) of this paragraph is the mortgage interest minus a sum calculated by applying the formula—

$$C \times \frac{B}{A}$$

[⁵where—

A = housing costs within the meaning of paragraph 1 of Schedule 3 to the Income Support Regulations [⁸or, as the case may be, paragraph 1 of Schedule 2 to the Jobseeker's Allowance Regulations];

B = the housing costs to be met in accordance with paragraphs 6 and 8 to 10 of Schedule 3 to the Income Support Regulations (housing costs) together with an amount (if any) determined under paragraph 7 of that Schedule (transitional protection) [⁸or, as the case may be, paragraphs 6 to 9 of Schedule 2 to the Jobseeker's Allowance Regulations]; and

C = the sum which is not allowed or falls to be deducted in accordance with paragraph 18 of Schedule 3 to the Income Support Regulations [⁸or, as the case may be, paragraph 4(8) or (11) or paragraph 17 of Schedule 2 to the Jobseeker's Allowance Regulations].]

(4) Where a payment is being made under a policy of insurance taken out by a beneficiary to insure against the risk of his being unable to maintain repayments of mortgage interest to a qualifying lender, then the amount of any relevant benefits payable to that lender shall be reduced by a sum equivalent to so much of the amount payable under the policy of insurance as represents payments in respect of mortgage interest.

(5) [⁹. . .]
(6) [⁹. . .]
(7) [⁵. . .]

(8) Where the amount of any relevant benefits to which a relevant beneficiary is entitled is less than the sum which would, but for this sub-paragraph, have been the specified part, then the specified part shall be the amount of any relevant benefits to which the relevant beneficiary is entitled less 10p.

Direct payment: more than one loan

4.179 4.—(1) This paragraph applies where the borrower is liable to pay mortgage interest in respect of two or more different loans.

[⁵(2) Subject to the following provisions of this paragraph, the Secretary of State shall pay to the qualifying lender or, if there is more than one qualifying lender, to each qualifying lender—

(a) a sum equal to the mortgage interest determined by reference to paragraph 12 of Schedule 3 to the Income Support Regulations [⁸or, as the case may be, paragraph 11 of Schedule 2 to the Jobseeker's Allowance Regulations] (standard rate) in respect of each loan made by that lender, plus

(S.I. 1987 No. 1968, Sched. 9A) (as amended)

(b) any amount payable in accordance with paragraph 7 of Schedule 3 to the Income Support Regulations (transitional protection) attributable to the particular loan; [⁹...]

(c) any additional amount attributable to a particular loan which may, under paragraph 3(5), have been taken into account in calculating the specified part.]

(3) If, by virtue of deductions made under either paragraph 3(2) or 3(3), the specified part is less than the amount payable by the borrower in respect of mortgage interest, then the sum payable under sub-paragraph (2)(a) shall be minus such proportion of the sum subtracted under those sub-paragraphs as is attributable to the particular loan.

(4) Paragraph 3(4) shall apply to reduce the amount payable to a qualifying lender mentioned in sub-paragraph (2) above as it applies to reduce the amount of any relevant benefits payable to a qualifying lender under paragraph 3.

(5) Where the specified part is the part referred to in paragraph 3(8), the Secretary of State shall pay the specified part directly to the qualifying lenders to whom mortgage interest is payable by the borrower in order of the priority of mortgages or (in Scotland) in accordance with the preference in ranking of heritable securities.

Relevant benefits

5.—[⁷...]   4.180

Time and manner of payments

6. Payments to qualifying lenders under regulation 34A and this Schedule shall be made in arrears at intervals of 4 weeks.   4.181

Fees payable by qualifying lenders

7. For the purposes of defraying the expenses of the Secretary of State in administering the making of payments under regulation 34A and this Schedule a qualifying lender shall pay to the Secretary of State a fee of [¹³£0.54] in respect of each payment made under regulation 34A and this Schedule.   4.182

Qualifying lenders

8. The following bodies and persons shall be qualifying lenders—   4.183
   (a) the Housing Corporation;
   (b) Housing for Wales;
   (c) Scottish Homes;
   (d) the Development Board for Rural Wales; and
   (e) any body incorporated under the Companies Act 1985 whose main objects include the making of loans secured by a mortgage of or a charge over land or (in Scotland) by a heritable security.

Election not to be regarded as a qualifying lender

9.—(1) A body which, or a person who, would otherwise be a qualifying lender may elect not to be regarded as such for the purposes of these Regulations by giving notice of election under this paragraph to the Secretary of State in accordance with sub-paragraphs (2) and (3).   4.184

(2) Subject to sub-paragraph (3), notice of election shall be given in writing—
   (a) in the case of the financial year 1992 to 1993, before 23rd May 1992 and shall take effect on that date; and
   (b) in the case of any other financial year, before 1st February in the preceding year and shall take effect on 1st April following the giving of the notice.

(3) A body which, or a person who, becomes a qualifying lender during a financial year and who wishes to elect not to be regarded as such for the purposes of these Regulations shall give notice of election in writing within a period of six weeks from the date on which the person or body becomes a qualifying lender.

(4) Regulation 34A shall not apply to a body which, or a person who, becomes a qualifying lender during a financial year for a period of six weeks from the date on which the person or body became a qualifying lender unless, either before the start of that period or at any time during that period, the person or body notifies the Secretary of State in writing that this sub-paragraph should not apply.

(5) A body which, or a person who, has made an election under this paragraph may revoke that election by giving notice in writing to the Secretary of State before 1st February in any financial year and the revocation shall take effect on the 1st April following the giving of the notice.

The Social Security (Claims and Payments) Regulations 1987

(6) Where a notice under this paragraph is sent by post it shall be treated as having been given on the day it was posted.

Provision of information

4.185   10.—(1) A qualifying lender shall provide the Secretary of State with information relating to—
- (a) the mortgage interest payable by a borrower;
- (b) the amount of the loan;
- (c) the purpose for which the loan is made;
- (d) the amount outstanding on the loan on which the mortgage interest is payable;
- (e) any change in the amount of interest payable by the borrower;

at the times specified in sub-paragraphs (2) and (3).

(2) [^{12}Subject to sub-paragraph (4),] the information referred to in heads (a), (b), (c) and (d) of sub-paragraph (1) shall be provided at the request of the Secretary of State when a claim for income support [^{8}or income-based jobseeker's allowance] is made and a sum in respect of mortgage interest is to be brought into account in determining the applicable amount.

(3) [^{12}Subject to sub-paragraph (4),] the information referred to in heads (d) and (e) of sub-paragraph (1) shall be provided at the request of the Secretary of State—
- (a) when a claim for income support [^{8}or income-based jobseeker's allowance] ceases to be paid to a relevant beneficiary; and
- (b) once every 12 months notwithstanding that, in relation to head (d), the information may already have been provided during the period of 12 months preceding the date of the Secretary of State's request.

[^{12}(4) Where a claimant or his partner is a person to whom either paragraph 1A of Schedule 3 to the Income Support (General) Regulations 1987 (housing costs) or paragraph 1A of Schedule 2 to the Jobseeker's Allowance Regulations 1996 (housing costs) refers, the information to which sub-paragraphs (2) and (3)(b) refer shall be provided at the request of the Secretary of State on the anniversary of the date on which the housing costs in respect of mortgage interest were first brought into account in determining the applicable amount of the person concerned.]

Recovery of sums wrongly paid

4.186   11—(1) Where sums have been paid to a qualifying lender under regulation 34A which ought not to have been paid for one or both of the reasons mentioned in sub-paragraph (2) of this paragraph, the qualifying lender shall, at the request of the Secretary of State, repay the sum overpaid.

(2) The reasons referred to in sub-paragraph (1) of this paragraph are—
- (a) that—
  - (i) the rate at which the borrower pays mortgage interest has been reduced [^{5} or the rate specified in paragraph 12 of Schedule 3 to the Income Support Regulations [^{8}or, as the case may be, paragraph 11 of Schedule 2 to the Jobseeker's Allowance Regulations] (standard rate) has been reduced] or the amount outstanding on the loan has been reduced, and
  - (ii) as a result of this reduction the applicable amount of the relevant beneficiary has also been reduced, but
  - (iii) no corresponding reduction was made to the specified part; or
- (b) subject to paragraph (3), that the relevant beneficiary has ceased to be entitled to any relevant benefits.

(3) A qualifying lender shall only repay sums which ought not to have been paid for the reason mentioned in sub-paragraph (2)(b) of this paragraph if the Secretary of State has requested that lender to repay the sums within a period of 4 weeks starting with the last day on which the relevant beneficiary was entitled to any relevant benefits.]

AMENDMENTS

1. The Social Security (Claims and Payments) Amendment Regulations 1992 (S.I. 1992 No. 1026), reg. 6 and Sched. (May 25, 1992).

2. The Social Security (Claims and Payments) Amendment (No. 3) Regulations 1993 (S.I. 1993 No. 2113), reg. 3 (September 27, 1993).

(S.I. 1987 No. 1968, Sched. 9A) (as amended)

3. The Social Security (Claims and Payments) Amendment (No. 3) Regulations 1994 (S.I. 1994 No. 2944), reg. 2 (April 1, 1995).
4. The Social Security (Claims and Payments) Amendment (No. 2) Regulations 1994 (S.I. 1994 No. 2943), reg. 16 (April 13, 1995).
5. The Social Security (Income Support and Claims and Payments) Amendment Regulations 1995 (S.I. 1995 No. 1613), reg. 3 and Sched. 2 (October 2, 1995).
6. The Social Security (Claims and Payments) Amendment (No. 2) Amendment Regulations 1996 (S.I. 1996 No. 2988), reg. 2 (April 1, 1997).
7. The Social Security (Claims and Payments etc.) Amendment Regulations 1996 (S.I. 1996 No. 672), reg. 2(8) (April 4, 1996).
8. The Social Security (Claims and Payments) (Jobseeker's Allowance Consequential Amendments) Regulations 1996 (S.I. 1996 No. 1460), reg. 2(27) (October 7, 1996).
9. The Social Security and Child Support (Miscellaneous Amendments) Regulations 1997 (S.I. 1997 No. 827), reg. 7(3) (April 7, 1997).
10. The Social Security (Child Maintenance Bonus) Regulations 1996 (S.I. 1996 No. 3195), reg. 16(2) (April 7, 1997).
11. The Social Security (Miscellaneous Amendments) Regulations 1997 (S.I. 1997 No. 454), reg. 8(10) (April 6, 1997).
12. The Social Security (Miscellaneous Amendments) (No. 4) Regulations 1997 (S.I. 1997 No. 2305), reg. 5 (October 22, 1997).
13. The Social Security (Claims and Payments) Amendment (No. 2) Regulations 1998 (S.I. 1998 No. 3039), reg. 2 (April 1, 1999).
14. The Social Security (Claims and Payments) Amendment Regulations 2000 (S.I. 2000 No. 1366), reg. 2, (June 14, 2000).

DEFINITIONS

"instrument for benefit payment"—see reg. 2(1).
"jobseeker's allowance"—*ibid.*
"mortgage interest"—see Administration Act, s.15A(4).
"qualifying lender"—see Administration Act, s.15A(3).
"relevant beneficiary"—see Administration Act, s.15A(1).

4.187

GENERAL NOTE

Para. 11 only authorises recovery of overpaid interest in the circumstances specified in sub-paras. (2) and (3).
In previous editions of this book it was suggested that it was not clear who decides that the interest has been overpaid, and that it was certainly arguable that this is the type of decision that should be made by an AO. *CIS 288/1994* and *CSIS 98/1994* hold that any decision regarding the recovery of any overpayment of mortgage interest from a qualifying lender is a matter for the Secretary of State, not the AO. The mortgage interest payment provisions are outside the scope of s.71 of the Administration Act (*CSIS 98/1994*). But in *CIS 5206/1995* the Commissioner reaches the opposite conclusion. He points out that under s.20 of the Administration Act all questions arising on claims or awards of benefit are to be determined by AOs, unless reserved to the Secretary of State (or other bodies). The question of whether the Secretary of State was *entitled to* recover a payment under para. 11 (which required consideration of whether the conditions in para. 11(2) were satisifed and also required calculation of the amount of the overpayment) was not reserved by para. 11 (or any other provision) to the Secretary of State. It therefore fell to be determined by an AO. Once it had been detemined that an overpayment was recoverable, the Secretary of State then had the discretion as to whether to request the lender to repay the

4.188

sum to him. The process of adjudication was thus the same as that under s.71 of the Act, even though the circumstances in which recovery could be sought were different. Furthermore, where any question of recovery under para. 11 arose, the claimant's award must first be reviewed and revised under s.25 (as had been accepted by the Court of Appeal in *Golding*, see below). If not, the Secretary of State would be bound to pay any overpayment recovered from the lender to the claimant, since the money recovered represented part of the benefit due to the claimant. There is thus a conflict between these decisions but *CIS 5206/1995* is cogently argued and it is suggested that it is to be preferred.

Note also that under para. 3(1) the amount that will be paid to the qualifying lender by the Secretary of State under reg. 34A (the "specified part") is defined by reference to the amount of mortgage interest met in the income support or JSA assessment. Thus, if the claimant disputes the amount that has been awarded for mortgage interest, or maintains that there are no grounds for reviewing the amount of an existing award, he will have a right of appeal to a SSAT in the normal way.

In *R. v. Secretary of State for Social Security, ex p. Golding, The Times*, March 15, 1996, there had been an overpayment of mortgage interest because the claimant's interest rate had reduced. Recovery of the overpayment was implemented by withholding current payments due to the claimant's building society. Brooke J. accepted the claimant's contention that the effect of sub-para. (2)(iii) was that the Secretary of State could only recover an overpayment where an AO had decided under sub-para. (2)(ii) that a claimant's applicable amount should be reduced but the amount paid to the lender had not changed. Thus the Secretary of State could not recover the overpayment from the lender under para. 11 in respect of the period before the AO's decision. Para. 11 only applied to overpayments made after that decision (*i.e.* as a result of the decision not being implemented). The result of this decision would have been that in effect recovery of any overpayment would be governed by s.71 of the Administration Act (since it would normally be the period between the reduction in the interest rate and the AO's review decision that would be in issue, assuming the AO's decision was implemented promptly).

The Court of Appeal on July 1, 1996 reversed Brooke J.'s decision. It was held that in sub-para. (2)(ii), the applicable amount means the amount as determined by the adjudication officer's assessment current at the date when the question is asked. Thus, once there had been a review with retrospective effect of Mr Golding's entitlement to take account of the reduction in interest rates, there was a reduction for that retrospective period in his applicable amount, so that sub-para. (2) (ii) was met. Sub-para. (2)(iii) was also met, because the "specified part" actually paid to the lender in that past period could not be reduced. Therefore the overpayment was repayable by the lender. The Court of Appeal rejected Mr Golding's argument that the condition in sub-para. (1) that the sums "ought not to have been paid" was not met, because the sums were paid under the current adjudication officer's assessment. The provisions were to be interpreted so as to be consistent with the clear statutory intention of dealing with the built-in problem under the direct payment scheme of annual retrospective notification of interest rate changes under para. 10. Note the circumstances in which there can be no review on a reduction in interest rates where the claimant's liability remains constant (Adjudication Regulations, reg. 63(7)).

The Court of Appeal did express concern over the method of recovery adopted by the Secretary of State, who had not asked the lender to repay the overpayment, but had made deductions from the amounts of mortgage interest currently being paid direct to the lender. The concern was that that might put the claimant into arrears. The Secretary of State accepted that he could only use the set-off method if it did not adversely affect the position of the claimant. The Court of Appeal considered that that would only be so if each deduction was accompanied in the lender's accounting system by a corresponding credit to the claimant's interest account. The DSS has apparently carried out a review of the arrangements for recovery of overpayments from lenders.

It should be noted that para. 11 only applies where the overpayment has occurred for the reasons specified in sub-para. (2) and not, for example, where it is due to an incorrect amount of capital being taken into account.

Until April 1997, deductions could be made from a claimant's benefit in respect of mortgage interest arrears under para. 3(5) (the April 1996 rate was £2.40). This is no longer possible if the lender is covered by the mortgage payments direct scheme. *CIS 15146/1996* holds that it was for the AO to decide whether such deductions were to be made and that a decision to alter the amount of a deduction had to be made by way of review, as this was not one of the up-rating changes which took effect automatically under section 159 of the Act without the need for a review decision. Furthermore, it was necessary to investigate whether there were in fact mortgage arrears, as the existence of arrears had to be proved in order to justify the deduction (see *R(IS)14/95* which had adopted the same approach in relation to deductions under para. 5 of Schedule 9). Adjudication officers and tribunals were not limited to determining whether there was sufficient income support in payment to sustain the direct payment.

The Social Security (Claims and Information) Regulations 1999

(S.I. 1999 No. 3108)

ARRANGEMENT OF REGULATIONS

1. Citation and commencement
2. Interpretation
3. Work-focused interview
4. Additional function of local authorities
5. Further provision as to claims
6. War pensions and child support
7. Holding information
8. Provision of information
9. Claims for Housing Benefit (*omitted*)
10. Consequential amendments to the Housing Benefit Regulations (*omitted*)
11. Claims for Council Tax Benefit (*omitted*)
12. Consequential amendments to the Council Tax Benefit Regulations (*omitted*)
13. Information
14. Purposes for which information may be used
15. Information supplied
16. Partners of claimants on jobseeker's allowance
17. Partners of claimants
18. Consequentials (*omitted*)

4.189

The Social Security (Claims and Information) Regulations 1999

SCHEDULES (*omitted*)

Citation and commencement

4.190　　1. These Regulations may be cited as the Social Security (Claims and Information) Regulations 1999 and shall come into force on 29th November 1999.

Interpretation

4.191　　2. In these Regulations,—
"the Act" means the Welfare Reform and Pensions Act 1999;
"the Child Support Acts" means the Child Support Act 1991 and the Child Support Act 1995;
"the Council Tax Benefit Regulations" means the Council Tax Benefit (General) Regulations 1992;
"the Housing Benefit Regulations" means the Housing Benefit (General) Regulations 1987;
"relevant authority" means a person within section 72(2) of the Act.

Work-focused interview

4.192　　3. A work-focused interview is an interview conducted for any or all of the following purposes—

(a) assessing a person's prospects for existing or future employment (whether paid or voluntary);

(b) assisting or encouraging a person to enhance his prospects of such employment;

(c) identifying activities which the person may undertake to strengthen his existing or future prospects of such employment;

(d) identifying current or future employment or training opportunities suitable to the person's needs; and

(e) identifying educational opportunities connected with the existing or future employment prospects or needs of the person.

Additional functions of local authorities

4.193　　4.—(1) A local authority to whom Part I of Schedule I to these Regulations applies may conduct a work-focused interview with, or provide assistance to, a person to whom paragraphs (2) and (3) apply, where the interview or assistance is requested or consented to by that person.

(2) This paragraph applies to a person who resides in a postcode district identified in Part I of Schedule 2 to these Regulations.

(3) This paragraph applies to any person making a claim for, or entitled to, any benefit specified in paragraph (4) and applies whether or not a person has had an interview in accordance with regulations made under section 2A of the Administration Act(d).

(4) The benefits specified in this paragraph are—

(a) income support;

(b) housing benefit;

(c) council tax benefit;

(d) widow's benefit;

(e) bereavement benefits;

(f) incapacity benefit;

(g) severe disablement allowance;

(h) invalid care allowance;

(i) a jobseeker's allowance;

(j) disability living allowance.

(5) For the purposes of paragraph (1), the request or consent may be made or given to—

(a) the local authority conducting the interview or giving the assistance;

(b) any person who, or authority which, may be specified as a designated authority for the purposes of section 2A(8) of the Administration Act; or

(c) a person designated an employment officer for the purposes of section 9 of the Jobseekers Act 1995.

(6) For the purposes of carrying out functions under paragraph (1), a local authority may in particular—

(a) obtain and receive information or evidence for the purpose of any work-focused interview to be conducted with that person;

(b) arrange for the work-focused interview to be conducted by one of the following—
   (i) the Secretary of State;
   (ii) a person providing services to the Secretary of State; or
   (iii) a person providing services to, or authorised to exercise any function of, the local authority;

(c) forward information supplied for the purpose of a work-focused interview to any person or authority conducting that interview;

(d) take steps to identify potential employment or training opportunities for persons taking part in work-focused interviews;

(e) conduct a work-focused interview;

(f) take steps to identify—
   (i) obstacles which may hinder a person in taking up employment or training opportunities;
   (ii) educational opportunities which may assist in reducing or removing such obstacles; and

(g) record information supplied at a work-focused interview.

The Social Security (Claims and Information) Regulations 1999

Further provisions as to claims

4.194   *Amends Claims as Payments Regulations 1987; the changes are incorporated in these regulations*

War Pensions and Child Support

4.195   **6.**—(1) Where a person resides in the area of an authority to which Part I or II of Schedule 1 to these Regulations refers, he may make a claim for a war pension, or submit an application under the Child Support Acts to any office displaying the one **one** logo (whether or not that office is situated within the area of the local authority in which the person resides).

(2) Any change of circumstances arising since a claim or application was made in accordance with paragraph (1) may be reported to the office to which that claim or application was made.

(3) The areas to which this paragraph refers are those areas which are within both—

(a) the area of a local authority identified in Part I or II of Schedule 1 to these Regulations, and

(b) a postcode area identified in Part I or II of Schedule 2 to these Regulations.

(4) A person making a claim or application to a participating authority in accordance with paragraph (1) shall comply with any requirements for the time being in force in relation to—

(a) claims for war pensions or applications under the Child Support Acts;

(b) the provision of information and evidence in support of such claims or applications,

as if those requirements also applied to the participating authority.

(5) A participating authority shall forward to the Secretary of State—

(a) any claim for a war pension or application under the Child Support Acts made in accordance with this regulation;

(b) details of changes of circumstances reported to the authority in accordance with this regulation; and

(c) any information or evidence—
   (i) given to the authority by the person making a claim or application or reporting the change of circumstances; or
   (ii) which is relevant to the claim or application or the change reported and which is held by the authority.

(6) For the purpose of this regulation, a "participating authority" means any authority or person to whom a claim or application may be made or change of circumstances reported in accordance with paragraphs (1) and (2).

(S.I. 1999 No. 3108, reg. 7)

Holding information

7. A relevant authority to whom information or evidence relating to social security matters is supplied or by whom such information or evidence is obtained, including information obtained under regulation 8(2), may—   4.196

(a) make a record of that information or evidence; and

(b) hold the information or evidence, whether as supplied or as recorded.

Provision of information

8.—(1) A relevant authority may give information or advice to any person, or to a person acting on his behalf, concerning—   4.197

(a) a claim he made, or a decision given on a claim he made, for a social security benefit or a war pension;

(b) an application he made, or a decision given on an application he made, under the Child Support Acts.

(2) For the purpose of giving information or advice in accordance with paragraph (1), a relevant authority may obtain information held by any other relevant authority.

Claims for Housing Benefit   4.198

Amends the Housing Benefit Regulations

10. Consequential Amendments to the Housing Benefit Regulations   4.199

Further amends the Housing Benefit Regulations

11. Claims for Council Tax Benefit   4.200

Amends the Council Tax Benefit Regulations

12. Consequential Amendments to the Council Tax Benefit Regulations   4.201

Further amends to the Council Tax Benefit Regulations

Information

13.—(1) A relevant authority which holds social security information may—   4.202

(a) use that information—
   (i) in connection with arrangements known as the New Deal and made under section 2 of the Employment and Training Act 1973(**a**);
   (ii) for any purpose to which regulations 3, 4 and 6 of these

Regulations, or any regulations inserted by these Regulations, apply; or

(iii) for purposes connected with the employment or training of the persons to whom it relates;

(b) supply the information—

(i) to any other relevant authority to enable that authority to carry out a work-focused interview or any function conferred upon it by these Regulations or by regulations inserted by these Regulations;

(ii) in so far as relevant for the purpose for which it is being provided, to any person in respect of whom the person undertaking the work-focused interview is notified has a vacancy or is about to have a vacancy in his employment or at his place of employment;

(iii) to any person (an "employment zone provider") to whom payments are made by the Secretary of State in accordance with section 60(5)(c)(i) of the Act (special schemes for claimants for jobseeker's allowance);

(iv) to any other relevant authority in connection with any scheme operated by, or any arrangements made by, the authority for purposes connected with employment or training;

(v) to any other relevant authority in connection with arrangements made under section 2 of the Employment and Training Act 1973 and known as the New Deal.

(2) An employment zone provider may supply to any other relevant authority information relating to any person participating in a scheme for which he receives a payment under section 60(5)(c)(i) of the Act where the information may be relevant to the person's benefit entitlement.

(3) Where the work-focused interview is undertaken by a relevant authority other than the authority which obtained the information, then the authority supplying the information shall, for the purposes of that interview, supply any other social security information held by them.

(4) A relevant authority which holds social security information may supply that information to any other relevant authority for the purposes of research, monitoring or evaluation in so far as it relates to any purpose specified in paragraph (5).

(5) The purposes specified in this paragraph are—

(a) work-focused interviews;

(b) any purpose for which regulations 3, 4 and 6 of these Regulations, or any regulations inserted by these Regulations, applies;

(c) any scheme or arrangements made by the Secretary of State connected with employment or training; and

(d) section 60 of the Act.

(S.I. 1999 No. 3108, reg. 13)

Purposes for which information may be used

14.—(1) The purposes for which information supplied in connection with matters referred to in paragraph (2) may be used are for— 4.203

(a) the processing of any claim for a social security benefit or a war pension or for an application for a maintenance assessment under the Child Support Act 1991;

(b) the consideration of any application for employment by a person to whom information is supplied in connection with any employment opportunity;

(c) the consideration of the training needs of the person who supplied the information;

(d) any purpose for which a work-focused interview may be conducted;

(e) the prevention, detection, investigation or prosecution of offences relating to social security matters.

(2) The matters referred to in this paragraph are—

(a) work-focused interviews; or

(b) any other provision in or introduced by these Regulations.

Information supplied

15. Information supplied to a person or authority under these Regulations— 4.204

(a) may be used for the purposes of amending or supplementing information held by the person or authority to whom it is supplied; and

(b) if it is so used, may be supplied to another person or authority, and used by him or it for any purpose, to whom or for which that other information could be supplied or used.

Partners of claimants on jobseeker's allowance

16.—(1) The social security information specified in paragraph (2) may be supplied by a relevant authority to the partner of a claimant for a jobseeker's allowance where— 4.205

(a) the allowance has been in payment to the claimant, or would have been in payment to him but for section 19 of the Jobseekers Act 1995 (circumstances in which jobseeker's allowance is not payable) for a period of six months or more;

(b) the allowance remains in payment or would be in payment but for that section; and

(c) the partner is being invited to attend the office of the relevant authority for purposes connected with employment or training.

The Social Security (Claims and Information) Regulations 1999

(2) The information which may be supplied is—

(a) that jobseeker's allowance is in payment to the claimant or would be in payment to him but for section 19 of the Jobseekers Act; and

(b) that payment has been made to the claimant or would have been so made but for section 19, for a period of at least six months.

(3) In this regulation, "partner" has the same meaning as in the Jobseeker's Allowance Regulations 1996 by virtue of section 1(3) of those Regulations.

Partners of claimants

4.206   **17.**—(1) The social security information specified in paragraph (4) may be supplied by a relevant authority to the partner of a claimant for a qualifying benefit where paragraph (3) is satisfied.

(2) The qualifying benefits are—

(a) a jobseeker's allowance;

(b) income support;

(c) incapacity benefit;

(d) severe disablement allowance.

(3) This paragraph is satisfied where—

(a) one or more of the qualifying benefits is or has been payable to the claimant;

(b) the benefit which is or has been payable includes an increase in respect of a partner; and

(c) the partner of the person entitled to the benefit payable is aged 50 or over.

(4) The information which may be supplied is—

(a) that a qualifying benefit is or has been payable to the claimant;

(b) the period for which the qualifying benefit has been payable.

(5) In this regulation, partner means one member of a married or unmarried couple of which the claimant is also a member.

Consequentials

4.207   **18.** *Omitted.*

(S.I. 1999 No. 1495)

Social Security Commissioners (Procedure) Regulations 1999

(S.I. 1999 No. 1495)

ARRANGEMENT OF REGULATIONS

PART I

GENERAL PROVISIONS

1. Citation and commencement
2. Revocation
3. Transitional provisions
4. Interpretation
5. General powers of a Commissioner.
6. Transfer of proceedings between Commissioners
7. Delegation of functions to authorised officers
8. Manner of and time for service of notices, etc.

PART II

APPLICATIONS FOR LEAVE TO APPEAL, APPEALS AND REFERENCES

9. Application to a Commissioner for leave to appeal
10. Notice of application to a Commissioner for leave to appeal
11. Determination of applications.
12. Notice of appeal
13. Time limit for appealing after leave obtained
14. References under the Forfeiture Act 1982.
15. Further provisions relating to references under the Forfeiture Act 1982
16. Acknowledgement of a notice of appeal or a reference and notification to each respondent

PART III

PROCEDURE

17. Represenation
18. Respondent's written observations
19. Written observations in reply
20. Directions
21. Procedure on linked case notice from the Secretary of State
22. Non-disclosure of medical evidence
23. Requests for hearings
24. Hearings
25. Summoning of witnesses
26. Withdrawal of applications for leave to appeal, appeals and references
27. Irregularities

PART IV

DECISIONS

28. Determinations and decisions of a Commissioner
29. Procedure after determination of a forfeiture rule question

30. Correction of accidental errors in decisions
31. Setting aside of decisions on certain grounds
32. Provisions common to regulations 30 and 31

PART V

APPLICATIONS FOR LEAVE TO APPEAL TO THE APPELLATE COURT

33. Application to a Commissioner for leave to appeal to the Appellate court

PART 1

GENERAL PROVISIONS

Citation and commencement

1. These Regulations may be cited as the Social Security Commissioners (Procedure) Regulations 1999 and shall come into force on June 1, 1999.

Revocation

2. The following Regulations are revoked to the extent that they relate to proceedings before the Social Security Commissioners—
   (a) the Social Security Commissioners Procedure Regulations 1987;
   (b) the Social Security Commissioners Procedure (Amendment) Regulations 1992; and
   (c) the Social Security (Adjudication) and Commissioners Procedure and Child Support Commissioners (Procedure) Amendment Regulations 1992; and

Transitional provisions

3—(1) Subject to paragraphs (2) to (3), these Regulations shall apply to all proceedings before the Commissioners on or after June 1, 1999.
  (2) In relation to any appeal or application for leave to appeal from any social security, disability or medical appeal tribunal constituted under Part II of the Social Security Administration Act 1992 these Regulations shall have effect with the modifications that—
   (a) "appeal tribunal" includes a reference to any such tribunal;
   (b) "chairman" includes a reference to a person authorised to deal with applications for leave to appeal under the Social Security (Adjudication) Regulations 1995;
   (c) "Secretary of State" includes a reference to an adjudication officer;
   (d) "section 14(7) of the Act" includes a reference to sections 23(6A) and 48(4A) of the Social Security Administration Act 1992, as modified by paragraph 4 of Schedule 6 to the Act;
   (e) "42 days" shall be substituted for "one month" in regulations 9(2) and 13(1); and
   (f) under regulation 9 a Commissioner may for special reasons

(S.I. 1999 No. 1495, reg. 3)

accept an application for leave to appeal even though the applicant has not sought to obtain leave to appeal from the chairman.

(3) Any transitional question arising under any application, appeal or reference in consequence of the coming into force of these Regulations shall be determined by a Commissioner who may for this purpose give such directions as he may think just, including modifying the normal requirements of these Regulations in relation to the application, appeal or reference.

Interpretation

4. In these Regulations, unless the context otherwise requires— 4.212
"the Act" means the Social Security Act 1998;
"appeal tribunal" means an appeal tribunal constituted under Chapter I of Part I of the Act;
"authorised officer" means an officer authorised by the Lord Chancellor, or in Scotland by the Secretary of State, in accordance with paragraph 6 of Schedule 4 to the Act;
"the chairman" for the purposes of regulations 9 and 10 means—
   (i) the person who was the chairman or sole member of the appeal tribunal which gave the decision against which leave to appeal is being sought; or
   (ii) any other person authorised to deal with applications for leave to appeal to a Commissioner against that decision under section 14 of the Act;
"Commissioner" has the meaning given in section 39 of the Act;
"forfeiture rule question" means any question referred to in section 4(1) or 4(1A) to 4(1H) of the Forfeiture Act 1982;
"legally qualified" means being a solicitor or barrister, or in Scotland, a solicitor or advocate;
"month" means a calendar month;
"office" means an Office of the Social Security Commissioners;
"party" means a party to the proceedings;
"proceedings" means any proceedings before a Commissioner, whether by way of an application for leave to appeal to, or from, a Commissioner, by way of an appeal or reference, or otherwise;
"respondent" means any person or organisation other than the applicant, appellant or person making the reference, who is one of the principal parties as defined in section 13 of the Act or is otherwise taking part in the proceedings in accordance with section 14 of the Act or regulation 24(6); and
"summons", in relation to Scotland, corresponds to "citation" and regulation 25 shall be construed accordingly.

General powers of a Commissioner

5.—(1) Subject to the provisions of these Regulations, a Commissioner may adopt any procedure in relation to proceedings before him. 4.213
(2) A Commissioner may—
(a) extend or abridge any time limit under these Regulations

(including, subject to regulations 9(3) and 13(2), granting an extension where the time limit has expired);
(b) expedite, postpone or adjourn any proceedings.

(3) Subject to paragraph (4), a Commissioner may, on or without the application of a party, strike out any proceedings for want of prosecution or abuse of process.

(4) Before making an order under paragraph (3), the Commissioner shall send notice to the party against whom it is proposed that it should be made giving him an opportunity to make representations why it should not be made.

(5) A Commissioner may, on application by the party concerned, give leave to reinstate any proceedings which have been struck out in accordance with paragraph (3) and, on giving leave, he may give directions as to the conduct of the proceedings.

(6) Nothing in these Regulations shall affect any power which is exercisable apart from these Regulations.

Transfer of proceedings between Commissioners

4.214 **6.** If it becomes impractical or inexpedient for a Commissioner to continue to deal with proceedings which are or have been before him, any other Commissioner may rehear or deal with those proceedings and any related matters.

Delegation of functions to authorised officers

4.215 **7.**—(1) The following functions of Commissioners may be exercised by legally qualified authorised officers, to be known as legal officers to the Commissioners—
 (a) giving directions under regulations 8 and 20;
 (b) determining requests for or directing hearings under regulation 23;
 (c) summoning witnesses, and setting aside a summons made by a legal officer, under regulation 25;
 (d) postponing a hearing under regulation 5;
 (e) giving leave to withdraw or reinstate applications, appeals or references under regulation 26;
 (f) waiving irregularities under regulation 27 in connection with any matter being dealt with by a legal officer;
 (g) extending or abridging time, directing expedition, giving notices, striking out and reinstating proceedings under regulation 5.

(2) Any party may, within 14 days of being sent notice of the direction or order of a legal officer, make a written request to a Commissioner asking him to reconsider the matter and confirm or replace the direction or order with his own, but, unless ordered by a Commissioner, a request shall not stop proceedings under the direction or order.

Manner of and time for service of notices, etc.

4.216 **8.**—(1) A notice to or other document for any party shall be deemed duly served if it is—

(S.I. 1999 No. 1495, reg. 8)

(a) delivered to him personally; or
(b) properly addressed and sent to him by prepaid post at the address last notified by him for this purpose, or to his ordinary address; or
(c) served in any other manner a Commissioner may direct.

(2) A notice to or other document for a Commissioner shall be delivered or sent to the office.

(3) For the purposes of any time limit, a properly addressed notice or other document sent by prepaid post, fax or email is effective from the date it is sent.

Part II

Applications for Leave to Appeal, Appeals and References

Application to a Commissioner for leave to appeal

9.—(1) An application to a Commissioner for leave to appeal against the decision of an appeal tribunal may be made only where the applicant has sought to obtain leave from the chairman and leave has been refused or the application has been rejected.

(2) Subject to paragraph (3) an application to a Commissioner shall be made within one month of notice of the refusal or rejection being sent to the applicant by the appeal tribunal.

(3) A Commissioner may for special reasons accept a late application or an application where the applicant failed to seek leave from the chairman within the specified time, but did so on or before the final date.

(4) In paragraph (3) the final date means the end of a period of 13 months from the date on which the decision of the appeal tribunal or, if later, any separate statement of the reasons for it, was sent to the applicant by the appeal tribunal.

4.217

General Note

Paragraph (1)
It may be arguable that a Commissioner could entertain an application from a claimant notwithstanding the claimant's failure to apply to a chairman if there was no full statement of reasons so that the chairman would be bound to refuse the application, particularly if further delay would mean that the claimant would miss "the final date", but see the wording of para. (3).

Paragraph (2)
A Commissioner may grant leave even if there is no full statement of the tribunal's reasons *(R(IS)11/99 CSDLA/536/99)*. However, the grounds upon which a tribunal may be found to have erred in law are limited in a case where there has been no request for a full statement of reasons and, in particular, a tribunal's decision cannot be set aside on the ground that the reasons given in the decision notice are inadequate *(R(IS)11/99)*.

Paragraph (3)
See the note to reg. 58(5) of the Social Security and Child Support (Decisions and Appeals) Regulations 1999.

Notice of application to a Commissioner for leave to appeal

10.—(1) An application to a Commissioner for leave to appeal shall be made by notice in writing, and shall contain—
  (a) the name and address of the applicant;
  (b) the grounds on which the applicant intends to rely;
  (c) if the application is made late, the grounds for seeking late acceptance; and
  (d) an address for sending notices and other documents to the applicant.

(2) The notice in paragraph (1) shall have with it copies of—
  (a) the decision against which leave to appeal is sought;
  (b) if separate, the written statement of the appeal tribunal's reasons for it; and
  (c) the notice of refusal or rejection sent to the applicant by the appeal tribunal.

(3) Where an application for leave to appeal is made by the Secretary of State he shall send each respondent a copy of the notice of application and any documents sent with it when they are sent to the Commissioner.

GENERAL NOTE

The requirements of this regulation are directory rather than mandatory and, although a failure to comply with them may delay a case or make it more difficult for the applicant to succeed, it will not invalidate the application *(R(IS)11/99)*. In particular, the requirement to send the written statement of the tribunal's reasons may be waived under reg. 27 if the applicant has not obtained one.

Determination of application

11.—(1) The office shall send written notice to the applicant and each respondent of the determination of an application for leave to appeal to a Commissioner.

(2) Subject to a direction by a Commissioner, where a Commissioner grants leave to appeal under regulation 9—
  (a) notice of appeal shall be deemed to have been sent on the date when notice of the determination is sent to the applicant; and
  (b) the notice of application shall be deemed to be a notice of appeal sent under regulation 12.

(3) If a Commissioner grants an application for leave to appeal he may, with the consent of the applicant and each respondent, treat and determine the application as an appeal.

Notice of appeal

12.—(1) Subject to regulation 11(2), an appeal shall be made by notice in writing and shall contain—
  (a) the name and address of the appellant;
  (b) the date on which the appellant was notified that leave to appeal had been granted;
  (c) the grounds on which the appellant intends to rely;

(d) if the appeal is made late, the grounds for seeking late acceptance; and
(e) an address for sending notices and other documents to the appellant.

(2) The notice in paragraph (1) shall have with it copies of—
(a) the notice informing the appellant that leave to appeal has been granted;
(b) the decision against which leave to appeal has been granted; and
(c) if separate, the written statement of the appeal tribunal's reasons for it.

GENERAL NOTE

As reg. 11(2) is invariably applied when a Commissioner grants leave, this regulation applies only where a chairman grants leave.

Time limit for appealing after leave obtained

13.—(1) Subject to paragraph (2), a notice of appeal shall not be valid unless it is sent to a Commissioner within one month of the date on which the appellant was sent written notice that leave to appeal had been granted.

(2) A Commissioner may for special reasons accept a late notice of appeal.

GENERAL NOTE

As reg. 11(2) is invariably applied when a Commissioner grants leave, this regulation applies only where a chairman grants leave.

References under the Forfeiture Act 1982

14.—(1) For the purposes of section 4(5) of the Forfeiture Act 1982, the Act shall be prescribed as a relevant enactment.

(2) Where in any case a forfeiture rule question arises, the Secretary of State shall refer it to a Commissioner to determine, and shall notify the person in relation to whom the question arises that he has done so.

(3) The reference shall be made in writing and shall include—
(a) a statement of the question for determination by the Commissioner and the relevant facts;
(b) the grounds upon which the reference is made; and
(c) the address for sending notices and other documents to the Secretary of State and to each respondent.

Further provisions relating to references under the Forfeiture Act 1982

15.—(1) Section 16(7) of the Act (tribunal of Commissioners to deal with cases involving questions of law of special difficulty) shall apply in relation to a forfeiture rule question as it applies in relation to an appeal under the Act.

(2) Sections 9 and 10 of the Act (revision and superseding of decisions) shall apply to a decision on a forfeiture rule question by a

Commissioner with the modification that those powers shall be exercisable only by a Commissioner, to whom any application for the purpose shall be made.

Acknowledgement of a notice of appeal or a reference and notification to each respondent

4.224   **16.** The office shall send—
(a) to the appellant or other person making the reference, an acknowledgement of the receipt of the notice of appeal or the reference;
(b) to each respondent, a copy of the notice of appeal or the reference.

GENERAL NOTE

In practice, whenever there is an appeal from a decision of a tribunal, the Office of the Social Security and Child Support Commissioners obtains the tribunal file from the clerk to the tribunal and a complete bundle of papers is made up from that file and copied to each party.

PART III

PROCEDURE

Representation

4.225   **17.** A party may conduct his case himself (with assistance from any person if he wishes) or be represented by any person whom he may appoint for the purpose.

Respondent's written observations

4.226   **18.**—(1) A respondent may submit to a Commissioner written observations on an appeal or reference within one month of being sent written notice of it.
(2) Written observations shall include—
(a) the respondent's name and address and address for sending documents;
(b) in the case of observations on an appeal, a statement as to whether or not he opposes the appeal, and
(c) in any case, the grounds upon which the respondent proposes to rely.
(3) The office shall send a copy of any written observations from a respondent to every other party.

Written observations in reply

4.227   **19.**—(1) Any party may submit to a Commissioner written observations in reply within one month of being sent written observations under regulation 18.

(2) The office shall send a copy of any written observations in reply to every other party.

(3) Where—

(a) written observations have been received from the respondent under regulation 18; and

(b) each of the principal parties expresses the view that the decision appealed against was erroneous in point of law,

a Commissioner may make an order under section 14(7) of the Act setting aside the decision and may dispense with the procedure in paragraphs (1) and (2).

Directions

20.—(1) Where a Commissioner considers that an application, appeal or reference made to him gives insufficient particulars to enable the question at issue to be determined, he may direct the party making the application, appeal or reference, or any respondent, to furnish any further particulars which may be reasonably required. 4.228

(2) In the case of an application for leave to appeal, or an appeal from an appeal tribunal, a Commissioner may, before determining the application or appeal, direct the tribunal to submit a statement of such facts or other matters as he considers necessary for the proper determination of that application or appeal.

(3) At any stage of the proceedings, a Commissioner may, on or without an application, give any directions as he may consider necessary or desirable for the efficient despatch of the proceedings.

(4) Without prejudice to regulations 18 and 19, or to paragraph (3), a Commissioner may direct any party before him to make any written observations as may seem to him necessary to enable the question at issue to be determined.

(5) An application under paragraph (3) shall be made in writing to a Commissioner and shall set out the direction which the applicant seeks.

(6) Unless a Commissioner shall otherwise determine, the office shall send a copy of an application under paragraph (3) to every other party.

Procedure on linked case notice from the Secretary of State

21. Any notice from the Secretary of State to a Commissioner under section 26 of the Act (Appeal involving issues that arise on appeal in other cases) shall be sent by notice in writing signed by or on behalf of the Secretary of State and shall identify, by its file reference or the names of the parties involved, each appeal or application to which it relates. 4.229

Non-disclosure of medical evidence

22.—(1) Where, in any proceedings, there is before a Commissioner medical evidence relating to a person which has not been disclosed to that person and in the opinion of the Commissioner the disclosure to that person of that evidence would be harmful to his health, such evidence shall not be disclosed to that person. 4.230

(2) Evidence such as is mentioned in paragraph (1)—

(a) shall not be disclosed to any person acting for or representing the person to whom it relates,
(b) in a case where a claim for benefit is made by reference to the disability of a person other than the claimant and the evidence relates to that other person, shall not be disclosed to the claimant or any person acting for or representing the claimant,

unless the Commissioner considers that it is in the interests of the person to whom the evidence relates to disclose it.

(3) Non-disclosure under paragraphs (1) or (2) does not preclude the Commissioner from taking the evidence concerned into account for the purpose of the proceedings.

GENERAL NOTE

See the note to reg. 42 of the Social Security and Child Support (Decisions and Appeals) Regulations 1999.

Requests for hearings

4.231
23.—(1) Subject to paragraphs (2), (3) and (4), a Commissioner may determine any proceedings without a hearing.

(2) Where a request for a hearing is made by any party, a Commissioner shall grant the request unless he is satisfied that the proceedings can properly be determined without a hearing.

(3) Where a Commissioner refuses a request for a hearing, he shall send written notice to the person making the request, either before or at the same time as making his determination or decision.

(4) A Commissioner may, without an application and at any stage, direct a hearing.

Hearings

4.232
24.—(1) This regulation applies to any hearing of an application, appeal or reference to which these Regulations apply.

(2) Subject to paragraph (3), the office shall give reasonable notice of the time and place of any hearing before a Commissioner.

(3) Unless all the parties concerned agree to a hearing at shorter notice, the period of notice specified under paragraph (2) shall be at least 14 days before the date of the hearing.

(4) If any party to whom notice of a hearing has been sent fails to appear at the hearing, the Commissioner may proceed with the case in that party's absence, or may give directions with a view to the determination of the case.

(5) Any hearing before a Commissioner shall be in public, unless the Commissioner for special reasons directs otherwise.

(6) Where a Commissioner holds a hearing the following persons or organisations shall be entitled to be present and be heard—
(a) the person or organisation making the application, appeal or reference;
(b) the claimant;
(c) the Secretary of State;

(d) a trade union, employers' association or other association which would have had a right of appeal under the Act;
(e) in cases concerning statutory sick pay and statutory maternity pay, the employer and the employee concerned;
(f) a person from whom it is determined that any amount is recoverable under or by virtue of section 71 or 74 of the Social Security Administration Act 1992; and
(g) with the leave of a Commissioner, any other person.

(7) Any person entitled to be heard at a hearing may—
(a) address the Commissioner;
(b) with the leave of the Commissioner, give evidence, call witnesses and put questions directly to any other person called as a witness.

(8) Nothing in these Regulations shall prevent a member of the Council on Tribunals or of the Scottish Committee of the Council in his capacity as such from being present at a hearing before a Commissioner which is not held in public.

Summoning of witnesses

25.—(1) Subject to paragraph (2), a Commissioner may summon any person to attend a hearing as a witness, at such time and place as may be specified in the summons, to answer any questions or produce any documents in his custody or under his control which relate to any matter in question in the proceedings.

(2) A person shall not be required to attend in obedience to a summons under paragraph (1) unless he has been given at least 14 days' notice before the date of the hearing or, if less than 14 days, has informed the Commissioner that he accepts such notice as he has been given.

(3) Upon the application of a person summoned under this regulation, a Commissioner may set the summons aside.

(4) A Commissioner may require any witness to give evidence on oath and for this purpose an oath may be administered in due form.

4.233

GENERAL NOTE

See the note to reg. 43 of the Social Security and Child Support (Decisions and Appeals) Regulations 1999.

Withdrawal of applications for leave to appeal, appeals and references

26.—(1) At any time before it is determined, an applicant may withdraw an application to a Commissioner for leave to appeal against a decision of an appeal tribunal by giving written notice to a Commissioner.

(2) At any time before the decision is made, the appellant or person making a reference to a Commissioner may withdraw his appeal or reference with the leave of a Commissioner.

(3) A Commissioner may, on application by the party concerned, give leave to reinstate any application, appeal or reference which has been

4.234

withdrawn in accordance with paragraphs (1) and (2) and, on giving leave, he may make directions as to the conduct of the proceedings.

GENERAL NOTE

Note that a Commissioner's approval is not required if an application for leave to appeal is to be withdrawn, whether it is an application for leave to appeal to a Commissioner or an application for leave to appeal to the Court of Appeal or Court of Session (see reg. 33(5)).

Irregularities

4.235   27. Any irregularity resulting from failure to comply with the requirements of these Regulations shall not by itself invalidate any proceedings, and the Commissioner, before reaching his decision, may waive the irregularity or take steps to remedy it.

Part IV

Decisions

Determinations and decisions of a Commissioner

4.236   28.—(1) The determination of a Commissioner on an application for leave to appeal shall be in writing and signed by him.

(2) The decision of a Commissioner on an appeal or reference shall be in writing and signed by him and, unless it was a decision made with the consent of the parties or an order setting aside a tribunal's decision under section 14(7) of the Act, he shall include the reasons.

(3) The office shall send a copy of the determination or decision and any reasons to each party.

(4) Without prejudice to paragraphs (2) and (3), a Commissioner may announce his determination or decision at the end of a hearing.

Procedure after determination of a forfeiture rule question

4.237   29. A Commissioner who has determined a forfeiture rule question shall remit the case to the Secretary of State for any necessary determination on entitlement to benefit to be made in the light of the decision on the forfeiture rule question.

Correction of accidental errors in decisions

4.238   30.—(1) Subject to regulations 6 and 32, the Commissioner who gave the decision may at any time correct accidental errors in any decision or record of a decision.

(2) A correction made to, or to the record of, a decision shall become part of the decision or record, and the office shall send a written notice of the correction to any party to whom notice of the decision has been sent.

(S.I. 1999 No. 1495, reg. 31)

Setting aside decisions on certain grounds

31.—(1) Subject to regulations 6 and 32, on an application made by any party, the Commissioner who gave the decision in proceedings may set it aside where it appears just to do so on the ground that—
  (a) a document relating to the proceedings was not sent to, or was not received at an appropriate time by, a party or his representative or was not received at an appropriate time by the Commissioner; or
  (b) a party or his representative was not present at a hearing before the Commissioner, or
  (c) there has been some other procedural irregularity or mishap.

(2) An application under this regulation shall be made in writing to a Commissioner within one month from the date on which the office gave written notice of the decision to the party making the application.

(3) Unless the Commissioner considers that it is unnecessary for the proper determination of an application made under paragraph (1), the office shall send a copy of it to each respondent, who shall be given a reasonable opportunity to make representations on it.

(4) The office shall send each party written notice of a determination of an application to set aside a decision and the reasons for it.

4.239

GENERAL NOTE

Paragraph (1)
It is a general principle that final decisions of courts cannot be set aside save for the purpose of correcting accidental error "which cannot really be disputed" and this approach was adopted in relation to Commissioners' decisions in *R(S) 3/89*. It is based on the view that it is in the interests of justice that there be finality to litigation. However, in *R(U) 3/89*, it was held that a decision could not be set aside unless there had been a procedural irregularity and that the power to set aside could not be used to correct other obvious errors. The phrase in the current legislation refers to "mishap" as well as "irregularity" and in, *CCS/910/99*, the Commissioner, following the analogy with the courts suggested in *R(S) 3/89*, drew a distinction between final decisions, which should be set aside only rarely, and refusals of leave to appeal which might more readily be set aside where a Commissioner recognised that he or she had overlooked a statutory provision or had based a decision on a misunderstanding of the evidence or where the applicant produced further evidence after the decision had been given which he or she could not reasonably have been expected to produce earlier.

Paragraph (2)
The time can be extended (see reg. 5(2)(a)).

Paragraph (3)
A Commissioner will usually regard it as necessary to obtain the views of the other parties unless he or she is minded to dismiss the application, in which case it is likely to be unnecessary.

Provisions common to regulations 30 and 31

32.—(1) In regulations 30 and 31, the word "decision" shall include determinations of applications for leave to appeal, orders setting aside

4.240

tribunal decisions under section 14(7) of the Act and decisions on appeals and references.

(2) There shall be no appeal against a correction or a refusal to correct under regulation 30 or a determination given under regulation 31.

PART V

APPLICATIONS FOR LEAVE TO APPEAL TO THE APPELLATE COURT

Application to a Commissioner for leave to appeal to the Appellate Court

4.241   **33.**—(1) Subject to paragraph (2), an application to a Commissioner under section 15 of the Act for leave to appeal against a decision of a Commissioner shall be made in writing, stating the grounds of the application, within three months from the date on which the applicant was sent written notice of the decision.

(2) Subject to a direction by a Commissioner, in calculating any time for applying for leave to appeal under paragraph (1), there shall be disregarded any day before the day—
  (a) on which notice was sent or a correction of a decision or the record of it under regulation 30; or
  (b) on which notice was sent of a determination that a decision shall not be set aside under regulation 31.

(3) Regulation 33 of the Social Security (Claims and Payments) Regulations 1987 (persons unable to act) shall apply to the right of appeal conferred by section 15 of the Act (appeal from Commissioner on point of law) as it applies to rights arising under the Social Security Acts generally.

(4) A person in respect of whom a forfeiture rule question arises and the Secretary of State, shall be authorised to apply for leave to appeal from a Commissioner's decision on a forfeiture rule question.

(5) Regulations 26(1) and 26(3) shall apply to an application to a Commissioner for leave to appeal from a Commissioner's decision as they apply to the proceedings in that regulation.

GENERAL NOTE

The three month time limit may be extended by the Commissioner under reg. 5(2)(a) but if the Commissioner refuses to do so, the court cannot extend the time (*White v. Chief Adjudication Officer* [1986] 2 All E.R. 905 (also reported as an appendix to *R(S) 8/85*)). It would be necessary to challenge the Commissioner's refusal by way of an application for judicial review. For the criteria for granting leave to appeal and the procedure for renewing an application in the court, see the note to s. 15 of the Social Security Act 1998.

(S.I. 1999 No. 991)

Social Security and Child Support (Decisions and Appeals) Regulations 1999

(S.I. 1999 No. 991)

ARRANGEMENT OF REGULATIONS

PART I

GENERAL

1. Citation, commencement and interpretation.   4.242
2. Service of notices or documents.

PART II

REVISIONS, SUPERSESSIONS AND OTHER MATTERS SOCIAL SECURITY

CHAPTER I

REVISIONS

3. Revision of decisions.
4. Late application for a revision.
5. Date from which a decision revised under section 9 takes effect.

CHAPTER II

SUPERSESSIONS

6. Supersession of decisions.
7. Date from which a decision superseded under section 10 takes effect.
8. Effective date for late notifications of change of circumstances.

CHAPTER III

OTHER MATTERS

9. Certificates of recoverable benefits.
10. Effect of a determination as to capacity for work.
11. Secretary of State to determine certain matters.
11A. Issues for decision by officers of Inland Revenue.
12. Decisions of the Secretary of State relating to industrial injuries benefits.
13. Income support and social fund determinations on incomplete evidence.
14. Effect of alteration in the component rates of income support and jobseeker's allowance.
15. Jobseeker's allowance determinations on incomplete evidence.

Social Security and Child Support (Decisions and Appeals) Regulations 1999

PART III

SUSPENSION, TERMINATION AND OTHER MATTERS

CHAPTER I

SUSPENSION AND TERMINATION

16. Suspension in prescribed cases.
17. Provision of information or evidence.
18. Termination in cases of failure to furnish information or evidence.
19. Suspension and termination for failure to submit to medical examination.
20. Making of payments which have been suspended.

CHAPTER II

OTHER MATTERS

21. Decisions involving issues that arise on appeal in other cases.
22. Appeals involving issues that arise in other cases.
23. *Omitted*
24. *Omitted*

PART IV

RIGHTS OF APPEAL AND PROCEDURE FOR BRINGING APPEALS

CHAPTER I

GENERAL

General appeals matters not including child support appeals

25. Other persons with a right of appeal.
26. Decisions against which an appeal lies.
27. Decisions against which no appeal lies.
28. Notice of decision against which appeal lies.
29. Further particulars required relating to certificate of recoverable benefits appeals or applications.

General appeals matters including child support appeals

30. Appeal against a decision which has been revised.
31. Time within which an appeal is to be brought.
32. Late appeals.
33. Making of appeals and applications.
34. Death of a party to an appeal.

(S.I. 1999 No. 991)

Part V

Appeal Tribunals for Social Security Contracting Out of Pensions, Vaccine Damage and Child Support

Chapter I

The Panel and Appeal Tribunals

35. Persons appointed to the panel.
36. Composition of appeal tribunals.
37. Assignment of clerks to appeal tribunals: function of clerks.

Chapter II

Procedure in Connection with Determination and Referrals of Appeals

38. Consideration and determination of appeals and referrals.
38A. Appeals raising issues for decision by officers of Inland Revenue.
39. Directions concerning oral hearings.
40. Withdrawal of appeal or referral.
41. Medical examination required by appeal tribunal.
42. Non-disclosure of medical advice or evidence.
43. Summoning of witnesses and administration of oaths.
44. *Omitted*
45. *Omitted*

Chapter III

Striking Out Appeals

46. Appeals which may be struck out.
47. Reinstatement of struck out appeals.
48. Misconceived appeals.

Chapter IV

Oral Hearings

49. Procedure at oral hearings.
50. Manner of providing expert assistance.
51. Postponement and adjournment.
52. Physical examination at oral hearings.

Social Security and Child Support (Decisions and Appeals) Regulations 1999

Chapter V

Decisions of Appeal Tribunals and Related Matters

Appeal tribunals decisions

53. Decisions of appeal tribunals.
54. Late applications for statement of reasons of tribunal decision.
55. Record of tribunal proceedings.
56. Correction of accidental errors.
57. Setting aside decisions on certain grounds.

Applications for leave to appeal to Commissioner (not including child support)

58. Application for leave to appeal to a Commissioner from an appeal tribunal.

Part VI

Revocations

59. Revocations.

Schedules

Schedule 1 Provisions conferring powers exercised in making these Regulations.
Schedule 2 Decisions against which no appeal lies.
Schedule 3 Qualifications of Persons Appointed to the Panel.
Schedule 4 Revocations.

Part I

General

Citation, commencement and interpretation

4.243   **1.**—(1) These Regulations may be cited as the Social Security and Child Support (Decisions and Appeals) Regulations 1999.
(2) These Regulations shall come into force—
(a) in so far as they relate to child support and for the purposes of this regulation and regulation 2 on June 1, 1999;
(b) in so far as they relate to—
   (i) industrial injuries benefit, guardian's allowance and child benefit; and
   (ii) a decision made under the Pension Schemes Act 1993 by virtue of section 170(2) of that Act;
on July 5, 1999;
(c) in so far as they relate to retirement pension, widow's benefit,

incapacity benefit, severe disablement allowance and maternity allowance, on September 6, 1999;

(d) in so far as they relate to [³ working families' tax credit and disabled person's tax credit], on October 5, 1999;

(e) in so far as they relate to attendance allowance, disability living allowance, invalid care allowance, jobseeker's allowance, credits of contributions or earnings, home responsibilities protection and vaccine damage payments, on October 18, 1999; and

(f) for all remaining purposes, on November 29, 1999.

(3) In these Regulations, unless the context otherwise requires—

"the Act" means the Social Security Act 1998;

"the 1997 Act" means the Social Security (Recovery of Benefits) Act 1997;

"the Claims and Payments Regulations" means the Social Security (Claims and Payments) Regulations 1987;

"appeal" means an appeal to an appeal tribunal;

[¹"the Board" means the Commissioners of Inland Revenue;]

"claimant" means—

(a) any person who is a claimant for the purposes of section 191 of the Administration Act or section 35(1) of the Jobseekers Act or any other person from whom benefit is alleged to be recoverable; and

(b) any person subject to a decision of [¹ an officer of the Board] under the Pension Schemes Act 1993;

"clerk to the appeal tribunal" means a clerk assigned to the appeal tribunal in accordance with regulation 37;

"the date of notification" means—

(a) the date that notification of a decision of the Secretary of State [³ or an officer of the Board] is treated as having been given or sent in accordance with regulation 2(b); or

(b) in the case of a social fund payment arising in accordance with regulations made under section 138(2) of the Contributions and Benefits Act—

  (i) the date seven days after the date on which the Secretary of State makes his decision to make a payment to a person to meet expenses for heating;

  (ii) where a person collects the instrument of payment at a post office, the date the instrument is collected;

  (iii) where an instrument of payment is sent to a post office for collection but is not collected and a replacement instrument is issued, the date on which the replacement instrument is issued; or

  (iv) where a person questions his failure to be awarded a payment for expenses for heating, the date on which the notification of the Secretary of State's decision given in response to that question is issued;

[⁴ "designated authority" has the meaning it has in regulation 2(1) of the Work-focused Interviews Regulations;]

"financially qualified panel member" means a panel member who satisfies the requirements of paragraph 4 of Schedule 3;

"the Income Support Regulations" means the Income Support (General) Regulations 1987;

"the Jobseeker's Allowance Regulations" means the Jobseeker's Allowance Regulations 1996;

"legally qualified panel member" means a panel member who satisfies the requirements of paragraph 1 of Schedule 3;

"medically qualified panel member" means a panel member who satisfies the requirements of paragraph 2 of Schedule 3;

"misconceived appeal" means an appeal which is—
  (a) frivolous or vexatious; or
  (b) obviously unsustainable and has no prospect of success.
other than an out of jurisdiction appeal;

[4 "official error" means an error made by—
  (a) an officer of the Department of Social Security, the Board or the Department for Education and Employment acting as such which no person outside any of those Departments caused or to which no person outside any of those Departments materially contributed;
  (b) a person employed by a designated authority acting on behalf of the authority, which no person outside that authority caused or to which no person outside that authority materially contributed;]

"out of jurisdiction appeal" means an appeal brought against a decision which is specified in Schedule 2 to the Act or a decision prescribed in regulation 27 (decisions against which no appeal lies);

"panel" means the panel constituted under section 6;

"panel member" means a person appointed to the panel;

"panel member with a disability qualification" means a panel member who satisfies the requirements of paragraph 5 of Schedule 3;

"party to the proceedings" means the Secretary of State [3 or, as the case may be, the Board or an officer of the Board,] and any other person—
  (a) who is one of the principal parties for the purposes of sections 13 and 14;
  (b) who has a right of appeal to an appeal tribunal under section 11(2) of the 1997 Act, section 20 of the Child Support Act as extended by paragraph 3 of Schedule 4C to that Act or section 12(2);

"President" means the President of appeal tribunals appointed under section 5;

"referral" means a referral of an application for a departure direction to an appeal tribunal under section 28D(1)(b) of the Child Support Act;

[3 "tax credit" means working families' tax credit or disabled person's tax credit, construing those terms in accordance with section 1(1) of the Tax Credits Act 1999;]

[2 "the Transfer Act" means the Social Security Contributions (Transfer of Functions, etc.) Act 1999.]

[4 "work-focused interview" has the meaning it has in regulation 3 of the Work-focused Interviews Regulations;

(S.I. 1999 No. 991, reg. 1)

"the Work-focused Interviews Regulations" means the Social Security (Work-focused Inteviews) Regulations 2000;]

[¹ (3A) In these Regulations as they relate to any decision made under the Pension Schemes Act 1993 by virtue of section 170(2) of that Act, any reference to the Secretary of State is to be construed as if it were a reference to an officer of the Board.]

(4) In these Regulations, unless the context otherwise requires, a reference—
   (a) to a numbered section is to the section of the Act bearing that number;
   (b) to a numbered Part is to the Part of these Regulations bearing that number;
   (c) to a numbered regulation or Schedule is to the regulation in, or Schedule to, these Regulations bearing that number;
   (d) in a regulation or Schedule to a numbered paragraph is to the paragraph in that regulation or Schedule bearing that number;
   (e) in a paragraph to a lettered or numbered sub-paragraph is to the sub-paragraph in that paragraph bearing that letter or number.

AMENDMENTS

1. Social Security Contributions (Transfer of Functions, etc.) Act 1999 (Commencement No. 2 and Consequential and Transitional Provisions) Order 1999 (S.I. 1999 No. 1662), art. 3(2) (July 5, 1999).
2. Social Security and Child Support (Decisions and Appeals) Amendment (No. 3) Regulations 1999 (S.I. 1999 No. 1670), reg. 2(2) (July 5, 1999).
3. Tax Credits (Decisions and Appeals) (Amendment) Regulations 1999 (S.I. 1999 No. 2570), regs 3 and 4 (October 5, 1999). Note that amendments made by these regulations only have effect with respect to tax credit (reg. 1(2) of the Amendment Regulations).
4. Social Security (Work-focused Interviews) Regulations 2000 (S.I. 2000 No. 897), reg. 16(5) and Sched. 6, para. 2 (April 3, 2000).

Service of notices or documents

2. Where, by any provision of the Act or of these Regulations— 4.244
   (a) any notice or other document is required to be given or sent to the clerk to the appeal tribunal or to an officer authorised by the Secretary of State [¹ or to an officer of the Board], that notice or document shall be treated as having been so given or sent on the day that it is received by the clerk to the appeal tribunal or by an officer authorised by the Secretary of State [¹ or by an officer of the Board], as the case may be, and
   (b) any notice (including notification of a decision of the Secretary of State [² or of an officer of the Board] or other document is required to be given or sent to any person other than the clerk to the appeal tribunal [¹ or an officer] authorised by the Secretary of State [¹ or an officer of the Board], as the case may be, that notice or document shall, if sent by post to that person's last known address, be treated as having been given or sent on the day that it was posted.

481

AMENDMENTS

1. Tax Credits (Decisions and Appeals) (Amendment) Regulations 1999 (S.I. 1999 No. 2570), reg. 5 (October 5, 1999). Note that amendments made by these regulations only have effect with respect to tax credit (reg. 1(2) of the Amendment Regulations).
2. Tax Credits (Decisions and Appeals) (Amendment) Regulations 2000 (S.I. 2000 No. 127), reg. 2 (February 14, 2000). This amendment has effect with respect only to tax credit (reg. 1(2) of the amending Regulations).

GENERAL NOTE

4.245   This regulation re-enacts reg. 1(3) of the Social Security (Adjudication) Regulations 1995.

PART II

REVISIONS, SUPERSESSIONS AND OTHER MATTERS SOCIAL SECURITY

CHAPTER I

REVISIONS

Revision of decisions

4.246   **3.**—(1) Subject to the following provisions of this regulation, any decision of the Secretary of State [³ or the Board or an officer of the Board] under section 8 or 10 ("the original decision") may be revised by him [³ or them] if—

[⁴ (a) he commences action leading to the revision within one month of the date of—
   (i) notification of the original decision; or
   (ii) the making of an appeal under section 12 provided that the appeal is made within the time prescribed in regulation 31 or, in a case to which regulation 32 applies, the time prescribed in that regulation; or]
(b) an application for a revision is received by the Secretary of State [³ or the Board or an officer of the Board] at the appropriate office—
   (i) within one month of the date of notification of the original decision,
   (ii) where a written statement is requested under paragraph (1)(b) of regulation 28, within 14 days of the expiry of the period specified in head (i), or
   (iii) within such longer period of time as may be allowed under regulation 4.

(2) Where the Secretary of State [³ or the Board or an officer of the Board] requires further evidence or information from the applicant in order to consider all the issues raised by an application under paragraph (1)(b) ("the original application"), he [³ or they] shall notify the applic-

ant that further evidence or information is required and the decision may be revised—
  (a) where the applicant provides further relevant evidence or information within one month of the date of notification or such longer period of time as the Secretary of State [³ or the Board or an officer of the Board] may allow; or
  (b) where the applicant does not provide such evidence or information within the time allowed under sub-paragraph (a), on the basis of the original application.

(3) In the case of a payment out of the social fund in respect of maternity or funeral expenses, a decision under section 8 may be revised where the application is made—
  (a) within one month of the date of notification of the decision, or if later
  (b) within the time prescribed for claiming such a payment under regulation 19 of, and Schedule 4 to, the Claims and Payments Regulations, or
  (c) within such longer period of time as may be allowed under regulation 4.

(4) In the case of a decision made under the Pension Schemes Act 1993 by virtue of section 170(2) of that Act, the decision may be revised at any time by [² an officer of the Board] where it contains an error.

(5) A decision of the Secretary of State [³ *Board or an officer of the Board*] under section 8 or 10—
  (a) which arose from an official error; or
  (b) [¹ except in the case of a disability decision or an incapacity benefit decision where there has been an incapacity determination (whether before or after the decision)] where the decision was made in ignorance of, or was based upon a mistake as to, some material fact and as a result of that ignorance of or mistake as to that fact, the decision was more advantageous to the claimant than it would otherwise have been but for that ignorance or mistake,

  [³ *(b) which was made in ignorance of, or was based on a mistake as to some material fact,*]
  (c) [¹ where the decision is a disability benefit decision, or is an incapacity benefit decision where there has been an incapacity determination (whether before or after the decision), which was made in ignorance of, or was based upon a mistake as to, some material fact in relation to a disability determination embodies in or necessary to the disability benefit decision, or the incapacity determination, and
    (i) as a result of that ignorance or mistake as to that fact the decision was more advantageous to the claimant than it would otherwise have been but for that ignorance or mistake and,
    (ii) the Secretary of State is satisfied that at the time the decision was made the claimant or payee knew or could reasonably have been expected to know of the fact in question and that it was relevant to the decision,]

may be revised at any time by the Secretary of State [³ *by the Board or an officer of the Board at any time not later than the end of the period of six years immediately following the date of the decision or, where ignorance of the material fact referred to in sub-paragraph (b) was caused by the fraudulent or negligent conduct of the claimant, not later than the end of the period of twenty years immediately following the date of the decision.*]

(6) A decision of the Secretary of State under section 8 or 10 that a jobseeker's allowance is not payable to a claimant for any period in accordance with section 19 of the Jobseekers Act may be revised at any time by the Secretary of State [⁵ (6A) A relevant decision within the meaning of section 2B(2) of the Administration Act may be revised at any time if it contains an error.]

(7) A decision under section 8 or 10 may be revised where—
(a) the Secretary of State [³ or the Board or an officer of the Board] awards entitlement to a relevant benefit; and
(b) on the date that entitlement arises, the claimant or a member of his family is entitled to another relevant benefit or to an increase in the rate of another benefit.

(8) A decision of the Secretary of State [³ or the Board of an officer of the Board] which is specified in Schedule 2 to the Act or is prescribed in regulation 27 (decisions against which no appeal lies) may be revised at any time.

[⁴ (9) Paragraph (1) shall not apply in respect of—
(a) a relevant change of circumstances which occurred since the decision was made or where the Secretary of State has evidence or information which indicates that a relevant change of circumstances will occur; nor
(b) a decision which relates to an attendance allowance or a disability living allowance where the person is terminally ill, within the meaning of section 66(2)(a) of the Contributions and Benefit Act, unless an application for revision which contains an express statement that the person is terminally ill is made either by—
  (i) the person himself; or
  (ii) any other person purporting to act on his behalf whether or not that other person is acting with his knowledge or authority,
but where such an application is received a decision may be so revised notwithstanding that no claim under section 66(1) or, as the case may be, 72(5) or 73(12) of that Act has been made.]

(10) The Secretary of State [³ or the Board] may treat an application for a supersession as an application for a revision.

(11) In this regulation and regulation 7, "appropriate office" means
(a) the office of the Department of Social Security or the Department for Education and Employment the address of which is indicated on the notification of the original decision; or
(b) in the case of a person who has claimed jobseeker's allowance, the office specified by the Secretary of State in accordance with regulation 23 of the Jobseeker's Allowance Regulations [²; or
(c) in the case of a contributions decision which falls within Part II of Schedule 3 to the Act, any National Insurance Contributions

office of the Board or any office of the Department of Social Security; or

(d) in the case of a decision made under the Pension Schemes Act 1993 by virtue of section 170(2) of that Act, any National Insurance Contributions office of the Board;] [³ or

(e) in the case of a person who has claimed working families' tax credit or disabled person's tax credit, a Tax Credits Office, the address of which is indicated on the notification of the original decision;] [⁵ or

(f) in the case of a relevant person within the meaning of regulation 2(2) of the Work-focused Interviews Regulations, an office of any designated authority which displays the one logo.]

AMENDMENTS

1. Social Security and Child Support (Decisions and Appeals) Amendment (No. 2) Regulations 1999 (S.I. 1999 No. 1623), reg. 2 (July 5, 1999).
2. Social Security Contributions (Transfer of Functions, etc.) Act 1999 (Commencement No. 2 and Consequential and Transitional Provisions) Order 1999 (S.I. 1999 No. 1662), art. 3(3) (July 5, 1999).
3. Tax Credits (Decisions and Appeals) (Amendment) Regulations 1999 (S.I. 1999 No. 2570), reg. 6 (October 5, 1999). Note that amendments made by these regulations only have effect with respect to tax credit (reg. 1(2) of the Amendment Regulations). In the case of para. (5) the amendments are substituted in relation to tax credit; for this reason the substituted words in relation to tax credit are shown in italics.
4. Social Security and Child Support (Decisions and Appeals), Vaccine Damage Payments and Jobseeker's Allowance (Amendment) Regulations 1999 (S.I. 1999 No. 2677), reg. 6 (October 18, 1999).
5. Social Security (Work-focused Interviews) Regulations 2000 (S.I. 2000 No. 897), reg. 16(5) and Sched. 6, para. 3 (April 3, 2000).

GENERAL NOTE

Revisions have effect from the date from which the decision being revised was effective (see s.9(3) of the Social Security Act 1998) unless a mistake was made in respect of that date, in which case the correct date is used (reg. 5). Supersessions are usually effective from a later date (reg. 7) and this distinction is the principal reason why it is necessary to distinguish between revision and supersession.

4.247

Paragraphs (1) to (3)

These allow a decision to be put right "on my ground" where the claimant applies for a revision within one month of the original decision being notified (but note the extension of time permitted where there has been a request for reasons (paras. (1)(b) and (3)(b)) or under reg. 4). They also allow revision where the Secretary of State notices the error within that time or, now that para. (1)(a) has been amended, within one month of the claimant bring an appeal that is made within the time-limit (including the time-limit as extended under reg. 32). The amendment makes it unnecessary for an appeal to be pursued where the Secretary of State accepts that it is well-founded. However, the amendment can also be used to the disadvantage of a claimant where an appeal has been brought against a decision which, upon reflection, the Secretary of State concludes was too generous although, in such a case, the appeal would not lapse (reg. 31(1)). Note that the time for appealing against the original

4.248

Social Security and Child Support (Decisions and Appeals) Regulations 1999

decision runs from the date the decision is revised *or is not revised* following an application under these paragraphs (reg. 31(2)), so that a claimant is not prejudiced by seeking a revision before appealing.

Paragraph (5)

4.249 Normally, a decision based on a mistake of law or fact made by the Secretary of State can only be superseded under reg. 6(2)(b) unless the error is detected in time to allow revision under paras (1) to (3). Supersession will be effective only from the date the application was made (see s.10(5) of the Social Security Act 1998). Para. (5) provides for such a decision to be revised rather than superseded where either there has been an official error or else there has been an overpayment (which might be recoverable under s.71 of the Social Security Administration Act 1992) due to a mistake of fact). In effect, the time limit is removed because revisions generally take effect from the same date as the original decision (see s.9(3) of the Social Security Act 1998). "Official error" is defined in reg. 1. Note that para. (5)(c) protects claimants of disability benefits or incapacity benefits from the full rigour of para. (b) and effectively prevents there from being a recoverable overpayment where a claimant could not reasonably have known a fact of which the Secretary of State was ignorant, or as to which he made a mistake, or could not reasonably have known that it was relevant. It does not protect the claimant who reasonably did not know that the Secretary of State was ignorant of, or had made a mistake as to, an obviously relevant fact of which he was aware, but that is presumably because in such cases any overpayment is unlikely to be recoverable anyway due to the lack of any misrepresentation or failure to disclose it.

Paragraph (7)

4.250 It is not immediately obvious either which of the two awards may be revised or the circumstances in which it may be revised. However, the paragraph presumably applies where entitlement to one benefit is relevant to entitlement to another that has been awarded earlier. It allows the earlier award to be revised from the date when it was first effective if the later award justifies such a revision. If the later award justifies adjusting the earlier award only from a later date, supersession will be appropriate (see regs. 6(2)(e) and 7(7)).

Paragraph (8)

4.251 See the note to reg. 6(2)(d).

Paragraph (10)

4.252 An application for supersession may be treated as an application for revision. On an appeal, this power may be exercised by an appeal tribunal or Commissioner. Reg. 6(5) provides that an application for revision may be treated as an application for supersession.

Late application for a revision

4.253 **4.**—(1) The time limit for making an application for a revision specified in regulation 3(1) or (3) may be extended where the conditions specified in the following provisions of this regulation are satisfied.

(2) An application for an extension of time shall be made by the claimant or a person acting on his behalf.

(3) An application shall—
(a) contain particulars of the grounds on which the extension of time is sought and shall contain sufficient details of the decision which it is sought to have revised to enable that decision to be identified; and

(b) be made within 13 months of the date of notification of the decision which it is sought to have revised.

(4) An application for an extension of time shall not be granted unless the applicant satisfies the Secretary of State [¹ or the Board or an officer of the Board] that—
   (a) it is reasonable to grant the application;
   (b) the application for revision has merit; and
   (c) special circumstances are relevant to the application and as a result of those special circumstances it was not practicable for the application to be made within the time limit specified in regulation 3.

(5) In determining whether it is reasonable to grant an application, the Secretary of State [¹ or the Board or an officer of the Board] shall have regard to the principle that the greater the amount of time that has elapsed between the expiration of the time specified in regulation 3(1) and (3) for applying for a revision and the making of the application for an extension of time, the more compelling should be the special circumstances on which the application is based.

(6) In determining whether it is reasonable to grant the application for an extension of time, no account shall be taken of the following—
   (a) that the applicant or any person acting for him was unaware of or misunderstood the law applicable to his case (including ignorance or misunderstanding of the time limits imposed by these Regulations); or
   (b) that a Commissioner or a court has taken a different view of the law from that previously understood and applied.

(7) An application under this regulation for an extension of time which has been refused may not be renewed.

AMENDMENT

1. Tax Credits (Decisions and Appeals) (Amendment) Regulations 1999 (S.I. 1999 No. 2570), reg. 7 (October 5, 1999). Note that amendments made by these regulations only have effect with respect to tax credit (reg. 1(2) of the Amendment Regulations).

GENERAL NOTE

Paragraph (6)(b)
See the note to reg. 32(8)(b) which is in similar terms.

Date from which a decision revised under section 9 takes effect

5. Where, on a revision under section 9, the Secretary of State [¹ or the Board or an officer of the Board] decides that the date from which the decision under section 8 or 10 ("the original decision") took effect was erroneous, the decision under section 9 shall take effect on the date from which the original decision would have taken effect had the error not been made.

AMENDMENT

1. Tax Credits (Decisions and Appeals) (Amendment) Regulations 1999 (S.I. 1999 No. 2570), reg. 8 (October 5, 1999). Note that amendments made by these regulations only have effect with respect to tax credit (reg. 1(2) of the Amendment Regulations).

GENERAL NOTE

4.256   This provides an exception to the general rule in s.9(3) of the Social Security Act 1998 that a revision takes effect from the same date as the original decision.

CHAPTER II

SUPERSESSIONS

Supersession of decisions

4.257   **6.**—(1) Subject to the following provisions of this regulation, for the purposes of section 10, the cases and circumstances in which a decision may be superseded under that section are set out in paragraphs (2) to (4).

(2) A decision under section 10 may be made on the Secretary of State's [² or the Board's] own initiative or on an application made for the purpose on the basis that the decision to be superseded—
  (a) is one in respect of which—
    (i) there has been a relevant change of circumstances since the decision was made; or
    (ii) it is anticipated that a relevant change of circumstances will occur;
  (b) is a decision of the Secretary of State [² or the Board or an officer of the Board] other than a decision to which sub-paragraph (d) refers and—
    (i) the decision was erroneous in point of law, or it was made in ignorance of, or was based upon a mistake as to, some material fact; and
    (ii) an application for a supersession was received by the Secretary of State [² or the Board], or the decision by the Secretary of State [² or the Board] to act on his [² or their] own initiative was taken, more than one month after the date of notification of the decision which is to be superseded or after the expiry of such longer period of time as may have been allowed under regulation 4;
  (c) is a decision of an appeal tribunal or of a Commissioner that was made in ignorance of, or was based upon a mistake as to, some material fact;
  (d) is a decision which is specified in Schedule 2 to the Act or is prescribed in regulation 27 (decisions against which no appeal lies); or
  (e) is a decision where—

(S.I. 1999 No. 991, reg. 6)

      (i) the Secretary of State [² or the Board or an officer of the Board] has awarded a relevant benefit; and

     (ii) on a date after the date that entitlement arises, the claimant or a member of his family becomes entitled to another relevant benefit or to an increase in the rate of another such benefit;

[³ (f) is a decision that a jobseeker's allowance is payable to a claimant where that allowance ceases to be payable by virtue of section 19(1) of the Jobseekers Act;

[¹

 (g) is an incapacity benefit decision where there has been an incapacity determination (whether before or after the decision) and where, since the decision was made, the Secretary of State has received medical evidence following an examination in accordance with regulation 8 of the Social Security (Incapacity for Work) (General) Regulations 1995 from a doctor referred to in paragraph (1) of that regulation;] [⁴ and

 (h) is one in respect of a person who—

     (i) is subsequently the subject of a separate decision or determination as to whether or not he took part in a work-focused interview;

    (ii) had been held not to have taken part in a work-focused interview but who had, subsequent to the decision to be superseded, attained the age of 60 or ceased to reside in an area in which there is a requirement to take part in a work-focused interview.]

(3) A decision which may be revised under regulation 3 may not be superseded under this regulation except where—

 (a) circumstances arise in which the Secretary of State [² or the Board or an officer of the Board] may revise that decision under regulation 3; and

 (b) further circumstances arise in relation to that decision which are not specified in regulation 3 but are specified in paragraph (2) or (4).

(4) Where the Secretary of State requires [² or the Board require] further evidence or information from the applicant in order to consider all the issues raised by an application under paragraph (2) ("the original application"), he [² or they] shall notify the applicant that further evidence or information is required and the decision may be superseded—

 (a) where the applicant provides further relevant evidence or information within one month of the date of notification or such longer period of time as the Secretary of State [² or the Board] may allow; or

 (b) where the applicant does not provide such evidence or information within the time allowed under sub-paragraph (a), on the basis of the original application.

(5) The Secretary of State [² or the Board] may treat an application for a revision or a notification of a change of circumstances as an application for a supersession.

Social Security and Child Support (Decisions and Appeals) Regulations 1999

(6) The following events are not relevant changes of circumstances for the purposes of paragraph (2)—
  (a) the repayment of a loan to which regulation 66A of the Income Support Regulations or regulation 136 of the Jobseeker's Allowance Regulations applies;
  (b) the absence from a nursing home or residential care home for a period of less than one week of a resident who is—
    (i) in receipt of income support or a jobseeker's allowance; and
    (ii) not a claimant to whom Part II of Schedule 4 to the Income Support Regulations applies
[³(c) the fact that a person has become terminally ill, within the meaning of section 66(2)(a) of the Contributions and Benefits Act, unless an application for supersession which contains an express statement that the person is terminally ill is made either by—
    (i) the person himself; or
    (ii) any other person purporting to act on his behalf whether or not that other person is acting with his knowledge or authority;
and where such an application is received a decision may be so superseded notwithstanding that no claim under section 66(1) or, as the case may be, 72(5) or 73(12) of that Act has been made.]

(7) In paragraph (6)(b), "nursing home" and "residential care home" have the same meanings as they have in regulation 19 of the Income Support Regulations.

AMENDMENTS

1. Social Security and Child Support (Decisions and Appeals) Amendment (No. 2) Regulations 1999 (S.I. 1999 No. 1623), reg. 2 (July 5, 1999).
2. Tax Credits (Decisions and Appeals) (Amendment) Regulations 1999 (S.I. 1999 No. 2570), reg. 9 (October 5, 1999). Note that amendments made by these regulations only have effect with respect to tax credit (reg. 1(2) of the Amendment Regulations).
3. Social Security and Child Support (Decisions and Appeals), Vaccine Damage Payments and Jobseeker's Allowance (Amendment) Regulations 1999 (S.I. 1999 No. 2677), reg. 7 (October 18, 1999).
4. Social Security (Work-focused Interviews) Regulations 2000 (S.I. 2000 No. 897), reg. 16(5) and Sched. 6, para. 4 (April 3, 2000).

GENERAL NOTE

Paragraph (2)

4.258   There is some degree of overlap between the subparagraphs (*e.g.*, (a)(i) and (e)) but this is not of particular significance. It is suggested that where two sub-paragraphs apply, the claimant is entitled to have the benefit of the more advantageous of the two as determined under reg. 7 (which provides numerous exceptions to the general rule under s.10(5) that a supersession is effective from the date it is made or the application for it was made).

Supersessions are effective from a later date (reg. 7) than revisions which are effective from the date the decision revised was, or should have been, effective (see s.9(3) of the Social Security Act 1998 and reg. 5) and that is the main reason for the distinction between supersession and revision. Whether the two concepts represent a simplification by comparison with the former concept of review seems doubtful.

Paragraph (2)(a)(i)

In *R(I) 56/54*, the Commissioner said: "A relevant change of circumstances postulates that the decision has ceased to be correct". This means that only an award may be superseded on the ground of change of circumstances. A decision that a claimant is not entitled to benefit at all may not be superseded on that ground. Instead, the claimant must make a new claim. However, in *R(A) 2/90*, the Commissioner considered *Saker v. Secretary of State for Social Services* (reported as an appendix to *R(I) 2/88*) in which Nicholls L.J. considered what might amount to a "material" fact for the purposes of a provision similar to para. (2)(b)(i) and said that a fact was material "if it was one which, had it been known to the medical board, would have called for serious consideration by the board and might well have affected its decision". In the light of that approach, the Commissioner held that a change of circumstances was relevant if it was necessary "to give those circumstances serious consideration to the extent that they might well affect [its] decision". In *Saker*, it made no practical difference whether or not the change of circumstances was regarded as "relevant" or not because, even if there were grounds requiring a review, there were no grounds for revision. However, it is important in cases where an element of judgement has been involved in the decision so that two decision-makers could reasonably hold different views as to the conclusion to be reached on the facts of the case. Paragraph (2) is intended to have the effect that, once benefit has been awarded, the Secretary of State cannot supersede the decision merely because a different judgement is now made on the same facts; it is necessary to show that the earlier decision was based on an erroneous appreciation of the facts or that the facts have changed. In *R(A) 2/90*, the claimant had been awarded the lower rate of attendance allowance based on satisfaction of the day supervision condition and he sought a review on the ground that there had been a change of circumstances justifying an award of the higher rate on the basis that he also satisfied the night attention condition. The Attendance Allowance Board decided that there had been a relevant change of circumstances even though it was not sufficient to justify a finding that the claimant satisfied the night attention condition. They then reached a different judgement in respect of the day supervision condition and decided that the claimant was not entitled to attendance allowance at all. It was not suggested that the facts on which that judgement was based were any different from the facts upon which the original award had been based. The Commissioner held that the Board were entitled to take that approach because the change of circumstances in respect of the night attention condition was "relevant" and so the Board was authorised to review the whole award and reach a fresh decision upon it. It is suggested that that approach is wrong and is liable to frustrate the purpose of the legislation which limits the circumstances in which a decision may be superseded. It may be significant that the legislation provides that the Secretary of State *may* supersede (formerly, review) a decision if the grounds are made out and, while he is no doubt bound to do so if the change of circumstances is sufficient to justify an alteration of the award, it seems equally appropriate that the award should *not* be superseded if the change of circumstances is not sufficient in itself to justify an alteration. In other words, while the Commissioner may have been correct to regard the change of circumstances as being "relevant", it still did not require the award to be reviewed and revised.

A new medical opinion is not itself a change of circumstances but a new medical report may reveal not only a new opinion but also new clinical findings which would show a change of circumstances (*R(IS) 2/97*). A change in legisla-

4.259

tion is a change of circumstances (*R(A) 4/81*) but an unexpected decision of a court (or a Commissioner) is not (*Chief Adjudication Officer v. McKiernon*, unreported, July 8, 1993). Para. (6) makes further provision as to matters that are not relevant changes of circumstances.

Paragraph (2)(a)(ii)

4.260   It is not clear on what ground a decision based on an anticipated change of circumstances could be superseded if the change did not materialise.

Paragraph (2)(b) and (c)

4.261   Para. (2)(b)(ii) exists to prevent there from being any overlap between supersession under para. (b) and revision under reg. 3(1). For the reasons given above, it is suggested that a decision ought not to be superseded under sub-paras. (b) or (c) if correcting the error of fact does not itself justify a different decision. Ignorance or mistake must be as to a primary fact and not merely as to an inference or conclusion of fact. Thus, a decision cannot be superseded simply on the ground that the Secretary of State now takes a different view of the case. "He must go further and assert and prove that the inference might not have been drawn, if the determining authority had not been ignorant of some specific fact of which it could have been aware, or had not been mistaken as to some specific fact which it took into consideration" (*R(I) 3/75*). It may be particularly difficult to show that a tribunal made a mistake of fact if neither party obtained a full statement of reasons and it may be equally difficult to show that a tribunal was ignorant of a material fact if neither party obtained a record of proceedings which would include a note of evidence.

Paragraph (2)(d)

4.262   This appears to overlap with reg. 3(8) but it is suggested that the first alteration of an unappealable decision must be made by revision under reg. 3(8) (due to the effect of para. (3)) but that thereafter no further revision is possible (see the note to s.9(1) of the Social Security Act 1998) so that the next alteration must be by way of supersession under para. (2)(d). Any alteration to the supersession must then be by way of revision and so on, with alternate supersessions and revisions.

Paragraph (2)(e)

4.263   See the note to reg. 3(7).
It is not clear why para. (2)(e) is confined to awards by the Secretary of State and does not include awards by appeal tribunals or Commissioners.

Date from which a decision superseded under section 10 takes effect

4.264   7.—(1) This regulation contains exceptions to the provisions of section 10(5) as to the date from which a decision under section 10 which supersedes an earlier decision is to take effect.

(2) Where a decision under section 10 is made on the ground that there has been, or it is anticipated that there will be, a relevant change of circumstances since the decision was made, the decision under section 10 shall take effect—

   (a) where the decision is advantageous to the claimant and the change was notified to an appropriate office within one month of the change occurring or within such longer period as may be allowed under regulation 8 for the claimant's failure to notify the change on an earlier data—

(i) subject to head (ii), from the date the change occurred or, where the change does not have effect until a later date, from the first date on which such effect occurs;
(ii) in a case where the date a change of circumstances is to take effect falls to be determined in accordance with regulation 26 or 26A of the Claims and Payments Regulations, the date so determined;
(b) where the decision is advantageous to the claimant and the change was notified to an appropriate office more than one month after the change occurred or after the expiry of any such longer period as may have been allowed under regulation 8—
  (i) in the case of a claimant who is in receipt of income support or a jobseeker's allowance and benefit is paid in arrears, from the beginning of the benefit week in which the notification was made;
  (ii) in the case of a claimant who is in receipt of income support or a jobseeker's allowance and benefit is paid in advance and the date of notification is the first day of a benefit week from that date and otherwise, from the beginning of the benefit week following the week in which the notification was made; or
  (iii) in any other case, the date of notification of the relevant change of circumstances; or
(c) where the decision is not advantageous to the claimant—
  (i) in a case where the date a change of circumstances is to take effect falls to be determined in accordance with regulation 26 or 26A of the Claims and Payments Regulations, the date so determined; or
  [1(ii) in the case of a disability benefit decision, or an incapacity benefit decision where there has been an incapacity determination (whether before or after the decision), where the Secretary of State is satisfied that in relation to a disability determination embodied in or necessary to the disability benefit decision, or the incapacity determination, the claimant or payee failed to notify an appropriate office of a change of circumstances which regulations under the Administration Act required him to notify, and the claimant or payee, as the case may be, knew or could reasonably have been expected to know that the change of circumstances should have been notified,
    (aa) from the date on which the claimant or payee, as the case may be, ought to have notified the change of circumstances, or
    (bb) if more than one change has taken place between the date from which the decision to be superseded took effect and the date of the superseding decision, from the date on which the first change ought to have been notified, or
  (iii) in any other case, except in the case of a decision which supersedes a disability benefit decision, or an incapacity benefit decision where there has been an incapacity deter-

mination (whether before or after the decision), from the date of change.]

(3) For the purposes of paragraphs (2) and (8) "benefit week" has the same meaning as in regulation 2(1) of the Income Support Regulations or, as the case may be, regulation 1(3) of the Jobseeker's Regulations.

(4) In paragraph (2) a decision which is to the advantage of the claimant includes a decision specified in regulation 30(2)(a) to (f).

(5) Where the Secretary of State supersedes [² or the Board supersede] a decision made by an appeal tribunal or a Commissioner on the grounds specified in regulation 6(2)(c) (grounds of ignorance of, or mistake as to, a material fact), the decision under section 10 shall take effect—

(a) in a case where, as a result of that ignorance of or mistake as to some material fact, the decision was more advantageous to the claimant than it would otherwise have been but for that ignorance or mistake, from the date on which the decision of the appeal tribunal or the Commissioner took, or was to take effect; or

(b) in any other case, from the date of the decision under section 10.

(6) Any decision made under section 10 in consequence of a decision which is a relevant determination for the purposes of section 27 shall take effect as from the date of the relevant determination.

(7) A decision to which regulation 6(2)(e) applies may be made so as to take effect as from the date on which the decision which has been superseded had effect, or at any time thereafter which is reasonable in the particular circumstances of the case.

[³(8) A decision to which regulation 6(2)(f) applies shall take effect—

(a) where section 19(2) of the Jobseekers Act applies, as from the beginning of the period specified in regulation 69 of the Jobseeker's Allowance Regulations; or

(b) where section 19(3) of the Jobseekers Act applies, as from the beginning of the period determined in accordance with that subsection.]

[⁴(9) A decision relating to attendance allowance or disability living allowance which is advantageous to the claimant and which is made under section 10 on the basis of a relevant change of circumstances shall take effect from—

(a) where the decision is made on the Secretary of State's own initiative, the date of that decision;

(b) where—

(i) the change is relevant to the question of entitlement to a particular rate of benefit; and

(ii) the claimant notifies the change before a date one month after he satisfied the conditions of entitlement to that rate or within such longer period as may be allowed under regulation 8,

the first pay day (as specified in Schedule 6 to the Claims and Payments Regulations) after he satisfied those conditions;

(c) where—

(i) the change is relevant to the question of whether benefit is payable; and
   (ii) the claimant notifies the change before a date one month after the change or within such longer period as may be allowed under regulation 8,
   the first pay day (as specified in Schedule 6 to the Claims and Payments Regulations) after the change occurred; or
(d) in any other case, the date of the application for the superseding decision.]

(10) A decision as to an award of incapacity benefit, which is made under section 10 because section 30B(4) of the Contributions and Benefits Act applies to the claimant, shall take effect as from the date on which he became entitled to the highest rate of the care component of disability living allowance.

(11) A decision as to an award of incapacity benefit or severe disablement allowance, which is made under section 10 because the claimant is to be treated as incapable of work under regulation 10 of the Social Security (Incapacity for Work) (General) Regulations 1995 (certain persons with a severe condition to be treated as incapable of work), shall take effect as from the date he is to be treated as incapable of work.

(12) Where this paragraph applies, a decision under section 10 may be made so as to take effect as from such date not more than eight weeks before—
(a) the application for supersession; or
(b) where no application is made, the date on which the decision under section 10 is made,
as is reasonable in the particular circumstances of the case.

(13) Paragraph (12) applies where—
(a) the effect of a decision under section 10 is that there is to be included in a claimant's applicable amount an amount in respect of a loan which qualifies under—
   (i) paragraph 15 or 16 of Schedule 3 to the Income Support Regulations; or
   (ii) paragraph 14 or 15 of Schedule 2 to the Jobseeker's Allowance Regulations; and
(b) that decision could not have been made earlier because information necessary to make that decision, requested otherwise than in accordance with paragraph 10(3)(b) of Schedule 9A to the Claims and Payments Regulations (annual requests for information), had not been supplied to the Secretary of State by the lender.

(14) Subject to paragraph (23), where a claimant is in receipt of income support and his applicable amount includes an amount determined in accordance with Schedule 3 to the Income Support Regulations (housing costs), and there is a reduction in the amount of eligible capital owing in connection with a loan which qualifies under paragraph 15 or 16 of that Schedule, a decision made under section 10 shall take effect—
(a) on the first anniversary of the date on which the claimant's housing costs were first met under that Schedule; or

(b) where the reduction in eligible capital occurred after the first anniversary of the date referred to in sub-paragraph (a), on the next anniversary of that date following the date of the reduction.

(15) Where a claimant is in receipt of income support and payments made to that claimant which fall within paragraph 29 or 30(1)(a) to (c) of Schedule 9 to the Income Support Regulations have been disregarded in relation to any decision under section 8 or 10 and there is a change in the amount of interest payable—

(a) on a loan qualifying under paragraph 15 or 16 of Schedule 3 to those Regulations to which those payments relate; or
(b) on a loan not so qualifying which is secured on the dwelling occupied as the home to which those payments relate,

a decision under section 10 which is made as a result of that change in the amount of interest payable shall take effect on whichever of the dates referred to in paragraph (16) is appropriate in the claimant's case.

(16) The date on which a decision under section 10 takes effect for the purposes of paragraph (15) is—

(a) the date on which the claimant's housing costs are first met under paragraph 6(1)(a), 8(1)(a) or 9(2)(a) of Schedule 3 to the Income Support Regulations; or
(b) where the change in the amount of interest payable occurred after the date referred to in sub-paragraph (a), on the date of the next alteration in the standard rate following the date of that change.

(17) In paragraph (16), "standard rate" has the same meaning as it has in paragraph 1(2) of Schedule 3 to the Income Support Regulations.

(18) Subject to paragraph (24) and, except in a case to which paragraph (23) applies, where a claimant is in receipt of a jobseeker's allowance and his applicable amount includes an amount determined in accordance with Schedule 2 to the Jobseeker's Allowance Regulations (housing costs), and there is a reduction in the amount of eligible capital owing in connection with a loan which qualifies under paragraph 14 or 15 of that Schedule, a decision under section 10 made as a result of that reduction shall take effect—

(a) on the first anniversary of the date on which the claimant's housing costs were first met under that Schedule; or
(b) where the reduction in eligible capital occurred after the first anniversary of the date referred to in sub-paragraph (a), on the next anniversary of that date following the date of the reduction.

(19) Where a claimant is in receipt of a jobseeker's allowance and payments made to that claimant which fall within paragraph 30 or 31(1)(a) to (c) of Schedule 7 to the Jobseeker's Allowance Regulations have been disregarded in relation to any decision under section 8 or 10 and there is a change in the amount of interest payable—

(a) on a loan qualifying under paragraph 14 or 15 of Schedule 2 to those Regulations to which those payments relate; or
(b) on a loan not so qualifying which is secured on the dwelling occupied as the home to which those payments relate,

any decision under section 10 which is made as a result of that change in the amount of interest payable shall take effect on whichever of the dates referred to in paragraph (20) is appropriate in the claimant's case.

(20) The date on which a decision under section 10 takes effect for the purposes of paragraph (19) is—
  (a) the date on which the claimant's housing costs are first met under paragraph 6(1)(a), 7(1)(a) or 8(2)(a) of Schedule 2 to the Jobseeker's Allowance Regulations; or
  (b) where the changes in the amount of interest payable occurred after the date referred to in sub-paragraph (a), on the date of the next alteration in the standard rate following the date of that change.

(21) In paragraph (20), "standard rate" has the same meaning as it has in paragraph 1(2) of Schedule 2 to the Jobseeker's Allowance Regulations.

(22) Where—
  (a) a claimant was paid benefit in respect of October 6, 1996 in accordance with an award of income support;
  (b) that claimant's applicable amount includes an amount determined in accordance with Schedule 3 to the Income Support Regulations (housing costs);
  (c) that claimant is treated as having been awarded a jobseeker's allowance by virtue of regulation 7 of the Jobseeker's Allowance (Transitional Provisions) Regulations 1996 (jobseeker's allowance to replace income support and unemployment benefit); and
  (d) a decision is made under section 10 in consequence of a reduction in the amount of eligible capital owing in connection with a loan which qualifies under paragraph 15 or 16 of Schedule 3 to the Income Support Regulations,
the decision under section 10 referred to in sub-paragraph (d) shall take effect on the next anniversary of the date on which housing costs were first met which occurs after the reduction.

(23) Where, in any case to which paragraph (14) or (18) applies, a claimant has been continuously in receipt of, or treated as having been continuously in receipt of income support or a jobseeker's allowance, or one of those benefits followed by the other, and he or his partner continues to receive either benefit, the anniversary to which those paragraphs refer shall be the anniversary of the earliest date on which benefit (whether income support or a jobseeker's allowance) in respect of those mortgage interest costs became payable.

(24) Where—
  (a) it has been determined that the amount of a jobseeker's allowance payable to a young person is to be reduced under regulation 63 of the Jobseeker's Allowance Regulations because paragraph (1)(b)(iii), (c), (d), (e) or (f) of that regulation (reduced payments under section 17 of the Jobseekers Act) applied in his case; and
  (b) the decision made in consequence of sub-paragraph (a) falls to be superseded by a decision under section 10 because the Secretary of State has subsequently issued a certificate under section 17(4) of the Jobseekers Act with respect to the failure in question,
the decision under section 10 shall take effect as from the same date as the decision made in consequence of sub-paragraph (a) has effect.

[5(25) In a case where a decision ("the first decision") has been made

Social Security and Child Support (Decisions and Appeals) Regulations 1999

that a person failed without good cause to take part in a work-focused interview, the decision under section 10 shall take effect as from the first day of the benefit week to commence for that person following the date of the first decision.

(26) In paragraph (25), "benefit week" means any period of 7 days corresponding to the week in respect of which the relevant social security benefit is due to be paid.]

AMENDMENTS

1. Social Security and Child Support (Decisions and Appeals) Amendment (No. 2) Regulations 1999 (S.I. 1999 No. 1623), reg. 4 (July 5, 1999).
2. Tax Credits (Decisions and Appeals) (Amendment) Regulations 1999 (S.I. 1999 No. 2570), reg. 10 (October 5, 1999). Note that amendments made by these regulations only have effect with respect to tax credit (reg. 1(2) of the Amendment Regulations).
3. Social Security and Child Support (Decisions and Appeals), Vaccine Damage Payments and Jobseeker's Allowance (Amendment) Regulations 1999 (S.I. 1999 No. 2677), reg. 8 (October 18, 1999).
4. Social Security and Child Support (Decisions and Appeals) Amendment Regulations 2000 (S.I. 2000 No. 119), reg. 2 (February 17, 2000).
5. Social Security (Work-focused Interviews) Regulations 2000 (S.I. 2000 No. 897), reg. 16(5) and Sched. 6, para. 5 (April 3, 2000).

GENERAL NOTE

Paragraph (2)

4.265   A supersession on the ground of change of circumstances advantageous to the claimant is effective from the date of the change if the change is notified within a month (or such longer period as is allowed under reg. 8) but is otherwise effective only from the date of notification. Where the change is not advantageous to the claimant, the supersession is generally effective from the date of change or, in the case of incapacity and disability cases, from the date when the change should have been reported. See reg. 7A for definitions material to para. (2)(c). Presumably, para. (2) does not apply to those attendance allowance and disability living allowance cases where para. (9) applies or, indeed, to any cases where any of paras (10) to (24) applies.

Paragraph (5)

4.266   This provides consistency between, on the one hand, revision and supersession of decisions of the Secretary of State on the ground of error of fact (under regs 3(5) and 6(2)(b)) and, on the other hand, supersession of decisions of appeal tribunals and Commissioners on the ground of error of fact (under reg. 6(2)(c)).

Paragraphs (12) to (23)

4.267   These contain provisions similar to those previously found in regs 63 and 63A of the Social Security (Adjudication) Regulations 1995.

[¹ **Definitions for the purposes of regulations 3(5)(c), 6(2)(g) and 7(2)(c) and ancillary provisions**

4.268   **7A.**—(1) For the purposes of regulations 3(5)(c), 6(2)(g) and 7(2)(c)—

"disability benefit decision" means a decision to award a relevant

(S.I. 1999 No. 991, reg. 7A)

benefit embodied in or necessary to which is a disability determination,

"disability benefit decision" means—
  (a) in the case of a decision as to an award of an attendance allowance or a disability living allowance, whether the person satisfies any of the conditions in section 64, 72(1) or 73(1) to (3), as the case may be, of the Contributions and Benefits Act,
  (b) in the case of a decision as to an award of severe disablement allowance, whether the person is disabled for the purpose of section 68 of the Contributions and Benefits Act, or
  (c) in the case of a decision as to an award of industrial injuries benefit, whether the existence or extent of any disablement is sufficient for the purposes of section 103 or 108 of the Contributions and Benefits Act or for the benefit to be paid at the rate which was in payment immediately prior to that decision;

"incapacity benefit decision" means a decision to award a relevant benefit embodied in or necessary to which is a determination that a person is or is to be treated as incapable of work under Part XIIA of the Contributions and Benefits Act,

"incapacity determination" means a determination whether a person is incapable of work by applying the all work test in regulation 24 of the Social Security (Incapacity for Work) (General) Regulations 1995 or whether a person is to be treated as incapable of work in accordance with regulation 10 (certain persons with a severe condition to be treated as incapable of work) or 27 (exceptional circumstances) of those Regulations, and

"payee" means a person to whom a benefit referred to in paragraph (a), (b) or (c) of the definition of "disability determination", or a benefit referred to in the definition of "incapacity benefit decision" is payable.

(2) Where a person's receipt of or entitlement to a benefit ("the first benefit") is a condition of his being entitled to any other benefit, allowance or advantage ("a second benefit") and a decision is revised under regulation 3(5)(c) or a superseding decision is made under regulation 6(2) to which regulation 7(2)(c)(ii) applies, the effect of which is that the first benefit ceases to be payable, or becomes payable at a lower rate than was in payment immediately prior to that revision or supersession, a consequent decision as to his entitlement to the second benefit shall take effect from the date of the change in his entitlement to the first benefit.]

AMENDMENT

1. Social Security and Child Support (Decisions and Appeals) Amendment (No. 2) Regulations 1999 (S.I. 1999 No. 1623), reg. 5 (July 5, 1999).

Effective date for late notifications of change of circumstances

8.—(1) For the purposes of regulation 7(2) [² and (9)], a longer period of time may be allowed for the notification of a change of circumstances in so far as it affects the effective date of the change where the

Social Security and Child Support (Decisions and Appeals) Regulations 1999

conditions specified in the following provisions of this regulation are satisfied.

(2) An application for the purposes of regulation 7(2) [² or (9)] shall be made by the claimant or a person acting on his behalf.

(3) The application referred to in paragraph (2) shall—
  (a) contain particulars of the relevant change of circumstances and the reasons for the failure to notify the change of circumstances on an earlier date; and
  (b) be made within 13 months of the date the change occurred.

(4) An application under this regulation shall not be granted unless the Secretary of State is satisfied [¹ or the Board are satisfied] that—
  (a) it is reasonable to grant the application;
  (b) the change of circumstances notified by the applicant is relevant to the decision which is to be superseded; and
  (c) special circumstances are relevant to the application and as a result of those special circumstances it was not practicable for the applicant to notify the change of circumstances within one month of the change occurring.

(5) In determining whether it is reasonable to grant the application, the Secretary of State [¹ or the Board] shall have regard to the principle that the greater the amount of time that has elapsed between the date one month after the change of circumstances occurred and the date the application for the purposes of regulation 7(2) [² or (9)] is made, the more compelling should be the special circumstances on which the application is based.

(6) In determining whether it is reasonable to grant an application, no account shall be taken of the following—
  (a) that the applicant or any person acting for him was unaware of, or misunderstood, the law applicable to his case (including ignorance or misunderstanding of the time limits imposed by these Regulations); or
  (b) that a Commissioner or a court has taken a different view of the law from that previously understood and applied.

(7) An application under this regulation which has been refused may not be renewed.

AMENDMENTS

1. Tax Credits (Decisions and Appeals) (Amendment) Regulations 1999 (S.I. 1999 No. 2570), reg. 11 (October 5, 1999). Note that amendments made by these regulations only have effect with respect to tax credit (reg. 1(2) of the Amendment Regulations).

2. Social Security and Child Support (Decisions and Appeals) Amendment Regulations 2000 (S.I. 2000 No. 119), reg. 3 (February 17, 2000).

GENERAL NOTE

Paragraph (6)(b)

4.270   See the note to reg. 32(8)(b) which is in similar terms.

(S.I. 1999 No. 991, reg. 9)

Chapter III

Other Matters

Certificates of recoverable benefits

9. A certificate of recoverable benefits may be reviewed under section 10 of the 1997 Act where the Secretary of State is satisfied that—
- (a) a mistake (whether in computation of the amount specified or otherwise) occurred in the preparation of the certificate;
- (b) the benefit recovered from a person who makes a compensation payment (as defined in section 1 of the 1997 Act) is in excess of the amount due to the Secretary of State;
- (c) incorrect or insufficient information was supplied to the Secretary of State by the person who applied for the certificate and in consequence the amount of benefit specified in the certificate was less than it would have been had the information supplied been correct or sufficient; or
- (d) a ground for appeal is satisfied under section 11 of the 1997 Act.

4.271

Effect of a determination as to capacity for work

10. A determination (including a determination made following a change of circumstances) whether a person is, or is to be treated as, capable or incapable of work which is embodied in or necessary to a decision under Chapter II of Part I of the Act or on which such a decision is based shall be conclusive for the purposes of any further such decision.

4.272

GENERAL NOTE

This re-enacts reg. 19 of the Social Security (Incapacity for Work) (General) Regulations 1995. Note that a decision that a person is *not*, or is not to be treated as, incapable of work is not of continuing effect. Consequently, it operates to allow supersession of any award of benefit current at the time it is made but it does not operate so as to prevent a person from making a new claim or a further application for supersession (although reg. 28 of the 1995 Regulations may not apply while a new assessment is arranged). See the Social Security Act 1998 (Commencement No. 9, and Savings and Consequential and Transitional Provisions) Order 1999, Sched. 14, paras 15 to 17 for transitional provisions relating to the determinations as to capacity for work.

4.273

Secretary of State to determine certain matters

11. Where, in relation to a determination for any purpose to which Part XIIA of the Contributions and Benefits Act applies, an issue arises as to—
- (a) whether a person is, or is to be treated as, capable or incapable of work in respect of any period; or
- (b) whether a person is terminally ill,

that issue shall be determined by the Secretary of State, notwithstanding that other matters fall to be determined by another authority.

4.274

Social Security and Child Support (Decisions and Appeals) Regulations 1999

[¹ **Issues for decision by officers of Inland Revenue**

11A.—(1) Where, on consideration of any claim or other matter, it appears to the Secretary of State that an issue arises which, by virtue of section 8 of the Transfer Act, falls to be decided by an officer of the Board, he shall refer that issue to the Board.

(2) Where—
  (a) the Secretary of State has decided any claim or other matter on an assumption of facts—
    (i) as to which there appeared to him to be no dispute, but
    (ii) concerning which, had an issue arisen, that issue would have fallen, by virtue of section 8 of the Transfer Act, to be decided by an officer of the Board; and
  (b) an application for revision or an application for supersession is made in relation to the decision of that claim or other matter; and
  (c) it appears to the Secretary of State on consideration of the application that such an issue arises,
he shall refer that issue to the Board.

(3) Pending the final decision of any issue which has been referred to the Board in accordance with paragraph (1) or (2) above, the Secretary of State may—
  (a) determine any other issue arising on consideration of the claim or other matter or, as the case may be, of the application,
  (b) seek a preliminary opinion of the Board on the issue referred and decide the claim or other matter or, as the case may be, the application in accordance with that opinion on that issue; or
  (c) defer making any decision on the claim or other matter or, as the case may be, the application.

(4) On receipt by the Secretary of State of the final decision of an issue which has been referred to the Board in accordance with paragraph (1) or (2) above, the Secretary of State that—
  (a) in a case to which paragraph (3)(b) above applies—
    (i) consider whether the decision ought to be revised under section 9 or superseded under section 10, and
    (ii) if so, revise it, or, as the case may be, make a further decision which supersedes it; or
  (b) in a case to which paragraph (3)(a) or (c) above applies, decide the claim or other matter or, as the case may be, the application,
in accordance with the final decision of the issue so referred.

(5) In paragraphs (3) and (4) above "final decision" means the decision of an officer of the Board under section 8 of the Transfer Act or the determination of any appeal in relation to that decision.]

AMENDMENT

1. Social Security and Child Support (Decisions and Appeals) Amendment (No. 3) Regulations 1999 (S.I. 1999 No. 1623), reg. 2(3) (July 5, 1999).

Decision of the Secretary of State relating to industrial injuries benefit

12.—(1) This regulation applies where, for the purpose of a decision of the Secretary of State relating to a claim for industrial injuries benefit

under Part V of the Contributions and Benefits Act an issue to be decided is—
  (a) the extent of a personal injury for the purposes of section 94 of that Act;
  (b) whether the claimant has a disease prescribed for the purposes of section 108 of that Act or the extent of any disablement resulting from such a disease; or
  (c) whether the claimant has a disablement for the purposes of section 103 of that Act or the extent of any such disablement.

(2) In connection with making a decision to which this regulation applies, the Secretary of State may refer an issue, together with any relevant evidence or information available to him, including any evidence or information provided by or on behalf of the claimant, to a medical practitioner who has experience in such of the issues specified in paragraph (1) as are relevant to the decision, for such report as appears to the Secretary of State to be necessary for the purpose of providing him with information for use in making the decision.

(3) In making a decision to which this regulation applies, the Secretary of State shall have regard to (among other factors)—
  (a) all relevant medical reports provided to him in connection with that decision; and
  (b) the experience, in such of the issues specified in paragraph (1) as are relevant to the decision, of any medical practitioner who has provided a report, including a medical practitioner who has provided a report following an examination required by the Secretary of State under section 19.

GENERAL NOTE

Adjudicating medical authorities have been abolished and so all decisions which an adjudication officer would, or might, have referred to such authorities under the Social Security Administration Act 1992 are now decided by the Secretary of State on the basis of medical advice. In practice, this is unlikely to make much difference in most cases but it does remove one level of decision-making in diagnosis and recrudescence cases where adverse decisions could be made by an adjudication officer and there was then a right of appeal to an adjudicating medical authority under regulation 48 of the Social Security (Adjudication) Regulations 1995.

See s. 30 of the Social Security Act 1998 for the effect of an earlier declaration that the claimant has suffered personal injury by accident.

4.277

Income support and social fund determinations on incomplete evidence

13.—(1) Where, for the purpose of a decision under section 8 or 10—
  (a) a determination falls to be made by the Secretary of State as to what housing costs are to be included in a claimant's applicable amount by virtue of regulation 17(1)(e) or 18(1)(f) of, and Schedule 3 to, the Income Support Regulations; and
  (b) it appears to the Secretary of State that he is not in possession of all of the evidence or information which is relevant for the purposes of such a determination,

4.278

he shall make the determination on the assumption that the housing costs to be included in the claimant's applicable amount are those that can be immediately determined.

(2) Where, for the purpose of a decision under section 8 or 10—
  (a) a determination falls to be made by the Secretary of State as to whether—
    (i) in relation to any person, the applicable amount falls to be reduced or disregarded to any extent by virtue of section 126(3) of the Contributions and Benefits Act (persons affected by trade disputes);
    (ii) for the purposes of regulation 12 of the Income Support Regulations, a person is by virtue of that regulation to be treated as receiving relevant education; or
    (iii) in relation to any claimant, the applicable amount includes severe disability premium by virtue of regulation 17(1)(d) or 18(1)(e), and paragraph 13 of Schedule 2 to, the Income Support Regulations; and
  (b) it appears to the Secretary of State that he is not in possession of all of the evidence or information which is relevant for the purposes of such a determination,

he shall make the determination on the assumption that the relevant evidence or information which is not in his possession is adverse to the claimant.

Effect of alteration in the component rates of income support and jobseeker's allowance

4.279

14.—(1) Section 159 of the Administration Act (effect of alteration in the component rates of income support) shall not apply to any award of income support in force in favour of a person where there is applicable to that person—
  (a) any amount determined in accordance with regulation 17(2) to (7) of the Income Support Regulations; or
  (b) any protected sum determined in accordance with Schedule 3A or 3B of those Regulations; or
  (c) any transitional addition, personal expenses addition or special transitional addition applicable under Part II of the Income Support (Transitional) Regulations 1987 (transitional protection).

(2) Where section 159 of the Administration Act does not apply to an award of income support by virtue of paragraph (1), a decision under section 10 may be made in respect of that award for the sole purpose of giving effect to any change made by an order under section 150 of the Administration Act.

(3) Section 159A of the Administration Act (effect of alterations in the component rates of jobseeker's allowance) shall not apply to any award of a jobseeker's allowance in force in favour of a person where there is applicable to that person any amount determined in accordance with regulations 87 of the Jobseeker's Allowance Regulations.

(4) Where section 159A of the Administration Act does not apply to an award of a jobseeker's allowance by virtue of paragraph (3), a

(S.I. 1999 No. 991, reg. 14)

decision under section 10 may be made in respect of that award for the sole purpose of giving effect to any change made by an order under section 150 of the Administration Act.

Jobseeker's allowance determinations on incomplete evidence

15. Where, for the purpose of a decision under section 8 or 10—
    (a) a determination falls to be made by the Secretary of State as to whether—
        (i) in relation to any person, the applicable amount falls to be reduced or disregarded to any extent by virtue of section 15 of the Jobseekers Act (persons affected by trade disputes); or
        (ii) for the purposes of regulation 54(2) to (4) of the Jobseeker's Allowance Regulations (relevant education), a person is by virtue of that regulation, to be treated as receiving relevant education; and
    (b) it appears to the Secretary of State that he is not in possession of all of the evidence or information which is relevant for the purposes of such a determination.

he shall make the determination on the assumption that the relevant evidence or information which is not in his possession is adverse to the claimant.

4.280

PART III

SUSPENSION, TERMINATION AND OTHER MATTERS

CHAPTER I

SUSPENSION AND TERMINATION

Suspension in prescribed cases

16.—(1) Subject to paragraph (2), the Secretary of State [¹ or the Board] may suspend payment of a relevant benefit, in whole or in part, in the circumstances prescribed in paragraph (3).

(2) The Secretary of State shall suspend payment of a jobseeker's allowance in the circumstances prescribed in paragraph (3)(a)(i) or (ii) where the issue or one of the issues is whether a person, who has claimed a jobseeker's allowance, is or was available for employment or whether he is or was actively seeking employment.

(3) The prescribed circumstances are that—
    (a) it appears to the Secretary of State [¹ or the Board] that—
        (i) an issue arises whether the conditions for entitlement to a relevant benefit are or were fulfilled;
        (ii) an issue arises whether a decision as to an award of a relevant

4.281

benefit should be revised under section 9 or superseded under section 10;
- (iii) an issue arises whether any amount paid or payable to a person by way of, or in connection with a claim for, a relevant benefit is recoverable under section 71(overpayments), 71A (recovery of jobseeker's allowance: severe hardship cases) or 74 (income support and other payments) of the Administration Act or regulations made under any of those sections; or
- (iv) the last address notified to him [¹ or them] of a person who is in receipt of a relevant benefit is not the address at which that person is residing; or
- (b) an appeal is pending against—
  - (i) a decision of an appeal tribunal, a Commissioner or a court;
  - (ii) a decision given in a different case by a Commissioner or a court, and it appears to the Secretary of State [¹ or the Board] that, if the appeal were to be determined in a particular way, an issue would arise as to whether the award of a relevant benefit (whether the same benefit or not) in the case itself ought to be revised or superseded.

(4) For the purposes of section 21(3)(c) an appeal is pending where the Secretary of State certifies [¹ or the Board certify] in writing that he proposes [¹ or they propose—
- (a) to make a request under regulation 53(4) for a statement of reasons for a decision of an appeal tribunal;
- (b) to bring an appeal against the decision; or
- (c) to bring an appeal against a decision in a different case and, if that appeal were to be allowed, an issue would arise as to whether the award of a relevant benefit (whether the same benefit or not) in the case itself ought to be revised or superseded.

AMENDMENT

1. Tax Credits (Decisions and Appeals) (Amendment) Regulations 1999 (S.I. 1999 No. 2570), reg. 12 (October 5, 1999). Note that amendments made by these regulations only have effect with respect to tax credit (reg. 1(2) of the Amendment Regulations).

Provision of information or evidence

17.—(1) This regulation applies where the Secretary of State requires information or evidence for a determination whether a decision awarding a relevant benefit should be—
- (a) revised under section 9; or
- (b) superseded under section 10.

(2) For the purposes of paragraph (1), the following persons must satisfy the requirements of paragraph (4)—
- (a) a person in respect of whom payment of a benefit has been suspended in the circumstances prescribed in regulation 16(3)(a);
- (b) a person who has made an application for a decision of the Secretary of State to be revised or superseded;

(c) a person who fails to comply with the provisions of regulation 32(1) of the Claims and Payments Regulations in so far as they relate to documents, information or facts required by the Secretary of State;
(d) a person who qualifies for income support by virtue of paragraph 7 of Schedule 1B to the Income Support Regulations;
(e) a person whose entitlement to benefit is conditional upon his being, or being treated as, incapable of work.

(3) The Secretary of State shall notify any person to whom paragraph (2) refers of the requirements of this regulation.

(4) A person to whom paragraph (2) refers must either—
(a) supply the information or evidence within—
   (i) a period of one month beginning with the date on which the notification under paragraph (3) was sent to him; or
   (ii) such longer period as he satisfies the Secretary of State is necessary in order to enable him to comply with the requirement; or
(b) satisfy the Secretary of State within the period of time specified in sub-paragraph (a)(i) that either—
   (i) the information or evidence required of him does not exist; or
   (ii) that it is not possible for him to obtain it.

(5) The Secretary of State may suspend the payment of a relevant benefit, in whole or in part, to any person to whom paragraph (2)(b) to (e) applies who fails to satisfy the requirements of paragraph (4).

(6) In this regulation, "evidence" includes evidence which a person is required to provide in accordance with regulation 2 of the Social Security (Medical Evidence) Regulations 1976.

[¹ *Provision of information or evidence*

17.—*(1) This regulation applies where the Board require information or evidence for a determination whether a decision awarding tax credit should be—*
   (a) revised under section 9; or
   (b) superseded under section 10.

(2) The relevant person shall furnish such certificates, documents, information and evidence as may be required by the Board for the purposes of paragraph (1), and shall do so within one month of being required to do so or such longer period as the Board may consider reasonable.

(3) In paragraph (2) "the relevant person" means any of the following—
(a) the claimant concerned;
(b) where the tax credit could have been claimed by either of two partners or where entitlement to or the amount of the tax credit was affected or liable to be affected by the circumstances of either partner, the partner other than the claimant;
(c) the employer of the claimant or, where sub-paragraph (b) applies, the employer of the partner other than the claimant.

(4) Where the claimant or any partner of the claimant is aged not less than 60 and is a member of, or a person deriving entitlement to a pension under,

a personal pension scheme, or is a party to, or a person deriving entitlement to a pension under, a retirement annuity contract, the claimant shall, where the Board so require and within one month of being required to do so or such longer period as the Board may consider reasonable, furnish the following information—
  (a) the name and address of the pension fund holder;
  (b) such other information, including any reference number or policy number, as is needed to enable the personal pension scheme or retirement annuity contract to be identified.

(5) A pension fund holder to whom paragraph (4) applies shall, where the Board so require and within one month of being required to do so or such longer period as the Board may consider reasonable, provide the Board with the information specified in paragraph (6).

(6) The information referred to in this paragraph is—
  (a) where the purchase of an annuity under a personal pension scheme has been deferred, the amount of any income which is being withdrawn from the personal pension scheme;
  (b) in the case of—
    (i) a personal pension scheme where income withdrawal is available, the maximum amount of income which may be withdrawn from the scheme; or
    (ii) a personal pension scheme where income withdrawal is not available, or a retirement annuity contract, the maximum amount of income which might be withdrawn from the fund if the fund were held under a personal pension scheme where income withdrawal was available,
calculated by or on behalf of the pension fund holder by means of tables prepared from time to time by the Government Actuary which are appropriate for this purpose.

(7) Every person providing childcare in respect of which a claimant to whom regulation 46A of the Family Credit (General) Regulations 1987 applies is incurring relevant childcare charges (within the meaning of that regulation), including a person providing childcare on behalf of a school, local authority, childcare scheme or establishment within paragraph (2)(b), (c) or (d) of that regulation, shall furnish such certificates, documents, information and evidence as may be required by the Board for the purposes of paragraph (1), and shall do so within one month of being required to do so or such longer period as the Board may consider reasonable.]

AMENDMENT

1. Tax Credits (Decisions and Appeals) (Amendment) Regulations 1999 (S.I. 1999 No. 2570), reg. 13 (October 5, 1999). Amendments made by these Regulations have effect only with respect to tax credit (reg. 1(2) of the Amendment Regulations). The form of reg. 17 in italics thus applies for the purposes of tax credit and the original form for other benefits.

Termination in cases of failure to furnish information or evidence

18.—(1) Subject to paragraphs (2), (3) and (4), the Secretary of State shall decide that where a person—

(S.I. 1999 No. 991, reg. 18)

    (a) whose benefit has been suspended in accordance with regulation 16 and who subsequently fails to comply with an information requirement made in pursuance of regulation 17; or

    (b) whose benefit has been suspended in accordance with regulation 17(5),

that person shall cease to be entitled to that benefit from the date on which payment was suspended except where entitlement to benefit ceases on an earlier date other than under this regulation.

    (2) Paragraph (1)(a) shall not apply where not more than one month has elapsed since the information requirement was made in pursuance of regulation 17.

    (3) Paragraph (1)(b) shall not apply where not more than one month has elapsed since the first payment was suspended in accordance with regulation 17.

    (4) Paragraph (1) shall not apply where benefit has been suspended in part under regulation 16 or, as the case may be, regulation 17.

[¹*Suspension and termination in cases of failure to furnish information or evidence*

18.—*(1) Where a claimant—*
    (a) is required by the Board under regulation 17 to furnish information, or evidence, and
    (b) fails to do so within the period specified by the Board in accordance with that regulation ("the suspension period"),
the Board may, subject to paragraphs (3) and (4), decide to suspend payment of tax credit to or on behalf of the claimant in whole or in part.

4.285

    (2) Where either—
    (a) a claimant whose benefit has been suspended in whole or in part in accordance with regulation 16 subsequently fails to comply with a requirement for information or evidence made under regulation 17, within the suspension period, or within the period of one month immediately following the suspension period; or
    (b)
        (i) a claimant has been required by the Board under regulation 17 to furnish information or evidence,
        (ii) the claimant has failed to do so within the suspension period and within the period of one month immediately following the suspension period, and
        (iii) the Board have suspended payment of tax credit to or on behalf of the claimant in whole or in part in accordance with paragraph (1) of this regulation.
the Board may, subject to paragraphs (3) to (5), decide that the claimant shall cease to be entitled to payment of tax credit with effect from a date not earlier than the date on which payment of tax credit was suspended.

    (3) No decision shall be taken by the Board pursuant to paragraph (1) or (2) where—
    (a) the failure to furnish information has been remedied; or
    (b) the Board have allowed a further period of time (in addition to the suspension period or the period of one month referred to in paragraph

(2)(a) or (b)(ii)) within which the claimant is required to furnish the information and the claimant has furnished the information within that further period.

(4) For the purposes of paragraphs (1) and (2), a claimant shall be deemed not to have failed to furnish information within the suspension period or within the period of one month referred to in paragraph (2)(a) or (b)(ii) if he had a reasonable excuse and that excuse has no ceased; and, where that excuse has ceased, he shall be deemed not to have failed to furnish information within either of those periods for those purposes if he furnished the information without unreasonable delay after the excuse had ceased.

(5) No decision shall be taken by the Board pursuant to paragraph (2) unless payment of the whole of the relevant tax credit to or on behalf of the claimant has been suspended, under regulation 16 or 17 or both of those regulations.]

AMENDMENT

1. Tax Credits (Decisions and Appeals) (Amendment) Regulations 1999 (S.I. 1999 No. 2570), reg. 13 (October 5, 1999). Amendments made by these Regulations have effect only with respect to tax credit (reg. 1(2) of the Amendment Regulations). The form of reg. 18 in italics thus applies for the purposes of tax credit and the original form for other benefits.

Suspension and termination for failure to submit to medical examination

19.—(1) Except where regulation 8 of the Social Security (Incapacity for Work) (General) Regulations 1995 applies (where a question arises as to whether a person is capable of work), the Secretary of State [¹or the Board] may require a person to submit to a medical examination by a medical practitioner where that person is in receipt of a relevant benefit, and either—
  (a) the Secretary of State considers [¹or the Board consider] it necessary to satisfy himself [¹or themselves] as to the correctness of the award of the benefit, or of the rate at which it was awarded; or
  (b) that person applies for a revision or supersession of the award and the Secretary of State considers [¹ or their] that the examination is necessary for the purpose of making his [¹ or the Board consider] decision.

(2) The Secretary of State [¹ or the Board] may suspend payment of a relevant benefit in whole or in part, to a person who fails, without good cause, on two consecutive occasions to submit to a medical examination in accordance with requirements under paragraph (1) except where entitlement to benefit is suspended on an earlier date other than under this regulation.

(3) Subject to paragraph (4), the Secretary of State [¹ or the Board] may determine that the entitlement to a relevant benefit of a person, in respect of whom payment of such a benefit has been suspended under paragraph (2), shall cease from a date not earlier than the date on which payment was suspended except where entitlement to benefit ceases on an earlier date other than under this regulation.

(4) Paragraph (3) shall not apply where not more than one month has elapsed since the first payment was suspended under paragraph (2).

AMENDMENT

1. Tax Credits (Decisions and Appeals) (Amendment) Regulations 1999 (S.I. 1999 No. 2570), reg. 14 (October 5, 1999). Note that amendments made by these Regulations have effect only with respect to tax credit (reg. 1(2) of the Amendment Regulations).

Making of payments which have been suspended

20.—(1) Subject to paragraphs (2) and (3), payment of a benefit suspended in accordance with regulation 16 [¹ or 17] shall be made where—
  (a) in a case to which regulation 16(2) or (3)(a)(i) to (iii) applies, the Secretary of State is satisfied [² or the Board are satisfied] that the benefit suspended is properly payable and no outstanding issues remain to be resolved;
  (b) in a case to which regulation 16(3)(a)(iv) applies, the Secretary of State is satisfied [² or the Board are satisfied] that the has [² or they have] been notified of the address at which the person is residing;
  (c) in a case to which regulation 16(3)(b) applies, an appeal is no longer pending and the benefit suspended remains payable following the determination of the appeal;
  (d) [¹ in a case to which regulation 17(5) applies, the Secretary of State is satisfied that the benefit is properly payable and the requirements of regulation 17(4) have been satisfied.]
[² (d) in a case to which regulation 18(1) applies, the Board are satisfied that the benefit suspended is properly payable and the requirements of regulation 17(2), (4), (5) or (7) have been satisfied.]

(2) Where regulation 16(4)(a) applies, payment of a benefit suspended shall be made if, within one month of the date on which he [² or they] received a copy of the tribunal's decision, the Secretary of State has not [², or the Board have not] notified the claimant in writing that he has [², or they have] requested, pursuant to regulation 53(4), a statement of the reasons for the decision.

(3) Where regulation 16(4)(b) or (c) applies, payment of a benefit suspended shall be made if the Secretary of State fails [² or the Board fail] to notify the claimant in writing, within one month of the date on which the Secretary of State receives [² or the Board receive] the reasons in writing for the decision on appeal which was pending for the purposes of regulation 16(3)(b), that an appeal or, as the case may be, an application for leave to appeal has been made against the decision.

(4) Payment of benefit which has been suspended in accordance with regulation 19 for failure to submit to a medical examination shall be made where the Secretary of State is satisfied [² or the Board are satisfied] that it is no longer necessary for the person referred to in that regulation to submit to a medical examination.

AMENDMENTS

1. Social Security and Child Support (Decisions and Appeals) Amendment (No. 2) Regulations 1999 (S.I. 1999 No. 1623), reg. 6 (July 5, 1999).
2. Tax Credits (Decisions and Appeals) (Amendment) Regulations 1999 (S.I. 1999 No. 2570), reg. 15 (October 5, 1999). Note that amendments made by these Regulations have effect only with respect to tax credit (reg. 1(2) of the Amendment Regulations). There are thus two forms of para. (1)(d) as the second form is only substituted for the purposes of tax credit.

CHAPTER II

OTHER MATTERS

Decisions involving issues that arise on appeal in other cases

4.288   21.—(1) For the purposes of section 25(3)(b) (prescribed cases and circumstances in which a decision may be made on a prescribed basis) a case which satisfies the condition in paragraph (2) is a prescribed case.

(2) The condition is that the claimant would be entitled to the benefit to which the decision which falls to be made relates, even if the appeal in the other case referred to in section 25(1)(b) were decided in a way which is the most unfavourable to him.

(3) For the purposes of section 25(3)(b), the prescribed basis on which the Secretary of State [¹ or the Board] may make the decision is as if—
  (a) the appeal in the other case which is referred to in section 25(1)(b) had already been determined; and
  (b) that appeal had been decided in a way which is the most unfavourable to the claimant.

(4) The circumstance prescribed under section 25(5)(c), where an appeal is pending against a decision for the purposes of that section, even though an appeal against the decision has not been brought (or, as the case may be, an application for leave to appeal against the decision has not been made) but the time for doing so has not yet expired, is where the Secretary of State [¹ or the Board—
  (a) certifies in writing that he is [¹, or certify in writing that they are,] considering appealing against that decision; and
  (b) considers [¹, or consider,] that, if such an appeal were to be determined in a particular way—
    (i) there would be no entitlement to benefit in a case to which section 25(1)(a) refers; or
    (ii) the appeal would affect the decision in that case in some other way.

AMENDMENT

1. Tax Credits (Decisions and Appeals) (Amendment) Regulations 1999 (S.I. 1999 No. 2570), reg. 16 (October 5, 1999). Note that amendments made

by these regulations only have effect with respect to tax credit (reg. 1(2) of the Amendment Regulations).

Appeals involving issues that arise in other cases

22. The circumstance prescribed under section 26(6)(c), where an appeal is pending against a decision in the case described in section 26(1)(b) even though an appeal against the decision has not been brought (or, as the case may be, an application for leave to appeal against the decision has not been made) but the time for doing so has not yet expired, is where the Secretary of State [¹ or the Board—
   (a) certifies in writing that he is [¹, or certify in writing that they are,] considering appealing against that decision; and
   (b) considers [¹, or consider,] that, if such an appeal were already determined, it would affect the determination of the appeal described in section 26(1)(a).

4.289

AMENDMENT

1. Tax Credits (Decisions and Appeals) (Amendment) Regulations 1999 (S.I. 1999 No. 2570), reg. 17 (October 5, 1999). Note that amendments made by these regulations only have effect with respect to tax credit (reg. 1(2) of the Amendment Regulations).

Regulation 23 Omitted 4.290

Regulation 24 Omitted 4.291

PART IV

RIGHTS OF APPEAL AND PROCEDURE FOR BRINGING APPEALS

CHAPTER I

GENERAL

General appeals matters not including child support appeals

Other persons with a right of appeal

25. For the purposes of section 12(2)(b), the following other persons have a right to appeal to an appeal tribunal—
   (a) any person appointed by the Secretary of State [¹ or the Board] under regulation 33(1) of the Claims and Payments Regulations (persons unable to act) to act on behalf of another;
   (b) any person claiming attendance allowance or disability living allowance on behalf of another under section 66(2)(b) of the

4.292

Contributions and Benefits Act or, as the case may be, section 76(3) of that Act (claims on behalf of terminally ill persons);

(c) in relation to a pension scheme, any person who, for the purposes of Part X of the Pension Schemes Act 1993, is an employer, member, trustee or manager by virtue of section 146(8) of that Act.

AMENDMENT

1. Tax Credits (Decisions and Appeals) (Amendment) Regulations 1999 (S.I. 1999 No. 2570), reg. 18 (October 5, 1999). Note that amendments made by these regulations only have effect with respect to tax credit (reg. 1(2) of the Amendment Regulations).

Decisions against which an appeal lies

4.293   **26.** An appeal shall lie to an appeal tribunal against a decision made by the Secretary of State [¹ or an officer of the Board]—
(a) as to whether a person is entitled to a relevant benefit for which no claim is required by virtue of regulation 3 of the Claims and Payments Regulations; or
(b) as to whether a payment be made out of the social fund to a person to meet expenses for heating by virtue of regulations made under section 138(2) of the Contributions and Benefits Act (payments out of the social fund).

AMENDMENT

1. Tax Credits (Decisions and Appeals) (Amendment) Regulations 1999 (S.I. 1999 No. 2570), reg. 19 (October 5, 1999). Note that amendments made by these regulations only have effect with respect to tax credit (reg. 1(2) of the Amendment Regulations).

Decisions against which no appeal lies

4.294   **27.**—(1) No appeal lies to an appeal tribunal against a decision set out in Schedule 2.
(2) In paragraph (1) and Schedule 2, "decision" includes determinations embodied in or necessary to a decision.
(3) An appeal made against a decision specified in paragraph (1) may be struck out in accordance with regulation 46.

4.295   GENERAL NOTE

See note to Sched. 2.

Notice of decision against which appeal lies

4.296   **28.**—(1) A person with a right of appeal under the Act or these Regulations against any decision of the Secretary of State [¹ or the Board or an officer of the Board] shall—
(a) be given written notice of the decision against which the appeal lies;
(b) be informed that, in a case where that written notice does not

include a statement of the reasons for that decision, he may, within one month of the date of notification of that decision, request that the Secretary of State [¹ or the Board or an officer of the Board] provide him with a written statement of the reasons for that decision; and

(c) be given written notice of his right of appeal against that decision.

(2) Where a written statement of the reasons for the decision is not included in the written notice of the decision and is requested under paragraph (1)(b), the Secretary of State [¹ or the Board or an officer of the Board] shall provide that statement within 14 days of receipt of the request.

AMENDMENT

1. Tax Credits (Decisions and Appeals) (Amendment) Regulations 1999 (S.I. 1999 No. 2570), reg. 20 (October 5, 1999). Note that amendments made by these regulations only have effect with respect to tax credit (reg. 1(2) of the Amendment Regulations).

GENERAL NOTE

Paragraph (1)
It is suggested that a failure to comply with any of these duties may invalidate the decision in some cases but not others. In particular, it is suggested that a failure to give notice of a decision at all may have the effect that there is no decision. On the other hand, subpara. (c) seems to be purely directory because a failure to comply with it appears not even to be a ground for appealing late (see the note to reg. 32(8)(a)). It is arguable that a statement of reasons only counts as such for the purposes of subpara. (b) if it is adequate but the adequacy of a statement of reasons is very much a matter of judgment and depends on the issues arising in the particular case. However, a request made under para. (1)(b) extends the time for appealing but, presumably, only if it is properly made and the notice really does not include an adequate statement of reasons. Accordingly, the cautious claimant will treat any purported statement of reasons as being adequate for the purpose and will ensure that the appeal is lodged within the usual one month time limit, even if a fuller explanation is expected in the Secretary of State's submission to the tribunal.

4.297

Paragraph (2)
The extension of time for applying for a revision under reg. 3(2) or appealing under reg. 31 assumes that the reasons are provided within 14 days of the usual month time limit expiring. If the statement of reasons is not received during that time, the cautious claimant will apply for revision or lodge the appeal before the 14-day extension expires rather than argue about whether the time should be further extended.

4.298

Further particulars required relating to certificate of recoverable benefits appeals or applications

29.—(1) An appeal or application under the 1997 Act relating to a certificate of recoverable benefits shall, in addition to any requirements imposed by regulations, include also the following particulars—

(a) in the case of an appeal, the date of the certificate of recoverable

4.299

benefits or the decision by the Secretary of State on review against which the appeal is brought, the question under section 11 of the 1997 Act to which the appeal relates and a summary of the arguments relied upon by the appellant to support his contention that the certificate is wrong;

(b) in the case of an application for an extension of time under regulation 32, in relation to the appeal which it is proposed to bring, the particulars required under sub-paragraph (a) together with particulars of the special circumstances on which the application is based.

(2) Where the appeal or the application for an extension of time is made by a person to whom a compensation payment has been made, a copy of the statement given to that person under section 9 of the 1997 Act or if that statement was not in writing, a written summary of it, shall be sent with that appeal or application.

(3) Where it appears to the Secretary of State that an appeal or application does not contain the further particulars required under paragraph (1) or is not accompanied by a written statement or summary as required under paragraph (2) he may direct the appellant or applicant to provide such particulars or such a statement or summary.

(4) Where paragraph (3) applies, the time specified for making the appeal or application may be extended by such period, not exceeding 14 days from the date of the Secretary of State's direction under paragraph (3), as the Secretary of State may determine.

(5) Where further particulars or a written statement or summary are required under paragraph (3) they shall be sent to or delivered to the Compensation Recovery Unit of the Department of Social Security at Reyrolle Building, Hebburn, Tyne and Wear, NE31 1XB within such period as the Secretary of State may direct.

(6) The Secretary of State may treat any appeal relating to the certificate of recoverable benefits as an application for review under section 10 of the 1997 Act.

General appeals matters including child support appeals

Appeal against a decision which has been revised

4.300 30.—(1) An appeal against a decision of the Secretary of State [¹ or the Board or an officer of the Board] shall not lapse where the decision is revised under section 16 of the Child Support Act or section 9 before the appeal is determined and the decision as revised is not more advantageous to the appellant than the decision before it was revised.

(2) Decisions which are more advantageous for the purposes of this regulation include decisions where—

(a) any relevant benefit paid to the appellant is greater or is awarded for a longer period in consequence of the decision made under section 9;

(b) it would have resulted in the amount of relevant benefit in payment being greater but for the operation of any provision of the

(S.I. 1999 No. 991, reg. 30)

Administration Act or the Contributions and Benefits Act restricting or suspending the payment of, or disqualifying a claimant from receiving, some or all of the benefit;
(c) as a result of the decision, a denial or disqualification for the receiving of any relevant benefit, is lifted, wholly or in part;
(d) it reverses a decision to pay benefit to a third party;
(e) in consequence of the revised decision, benefit paid is not recoverable under section 71, 71A or 74 of the Administration Act or regulations made under any of those sections, or the amount so recoverable is reduced; or
(f) a financial gain accrued or will accrue to the appellant in consequence of the decision.

(3) Where a decision as revised under section 16 of the Child Support Act or under section 9 is not more advantageous to the appellant than the decision before it was revised, the appeal shall be treated as though it had been brought against the decision as revised.

(4) The appellant shall have a period of one month from the date of notification of the decision as revised to make further representations as to the appeal.

(5) After the expiration of the period specified in paragraph (4), or within that period if the appellant consents in writing, the appeal to the appeal tribunal shall proceed except where, in the light of the further representations from the appellant, the Secretary of State [¹ or the Board or an officer of the Board] further revises his [¹, or revise their,] decision and that decision is more advantageous to the appellant than the decision before it was revised.

AMENDMENT

1. Tax Credits (Decisions and Appeals) (Amendment) Regulations 1999 (S.I. 1999 No. 2570), reg. 21 (October 5, 1999). Note that amendments made by these regulations only have effect with respect to tax credit (reg. 1(2) of the Amendment Regulations).

GENERAL NOTE

This provides an exception to the general rule that an appeal lapses when the decision under appeal is revised (see s.9(6) of the Social Security Act 1998 and the note to s.9(5)).

4.301

Time within which an appeal is to be brought

31.—(1) Where an appeal lies from a decision of the Secretary of State [¹ or the Board or an officer of the Board] to an appeal tribunal, except in the case of a decision of the Secretary of State under section 3 or 3A of the Vaccine Damage Payments Act, the time within which that appeal must be brought is, subject to the following provisions of this Part—
(a) within one month of the date of notification of the decision against which the appeal is brought; or
(b) where a written statement of reasons for that decision is

4.302

requested, within 14 days of the expiry of the period specified in sub-paragraph (a).

(2) Where the Secretary of State [¹ or the Board or an officer of the Board]—
- (a) revises, or following an application for a revision under regulation 3(1) or (3) does not revise, a decision under section 16 of the Child Support Act or under section 9, or
- (b) supersedes a decision under section 17 of the Child Support Act or under section 10,

the period of one month specified in paragraph (1) shall begin to run from the date of notification of the revision or supersession of the decision, or following an application for a revision under regulation 3(1) or (3), the date the Secretary of State [¹ or the Board or an officer of the Board] issues a notice that he is [¹ or they are] not revising the decision.

(3) An appeal against a certificate of recoverable benefits must be brought—
- (a) not later than one month after the date a person making a compensation payment discharges his liability under section 6 of the 1997 Act;
- (b) where the certificate is reviewed by the Secretary of State [¹ or the Board or an officer of the Board] in accordance with regulations made under section 11(5)(c) of the 1997 Act, not later than one month after the date the certificate is confirmed, or, as the case may be, a fresh certificate is issued; or
- (c) where an agreement is made under which an earlier compensation payment is treated as having been made in final discharge of a claim made by or in respect of an injured person and arising out of the accident, injury or disease, not later than one month after the date of that agreement.

(4) Where a dispute arises as to whether an appeal was brought within the time limit specified in this regulation, the dispute shall be referred to, and be determined by, a legally qualified panel member.

(5) The time limit specified in this regulation for bringing an appeal may be extended in accordance with regulation 32.

AMENDMENT

1. Tax Credits (Decisions and Appeals) (Amendment) Regulations 1999 (S.I. 1999 No. 2570), reg. 22 (October 5, 1999). Note that amendments made by these regulations only have effect with respect to tax credit (reg. 1(2) of the Amendment Regulations).

GENERAL NOTE

Paragraph (4)

4.303   It may be arguable that a decision of a legally qualified panel member is a decision of an appeal tribunal for the purposes of permitting an appeal against it to be brought before a Commissioner under section 14 of the Social Security Act 1998.

(S.I. 1999 No. 991, reg. 31)

Late appeals

32.—(1) The time within which an appeal must be brought may be extended where the conditions specified in paragraphs (2) to (8) are satisfied, but no appeal shall in any event be brought more than one year after the expiration of the last day for appealing under regulation 31.

(2) An application for an extension of time under this regulation shall be made in accordance with regulation 33 and shall be determined by a legally qualified panel member.

(3) An application under this regulation shall contain particulars of the grounds on which the extension of time is sought, including details of any relevant special circumstances for the purposes of paragraph (4).

(4) An application for an extension of time shall not be granted unless the panel member is satisfied that—
  (a) if the application is granted there are reasonable prospects that the appeal will be successful;
  (b) it is in the interests of justice for the application to be granted.

(5) For the purposes of paragraph (4) it is not in the interests of justice to grant an application unless the panel member is satisfied that—
  (a) the special circumstances specified in paragraph (6) are relevant to the application; or
  (b) some other special circumstances exist which are wholly exceptional and relevant to the application.
and as a result of those special circumstances, it was not practicable for the application to be made within the time limit specified in regulation 31.

(6) For the purposes of paragraph (5)(a), the special circumstances are that—
  (a) the applicant or a spouse or dependant of the applicant has died or suffered serious illness;
  (b) the applicant is not resident in the United Kingdom; or
  (c) normal postal services were disrupted.

(7) In determining whether it is in the interests of justice to grant the application, the panel member shall have regard to the principle that the greater the amount of time that has elapsed between the expiration of the time within which the appeal is to be brought under regulation 31 and the making of the application for an extension of time, the more compelling should be the special circumstances on which the application is based.

(8) In determining whether it is in the interestss of justice to grant an application, no account shall be taken of the following—
  (a) that the applicant or any person acting for him was unaware of or misunderstood the law applicable to his case (including ignorance or misunderstanding of the time limits imposed by these Regulations); or
  (b) that a Commissioner or a court has taken a different view of the law from that previously understood and applied.

(9) An application under this regulation for an extension of time which has been refused may not be renewed.

(10) The panel member who determines an application under this regulation shall record a summary of his decision in such written form as has been approved by the President.

(11) As soon as practicable after the decision is made a copy of the decision shall be sent or given to every party to the proceedings.

GENERAL NOTE

4.305   These very stringent conditions are similar to those imposed under reg. 3 of the Social Security (Adjudication) Regulations 1995 but para. (5)(a) is new and the test of practicality imposed by para. (5) is simpler than the previous test but no more generous.

Paragraph (2)
4.306   It is arguable that the decision of the panel member is a decision of an appeal tribunal for the purpose of permitting an appeal to be brought against it under s.14 of the Social Security Act 1998.

Paragraph (8)(a)
4.307   The simple failure of the Secretary of State to comply with reg. 28(1) and inform the claimant of his or her right of appeal will presumably be enough to amount to special circumstances for the purposes of para. (5) and the resulting ignorance would mean that it was not practical for the claimant to make the application in time (see *R(I) 1/90*). However, para. 8(a) appears to have the effect that that ignorance must be ignored so that the claimant cannot be allowed to appeal late. If that is right, it seems monstrously unfair.

Paragraph (8)(b)
4.308   Understood by whom? Presumably not the applicant because the view must also be different from that previously applied. But is it the understanding of the Benefits Agency as a whole that matters or of the particular local office or of the panel member considering the application? Whatever the answer, it is not easy to see what subpara. (b) adds to subpara. (a).

Making of appeals and applications

4.309   **33.**—(1) An appeal, or an application for an extension of time for making an appeal to an appeal tribunal shall be in writing either on a form approved for the purpose by the Secretary of State [² or the Board] or in such other format as the Secretary of State accepts [² or the Board accepts] as sufficient for the purpose and shall—
  (a) be signed by—
    (i) the person who, under [³ section 4(1) of the Vaccine Damage Payments Act], section 20 of the Child Support Act as extended by paragraph 3 of Schedule 4C to that Act, section 11(2) of the 1997 Act or section 12(2), has a right of appeal; or
    (ii) where the person in head (I) has provided written authority to a representative to act on his behalf, by that representative;
  (b) be sent or delivered to an appropriate office;
  (c) contain particulars of the grounds on which it is made; and
  (d) contain sufficient particulars of the decision, the certificate of recoverable benefits or the subject of the application, as the case

may be, to enable that decision, certificate or subject of the application to be identified.

(2) In this regulation, "an appropriate office" means—

(a) in the case of an appeal under the 1997 Act against a certificate of recoverable benefits, the Compensation Recovery Unit of the Department of Social Security at Reyrolle Building, Hebburn, Tyne and Wear, NE31 1XB;

(b) in the case of an appeal against a decision relating to a jobseeker's allowance, an office of the Department of Social Security or of the Department for Education and Employment;

(c) in the case of a contributions decision which falls within Part II of Schedule 3 to the Act, any National Insurance Contributions office [¹ of the Board, or any office of the Department of Social Security];

[¹(cc) in the case of a decision made under the Pension Schemes Act 1993 by virtue of section 170(2) of that Act, any National Insurance Contributions office of the Board;]

(d) in the case of an appeal under section 20 of the Child Support Act as extended by paragraph 3 of Schedule 4C to that Act, an office of the Child Support Agency; [². . .]

]²(dd) in the case of an appeal against a decision relating to working families' tax credit or disabled person's tax crdit, a Tax Credits Office of the Board;

[⁴(ddd) in a case where the decision appealed against was a decision arising from a claim to a designated office, an office of a designated authority;] and

(e) in any other case, an office of the Department of Social Security.

(3) A form which is not completed in accordance with the instructions on the form—

(a) except where paragraph (4) applies, does not satisfy the requirements of paragraph (1), and

(b) may be returned by the Secretary of State [² or the Board] to the sender for completion in accordance with those instructions.

(4) Where the Secretary of State is satisfied [² or the Board are satisfied] that the form, although not completed in accordance with the instructions on it, includes sufficient information to enable the appeal or application to proceed, he [² or they] may treat the form as satisfying the requirements of paragraph (1).

(5) Where an appeal or application is made in writing otherwise than on the approved form ("the letter"), and the letter includes sufficient information to enable the appeal or application to proceed, the Secretary of State [² or the Board] may treat the letter as satisfying the requirements of paragraph (1).

(6) Where the letter does not include sufficient information to enable the appeal or application to proceed, the Secretary of State [² or the Board] may request further information in writing ("further particulars") from the person who wrote the letter.

(7) Where a person to whom a form is returned or from whom further particulars are requested duly completes and returns the form or sends

Social Security and Child Support (Decisions and Appeals) Regulations 1999

the further particulars and the form or particulars (as the case may be) are received by the Secretary of State [² or the Board] within—
(a) 14 days of the date on which the form was returned to him by the Secretary of State [² or the Board],
(b) 14 days of the date on which the Secretary of State's [² or the Board's] request was made ("the date of request"), or
(c) such longer period as the Secretary of State [² or the Board] may direct,

the time for making the appeal shall be extended by 14 days from the date the form was returned, the date of request or the date of the Secretary of State's [² or the Board's] direction, as the case may be.

(8) Where a person to whom a form is returned or from whom further particulars are requested does not complete and return the form or send further particulars within the period of time specified in paragraph (7)—
(a) the Secretary of State [² or the Board] shall forward a copy of the form, or as the case may be, the letter, together with any other relevant documents or evidence to a legally qualified panel member, and
(b) the panel member shall determine whether the form or the letter satisfies the requirement of paragraph (1), and shall inform the appellant or applicant and the Secretary of State [² or the Board] of his determination.

(9) Where—
(a) a form is duly completed and returned or further particulars are sent after the expiry of the period of time allowed in accordance with paragraph (7), and
(b) no decision has been made under paragraph (8) at the time the form or the further particulars are received by the Secretary of State [² or the Board],

that form or further particulars shall also be forwarded to the legally qualified panel member who shall take into account any further information or evidence set out in the form or further particulars.

AMENDMENTS

1. Social Security Contributions (Transfer of Functions, etc.) Act 1999 (Commencement No. 2 and Consequential and Transitional Provisions) Order 1999 (S.I. 1999 No. 1662), art. 3(4) (July 5, 1999).
2. Tax Credits (Decisions and Appeals) (Amendment) Regulations 1999 (S.I. 1999 No. 2570), reg. 23 (October 5, 1999). Note that amendments made by these regulations only have effect with respect to tax credit (reg. 1(2) of the Amendment Regulations).
3. Social Security and Child Support (Decisions and Appeals), Vaccine Damage Payments and Jobseeker's Allowance (Amendment) Regulations 1999 (S.I. 1999 No. 2677), reg. 9 (October 18, 1999).
4. Social Security (Work-focused Interviews) Regulations 2000 (S.I. 2000 No. 897), reg. 16(5) and Sched. 6, para. 6 (April 3, 2000).

GENERAL NOTE

Paragraph (1)

4.310   At first sight it is surprising that it should be the Secretary of State who decides whether the appeal is in a sufficient format, but it is implicit in paras

(4) and (5) that a technically deficient appeal should be allowed to proceed provided that it includes sufficient information to make that possible and the final decision not to admit an appeal is made by a legally qualified panel member under para. (8).

Death of a party to an appeal

34.—(1) In any proceedings, on the death of a party to those proceedings (other than the Secretary of State [¹ or the Board]), the Secretary of State [¹ or the Board] may appoint such person as he thinks [¹ or they think] fit to proceed with the appeal in the place of such deceased party.

(2) A grant of probate, confirmation or letters of administration to the estate of the deceased party, whenever taken out, shall have no effect on an appointment made under paragraph (1).

(3) Where a person appointed under paragraph (1) has, prior to the date of such appointment, taken any action in relation to the appeal on behalf of the deceased party, the effective date of appointment by the Secretary of State [¹ or the Board] shall be the day immediately prior to the first day on which such action was taken.

AMENDMENT

1. Tax Credits (Decisions and Appeals) (Amendment) Regulations 1999 (S.I. 1999 No. 2570), reg. 24 (October 5, 1999). Note that amendments made by these regulations only have effect with respect to tax credit (reg. 1(2) of the Amendment Regulations).

PART V

APPEAL TRIBUNALS FOR SOCIAL SECURITY CONTRACTING OUT OF PENSIONS, VACCINE DAMAGE AND CHILD SUPPORT

CHAPTER I

THE PANEL AND APPEAL TRIBUNALS

Persons appointed to the panel

35. For the purposes of section 6(3), the panel shall include persons with the qualifications specified in Schedule 3.

Composition of appeal tribunals

36.—(1) Subject to the following provisions of this regulation, an appeal tribunal, including an appeal tribunal determining a misconceived appeal as a preliminary issue in accordance with regulation 48, shall consist of a legally qualified panel member.

[¹ (2) Subject to paragraphs (3) to (5), an appeal tribunal shall consist of a legally qualified panel member and—
  (a) a medically qualified panel member where—
    (i) the issue, or one of the issues, raised on the appeal is whether the all work test is satisfied, or
    (ii) the appeal is made under section 11(1)(b) of the 1997 Act; or
  (b) one medically qualified panel member or two such members or one medically qualified panel member and an additional member drawn from the panel for the purposes described in paragraph (5) below where—
    (i) the issue, or one of the issues, raised on the appeal relates to either industrial injuries benefit under Part V of the Contributions and Benefits Act or severe disablement allowance under section 68 of that Act; or
    (ii) the appeal is made under section 4 of the Vaccine Damage Payments Act.";
(3) An appeal tribunal shall consist of a financially qualified panel member and a legally qualified panel member where—
  (a) the issue raised, or one of the issues raised on appeal or referral, relates to child support or a relevant benefit; and
  (b) the appeal or referral may require consideration by members of the appeal tribunal of issues which are, in the opinion of the President, difficult and which relate to—
    (i) profit and loss accounts, revenue accounts or balance sheets relating to any enterprise;
    (ii) an income and expenditure account in the case of an enterprise not trading for profit; or
    (iii) the accounts of any trust fund.
(4) Where the composition of an appeal tribunal would fall to be prescribed under both paragraphs (2) and (3), it shall consist of a medically qualified panel member, a financially qualified panel member and a legally qualified panel member.
(5) Where the composition of an appeal tribunal is prescribed under [¹paragraph (1), (2)(a) or] (3), the President may determine that the appeal tribunal shall include such an additional member drawn from the panel constituted under section 6 as he considers appropriate for the purposes of providing further experience for that additional member or for assisting the President in the monitoring of standards of decision making by panel members.
(6) An appeal tribunal shall consist of a legally qualified panel member, a medically qualified panel member and a panel member with a disability qualification in any appeal which relates to an attendance allowance or a disability living allowance under Part III of the Contributions and Benefits Act or a disability working allowance under section 129 of that Act.
[¹(7) In paragraph (2)(a)(i) above, "all work test" has the meaning it bears in regulation 2(1) of the Social Security (Incapacity for Work) (General) Regulations 1995.]

(S.I. 1999 No. 991, reg. 36)

AMENDMENT

1. Social Security and Child Support (Decisions and Appeals) (Amendment) Regulations 1999 (S.I. 1999 No. 1466), reg. 2 (June 1, 1999).

GENERAL NOTE

Paragraph (1)
As this paragraph is subject to the others, a tribunal considering whether to strike out a misconceived industrial injuries case would have to include at least one doctor among its members.

4.314

Paragraph (2)
The unsatisfactory experiment of having medical assessors in incapacity benefit cases is abandoned in favour of having a doctor as a member of a tribunal. Some cases previously heard by a medical appeal tribunal will now be heard by a tribunal with only one medical member. Most will continue to have two. The fact that all cases concerning disablement benefit now include a doctor is generally to be welcomed, although there may be a few cases where the need for a doctor is not immediately obvious. Even a tribunal hearing an appeal concerned solely with the question whether a person had good cause for delaying a claim for disablement benefit must have a medical member (*CI/4781/98*). The potential advantage of the new provision is that the jurisdictional difficulties caused by the overlapping roles of the different adjudicating authorities under the previous legislation no longer arise in the same form, although different problems may arise if the various issues arising on a claim are determined by different decision-makers. In *CI/1327/98* it was said that *R(I) 4/91* had been superseded because the difficulties relating to the distinction between the diagnosis question and the prescription question in industrial disease cases had been removed. There is often an advantage in having a doctor considering whether a person has suffered an industrial accident and there is even more advantage in having that issue considered at the same time as the question whether the claimant has suffered a loss of faculty as the result of an accident. Note, however, that an appeal in respect of an industrial accident declaration under section 29(2) of the Social Security Act 1998, where there has been *no* claim for benefit, must be considered by a tribunal without a medical member (although s.30 limits the effect of such a decision). Note also, that the circumstances in which the medical member or members of a tribunal may physically examine a claimant are limited by reg. 52. As the power to examine a claimant is no longer related to the constitution of the tribunal, tribunals will have to consider in each case whether or not they are entitled to examine the claimant.

4.315

There is no statutory requirement that the legally qualified panel member be the chairman, although that is currently the invariable practice.

Paragraph (6)
This effectively preserves disability appeal tribunals and transfers to them the limited jurisdiction of social security appeal tribunals in respect of attendance allowance, disability living allowance and disability working allowance.

4.316

Assignment of clerks to appeal tribunals: function of clerks

37. The Secretary of State shall assign a clerk to service each appeal tribunal and the clerk so assigned shall be responsible for summoning members of the panel constituted under section 6 to serve on the tribunal.

4.317

Social Security and Child Support (Decisions and Appeals) Regulations 1999

CHAPTER II

PROCEDURE IN CONNECTION WITH DETERMINATION OF APPEALS AND REFERRALS

Consideration and determination of appeals and referrals

4.318   **38.**—(1) The procedure in connection with the consideration and determination of an appeal or a referral shall, subject to the following provisions of these Regulations, be such as a legally qualified panel member shall determine.

(2) A legally qualified panel member may give directions requiring a party to the proceedings to comply with any provision of these Regulations and may at any stage of the proceedings, either of his own motion or on a written application made to the clerk to the appeal tribunal by any party to the proceedings, give such directions as he may consider necessary or desirable for the just, effective and efficient conduct of the proceedings and may direct any party to the proceedings to provide such particulars or to produce such documents as may be reasonably required.

(3) Where a clerk to the appeal tribunal is authorised to take steps in relation to the procedure of the tribunal he may give directions requiring any party to the proceedings to comply with any provision of these Regulations.

GENERAL NOTE

4.319   If an appellant is given due warning, an appeal may be struck out under reg. 46(1)(c) for failure to comply with a direction.

[¹Appeals raising issues for decision by officers of Inland Revenue

4.320   **38A.**—(1) Where, on consideration of any appeal, it appears to an appeal tribunal that an issue arises which, by virtue of section 8 of the Transfer Act, falls to be decided by an officer of the Board, that tribunal shall—
   (a) refer the appeal to the Secretary of State pending the decision of that issue by an officer of the Board; and
   (b) require the Secretary of State to refer that issue to the Board;
and the Secretary of State shall refer that issue accordingly.

(2) Pending the final decision of any issue which has been referred to the Board in accordance with paragraph (1) above, the Secretary of State may revise the decision under appeal, or make a further decision superseding that decision, in accordance with his determination of any issue other than one which has been so referred.

(3) On receipt by the Secretary of State of the final decision of an issue which has been referred in accordance with paragraph (1) above, he shall consider whether the decision under appeal ought to be revised under section 9 or superseded under section 10, and—

(S.I. 1999 No. 991, reg. 38A)

(a) if so, revise it or, as the case may be, make a further decision which supersedes it; or
(b) if not, forward the appeal to the appeal tribunal which shall determine the appeal in accordance with the final decision of the issue so referred.

(4) In paragraphs (2) and (3) above, "final decision" has the same meaning as in regulation 11A(3) and (4).]

AMENDMENT

1. Social Security and Child Support (Decisions and Appeals) Amendment (No. 3) Regulations 1999 (S.I. 1999 No. 1670), reg. 2(4) (July 5, 1999).

Directions concerning oral hearings

39.—(1) Where an appeal or a referral is made to an appeal tribunal, the clerk to the appeal tribunal shall direct the appellant and any other party to the proceedings to notify the clerk to the appeal tribunal in writing whether he wishes to have an oral hearing of the appeal or whether he is content for the appeal or referral to proceed without an oral hearing.

(2) Except in the case of a referral, a direction under paragraph (1) shall include a statement informing the appellant that, if he does not respond in writing to the direction within the period specified in paragraph (3), the appeal may be struck out in accordance with regulation 46.

(3) A notification given in accordance with paragraph (1) must be received by the clerk to the appeal tribunal within 14 days of the date of issue of the direction of the clerk to the appeal tribunal under paragraph (1) or within such longer period as the clerk to the appeal tribunal may direct.

(4) Where a party to the proceedings notifies the clerk to the appeal tribunal in accordance with paragraph (3) that he wishes to have an oral hearing of the appeal or referral, the appeal tribunal shall hold an oral hearing.

(5) The chairman, or in the case of an appeal tribunal which has only one member, that member, may of his own motion direct that an oral hearing of the appeal or referral be held if he is satisfied that such a hearing is necessary to enable the appeal tribunal to reach a decision.

4.321

GENERAL NOTE

Unless a claimant positively opts either for an oral hearing or what is known colloquially as a "paper hearing", the appeal is liable to be struck out altogether under reg. 46(1)(c). There are many cases where a claimant really has no realistic prospects of success unless he or she attends an oral hearing and gives evidence. Even though claimants are advised in general terms that the chances of success may be greater at an oral hearing, it may be thought that the mere fact that they are offered the choice will suggest to many that a paper hearing is a not a foolish option. In *CDLA/1347/99*, it was said that, if a tribunal was wholly unable to do justice without there being an oral hearing, it ought to adjourn the proceedings, and direct that there be one (see reg. 39(5)) but that, otherwise, a tribunal was generally entitled to take the view that a claimant who

4.322

had rejected the option of an oral hearing having had notice of the issues in the case had had an adequate opportunity to put his case and had lost the chance of strengthening it by giving oral evidence.

Withdrawal of appeal or referral

4.323   **40.**—(1) An appeal may be withdrawn by the appellant or an authorised representative of the appellant and a referral may be withdrawn by the Secretary of State [¹the Board or an officer of the Board], as the case may be, either—
  (a) at an oral hearing; or
  (b) at any other time before the appeal or referral is determined, by giving notice in writing of withdrawal to the clerk to the appeal tribunal.

(2) If an appeal or a referral is withdrawn (as the case may be) in accordance with paragraph (1)(a), the clerk to the appeal tribunal shall send a notice in writing to any party to the proceedings who is not present when the appeal or referral is withdrawn, informing him that the appeal or referral (as the case may be) has been withdrawn.

(3) If an appeal or a referral is withdrawn (as the case may be) in accordance with paragraph (1)(b), the clerk to the appeal tribunal shall send a notice in writing to every party to the proceedings informing them that the appeal or referral (as the case may be) has been withdrawn.

AMENDMENT

1. Tax Credits (Decisions and Appeals) (Amendment) Regulations 1999 (S.I. 1999 No. 2570), reg. 25 (October 5, 1999). Note that amendments made by these regulations only have effect with respect to tax credit (reg. 1(2) of the Amendment Regulations).

Medical examination required by appeal tribunal

4.324   **41.**—For the purposes of section 20(2) (medical examination required by appeal tribunal) the prescribed condition which must be satisfied is that the issue, or one of the issues, raised on the appeal—
  (a) is whether the claimant satisfies the conditions for entitlement to—
    (i) the care component of a disability living allowance specified in section 72(1) and (2) of the Contributions and Benefits Act;
    (ii) the mobility component of a disability living allowance specified in section 73(1), (8) and (9) of that Act;
    (iii) an attendance allowance specified in section 64 and 65(1) of that Act;
    (iv) a [²disabled person's tax credit] specified in section 129(1)(b) of that Act;
    (v) [¹. . .]; or
    (vi) severe disablement allowance under section 68 of that Act;
  (b) relates to the period throughout which the claimant is likely to

satisfy the conditions for entitlement to an attendance allowance or a disability living allowance;
(c) is the rate at which an attendance allowance is payable;
(d) is the rate at which the care component or the mobility component of a disability living allowance is payable;
([¹(dd) is whether a person is incapable of work for the purposes of the Contributions and Benefits Act;]
(e) [¹ . . .];
(f) relates to the extent of a person's disablement and its assessment in accordance with Schedule 6 to the Contributions and Benefits Act;
(g) is whether the claimant suffers a loss of physical or mental faculty as a result of the relevant accident for the purposes of section 103 of the Contributions and Benefits Act;
(h) relates to any disease or injury prescribed for the purposes of section 108 of the Contributions and Benefits Act; or
(i) relates to any payment arising under, or by virtue of a scheme having effect under, section 111 of, and Schedule 8 to, the Contributions and Benefits Act (workmen's compensation).

AMENDMENTS

1. Social Security and Child Support (Decisions and Appeals) Amendment (No. 3) Regulations 1999 (S.I. 1999 No. 1670), reg. 2(5) (July 5, 1999).
2. Tax Credits (Decisions and Appeals) (Amendment) Regulations 1999 (S.I. 1999 No. 2570), reg. 26 (October 5, 1999). Note that amendments made by these regulations only have effect with respect to tax credit (reg. 1(2) of the Amendment Regulations).

GENERAL NOTE

These are the only circumstances in which a tribunal may refer a person for medical examination (although it is just arguable that s.7(4) of the Social Security Act 1998 and reg. 50 are in broad enough terms to permit an examination in other cases). See reg. 52 for the circumstances in which the tribunal may themselves carry out an examination.

4.325

Non-disclosure of medical advice or evidence

42.—(1) Where, in connection with the consideration and determination of an appeal or referral there is before an appeal tribunal medical advice or medical evidence relating to a person which has not been disclosed to him and in the opinion of the chairman, or in the case of an appeal tribunal which has only one member, in the opinion of that member, the disclosure to that person of that advice or evidence would be harmful to his health, such advice or evidence shall not be required to be disclosed to that person.

(2) Advice or evidence such as is mentioned in paragraph (1) shall not be disclosed to any person acting for or representing the person to whom it relates or, in a case where a claim for benefit is made by reference to the disability of a person other than the claimant and the advice or evidence relates to that other person, shall not be disclosed to the

4.326

claimant or any person acting for or representing him, unless the chairman, or in the case of an appeal tribunal which has only one member, that member, is satisfied that it is in the interests of the person to whom the advice or evidence relates to do so.

(3) A tribunal shall not be precluded from taking into account for the purposes of the determination advice or evidence which has not been disclosed to a person under the provisions of paragraph (1) or (2).

GENERAL NOTE

4.327 In *R(A) 4/89*, the Attendance Allowance Board withheld from a claimant "additional information" supplied by a doctor who in effect said that when he arrived outside the claimant's house the claimant was sitting with his back to a window but when he went in the claimant was lying on a couch claiming to be unable to respond to the doctor's questions. The doctor was therefore implying that the claimant was a fraud. The Commissioner held that this was not "medical evidence", but was factual evidence and that, in any event, the power to withhold evidence that was prejudicial, rather than helpful, to a claimant should be exercised with caution. He held the Board to have erred in law because it was common fairness to let the claimant be aware of the allegation that he was a fraud. It is difficult to see how evidence of the sort considered in that case could possibly be harmful to the claimant's health. A doctor's wish to avoid embarrassment is not a ground for withholding evidence.

In *CSDLA/5/95*, there was withheld evidence that the child claimant was not seriously ill but that her mother, who was acting on her behalf, was suffering from Munchausen By Proxy Syndrome. The Deputy Commissioner pointed out that the fact a senior medical officer was of the view that disclosure would cause "considerably difficulty and distress" did not mean that it would be harmful to the health of any person. However, more fundamentally, he held that, while a claimant was not necessarily entitled to see the whole evidence in the case:

". . . . no adversarial dispute should be decided against a party on the basis of evidence not disclosed to them unless that party has been given sufficient indication of the gist of that evidence to give them a proper opportunity to put forward their case."

He added that non-disclosure to a representative must be considered "quite separately to, and perhaps even more cautiously than, non-disclosure to a claimant" and that the regulation should be operated "in a manner consistent with the principles of natural justice". Further, he held that a claimant to whom material is not being disclosed should be told that fact, and the tribunal's record of reasons should refer to it and no part of that reasoning should not be disclosed to the claimant.

In *CDLA/1347/99*, the Commissioner disagreed with that approach, holding that the statutory provision expressly authorised a breach of the rules of natural justice and that, in exercising the discretion to withhold evidence, a tribunal should consider whether the authorised breach would be a lesser evil than revealing the information. If minded to reveal evidence that had been withheld on medical advice, he suggested that it might be prudent to give the medical advisor the opportunity of justifying the advice before revealing the evidence. The Commissioner also agreed with a suggestion that, if reasons for a decision were being given, withheld evidence should be referred to in a supplementary statement of reasons given to the Secretary of State (and the claimant's representative if the evidence had been revealed to him or her) but not given to the claimant. That would have the effect that, in the event of an appeal, the Commissioner would know how the evidence had been approached.

(S.I. 1999 No. 991, reg. 41)

In *CDLA/1347/99* (as in *R(A) 4/89*), the withheld evidence was not even "medical advice or medical evidence". In *CSDLA/5/95*, the evidence was undoubtedly "medical evidence" but it is not clear why it was regarded as harmful. Indeed, in most cases concerning attendance allowance or disability living allowance, this regulation will not give rise to great problems because evidence that a claimant is seriously ill, which is the sort of evidence that would normally be withheld, is evidence that is likely to assist the claimant rather than the reverse. It is in cases concerning disablement benefit, where causation is often in issue, that the problem arises most acutely. There, if a tribunal are satisifed that evidence should be withheld but would be likely to be contested by a claimant if he or she knew of it, it is suggested that they should take care to ensure that it is properly tested by, for example, obtaining a second opinion. If proceedings cannot properly be adversarial, they must be truly inquisitorial. Indeed, if there were contradictory evidence and the claimant would be likely to contest the withheld evidence, a tribunal might well be particularly slow to conclude that reg. 42 should be applied and might choose either to disclose the evidence or else to disregard it.

Summoning of witnesses and administration of oaths

43.—(1) A chairman, or in the case of an appeal tribunal which has only one member, that member, may by summons, or in Scotland, by citation, require any person in Great Britain to attend as a witness at a hearing of an appeal, application or referral at such time and place as shall be specified in the summons or citation and, subject to paragraph (2), at the hearing to answer any question or produce any documents in his custody or under his control which relate to any matter in question in the appeal, application or referral but—

(a) no person shall be required to attend in obedience to such summons or citation unless he has been given at least 14 days' notice of the hearing or, if less than 14 days' notice is given, he has informed the tribunal that the notice given is sufficient; and

(b) no person shall be required to attend and give evidence or to produce any document in obedience to such summons or citation unless the necessary expenses of attendance are paid or tendered to him.

(2) No person shall be compelled to give any evidence or produce any document or other material that he could not be compelled to give or produce on a trial of an action in a court of law in that part of Great Britain where the hearing takes place.

(3) In exercising the powers conferred by this regulation, the chairman, or in the case of an appeal tribunal which has only one member, that member, shall take into account the need to protect any matter that relates to intimate personal or financial circumstances, is commercially sensitive, consists of information communicated or obtained in confidence or concerns national security.

(4) Every summons or citation issued under this regulation shall contain a statement to the effect that the person in question may apply in writing to a chairman to vary or set aside the summons or citation.

(5) A chairman, or in the case of an appeal tribunal which has only one member, that member, may require any witness, including a witness summoned under the powers conferred by this regulation, to give evid-

4.328

ence on oath or affirmation and for that purpose there may be administered an oath or affirmation in due form.

GENERAL NOTE

4.329   The power to summons witnesses is not backed by any power to punish for non-compliance. A summons issued under this regulation therefore amounts to no more than a very formal request. This would not have mattered had R.S.C. Ord. 38, r. 19 remained in force because that enabled the High Court to issue a subpoena in aid of a tribunal who could not themselves compel attendance and a failure to comply with it would have been punishable in the High court as contempt of court. C.P.R. rule 34.4 now enables the High Court to issue a summons in aid of a tribunal but only if the tribunal has no power to issue a summons itself. In the light of this regulation, it seems doubtful that a summons can be issued by the High Court in aid of an appeal tribunal constituted under the Social Security Act 1998. The Civil Procedure Rules Committee probably did not contemplate the possibility of a tribunal having the power to issue an unenforceable summons.

4.330   *Regulation 44 Omitted*

4.331   *Regulation 45 Omitted*

CHAPTER III

STRIKING OUT APPEALS

Appeals which may be struck out

4.332   **46.**—(1) Subject to paragraphs (2) and (3), an appeal may be struck out by the clerk to the appeal tribunal—
 (a) where it is an out of jurisdiction appeal and the appellant has been notified by the Secretary of State that an appeal brought against such a decision may be struck out;
 (b) for want of prosecution including an appeal not made within the time specified in these Regulations; or
 (c) subject to regulation 39(4), for failure of the appellant to comply with a direction given under these Regulations where the appellant has been notified that failure to comply with the direction could result in the appeal being struck out.

(2) Where the clerk to the appeal tribunal determines to strike out the appeal, he shall notify the appellant that his appeal has been struck out and of the procedure for reinstatement of the appeal as specified in regulation 47.

(3) The clerk to the appeal tribunal may refer any matter for determination under this regulation to a legally qualified panel member for decision by the panel member rather than the clerk to the appeal tribunal.

(4) Subject to regulation 48, a misconceived appeal may be struck

out by a legally qualified panel member but such an appeal shall not be struck out unless the appellant has been given notice of—
  (a) the intention to strike out the appeal,
  (b) the ground on which the intention to strike out is based, and
  (c) the requirement to notify the clerk to the appeal tribunal in writing of the matters specified in regulation 48(1)(a) or (b) and that failure to comply with this requirement may result in the appeal being struck out.

GENERAL NOTE

The terms "out of jurisdiction appeal" and "misconceived appeal" are defined in reg. 1. Given that what is being struck out is an appeal to a tribunal, it is arguable that a decision of a legally qualified panel member to strike out an appeal, or to refuse to reinstate under reg. 47 an appeal struck out by a clerk, is a decision of a tribunal against which an appeal might be brought to a Commissioner under s. 14 of the Social Security Act 1998. Plainly there are few cases when leave to appeal would be given but it would be odd if there were no means, short of an application for judicial review, by which a panel member's view as to whether or not an appeal was "out of jurisdiction" might be challenged.

Reinstatement of struck out appeals

47. A legally qualified panel member may reinstate an appeal which has been struck out in accordance with regulation 46 or regulation 48(2) where—
  (a) the appellant has made representations, or as the case may be, further representations in support of his appeal with reasons why he considers that his appeal should not have been struck out, to the clerk to the appeal tribunal, in writing within one month of the order to strike out the appeal being issued, and the panel member is satisfied in the light of those representations that there are reasonable grounds for reinstating the appeal;
  (b) the panel member is satisfied that the appellant did not receive the notification required under regulation 46(4);
  (c) the panel member is satisfied that the appeal is not an appeal which may be struck out under regulation 46; or
  (d) the panel member is satisfied that notwithstanding that the appeal is one which may be struck out under regulation 46, it is not in the interests of justice for the appeal to be struck out.

4.333

Misconceived appeals

48.—(1) Where the appellant has been given notice under regulation 46(4) of intention to strike out an appeal on the ground that it is a misconceived appeal that person must within 14 days of the issue of such notice notify the clerk to the appeal tribunal in writing that—
  (a) he wishes the question of whether his appeal is misconceived to be determined by an appeal tribunal as a preliminary issue at an oral hearing, or
  (b) he is content for an appeal tribunal to consider the question of

4.334

whether his appeal is misconceived as a preliminary issue without an oral hearing and make representations in writing to the clerk to the appeal tribunal as to why he considers that the appeal is not misconceived.

(2) Where the appellant fails to notify or to make representations to the clerk to the appeal tribunal in writing as required in paragraph (1) within the period specified in that paragraph, a legally qualified panel member may strike out the appeal.

(3) Where the appellant notifies the clerk to the appeal tribunal under paragraph (1) within the period specified in that paragraph that he wishes an appeal tribunal to determine the question of whether his appeal is misconceived as a preliminary issue at an oral hearing, the appeal tribunal shall hold an oral hearing for that preliminary issue.

(4) Where the appeal tribunal determine as a preliminary issue that the appeal is a misconceived appeal, the appeal shall be struck out and the clerk to the appeal tribunal shall notify the appellant that the appeal is struck out.

(5) Where the appeal tribunal determine as a preliminary issue that the appeal is not a misconceived appeal—
  (a) the appeal tribunal shall refer the appeal and all the supporting documentation to the Secretary of State together with a statement of the reasons why the appeal tribunal considers that the appeal is not misconceived;
  (b) the clerk to the appeal tribunal shall notify the appellant of the referral of the appeal to the Secretary of State and send the appellant a copy of the reasons why the appeal tribunal considers that the appeal is not misconceived;
  (c) the Secretary of State may revise or supersede the decision against which the appeal is brought; and
  (d) if the Secretary of State does not revise or supersede the decision against the appeal is brought in the appellant's favour, the Secretary of State shall refer the appeal for determination by an appeal tribunal.

(6) Chapter IV of this Part shall apply to an oral hearing held under this regulation.

Chapter IV

Oral Hearings

Procedure at oral hearings

4.335   49.—(1) Subject to the following provisions of this Part, the procedure for an oral hearing shall be such as the chairman, or in the case of an appeal tribunal which has only one member, such as that member, shall determine.

(2) Except where paragraph (3) applies, not less than 14 days notice

Enactment = Acts of Parliament

(S.I. 1999 No. 991, reg. 49)

(beginning with the day on which the notice is given and ending on the day before the hearing of the appeal is to take place) of the time and place of any oral hearing of an appeal shall be given to every party to the proceedings, and if such notice has not been given to a person to whom it should have been given under the provisions of this paragraph the hearing may proceed only with the consent of that person.

(3) Any party to the proceedings may waive his right to receive not less than 14 days notice of the time and place of any oral hearing by giving notice to the clerk to the appeal tribunal.

(4) If a party to the proceedings to whom notice has been given under paragraph (2) fails to appear at the hearing the chairman, or in the case of an appeal tribunal which has only one member, that member, may, having regard to all the circumstances including any explanation offered for the absence, proceed with the hearing notwithstanding his absence, or give such directions with a view to the determination of the appeal as he may think proper.

(5) If a party to the proceedings has waived his right to be given notice under paragraph (2) the chairman, or in the case of an appeal tribunal which has only one member, that member, may proceed with the hearing notwithstanding his absence.

(6) Any oral hearing shall be in public except—
(a) where the appellant requests a private hearing, or
(b) where the chairman, or in the case of an appeal tribunal which has only one member, that member, is satisfied that intimate personal or financial circumstances may have to be disclosed or that considerations of national security are involved, in which case the hearing shall be in private.

(7) Any party to the proceedings shall be entitled to be present and be heard at an oral hearing.

(8) A person who has the right to be heard at a hearing may be accompanied and may be represented by another person whether having professional qualifications or not and, for the purposes of the proceedings at the hearing, any such representative shall have all the rights and powers to which the person whom he represents is entitled.

(9) The following persons shall also be entitled to be present at an oral hearing (whether or not it is otherwise in private) but shall take no part in the proceedings—
(a) the President;
(b) any person undergoing training as a chairman or panel member of an appeal tribunal or as a clerk to an appeal tribunal;
(c) any person acting on behalf of the President in the training or supervision of panel members or in the monitoring of standards of decision-making by panel members;
(d) with the leave of the chairman, or in the case of an appeal tribunal which has only one member, with the leave of that member, and the consent of every party to the proceedings actually present, any other person; and
(e) a member of the Council on Tribunals or of the Scottish Committee of the Council on Tribunals.

(10) Nothing in paragraph (9) affects the rights of any person men-

tioned in sub-paragraphs (a) and (b) of that paragraph at any oral hearing where he is sitting as a member of the tribunal or acting as its clerk, and nothing in this regulation prevents the presence at an oral hearing of any witness.

(11) Any person entitled to be heard at an oral hearing may address the tribunal, may give evidence, may call witnesses and may put questions directly to any other person called as a witness.

(12) For the purpose of arriving at its decision an appeal tribunal shall, and for the purpose of discussing any question of procedure may, notwithstanding anything contained in these Regulations, order all persons not being members of the tribunal, other than the person acting as clerk to the appeal tribunal, to withdraw from the hearing except that—
- (a) a member of the Council on Tribunals or of the Scottish Committee of the Council on Tribunals, the President or any person mentioned in paragraph (9)(c); and
- (b) with the leave of the chairman, or in the case of an appeal tribunal which has only one member, with the leave of that member, any person mentioned in paragraph (9)(b) or (d),

main remain present at any such sitting.

GENERAL NOTE

Paragraph (2)

4.336   The inadequate period of notice previously required has been doubled to 14 days.

Manner of providing expert assistance

4.337   **50.**—(1) Where an appeal tribunal require one or more experts to provide assistance to it in dealing with a question of fact of special difficulty under section 7(4), such an expert shall, if the chairman, or in the case of a tribunal with only one member, that member, so requests, attend at the hearing and give evidence and if the chairman or member sitting alone considers it appropriate, the expert shall enquire into and provide a written report on the question.

(2) A copy of any written report received from an expert in accordance with paragraph (1) shall be supplied to every party to the proceedings.

GENERAL NOTE

4.338   The expert may assist the tribunal as a witness, which implies that the parties may cross-examine him or her. There is no provision for an expert to sit as an assessor.

Postponement and adjournment

4.339   **51.**—(1) Where a person to whom notice of an oral hearing is given wishes to request a postponement of that hearing he shall do so in writing to the clerk to the appeal tribunal stating his reasons for the request, and the clerk to the appeal tribunal may grant or refuse the request as he thinks fit or may pass the request to a legally qualified panel member who may grant or refuse the request as he thinks fit.

(2) Where the clerk to the appeal tribunal or the panel member, as the case may be, refuses a request to postpone the hearing he shall—
  (a) notify in writing the person making the request of the refusal; and
  (b) place before the appeal tribunal at the hearing both the request for the postponement and notification of its refusal.

(3) A panel member or the clerk to the appeal tribunal may of his own motion at any time before the beginning of the hearing postpone the hearing.

(4) An oral hearing may be adjourned by the appeal tribunal at any time on the application of any party to the proceedings or of its own motion.

(5) Where a hearing has been adjourned and it is not practicable, or would cause undue delay, for it to be resumed before a tribunal consisting of the same member or members, the appeal or referral shall be heard by a differently constituted tribunal and the proceedings shall be by way of a complete rehearing.

GENERAL NOTE

The distinction between a postponement and an adjournment is that the former occurs before the beginning of the hearing and the latter occurs once the hearing has begun, although an application for an adjournment may be made right at the beginning of a hearing. In *CDLA/3680/97*, the Commissioner said that "[w]here an application for a postponement is refused—or no reply is received to such an application—it is incumbent on the claimant to take all possible steps to appear, or to have someone appear on his or her behalf, before the tribunal in order to assist the tribunal in considering whether there should be an adjournment". A representative should be ready to argue the case as well as possible if the application for an adjournment is refused. In *CSDLA/90/98*, the Commissioner was highly critical of a local authority representative who had represented a claimant before a tribunal on an application for an adjournment. The claimant had had a prior engagement and the Commissioner found that the representative had indicated to her that she need not attend the tribunal hearing without asking her why the other engagement should take priority. When the tribunal refused to adjourn the hearing the representative had withdrawn. The Commissioner said that the nature of the other engagement should have been explained to the tribunal, that it was not for a representative to tell a claimant not to attend a hearing (because a tribunal were not bound to grant an adjournment merely because the claimant was not there) and that a representative who wished to withdraw should obtain the leave of the tribunal to do so. The claimant had been entitled to expect her representative to argue her case on the basis of the evidence available to him and doing so would not have prevented him from arguing on appeal that the tribunal had erred in refusing the adjournment.

Physical examinations at oral hearings

52. For the purposes of section 20(3) an appeal tribunal may not carry out a physical examination except in a case which relates to—
  (a) the extent of a person's disablement and its assessment in accordance with section 68(6) of, and Schedule 6 to, the Contributions and Benefits Act;
  (b) the extent of a person's disablement and its assessment in accordance with section 103 of that Act;

4.340

(c) diseases or injuries prescribed for the purposes of section 108 of that Act.

GENERAL NOTE

4.341 See reg. 41 for the circumstances in which a tribunal may refer a claimant for medical examination.

CHAPTER V

DECISIONS OF APPEAL TRIBUNALS AND RELATED MATTERS

Appeal tribunal decisions

Decisions of appeal tribunals

4.342 **53.**—(1) Every decision of an appeal tribunal shall be recorded in summary by the chairman, or in the case of an appeal tribunal which has only one member, by that member.

(2) The decision notice specified in paragraph (1) shall be in such written form as shall have been approved by the President and shall be signed by the chairman, or in the case of an appeal tribunal which has only one member, by that member.

(3) As soon as may be practicable after an appeal or referral has been decided by an appeal tribunal, a copy of the decision notice prepared in accordance with paragraph (1) and (2) shall be sent or given to every party to the proceedings who shall also be informed of—

(a) his right under paragraph (4); and

[¹(b) except in the case of an appeal under the Vaccine Damage Payments Act, the conditions governing appeals to a Commissioner.]

(4) A party to the proceedings may apply in writing to the chairman, or in the case of a tribunal with only one member, to that member, for a copy of a statement of the reasons for the tribunal's decision within one month of the sending or giving of the decision notice to every party to the proceedings or within such longer period as may be allowed in accordance with regulation 54.

(5) If the decision is not unanimous, the decision notice specified in paragraph (1) shall record that one of the members dissented and the statement of reasons referred to in paragraph (4) shall include the reasons given by the dissenting member for dissenting.

AMENDMENT

1. Social Security and Child Support (Decisions and Appeals), Vaccine Damage Payments and Jobseeker's Allowance (Amendment) Regulations 1999 (S.I. 1999 No. 2677), reg. 10 (October 18, 1999).

GENERAL NOTE

Paragraph (2)

The form prescribed by the President includes a space where there may be written summary grounds for the decision. In *CIB/668/98*, the Commissioner

(S.I. 1999 No. 991, reg. 53)

held that it followed that a failure to include a proper reason for a decision on the decision notice was a breach of procedure rendering the decision liable to be set aside on appeal. However, in *CIB/4497/98*, it was held that the remedy for any inadequacy in the reasons given on a decision notice was to apply for a full statement of reasons under what is now para. (4).

Paragraph (4)

There is no express provision for the giving of a statement of reasons in the absence of a request but there is no reason in principle why a chairman should not do so. It is also suggested that, although a party has no right to a decision if no application is made within a month or such further time as may be allowed under reg. 54, a chairman remains able to issue a statement if satisfied that it is right to do so. A chairman's power to write a statement of reasons survives the termination of his or her appointment to the panel. The statement must at least be adopted by the chairman (or possibly another member) of the tribunal who heard the appeal. Therefore a statement written by a regional chairman in the erroneous belief that it could not be written by the chairman who heard the appeal because her appointment had come to an end, was not valid (*CIS/2132/98*). It is usually an error of law to fail to issue a statement of reasons when a request is made within the prescribed time and there are occasions when an application for leave to appeal should be treated as such a request *(R(IS) 11/99)*. In *CDLA/5793/97*, it was suggested that there would be such an implied request "whenever the claimant's application for leave to appeal raises an issue that is not fully explained in the summary grounds issued as part of a decision notice or by the other documents in the case". However, a tribunal's decision will not be erroneous in law for breach of the duty to imposed by this paragraph if the decision notice issued under para. (1) in fact contains all that would be required in a full statement of reasons *R(IS) 11/99)*, although the practice of some chairman of stating that the summary reasons on a decision notice amount to a full statement of reasons has been frowned upon, on the basis that such summary reasons are more likely to contain errors than fuller statements produced in response to a request, and held to be of no effect *(CSDLA/551/99)*. Unlike its predecessors, this paragraph includes no express duty to record the tribunal's findings but it is suggested that this makes no practical difference because it is necessary to record a tribunal's findings on any matters in dispute as part of the explanation for its decision. Indeed, it has been said in *Evans* (below) that there are occasions when a record of the tribunal's findings provides a complete explanation for the decision. The inadequacy of tribunal's reasons is probably the most common ground upon which tribunals' decsions are set aside by Commissioners. The superficiality of many submissions made by both claimant's representatives and the Secretary of State's representatives have been the subject of adverse comment by Commissioners (see, for example, *CIB/4497/98* in which it was said that there is no simple formula for writing reasons for a decision).

In *In re Poyser and Mills' Arbitration* [1964] 2 Q.B. 467, 478, Megaw J. said:

"Parliament provided that reasons shall be given, and in my view that must be read as meaning that proper, adequate reasons must be given. The reasons that are set out must be reasons that will not only be intelligible, but which deal with the substantial points that have been raised."

In *R(A) 1/72*, the Chief Commissioner, considering an appeal from a delegated medical practitioner acting on behalf of the Attendance Allowance Board, said:

"The obligation to give reasons for the decision in [a case involving a conflict of evidence] imports a requirement to do more than only to state the conclusion, and for the determining authority to state that on the evidence the

4.343

authority is not satisfied that the statutory conditions are met, does no more than this. It affords no guide to the selective process by which the evidence has been accepted, rejected, weighed or considered, or the reasons for any of these things. It is not, of course, obligatory thus to deal with every piece of evidence or to over elaborate, but in an administrative quasi-judicial decision the minimum requirement must at least be that the claimant, looking at the decision should be able to discern on the face of it the reasons why the evidence has failed to satisfy the authority. For the purpose of the regulation which requires the reasons for the review decision to be set out, a decision based, and only based, on a conclusion that the total effect of the evidence fails to satisfy, without reasons given for reaching that conclusion, will in many cases be no adequate decision at all."

On the other hand, it is acknowledged in *Baron v. Secretary of State for Social Services* (reported as an appendix to *R(M) 6/86*) that there are limits to the extent to which a tribunal can be expected to give reasons for decisions on matters of judgment, such as the distance a claimant could walk without having to stop or the extent of breathlessness and pain which caused him to stop. Assessments of disablement also give rise to difficult judgments. In *CI/636/93*, the Commissioner said:

"Whether or how far the duty in law to give reasons for their decision extends beyond saying that the particular percentage arrived at is in the medical judgment of the tribunal a fair one on these particular facts must depend on the nature of the individual case and the issues that have been raised in it. It seems to me that the position is correctly summarised by the Commissioner in *R(I) 30/61* at paragraph 8: there may well be cases where a mere statement that the tribunal makes an assessment at a particular percentage is in itself a sufficient record, since it implies that they think that is a fair assessment; but in other cases findings of fact and an explanation of reasons will be needed to show that evidence they have accepted or rejected as justifying the making of a smaller or larger assessment, since otherwise the claimant will be left guessing as to the basis on which the decision has been arrived at. And in a case where specific submissions backed with expert medical evidence have been addressed to them on the basis of assessment to be used, it will normally be an error of law for the tribunal simply to state their conclusion in the form of a percentage without making it clear to what extent and for what reasons they are accepting or rejecting the suggested basis, since they will not have carried out the general duty to give reasons on a material issue raised before them: see *R(I) 18/61* para. 13."

Further guidance in medical cases has been given by the Court of Appeal in *Evans v. Secretary of State for Social Services* (reported as *R(I) 5/94*) where it was said:

"1. The decision should record the medical question or questions which the tribunal is required to answer. Provided the questions are set out and the are set out and the answers are directed to the questions it should then be possible for the parties to know the issues to which the tribunal have addressed themselves.
2. In cases where the tribunal have medically examined the claimant they should record their findings. These findings by themselves may be sufficient to demonstrate the reason why they have reached a particular conclusion.
3. Where, however, the clinical findings do not point to some obvious diagnosis it may be necessary to give a short explanation as to why they have made one diagnosis rather than another. Such an explanation will be

important in cases where the tribunal's diagnosis differs from a reasoned diagnosis of another qualified practitioner who has examined the claimant on an earlier occasion.

4. A decision on a question of causation may pose particular difficulties when one is examining the adquacy of the reasons for a decision. In some cases it may be sufficient for the tribunal to record that it was not satisfied that the present condition was caused by the relevant trauma. Where, however, a claimant has previously been in receipt of some benefit or allowance (particularly if paid over a long period of time) and there is no question of malingering or bad faith then . . . the tribunal should go further than merely to state a conclusion. If one accepts that the underlying principle is fairness the claimant should be given some explanation, which may be very short, to enable him or his advisors to know where the break in causation has been found. Thus it may well be that the claimant will wish to reapply and for this purpose fairness requires that, if possible, he should be told why his claim has failed."

In *Baron v. Secretary of State for Social Services* (reported as an appendix to *R(M) 6/86*), it was said that:

"The overriding test must always be: is the tribunal providing both parties with the materials which will enable them to know that the tribunal has made no error of law in reaching its findings of fact?"

Late applications for a statement of reasons of tribunal decision

54.—(1) The time for making an application for a copy of the statement of the reasons for a tribunal's decision may be extended where the conditions specified in paragraphs (2) to (8) are satisfied, but no application shall in any event be brought more than three months after the date of the sending or giving of the notice of the decision of the appeal tribunal.

(2) An application for an extension of time under this regulation shall be made in writing and shall be determined by a legally qualified panel member.

(3) An application under this regulation shall contain particulars of the grounds on which the extension of time is sought, including details of any relevant special circumstances for the purposes of paragraph (4).

(4) The application for an extension of time shall not be granted unless the panel member is satisfied that it is in the interests of justice for the application to be granted.

(5) For the purposes of paragraph (4) it is not in the interests of justice to grant the application unless the panel member is satisfied that—

(a) the special circumstances specified in paragraph (6) are relevant to the application; or

(b) some other special circumstances are relevant to the application, and as a result of those special circumstances it was not practicable for the application to be made within the time limit specified in regulation 53(4).

(6) For the purposes of paragraph (5)(a), the special circumstances are that—

4.344

Social Security and Child Support (Decisions and Appeals) Regulations 1999

(a) the applicant or a spouse or dependant of the applicant has died or suffered serious illness;
(b) the applicant is not resident in the United Kingdom; or
(c) normal postal services were adversely disrupted.

(7) In determining whether it is in the interests of justice to grant the application, the panel member shall have regard to the principle that the greater the amount of time that has elapsed between the expiration of the time within which the application for a copy of the statement of reasons for a tribunal's decision is to be made and the making of the application for an extension of time, the more compelling should be the special circumstances on which the application is based.

(8) In determining whether it is in the interests of justice to grant the application, no account shall be taken of the following—
(a) that the person making the application or any person acting for him was unaware of, or misunderstood, the law applicable to his case (including ignorance or misunderstanding of the time limits imposed by these Regulations); or
(b) that a Commissioner or a court has taken a different view of the law from that previously understood and applied.

(9) An application under this regulation for an extension of time which has been refused may not be renewed.

(10) The panel member who determines the application shall record a summary of his decision in such written form as has been approved by the President.

(11) As soon as practicable after the decision is made a copy of the decision shall be sent or given to every party to the proceedings.

(12) Any person who under paragraph (11) receives a copy of the decision may, within one month of the decision being sent to him, apply in writing for a copy of the reasons for that decision and a copy shall be supplied to him.

Record of tribunal proceedings

4.345   **55.**—(1) A record of the proceedings at an oral hearing, which is sufficient to indicate the evidence taken, shall be made by the chairman, or in the case of an appeal tribunal which has only one member, by that member, in such medium as he may direct.

(2) Such record shall be preserved by the clerk to the appeal tribunal for six months from the date of the decision made by the appeal tribunal to which the record relates and any party to the proceedings may within that period apply in writing for a copy of that record and a copy shall be supplied to him.

GENERAL NOTE

4.346   The failure to make or preserve a record of proceedings may result in a tribunal's decision being held to be erroneous in law but it does not necessarily do so. The reduction in the period for which the record must be preserved from 18 months to 6 months seems undesirable when an application for leave to appeal may be made as much as 13 months after the date of the tribunal's decision. The duty to provide a record of proceedings is a duty to provide one that is comprehensible without some other person's assistance *(CIB/3013/97)* in order that people may understand what happened on the hearing on the appeal *(CDLA/4110/97)*, so that providing an illegible document is not sufficient. A failure to comply with this duty will not always render the tribunal's decision erroneous in point of law but it will do so if, in a particular case, it is necessary to have regard to the evidence given at the hearing or to any contention put forward at the hearing in order to decide whether some other ground of appeal is made out *(CDLA/1389/97)*.

Correction of accidental errors

56.—(1) The clerk to the appeal tribunal, or where the clerk refers the matter to a legally qualified panel member, that member, may at any time correct accidental errors in any decision, or the record of any such decision, of an appeal tribunal made under a relevant enactment, the Child Support Act or the Vaccine Damage Payments Act.

(2) A correction made to, or to the record of, a decision shall be deemed to be part of the decision or record of that decision and written notice of it shall be given as soon as practicable to every party to the proceedings.

(3) In this regulation and regulation 57, "relevant enactment" has the same meaning as in section 28(3).

4.347

GENERAL NOTE

The fact that it is necessary to have this provision suggests that the accidental errors that may be corrected may be significant even though they may be only slips of the pen. It is therefore disconcerting to find that the correction may be made at any time but no provision is made for extending the time for requesting a statement of reasons or appealing against the decision when a significant correction is made late.

A decision is only effective when it is sent out *(R(I) 14/74)*. Until then, it may be altered informally. Even if an oral "decision" has been given, the case may be recalled by the tribunal before it is sent out, if it appears to them that they have made a serious mistake *(CI/141/87*, applying *Re Harrison's Share* [1955] Ch. 260). Generally it would then be necessary to have a rehearing.

4.348

Setting aside decisions on certain grounds

57.—(1) On an application made by a party to the proceedings, a decision of an appeal tribunal made under a relevant enactment, the Child Support Act or the Vaccine Damage Payments Act, may be set aside by a legally qualified panel member in a case where it appears just to set the decision aside on the ground that—

(a) a document relating to the proceedings in which the decision was made was not sent to, or was not received at an appropriate time by, a party to the proceedings or the party's representative or was not received at an appropriate time by the person who made the decision;

(b) a party to the proceedings in which the decision was made or the party's representative was not present at a hearing relating to the proceedings.

(2) In determining whether it is just to set aside a decision on the ground set out in paragraph (1)(b), the panel member shall determine

4.349

whether the party making the application gave notice that he wished to have an oral hearing, and if that party did not give such notice the decision shall not be set aside unless the chairman, or in the case of an appeal tribunal which has only one member, unless that member is satisfied that the interests of justice manifestly so require.

(3) An application under this regulation shall be made in accordance with regulations 31 to 33.

(4) Where an application to set aside a decision is entertained under paragraph (1), every party to the proceedings shall be sent a copy of the application and shall be afforded a reasonable opportunity of making representations on it before the application is determined.

(5) Notice in writing of a determination on an application to set aside a decision shall be sent or given to every party to the proceedings as soon as may be practicable and the notice shall contain a statement giving the reasons for the determination.

GENERAL NOTE

Paragraph (1)

4.350
Reg. 10(1)(c) of the Social Security (Adjudication) Regulations 1995 provided for a third ground for setting aside when "the interests of justice so require" which had been held to be limited to procedural errors and mishaps. It seems odd that that ground should have been dropped when s.13 of the Social Security Act 1998 has so expanded the grounds upon which a decision may be set aside. Section 13(2) is not a complete substitute because there are cases when there has been a procedural slip and the interests of justice might require a decision to be set aside even though, strictly speaking, there has been no breach of the rules of natural justice and the tribunal's decision is not erroneous in point of law. The most obvious example is where a tribunal has quite properly decided to proceed with a case in the unexplained absence of a material witness and it subsequently transpires that the witness had a very good reason for not appearing and for not informing the tribunal or the party intending to call him or her. However, if a power to set aside a decision to remedy an obvious unfairness may be regarded as a "procedural safeguard", such a power may be implied notwithstanding its absence from the statutory scheme (see *per* Lord of Harwich in *Lloyd v. McMahon* [1987] A.C. 625, 702–3). S.28(2) of the 1998 Act appears to anticipate the existence of implied powers of this nature. The loss of regulation 10(1)(c) of the 1995 Regulations may therefore be immaterial.

In *CSB/15394/96* and *CSB/574/97*, a tribunal refused to set aside a decision on the ground that the claimant's case for the setting aside amounted to an allegation that there had been a breach of the rules of natural justice which was an error of law so that an appeal to a Commissioner was the appropriate course for the claimant to take. The Commissioner hearing the appeal disagreed. He pointed out that most grounds for setting aside would also be proper grounds for appeal and that the regulation existed to provide an expeditious alternative to an appeal. On the other hand, in *CSDLA/303/98*, the Commissioner held that a claimant was not entitled to raise by way of appeal an issue of fact determined under the forerunner of this regulation. The tribunal considering the application for setting aside had found as a fact that a fax allegedly sent to the Independent Tribunal Service had not in fact been sent. The Commissioner held that that question of fact could not be considered on an appeal because "there could be no question of unfairness arising as the claimant had been provided with the remedy of seeking set aside". It is not recorded whether or not the claimant was offered an oral hearing of the application for setting aside, which would have been unusual. It may still be arguable that a finding made on such an application without an oral hearing is not sufficient to remove a Commissioner's jurisdiction to consider the same issue on an appeal.

Applications for leave to appeal to a Commissioner
(not including child support)

Application for leave to appeal to a Commissioner from an appeal tribunal

58.—(1) An application for leave to appeal to a Commissioner from a decision of an appeal tribunal under section 12 or 13 shall—
  (a) be made within the period of one month commencing on the date the applicant is sent a written statement of the reasons for the decision against which leave to appeal is sought; and
  (b) have annexed to it a copy of that written statement of the reasons for the decision.

(2) Where an application for leave to appeal to a Commissioner is made by the Secretary of State [¹or the Board], the clerk to an appeal tribunal shall, as soon as may be practicable, send a copy of the application to every other party to the proceedings.

(3) Any party to the proceedings who is sent a copy of an application for leave to appeal in accordance with paragraph (2) may make representations in writing within one month of the date the application is sent.

(4) A person determining an application for leave to appeal to a Commissioner, shall take into account any further representations received from the applicant before the determination is made, and shall record his decision in writing and send a copy to every party to the proceedings.

(5) Where there has been a failure to apply for leave to appeal within the period of time specified in paragraph (1)(a) but an application is made within one year of the last date for making an application within that period, a legally qualified panel member may, if for special reasons he thinks fit, accept and proceed to consider and determine the application.

(6) Where in any case it is impracticable, or it would be likely to cause undue delay for an application for leave to appeal against a decision of an appeal tribunal to be determined by the person who was the chairman, or in the case of an appeal tribunal which has only one member, the member, of that tribunal, the application shall be determined by a legally qualified panel member.

AMENDMENT

1. Tax Credits (Decisions and Appeals) (Amendment) Regulations 1999 (S.I. 1999 No. 2570), reg. 27 (October 5, 1999). Note that amendments made by these regulations only have effect with respect to tax credit (reg. 1(2) of the Amendment Regulations).

GENERAL NOTE

No provision is made for an appeal to be brought against a decision when there is no statement of reasons. In practice, if the application is made within the time for requesting a statement of reasons, the application will be treated as such a request. The problems arise where the application is received too late and no statement of reasons is issued. In *R(IS) 11/99*, it was held that a tribunal chairman had no jurisdiction under the previous legislation to consider an application for leave to appeal if there was no full statement of the tribunal's decision. It was also held that a Commissioner did have jurisdiction, but that was doubted in *CIS/4437/98*. Under the new legislation the position is clearer. A panel member cannot grant leave to appeal if there is no written statement of reasons (because the date of issue of such a statement is the date from which time runs) but, under reg. 9 of the Social Security Commissioners (Procedure) Regulations 1999, an application may be made to a Commissioner not only when one has been "refused" by a panel member but also when one has been "rejected" (e.g. for want of jurisdiction) *(CSDLA/536/99)*.

Paragraph (5)
There is a broad discretion to extend the time for appealing where that is necessary to enable justice to be done. The approach of the Court of Appeal in *Regina v. Secretary of State for the Home Department, ex parte Mehta* [1975] 1 W.L.R. 1087 was followed in *R(M) 1/87* and it was held that it was wrong to consider only whether there were special reasons for the delay in applying for leave to appeal. In *CCS/2064/99*, it was suggested that relevant factors included the strength of the grounds of appeal, the amount of money involved, whether the decision affected current entitlement, whether there was an adequate alternative remedy, the difficulties that the lapse of time might create for making any further findings of fact and the way in which the parties had conducted the case, including their respective contributions to delay. The amount of delay is also relevant but, in *CSDLA/71/99*, the Commissioner made it plain that "special reasons" for admitting a late application for leave to appeal would not necessarily be found merely because the application was made only two or three days late, even if the applicant had an arguable case on the merits. In that case, the applicant was not helped by the fact that the original explanation for the delay advanced by his representative turned out not to be true and leave to appeal was refused.

Part VI

Revocations

Recovations

4.353   59.—(1) The Regulations listed in column (2) of Schedule 4 are hereby revoked to the extent specified in column (3) of that Schedule.

(2) Notwithstanding their revocation for particular purposes, the Regulations listed in column (2) of Schedule 4 shall continue to have full effect up to and including November 28, 1999 in relation to any benefit to which these Regulations do not apply for the time being by virtue of regulation 1(2).

(3) So much of any document as refers expressly or by implication to any regulation revoked by paragraph (1) shall, in so far as the context permits, for the purposes of these Regulations be treated as referring to the corresponding provision of these Regulations.

(S.I. 1999 No. 991, Sched. 1)

SCHEDULE 1

PROVISIONS CONFERRING POWERS EXERCISED IN MAKING THESE REGULATIONS 4.354

Column (1) Provision		Column (2) Relevant Amendments
Vaccine Damage Payments Act 1979	Section 4(2) and (3)	The Act, Section 46
	Section 7A(1)	The Act, Section 47
Child Support Act 1991	Section 16(6)	The Act, Section 40
	Section 20(5) and (6)	The Act, Section 42
	Section 28ZA(2)(b) and (4)(c)	The Act, Section 43
	Section 28ZB(6)(c)	The Act, Section 43
	Section 28ZC(7)	The Act, Section 44
	Section 28ZD(1) and (2)	The Act, Section 44
	Section 46B	The Act, Schedule 7, paragraph 44
	Section 51(2)	The Act, Schedule 7, paragraph 46
	Schedule 4A, paragraph 8	The Act, Schedule 7, paragraph 53
Social Security Administration Act 1992	Section 5(1)(hh)	The Act, Section 74
	Section 159	The Act, Schedule 7, paragraph 95
	Section 159A	The Act, Schedule 7, paragraph 96
Pension Schemes Act 1993	Section 170(3)	The Act, Schedule 7, paragraph 131
Social Security (Recovery of Benefits) Act 1997	Section 10	The Act, Schedule 7, paragraph 149
	Section 11(5)	
Social Security Act 1998	Section 6(3)	
	Section 7(6)	
	Section 9(1), (4) and (6)	
	Section 10(3) and (6)	
	Section 11(1)	
	Section 12(2) and (3), (6) and (7)	
	Section 14(10)(a) and (11)	
	Section 16(1) and Schedule 5	
	Section 17	
	Section 18(1)	
	Section 20	
	Section 21(1) to (3)	
	Section 22	
	Section 23	
	Section 24	
	Section 25(3)(b) and (5)(c)	
	Section 26(6)(c)	
	Section 28(1)	
	Section 31(2)	
	Section 79(1) and (3) to (7)	
	Section 84	
	Schedule 1, paragraphs 7, 11 and 12	
	Schedule 2, paragraph 9	
	Schedule 3, paragraphs 1, 4 and 9	

Social Security and Child Support (Decisions and Appeals) Regulations 1999

SCHEDULE 2   **Regulation 27**

DECISIONS AGAINST WHICH NO APPEAL LIES

Child benefit

4.355   **1.** A decision of the Secretary of State as to whether an educational establishment be recognised for the purposes of Part IX of the Contributions and Benefits Act.

2. A decision of the Secretary of State to recognise education provided otherwise than at a recognised educational establishment.

3. A decision of the Secretary of State made in accordance with the discretion conferred upon him by the following provisions of the Child Benefit (Residence and Persons Abroad) Regulations 1976—
 (a) regulation 2(2)(c)(iii) (decision relating to a child's temporary absence abroad);
 (b) regulation 7(3) (certain days of absence abroad disregarded).

4. A decision of the Secretary of State made in accordance with the discretion conferred upon him by regulation 2(1) or (3) of the Child Benefit (General) Regulations 1976 (provisions relating to contributions and expenses in respect of a child).

Claims and payments

4.356   **5.** A decision of the Secretary of State under the Claims and Payments Regulations except a decision under—
 (a) regulation 19 as to the time for claiming benefit;
 (b) regulation 37AB as to the payment of withheld benefit;
 (c) regulation 38 as to the extinguishment of the right to payment of sums by way of benefit where payment is not obtained within the prescribed period; and
 (d) the following provisions of Schedule 9 and regulation 35(1) in so far as it relates to them—
  (i) paragraph 3 relating to the amount deductible by way of housing costs;
  (ii) paragraph 4 relating to the amount of miscellaneous housing costs payable direct to a third party;
  (iii) paragraph 4A relating to the direct payment to a third party of benefit payable to or in respect of persons resident in hostels;
  (iv) paragraph 5 relating to payments of benefit direct to the claimant's or his partner's landlord;
  (v) paragraph 6 relating to the payment out of benefit of fuel costs;
  (vi) paragraph 7 relating to the payment out of benefit of water charges;
  (vii) paragraph 7A in connection with amounts payable in place of child support maintenance;
  (viii) paragraph 7B as to whether an amount in respect of arrears of child support maintenance is to be deducted from a person's jobseeker's allowance; and
  (ix) paragraph 9(3) as to the priority between liabilities for items of gas and electricity.

CONTRACTED OUT PENSION SCHEMES

4.357   **6.** A decision of the Secretary of State under section 109 of the Pension Schemes Act 1993 or any Order made under it (annual increase of guaranteed minimum pensions).

DECISIONS DEPENDING ON OTHER CASES

4.358   **7.** A decision of the Secretary of State under section 25 or 26 (decisions and appeals depending on other cases).

DEDUCTIONS

4.359   **8.** A decision which falls to be made by the Secretary of State under the Fines (Deductions from Income Support) Regulations 1992, other than one falling within regulation 4 of those Regulations.

9.—(1) Except in relation to a decision to which sub-paragraph (2) applies, any decision

(S.I. 1999 No. 991, Sched. 2)

of the Secretary of State under the Community Charges (Deductions from Income Support) (No. 2) Regulations 1990, the Community Charges (Deductions from Income Support) (Scotland) Regulations 1989 or the Council Tax (Deductions from Income Support) Regulations 1993.

(2) This sub-paragraph applies to a decision—
  (a) whether there is an outstanding sum due of the amount sought to be deducted;
  (b) whether benefit is sufficient for a deduction to be made; and
  (c) on the priority to be given to any deduction.

European Community regulations

10. An authorization given by the Secretary of State in accordance with article 22(1) or (1) of Council Regulation (EEC) No. 1408/71 on the application of social security schemes to employed persons, to self-employed persons and to members of their families moving within the Community.   **4.360**

Expenses

11. A decision of the Secretary of State whether to pay expenses to any person under section 180 of the Administration Act.   **4.361**

Guardian's allowance

12. A decision of the Secretary of State relating to the giving of a notice under regulation 5(8) of the Social Security (Guardian's Allowance) Regulations 1975 (children whose surviving parents are in prison or legal custody).   **4.362**

Income support

13. A decision of the Secretary of State which embodies a determination made in accordance with paragraph (1) or (2) of regulation 13 (income support and social fund determinations on incomplete evidence).   **4.363**

Industrial injuries benefit

14. A decision of the Secretary of State relating to the question whether—   **4.364**
  (a) disablement pension be increased under section 104 of the Contributions and Benefits Act (constant attendance); or
  (b) disablement pension be further increased under section 105 of the Contributions and Benefits Act (exceptionally severe disablement);
and if an increase is to be granted or renewed, the period for which and the amount at which it is payable.

15. A decision of the Secretary of State under regulation 2(2) of the Social Security (Industrial Injuries and Diseases) Miscellaneous Provisions Regulations 1986 as to the length of any period of interruption of education which is to be disregarded.

16. A decision of the Secretary of State to approve or not to approve a person undertaking work for the purposes of regulation 17 of the Social Security (General Benefit) Regulations 1982.

17. A decision of the Secretary of State as to how the limitations under Part VI of Schedule 7 to the Contributions and Benefits Act on the benefit payable in respect of any death are to be applied in the circumstances of any case.

Invalid vehicle scheme

18. A decision of the Secretary of State relating to the issue of certificates under regulation 13 of, and Schedule 2 to, the Social Security (Disability Living Allowance) Regulations 1991.   **4.365**

Social Security and Child Support (Decisions and Appeals) Regulations 1999

JOBSEEKER'S ALLOWANCE

4.366   **19.**—(1) A decision of the Secretary of State under Chapter IV of Part II of the Jobseeker's Allowance Regulations as to the day and the time a claimant is to attend at a job centre.

(2) A decision of the Secretary of State as to the day of the week on which a claimant is required to provide a signed declaration under regulation 24(10) of the Jobseeker's Allowance Regulations.

(3) A decision of the Secretary of State which embodies a determination made in accordance with regulation 15 (Jobseeker's allowance determinations on incomplete evidence).

PAYMENTS ON ACCOUNT, OVERPAYMENTS AND RECOVERY

4.367   **20.** A decision of the Secretary of State under the Social Security (Payments on account, Overpayments and Recovery) Regulations 1988, except a decision of the Secretary of State under the following provisions of those Regulations—
   (a) regulation 3(1)(a) to offset any interim payment made in anticipation of an award of benefit;
   (b) regulation 4(1) as to the overpayment of an interim payment;
   (c) regulation 5 as to the offsetting of a prior payment against a subsequent award;
   (d) regulation 11(1) as to whether a payment in excess of entitlement has been credited to a bank or other account;
   (e) regulation 13 as to the sums to be deducted in calculating recoverable amounts;
   (f) regulation 14(1) as to the treatment of capital to be reduced;
   (g) regulation 19 determining a claimant's protected earnings; and
   (h) regulation 24 whether a determination as to a claimant's protected earnings is revised or superseded.

PERSONS ABROAD

4.368   **21.** A decision of the Secretary of State made under—
   (a) regulation 2(1)(a) of the Social Security Benefit (Persons Abroad) Regulations 1975 whether to certify that it is consistent with the proper administration of the Contributions and Benefits Act that a disqualification under section 113(1)(a) of that Act should not apply;
   (b) regulation 9(4) or (5) of those Regulations whether to allow a person to avoid disqualification for receiving benefit during a period of temporary absence from Great Britain longer than that specified in the regulation.

RECIPROCAL AGREEMENTS

4.369   **22.** A decision of the Secretary of State made in accordance with an Order made under section 179 of the Administration Act (reciprocal agreements with countries outside the United Kingdom).

SOCIAL FUND AWARDS

4.370   **23.** A decision of the Secretary of State under section 78 of the Administration Act relating to the recovery of social fund awards.

SUPSENSION

4.371   **24.** A decision of the Secretary of State relating to the suspension of a relevant benefit or to the payment of such a benefit which has been suspended under Part III.

UP-RATING

4.372   **25.** A decision of the Secretary of State relating to the up-rating of benefits under Part X of the Administration Act.

(S.I. 1999 No. 991, Sched. 2)

[¹**26.** Any decision treated as a decision of the Secretary of State whether or not to waive or defer a work-focused interview.]   4.373

AMENDMENT

1. Social Security (Work-focused Interviews) Regulations 2000 (S.I. 2000 No. 897), reg. 16(5) and Sched. 6, para. 7 (April 3, 2000).

GENERAL NOTE

If reg. 27 if made under s.12(2) of the Social Security Act 1998, it is arguable that much of Sched. 2 to the Regulations is *ultra vires*, having regard to s.12(3). It is not easy to see why, for instance, a decision of the Secretary of State that an educational establishment be recognised for the purposes of child benefit or to recognise education provided otherwise that at such a recognised establishment (paras 1 and 2 of Sched. 2) is not a decision "that relates to the conditions of entitlement" to child benefit. The fact that a large element of discretion is involved is not material. There is no reason in principle why such a discretion should not be exercised by a tribunal. There may be sound reasons for restricting the rights of appeal in cases where there is a large element of pure discretion, so that any challenge has to be by way of application for revision under s.9 or for judicial review, and, of course, there was no right of appeal under the old legislation, but it is arguable that neither of those considerations carries much weight against the clear language of s.12(3). On the other hand, it is arguable that reg. 27 is made under para. 9 of Sched. 2 to the Act, which is in much broader terms than s.12. Both regulation-making powers are to be found in Sched. 1 to the Regulations. What the point is in having s.12(2) qualified by s.12(3) when there is the broader unqualified power in the same Act is unclear but an argument that a broad power should be regarded as qualified by the scope of the narrower power found little sympathy in *R. v. Secretary of State for Social Security, ex parte Moore* (1993).   4.374

In this Schedule, "decision" includes determinations embodied in or necessary to a decision (see reg. 27(2)).

SCHEDULE 3   Regulations 1(3) and 35

QUALIFICATIONS OF PERSONS APPOINTED TO THE PANEL

Legal Qualifications

1. Persons who—   4.375
   (a) have a general qualification (construed in accordance with section 71 of the Courts and Legal Services Act 1990); or
   (b) are advocates or solicitors in Scotland.

Medical Qualifications

2. Fully registered medical practitioners, where—   4.376
   (a) the practitioner's name appears on a medical specialist register maintained in any EEA State in accordance with the Medical Directive; or
   (b) the practitioner holds a vocational training certificate or a certificate of acquired rights in an EEA State other than the United Kingdom which must in his case be recognised in the United Kingdom by virtue of the Medical Directive (whether or not as read with the EEA Agreement) or by virtue of an enforceable community right; or
   (c) the practitioner does not satisfy the requirements of sub-paragraphs (a) or (b) above, but has not less than 10 years experience in clinical practice, or as a medical analyst or research worker in disciplines which are the same or similar to those undertaken by practitioners to whom those sub-paragraphs apply.

Social Security and Child Support (Decisions and Appeals) Regulations 1999

3. In paragraph 2 above and in this paragraph—

"EEA Agreement" means the Agreement of the European Economic Area signed at Oporto on May 2, 1992 as adjusted by the Protocol signed at Brussels on March 17, 1993;

"EEA State" means a state which is a contracting party to the EEA Agreement;

"Medical Directive" means Council Directive 93/16/EEC of April 5, 1993 to facilitate the free movement of doctors and the mutual recognitions of their diplomas, certificates and other evidence of formal qualifications, as amended by Council Directive 97/50/EC of October 6, 1997;

"Vocational training certificate" means a diploma, certificate or other evidence of formal qualifications awarded on completion of a course of specific training in general medical practice and referred to in article 30 of the Medical Directive.

Financial Qualifications

4.377   4. Accountants who are members of—
   (a) the Institute of Chartered Accountants in England and Wales;
   (b) the Institute of Chartered Accountants in Scotland;
   (c) the Institute of Chartered Accountants in Ireland;
   (d) the Association of Chartered Certified Accountants;
   (e) the Chartered Institute of Management Accountants; or
   (f) the Chartered Institute of Public Finance and Accountancy.

Disability Qualifications

4.378   5. Persons, other than registered medical practitioners, who are experienced in dealing with the needs of disabled persons—
   (a) in a professional or voluntary capacity; or
   (b) because they are themselves disabled.

SCHEDULE 4 — Regulation 59

4.379   REVOCATIONS

Column 1 Statutory Instrument Number	Column 2 Statutory Instrument	Column 3 Provision Revoked
1979/432	The Vaccine Damage Payments Regulations 1979	Part III
1992/2641	The Child Support Appeal Tribunals (Procedure) Regulations 1992	The whole Regulations
1995/311	The Social Security (Incapacity for Work) (General) Regulations 1995	Regulations 19 and 20 to 22
1995/1801	The Social Security (Adjudication) Regulations 1995	The whole Regulations
1996/182	The Social Security (Adjudication) and Child Support Amendment Regulations 1996	Regulation 2
1996/425	The Social Security (Industrial Injuries and Diseases) (Miscellaneous Amendments) Regulations 1996	Regulation 2
1996/1518	The Social Security (Adjudication) Amendment Regulations 1996	The whole Regulations
1996/2306	The Social Security (Claims and Payments and Adjudication) Amendment Regulations 1996	Regulations 8 and 9
1996/2450	The Social Security (Adjudication) and Child Support Amendment (No. 2) Regulations 1996	Regulations 2 to 13

(S.I. 1999 No. 991, Sched. 4)

Column 1 Statutory Instrument Number	Column 2 Statutory Instrument	Column 3 Provision Revoked
1996/2659	The Social Security (Adjudication) Amendment (No. 2) Regulations 1996	The whole Regulations
1997/65	The Income-Related Benefits and Job-seeker's Allowance (Miscellaneous Amendments) Regulations 1997	Regulation 16
1997/793	The Social Security (Miscellaneous Amendments) (No. 2) Regulations 19987	Regulations 1(2)(a) and 8 to 17
1997/810	The Social Security (Industrial Injuries) (Miscellaneous Amendments) Regulations 1997	Regulations 2, 3 and 4
[¹ 1997/955]	The Social Security (Adjudication) and Commissioners Procedure and Child Support Commissioners (Procedure) Amendment Regulations 1997	In regulation 1(2), the definition of "the Adjudication Regulations" and regulations 2 to 6
1997/1839	The Social Security (Attendance Allowance and Disability Living Allowance) (Miscellaneous Amendments) Regulations 1997	In regulation 1(2) the definition of "the Adjudication Regulations" and regulation 4
1997/2237	The Social Security (Recovery of Benefits) (Appeals) Regulations 1997	The whole Regulations
1997/2305	The Social Security (Miscellaneous Amendments) (No. 4) Regulations 1997	Regulation 4

The Social Security (General Benefit) Regulations 1982

(S.I. 1982 No. 1408) *(as amended)*

ARRANGEMENT OF REGULATIONS

PART I

General

1. Citation, commencement and interpretation   **4.380**
2. Exceptions from disqualification for imprisonment etc.
3. Suspension of payment of benefit during imprisonment etc.
4. Interim payments by way of benefit under the Act
5. Deduction of benefit required to be repaid (*revoked*)
6. Set-off of benefit against earlier payment of dependency benefit (*revoked*)
7. Repayment by a person who has received payment of benefit on behalf of a beneficiary (*revoked*)
8. Rounding of sums payable by way of benefit (*revoked*)

The Social Security (General Benefit) Regulations 1982

Part II

Provisions Relating To Benefit Other Than Industrial Injuries Benefit

9. Payments of benefit and suspension of payments pending a decision on appeals or references, arrears and repayments
10. Disqualifications to be disregarded for certain purposes

Part III

Provisions Relating To Industrial Injuries Benefit Only

PRINCIPLES OF ASSESSMENT
11. Further definition of the principles of assessment of disablement and prescribed degrees of disablement

INJURY AND DISABLEMENT BENEFIT
14. Amount of disablement gratuities
15. Weekly value of gratuity for purposes of reduction of increase of disablement benefit during hospital treatment
16. Earnings level for the purposes of unemployability supplement under section 58 of the Act

INCREASE OF INJURY AND DISABLEMENT BENEFIT
17. Circumstances in which, for the purposes of section 60, a beneficiary may be treated as being incapable of following an occupation or employment notwithstanding that he has worked thereat
18. Payments in respect of special hardship where beneficiary is entitled to a gratuity
19. Increase of disablement pension for constant attendance
20. Determination of degree of disablement for constant attendance allowance
21. Condition for receipt of increase of disablement pension for constant attendance under section 61 while receiving medical treatment as an inpatient
22. Treatment of distinct periods of hospital in-patient treatment as continuous for the purposes of section 62 of the Act

INDUSTRIAL DEATH BENEFIT
Regulations 23-37 omitted

ADJUSTMENT OF BENEFIT FOR SUCCESSIVE ACCIDENTS
38. Adjustment of benefit for successive accidents where a disablement gratuity is payable
39. Adjustment of increase of benefit in respect of successive accidents

DISQUALIFICATION FOR RECEIPT OF BENEFIT AND SUSPENSION OF BENEFIT PENDING APPEALS ETC.
40. Disqualification for receipt of benefit, suspension of proceedings on claims and suspension of payment of benefit

(S.I. 1982 No. 1408) (as amended)

PAYMENTS UNDER THE ACT TO CERTAIN PERSONS WHO CONTRACTED DISEASES OR WHO WERE INJURED BEFORE 5 JULY 1948
Regulations 42-45 omitted

MISCELLANEOUS PROVISIONS
46. Conditions relating to payment of additional benefit under awards made before the day appointed for any increase of benefit under any Act amending the Act or under any up-rating order

PART IV

47. Revocation and transitional provisions

SCHEDULES

SCHEDULE 1—Provisions for the purpose of which disqualifications under the Act are to be disregarded
SCHEDULE 2—Prescribed degrees of disablement
SCHEDULE 3—Scale of disablement gratuities
Schedule 4—Rate of disablement pension payable in lieu of disablement gratuity in accordance with regulation 18

Schedules 5-9 Omitted

PART I

GENERAL

Citation, commencement and interpretation

1—(1) These regulations may be cited as the Social Security (General Benefit) Regulations 1982 and shall come into operation on 4th November, 1982.
(2) In these regulations, unless the context otherwise requires—
"the Act" means the Social Security Act 1975;
"the Child Benefit Act" means the Child Benefit Act 1975;
"child benefit" means benefit under Part I of the Child Benefit Act;
[¹ "determining authority" means, as the case may require, the Secretary of State, an appeal tribunal constituted under section 7 of the Social Security Act 1998, the Chief or any other Social Security Commissioner appointed under Schedule 4 to that Act, or a tribunal consisting of any three or more such Commissioners constituted in accordance with section 16(7) of that Act;]
"entitled to child benefit" includes treated as so entitled;
"industrial injuries benefit" means [²...] disablement benefit and industrial death benefit payable under section 50 of the Act;
"parent" has the meaning assigned to it by section 24(3) of the Child Benefit Act;
"standard rate of increase" means the amount specified in Part IV or Part V of Schedule 4 to the Act as the amount of an increase of the benefit in question for an adult dependant;

"the Workmen's Compensation Act" means the Workmen's Compensation Acts 1925 to 1945, or the enactments repealed by the Workmen's Compensation Act 1925 or the enactments repealed by the Workmen's Compensation Act 1906;
and other expressions have the same meanings as in the Act.

(3) Unless the context otherwise requires, any reference in these regulation—
  (a) to a numbered section is to the section of the Act bearing that number;
  (b) to a numbered regulation is a reference to the regulation bearing that number in these regulations and any reference in a regulation to a numbered paragraph is a reference to the paragraph of that regulation bearing that number.

AMENDMENTS

1. The Social Security Act 1998 (Commencement No. 8, and Savings and Consequential and Transitional Provisions) Order 1999 (S.I. 1999 No 1958), Sched. 5 (July 4, 1999)
2. The Social Security (Abolition of Injury Benefit) (Consequential) Regulations 1983 (S.I. 1983 No 186), reg. 13 (April 6, 1983)

Exceptions from disqualification for imprisonment etc.

4.382   **2.**—(1) The following provisions of this regulation shall have effect to except benefit from the operation of [section 113(1)(b) of the Social Security Contributions and Benefits Act 1992] which provides that (except where regulations otherwise provide) a person shall be disqualified for receiving any benefit and an increase of benefit shall not be payable in respect of any person as the beneficiary's wife or husband, for any period during which that person is undergoing imprisonment or detention in legal custody (hereinafter in this regulation referred to as "the said provisions").

(2) The said provisions shall not operate to disqualify a person for receiving [¹incapacity benefit], [²attendance allowance, disability living allowance], widow's benefit, child's special allowance, maternity allowance, retirement pension of any category, age addition, [³severe disablement allowance], [⁴...disablement benefit], [⁵...reduced earnings allowance, retirement allowance] or industrial death benefit or to make an increase of benefit not payable in respect of a person as the beneficiary's wife or husband, for any period during which that person is undergoing imprisonment or detention in legal custody in connection with a charge brought or intended to be brought against him in criminal proceedings, or pursuant to any sentence or order for detention made by a court in such proceedings, unless, in relation to him, a penalty is imposed at the conclusion of those proceedings or, in the case of default of payment of a sum adjudged to be paid on conviction, a penalty is imposed in respect of such default.

(3) The said provisions shall not operate to disqualify a person for receiving any benefit (not being a guardian's allowance or death grant), or to make an increase of benefit not payable in respect of a person as

the beneficiary's wife or husband, for any period during which that person is undergoing detention in legal custody after the conclusion of criminal proceedings if it is a period during which he is liable to be detained in a hospital or similar institution in Great Britain as a person suffering from mental disorder unless—
  (a) pursuant to any sentence or order for detention made by the court at the conclusion of those proceedings, he has undergone detention by way of penalty in a prison, a detention centre, a Borstal institution or a young offenders institution; and
  (b) he was removed to the hospital or similar institution while liable to be detained as a result of that sentence or order, and, in the case of a person who is liable to be detained in the hospital or similar institution by virtue or any provision of the Mental Health Act 1959 or the Mental Health (Scotland) Act 1960, a direction restricting his discharge has been given under either of those Acts and is still in force.

(4) Where, as respects a person in relation to whom each of the conditions specified in paragraph (3)(a) and (b) is satisfied, a certificate given by or on behalf of the Secretary of State for the Home Department or the Secretary of State for Scotland and furnished to the Secretary of State for Social Services shows the earliest date on which that person would have been expected to be discharged from the detention pursuant to the said sentence or order if he had not been transferred to a hospital or similar institution, the said conditions shall be deemed not to be satisfied in relation to that person as from the day next following that date.

(5) The said provisions shall not operate to disqualify a person for receiving a guardian's allowance or death grant.

[^{5}(6) Subject to paragraph (7), the said provisions shall not operate to disqualify a person for receiving disablement benefit, other than any increase of that benefit, for any period during which he is undergoing imprisonment or detention in legal custody.]

(7) The amount payable by virtue of the last preceding paragraph by way of any disablement pension or pensions in respect of any period, other than a period in respect of which that person is excepted from disqualification by virtue of the provisions of paragraph (3) of this regulation, during which that person is and has continuously been undergoing imprisonment or detention in legal custody, shall not exceed the total amount payable by way of such pension or all such pensions for a period of one year.

(8) For the purposes of this regulation—
  (a) "court" means any court in the United Kingdom, the Channel Islands or the Isle of Man or in any place to which the Colonial Prisoners Removal Act 1884 applies or any naval court-martial, army court-martial or air force court-martial within the meaning of the Courts-Martial (Appeals) Act 1968, or the Courts-Martial Appeal Court;
  (b) "hospital or similar institution" means any place (not being a prison, a detention centre, a Borstal institution, a young offenders institution or a remand centre, and not being at or in any such

place) in which persons suffering from mental disorder are or may be received for care or treatment;
  (c) "penalty" means a sentence of imprisonment, Borstal training or detention under section 53 of the Children and Young Persons Act 1933 or under section 57(3) of the Children and Young Persons (Scotland) Act 1937 or under section 208(3) and 416(4) of the Criminal Proceedings (Scotland) Act 1975 or an order for detention in a detention centre;
  (d) in relation to a person who is liable to be detained in Great Britain as a result of any order made under the Colonial Prisoners Removal Act 1884, references to a prison shall be construed as including references to a prison within the meaning of that Act;
  (e) a person who is liable to be detained by virtue of any provision of the Mental Health Act 1959 or the Mental Health (Scotland) Act 1960 shall be treated as if a direction restricting his discharge had been given under one or other of those Acts if for the purposes thereof he is to be so treated;
  (f) references to mental disorder shall be construed as including references to any mental disorder within the meaning of the Mental Health Act 1959 or the Mental Health (Scotland) Act 1960;
  (g) criminal proceedings against any person shall be deemed to be concluded upon his being found insane in those proceedings so that he cannot be tried or his trial cannot proceed.
(9) Where a person outside Great Britain is undergoing imprisonment or detention in legal custody and, in similar circumstances in Great Britain, he would have been excepted, by the operation of any of the preceding paragraphs of this regulation, from disqualification under the said provisions (referred to in paragraph (1)) for receiving the benefit claimed, he shall not be disqualified for receiving that benefit by reason only of his said imprisonment or detention.
(10) Paragraph (9) applies to increases of benefit not payable under the said provisions as it applied to disqualification for receiving benefit.

AMENDMENTS

1. The Social Security (Incapacity Benefit) (Consequential and Transitional Amendments and Savings) Regulations 1995 (S.I. 1995 No 829), reg. 16 (April 13, 1995)
2. The Disability Living Allowance and Disability Working Allowance (Consequential Provisions) Regulations 1991 (S.I. 1991 No 2742), reg. 11 (April 6, 1992)
3. The Social Security (Severe Disablement Allowance) Regulations 1984 (S.I. 1984 No 1303), reg. 11 (November 29, 1984)
4. The Social Security (Abolition of Injury benefit) (Consequential) Regulations 1983 (S.I. 1983 No 186), reg. 13 (April 6, 1983)
5. The Social Security (Industrial Injuries and Diseases) (Miscellaneous Amendments) Regulations 1996 (S.I. 1996 No 425), reg. 4 (March 24, 1996)

DEFINITIONS

"the Act": reg. 1.
"benefit": C & BA 1992, s.122.

(S.I. 1982 No. 1408, Reg. 2) (as amended)

"court": para. (8)(a).
"Great Britain": by Art. 1 of the Union with Scotland Act 1706, this means England, Scotland and Wales.
"hospital or similar institution": para.(8)(b).
"penalty": para. (8)(c).
"the said provisions": para. (1).

GENERAL NOTE

Persons who can bring themselves within the terms of this regulation can escape the disqualification from benefit provided for in s.113(1)(b) of the Contributions and Benefits Act. Different rules apply to different benefits.

Under para. (2) the disqualification applies in cases of imprisonment in connection with criminal proceedings where such penalty is imposed at the conclusion of proceedings. Imprisonment outside the exercise of criminal jurisdiction does not disqualify from benefit: *R(S)8/79*. It is now established that "penalty" in this paragraph includes the imposition of a suspended sentence and that a suspended sentence amounts to a sentence of imprisonment: *R(S)1/71*.

Paragraph (3) deals with the transfer of offenders from prison to hospital as mental patients under the mental health legislation. The disqualification in such circumstances exists only for the length of the original sentence: *R(P)2/57* reversing *R(S)9/56*. Provision is made for the Secretary of State to issue a certificate which is conclusive as to the earliest date on which the original sentence would come to an end had the person not been transferred to hospital.

References to the Mental Health Act 1959 should now be read as references to the Mental Health Act 1983.

Suspension of payment of benefit during imprisonment etc.

3.—(1) Subject to the following provisions of this regulation, the payment to any person of any benefit—
   (a) which is excepted from the operation of [section 113(1)(b) of the Social Security Contributions and Benefits Act 1992] by virtue of the provisions of regulation 2(2), (5) and (6) or by any of those paragraphs as applied by regulation 2(9); or
   (b) which is payable otherwise than in respect of a period during which he is undergoing imprisonment or detention in legal custody; shall be suspended while that person is undergoing imprisonment or detention in legal custody.

(2) Paragraph (1) shall not operate to require the payment of any benefit to be suspended while the beneficiary is liable to be detained in a hospital or similar institution as defined in regulation 2(8)(b) during a period for which in his case, benefit to which regulation 2(3) applies is or would be excepted from the operation of the said [section 113(1)] by virtue of the provision of regulation 2(3).

(3) A guardian's allowance or death grant, or any benefit to which paragraph (1)(b) applies may nevertheless be paid while the beneficiary is undergoing imprisonment or detention in legal custody to any person appointed for the purpose by the Secretary of State to receive and deal with any sums payable on behalf of the beneficiary on account of that benefit, and the receipt of any person so appointed shall be a good discharge to the Secretary of State and the National Insurance Fund for any sum so paid.

4.384

The Social Security (General Benefit) Regulations 1982

(4) Where, by virtue of this regulation, payment of benefit under [Part V of the Social Security Contribution and Benefits Act 1992] is suspended for any period, the period of suspension shall not be taken into account in calculating any period under the provisions of regulation 22 of the Social Security (Claims and Payments) Regulations 1979 (extinguishment of right to sums payable by way of benefit which are not obtained within the prescribed time).

Interim payments by way of benefit under the Act

4.385 **4.**—(1) Where, under arrangements made by the Secretary of State with the consent of the Treasury, payment by way of benefit has been made pending determination of a claim for it without due proof of the fulfilment of the relevant conditions or otherwise than in accordance with the provisions of the Act and orders and regulations made under it, the payment so made shall, for the purposes of those provisions, but subject to the following provisions of this regulation, be deemed to be a payment of benefit duly made.

(2) When a claim for benefit in connection with which a payment has been made under arrangements such as are referred to in paragraph (1) above is determined by a determining authority—
  (a) if that authority decides that nothing was properly payable by way of the benefit in respect of which the payment was made or that the amount properly payable by way of that benefit was less than the amount of the payment, it may, if appropriate, direct that the whole or part of the overpayment be treated as paid on account of benefit (whether benefit under the Act or the Supplementary Benefits Act 1976) which is properly payable, but subject as aforesaid shall require repayment of the overpayment; and
  (b) if that authority decides that the amount properly payable by way of the benefit in respect of which the payment was made equals or exceeds the amount of that payment, it shall treat that payment as paid on account of the benefit properly payable.

(3) Unless before a payment made under arrangements such as are mentioned in paragraph (1) above has been made to a person that person had been informed of the effect of sub-paragraph (a) of paragraph (2) above as it relates to repayment of an overpayment, repayment of an overpayment shall not be required except where the determining authority is satisfied that[1] he, or any person acting for him, has, whether fraudulently or otherwise, misrepresented or failed to disclose any material fact and that the interim payment has been made in consequence of the misrepresentation or failure.]

(4) An overpayment required to be repaid under the provisions of this regulation shall, without prejudice to any other method of recovery, be recoverable by deduction from any benefit then or thereafter payable to the person by whom it is to be repaid or any persons entitled to receive his benefit on his death.

AMENDMENT

1. The Social Security (Payments on account, Overpayment and Recovery) Regulations 1987 (S.I. 1987 No 491), reg. 19 (April 6, 1987.

(S.I. 1982 No. 1408, Reg. 4) (as amended)

GENERAL NOTE

This regulation has not been repealed by the Overpayments Regulations because its provisions will still be needed for cases where the relevant determination was made before April 6, 1987. As time passes the provision will fall into disuse, and will in due course be revoked.

4.386

Regulations 5-7 revoked by *The Social Security (Payments on account, Overpayment and Recovery) Regulations 1987 (S.I. 1987 No 491)*, reg. 19 *(April 6, 1987)*

4.387

Regulation 8 revoked by *The Social Security (Claims and Payments) Regulations 1987 (S.I. 1987 No 1968)*, reg. 48 *(April 11, 1988)*

4.388

PART II

PROVISIONS RELATING TO BENEFIT OTHER THAN INDUSTRIAL INJURIES BENEFIT

Payment of benefit and suspension of payments pending a decision on appeals or references, arrears and repayments

9. (1)–(4) [¹ . . .]
(5) [² . . .]
[³ (5A) Where a person—

(a) has received a contribution-based jobseeker's allowance in respect of one or more days in one or more periods of entitlement to a jobseeker's allowance; and
(b) is subsequently awarded a contribution-based jobseeker's allowance in respect of one or more days which fell before the days mentioned in sub-paragraph (a) ("the earlier period"); and
(c) in consequence of the award mentioned in sub-paragraph (b) the number of days on which a person was entitled to a contribution-based jobseeker's allowance exceeds the number of days specified for the purposes of section 5(1) of the Jobseekers Act 1995 (duration of a contribution-based jobseeker's allowance).

then any benefit which would, but for this provision, have become overpaid if the amount due under the subsequent award was paid shall be treated as having been paid in respect of the earlier period and the amount due to be paid under the subsequent award shall be reduced accordingly.

(5B) Where a person—
(a) has received a contribution-based jobseeker's allowance in respect of one or more days in one or more periods of entitlement to a jobseeker's allowance;
(b) is subsequently awarded unemployment benefit in respect of one or more days that fell before 7th October 1996 or in the benefit week that includes 7th October 1996 ("the earlier period"); and
(c) in consequence of the award mentioned in sub-paragraph (b) the number of days on which a person was entitled to a contribution-

4.389

The Social Security (General Benefit) Regulations 1982

based jobseeker's allowance exceeds the number of days specified for the purposes of section 5(1) of the Jobseekers Act 1995 (duration of a contribution-based jobseeker's allowance) or regulation 7(3) (claims for entitlement to a jobseeker's allowance) of the Jobseeker's Allowance (Transitional Provisions) Regulations 1995,
then any benefit which would, but for this provision, have become overpaid if the amount due under the subsequent award was paid shall be treated as having been paid in respect of the earlier period and the amount due under the subsequent award shall be reduced accordingly.

(5c) Where on appeal or review a decision is reversed or varied or revised and by reason thereof any sum on account of a contribution-based jobseeker's allowance is shown to have been paid to any person in respect of days for which he was not entitled to it, then, in determining for the purposes of section 5(1) of the Jobseekers Act 1995 whether that person has exhausted his right to that benefit and what is the last day for which he was entitled to it—

(a) any period for which such sum has been paid in pursuance of the original decision shall be treated as if it was a period for which that person was entitled to that benefit notwithstanding that that period is not a period of entitlement to a contribution-based jobseeker's allowance;

(b) where any sum has been so paid to such a person and that sum or any part thereof is recovered, then there shall be excluded for the purposes of the said determination under section 5(1) of the Jobseekers Act 1995 a number of days (to the nearest whole number) equal to the number to be obtained by dividing the amount recovered by one seventh (rounded to the nearest penny) of the weekly rate at which benefit was paid.

(5D) Paragraph (5C) shall not apply to a period for which there would have been entitlement to a contribution-based jobseeker's allowance but for a payment by the Secretary of State in accordance with section 182 of the Employment Rights Act 1996(b) (employee's rights or insolvency of employer), in respect of a sum owed by that person's former employer, where the Secretary of State, in calculating the payment, has made a deduction from that sum on account of any contribution-based jobseeker's allowance received.]

(6)–(6k) [4...]

(7)–(9) [5...]

AMENDMENTS

1. The Social Security (Claims and Payments) Regulations 1987 (S.I. 1987 No 1968), reg. 48 (April 11, 1988)
2. The Social Security (Miscellaneous Amendments) Regulations 1997 (S.I. 1997 No 454), reg. 6 (April 7, 1997)
3. The Social Security and Child Support (Jobseeker's Allowance)

(S.I. 1982 No. 1408, Reg. 9) (as amended)

(Miscellaneous Amendments) Regulations 1996 (S.I. 1996 No 2538), reg. 5 (October 28, 1996)

4. The Social Security (Miscellaneous Amendments) Regulations 1997 (S.I. 1997 No 454), reg. 6 (April 7, 1997)

5. The Social Security (Claims and Payments) Regulations 1987 (S.I. 1987 No 1968), reg. 48 (April 11, 1988)

Disqualifications to be disregarded for certain purposes

10.—(1) Subject to paragraph (2), where a person of any class mentioned in column (1) of Schedule 1 to these regulations would be entitled to the benefit set opposite that class in column (2) of that Schedule but for the operation of any provision of the Act disqualifying him for the receipt of that benefit, that person shall be treated as if entitled to that benefit for the purpose of the provisions of the Act set opposite thereto in column (3) of the said Schedule and of any regulations made thereunder.

(2) For the purposes of determining whether the condition contained in section 79(1) of the Act (which makes a claim a condition of any person's right to any benefit) is satisfied, a person who would be entitled to any benefit but for the operation of any provision of the Act disqualifying him for the receipt of it, and who ceases to be so disqualified within a period of 3 months from the commencement of the disqualification, shall be treated as if entitled to it.

4.390

PART III

PROVISIONS RELATING TO INDUSTRIAL INJURIES BENEFIT ONLY

Principles of Assessment

Further definition of the principles of assessment of disablement and prescribed degrees of disablement

11.—(1) Schedule 8 to the Act (general principles relating to the assessment of the extent of disablement) shall have effect subject to the provisions of this regulation.

(2) When the extent of disablement is being assessed for the purposes of section 57, any disabilities which, though resulting from the relevant loss of faculty, also result, or without the relevant accident might have been expected to result, from a cause other than the relevant accident (hereafter in this regulation referred to as "the other effective cause") shall only be taken into account subject to and in accordance with the following provisions of this regulation.

(3) [¹ Subject to paragraphs(5A) and (5B)] an assessment of the extent of disablement made by reference to any disability to which paragraph (2) applies, in a case where the other effective cause is a congenital defect or is an injury or disease received or contracted before the relevant accident, shall take account of all such disablement except to the extent to which the claimant would have been subject thereto during

4.391

the period taken into account by the assessment if the relevant accident had not occurred.

(4) [Subject to paragraphs (5A) and (5B)] any assessment of the extent of disablement made by reference to any disability to which paragraph (2) applies, in a case where the other effective cause is an injury or disease received or contracted after and not directly attributable to the relevant accident, shall take account of all such disablement to the extent to which the claimant would have been subject thereto during the period taken into account by the assessment if that other effective cause had not arisen and where, in any such case, the extent of a disablement would be assessed at not less than 11 per cent if that other effective cause had not arisen, the assessment shall also take account of any disablement to which the claimant may be subject as a result of that other effective cause except to the extent to which he would have been subject thereto if the relevant accident had not occurred.

(5) [Subject to paragraphs (5A) and (5B)] any disablement to the extent to which the claimant is subject thereto as a result both of an accident and a disease or two or more accidents or diseases (as the case may be), being accidents arising out and in the course of, or diseases due to the nature of, employed earners' employment, shall only be taken into account in assessing the extent of disablement resulting from one such accident or disease being the one which occurred or developed last in point of time.

[^{1} (5A) Where—
(a) a person has an award of industrial injuries disablement benefit in respect of the disease specified in paragraph D1 of Part I of Schedule 1 to the Social Security (Industrial Injuries) (Prescribed Diseases) Regulations 1985 (in this paragraph and paragraph (5B) referred to as "disease D1"); and
(b) by virtue of either paragraph (3 or (4) that award takes account of disablement resulting from the effects of chronic bronchitis or emphysema, not being chronic bronchitis or emphysema prescribed in paragraph D12 or Part I of Schedule 1 to the Social Security (Industrial Injuries) (Prescribed Diseases) Regulations 1985 (in this paragraph and paragraph (5B) referred to as "disease D12"); and
(c) after the date on which the award referred to in sub-paragraph (a) of this paragraph was made the person becomes entitled to industrial injuries disablement benefit in respect of disease D12,

then, during any period when such disablement benefit is payable in respect of disease D12, paragraphs (3), (4) and (5) shall not apply to the assessment in respect of disease D1 for the purpose of assessing the extent of disablement resulting from disease D12.

(5B) where:
(a) a person has an award of industrial injuries disablement benefit in respect of the disease D12; and
(b) by virtue of either paragraph (3) or (4) that award takes account of disablement resulting from the effects of pneumoconiosis, not being disease D1; and
(c) after the date on which the award referred to in sub-paragraph

(S.I. 1982 No. 1408, Reg. 11) (as amended)

(a) of this paragraph was made the person becomes entitled to industrial injuries disablement benefit in respect of disease D1, then, during any period when such disablement benefit is payable in respect of disease D1, paragraphs (3),(4) and (5) shall not apply to the assessment in respect of disease D12 for the purpose of assessing the extent of disablement resulting from disease D1.]

(6) Where the sole injury which a claimant suffers as a result of the relevant accident is one specified in column 1 of Schedule 2 to these regulations, whether or not such injury incorporates one or more other injuries so specified, the loss of faculty suffered by the claimant as a result of that injury shall be treated for the purposes of section 57 of, and Schedule 8 to, the Act as resulting in the degree of disablement set against such injury in column 2 of the said Schedule 2 subject to such increase or reduction of that degree of disablement as may be reasonable in the circumstances of the case where having regard to the provisions of the said Schedule 8 to the Act and to the foregoing paragraphs of this regulation, that degree of disablement does not provide a reasonable assessment of the extent of disablement resulting from the relevant loss of faculty.

(7) For the purposes of paragraph (6) where the relevant injury is one so specified in the said column 1 against which there is set in the said column 2 the degree of disablement of 100 per cent and the claimant suffers some disablement to which he would have been subject whether or not the relevant accident had occurred, no reduction of that degree of disablement shall be required if the [^{2} the Secretary of State or, as the case may be, an appeal tribunal] is satisfied that, in the circumstances of the case, 100 per cent is a reasonable assessment of the extent of disablement from the relevant loss of faculty.

(8) For the purposes of assessing, in accordance with the provisions of Schedule 8 to the Act, the extent of disablement resulting from the relevant injury in any case which does not fall to be determined under paragraph (6) or (7), [the Secretary of State or, as the case may be, an appeal tribunal] may have such regard as may be appropriate to the prescribed degrees of disablement set against the injuries specified in the said Schedule 2.

AMENDMENTS

1. The Social Security (Industrial Injuries) (Prescribed Diseases) Amendment (No. 2) Regulations 1993 (S.I. 1993 No 1985), reg. 7 (September 13, 1993)

2. The Social Security Act 1998 (Commencement No. 8, and Savings and Consequential and Transitional Provisions) Order 1999 (S.I. 1999 No 1958), Sched. 5 (July 4, 1999)

[¹ . . .] Disablement benefit

4.392 Regulations 12 and 13 revoked by S.I. 1983 No 186, reg. 13 (April 6, 1983)

Amount of disablement gratuities

4.393 **14.**—(1) Where the extent of a claimant's disablement is assessed at any of the degrees of disablement severally specified in column 1 of Schedule 3 to these regulations, the amount of any disablement gratuity payable shall
   (a) if the period taken into account by that assessment is limited by reference to the claimant's life or is not less than 7 years, be the amount calculated as the percentage of the maximum disablement gratuity (specified in paragraph 2 of Part V of Schedule 4 to the Act) which is shown in column 2 of Schedule 3 to these regulations as being appropriate to that degree of disablement;
   (b) in any other case, be the amount calculated as such a percentage of the maximum disablement gratuity as bears the same proportion to the percentage shown in column 2 of Schedule 3 to these regulations as being appropriate to that degree of disablement as the period taken into account by the assessment bears to a period of 7 years, a fraction of 5 pence being, for this purpose, treated as 5 pence.

[¹ (1A) Paragraph (1) applies in relation to cases where the claim for benefit was made before 1st October 1986.]

(2) For the purposes of this regulation, whenever such maximum disablement gratuity is altered by virtue of the passing of an Act or the making of an up-rating order, corresponding variations in the scale of gratuities payable under this regulation shall be payable only where the period taken into account by the assessment of the extent of disablement in respect of which the gratuity is awarded begins on or after the date of coming into operation of the provision altering the amount of the maximum disablement gratuity.

AMENDMENT

1. The Social Security (Industrial Injuries and Diseases) Miscellaneous Provisions Regulations 1986 (S.I. 1986 No 1561), reg.7 (October 1, 1986)

Weekly value of gratuity for purposes of reduction of increase of disablement benefit during hospital treatment

4.394 **15.** For the purpose of reducing the weekly rate of disablement pension payable by virtue of section 62 to a person awarded a disablement gratuity wholly or partly in respect of the same period, the weekly value of the gratuity shall be the weekly rate of disablement pension which would be payable to that person in lieu thereof in accordance with regulation 18(2) if that regulation applied to his case.

(S.I. 1982 No. 1408, Reg. 15) (as amended)

Earnings level for the purpose of unemployability supplement under section 58 of the Act

16. [¹ For the purpose of section 58(3) (earnings level that does not disqualify for unemployability supplement) the prescribed amount of earnings in a year shall be 3,042.]

AMENDMENT

1. The Social Security Benefits Up-rating Regulations 2000 (S.I. 2000 No 526), reg.4 (April 10, 2000)

Increase of [¹ . . .] Disablement Benefit

Circumstances in which, for the purposes of section 59A, a beneficiary may be treated as being incapable of following an occupation or employment notwithstanding that he has worked thereat

17.—(1) For the purposes of [² section 59A (reduced earnings allowance)], when it is being determined whether a beneficiary has at all times since the end of [² the period of 90 days referred to in section 57(4) been incapable of following his regular occupation or employment of an equivalent standard which is suitable in his case, and in determining that question only, the fact that since the end of that period of 90 days] such beneficiary had worked at that occupation or any such employment (as the case may be)—
  (a) for the purpose of rehabilitation or training or of ascertaining whether he had recovered from the effects of the relevant injury; or
  (b) before obtaining surgical treatment for the effects of the said injury; shall be disregarded in respect of the periods specified in the next following paragraph.

(2) The periods during which the beneficiary worked at his regular occupation or at employment of equivalent standard, which shall be disregarded in accordance with the provision of the preceding paragraph, shall be—
  (a) in any case to which sub-paragraph (a) of that paragraph applies—
    (i) any period during which he worked thereat for any of the said purposes with the approval of the Secretary of State or on the advice of a medical practitioner, and
    (ii) any other period or periods during which he worked thereat for any of the said purposes and which did not exceed six months in the aggregate, and
  (b) in any case to which sub-paragraph (b) of that paragraph applies—
    (i) any period during which he worked thereat and throughout which it is shown that having obtained the advice of a medical practitioner to submit himself to such surgical treatment

he was waiting to undergo the said treatment in accordance therewith, and

(ii) any other period during which he worked thereat and throughout which is shown that he was in process of obtaining such advice.

AMENDMENTS

1. The Social Security (Abolition of Injury Benefits) (Consequential) Regulations 1983 (S.I. 1983 No 186), reg. 13 (April 6, 1983)
2. The Social Security (Industrial Injuries and Diseases) Miscellaneous Provisions Regulations 1986 (S.I. 1986 No 1561), reg. 7 (October 1, 1986)

GENERAL NOTE

4.397 The regulation permits both the fact of work and the period for which it has been undertaken to be disregarded where the claimant seeks to establish entitlement to reduced earnings allowance under the "continuous condition", so long as the work is undertaken for either of the purposes specified in the regulation. (See generally, *R(I)1/51, R(I)35/55, R(I)35/58)*.

If the claimant relies upon the purpose in para. (1)(a), the extent of the qualifying period depends upon whether the return to work is upon the advice of a medical practitioner or with the approval of the Secretary of State—without such authorisation the period (or aggregate periods) may not exceed six months. "Rehabilitation", means getting better *(R(I)69/53)*, but "ascertaining the results of the relevant injury" has been more widely interpreted to mean discovering whether the claimant can still do the job *(R(I)1/69)*. The "advice" of the doctor referred to in the paragraph does not have to be specifically directed to value of a resumption of work, but there must be something which the claimant can point to in the general advice he receives which is relevant to one of the specified purposes—the "general approval and consent of his doctor" *(R(I)93/53)*, or "in allowing the claimant to continue at work while in receipt of treatment the doctor must be taken to have advised him to remain at work" *(R(I)69/53)*.

If the claimant relies upon the purpose in para. (1)(b), the periods he may use depend upon whether he has actually received advice on surgical treatment, or is in the process of obtaining it. Note that, in this paragraph, the advice must be much more clear and the doctor must have given a specific opinion that surgical treatment should be carried out—further, the claimant must intend to give up work and undergo the treatment as soon as it can be arranged *(R(I)81/53)*. The claimant can only avail himself of this paragraph if he has been seeking advice "throughout" the period he has been working, or he has been waiting for the treatment "throughout" the period, and he is not entitled to delay unduly in seeking treatment. He must use "reasonable zeal and expedition" to secure the treatment *(R(I)35/57)*.

Payments in respect of special hardship where beneficiary is entitled to a gratuity

4.398 **18.**—(1) Where in any case a beneficiary is entitled to or has received a disablement gratuity, such beneficiary shall as respects that gratuity have the like rights to payments in respect of special hardship as he would have had by way of increase of disablement pension under section 60 if the disablement gratuity had been a disablement pension payable during the period taken into account by the assessment.

(S.I. 1982 No. 1408, Reg. 18) (as amended)

(2) A beneficiary who is entitled as respects a disablement gratuity to payments in respect of special hardship by virtue of the preceding paragraph shall, if he makes an application in that behalf at any time before that gratuity or any part thereof has been paid to him, be entitled, subject to the proviso to section 57(6), to a disablement pension in lieu of such gratuity for any part of the period taken into account by the assessment during which he may be entitled to an increase of such pension in respect of special hardship under section 60, and the weekly rate of such pension shall be determined in accordance with Schedule 4 of these regulations.

(3) For the purposes of paragraph (2) and notwithstanding the provisions of regulation 14(2) whenever the weekly rate of such pension is altered consequent upon the passing of an Act or the making of an uprating order, such variation shall have effect as from the date on which the provision varying the amount of the disablement pension specified in paragraph 3 of Part V of Schedule 4 to the Act comes into force, whether the period taken into account by the assessment began before or after that date.

(4) Where a pension has been payable under paragraph (2) in lieu of a gratuity for any period and the beneficiary ceases to be entitled to an increase of such pension under the provisions of section 60, the amount of that gratuity shall be treated as reduced by the amounts which have been paid to the beneficiary by way of such pension, other than an increase thereof under the said section 60 and, subject to the provisions of these regulations, the balance (if any) shall then be payable accordingly.

General Note

This regulation will only continue in force to cover those claimants who were in receipt of special hardship allowance under this regulation as at October 1, 1986. A claimant in that group became entitled to reduced earnings allowance on that day and will remain so entitled under this regulation until either the period of assessment has expired or the assessment is reviewed, or until reduced earnings allowance has ceased to be payable (whichever is the earlier). See the Social Security (Industrial Injuries and Diseases) Miscellaneous Provisions Regulations 1986 (S.I. 1986 No. 1561), reg. 7(5), (6).

4.399

Increase of disablement pension for constant attendance

19. The amount by which the weekly rate of disablement pension may be increased under [section 104 of the Social Security Contributions and Benefits Act 1992] where constant attendance is required by a beneficiary as a result of the relevant loss of faculty shall—
   (a) where the beneficiary (not being a case to which paragraph (b) of this regulation relates) is to a substantial extent dependent on such attendance for the necessities of life and is likely to remain so dependent for a prolonged period, be the amount specified in paragraph [2](a) of Part V of Schedule 4 to the Act (unless the attendance so required is part-time only, in which case the amount shall be such sum as may be reasonable in the

4.400

circumstances) or, where the extent of such attendance is greater by reason of the beneficiary's exceptionally severe disablement, a sum not exceeding one and a half times the amount specified in paragraph [2](a) of Part V of the said Schedule, a fraction of five pence being for this purpose treated as five pence;

(b) where the beneficiary is so exceptionally severely disabled as to be entirely, or almost entirely, dependent on such attendance for the necessities of life, and is likely to remain so dependent for a prolonged period and the attendance so required is whole-time, be the amount specified in paragraph [2](b) of Part V of Schedule 4 to the Act.

Determination of degree of disablement for constant attendance allowance

20.—(1) For the purpose of determining whether a person is entitled to an increase by way of constant attendance allowance under section 61 or to a corresponding increase by virtue of section 159(3)(b) of the Act or section 7(3)(b) of the Industrial Injuries and Diseases (Old Cases) Act 1975 of any other benefit, the Secretary of State shall, in a case where that person is subject to disabilities in respect of which payments of two or more of the descriptions set out in the next following paragraph of this regulation fall to be made, determine the extent of that person's disablement by taking into account all such disabilities to which that person is subject.

(2) The payments which may be taken into account are those of the following descriptions:

(a) payments by way of disablement pensions under the Act;

(b) weekly payments to which that person is or has been at any time after 4 July 1948 entitled in respect of injury or disease being payments by way of compensation under the Workmen's Compensation Acts or under any contracting-out scheme duly certified thereunder;

(c) payments to which that person is or has been at any time after 4 July 1948 entitled as a former constable or fireman on account of an injury pension under or by virtue of any enactment in respect of an injury received or disease contracted by that person before 5 July 1948 or in respect of his retirement in consequence of such an injury or disease;

(d) payments by way of benefit under the Industrial Injuries and Diseases (Old Cases) Act 1975; and

(e) payments of personal benefit by way of disablement pension or gratuity under any Personal Injuries Scheme or Service Pensions Instrument or 1914-18 War Injuries Scheme.

(3) In sub-paragraph (2)(e) the expressions "personal benefit", "disablement pension", "Personal Injuries Scheme" and "Service Pensions Instrument" have the meanings which are assigned to them by the Social Security (Overlapping Benefits) Regulations 1979 for the purposes of those regulations.

(S.I. 1982 No. 1408, Reg. 20) (as amended)

Condition for receipt of increase of disablement pension for constant attendance under section 61 while receiving medical treatment as an in-patient

21.—(1) For the purposes of section 61 (increase of disablement pension in respect of the need of constant attendance), subject to paragraph (2) it shall be a condition for the receipt of an increase of disablement pension under the said section 61 for any period in respect of any person that during that period he is not receiving, or has not received, free in-patient treatment, and for this purpose a person shall be regarded as receiving or having received free in-patient treatment if he would be so regarded for the purposes of the Social Security (Hospital In-Patients) Regulations 1975

(2) Where a person was entitled to an increase of disablement pension under the said section 61 in respect of the period immediately before he commenced to undergo any treatment mentioned in paragraph (1), that paragraph shall not apply in respect of the first 4 weeks of any continuous period during which he is undergoing such treatment.

(3) For the purposes of paragraph (2), 2 or more distinct periods separated by an interval not exceeding 28 days, or by 2 or more such intervals, shall be treated as a continuous period equal in duration to the total of such distinct periods and ending on the last day of the later or last such period.

Treatment of distinct periods of hospital in-patient treatment as continuous for the purposes of section 62 of the Act

22. For the purposes of section 62 (increase of disablement benefit during hospital treatment) a person who receives medical treatment as an in-patient for 2 or more distinct periods separated by an interval of less than a week in each case shall be treated as receiving such treatment continuously from the beginning of the first period until the end of the last.

GENERAL NOTE

Section 62 of the Social Security Act 1975 has been replaced by para. 10 of Schedule 7 to the Social Security Contributions and Benefits Act 1992.

Regulations 23–37 omitted.

Adjustment of Benefit for Successive Accidents

Adjustment of benefit for successive accidents where a disablement gratuity is payable

38.—(1) In a case where—
(a) a person who is entitled, as a result of an accident, to a disablement pension (hereafter in this paragraph referred to as an "existing pension") which is payable in respect of an assessment for a period which is limited by reference to that person's life,

becomes as a result of any other accident, entitled to an award as a result of an assessment of disablement in respect of which a disablement gratuity would, but for this regulation, be payable; and

(b) the aggregate amount of the assessment in respect of the existing pension and of the assessment in respect of which such disablement gratuity would be payable would, if it were the amount of the assessment of the extent of the disablement resulting from any one accident suffered by that person, have entitled him to receive a disablement pension at a higher rate than the rate of such existing pension;

then, if at any time before his claim for disablement benefit is determined, he so elects, that person shall be entitled to a disablement pension in lieu of the said disablement gratuity at a rate equal to the difference between the said higher rate and the rate of the existing pension.

(2) In a case in which a person who is entitled as a result of any accident to a disablement pension would but for the provisions of this paragraph become entitled in respect of any other accident to a disablement gratuity (not being a case in which he is entitled to a disablement pension in lieu of such gratuity)—

(a) if the assessment in respect of which such pension is payable to him amounts to not less than 100 per cent, such person shall not be entitled to receive any disablement gratuity in respect of such other accident;

(b) in any other case, such person shall not be entitled to receive, by way of disablement gratuity in respect of such other accident, an amount exceeding that which would be payable in respect of an assessment equal to the difference between 100 per cent. and the percentage of the assessment in respect of which such pension is payable to him.

(3) For the respective purposes of the two preceding paragraphs of this regulation—

(a) references to an existing pension within the meaning of paragraph (1) and to any disablement pension in paragraph (2) respectively shall include references to all such pensions which may be payable to the person concerned, and references to the amount of the assessment in respect of which, and the rate at which, any such pension is payable shall include references to the aggregate amount of the assessments in respect of which or the aggregate of the rates at which all such pensions are payable as aforesaid;

(b) the extent by which an assessment is increased by virtue of the provisions of section 62 of the Act (increase of disablement benefit during hospital treatment) shall be disregarded;

(c) for the purposes of paragraph (1)(a) a person shall be deemed to be entitled to a disablement pension and to an award as described in the said sub-paragraph from the respective dates of commencement of the periods taken into account by the assessments relating to such pension and to such award.

(S.I. 1982 No. 1408, Reg. 20) (as amended)

Adjustment of increase of benefit of successive accidents

39.—(1) Where a person who is entitled to a disablement pension in respect of any accident suffered by him—
  (a) has received, or is entitled to, a disablement gratuity in respect of any other accident; and
  (b) as a result of the loss of faculty in respect of which he has received, or is entitled to that gratuity, is incapable of work and is likely to remain permanently so incapable;
the provisions of section 58 (increase of disablement pension by way of unemployability supplement) shall apply as if that loss of faculty resulted from the accident in respect of which such disablement pension is payable.

(2) Where a person—
  (a) would be entitled to a disablement pension in respect of any accident but for the provisions of section 91(1)(a) (limitations on the aggregate weekly rates of benefit payable for the same period in respect of successive accidents); and
  (b) by reason only of those provisions, is unable to satisfy the conditions for the receipt of an increase of that pension by way of unemployability supplement under section 58;
the provisions of the said section 58 shall apply as if such disablement pension were payable to that beneficiary.

(3) At any time at which the sum total of the several assessments in respect of two or more accidents suffered by any person amounts to not less than 100 per cent. during the continuance of the periods respectively taken into account thereby, the weekly rate of any disablement pension which is payable to him may be increased in accordance with the provisions of section 61 if he requires constant attendance as a result of the loss of faculty resulting from any one or more of such accidents, whether or not that pension is payable in respect of an assessment of 100 per cent or in respect of that loss of faculty.

(4) A beneficiary who has suffered two or more accidents shall not be entitled at any time to more than one of each of the following increases of benefit, that is to say—
  (a) by way of unemployability supplement under section 58;
  (b) in respect of the need of constant attendance under section 61;
  (c) in respect of a child, under section 64;
  (d) in respect of an adult dependant, under section 66.

Disqualification for Receipt of Benefit and Suspension of Benefit Pending Appeals etc.

Disqualification for receipt of benefit, suspension of proceedings on claims and suspension of payment of benefit

40.—(1)[^{1}. . .]
(2) If, without good cause—
  (a) a claimant fails to furnish to the prescribed person any informa-

tion required for the determination of the claim or of any question arising in connection therewith; or

(b) a beneficiary fails to give notice to the prescribed person of any change of circumstances affecting the continuance of the right to benefit or to the receipt thereof, or to furnish as aforesaid any information required for the determination of any question arising in connection with the award; or

(c) a claimant for, or a beneficiary in receipt of, disablement benefit fails to comply with any requirement of regulation 26 of the Social Security (Claims and Payments) Regulations 1979 (obligations of claimants for, and beneficiaries in receipt of [1. . .] disablement benefit);

he shall, subject to the following provisions of this regulation, if the [2 the Secretary of State, an appeal tribunal] or the Commissioner so decide, be disqualified for receiving any benefit claimed in respect of the period of such failure.

(3) If a claimant or beneficiary wilfully obstructs, or is guilty of other misconduct in connection with any examination or treatment to which he is required under regulation 26 of the Social Security (Claims and Payments) Regulation 1979 to submit himself, or any proceedings under the Act for the determination of his right to benefit or to the receipt thereof, he shall, subject to the provisions of this regulation, be disqualified for receiving any benefit claimed for such period as the insurance officer, a local tribunal or the Commissioner shall determine.

(4) In any case to which any of the foregoing paragraphs of this regulation relates, proceedings on the claim or payment of benefit, as the case may be, may be suspended for such period as the insurance officer, a local tribunal or the Commissioner may determine.

(5) Nothing in this Regulation providing for the disqualification for the receipt of benefit for any of the following matters, that is to say—

(a) [1. . .]
(b) for failure to comply with the requirements of regulation 26 of the Social Security (Claims and Payments) Regulation 1979;
(c) for obstruction of, or misconduct in connection with, medical examination or treatment;

shall authorise the disentitlement of a claimant or beneficiary to benefit for a period exceeding six weeks on any disqualification.

(6) No person shall be disqualified for receiving any benefit for refusal to undergo a surgical operation not being one of minor character.

(7) A person who would be entitled to any benefit but for the operation of any of the foregoing provisions of this regulation shall be treated as if he were entitled thereto for the purpose of any rights or obligations under the Act (whether of himself or any other person) which depend on his being so entitled other than the right to payment of that benefit.

AMENDMENTS

1. The Social Security (Abolition of Injury Benefit) (Consequential) Regulations 1983 (S.I. 1983, No 186), reg. 13 (April 6, 1983)
2. The Social Security Act 1998 (Commencement No. 8, and Savings and

(S.I. 1982 No. 1408, Reg. 40) (as amended)

Consequential and Transitional Provisions) Order 1999 (S.I. 1999 No 1958), Sched. 5 (July 4, 1999)

Regulation 41 revoked by The Social Security (Claims and Payments) Regulations 1987 (S.I. 1987 No 1968), reg. 48 (April 11, 1988)   4.409

Regulations 42–45 omitted.   4.410

Miscellaneous Provisions

Conditions relating to payment of additional benefit under awards made before the day appointed for an increase of benefit under any Act amending the Act or under any up-rating order

46. Where an award of any benefit under Chapter IV or V Part II of the Act has been made before the day appointed for the payment of benefit of the description to which the award relates at a higher rate by virtue of an Act or up-rating order which increases benefit payable under the Act, paragraph 2(1) of Schedule 14 to the Act (which relates to the effect of any such award) shall, if the period to which the award relates has not ended before that day, have effect subject to the condition that if the award has not been made in accordance with the provisions of sub-paragraph (2) of that paragraph which authorise the making of such an award providing for the payment of the benefit at the higher rate as from that day and a question as to—   4.411

(a) the weekly rate at which the benefit is payable by virtue of the Act or up-rating order which so increases benefit or of these regulations, or

(b) whether the conditions for the receipt of the benefit at the higher rate are satisfied;

the benefit shall be or continue to be payable at the weekly rate specified in the award until the said question shall have been determined in accordance with the provisions of the Act.

Regulation 47 omitted.   4.412

The Social Security (General Benefit) Regulations 1982

SCHEDULE 1 — Regulation 10

PROVISIONS FOR THE PURPOSE OF WHICH DISQUALIFICATIONS UNDER THE ACT ARE TO BE DISREGARDED

Class of persons (1)	Benefit for which person is disqualified (2)	Section of the Act for the purpose of which disqualification is to be disregarded (3)	Subject matter (4)
A widow	Widow's allowance	25(3)	Period for which a widowed mother's allowance is payable (being a period for which she is not entitled to widow's allowance).
	Widow's allowance or widowed mother's allowance	26(3)	Period for which a widow's pension is payable (being a period for which she is not entitled to a widow's allowance or a widowed mother's allowance).
	Widowed mother's allowance	26(1)(b)	Widow's pension for certain widows ceasing to be entitled to widowed mother's allowance.
The husband of a widow	Category A retirement pension	24(1)(a)	Widow's allowance for widow of husband who at the date of his death was not entitled to a Category A retirement pension

In this Schedule "widowed mother's allowance" and "widow's pension" include benefit under section 39(4) corresponding to a widowed mother's allowance and a widow's pension respectively

SCHEDULE 2 — Regulation 11

PRESCRIBED DEGREES OF DISABLEMENT

Description of injury	Degree of disablement per cent
1. Loss of both hands or amputation at higher sites	100
2. Loss of a hand and a foot	100
3. Double amputation through leg or thigh, or amputation through leg or thigh on one side and loss of other foot	100
4. Loss of sight to such an extent as to render the claimant unable to perform any work for which eyesight is essential	100
5. Very severe facial disfiguration	100
6. Absolute deafness	100
7. Forequarter or hindquarter amputation	100
Amputation cases-upper limbs (either arm)	
8. Amputation through shoulder joint	90
9. Amputation below shoulder with stump less than 20.5 centimetres from tip of acromion	80

(S.I. 1982 No. 1408, Sched. 2) (as amended)

Description of injury	Degree of disablement per cent	
10. Amputation from 20.5 centimetres from tip of acromion to less than 11.5 centimetres below tip of olecranon	70	
11. Loss of a hand or of the thumb and four fingers of one hand or amputation from 11.5 centimetres below tip of olecranon	60	
12. Loss of thumb	30	
13. Loss of thumb and its metacarpal bone	40	
14. Loss of four fingers of one hand	50	
15. Loss of three fingers of one hand	30	
16. Loss of two fingers of one hand	20	
17. Loss of terminal phalanx of thumb	20	
Amputation cases-lower limbs		
18. Amputation of both feet resulting in end-bearing stumps	90	**4.417**
19. Amputation through both feet proximal to the metatarso-phalangeal joint	80	
20. Loss of all toes of both feet through the metatarso-phalangeal joint	40	
21. Loss of all toes of both feet proximal to the proximal inter-phalangeal joint	30	
22. Loss of all toes of both feet distal to the proximal inter-phalangeal joint	20	
23. Amputation at hip	90	
24. Amputation below hip with stump not exceeding 13 centimetres in length measured from tip of great trochanter	80	
25. Amputation below hip and above knee with stump exceeding 13 centimetres in length measured from tip of great trochanter, or at knee not resulting in end-bearing stump	70	
26. Amputation at knee resulting in end-bearing stump or below knee with stump not exceeding 9 centimetres	60	
27. Amputation below knee with stump exceeding 9 centimetres but not exceeding 13 centimetres	50	
28. Amputation below knee with stump exceeding 13 centimetres	40	
29. Amputation of one foot resulting in end-bearing stump	30	
30. Amputation through one foot proximal to the metatarso-phalangeal joint	30	
31. Loss of all toes of one foot through the metatarso-phalangeal joint	20	
Other injuries		
32. Loss of one eye, without complications, the other being normal	40	**4.418**
33. Loss of vision of one eye, without complications or disfigurement of the eyeball, the other being normal	30	
Loss of:		
A Fingers of right or left hand		
Index finger:		
34. Whole	14	**4.419**
35. Two phalanges	11	
36. One phalanx	9	
37. Guillotine amputation of tip without loss of bone	5	
Middle finger:		
38. Whole	12	**4.420**
39. Two phalanges	9	
40. One phalanx	7	
41. Guillotine amputation of tip without loss of bone	4	
Ring or little finger:		
42. Whole	7	

577

The Social Security (General Benefit) Regulations 1982

Description of injury	Degree of disablement per cent
43. Two phalanges	6
44. One phalanx	5
45. Guillotine amputation of tip without loss of bone	2
B Toes of right or left foot	
Great toe:	
46. Through metatarso-phalangeal joint	14
47. Part, with some loss of bone	3
Any other toe:	
48. Through metatarso-phalangeal joint	3
49. Part, with some loss of bone	1
Two toes of one foot, excluding great toe:	
50. Through metatarso-phalangeal joint	5
51. Part, with some loss of bone	2
Three toes of one foot, excluding great toe:	
52. Through metatarso-phalangeal joint	6
53. Part, with some loss of bone	3
Four toes of one foot, excluding great toe:	
54. Through metatarso-phalangeal joint	9
55. Part, with some loss of bone	3

SCHEDULE 3   **Regulation 14**

SCALE OF DISABLEMENT GRATUITIES

Degree of disablement (1)	Appropriate proportion of maximum disablement gratuity (as specified in paragraph 2 of Part V of Schedule 4 to the Act) (2)
	per cent
1 per cent	10
2 per cent	15
3 per cent	20
4 per cent	25
5 per cent	30
6 per cent	35
7 per cent	40
8 per cent	45
9 per cent	50
10 per cent	55
11 per cent	60
12 per cent	65
13 per cent	70
14 per cent	75
15 per cent	80
16 per cent	85
17 per cent	90
18 per cent	95
19 per cent	100

(S.I. 1982 No. 1408, Sched. 4) (as amended)

SCHEDULE 4   **Regulation 18**

[*Schedule 4 saved for certain purposes by regulation 7(5) and (6) of The Social Security (Industrial Injuries and Diseases) Miscellaneous Provisions Regulations 1986, S.I. 1986/1561.*]   4.423

Rate of Disablement Payable in Lieu of Disablement Gratuity in Accordance with Regulation 18

Where the degree of disablement is as specified in column (1) of the following table, the weekly rate of the pension shall be determined in accordance with column (2) of that table:

Degree of disablement (1)	Rate of pension (2)
less than 20 per cent but not less than 16 per cent	the appropriate weekly amount of disablement pension payable in respect of a degree of disablement of 20 per cent as specified in paragraph 3 of Part V of Schedule 4 to the Act;
less than 16 per cent but not less than 11 per cent	75 per cent of the appropriate weekly amount of disablement pension payable in respect of a degree of disablement of 20 per cent as specified in the said paragraph 3:

Degree of disablement (1)	Rate of pension (2)
less than 11 per cent but not less than 6 per cent	50 per cent of the appropriate weekly amount of disablement pension payable in respect of a degree of disablement of 20 per cent as specified in the said paragraph 3:
less than 6 per cent	25 per cent of the appropriate weekly amount of disablement pension payable in respect of a degree of disablement of 20 per cent as specified in the said paragraph 3: a fraction of a penny, being for this purpose treated as a penny.

Schedules 5–9 omitted

Social Security (Medical Evidence) Regulations 1976

(S.I. 1976 No. 615) (*as amended*)

Arrangement of Regulations

1. Citation, commencement and interpretation.   4.424
2. Evidence of incapacity for work and confinement.
3. *Revoked.*
4. *Revoked.*
5. Self-certificate for first seven days of a spell of incapacity for work.

Schedules

Schedule 1
    Part I:—Rules

Part II:—Form of Doctor's Statement
Part III:—The Notes
Schedule 1A
  Part I: Rules
  Part II: Form of Special Statement
Schedule 1B
  Part I: Rules
  Part II: Form of Doctor's Statement
Schedule 2
  Part I Rules
  Part II Form of Certificate

Citation, commencement, and interpretation

1.—(1) These regulations may be cited as the Social Security (Medical Evidence) Regulations 1976, and shall come into operation on 4th October,

(2) In these regulations, unless the context otherwise requires—

"the Act" means the Social Security Act 1975;

[1"the Contributions and Benefits Act" means the Social Security Contributions and Benefits Act 1992;

"the all work test" means the test provided for in section 171C of the Contributions and Benefits Act;]

[2"registered midwife" means a midwife who is registered as a midwife with the United Kingdom Central Council for Nursing, Midwifery and Health Visiting under the Nurses, Midwives and Health Visitors Act 1979;

"doctor" means a registered medical practitioner;]

"signature" means, in relation to any statement or certificate given in accordance with these regulations, the name by which the person giving that statement or certificate, as the case may be, is usually known (any name other than the surname being either in full or otherwise indicated) written by that person in his own handwriting; and "signed" shall be construed accordingly.

(3) Any reference in these regulations to any provisions made by or contained in any enactment or instrument shall, except in so far as the context otherwise requires, be construed as a reference to that provision as amended or extended by any enactment or instrument and as including a reference to any provision which it re-enacts or replaces, or which may re-enact or replace it, with or without modification.

(4) The rules for the construction of Acts of Parliament contained in the Interpretation Act 1889 shall apply in relation to this instrument and in relation to the revocation effected by it as if this instrument, the regulations revoked by it and regulations revoked by the regulations so revoked were Acts of Parliament, and as if each revocation were a repeal.

AMENDMENTS

1. The Social Security (Medical Evidence) Amendment Regulations 1994 (S.I. 1994 No 2975), reg. 2 (April 13, 1995).

2. The Social Security (Medical Evidence) Amendment Regulations 1987 (S.I. 1987 No 409), ref. 2 (April 6, 1987).

(S.I. 1976 No. 615, Reg. 1) (as amended)

Evidence of incapacity for work and confinement

2.—(1) [¹Subject to regulation 5] [³where a person claims he is entitled to any benefit, allowance or advantage I (other than industrial injuries benefit or statutory sick pay), and his entitlement to that benefit, allowance or advantage depends on his being incapable of work, then in respect of each day until he has been assessed for the purposes of the [⁶personal capability assessment], he shall provide evidence of such incapacity—]

[³(a) by means of a certificate in the form of a statement in writing given by a doctor in accordance with the rules set out in Part I of Schedule 1 to these Regulations on the form set out in Part II of that Schedule; or

(b) where a doctor—
  (i) has not given a statement under sub-paragraph (a) of this paragraph since the patient was examined and wishes to give such a statement but more than one day has passed since the examination; or
  (ii) advises that the patient should refrain from work on the basis of a written report from another doctor,

by means of a special statement given in accordance with the rules set out in Part I of Schedule 1A to these Regulations on the form set out in Part II of that Schedule;] or

[²](c) [⁶where the question of whether a person is capable or incapable of work falls to be determined in accordance with the personal capability assessment] and the Secretary of State so requests, a statement in writing given by a doctor in accordance with the rules set out in Part I of Schedule 1B to these Regulations on the form set out in Part II of that Schedule; or

(d) where it would be unreasonable to require a person to provide a statement [⁴in accordance with sub-paragraphs (a) to (c),] such other evidence as may be sufficient to show that he should refrain [⁴(or should have refrained)] from work by reason of some specific disease or bodily or mental disablement.]

(2) Every person to whom paragraph (1) applies [²who has not been assessed for the purposes of the all work test] shall, before he returns to work, furnish evidence of the date on which he will become fit to resume work either in accordance with rule 10 of Part I of Schedule 1 to these regulations, or by such other means as may be sufficient in the circumstances of the case.

(3) Every woman who claims maternity benefit shall furnish evidence—

(a) where the claim is made in respect of expectation of confinement, that she is pregnant and as to the stage which she has reached in her pregnancy; or

(b) where the claim is made by virtue of the fact of confinement, that she has been confined;

and shall furnish such evidence [⁵by means of a maternity certificate] given by a doctor or by a registered midwife in accordance with the rules set out in Part I of Schedule 2 to these regulations in the appropriate

Social Security (Medical Evidence) Regulations 1976

form as set out in Part II of that Schedule or by such other means as may be sufficient in the circumstances of any particular case.

AMENDMENTS

1. The Social Security (Medical Evidence, Claims and Payments) Amendments Regulations 1982 (S.I. 1982 No 699), reg.2 (June 14, 19820
2. The Social Security (Medical Evidence) Amendment Regulations 1994 (S.I. 1994 No 2975), reg.2 (April 13, 1995)
3. The Social Security (Medical Evidence) Amendment Regulations 1992 (S.I. 1992 No 2471), reg.3 (March 9, 1992)
4. The Social Security (Incapacity for Work) Miscellaneous Amendments Regulations 1995 (S.I. 1995 No 987), reg.4 (April 13, 1995)
5. The Social Security (Medical Evidence) Amendment Regulations 1987 (S.I. 1987 No 409), reg.3 (April 6, 1987)
6. The Social Security (Incapacity) Miscellaneous Amendments Regulations 2000 (S.I. 2000 No 590), reg.6 (April 3, 2000)

4.427 GENERAL NOTE

In *CSIS/065/1991*, the Commissioner—ruled that the reference in the regulation to "such other means as may be sufficient in the particular circumstances of any particular case" meant that evidence of incapacity need not be in the form of a medical certificate. This means that medical certificates other than in the form set out in the Schedule may be acceptable as well as evidence from the claimant himself or herself (para. 14). Whether such evidence is sufficient is a matter for determination by the adjudication officer or tribunal and not the Secretary of State (para. 15).

In *CIB/17533/1996* (starred as *98/97*) the Commissioner addressed an issue which was being argued by a number of representatives, namely that there was no jurisdiction to make an all work test determination where the adjudication officer had requested the claimant to obtain the special Form Med. 4 and this form was not available to the adjudication officer when the decision was made. Form Med. 4 is the special form which specifically directs doctors to consider capacity for *all* work in certifying incapacity for work. The Commissioner concludes that it "the somewhat legalistic proposition that a decision by an adjudication officer made without a form MED4 is a nullity or is erroneous in law cannot in my view be sustained" (para. 8 of Common Appendix).

4.428 *Regulation 3 revoked by The Social Security (Claims and Payments) Regulations 1979 (S.I. 1979 No 628), reg. 32 (July 9, 1979).*

4.429 *Regulation 4 revoked by The Social Security (Medical Evidence, Claims and Payments) Amendments Regulations 1982 (S.I. 1982 No 699), reg. 2 (June 14, 1982).*

[1]Self-certificate for first 7 days of a spell of incapacity for work

4.430 **5.**—[2(1)[3The evidence of incapacity required for the purposes of determining entitlement to a benefit, allowance or advantage referred to in regulation 2(1)]—

(a) for a spell of incapacity which lasts less than 8 days, or

(b) in respect of any of the first 7 days of a longer spell of incapacity;

may consist of a self certificate instead of a certificate in the form of a

(S.I. 1976 No. 615, Reg. 5) (as amended)

statement in writing given by a doctor in accordance with regulation 2(1).]

(2) For the purpose of this regulation:

a "self-certificate" means a declaration made by the claimant in writing, in a form approved for the purpose by the Secretary of State, that he has been unfit for work from a date or for a period specified in the declaration and may include a statement that the claimant expects to continue to be unfit for work on days subsequent to the date on which it is made";

[³ "spell of incapacity" has the meaning given to it by section 171B(3) of the Contributions and Benefits Act.]]

AMENDMENTS

1. The Social Security (Medical Evidence, Claims and Payments) Amendments Regulations 1982 (S.I. 1982 No 699), reg. 2 (June 14, 1982)
2. The Social Security (Medical Evidence, Claims and Payments) Amendment Regulations 1989 (S.I. 1989 No 1686), reg. 2 (October 9, 1989)
3. The Social Security (Medical Evidence) Amendment Regulations 1994 (S.I. 1994 No 2975), reg. 2 (April 13, 1995)

SCHEDULE 1   **Regulation 2(1)**

PART I

RULES

1. In these rules, unless the context otherwise requires—   4.431

"claimant" means the person in respect of whom a statement is given in accordance with these rules;
"doctor" means a registered medical practitioner not being the claimant;
"doctor's statement" means a statement given in accordance with these rules;
"2 weeks" means any period of 14 consecutive days.

2. The doctor's statement shall be in the form set out in Part II of this Schedule.
3. Where the claimant is on the list of a doctor providing general medical services under the National Health Service Act 1946, or the National Health Service (Scotland) Act 1947, and is being attended by such a doctor, the doctor's statement shall be on a form provided by the Secretary of State for the purpose and shall be signed by that doctor.
4. In any other case, the doctor's statement shall be either on a form provided by the Secretary of State for the purpose or in a form substantially to the like effect, and shall be signed by the doctor attending the claimant.
5. Every doctor's statement shall be completed in ink or other indelible substance, and shall contain the following particulars—
    (a) the claimant's name;
    (b) the date of the examination on which the doctor's statement is based;
    (c) the diagnosis of the claimant's disorder in respect of which the doctor is advising the claimant to refrain from work or, as the case may be, which has caused the claimant's absence from work;
    (d) the date on which the doctor's statement is given;
    (e) the address of the doctor.

and shall bear, opposite the words "Doctor's signature," the signature of the doctor making the statement written after there have been entered the claimant's name and the doctor's diagnosis.

6. Subject to rules 7 and 8 below, the diagnosis of the claimant's disorder in respect of which the doctor is advising the claimant to refrain from work or, as the case may be, which has caused the claimant's absence from work shall be specified as precisely as the doctor's knowledge of the claimant's condition at the time of the examination permits.

Social Security (Medical Evidence) Regulations 1976

7. Where, in the doctor's opinion, a disclosure to the claimant of the precise disorder would be prejudicial to his well-being, the diagnosis may be specified less precisely.

8. In the case of an initial examination by a doctor in respect of a disorder stated by the claimant to have caused incapacity for work, where—
  (a) there are no clinical signs of that disorder, and
  (b) in the doctor's opinion, the claimant need not refrain from work,
instead of specifying a diagnosis "unspecified" may be entered.

9. A doctor's statement must be given on a date not later than one day after the date of the examination on which it is based, and no further doctor's statement based on the same examination shall be furnished other than a doctor's statement by way of replacement of an original which has been lost or mislaid, in which case it shall be clearly marked "duplicate."

10. Where, in the doctor's opinion, the claimant will become fit to resume work on a day not later than 2 weeks after the date of the examination on which the doctor's statement is based, the doctor's statement shall specify that day.

11. Subject to rules 12 and 13 below, the doctor's statement shall specify the minimum period during which, in the doctor's opinion, the claimant should, by reason of his disorder, refrain from work.

12. The period specified shall begin on the date of the examination on which the doctor's statement is based and shall not exceed 6 months unless the claimant has, on the advice of a doctor, refrained from work for at least 6 months immediately preceding that date.

13. Where—
  (a) the claimant has, on the advice of a doctor, refrained from work for at least 6 months immediately preceding the date of the examination on which the doctor's statement is based, and
  (b) in the doctor's opinion, it will be necessary for the claimant to refrain from work for the foreseeable future, instead of specifying a period, the doctor may, having regard to the circumstances of the particular case, enter the words "until further notice."

14. The Notes set out in Part III of this Schedule shall accompany the form of doctor's statement provided by the Secretary of State.

15. A doctor may, having regard to the circumstances of the particular case, indicate on the doctor's statement that the claimant should be considered for vocational rehabilitation.

PART II

FORM OF DOCTOR'S STATEMENT

DOCTOR'S STATEMENT

In confidence to

Mr./Mrs./Miss ....

I examined you today/yesterday and advised you that:

(a) you need not   (b) you should refrain from work
    refrain from work
                              for ....

                              OR until ....

Diagnosis of your disorder
causing absence from work ....

(S.I. 1976 No. 615, Sched. 1) (as amended)

Doctor's remarks

Doctor's signature

Date of signing

Recommendation for vocational rehabilitation

Part III

THE NOTES 4.433

The following notes shall accompany the form of doctor's statement provided by the Secretary of State—
On the doctor's statement—
(1) After the words "you should refrain from work for", the period entered must not exceed 6 months unless the patient has, on the advice of a doctor, already refrained from work for a continuous period of 6 months.
(2) After the words "you should refrain from work until"—
   (a) if the patient is being given a date when he can return to work the date entered should not be more than 2 weeks after the date of the examination;
   (b) if the patient has already been incapable of work for at least 6 months and recovery of capacity for work in the foreseeable future is not expected "further notice" may be entered.

SCHEDULE 1A **Regulation 2(1)**

Part I

RULES

1.—In these rules, unless the context otherwise requires— 4.434

"claimant" means the person in respect of whom a statement is given in accordance with these rules;
"doctor" means a registered medical practitioner not being the claimant;
"special statement" means the form prescribed in Part II of this Schedule.

2. Where a doctor advises a claimant to refrain from work on the basis of a written report which he has received from another doctor or where a doctor has not issued a statement since the claimant was examined and he wishes to issue a statement more than a day after the examination he shall use the special statement.
3. The special statement shall be completed in the manner described in paragraph 5 of Part I to Schedule 1.

Social Security (Medical Evidence) Regulations 1976

4. Subject to rules 5 and 6 below, the diagnosis of the claimant's disorder in respect of which the doctor is advising the claimant to refrain from work or as the case may be, which has caused the claimant's absence from work shall be specified as precisely as the doctor's knowledge of the claimant's condition permits.

5. Where, in the doctor's opinion, a disclosure to the claimant of the precise disorder would be prejudicial to his well being, the diagnosis may be specified less precisely.

6. In a case of a disorder stated by the claimant to have caused incapacity for work, where—
    (a) no clinical signs have been found of that disorder, and
    (b) in the doctor's opinion, the claimant need not refrain from work, instead of specifying a diagnosis "unspecified" may be entered.

7. Part B of the special statement must only be given on a date not later than one month after the date of the written report on which the special statement is based and that part shall only be used where the claimant is being advised to refrain from work for a specified period of not more than one month.

PART II

FORM OF SPECIAL STATEMENT

FOR SOCIAL SECURITY AND
STATUTORY SICK PAY
PURPOSES ONLY

Special Statement
by the Doctor

In confidence to

Mr./Mrs./Miss/Ms ....

(A) I have examined you on the following dates ....
....
....

(B) I have not examined you but, on the basis of a recent written report from—
Doctor .... (Name if known)
of ....
....
.... (Address)

and advised you that you should refrain from work

I have advised you that should refrain

From .... to ....

from work for/until ....

Diagnosis of your disorder
causing absence from work ....

Doctor's remarks

Doctor's
signature

Date of
signing

The special circumstances in which this form may be used are described in the handbook "Medical Evidence for Social Security and Statutory Sick Pay purposes".

(S.I. 1976 No. 615, Sched. 1A) (as amended)

AMENDMENT

1. The Social Security (Miscellaneous provisions) Amendments Regulations 1992 (S.I. 1992 No 247), reg. 3 (March 9, 1992)

SCHEDULE 1B   Regulation 2(1)(c)

PART I

RULES

1. In these rules, unless the context otherwise requires—

"claimant" means the person in respect of whom a statement is given in accordance with these rules;
"doctor" means a registered medical practitioner not being the claimant;
"all work test statement" means a statement given by a doctor in accordance with these rules.

2. Where the Secretary of State has requested that the claimant provide an all work test statement, that statement shall be provided in the form prescribed in Part II of this Schedule notwithstanding that the claimant has already provided a statement in accordance with Schedule 1 or 1A.

3. The all work test statement shall be completed in accordance with rules 3, 4, 5 [²and 9 to 13] of Part I to Schedule 1.

4. Subject to rule 5 below, the diagnosis of—
   (a) the disorder in respect of which the doctor is advising the claimant to refrain from work or, as the case may be, which has caused the claimant's absence from work; and
   (b) any other condition which could affect the claimant's capacity for work, shall be specified as precisely as the doctor's knowledge of the claimant's condition at the time of the examination permits.

5. Where, in the doctor's opinion, a disclosure to the claimant of the precise disorder would be prejudicial to his well being, the diagnosis may be specified less precisely.

6. The notes set out in Part III of this Schedule shall accompany the form of doctor's statement provided by the Secretary of State.

PART II

FORM OF DOCTOR'S STATEMENT

THIS STATEMENT SHOULD <u>NOT</u> BE USED FOR PEOPLE CLAIMING STATUTORY SICK PAY FROM THEIR EMPLOYER.

Doctor's Statement

In confidence to
Mr/Mrs/Miss/Ms ....

Note for Doctor—We are making an assessment of your patient's eligibility for incapacity Benefit and other state benefits under the terms of the all work test. Please complete the following boxes.

Main diagnosis *(be as precise as possible)* ....

Social Security (Medical Evidence) Regulations 1976

Other diagnoses ....

Doctor's remarks
(Including comments on the disabling effects of the condition, treatment and progress—accuracy and detail will avoid requests for completion of a medical report).

Note for Doctor—While the all work test is being carried out, we need evidence that your patient should refrain from <u>his usual occupation</u>. Please provide the following information (which will not be part of the [³perpetual capability assessment).

I am issuing the following statement based upon the current guidance to certifying medical practitioners. I examined you today/yesterday and advised you that:

(a) You need not refrain from your usual occupation

(b) You should refrain from your usual occupation

    for (*insert period*) ....

    OR until ....

Doctor's signature

Date of signing

Form Med 4

PART III

THE NOTES

The following notes shall accompany the form of doctor's statement provided by the Secretary of State:

4.438   1. After the words on the doctor's statement "you should refrain from your usual occupation"—
    (i) if the patient is being given a date when he can return to work, the date entered should not be more than 2 weeks after the date on which the statement is issued;
    (ii) if recovery of capacity for work in the foreseeable future is not expected, "further notice" may be entered.

2. The "remarks" box should be used to provide additional information; including

(S.I. 1976 No. 615, Sched. 1B) (as amended)

further details of diagnosed conditions, the disabling effect of such conditions, and notes on the patient's treatment and progress. Accuracy and detail will avoid requests for completion of a medical report.

3. The "remarks" box should also be used to state whether or not the patient is able to travel a reasonable distance to a medical examination as a result of his condition. If no entry is made, it will be assumed that the patient can travel.

4. This form of doctor's statement should not be used where the patient is claiming statutory sick pay from their employer. Form Med 3 should be used for that purpose.

AMENDMENTS

1. The Social Security (Medical Evidence) Amendment Regulations 1994 (S.I. 1994 No 2975), reg. 3 (April 13, 1995)
2. The Social Security (Incapacity for Work) Miscellaneous Amendments Regulations 1995 (S.I. 1995 No 987), reg. 4 (April 13, 1995)
3. The Social Security (Incapacity) Miscellaneous Amendments Regulations 2000 (S.I. 2000 No 590), reg. 6 (April 3, 2000)

[^{1}]SCHEDULE 2   Regulation 2(3)

PART I

RULES

1. In these rules any reference to a woman is a reference to the woman in respect of whom a maternity certificate is given in accordance with these rules.   **4.439**

2. A maternity certificate shall be given by a doctor or registered midwife attending the woman and shall not be given by the woman herself.

3. The maternity certificate shall be on a form provided by the Secretary of State for the purpose and the wording shall be that set out in the appropriate part of the form specified in Part II of this Schedule.

4. Every maternity certificate shall be completed in ink or other indelible substance and shall contain the following particulars—
  (a) the woman's name;
  (b) the week in which the woman is expected to be confined or, if the maternity certificate is given after confinement, the date of that confinement and the date the confinement was expected to take place [^{2} . . .];
  (c) the date of the examination on which the maternity certificate is based;
  (d) the date on which the maternity certificate is signed; and
  (e) the address of the doctor or where the maternity certificate is signed by a registered midwife the personal identification number given to her by the United Kingdom Central Council for Nursing, Midwifery and Health Visiting ("UKCC") on her registration in Part 10 of the register maintained under section 10 of the Nurses, Midwives and Health Visitors Act 1979 and the expiry date of that registration,

and shall bear opposite the word "Signature", the signature of the person giving the maternity certificate written after there has been entered on the maternity certificate the woman's name and the expected date or, as the case may be, the date of the confinement.

5. After a maternity certificate has been given, no further maternity certificate based on the same examination shall be furnished other than a maternity certificate by way of replacement of an original which has been lost or mislaid, in which case it shall be clearly marked "duplicate".

Social Security (Medical Evidence) Regulations 1976

[²]PART II

FORM OF CERTIFICATE

4.440   **MATERNITY CERTIFICATE**

Please fill in this form in ink

Name of patient

Fill in this part if you are giving the certificate before the confinement. *Do not fill this in more that 14 weeks before the week the baby is expected.*	*Fill in this part if you are giving the certificate after the confinement.* I certify that I attended you in connection with the birth which took place on
I certify that I examined you on the date given below. In my opinion you can expect to have your baby in the week that includes ..../........../........	......./.........../......... when you were delivered of a child [ ] children. In my opinion your baby was expected in the week that includes ..../........../........
Week means a period of 7 days starting on a Sunday and ending on a Saturday.	

Date of examination ..../........../........

Date of signing ..../........../........

Signature

Registered midwives

Please give your UKCC Personal Identification Number and the expiry date of your registration with the UKCC.

Doctors
Please stamp your name and address here if the form has not been stamped by the Family Health Service Authority in whose medical list you are included.

(S.I. 1976 No. 615, Sched. 2) (as amended)

AMENDMENTS

1. The Social Security (Medical Evidence) Amendment Regulations 1987 (S.I. 1987 No 409), ref.4 (April 6, 1987)
2. The Social Security (Miscellaneous Provisions) Amendment Regulations 1991 (S.I. 1991 No 2284), reg.21 (November 1, 1991)

Social Security (Payments on Account, Overpayments and Recovery) Regulations 1988

(S.I. 1988 No. 664) *(as amended)*

ARRANGEMENT OF REGULATIONS

PART I

GENERAL

1. Citation, commencement and interpretation.   4.441

PART II

INTERIM PAYMENTS

2. Making of interim payments.
3. Bringing interim payments into account.
4. Recovery of overpaid interim payments.

PART III

OFFSETTING

5. Offsetting prior payment against subsequent award.
6. Exception from offset of recoverable overpayment.

PART IV

PREVENTION OF DUPLICATION OF PAYMENTS

7. Duplication and prescribed income.
8. Duplication and prescribed payments.
9. Duplication and maintenance payments.
10. Conversion of payments made in a foreign currency.

PART V

DIRECT CREDIT TRANSFER OVERPAYMENTS

11. Recovery of overpayments by automated or other direct credit transfer.

Part VI

Revision of Determination and Calculation of Amount Recoverable

12. Circumstances in which determination need not he revised.
13. Sums to be deducted in calculating recoverable amounts.
14. Quarterly diminution of capital resources.

Part VII

The Process of Recovery

15. Recovery by deduction from prescribed benefits.
16. Limitations on deductions from prescribed benefits.
17. Recovery from couples.

Part VIII

Recovery by Deductions from Earnings Following Trade Dispute

18. Recovery by deductions from earnings.
19. Award and protected earnings.
20. Service and contents of deduction notices.
21. Period for which deduction notice has effect.
22. Effect of deduction notice.
23. Increase of amount of award on appeal or review.
24. Review of determination of protected earnings.
25. Power to serve further deduction notice on resumption of employment.
26. Right of Secretary of State to recover direct from claimant.
27. Duties and liabilities of employers.
28. Claimants to give notice of cessation or resumption of employment.
29. Failure to notify.

Part IX

Revocations, Transitional Provisions and Savings

30. Revocations.
31. Transitional provisions and savings.

Part I

General

Citation, commencement and interpretation

1.—(1) These regulations may be cited as the Social Security (Payments on account, Overpayments and Recovery) Regulations 1988 and shall come into force on 6th April 1988.

(2) In these Regulations, unless the context otherwise requires—

"the Act" means the Social Security Act 1986;

[⁵"adjudicating authority" means, as the case may require, the Secretary of State, an appeal tribunal constituted under Chapter 1 of Part I of the Social Security Act 1998, the Chief or other Commissioner, or a tribunal consisting of any three or more Commissioners constituted in accordance with section 16(7) of that Act]

[⁶"adjudicating authority" means, as the case may require, the Board, an officer of the Board, an appeal tribunal constituted under section 7 of the Social Security Act 1998, the Chief Social Security Commissioner or any other Social Security Commissioner, or a tribunal of three or more such Commissioners constituted in accordance with section 16(7) of that Act]

"benefit" means [⁴a jobseeker's allowance and] any benefit under the Social Security Act 1975 [SSCBA, Parts II to V], child benefit, family credit, income support and [¹any social fund payment under sections 32(2)(a) and 32(2A) of the Act [SSCBA, s.138(1)(a) and (2)] [³and any incapacity benefit under sections 30A(1) and (5) of the Contributions and Benefits Act]];

[⁶"the Board" means the Commissioners of Inland Revenue]

"child benefit" means benefit under Part I of the Child Benefit Act 1975 [SSCBA, Part IX];

"the Claims and Payments Regulations" means the Social Security (Claims and Payments) Regulations 1987;

[³"the Contributions and Benefits Act" means the Social Security Contributions and Benefits Act 1992;]

[²"disability living allowance" means a disability living allowance under section 37ZA of the Social Security Act 1975 [SSCBA, s.71];

[⁷ "disabled person's tax credit" means a disabled person's tax credit under section 129 of the Contributions and Benefits Act and, in relation to things done, or falling to be done, prior to 5th October 1999, shall include a reference to disability working allowance;] [⁷. . .]

"guardian's allowance" means an allowance under section 38 of the Social Security Act 1975 [SSCBA, s.77];

"income support" means income support under Part II of the Act [SSCBA, Part VII] and includes personal expenses addition, special transitional addition and transitional addition as defined in the Income Support (Transitional) Regulations 1987;

"Income Support Regulations" means the Income Support (General) Regulations 1987;

[⁴ "Jobseeker's Allowance Regulations" means the Jobseeker's Allowance Regulations 1996;]

"severe disablement allowance" means an allowance under section 36 of the Social Security Act 1975 [SSCBA, s.68].

[⁷ "start notification" means a notification of entitlement to tax credit furnished to an employer by the Board, referred to in section 6(2)(a) of the Tax Credits Act 1999;

"tax credit" means working families' tax credit or disabled person's tax credit;

"working families' tax credit" means working families' tax credit under section 128 of the Contributions and Benefits Act and, in relation to things done, or falling to be done, prior to 5th October 1999 shall include a reference to family credit.]

(3) Unless the context otherwise requires, any reference in these regulations to a numbered Part or regulation is a reference to the Part or regulation bearing that number in these Regulations and any reference in a regulation to a numbered paragraph is a reference to the paragraph of that regulation bearing that number.

AMENDMENTS

1. The Social Security (Payments on account, Overpayments and Recovery) Amendments Regulations 1989 (S.I. 1989 No. 136), reg. 3 (February 27, 1989).

2. The Disability Living Allowance and Disability Working Allowance (Consequential Provisions) Regulations 1991 (S.I. 1991 No. 2742), reg. 15 (April 6, 1992).

3. The Social Security (Incapacity Benefit) (Consequential and Transitional Amendments and Savings) Regulations 1995 (S.I. 1995 No. 829), reg. 21(2) (April 13, 1995).

4. The Social Security and Child Support (Jobseeker's Allowance) (Consequential Amendments) Regulations 1996 (S.I. 1996 No. 1345), reg. 23(2) (October 7, 1996).

5. The Tax Credits (Payments on Account, Overpayments and Recovery) (Amendment) Regulations 1999 (S.I. 1999 No 2571), reg. 3 (October 5, 1999)

6. For tax credits purposes only these words substituted by The Tax Credits (Payments on Account, Overpayments and Recovery) (Amendment) Regulations 1999 (S.I. 1999 No 2571), reg. 3 (October 5, 1999)

7. The Tax Credits (Payments on Account, Overpayments and Recovery) (Amendment) Regulations 1999 (S.I. 1999 No 2571), reg. 3 (October 5, 1999)

PART II

INTERIM PAYMENTS

Making of interim payments

4.443

2.—(1) [³Subject to paragraph (1A),] the Secretary of State may, in his discretion, [⁴ the Board may in their discretion] make an interim payment, that is to say a payment on account of any benefit to which it appears to him [⁴ them] that a person is or may be entitled, in the following circumstances—
  (a) a claim for that benefit has not been made in accordance with the Claims and Payments Regulations and it is impracticable for such a claim to be made immediately; or
  (b) a claim for that benefit has been so made, but it is impracticable for it or [⁵ an] application or appeal which relates to it to be determined immediately; or
  (c) an award of that benefit has been made but it is impracticable for the beneficiary to be paid immediately, except by means of an interim payment.

(S.I. 1988 No. 664, Reg. 2) (as amended)

[³(1A) Paragraph (1) shall not apply pending the determination of an appeal unless the Secretary of State [⁴ the Board] is of the opinion that there is entitlement to benefit.]

(2) [¹Subject to paragraph (3)] on or before the making of an interim payment the recipient shall be given notice in writing of his liability under this Part to have it brought into account and to repay any overpayment.

(3) Where the recipient of an interim payment of disability living allowance—
   (a) is terminally ill within the meaning of [section 66(2) of the Social Security Contributions and Benefits Act 1992]; or
   (b) had an invalid carriage or other vehicle provided by the Secretary of State under section 5(2)(a) of the National Health Service Act 1977 and Schedule 2 to that Act or under section 46 of the National Health Service (Scotland) Act 1978,

the requirement to give notice in paragraph (2) of this regulation shall be omitted.

[²(4) Where an interim payment of income support is made because a payment to which the recipient is entitled by way of child support maintenance under the Child Support Act 1991, or periodical payments under a maintenance agreement within the meaning of section 9(1) of that Act or under a maintenance order within the meaning of section 107(15) of the Social Security Administration Act 1992, has not been made, the requirement in paragraph (2) of this regulation to give notice shall be omitted.]

AMENDMENTS

1. The Disability Living Allowance and Disability Working Allowance (Consequential Provisions) Regulations 1991 (S.I. 1991 No. 2742), reg. 15 (April 6, 1992).
2. The Social Security (Payments on account, Overpayments and Recovery) Amendment Regulations 1993 (S.I. 1993 No. 650), reg. 2 (April 5, 1993).
3. The Social Security (Persons from Abroad) Miscellaneous Amendments Regulations 1996 (S.I. 1996 No. 30), reg. 10 (February 5, 1996).
4. For tax credits purposes only The Tax Credits (Payments on Account, Overpayments and Recovery) (Amendment) Regulations 1999 (S.I. 1999 No 2571), reg. 4 (October 5, 1999)
5. The Social Security Act 1998 (Commencement No. 9, and Savings and Consequential and Transitional Provisions) Order 1999 (S.I. 1999 No 2422), Sched. 8 (September 6, 1999)

GENERAL NOTE

Interim payments are made at the discretion of the Secretary of State. Thus there is no right of appeal and any refusal can only be challenged (other than by making further representations) by judicial review. The test under para. (1) is not whether it is "clear" that the person will qualify for a particular benefit, but whether it appears to the Secretary of State that he "is or may be entitled" to that benefit (*R. v. Secretary of State for Social Security, ex parte Sarwar Getachew and Urbanek*, High Court, April 11, 1995). Thus the Secretary of State can decide to make interim payments even where entitlement to, for example,

4.444

Social Security (Payments on Account, etc.) Regulations 1988

income support is not certain. Interim payments are recoverable if the person is subsequently found not to be entitled to the benefit claimed (see reg. 4).

The introduction of an habitual residence rule for income support from August 1, 1994 (see the additional definition of "person from abroad" in reg. 21(3) of the Income Support Regulations) focussed fresh attention on this regulation. Most claimants who fail the test were not eligible for urgent cases payments under reg. 70(3) of the Income Support Regulations, even before the February 1996 changes, and so face a delay of what can be several months until their appeal is heard without any benefit. This led to many claimants asking for interim payments pending the hearing of their appeals which in a few cases at least were paid. But this in turn precipitated the introduction of para. (1A).

Under para. (1A), in force from February 5, 1996, an interim payment will not be made if an appeal is pending unless the Secretary of State considers that there *is* entitlement to benefit. (See *R. v. Secretary of State for Social Security ex parte Grant* (High Court, July 31, 1997.)) This change is apparently to restore the original policy intention that interim payments could be made where entitlement was clear but the amount of benefit due was not (para. 46 of the DSS Explanatory Memorandum to the Social Security Advisory Committee (Cm.3062/1996)). But the wording of para. (1)(b) and the first part of reg. 4(3)(ii) somewhat belies this. Moreover, if the case involves a point of E.C. law (as, *e.g.* an appeal concerning the habitual residence test may do), para. (1A) could be in breach of E.C. law in so far as it prevents the Secretary of State from having the power to grant interim relief (see *Factortame Ltd and others v. Secretary of State for Transport (No. 2)* [1991] 1 A.C. 603, [1991] 1 All E.R. 70).

In a ruling made in the appeal *CDLA/913/1994*, the Commissioner held that he had no jurisdiction to order interim payment of benefit where a question had been referred to the European Court of Justice for a preliminary ruling. The case in which the question arose was concerned with entitlement, not payment, and to make such an order would go beyond what was required by Community law. The Commissioner left it open whether there was jurisdiction to make an interim or provisional award of benefit in such circumstances, since he was satisfied that, even if such a power exists, he would not exercise his discretion to make an award.

That ruling was challenged by way of judicial review. In *R. v. Social Security Commissioner, ex parte Snares*, March 24, 1997, Popplewell J. rejected the challenge. He decided that the exercise of discretion by the Commissioner could not be impugned. Unfortunately, however, Popplewell J. did not adopt the distinction made by the Commissioner between an award of entitlement and an order for payment and tended to run the two issues together. If it had been necessary to the determination, he would have regarded the question of the interim remedies available pending a ruling by the Court of Justice as not *acte claire* and would have made a further reference to the Court of Justice.

Bringing interim payments into account

4.445

[¹3. [²Subject to paragraph (2)] where it is practicable to do so and, where notice is required to be given under regulation 2(2), such notice has been given—
   (a) any interim payment, other than an interim payment made in the circumstances mentioned in regulation 2(4),—
      (i) which was made in anticipation of an award of benefit shall be offset by the adjudicating authority in reduction of the benefit to be awarded; and

(S.I. 1988 No. 664, Reg. 3) (as amended)

    (ii) whether or not made in anticipation of an award, which is not offset under sub-paragraph (i) shall be deducted by the Secretary of State from—
        (a) the sum payable under the award of benefit on account of which the interim payment was made; or
        (b) any sum payable under any subsequent award of the same benefit to the same person; and
(b) any interim payment made in the circumstances mentioned in regulation 2(4) shall be offset by the Secretary of State against any sum received by him in respect of arrears of child support maintenance payable to the person to whom the interim payment was made.]

[²(2) Where the interim payment in paragraph (1)(a) is a payment on account of tax credit, paragraph (1)(a), but not paragraph (1)(b), shall apply with the modification that, for the words "Secretary of State" there is substituted the word "Board".]

AMENDMENTS

    1. The Social Security (Payments on account, Overpayments and Recovery) Amendment Regulations 1993 (S.I. 1993 No. 650), reg. 2 (April 5, 1993).
    2. The Tax Credits (Payments on Account, Overpayments and Recovery) (Amendment) Regulations 1999 (S.I. 1999 No 2571), reg. 5 (October 5, 1999)

Recovery of overpaid interim payments

4.446

    4.—(1) Where the adjudicating authority has determined that an interim payment has been overpaid in circumstances which fall within paragraph (3) and [¹where notice is required to be given under regulation 2(2), such notice has been given], that authority shall determine the amount of the overpayment.

    (2) The amount of the overpayment shall be recoverable by the Secretary of State, by the same procedures and subject to the same conditions as if it were recoverable under section 53(1) of the Act [SSAA, s.71(1)].

    (3) The circumstances in which an interim payment may be determined to have been overpaid are as follows—
(a) an interim payment has been made under regulation 2(1)(a) or (b) but—
    (i) the recipient has failed to make a claim in accordance with the Claims and Payments Regulations as soon as practicable, or has made a claim which is either defective or is not made on the form approved for the time being by the Secretary of State and the Secretary of State has not treated the claim as duly made under regulation 4(7) of the Claims and Payments Regulations; or
    (ii) it has been determined that there is no entitlement on the claim, or that the entitlement is less than the amount of the interim payment or that benefit is not payable; or
    (iii) the claim has been withdrawn under regulation 5(2) of the Claims and Payments Regulations; or

(b) an interim payment has been made under regulation 2(1)(c) which exceeds the entitlement under the award of benefit on account of which the interim payment was made[¹; or
(c) an interim payment of income support has been made under regulation 2(1)(b) in the circumstances mentioned in regulation 2(4).]

(4) For the purposes of this regulation a claim is defective if it is made on the form approved for the time being by the Secretary of State but is not completed in accordance with the instructions on the form.

[²(5) Where the interim Where the interim payment in paragraph (1)(a) is a payment on a ccount of tax credit, paragraph (1)(a), but not paragraph (1)(b), shall apply with the modification that, for the words "Secretary of State" there is substituted the word "Board".]

AMENDMENTS

1. The Social Security (Payments on account, Overpayments and Recovery) Amendment Regulations 1993 (S.I. 1993 No. 650), reg. 2 (April 5, 1993).
2. The Tax Credits (Payments on Account, Overpayments and Recovery) (Amendment) Regulations 1999 (S.I. 1999 No 2571), reg. 5 (October 5, 1999)

PART III

OFFSETTING

Offsetting prior payment against subsequent award

5.—(1) Subject to regulation 6 (exception from offset of recoverable overpayment), any sum paid in respect of a period covered by a subsequent determination in any of the cases set out in paragraph (2) shall be offset against arrears of entitlement under the subsequent determination and, except to the extent that the sum exceeds the arrears, shall be treated as properly paid on account of them.

[²(1A) In paragraph (1) the reference to "any sum paid" shall, in relation to tax credit, include a reference to any amount or calculation of tax credit payable in respect of a period to the date of subsequent determination, which is included in a start notification given by the Board to an employer, and for the payment of which the employer remains responsible.]

(2) Paragraph (1) applies in the following cases—

[³*Case 1: Payment pursuant to a decision which is revised or superseded, or overturned on appeal*
Where a person has been paid a sum by way of benefit pursuant to a decision which is subsequently revoked under section 9 of the Social Security Act 1998, superseded under Section 10 of that Act or overturned on appeal]

Case 2: Award or payment of benefit in lieu
Where a person has been paid a sum by way benefit under the original award and it is subsequently determined, . . ., that another benefit should be awarded or is payable in lieu of the first.

(S.I. 1988 No. 664, Reg. 5) (as amended)

Case 3: Child benefit and severe disablement allowance
Where either—
  (a) a person has been awarded and paid child benefit for a period in respect of which severe disablement allowance is subsequently determined to be payable to the child concerned, or
  (b) severe disablement allowance is awarded and paid for a period in respect of which child benefit is subsequently awarded to someone else, the child concerned in the subsequent determination being the beneficiary of the original award.

Case 4: Increase of benefit for dependant
Where a person has been paid a sum by way of an increase in respect of a dependent person under the original award and it is subsequently determined that that other person is entitled to benefit for that period, or that a third person is entitled to the increase for that period in priority to the beneficiary of the original award.

Case 5: Increase of benefit for partner
Where a person has been paid a sum by way of an increase in respect of a partner (as defined in regulation 2 of the Income Support Regulations) and it is subsequently determined that that other person is entitled to benefit for that period.

[² (2A) In paragraph (2), Case 2 shall not apply where either—
  (a) the sum paid under the original award, or
  (b) the subsequent decision on the revision, supersession or appeal,
referred to in the Case (but not both) is or relates to tax credit.]

(3) Where an amount has been deducted under regulation 13(b) (sums to be deducted in calculating recoverable amounts) an equivalent sum shall be offset against any arrears of entitlement of that person under a subsequent award of income support[¹, or income-based jobseeker's allowance] for the period to which the deducted amount relates.

(4) Where child benefit which has been paid under an award in favour of a person (the original beneficiary) is subsequently awarded to someone else for any week, the benefit shall nevertheless be treated as properly paid if it was received by someone other than the original beneficiary, who—
  (a) either had the child living with him or was contributing towards the cost of providing for the child at a weekly rate which was not less than the weekly rate under the original award, and
  (b) could have been entitled to child benefit in respect of that child for that week had a claim been made in time.

(5) Any amount which is treated, under paragraph (4), as properly paid shall be deducted from the amount payable to the beneficiary under the subsequent award.

AMENDMENTS

1. The Social Security and Child Support (Jobseeker's Allowance) (Consequential Amendments) Regulations 1996 (S.I. 1996 No. 1345), reg. 23(5) and (6) (October 7, 1996).

2. The Tax Credits (Payments on Account, Overpayments and Recovery) (Amendment) Regulations 1999 (S.I. 1999 No 2571), reg. 7 (October 5, 1999)

3. The Social Security Act 1998 (Commencement No. 11 and Transitional Provisions) Order 1999 (S.I. 1999 No 2860), Sched 4, (October 18, 1999)

GENERAL NOTE

4.449 This regulation contains important powers to deal with cases where a subsequent award of one benefit replaces an earlier award of a different benefit. It enables the benefit originally awarded to be treated as paid on account of the benefit subsequently awarded. The circumstances in which the power is available are spelled out in the five cases listed in the regulation. Tribunals may need to refer to this power when the result of their decision is to substitute one benefit for another which has already been awarded.

Exception from offset of recoverable overpayment

4.448 **6.** No amount may be offset under regulation 5(1) which has been determined to be a recoverable overpayment for the purposes of section 53(1) of the Act [SSAA, s.71(1)].

PART IV

PREVENTION OF DUPLICATION OF PAYMENTS

Duplication and prescribed income

4.450 **7.**—[¹ (1) For the purposes of section 74(1) of the Social Security Administration Act 1992 (income support [³ and income-based jobseeker's allowance] and other payments), a person's prescribed income is—
   (a) income required to be taken into account in accordance with Part V of the Income Support Regulations [³or, as the case may be, Part VIII of the Jobseeker's Allowance Regulations], except for the income specified in sub-paragraph (b); and]
[²(b) income which, if it were actually paid, would be required to be taken into account in accordance with Chapter VIIA of Part V of the Income Support Regulations [³or, as the case may be, Chapter VIII of Part VIII of the Jobseeker's Allowance Regulations] (child support maintenance); but only in so far as it relates to the period beginning with the effective date of the maintenance assessment under which it is payable, as determined in accordance with regulation 30 of the Child Support (Maintenance Assessment Procedure) Regulations 1992, and ending with the first day which is a day specified by the Secretary of State under regulation 4(1) of the Child Support (Collection and Enforcement) Regulations 1992 as being a day on which payment of child support maintenance under that maintenance assessment is due.]
  (2) The prescribed date in relation to any payment of income prescribed by [¹paragraph (1)(a)] is—
   (a) where it is made in respect of a specific day or period, that day or the first day of the period;
   (b) where it is not so made, the day or the first day of the period to which it is fairly attributable.

(S.I. 1988 No. 664, Reg. 7) (as amended)

[²(3) Subject to paragraph (4), the prescribed date in relation to any payment of income prescribed by paragraph (1)(b) is the last day of the maintenance period, determined in accordance with regulation 33 of the Child Support (Maintenance Assessment Procedure) Regulations 1992, to which it relates.

(4) Where the period referred to in paragraph (1)(b) does not consist of a number of complete maintenance periods the prescribed date in relation to income prescribed by that sub-paragraph which relates to any part of that period which is not a complete maintenance period is the last day of that period.]

AMENDMENTS

1. The Social Security (Payments on account, Overpayments and Recovery) Amendment Regulations 1993 (S.I. 1993 No. 650), reg. 2, as amended by The Social Security (Miscellaneous Provisions) Amendment Regulations 1993 (S.I. 1993 No. 846), reg. 4 (April 5, 1993).
2. The Social Security (Payments on account, Overpayments and Recovery) Amendment Regulations 1993 (S.I. 1993 No. 650), reg. 2, as amended by The Social Security (Miscellaneous Provisions) Amendment Regulations 1993 (S.I. 1993 No. 846), reg. 4 (April 5, 1993).
3. The Social Security and Child Support (Jobseeker's Allowance) (Consequential Amendments) Regulations 1996 (S.I. 1996 No. 1345), reg. 23(3) (October 7, 1996).

GENERAL NOTE

See the notes to s.74(1) of the Administration Act. 4.451

Under s.54 of the Child Support Act 1991 "maintenance assessment" means an assessment of maintenance made under that Act, including, except where regulations prescribe otherwise, an interim assessment. Under reg. 30 of the Child Support (Maintenance Assessment Procedure) Regulations 1992, the effective date of a new assessment is usually, when the application was made by the person with care of the child, the date on which a maintenance enquiry form was sent to the absent parent or, where the application was made by the absent parent, the date on which an effective maintenance form was received by the Secretary of State. Arrears will inevitably accrue while the assessment is being made. In the meantime income support or income-based JSA can be paid in full to the parent with care. When the arrears are paid, the amount of "overpaid" income support or JSA is recoverable under s.74(1) of the Administration Act.

See the notes to reg. 60C of the Income Support (General) Regulations for the interaction with payments of other arrears of child support maintenance, which are excluded from the operation of s.74(1). Note also s.74A of the Administration Act and regs. 55A and 60E of the Income Support Regulations and regs. 119 and 127 of the Jobseeker's Allowance Regulations.

Duplication and prescribed payments

8.—(1) For the purposes of section 27(2) of the Act [SSAA, s.74(2)] 4.452 (recovery of amount of benefit awarded because prescribed payment not made on prescribed date), the payment of any of the following is a prescribed payment—

Social Security (Payments on Account, etc.) Regulations 1988

    (a) any benefit under the Social Security Act 1975 [SSCBA, Parts II to V] other than any grant or gratuity or a widow's payment;
    (b) any child benefit;
    (c) any family credit;
    (d) any war disablement pension or war widow's pension which is not in the form of a gratuity and any payment which the Secretary of State accepts as analogous to any such pension;
    (e) any allowance paid under the Job Release Act 1977;
    (f) any allowance payable by or on behalf of [²Scottish Enterprise Highlands and Islands Enterprise or] [¹the Secretary of State] to or in respect of a person for his maintenance for any period during which he is following a course of training or instruction provided or approved by [²Scottish Enterprise Highlands and Islands Enterprise or] [¹the Secretary of State]
    (g) any payment of benefit under the legislation of any member State other than the United Kingdom concerning the branches of social security mentioned in Article 4(1) of Regulation (EEC) No. 1408/71 on the application of social security schemes to employed persons, to self-employed persons and to members of their families moving within the Community, whether or not the benefit has been acquired by virtue of the provisions of that Regulation;

[³. . .]
    (2) The prescribed date, in relation to any payment prescribed by paragraph (1) is the date by which receipt of or entitlement to that benefit would have to be notified to the Secretary of State if it were to be taken into account in determining, whether [⁵by way of revision or supersession], the amount of or entitlement to income support [⁴, or income-based jobseeker's allowance].

AMENDMENTS

    1. Employment Act 1989, Sched. 5, paras. 1 and 4 (November 16, 1989).
    2. The Enterprise (Scotland) Consequential Amendments Order 1991 (S.I. 1991 No. 387), art. 14 (April 1, 1991).
    3. The Tax Credits (Payments on Account, Overpayments and Recovery) (Amendment) Regulations 1999 (S.I. 1999 No 2571), reg. 8 (October 5, 1999)
    4. The Social Security and Child Support (Jobseeker's Allowance) (Consequential Amendments) Regulations 1996 (S.I. 1996 No. 1345), reg. 23(5) and (6) (October 7, 1996).
    5. The Social Security Act 1998 (Commencement No. 11 and Transitional Provisions) Order 1999 (S.I. 1999 No 2680), Sched. 4 (October 18, 1999)

4.453   GENERAL NOTE

    See the notes to s.74(2) of the Administration Act.
    R(IS)14/94 concerned an overpayment of income support which arose from the award of invalid care allowance. The claimant was an elderly widow, whose daughter was her appointee. Income support was paid to the widow. The daughter was in receipt of invalid care allowance in respect of her mother. Recovery was sought under s.27 of the Social Security Act 1986 (now s.74 of the Administration Act) from the widow.
    The claimant argued that the words in reg. 8(2) "taken into account" meant

that only the claimant's resources and requirements were to be considered. The Commissioner rejects such a narrow reading of the words and says that "the words 'into account' should be given a wide interpretation and in the context include 'take notice of'."

Duplication and maintenance payments

9. For the purposes of section 27(3) of the Act [SSAA, s.74(3)] (recovery of amount of benefit awarded because maintenance payments not made), the following benefits are prescribed—
  (a) child benefit;
  (b) increase for dependants of any benefit under the Social Security Act 1975 [SSCBA, Parts II to V];
  (c) child's special allowance under section 31 of the Social Security Act 1975 [SSCBA, s.56]; and
  (d) guardian's allowance.

GENERAL NOTE

See the notes to s.74(3) of the Administration Act.

Conversion of payments made in a foreign currency

10. Where a payment of income prescribed by regulation 7(1), or a payment prescribed by regulation 8(1), is made in a currency other than sterling, its value in sterling, for the purposes of section 27 of the Act [SSAA, s.74] and this Part, shall be determined, after conversion by the Bank of England, or by [¹any institution which is authorised under the Banking Act 1987], as the net sterling sum into which it is converted, after any banking charge or commission on the transaction has been deducted.

AMENDMENT

1. The Social Security (Payments on Account, Overpayments and Recovery) (Amendment) Regulations 1988 (S.I. 1988 No 688), reg. 2(2) (April 11, 1988).

PART V

DIRECT CREDIT TRANSFER OVERPAYMENTS

Recovery of overpayments by automated or other direct credit transfer

11.(1) [¹ Subject to paragraph (4)] where it is determined by the adjudicating authority that a payment in excess of entitlement has been credited to a bank or other account under an arrangement for automated or other direct credit transfer made in accordance with regulation 21 of the Claims and Payments Regulations and that the conditions prescribed by paragraph (2) are satisfied, the excess, or the specified part of it to which the Secretary of State's certificate relates, shall be recoverable under this regulation.

(2) The prescribed conditions for recoverability under paragraph (1) are as follows—

(a) the Secretary of State has certified that the payment in excess of entitlement, or a specified part of it, is materially due to the arrangements for payments to be made by automated or other direct credit transfer; and

(b) notice of the effect which this regulation would have, in the event of an overpayment, was given in writing to the beneficiary, or to a person acting for him, before he agreed to the arrangement.

(3) Where the arrangement was agreed to before April 6, 1987 the condition prescribed by paragraph (2)(b) need not be satisfied in any case where the application for benefit to be paid by automated or other direct credit transfer contained a statement, or was accompanied by a written statement made by the applicant, which complied with the provisions of regulation 16A(3)(b) and (8) of the Social Security (Claims and Payments) Regulations 1979 or, as the case may be, regulation 7(2)(b) and (6) of the Child Benefit (Claims and Payments) Regulations 1984.

[¹ Where the payment mention in paragra[h (1) is a payment of tax credit, paragraphs (1) and (2) shall apply with the modifications that—

(a) in paragraph (1) for the words "Secretary of State" there is substituted the words "Board's", and

(b) in paragraph (2) for the words "Secretary of State" there is substituted the word "Board".]

AMENDMENT

1. The Tax Credits (Payments on Account, Overpayments and Recovery) (Amendment) Regulations 1999 (S.I. 1999 No 2571), reg. 9 (October 5, 1999)

PART VI

CALCULATION OF AMOUNT RECOVERABLE

AMENDMENT

1. S.I. 1999 No 2422, Sched. 8 (September 6, 1999)

Circumstances in which determination need not be revised

4.458
12. Section 53(4) of the Act [SSAA, s.71(5)] (recoverability dependent on reversal, variation, revision [¹ or supersession] of determination) shall not apply where the fact and circumstances of the misrepresentation or non-disclosure do not provide a basis for [¹ the decision pursuant to which the payment who made to be versed under section 9 of the Social Security Act 1998 or superseded under section 10 of that Act.]

(S.I. 1988 No. 664, Reg. 12) (as amended)

AMENDMENT

1. The Social Security Act 1998 (Commencement No. 9, and Savings and Consequential and Transitional Provisions) Order 1999 (S.I. 1999 No. 2422), Sched. 8 (September 6, 1999)

GENERAL NOTE 4.459

See the notes to s.71(5A) of the Administration Act.

Sums to be deducted in calculating recoverable amounts

13. [² Subject to paragraph (2)] in calculating the amounts recoverable under section 53(1) of the Act [SSAA, s.71(1)] or regulation 11, where there has been an overpayment of benefit, the adjudicating authority shall deduct— 4.460
(a) any amount which has been offset under Part III;
(b) any additional amount of income support[¹, or income-based jobseeker's allowance] which was not payable under the original, or any other, determination, but which should have been determined to be payable—
  (i) on the basis of the claim as presented to the adjudicating authority, or
  (ii) on the basis of the claim as it would have appeared had the misrepresentation or non-disclosure been remedied before the determination;
but no other deduction shall be made in respect of any other entitlement to benefit which may be, or might have been, determined to exist.
[² (2) Paragraph (1) shall apply to tax credit only where both—
(a) The overpayment of benefit referred to in paragraph (1), and
(b) The amount referred to in sub-paragraph (a) of that paragraph,
Are tax credit, and with the modification that sub-paragraph (b) of that paragraph is omitted.]

AMENDMENTS

1. The Social Security and Child Support (Jobseeker's Allowance) (Consequential Amendments) Regulations 1996 (S.I. 1996 No. 1345), reg. 23(5) and (6) (October 7, 1996).
2. The Tax Credits (Payments on Account, Overpayments and Recovery) (Amendment) Regulations 1999 (S.I. 1999 No 2571), reg 11 (October 5, 1999)

GENERAL NOTE

See the notes to s.71(1) and (2) of the Administration Act, 1992. 4.461
In calculating the amount of overpaid benefit, provision is made for deducting amounts of benefit treated as paid on account of subsequent awards under Pt III and underpaid income support. There does not appear to be any power to bring into account underpayments of other benefits found to have arisen during the period to which the overpayment relates. See also *CIS/5/92*.

Quarterly diminution of capital resources

14.—(1) For the purposes of section 53(1) of the Act [SSAA, s.71(1)], where income support[², or income-based jobseeker's allow- 4.462

Social Security (Payments on Account, etc.) Regulations 1988

ance][¹, working families tax credit or disabled pension's tax credit] has been overpaid in consequence of a misrepresentation as to the capital a claimant possesses or a failure to disclose its existence, the adjudicating authority shall treat that capital as having been reduced at the end of each quarter from the start of the overpayment period by the amount overpaid by way of income support[², or income-based jobseeker's allowance] [¹, working families tax credit or disabled pension's tax credit] within that quarter.

(2) Capital shall not be treated as reduced over any period other than a quarter or in circumstances other than those for which paragraph (1) provides.

(3) In this regulation—

"a quarter" means a period of 13 weeks starting with the first day on which the overpayment period began and ending on the 90th consecutive day thereafter.

"overpayment period" is a period during which income support [³or an income-based jobseeker's allowance,] [¹ working families tax credit or disabled pension's tax credit] is overpaid in consequence of a misrepresentation as to capital or a failure to disclose its existence.

AMENDMENTS

1. The Tax Credits (Payments on Account, Overpayments and Recovery) (Amendment) Regulations 1999 (S.I. 1999 No 2571), reg.12 (October 5, 1999).
2. The Tax Credits (Payments on Account, Overpayments and Recovery) (Amendment) Regulations 1999 (S.I. 1996 No. 2571), reg. 23(5) and (6) (October 7, 1996).
3. The Social Security (Jobseeker's Allowance and Payments on account) (Miscellaneous Amendments) Regulations 1996 (S.I. 1996 No. 2519), reg. 3(2) (October 7, 1996).

4.463   GENERAL NOTE

See the notes to s.71(1) and (2) of the Administration Act,

PART VII

THE PROCESS OF RECOVERY

Recovery by deduction from benefits

4.464   **15.**—(1) Subject to regulation 16, where any amount is recoverable under sections 27 or 53(1) of the Act [SSAA, ss.74 or 71(1)], or under these Regulations, that amount shall be recoverable by the Secretary of State from any of the benefits prescribed by the next paragraph, to which the person from whom [¹the amount is determined] to be recoverable is entitled.

(S.I. 1988 No. 664, Reg. 15) (as amended)

(2) The following benefits are prescribed for the purposes of this regulation—
- (a) subject to paragraphs (1) and (2) of regulation 16, any benefit under the Social Security Act 1975 [SSCBA, Parts II to V];
- (b) subject to paragraphs (1) and (2) of regulation 16, any child benefit;
- (c) [⁵. . .]
- (d) subject to regulation 16, any income support, [⁴or a jobseeker's allowance].

[²(e) [⁵. . .];
[³(f) any incapacity benefit.]

AMENDMENTS

1. The Social Security (Payments on account, Overpayments and Recovery) Amendments Regulations 1988 (S.I. 1988 No. 688), reg. 2(3) (April 11, 1988).
2. The Disability Living Allowance and Disability Working Allowance (Consequential Provisions) Regulations 1991 (S.I. 1991 No. 2742), reg. 15 (April 6, 1992).
3. The Social Security (Incapacity Benefit) (Consequential and Transitional Amendments and Savings) Regulations 1991 (S.I. 1995 No. 829), reg. 21(3) (April 13, 1995).
4. The Social Security (Jobseeker's Allowance and Payments on account) (Miscellaneous Amendments) Regulations 1996 (S.I. 1996 No. 2519), reg. 3(3) (October 7, 1996).
5. The Social Security (Jobseeker's Allowance and Payments on account) (Miscellaneous Amendments) Regulations 1996 (S.I. 1996 No 2519), reg 13 (October 5, 1999)

Limitations on deductions from prescribed benefits

16.—(1) Deductions may not be made from entitlement to the benefits prescribed by paragraph (2) except as a means of recovering an overpayment of the benefit from which the deduction is to be made.

(2) The benefits [¹prescribed] for the purposes of paragraph (1) are guardian's allowance, [². . .] and child benefit.

(3) Regulation 15 shall apply without limitation to any payment of arrears of benefit other than any arrears caused by the operation of regulation 37(1) of the Claims and Payments Regulations (suspension of payments).

(4) Regulation 15 shall apply to the amount of [⁵benefit] to which a person is presently entitled only to the extent that there may, subject to paragraphs 8 and 9 of Schedule 9 to the Claims and Payments Regulations, be recovered in respect of any one benefit week—
- (a) in a case to which paragraph (5) applies, not more than the amount there specified; and
- (b) in any other case, 3 times 5 per cent of the personal allowance for a single claimant aged not less than 25, that 5 per cent being, where it is not a multiple of 5 pence, rounded to the next higher such multiple.

[⁶(4A) Paragraph (4) shall apply to the following benefits—
- (a) income support;

Social Security (Payments on Account, etc.) Regulations 1988

   (b) an income-based jobseeker's allowance;
   (c) where, if there was no entitlement to a contribution-based jobseeker's allowance, there would be entitlement to an income-based jobseeker's allowance at the same rate, a contribution-based jobseeker's allowance.]

(5) Where the person responsible for the misrepresentation of or failure to disclose a material fact has, by reason thereof, been found guilty of an offence under section 55 of the Act [SSAA, s.112] or under any other enactment, or has made a written statement after caution in admission of deception or fraud for the purpose of obtaining benefit, the amount mentioned in paragraph (4)(a) shall be 4 times 5 per cent. of the personal allowance for a single claimant aged not less than 25, that 5 per cent being, where it is not a multiple of 10 pence, rounded to the nearest such multiple or, if it is a multiple of 5 pence but not of 10 pence, the next higher multiple of 10 pence.

[⁶(5A) Regulation 15 shall apply to an amount of a contribution-based jobseeker's allowance, other than a contribution-based jobseeker's allowance to which paragraph (4) applies in accordance with paragraph (4A)(c), to which a person is presently entitled only to the extent that there may, subject to paragraphs 8 and 9 of Schedule 9 to the Claims and Payments Regulations be recovered in respect of any one benefit week a sum equal to one third of the age-related amount applicable to the claimant under section 4(1)(a) of the Jobseekers Act 1995.

(5B) For the purposes of paragraph (5A) where the sum that would otherwise fall to be deducted includes a fraction of a penny, the sum to be deducted shall be rounded down to the nearest whole penny.]

   (6) [⁵Where—
   (a) in the calculation of the income of a person to whom income support is payable, the amount of earnings or other income falling to be taken into account is reduced by paragraphs 4 to 9 of Schedule 8 to the Income Support Regulations (sums to be disregarded in the calculation of earnings) or paragraphs 15 and 16 of Schedule 9 to those Regulations (sums to be disregarded in the calculation of income other than earnings); or
   (b) in the calculation of the income of a person to whom income-based jobseeker's allowance is payable, the amount of earnings or other income falling to be taken into account is reduced by paragraphs 5 to 12 of Schedule 6 to the Jobseeker's Allowance Regulations (sums to be disregarded in the calculation of earnings) or paragraphs 15 and 17 of Schedule 7 to those Regulations (sums to be disregarded in the calculation of income other than earnings),

the weekly amount] applicable under paragraph (4) may be increased by not more than half the amount of the reduction, and any increase under this paragraph has priority over any increase which would, but for this paragraph, be made under paragraph 6(5) of Schedule 9 to the Claims and Payments Regulations.

(7) Regulation 15 shall not be applied to a specified benefit so as to reduce the benefit in any one benefit week to less than 10 pence.

(8) In this regulation—

(S.I. 1988 No. 664, Reg. 16) (as amended)

"benefit week" means the week corresponding to the week in respect of which the benefit is paid;

"personal allowance for a single claimant aged not less than 25" means the amount specified in paragraph 1(1)(c) of column 2 of Schedule 2 to the Income Support Regulations [⁵or, in the case of a person who is entitled to income-based jobseeker's allowance, the amount for the time being specified in paragraph 1(1)(e) of column (2) of Schedule 1 to the Jobseeker's Allowance Regulations;]

[⁴"specified benefit" means—
- (a) in respect of any period during which benefit is paid by means of an instrument of payment, [⁶a jobseeker's allowance, or] income support either alone or together with any [⁵ . . .] [⁶ . . .] incapacity benefit, retirement pension or severe disablement allowance which is paid by means of the same instrument of payment; and
- (b) in respect of any period during which benefit is paid by means of an instrument for benefit payment, [⁶a jobseeker's allowance] income support and, where paid concurrently with income support, [⁵ . . .] [⁶ . . .] incapacity benefit, retirement pension or severe disablement allowance [⁶ . . .];

[⁷but does not include any sum payable by way of child maintenance bonus in accordance with section 10 of the Child Support Act 1995 and the [⁸Social Security (Child Maintenance Bonus)] Regulations 1996;]]

"written statement after caution" means—
- (i) in England and Wales, a written statement made in accordance with the Police and Criminal Evidence Act 1984 (Codes of Practice) (No. 1) Order 1985, or, before that Order came into operation, the Judges Rules;
- (ii) in Scotland, a written statement duly witnessed by two persons.

AMENDMENTS

1. The Social Security (Payments on account, Overpayments and Recovery) Amendments Regulations 1988 (S.I. 1988 No. 688), reg. 2(4) (April 11, 1988).

2. The Disability Living Allowance and Disability Working Allowance (Consequential Provisions) Regulations 1991 (S.I. 1991 No. 2742), reg. 15 (April 6, 1992).

3. The Social Security (Incapacity Benefit) (Consequential and Transitional Amendments and Savings) Regulations 1995 (S.I. 1995 No. 829), reg. 21(4) (April 13, 1995).

4. The Social Security (Claims and Payments, etc.) Amendment Regulations 1996 (S.I. 1996 No. 672), reg. 4 (April 4, 1996).

5. The Social Security and Child Support (Jobseeker's Allowance) (Consequential Amendments) Regulations 1996 (S.I. 1996 No. 1345), reg. 23(4) (October 7, 1996).

6. The Social Security (Jobseeker's Allowance and Payments on account) (Miscellaneous Amendments) Regulations 1996 (S.I. 1996 No. 2519), reg. 3(4) (October 7, 1996).

7. The Social Security (Child Maintenance Bonus) Regulations 1996 (S.I. 1996 No. 3195), reg. 16(3) (April 7, 1997).

8. The Social Security (Miscellaneous Amendments) Regulations 1997 (S.I. 1997 No. 454), reg. 8(10) (April 6, 1997).

Recovery from couples

4.466 **17.** In the case of an overpayment of income support [², or income-based jobseeker's allowance] [¹, family credit or disability working allowance] to one of a married or unmarried couple, the amount recoverable by deduction, in accordance with regulation 15, may be recovered by deduction from income support [², or income-based jobseeker's allowance] [¹, family credit or disability working allowance] payable to either of them, provided that the two of them are a married or unmarried couple at the date of the deduction.

AMENDMENTS

1. The Disability Living Allowance and Disability Working Allowance (Consequential Provisions) Regulations 1991 (S.I. 1991 No. 2742), reg. 15 (April 6, 1992).
2. The Social Security and Child Support (Jobseeker's Allowance) (Consequential Amendments) Regulations 1996 (S.I. 1996 No. 1345), reg. 23(5) and (6) (October 7, 1996).

PART VIII

RECOVERY BY DEDUCTIONS FROM EARNINGS FOLLOWING TRADE DISPUTE

Recovery by deductions from earnings

4.467 **18.**—(1) Any sum paid to a person on an award of income support made to him by virtue of section 23(8) of the Act [SSCBA, s.127] (effect of return to work after a trade dispute) shall be recoverable from him in accordance with this Part of these Regulations.

(2) In this Part, unless the context otherwise requires—

"available earnings" means the earnings, including any remuneration paid by or on behalf of an employer to an employee who is for the time being unable to work owing to sickness, which remain payable to a claimant on any pay-day after deduction by his employer of all amounts lawfully deductible by the employer otherwise than by virtue of a deduction notice;

"claimant" means a person to whom an award is made by virtue of section 23(8) of the Act [SSCBA, s.127];

"deduction notice" means a notice under regulation 20 or 25;

"employment" means employment (including employment which has been suspended but not terminated) in remunerative work, and related expressions shall be construed accordingly;

"pay-day" means an occasion on which earnings are paid to a claimant;

"protected earnings" means protected earnings as determined by an adjudicating authority, in accordance with regulation 19(2), under regulation 19(1)(a) or 24;

"recoverable amount" means the amount (determined in accordance with regulation 20(3) or (5) or regulation 25(2)(a)) by reference to which deductions are to be made by an employer from a claimant's earnings by virtue of a deduction notice;

"repaid by the claimant" means paid by the claimant directly to the Secretary of State by way of repayment of income support otherwise recoverable under this Part of these Regulations.

(3) Any notice or other document required or authorised to be given or sent to any person under the provisions of this Part shall be deemed to have been given or sent if it was sent by post to that person in accordance with paragraph (6) of regulation 27 where that regulation applies and, in any other case, at his ordinary or last known address or in the case of an employer at the last place of business where the claimant to which it relates is employed, and if so sent to have been given or sent on the day on which it was posted.

Award and protected earnings

19.—(1) Where an adjudicating authority determines that a person claiming income support is entitled by virtue of section 23(8) of the Act [SSCBA, s.127] (effect of return to work after a trade dispute) and makes an award to him accordingly he shall determine the claimant's protected earnings (that is to say the amount below which his actual earnings must not be reduced by any deduction made under this Part).

(2) The adjudicating authority shall include in his decision—
  (a) the amount of income support awarded together with a statement that the claimant is a person entitled by virtue of section 23(8) of the Act [SSCBA, s.127] and that accordingly any sum paid to him on that award will be recoverable from him as provided in this Part;
  (b) the amount of the claimant's protected earnings, and
  (c) a statement of the claimant's duty under regulation 28 (duty to give notice of cessation or resumption of employment).

[¹(3) The protected earnings of the claimant shall be the sum determined by—
  (a) taking the sum specified in paragraph (4),
  (b) adding the sum specified in paragraph (5), and
  (c) subtracting from the result any child benefit which falls to be taken into account in calculating his income for the purposes of Part V of the Income Support Regulations.]

(4) The sum referred to in paragraph (3)(a) shall be the aggregate of the amounts calculated under regulation 17(a) to (d), 18(a) to (e), 20 or 21, as the case may be, of the Income Support Regulations.

(5) The sum referred to in paragraph (3)(b) shall be £27 except where the sum referred to in paragraph (3)(a) includes an amount calculated under regulation 20 in which case the sum shall be £8.00.

AMENDMENT

1. The Social Security (Payments on account, Overpayments and Recovery) Amendments Regulations 1988 (S.I. 1988 No. 688), reg. 2(5) (April 11, 1988).

Service and contents of deduction notices

4.469

20.—(1) Where the amount of income support has not already been repaid by the claimant, the Secretary of State shall serve a deduction notice on the employer of the claimant.

(2) A deduction notice shall contain the following particulars—
  (a) particulars enabling the employer to identify the claimant;
  (b) the recoverable amount;
  (c) the claimant's protected earnings as specified in the notification of award.

(3) Subject to paragraph (5) the recoverable amount shall be—
  (a) the amount specified in the decision as having been awarded to the claimant by way of income support; reduced by
  (b) the amount (if any) which has been repaid by the claimant before the date of the deduction notice.

(4) If a further award relating to the claimant is made the Secretary of State shall cancel the deduction notice (giving written notice of the cancellation to the employer and the claimant) and serve on the employer a further deduction notice.

(5) The recoverable amount to be specified in the further deduction notice shall be the sum of—
  (a) the amount determined by applying paragraph (3) to the further award; and
  (b) the recoverable amount specified in the cancelled deduction notice less any part of that amount which before the date of the further notice has already been deducted by virtue of the cancelled notice or repaid by the claimant.

Period for which deduction notice has effect

4.470

21.—(1) A deduction notice shall come into force when it is served on the employer of the claimant to whom it relates and shall cease to have effect as soon as any of the following conditions is fulfilled—
  (a) the notice is cancelled by virtue of regulation 20(4) or paragraph (2) of this regulation;
  (b) the claimant ceases to be in the employment of the person on whom the notice was served;
  (c) the aggregate of—
    (i) any part of the recoverable amount repaid by the claimant on or after the date of the deduction notice, and
    (ii) the total amount deducted by virtue of the notice, reaches the recoverable amount;
  (d) there has elapsed a period of 26 weeks beginning with the date of the notice.

(2) The Secretary of State may at any time give a direction in writing cancelling a deduction notice and—
  (a) he shall cause a copy of the direction to be served on the employer concerned and on the claimant;
  (b) the direction shall take effect when a copy of it is served on the employer concerned.

(S.I. 1988 No. 664, Reg. 21) (as amended)

Effect of deduction notice

22.—(1) Where a deduction notice is in force the following provisions of this regulation shall apply as regards any relevant pay-day.

(2) Where a claimant's earnings include any bonus, commission or other similar payment which is paid other than on a day on which the remainder of his earnings is paid, then in order to calculate his available earnings for the purposes of this regulation any such bonus, commission or other similar payment shall be treated as being paid to him on the next day of payment of the remainder of his earnings instead of on the day of actual payment.

(3) If on a relevant pay-day a claimant's available earnings—
(a) do not exceed his protected earnings by at least £1, no deduction shall be made;
(b) do exceed his protected earnings by at least £1, his employer shall deduct from the claimant's available earnings one half of the excess over his protected earnings,

so however that where earnings are paid other than weekly the amount of the protected earnings and the figure of £1 shall be adjusted accordingly, in particular—
(c) where earnings are paid monthly, they shall for this purpose be treated as paid every five weeks (and the protected earnings and the figure of £1 accordingly multiplied by five);
(d) where earnings are paid daily, the protected earnings and the figure of £1 shall be divided by five,

and if, in any case to which sub-paragraph (c) or (d) does not apply, there is doubt as to the adjustment to be made this shall be determined by the Secretary of State on the application of the employer or the claimant.

(4) Where on a relevant pay-day earnings are payable to the claimant in respect of more than one pay-day the amount of the protected earnings and the figure of £1 referred to in the preceding paragraph, adjusted where appropriate in accordance with the provisions of that paragraph, shall be multiplied by the number of pay-days to which the earnings relate.

(5) Notwithstanding anything in paragraph (3)—
(a) the employer shall not make a deduction on a relevant pay-day if the claimant satisfies him that up to that day he has not obtained payment of the income support to which the deduction notice relates;
(b) the employer shall not on any relevant pay-day deduct from the claimant's earnings by virtue of the deduction notice an amount greater than the excess of the recoverable amount over the aggregate of all such amounts as, in relation to that notice, are mentioned in regulation 21(1)(c)(i) and (ii); and
(c) where the amount of any deduction which by this regulation the employer is required to make would otherwise include a fraction of 1p, that amount shall be reduced by that fraction.

(6) For the purpose of this regulation "relevant pay-day" means any pay-day beginning with—

4.471

(a) the first pay-day falling after the expiration of the period of one month from the date on which the deduction notice comes into force; or
(b) if the employer so chooses, any earlier pay-day after the notice has come into force.

Increase of amount of award on appeal or [¹ otherwise]

4.472   23. If the amount of the award is increased, whether on appeal or [¹ otherwise], this Part shall have effect as if on the date on which the amount of the award was increased—
(a) the amount of the increase was the recoverable amount; and
(b) the claimant's protected earnings [¹, where a notice of variation of protected earnings is given under regulation 24, were the earnings stated in the notice]

AMENDMENTS

1. The Social Security Act 1998 (Commencement No. 12, and Consequential and Transitional Provisions) Order 1999 (S.I. 1999 No 3178), sched.9 (November 29, 1999)

A [¹ Notice of variation] of protected earnings

4.473   [¹ . . .]   24.—(1) [¹. . .]
[¹ (2) The Secretary of State shall give a claimant's employer written notice varying the deduction notice where a decision as to a claimant's protected earnings is revised or superseded.]
(3) Variation of a deduction notice under paragraph (2) shall take effect either from the end of the period of 10 working days beginning with the day on which notice of the variation is given to the employer or, if the employer so chooses, at any earlier time after notice is given.

AMENDMENT

1. The Social Security Act 1998 (Commencement No. 12 and Consequential and Transitional Provisions) Order 1999 (S.I. 1999 No 3178), Sched. 9 (November 29, 1999)

Power to serve further deduction notice on resumption of employment

4.474   25.—(1) Where a deduction notice has ceased to have effect by reason of the claimant ceasing to be in the employment of the person on whom the notice was served, the Secretary of State may, if he thinks fit, serve a further deduction notice on any person by whom the claimant is for the time being employed.
(2) Notwithstanding anything in the foregoing provisions of these Regulations, in any such deduction notice—
(a) the recoverable amount shall be equal to the recoverable amount as specified in the previous deduction notice less the aggregate of—

(i) the total of any amounts required to be deducted by virtue of that notice, and
(ii) any additional part of that recoverable amount repaid by the claimant on or after the date of that notice,

or, where this regulation applies in respect of more than one such previous notice, the aggregate of the amounts as so calculated in respect of each such notice;

(b) the amount specified as the claimant's protected earnings shall be the same as that so specified in the last deduction notice relating to him which was previously in force or as subsequently [¹ raned].

AMENDMENT

1. The Social Security Act 1998 (Commencement No. 12 and Consequential and Transitional Provisions) Order 1999 (S.I. 1999 No 3178), Sched 9 (November 29, 1999)

Right of Secretary of State to recover direct from claimant

26. Where [¹, at any time, it is not practicable for the Secretary of State] by means of a deduction notice, to effect recovery of the recoverable amount or of so much of that amount as remains to be recovered from the claimant, the amount which remains to be recovered shall, by virtue of this regulation, be recoverable from the claimant by the Secretary of State.

AMENDMENT

1. The Social Security Act 1998 (Commencement No. 12 and Consequential and Transitional Provisions) Order 1999 (S.I. 1999 No 3178), Sched. 9 (November 29, 1999).

Duties and liabilities of employers

27.—(1) An employer shall keep a record of the available earnings of each claimant who is an employee in respect of whom a deduction notice is in force and of the payments which he makes in pursuance of the notice.

(2) A record of every deduction made by an employer under a deduction notice on any pay-day shall be given or sent by him to the Secretary of State, together with payment of the amount deducted, by not later than the 19th day of the following month.

(3) Where by reason only of the circumstances mentioned in regulation 22(5)(a) the employer makes no deduction from a claimant's weekly earnings on any pay-day he shall within 10 working days after that pay-day give notice of that fact to the Secretary of State.

(4) Where a deduction notice is cancelled by virtue of regulation 20(4) or 21(2) or ceases to have effect by virtue of regulation 21(1) the employer shall within 10 working days after the date on which the notice is cancelled or, as the case may be, ceases to have effect—

(a) return the notice to the Secretary of State and, where regulation 21(1) applies, give notice of the reason for its return;

Social Security (Payments on Account, etc.) Regulations 1988

(b) give notice, in relation to each relevant pay-day (as defined in regulation 22(6)), of the available earnings of the claimant and of any deduction made from those earnings.

(5) If on any pay-day to which regulation 22(3)(b) applies the employer makes no deduction from a claimant's available earnings, or makes a smaller deduction than he was thereby required to make, and in consequence any amount is not deducted while the deduction notice, or any further notice which under regulation 20(4) cancels that notice, has effect—

(a) the amount which is not deducted shall, without prejudice to any other method of recovery from the claimant or otherwise, be recoverable from the employer by the Secretary of State; and

(b) any amount so recovered shall, for the purposes of these Regulations, be deemed to have been repaid by the claimant.

(6) All records and notices to which this regulation applies shall given or sent to the Secretary of State, on a form approved by him, at such office of the [¹Department of Social Security] as he may direct.

AMENDMENT

1. The Transfer of Functions (Health and Social Security) Order 1988 (S.I. 1988 No. 1843), art. 3(4) (November 28, 1988).

Claimants to give notice of cessation or resumption of employment

4.477   **28.**—(1) Where a claimant ceases to be in the employment of a person on whom a deduction notice relating to him has been duly served knowing that the full amount of the recoverable amount has not been deducted from his earnings or otherwise recovered by the Secretary of State, he shall give notice within 10 working days to the Secretary of State of his address and of the date of such cessation of employment.

(2) Where on or after such cessation the claimant resumes employment (whether with the same or some other employer) he shall within 10 working days give notice to the Secretary of State of the name of the employer and of the address of his place of employment.

Failure to notify

4.478   **29.** If a person fails to comply with any requirement under regulation 27 or 28 to give notice of any matter to the Secretary of State he shall be guilty of an offence and liable on summary conviction to a fine not exceeding—

(a) for any one offence, level 3 on the standard scale; or

(b) for an offence of continuing any such contravention, £40 for each day on which it is so continued.

(S.I. 1988 No. 664, Reg. 30) (as amended)

PART IX

REVOCATION, TRANSITIONAL PROVISIONS AND SAVINGS

Revocation

30. Subject to regulation 31(3), the Social Security (Payments on account, Overpayments and Recovery) Regulations 1987 are hereby revoked except for regulations 19 and the Schedule thereto and 20(2) and (3) which shall continue in force.

4.479

Transitional provisions and savings

31.—(1) These Regulations shall apply to any question relating to the repayment or recoverability of family income supplement and supplementary benefit as though the definition of "benefit" in regulation 1(2) included references to both those benefits and as though any reference in Part VIII to income support was a reference to income support and supplementary benefit.

4.480

(2) Anything done or begun under the Social Security (Payments on account, Overpayments and Recovery) Regulations 1987 or Part IV of the Supplementary Benefit (Trade Disputes and Recovery from Earnings) Regulations 1980 shall be deemed to have been done or, as the case may be, continued under the corresponding provisions of these Regulations.

(3) Where this regulation applies—
(a) regulation 3(b)(ii) shall have effect as though for the words "the same benefit" there were substituted the words "income support" if the interim payment was of supplementary benefit and "family credit" if the interim payment was of family income supplement;
(b) regulation 13(b) shall have effect as though for the words "income support" there were substituted the words "supplementary benefit".

(4) In this Part—
"family income supplement" means benefit under the Family Income Supplements Act 1970;
"supplementary benefit" means benefit under Part I of the Supplementary Benefits Act 1976.

The Social Security (Recovery of Benefits) Regulations 1997

(S.I. 1997 No. 2205) *(as amended)*

ARRANGEMENT OF REGULATIONS

1. Citation, commencement and interpretation.
2. Exempted trusts and payments.

4.481

The Social Security (Recovery of Benefits) Regulations 1997

3. Information to be provided by the compensator.
4. Information to be provided by the injured person.
5. Information to be provided by the employer.
6. Provision of information.
7. Application for a certificate of recoverable benefits.
8. Payments into court.
9. Reduction of compensation: complex cases.
10. Structured settlements.
11. Adjustments.
12. Transitional provisions.

The Secretary of State for Social Security, in exercise of the powers conferred by section 189(4), (5) and (6) of the Social Security Administration Act 1992 and sections 4(9), 14(2), (3) and (4), 16(1) and (2), 18, 19, 21(3), 23(1), (2), (5) and (7), 29 and 32 of, and paragraphs 4 and 8 of Schedule 1 to, the Social Security (Recovery of Benefits) Act 1997, and of all other powers enabling her in that behalf, hereby makes the following Regulations:

Citation, commencement and interpretation

4.482 1.—(1) These Regulations may be cited as the Social Security (Recovery of Benefits) Regulations 1997 and shall come into force on 6th October 1997.

(2) In these Regulations—

"the 1992 Act" means the Social Security Administration Act 1992;

"the 1997 Act" means the Social Security (Recovery of Benefits) Act 1997;

"commencement day" means the day these Regulations come into force;

"compensator" means a person making a compensation payment;

"Compensation Recovery Unit" means the Compensation Recovery Unit of the Department of Social Security at Reyrolle Building, Hebburn, Tyne and Wear NE31 1XP.

(3) A reference in these Regulations to a numbered section or Schedule is a reference, unless the context otherwise requires, to that section of or Schedule to the 1997 Act.

Exempted trusts and payments

4.483 2.—(1) The following trusts are prescribed for the purposes of paragraph 4 of Schedule 1—

(a) the Macfarlane Trust established on 10th March 1988 partly out of funds provided by the Secretary of State to the Haemophilia Society for the relief of poverty or distress among those suffering from haemophilia;

(b) the Macfarlane (Special Payments) Trust established on 29th January 1990 partly out of funds provided by the Secretary of State, for the benefit of certain persons suffering from haemophilia;

(c) the Macfarlane (Special Payments) (No. 2) Trust established on

(S.I. 1997 No. 2205, Reg. 2) (as amended)

3rd May 1991 partly out of funds provided by the Secretary of State, for the benefit of certain persons suffering from haemophilia and other beneficiaries;
(d) the Eileen Trust established on 29th March 1993 out of funds provided by the Secretary of State for the benefit of persons eligible for payment in accordance with its provisions.

(2) The following payments are prescribed for the purposes of paragraph 8 of Schedule 1—
(a) any payment to the extent that it is made—
   (i) in consequence of an action under the Fatal Accidents Act 1976; or
   (ii) in circumstances where, had an action been brought, it would have been brought under that Act;
(b) any payment to the extent that it is made in respect of a liability arising by virtue of section 1 of the Damages (Scotland) Act 1976;
(c) any payment made under the Vaccine Damage Payments Act 1979 to or in respect of the injured person;
(d) any award of compensation made to or in respect of the injured person under the Criminal Injuries Compensation Act 1995 or by the Criminal Injuries Compensation Board under the Criminal Injuries Compensation Scheme 1990 or any earlier scheme;
(e) any compensation payment made by British Coal in accordance with the NCB Pneumoconiosis Compensation Scheme set out in the Schedule to an agreement made on the 13th September 1974 between the National Coal Board, the National Union of Mine Workers, the National Association of Colliery Overmen Deputies and Shot-firers and the British Association of Colliery Management;
(f) any payment made to the injured person in respect of sensorineural hearing loss where the loss is less than than 50 dB in one or both ears;
(g) any contractual amount paid to an employee by an employer of his in respect of a period of incapacity for work;
(h) any payment made under the National Health Service (Injury Benefits) Regulations 1995 or the National Health Service (Scotland) (Injury Benefits) Regulations 1974;
(i) any payment made by or on behalf of the Secretary of State for the benefit of persons eligible for payment in accordance with the provisions of a scheme established by him on 24th April 1992 or, in Scotland, on 10th April 1992.

Information to be provided by the compensator

3.—The following information is prescribed for the purposes of section 23(1):
(a) the full name and address of the injured person;
(b) where known, the date of birth or national insurance number of that person, or both if both are known;
(c) where the liability arises, or is alleged to arise, in respect of an accident or injury, the date of the accident or injury;

(d) the nature of the accident, injury or disease; and
(e) where known, and where the relevant period may include a period prior to 6th April 1994, whether, at the time of the accident or injury or diagnosis of the disease, the person was employed under a contract of service, and, if he was, the name and address of his employer at that time and the person's payroll number.

Information to be provided by the injured person

4.485 **4.** The following information is prescribed for the purposes of section 23(2):
(a) whether the accident, injury or disease resulted from any action taken by another person, or from any failure of another person to act, and, if so, the full name and address of that other person;
(b) whether the injured person has claimed or may claim a compensation payment, and, if so, the full name and address of the person against whom the claim was or may be made;
(c) the amount of any compensation payment and the date on which it was made;
(d) the listed benefits claimed, and for each benefit the date from which it was first claimed and the amount received in the period beginning with that date and ending with the date the information is sent;
(e) in the case of a person who has received statutory sick pay during the relevant period and prior to 6th April 1994, the name and address of any employer who made those payments to him during the relevant period and the dates the employment with that employer began and ended; and
(f) any changes in the medical diagnosis relating to the condition arising from the accident, injury or disease.

Information to be provided by the employer

4.486 **5.** The following information is prescribed for the purposes of section 23(5):
(a) the amount of any statutory sick pay the employer has paid to the injured person since the first day of the relevant period and before 6th April 1994;
(b) the date the liability to pay such statutory sick pay first arose and the rate at which it was payable;
(c) the date on which such liability terminated; and
(d) the causes of incapacity for work during any period of entitlement to statutory sick pay during the relevant period and prior to 6th April 1994.

Provision of information

4.487 **6.** A person required to give information to the Secretary of State under regulations 3 to 5 shall do so by sending it to the Compensation Recovery Unit not later than 14 days after—
(a) where he is a person to whom regulation 3 applies, the date on

(S.I. 1997 No. 2205, Reg. 6) (as amended)

which he receives a claim for compensation from the injured person in respect of the accident, injury or disease;
(b) where he is a person to whom regulation 4 or 5 applies, the date on which the Secretary of State requests the information from him.

Application for a certificate of recoverable benefits

7.—(1) The following particulars are prescribed for the purposes of section 21(3)(a) (particulars to be included in an application for a certificate of recoverable benefits):   4.488
  (a) the full name and address of the injured person;
  (b) the date of birth and, where known, the national insurance number of that person;
  (c) where the liability arises or is alleged to arise in respect of an accident or injury, the date of the accident or injury;
  (d) the nature of the accident, injury or disease;
  (e) where the person liable, or alleged to be liable, in respect of the accident, injury or disease, is the employer of the injured person, or has been such an employer, the information prescribed by regulation 5.
(2) An application for a certificate of recoverable benefits is to be treated for the purposes of the 1997 Act as received by the Secretary of State on the day on which it is received by the Compensation Recovery Unit, or if the application is received after normal business hours, or on a day which is not a normal business day at that office, on the next such day.

Payments into court

8.—(1) Subject to the provisions of this regulation, where a party to an action makes a payment into court which, had it been paid directly to another party to the action ("the relevant party"), would have constituted a compensation payment—   4.489
  (a) the making of that payment shall be treated for the purposes of the 1997 Act as the making of a compensation payment;
  (b) a current certificate of recoverable benefits shall be lodged with the payment; and
  (c) where the payment is calculated under section 8, the compensator must give the relevant party the information specified in section 9(1), instead of the person to whom the payment is made.
(2) The liability under section 6(1) to pay an amount equal to the total amount of the recoverable benefits shall not arise until the person making the payment into court has been notified that the whole or any part of the payment into court has been paid out of court to or for the relevant party.
(3) Where a payment into court in satisfaction of his claim is accepted by the relevant party in the initial period, then as respects the compensator in question, the relevant period shall be taken to have ended, if it has not done so already, on the day on which the payment into court

(or if there were two or more such payments, the last of them) was made.

(4) Where, after the expiry of the initial period, the payment into court is accepted in satisfaction of the relevant party's claim by consent between the parties, the relevant period shall end, if it has not done so already, on the date on which application to the court for the payment is made.

(5) Where, after the expiry of the initial period, payment out of court is made wholly or partly to or for the relevant party in accordance with an order of the court and in satisfaction of his claim, the relevant period shall end, if it has not done so already, on the date of that order.

(6) In paragraphs (3), (4) and (5), "the initial period" means the period of 21 days after the receipt by the relevant party to the action of notice of the payment into court having been made.

(7) Where a payment into court is paid out wholly to or for the party who made the payment (otherwise than to or for the relevant party to the action) the making of the payment into court shall cease to be regarded as the making of a compensation payment.

(8) A current certificate of recoverable benefits in paragraph (1) means one that is in force as described in section 4(4).

Reduction of compensation: complex cases

4.490   9.—(1) This regulation applies where—
(a) a compensation payment in the form of a lump sum (an "earlier payment") has been made to or in respect of the injured person; and
(b) subsequently another such payment (a "later payment") is made to or in respect of the same injured person in consequence of the same accident, injury or disease.

(2) In determining the liability under section 6(1) arising in connection with the making of the later payment, the amount referred to in that subsection shall be reduced by any amount paid in satisifaction of that liability as it arose in connection with the earlier payment.

(3) Where—
(a) a payment made in satisfaction of the liability under section 6(1) arising in connection with an earlier payment is not reflected in the certificate of recoverable benefits in force at the time of a later payment, and
(b) in consequence, the aggregate of payments made in satisifaction of the liability exceeds what it would have been had that payment been so reflected,
the Secretary of State shall pay the compensator who made the later payment an amount equal to the excess.

(4) Where—
(a) a compensator receives a payment under paragraph (3), and
(b) the amount of the compensation payment made by him was calculated under section 8,
then the compensation payment shall be recalculated under section 8, and the compensator shall pay the amount of the increase (if any) to the person to whom the compensation payment was made.

(5) Where both the earlier payment and the later payment are made by the same compensator, he may—
   (a) aggregate the gross amounts of the payments made by him;
   (b) calculate what would have been the reduction made under section 8(3) if that aggregate amount had been paid at the date of the last payment on the basis that—
      (i) so much of the aggregate amount as is attributable to a head of compensation listed in column (1) of Schedule 2 shall be taken to be the part of the gross amount which attributable to that head, and
      (ii) the amount of any recoverable benefits shown against any head in column (2) of that Schedule shall be taken to be the amount determined in accordance with the most recent certificate of recoverable benefits;
   (c) deduct from that reduction calculated under sub-paragraph (b) the amount of the reduction under section 8(3) from any earlier payment; and
   (d) deduct from the latest gross payment the net reduction calculated under sub-paragraph (c) (and accordingly the latest payment may be nil).

(6) Where the Secretary of State is making a refund under paragraph (3), he shall send to the compensator (with the refund) and to the person to whom the compensation payment was made a statement showing—
   (a) the total amount that has already been paid by that compensator to the Secretary of State;
   (b) the amount that ought to have been paid by that compensator; and
   (c) the amount to be repaid to that compensator by the Secretary of State.

(7) Where the reduction of a compensation payment is recalculated by virtue of paragraph (4) or (5) the compensator shall give notice of the calculation to the injured person.

Structured settlements

10.—(1) This regulation applies where—
   (a) in final settlement of an injured person's claim, an agreement is entered into—
      (i) for the making of periodical payments (whether of an income or capital nature); or
      (ii) for the making of such payments and lump sum payments; and
   (b) apart from the provisions of this regulation, those payments would fall to be treated for the purposes of the 1997 Act as compensation payments.

(2) Where this regulation applies, the provisions of the 1997 Act and these Regulations shall be modified in the following way—
   (a) the compensator in question shall be taken to have made on that day a single compensation payment;

(b) the relevant period in the case of the compensator in question shall be taken to end (if it has not done so already) on the day of settlement;
(c) payments under the agreement referred to in paragraph (1)(a) shall be taken not to be compensation payments;
(d) paragraphs (5) and (7) of regulation 11 shall not apply.

(3) Where any further payment falls to be made to or in respect of the injured person otherwise than under the agreement in question, paragraph (2) shall be disregarded for the purpose of determining the end of the relevant period in relation to that further payment.

(4) In any case where—
(a) the person making the periodical payments ("the secondary party") does so in pursuance of arrangements entered into with another ("primary party") (as in a case where the primary party purchases an annuity for the injured person from the secondary party), and
(b) apart from those arrangements, the primary party would have been regarded as the compensator,

then for the purposes of the 1997 Act, the primary party shall be regarded as the compensator and the secondary party shall not be so regarded.

(5) In this regulation "the day of settlement" means—
(a) if the agreement referred to in paragraph (1)(a) is approved by a court, the day on which that approval is given; and
(b) in any other case, the day on which the agreement is entered into.

Adjustments

11.—(1) Where the conditions specified in subsection (1) and paragraphs (a) and (b) of subsection (2) of section 14 are satisfied, the Secretary of State shall pay the difference between the amount that has been paid and the amount that ought to have been paid to the compensator.

(2) Where the conditions specified in subsection (1) and paragraphs (a) and (b) of subsection (3) of section 14 are satisfied, the compensator shall pay the difference between the total amounts paid and the amount that ought to have been paid to the Secretary of State.

(3) Where the Secretary of State is making a refund under paragraph (1), or demanding payment of a further amount under paragraph (2), he shall send to the compensator (with the refund or demand) and to the person to whom the compensation payment was made a statement showing—
(a) the total amount that has already been paid to the Secretary of State;
(b) the amount that ought to have been paid; and
(c) the difference, and whether a repayment by the Secretary of State or a further payment to him is required.

(4) This paragraph applies where—
(a) the amount of the compensation payment made by the compensator was calculated under section 8; and
(b) the Secretary of State has made a payment under paragraph (1).

(S.I. 1997 No. 2205, Reg. 11) (as amended)

(5) Where paragraph (4) applies, the amount of the compensation payment shall be recalculated under section 8 to take account of the fresh certificate of recoverable benefits and the compensator shall pay the amount of the increase (if any) to the person to whom the compensation payment was made.

(6) This paragraph applies where—
(a) the amount of the compensation payment made by the compensator was calculated under section 8;
(b) the compensator has made a payment under paragraph (2); and
(c) the fresh certificate of recoverable benefits issued after the review or appeal was required as a result of the injured person or other person to whom the compensation payment was made supplying to the compensator information knowing it to be incorrect or insufficient with the intent of enhancing the compensation payment calculated under section 8, and the compensator supplying that information to the Secretary of State without knowing it to be incorrect or insufficient.

(7) Where paragraph (6) applies, the compensator may recalculate the compensation payment under section 8 to take account of the fresh certificate of recoverable benefits and may require the repayment to him by the person to whom he made the compensation payment of the difference (if any) between the payment made and the payment as so recalculated.

Transitional provisions

12.—(1) In relation to a compensation payment to which by virtue of section 2 the 1997 Act applies and subject to paragraph (2), a certificate of total benefit issued under Part IV of the 1992 Act shall be treated on or after the commencement date as a certificate of recoverable benefits issued under the 1997 Act and the amount of total benefit treated as that of recoverable benefits.

(2) Paragraph (1) shall not apply to a certificate of total benefit which specifies an amount in respect of disability living allowance without specifying whether that amount was, or is likely to be, paid wholly by way of the care component or the mobility component or (if not wholly one of them) specifying the relevant amount for each component.

[¹(3) Any appeal under section 98 of the 1992 Act made on or after 6th October 1997 which has not been determined before 29th November 1999 shall be referred to an appeal tribunal constituted in accordance with paragraph (3I) below.

(3A) Any appeal duly made before 6th October 1997 which has not been referred to a medical appeal tribunal or a social security appeal tribunal shall be referred to and determined by an appeal tribunal constituted in accordance with paragraph (3I) below.

(3B) Any appeal duly made before 6th October 1997 and referred to a medical appeal tribunal shall be determined by an appeal tribunal constituted in accordance with paragraph (3I) below which shall determine all issues.

(3C) Any appeal duly made before 6th October 1997 and referred to

4.493

a social security appeal tribunal shall be determined by an appeal tribunal which shall consist of a legally qualified panel member and in making its determination, the appeal tribunal shall be bound by any decision of a medical appeal tribunal to which a question under section 98(5) of the 1992 Act was referred.

(3D) An appeal tribunal constituted in accordance with paragraph (3I) below shall completely rehear any appeal made under section 98 of the 1992 Act which stands adjourned immediately before 29th November 1999.

(3E) Where a Commissioner holds that the decision of a medical appeal tribunal or a social security appeal tribunal on an appeal made before 6th October 1997 was erroneous in law and refers the case to an appeal tribunal, that appeal tribunal shall be constituted in accordance with paragraph (3I) below and shall determine all issues in accordance with the Commissioner's direction.

(3F) Regulation 11 of the Social Security (Recoupment) Regulations 1990 ("the 1990 Regulations") and regulation 12 of those Regulations shall have effect in relation to any appeal under section 98 of the 1992 Act made on or after 6th October 1997 with the modification that for the word "chairman" in each place in which it occurs there were substituted the words "legally qualified panel member".

(3G) Regulation 13 of the 1990 Regulations shall have effect in relation to any appeal under section 98 of the 1992 Act made on or after 6th October 1997.

(3H) Any other transitional question arising from an appeal made under section 98 of the 1992 Act in consequence of the coming into force of the Social Security and Child Support (Decisions and Appeals) Regulations 1999 ("the 1999 Regulations") shall be determined by a legally qualified panel member who may for this purpose give such directions consistent with these regulations as are necessary.

(3I) For the purposes of paragraphs (3) to (3B) and (3E) above an appeal tribunal shall be constituted under Chapter I of Part I of the Social Security Act 1998 as though the appeal were made under section 11(1)(b) of the 1997 Act.

(3J) In this regulation, "legally qualified panel member" has the meaning it bears in regulation 1(3) of the 1999 Regulations.]

(4) Paragraph (5) applies where—
(a) an amount has been paid to the Secretary of State under section 82(1)(b) of the 1992 Act,
(b) liability arises on or after the commencement day to make a payment under section 6(1), and
(c) the compensation payments which give rise to the liability to make both payments are to or in respect of the same injured person in consequence of the same accident, injury or disease.

(5) Where this paragraph applies, the liability under section 6 shall be reduced by the payment (or aggregate of the payments, if more than one) described in paragraph (4)(a).

(6) Where—
(a) a payment into court has been made on a date prior to the com-

(S.I. 1997 No. 2205, Reg. 11) (as amended)

mencement day but the initial period, as defined in section 93(6) of the 1992 Act, in relation to that payment, expires on or after the commencement day; and

(b) the payment into court is accepted by the other party to the action in the initial period,

that payment into court shall be treated as a compensation payment to which the 1992 Act, and not the 1997 Act, applies.

(7) Where a payment into court has been made prior to the commencement day, remains in court on that day and paragraph (6) does not apply, that payment into court shall be treated as a payment to which the 1997 Act applies, but paragraph (1) (b) and (c) of regulation 8 shall not apply.

AMENDMENT

1. Social Security Act 1998 (Commencement No. 12 and Consequential and Transitional Provisions) Order 1999 (S.I. 1999 No. 3178), Art. 3(17) and Sched. 17 (November 29, 1999).

INDEX

Abuse of rights, prohibition of
human rights, 3.83
Accident, notification of
industrial injuries benefit, and
generally, 1.21–1.22
Regulations, 4.6, 4.11
Accommodation costs
payment of benefit, 4.166
Adjudication of benefits
introduction, 1.46
supplementary benefits, and, 1.177
Adjustment of benefits
and see under individual benefit headings
child benefit, 1.92–1.93
child maintenance, 1.82–1.83
income support, 1.76–1.81
industrial injuries benefit
successive accidents, 4.406–4.407
overlapping benefits, 1.74–1.75
Advance claims
disability living allowance, 4.64–4.65
disability working allowance, 4.62–4.63
generally, 4.60–4.61
maternity allowance, 4.66
retirement pension, 4.67–4.68
Age addition
claims for benefit, 4.16–4.17
imprisonment, 4.382–4.383
Alienation of benefit
generally, 1.165–1.166
All work test certificate
form, 4.437–4.438
rules, 4.436
Alternative, payment in the
claims for benefit
generally, 4.54–4.55
list of benefits, 4.140
Amendment of claim
generally, 4.16–4.17
Another natural person
payment of benefits, 4.114–4.115
Appeal, notice of
acknowledgment, 4.224
decisions
correction of errors, 4.238
forfeiture rule questions, 4.237
generally, 4.236
setting aside, 4.239
supplementary, 4.240

Appeal, notice of—*cont.*
directions, 4.228
generally, 4.220
medical evidence, 4.230
response to notice or reference,
generally, 4.226
reply, 4.227
time limits, 4.221
withdrawal, 4.234
Appeals from appeals tribunal
generally, 1.309–1.313
procedure
generally, 1.316–1.324
regulations, 4.351–4.352
Appeals to appeals tribunal
appealable decisions
generally, 1.422
regulations, 4.293
appellants, 4.292
certificates of recoverable benefits, 4.299
correction of errors, 4.347–4.348
death of party, 4.311
decisions
correction of errors, 4.347–4.348
generally, 4.342–4.343
late application for statement of reasons, 4.344
record of proceedings, 4.345–4.346
setting aside, 4.349–4.350
dependant upon appeal in other cases
generally, 1.346–1.352
regulations, 4.289
extension of time limits, 4.304–4.308
generally, 1.299–1.305
issues determinable by Revenue
generally, 1.339–1.340
regulations, 4.320
medical examination
generally, 1.328–1.330
regulations, 4.324–4.325
non-disclosure of medical evidence, 4.326–4.327
oral hearings
adjournment, 4.339
directions, 4.321–4.322
expert assistance, 4.337–4.338
physical examinations, 4.340–4.341
postponement, 4.339
procedure, 4.335–4.336
record of proceedings, 4.345–4.346

629

Index

Appeals to appeals tribunal—*cont.*
  oral hearings—*cont.*
  procedure
    applications, 4.309–4.310
    determination, 4.318–4.319
    generally, 1.316–1.324
    medical examination, 4.324–4.327
    oral hearings, 4.321–4.322
    withdrawal, 4.323
    witness summons, 4.328–4.329
  record of proceedings, 4.345–4.346
  recovery of benefit, and
    generally, 1.200–1.203
    reference of questions, 1.204–1.206
    supplementary, 1.210–1.211
  re-determination, 1.306–1.308
  revision of decisions, 4.300–4.301
  setting aside decisions, 4.349–4.350
  statement of reasons
    generally, 4.342–4.343
    late application, 4.344
  striking out
    generally, 4.332
    misconceived applications, 4.334
    reinstatement, 4.333
  time limits, 4.302–4.303
  unappealable decisions
    generally, 1.411–1.421
    regulations, 4.294–4.295, 4.355–4.374
  withdrawal, 4.323
  witness summons, 4.328–4.329
Appeals from Commissioner
  generally, 1.314–1.315
Appeals to Commissioners
  applications for leave, 4.351–4.352
  dependant upon appeal in other cases
    generally, 1.346–1.352
    regulations, 4.288
  generally, 1.309–1.313
  issues determinable by Revenue, 1.339–1.340
  medical examination, 1.325–1.327
  procedure, 1.316–1.324
  recovery of benefit, and, 1.207–1.209
  unappealable decisions, 1.411–1.421
Appeals tribunals
  appointment panel
    generally, 1.274–1.275
    qualifications, 4.312, 4.375–4.378
  clerks
    functions, 4.317
    generally, 1.401
  composition, 4.313–4.316
  constitution, 1.276–1.278
  definition, 1.384
  delegation of functions, 1.406
  officers, 1.403
  President
    functions, 1.404
    generally, 1.272–1.273

Appeals tribunals—*cont.*
  remuneration, 1.402
  tenure of office, 1.401
  remuneration, 1.402
  staff, 1.403
  unification, 1.270–1.271
Application for leave to appeal
  acknowledgment, 4.224
  courts, to, 4.241
  decisions
    correction of errors, 4.238
    forfeiture rule questions, 4.237
    generally, 4.236
    setting aside, 4.239
    supplementary, 4.240
  determination, 4.219
  directions, 4.228
  generally, 4.220
  medical evidence, 4.230
  notice, 4.218
  response to notice or reference,
    generally, 4.226
    reply, 4.227
  time limits, 4.221
  withdrawal, 4.234
Appointment of third parties
  claims for benefit, 4.112–4.121
Assembly, freedom of
  human rights, 3.78
Assessment of damages
  recovery of benefit, 1.218–1.219
Assignment of benefit
  generally, 1.165–1.166
Attendance allowance
  imprisonment, 4.382–4.383
  payment of benefit, 4.96
Attendance in person
  claims for benefit, 4.52–4.53
Automated credit transfers
  overpayment of benefit, 1.66

Board of Inland Revenue
  decisions by officers, 1.256–1.257

Category A retirement pensions
  claims for benefit
    and see **Claims for benefit**
    advance claim, 4.67–4.68
    generally, 4.16–4.17
  imprisonment, 4.382–4.383
Category B retirement pensions
  claims for benefit
    and see **Claims for benefit**
    advance claim, 4.67–4.68
    generally, 4.16–4.17
  imprisonment, 4.382–4.383
Category C retirement pensions
  claims for benefit
    and see **Claims for benefit**

Index

Category C retirement pensions—*cont.*
  advance claim, 4.67–4.68
  generally, 4.16–4.17
  imprisonment, 4.382–4.383
Category D retirement pensions
  claims for benefit
  and see **Claims for benefit**
  advance claim, 4.67–4.68
  generally, 4.16–4.17
  imprisonment, 4.382–4.383
Causation
  overpayment of benefits, 1.64
Certificate of recoverable benefits
  appeals to Commissioners, 1.207–1.209
  appeals to tribunal
    generally, 1.200–1.203, 4.299
    reference of questions, 1.204–1.206
    supplementary, 1.210–1.211
  applications
    generally, 1.186–1.187
    regulations, 4.488
  contents, 1.188–1.189
  review
    generally, 1.197–1.199
    regulations, 4.271
    supplementary, 1.210–1.211
Charges on benefit
  generally, 1.165–1.166
Child benefit
  claims for payment
  and see **Claims for benefit**
    generally, 1.36–1.37
    'one' office, and, 4.195
  overpayment of benefit
    generally, 1.73
    prescribed payments, 4.452–4.455
  payment of benefit
    election, 4.162
    generally, 4.94
Child's special allowance
  imprisonment, 4.382–4.383
Christmas bonus
  generally, 1.372–1.373, 1.412
Claims for benefit
  adjudication of,
  and see **Adjudication of benefit**
    introduction, 1.46
  advance, in
    disability living allowance, 4.64–4.65
    disability working allowance, 4.62–4.63
    generally, 4.60–4.61
    maternity allowance, 4.66
    retirement pension, 4.67–4.68
  age addition, 4.16–4.17
  alternative, in the
    generally, 4.54–4.55
    list of benefits, 4.139
  amendment of claims, 4.33–4.34
  attendance in person, 4.52–4.53

Claims for benefit—*cont.*
  child benefit
    generally, 1.36–1.37
    'one' office, and, 4.195
  cold weather payments, 4.69–4.70
  council tax benefits, 1.17–1.20
  date of claim, 4.35–4.48
  date of entitlement, 4.71–4.72
  disabled person's tax credit,
    initial claims, 1.27–1.31
    repeat claims, 1.27–1.31
  disability living allowance
    advance payments, 4.64–4.65
    generally, 4.24
  disability working allowance
    advance payments, 4.62–4.63
    generally, 4.24
  duration of award,
    generally, 4.73–4.78
  emergency payments, 1.44–1.45
  evidence, 4.50–4.51
  exemptions from, 4.16–4.17
  holding information, 4.196
  incapacity benefit, 4.56
  income support
    exempt claims, 4.16–4.17
    generally, 4.18–4.19
    method, 4.23
  industrial injuries benefits
    accident notification, 1.21–1.22, 4.6, 4.11
    claimant obligations, 1.25–1.26, 4.8
    employers obligations, 4.7
    medical examination, 1.23–1.24, 4.8
    notification obligations, 1.21–1.22, 4.6
  information, provision of
    generally, 4.50–4.51
    local authorities, by, 4.197
  interchange of benefits
    generally, 4.54–4.55
    list of benefits, 4.140
  jobseeker's allowance
    exempt claims, 4.16–4.17
    generally, 4.18–4.19
    method, 4.25
    special provisions, 4.141
  local authorities, and
    child support, 4.195
    functions, 4.193–4.194
    holding information, 4.196
    provision of information, 4.197
    use and supply of information, 4.202–4.206
    war pensions, 4.195
  maternity allowance,
    advance claim, 4.66
    generally, 4.57–4.59
  maternity pay, 1.40–1.41
  method, 4.18–4.30

631

Index

Claims for benefit—*cont.*
  mortgage interest, 1.42–1.43
  necessity
    generally, 1.2–1.8
    retrospective effect, 1.9
  'one' offices
    child benefit, 4.195
    generally, 4.31–4.32
    war pensions, 4.195
  procedure
    advance claims, 4.60–4.68
    alternate claims, 4.54–4.55
    amendment, 4.33–4.34
    attendance in person, 4.52–4.53
    date of claim, 4.35–4.48
    date of entitlement, 4.71–4.72
    duration of award, 4.73–4.78
    evidence, 4.50–4.51
    generally, 4.16–4.17
    information, 4.50–4.51
    interchange of benefits, 4.54–4.55
    method, 4.18–4.30
    'one' offices, 4.31–4.32
    time of claim, 4.79–4.86
    withdrawal, 4.33–4.34
    work-focused interviews, 4.49
  retirement pensions,
    advance claim, 4.67–4.68
    generally, 4.16–4.17
  severe disablement allowance, 4.56
  sick pay, 1.38–1.39
  social fund, 1.32–1.35
  statutory maternity pay, 1.40–1.41
  statutory sick pay, 1.38–1.39
  supplementary benefits, and, 1.177
  time of claim
    generally, 4.79–4.86
    prescribed period, 4.143–4.145
  war pensions, 4.195
  widowed mother's allowance, 1.12–1.13
  widowhood benefits, 1.10–1.11
  widow's benefit, 1.12–1.13
  withdrawal of claim, 4.33–4.34
  work-focused interviews
    generally, 4.49
    local authorities, by, 4.193
    nature, 4.192
  working families tax credit, 4.22

Commissioners of Inland Revenue
  appeals from, 4.241
  appeals to
    recovery of benefit, 1.207–1.209
  application for leave to appeal
    decisions, 4.236–4.240
    determination, 4.219
    directions, 4.228
    generally, 4.217
    medical evidence, 4.230
    notice, 4.218
    withdrawal, 4.234

Commissioners of Inland Revenue—*cont.*
  application for leave to appeal to courts, 4.241
  appointment, 1.424
  correction of errors, 4.238
  decisions
    correction of errors, 4.238
    forfeiture rule questions, 4.237
    generally, 1.256–1.257, 4.236
    setting aside, 4.239
    supplementary, 4.240
  delegation of functions
    generally, 4.215
    supplementary, 1.427
  directions, 4.228
  forfeiture rule questions
    meaning, 4.212
    post-decision procedure, 4.237
  hearings
    generally, 4.232
    request for, 4.231
  irregularities, effect of, 4.235
  linked case notice, 4.229
  medical evidence, non-disclosure of, 4.230
  notice of appeal
    acknowledgment, 4.224
    decisions, 4.236–4.240
    directions, 4.228
    generally, 4.220
    medical evidence, 4.230
    reply to response, 4.227
    response, 4.226
    service, 4.216
    time limits, 4.221
    withdrawal, 4.234
  powers, 4.213
  procedure
    regulations, 4.225–4.235
  recovery of benefit
    generally, 1.200–1.203
    reference of questions, 1.204–1.206
    supplementary, 1.210–1.211
  reference
    acknowledgment, 4.224
    decisions, 4.236–4.240
    directions, 4.228
    Forfeiture Act 1982, under, 4.223
    generally, 4.222
    medical evidence, 4.230
    reply to response, 4.227
    response, 4.226
    withdrawal, 4.234
  remuneration, 1.425
  reply to response, 4.227
  representation, 4.225
  request for hearings, 4.231
  response to notice or reference
    generally, 4.226
    reply, 4.227

Index

Commissioners of Inland Revenue— *cont.*
service of notices, 4.216
setting aside decisions, 4.239
tenure of office, 1.426
transfer of proceedings, 4.214
witness summons, 4.233
Compensation payments, recovery of
introduction, 1.94
Computation of benefits
alteration of rates of benefit
age-related benefits, 1.142–1.145
child benefit, 1.134–1.137
contributory benefits, 1.129–1.130
effect, 1.138
job-seeker's allowance, 1.140–1.141
up-rating of pensions, 1.131–1.133
Computers, use of
decisions, 1.268
Conscience, freedom of
human rights, 3.75–3.76
Constant attendance allowance
increase, 4.400–4.404
payment of benefit, 4.96
Contributory benefits
claims for benefit
and see **Claims for benefit**
generally, 1.2–1.31
procedure, 4.16–4.86
payment of benefit, 4.87–4.111
Correction of errors in decisions
appeals procedure, 4.347–4.348
Commissioners procedure, 4.238
decisions, 1.360–1.362
Council Directive on equal treatment
operative provisions, 2.119–2.137
recitals, 2.118
Council Regulations on application of social security schemes (1972)
contents, 2.107–2.108
implementation, 2.109–2.117
Council Regulations on application of social security schemes (1997)
contents, 2.44
determination of applicable legislation, 2.62–2.72
general provisions
declarations on scope, 2.53
definitions, 2.45–2.46
equality of treatment, 2.49–2.50
matters covered, 2.51–2.52
non-contributory benefits, 2.57–2.58
overlapping of benefits, 2.60–2.61
persons covered, 2.47–2.48
waiver of residence, 2.55–2.56
special provisions
family benefits, 2.93–2.102
non-contributory benefits, 2.105
sickness and maternity, 2.73–2.81
unemployment benefits, 2.83–2.91

Court orders
recovery of benefits, 1.212–1.213

Date of claim
generally, 4.35–4.48
Date of entitlement
generally, 4.71–4.72
Death of claimant
appeals procedure, 4.311
payment of benefit, 4.105–4.106
Decisions
appeals from appeals tribunal
generally, 1.309–1.313
procedure, 1.316–1.324
appeals to appeals tribunal
appealable decisions, 1.422, 4.293
appellants, 4.292
certificates of recoverable benefits, 4.299
death of party, 4.311
decisions, 4.342–4.350
dependant upon appeal in other cases, 1.346–1.352, 4.289
extension of time limits, 4.304–4.308
generally, 1.299–1.305
issues determinable by Revenue, 1.339–1.340, 4.320
medical examination, 1.328–1.330, 4.324–4.325
non-disclosure of medical evidence, 4.326–4.327
oral hearings, 4.321–4.322, 4.335–4.341
procedure, 1.316–1.324, 4.309–4.310, 4.318–4.319
re-determination, 1.306–1.308
revision of decisions, 4.300–4.301
striking out, 4.332–4.334
time limits, 4.302–4.303
unappealable decisions, 1.411–1.421, 4.294–4.295, 4.355–4.374
withdrawal, 4.323
witness summons, 4.328–4.329
appeals from Commissioner, 1.314–1.315
appeals to Commissioner
applications for leave, 4.351–4.352
dependant upon appeal in other cases, 1.346–1.352, 4.288
generally, 1.309–1.313
issues determinable by Revenue, 1.339–1.340
medical examination, 1.325–1.337
procedure, 1.316–1.324
unappealable decisions, 1.411–1.421
appeals tribunals
appointment panel, 1.274–1.275, 4.312, 4.375–4.378
clerks, 4.317
composition, 4.313–4.316

633

Decisions—*cont.*
  appeals tribunals—*cont.*
    constitution, 1.276–1.278
    definition, 1.384
    President, 1.272–1.273
    supplementary, 1.401–1.410
    unification, 1.270–1.271
  certificates of recoverable benefits
    appeals, 4.299
    review, 4.271
  Christmas bonus, 1.372–1.373, 1.412
  Commissioners, by
    correction of errors, 4.238
    forfeiture rule questions, 4.237
    generally, 4.236
    reference of issues, 4.275
    setting aside, 4.239
    supplementary, 4.240
  computers, use of, 1.268
  correction of error, 1.360–1.362
  error, cases of
    restriction of benefit, 1.353–1.359
    setting aside decisions, 1.360–1.362
    failure to furnish information, 1.335–1.336
    failure to submit to medical, 1.337–1.338
  incapacity for work
    generally, 1.367–1.369
    regulations, 4.272–4.274
  income support
    alteration in component rates, 4.279
  industrial accidents, as to
    effect, 1.365–1.366
    generally, 1.363–1.364
  industrial diseases, 1.370–1.371
  industrial injuries benefit
    generally, 1.422
    regulations, 4.276–4.277
  information, use of, 1.269
  jobseeker's allowance
    alteration in component rates, 4.279
    incomplete evidence, 4.280
  medical examination
    appeal tribunal, for, 1.328–1.330, 4.324–4.325
    failure to submit to, 1.337–1.338
    Secretary of State, for, 1.325–1.327
  notice of decision, 4.296–4.298
  pilot schemes, 1.388–1.389
  procedure
    finality of decisions, 1.321–1.323
    generally, 1.316–1.320
    matters arising, 1.324
    medical examination, 1.325–1.330
    regulations, 1.432–1.433
  recovery of benefits, 1.422
  re-determination of appeals, 1.306–1.308
  reference of issues to Revenue
    appeals, 1.339–1.340

Decisions—*cont.*
  reference of issues to Revenue—*cont.*
    generally, 1.294–1.295
  revision of decisions
    appeals, 4.300–4.301
    definitions, 4.268
    effective date, 4.255–4.256
    generally, 1.283–1.288
    procedure, 4.246–4.252
    extension of time limits, 4.253–4.254
  Secretary of State, by
    appeals, 1.299–1.315
    dependant upon appeal in other cases, 1.341–1.345
    generally, 1.279–1.282
    industrial injuries benefit, 4.276–4.277
    reference of issues to Revenue, 1.294–1.295
    regulations, 1.296–1.298
    review of decisions, 1.283–1.288
    superseding earlier decisions, 1.289–1.293
  service of notices, 4.244–4.245
  setting aside decisions, 1.360–1.362
  social fund payments
    appropriate officers, 1.375–1.376
    review of determinations, 1.380–1.383
    social fund Commissioner, 1.378–1.379
  supersession of decisions
    change of circumstances, 4.269–4.270
    definitions, 4.268
    effective date, 4.264–4.267
    generally, 1.289–1.293
    procedure, 4.257–4.263
  suspension of benefit
    failure to furnish information, 1.333–1.334, 4.285
    failure to submit to medical, 1.337–1.338, 4.286
    information, provision of, 4.282–4.283
    prescribed circumstances, 1.331–1.332, 4.281
    recommencement of payments, 4.287
  termination of benefit
    failure to furnish information, 1.335–1.336, 4.284–4.285
    failure to submit to medical, 1.337–1.338, 4.286
  third parties, payments to, 1.422
  transfer of functions, and, 1.266–1.267
  work-focused interviews, 1.416

Declaration of incompatibility
  generally, 3.11–3.12
  intervention by Crown, 3.13–3.14
  remedial action, 3.29–3.30

Deduction from compensation payments
appeals to Commissioners, 1.207–1.209
appeals to tribunal
  generally, 1.200–1.203
  reference of questions, 1.204–1.206
  supplementary, 1.210–1.211
assessment of damages, and, 1.218–1.219
certificate of recoverable benefits
  appeals, 1.200–1.211
  applications, 1.186–1.187
  contents, 1.188–1.189
  review, 1.197–1.199
court orders, 1.212–1.213
disregarded payments, 1.227–1.231
income support, and
  diversion of arrested earnings, 1.107–1.108
  generally, 1.95–1.98
  recovery of benefit, 1.99–1.100
  recovery of income support, 1.101–1.104
information, provision of, 1.233–1.237
introduction, 1.181
liability of compensator
  generally, 1.190–1.191
  overpayments, and, 1.225–1.226
  recovery procedure, 1.192–1.193
  wrongly-made payments, 1.227–1.231
overpayments
  disregards, 1.227–1.231
  generally, 1.225–1.226
payments into court, 1.214–1.216
recoverable benefits, 1.182–1.183
recoverable payments
  exempt payments, 1.248
  generally, 1.182–1.183
  list, 1.251–1.253
  small payments, 1.249–1.250
reduction of compensation payment
  complex cases, 1.220–1.224
  generally, 1.194–1.195
  lump sum payments, 1.220–1.222
  more than one person, payments by, 1.223–1.224
  periodical payments, 1.220–1.222
  supplementary, 1.196
reference of questions, 1.204–1.206
relevant cases, 1.180–1.181
relevant payments
  exempt payments, 1.248
  generally, 1.182–1.183
  list, 1.251–1.253
  small payments, 1.249–1.250
relevant period, 1.184–1.185
review of certificates
  generally, 1.197–1.199
  supplementary, 1.210–1.211

Dependency benefits
claims for benefit
  and see **Claims for benefit**
  generally, 1.2–1.31
  procedure, 4.16–4.86
payment of benefit, 4.87–4.111

Direct credit transfers
overpayment of benefits
  generally, 1.66
  regulations, 4.457
payment of benefits, 4.91–4.92

Direct payments
accommodation costs, 4.166
another natural person, to, 4.114–4.115
appointee, to, 4.112–4.113
funeral providers, to, 4.118–4.119
hostels, to
  generally, 4.120–4.121
  miscellaneous, 4.167
housing costs, 4.165
maternity expenses, 4.118–4.119
maximum amounts, 4.173
mortgage lenders, to
  generally, 4.116–4.117
  miscellaneous, 4.176–4.186
partner, to, 4.122–4.123
priority, 4.174
utility companies, to
  generally, 4.118–4.119
  miscellaneous, 4.169
  service charges, 4.168
water charges, 4.170

Disability living allowance (DLA)
claims for benefit
  and see **Claims for benefit**
  advance payments, 4.64–4.65
  generally, 4.24
imprisonment, 4.382–4.383
mobility component
  children, 4.130
  exempt cases, 4.129
  payment to Motability, 4.131–4.133
payment of benefit
  attendance allowance, 4.96
  Motability, to, 4.131–4.133
payment to Motability
  generally, 4.131
  restriction, 4.133
  termination, 4.132

Disability working allowance (DWA)
claims for benefit
  and see **Claims for benefit**
  advance payments, 4.62–4.63
  generally, 4.24

Disabled person's tax credit (DPTC)
claims for benefit
  and see **Claims for benefit**
  initial claims, 1.27–1.31
  repeat claims, 1.27–1.31

Index

Disabled person's tax credit (DPTC)—*cont.*
overpayment of benefit, 1.52
payment of benefit, 4.100
Disablement, assessment of
prescribed degrees, 4.391, 4.414–4.421
principles, 4.391
Disablement benefit
imprisonment, 4.382–4.383
Disablement gratuity
amount, 4.393
rates in lieu, 4.423
scale, 4.422
special hardship, 4.398–4.399
successive accidents, 4.406
weekly value, 4.394
Disablement pension
constant attendance,
  increase of benefit, 4.400–4.404
increase,
  constant attendance, 4.400–4.404
  special hardship, 4.398–4.399
Disclosure
overpayment of benefit, 1.60
Discrimination, prohibition of
human rights, 3.80–3.81
Disqualification from benefit
disregards, 4.390, 4.413
generally, 4.408
imprisonment, 4.382–4.383
Duplication of payments, prevention of
maintenance payments, 4.454–4.456
prescribed income, 4.450–4.451
prescribed payments
  foreign currency payments, 4.456
  generally, 4.452–4.453
Duration of award
generally, 4.73–4.78

EC Court of Justice
generally, 2.38–2.39
guidance for references, 2.40–2.41
EC law
binding nature, 2.7
Council Directive
  equal treatment, 2.118–2.137
Council Regulations
  application of social security schemes, 2.44–2.117
EC Treaty
  citizenship, 2.26–2.31
  Court of Justice, 2.38–2.41
  final provisions, 2.42–2.
  freedom of movement, 2.32–2.37
  principles, 2.16–2.25
implementation of Treaties
  direct effect, 2.10
  generally, 2.6
  indirect effect, 2.11

EC law—*cont.*
implementation of treaties—*cont.*
  liability for breach, 2.12
  supremacy, 2.9
interim relief, 2.13
proof of Treaties, 2.14–2.15
supremacy, 2.9
types, 2.8
EC Treaty
citizenship, 2.26–2.31
Court of Justice
  generally, 2.38–2.39
  guidance for references, 2.40–2.41
final provisions, 2.42–2.
freedom of movement, 2.32–2.37
principles, 2.16–2.25
Education, right to
human rights, 3.87–3.88
Emergency payments
claims for benefit, 1.44–1.45
Equal treatment, Council Directive on
operative provisions, 2.119–2.137
recitals, 2.118
Error, cases of
restriction of benefit, 1.353–1.359
setting aside decisions, 1.360–1.362
Errors, correction of
appeals procedure, 4.347–4.348
Commissioners procedure, 4.238
decisions, 1.360–1.362
European Communities Act 1972
and see **EC law**
arrangement of sections, 2.1
citation, 2.2
commencement, 2.2
definitions, 2.2–2.5
general provisions
  implementation of Treaties, 2.6–2.13
  proof of Treaties, 2.14–2.15
European Convention on Human Rights
and see **Human rights**
First Protocol
  education, right to, 3.87–3.88
  free elections, right to, 3.89
  property, protection of, 3.85–3.86
freedoms
  assembly, of, 3.78
  conscience, of, 3.75–3.76
  expression, of, 3.77
  religion, of, 3.75–3.76
  thought, of, 3.75–3.76
prohibitions
  abuse of rights, of, 3.83
  discrimination, of, 3.80–3.81
  forced labour, of, 3.56–3.57
  punishment without law, on, 3.70
  slavery, of, 3.56–3.57
  torture, of, 3.54–3.55

Index

European Convention on Human Rights—cont.
protections
property, of, **3.85–3.86**
restrictions
limitation on use, **3.84**
political activity of aliens, **3.82**
rights
education, to, **3.87–3.88**
fair trial, **3.60–3.69**
free elections, to, **3.89**
liberty, to, **3.58–3.59**
life, to, **3.52–3.53**
marriage, to, **3.79**
private life, to respect for, **3.71–3.74**
security, **3.58–3.59**
Sixth Protocol, **3.90**
Evidence for claim
generally, **4.50–4.51**
Expression, freedom of
human rights, **3.77**
Extension of time limits
appeals procedure, **4.304–4.308**
revision of decisions, **4.253–4.254**
Extinguishment of benefit
generally, **4.124–4.127**

Failure to disclose
overpayment of benefits
generally, **1.59**
material fact, **1.62**
mental capacity, **1.61**
missing documents, **1.63**
suspension of benefit
generally, **1.333–1.334**
regulations, **4.285**
Failure to furnish information
suspension of benefit
generally, **1.335–1.336**
regulations, **4.285**
Failure to maintain
diversion of arrested earnings, **1.107–1.108**
generally, **1.95–1.98**
recovery of benefit, **1.99–1.100**
recovery of income support, **1.101–1.104**
reduction of income support, **1.105–1.106**
Failure to submit to medical
suspension of benefit
generally, **1.337–1.338**
regulations, **4.286**
Fair trial, right to
human rights, **3.60–3.69**
Forced labour, prohibition of
human rights, **3.56–3**.
Forfeiture rule questions
meaning, **4.212**
post-decision procedure, **4.237**

Fractional sums
payment of benefit, **4.101–4.10257**
Free elections, right to
human rights, **3.89**
Funeral expenses
payment of benefit, **4.118–4.119**

Guardian's allowance
payment of benefit, **4.94**

Heating expenses
payment of benefit, **4.118–4.119**
Holding information
local authorities, and, **4.196**
Hostels, to
payment of benefit
generally, **4.120–4.121**
miscellaneous, **4.167**
Housing costs
payment of benefit, **4.165**
Human rights
Convention rights
generally, **3.2–3.3**
interpretation, **3.4–3.8A**
declaration of incompatibility
generally, **3.11–3.12**
intervention by Crown, **3.13–3.14**
remedial action, **3.29–3.30**
derogations
duration, **3.41–3.42**
generally, **3.37–3.44**
1988 notification, **3.91**
1989 notification, **3.92**
periodic review, **3.43–3.44**
ECHR judges, **3.45**
European Convention on Human Rights
Articles, **3.52–3.84**
First Protocol, **3.85–3.89**
Sixth Protocol, **3.90**
existing human rights, safeguards for
conscience, freedom of, **3.35–3.36**
expression, freedom of, **3.33–3.34**
generally, **3.31–3.32**
religion, freedom of, **3.35–3.36**
thought, freedom of, **3.35–3.36**
legislation
declaration of incompatibility, **3.11–3.12**
interpretation, **3.9–3.10**
intervention by Crown, **3.13–3.14**
remedial action, **3.29–3.30**
Parliamentary procedure, **3.46–3.47**
public authorities, acts of
generally, **3.15–3.16**
judicial acts, **3.27–3.28**
judicial remedies, **3.24–3.26**
proceedings, **3.17–3.23**
remedial action, **3.29–3.30**

Index

Human rights—*cont.*
reservations
generally, **3**.39–**3**.40
1952 text, **3**.93–**3**.94
statements of compatibility, **3**.46–**3**.47
Human Rights Act 1998
arrangement of sections, **3**.1
citation, **3**.50
commencement, **3**.50–**3**.51
definitions, **3**.49
general provisions
derogations, **3**.37–**3**.44
ECHR judges, **3**.45
legislation, **3**.9–**3**.14
other rights, **3**.31–**3**.36
Parliamentary procedure, **3**.46–**3**.47
public authorities, **3**.15–**3**.28
remedial action, **3**.29–**3**.30
reservations, **3**.39–**3**.40
introductory provisions, **3**.2–**3**.8
schedules
derogations, **3**.91–**3**.92
European Convention, **3**.52–**3**.90
reservations, **3**.93–**3**.94
supplementary provisions, **3**.48

Imprisonment, persons serving term of
disqualification from benefit, **4**.382–**4**.383
suspension of benefit, **4**.384
Inalienability of benefit
generally, **1**.165–**1**.166
Incapacity benefit
claims for benefit
and see **Claims for benefit**
generally, **4**.56
imprisonment, **4**.382–**4**.383
payment of benefit, **4**.95
Incapacity for work, medical evidence of
forms
all work test statement, **4**.437–**4**.438
general certificate, **4**.432–**4**.433
maternity certificate, **4**.440
special statement, **4**.435
generally, **4**.426–**4**.429
rules
all work test statement, **4**.436
general certificate, **4**.431
maternity certificate, **4**.439
special statement, **4**.434
self-certification, **4**.430
Income support
claims for benefit
and see **Claims for benefit**
exempt claims, **4**.16–**4**.17
generally, **4**.18–**4**.19
method, **4**.23
decisions

Income support—*cont.*
alteration in component rates, **4**.279
failure to maintain
diversion of arrested earnings, **1**.107–**1**.108
generally, **1**.95–**1**.98
recovery of benefit, **1**.99–**1**.100
recovery of income support, **1**.101–**1**.104
reduction of income support, **1**.105–**1**.106
liability to maintain, **1**.98
overpayment of benefit
generally, **1**.73
prescribed income, **4**.450–**4**.451
payment of benefit **4**.97
Increase in benefit
industrial injuries benefit
disablement gratuity, **4**.398–**4**.399
disablement pension, **4**.400
reduced earnings allowance, **4**.396–**4**.397
Industrial accidents, decisions as to
effect, **1**.365–**1**.366
generally, **1**.363–**1**.364
Industrial diseases
decisions, **1**.370–**1**.371
Industrial death benefit
imprisonment, **4**.382–**4**.383
Industrial injuries benefit
accident notification
generally, **1**.21–**1**.22
Regulations, **4**.6, **4**.11
adjustment,
successive accidents, **4**.406–**4**.407
claimant obligations
generally, **1**.25–**1**.26
Regulations, **4**.8
claims for benefit
and see **Claims for benefit**
accident notification, **1**.21–**1**.22, **4**.6, **4**.11
claimant obligations, **1**.25–**1**.26, **4**.8
employers obligations, **4**.7
medical examination, **1**.23–**1**.24, **4**.8
notification obligations, **1**.21–**1**.22, **4**.6, **4**.11
constant attendance allowance
increase, **4**.400–**4**.404
decisions
generally, **1**.422
regulations, **4**.276–**4**.277
disablement, assessment of
prescribed degrees, **4**.391, **4**.414–**4**.421
principles, **4**.391
disablement gratuity
amount, **4**.393
rates in lieu, **4**.423
scale, **4**.422

Index

Industrial injuries benefit—*cont.*
disablement gratuity—*cont.*
special hardship, 4.398–4.399
successive accidents, 4.406
weekly value, 4.394
disablement pension
constant attendance, 4.400–4.404
successive accidents, 4.407
increase in benefit
disablement gratuity, 4.398–4.399
disablement pension, 4.400
reduced earnings allowance, 4.396–4.397
medical examination
generally, 1.23–1.24
Regulations, 4.8
notification obligations
generally, 1.21–1.22
Regulations, 4.6, 4.11
payment of benefits, 4.107
reduced earnings allowance
incapacity for work, 4.396–4.397
successive accidents
disablement gratuity, 4.406
disablement pension, 4.407
unemployability supplement,
earnings level, 4.395
Industrial injuries gratuities
payment of benefit, 4.107
Information, provision of
age, 1.111–1.112
claims for benefit
generally, 4.50–4.51
local authorities, by, 4.197
death
generally, 1.111–1.112
notification, 1.113–1.114
incapacity benefit
employer, by, 1.121–1.122, 1.124–1.125
industrial injuries benefit, 1.121–1.122
jobseeker's allowance
regulations, 873-876
statutory basis, 314-315
transitional provisions, and, 969-970
maintenance proceedings, 1.126–1.127
marriage, 1.111–1.112
maternity allowance, 1.121–1.122
payment of benefit, 4.108–4.111
personal representatives, by, 1.115–1.116
recovery of benefits
compensator, by, 4.484
employer, by, 4.486
generally, 1.233–1.237
injured person, by, 4.485
procedure, 4.487
severe disablement allowance, 1.121–1.122, 1.124–1.125
statutory maternity pay

Information, provision of—*cont.*
statutory maternity pay—*cont.*
employer, by, 1.124–1.125
Secretary of State, by, 1.123
statutory sick pay
employer, by, 1.121–1.122
Secretary of State, by, 1.119–1.120
suspension of benefit, 4.282–4.283
Information, use of
decisions, 1.269
local authorities, and
generally, 4.202
partner of claimant, 4.205–4.206
purpose, 4.203–4.204
Instruments of payment
generally, 4.134–4.135
presentation, 4.89–4.90
Interchange of benefits
claims for benefit
generally, 4.54–4.55
list of benefits, 4.140
Interim payments
benefit under Act, by way of, 4.385–4.386
bringing into account, 4.445
generally, 4.443–4.444
overpayment, 4.446
Irregularities, effect of
Commissioners procedure, 4.235

Jobseeker's allowance
claims for benefit
and see **Claims for benefit**
exempt claims, 4.16–4.17
generally, 4.18–4.19
method, 4.25
special provisions, 4.141
decisions
alteration in component rates, 4.279
incomplete evidence, 4.280
overpayment of benefit
generally, 1.71–1.72
prescribed income, 4.450–4.451
payment of benefit, 4.98–4.99

Legislation
declaration of incompatibility, 3.11–3.12
interpretation, 3.9–3.10
intervention by Crown, 3.13–3.14
remedial action, 3.29–3.30
Liberty, right to
human rights, 3.58–3.59
Life, right to
human rights, 3.52–3.53
Limitation period
overpayment of benefits, 1.50–1.51

Index

Local authorities
claims for payment, and
child support, 4.195
functions, 4.193–4.194
holding information, 4.196
provision of information, 4.197
use and supply of information,
4.202–4.206
war pensions, 4.195
Long term benefits
payment of benefit, 4.93

Marriage, right to
human rights, 3.79
Maternity allowance (SMA)
claims for benefit
and see **Claims for benefit**
advance claim, 4.66
generally, 4.57–4.59
imprisonment, 4.382–4.383
payment of benefit, 4.95
Maternity expenses
payment of benefit, 4.118–4.119
Maternity pay
claims for benefit
and see **Claims for benefit**
generally, 1.40–1.41
medical evidence
form, 4.440
rules, 4.439
Medical evidence
Commissioners procedure, 4.216
Medical evidence of incapacity for work
forms
all work test statement, 4.437–4.438
general certificate, 4.432–4.433
maternity certificate, 4.440
special statement, 4.435
generally, 4.426–4.429
rules
all work test statement, 4.436
general certificate, 4.431
maternity certificate, 4.439
special statement, 4.434
self-certification, 4.430
Medical examination
appeals procedure
generally, 1.328–1.330
regulations, 4.324–4.325
failure to submit to, 1.337–1.338
industrial injuries benefit, and
generally, 1.23–1.24
Regulations, 4.8
Secretary of State, for, 1.325–1.327
Misrepresentation
overpayment of benefits
fraudulently or otherwise, 1.57
generally, 1.53

Misrepresentation—*cont.*
overpayment of benefits—*cont.*
material fact, 1.62
mental capacity, 1.61
misrepresents, 1.58
missing documents, 1.63
Mobility component
payment of benefit
children, 4.130
exempt cases, 4.129
payment to Motability, 4.131–4.133
payment to Motability
generally, 4.131
restriction, 4.133
termination, 4.132
Mortgage interest
claims for benefit, 1.42–1.43
Mortgage lenders, payment to
generally, 4.116–4.117
miscellaneous, 4.176–4.186
Motability payment to
generally, 4.131
restriction, 4.133
termination, 4.132

National insurance number
application for, 1.161–1.162
Non-contributory benefits
claims for benefit
and see **Claims for benefit**
generally, 1.2–1.31
procedure, 4.16–4.86
payment of benefit, 4.87–4.111
Notice of appeal
acknowledgment, 4.224
decisions
correction of errors, 4.238
forfeiture rule questions, 4.237
generally, 4.236
setting aside, 4.239
supplementary, 4.240
directions, 4.228
generally, 4.220
medical evidence, 4.230
response to notice or reference,
generally, 4.226
reply, 4.227
time limits, 4.221
withdrawal, 4.234
Notification of accidents
industrial injuries benefit, and
generally, 1.21–1.22
Regulations, 4.6, 4.11

Offsetting
generally, 1.56
regulations
exceptions, 4.448
generally, 4.447

Index

'One' offices
claims for benefit
child benefit, 4.195
generally, 4.31–4.32
war pensions, 4.195

Oral hearings
appeals procedure
adjournment, 4.339
directions, 4.321–4.322
expert assistance, 4.337–4.338
physical examinations, 4.340–4.341
postponement, 4.339
procedure, 4.335–4.336
record of proceedings, 4.345–4.346

Overpayments of benefit
automated credit transfers, by
generally, 1.66
regulations, 4.457
calculation of amount, 1.65
causation, 1.64
child benefit, and
generally, 1.73
prescribed payments, 4.452–4.455
deduction from benefits, and
generally, 4.464
limitations, 4.465
direct credit transfer, by
generally, 1.66
regulations, 4.457
disclosure, 1.60
failure to disclose
generally, 1.59
material fact, 1.62
mental capacity, 1.61
missing documents, 1.63
generally, 1.47–1.49
guide, 1.68
income support, and
generally, 1.73
prescribed income, 4.450–4.451
interim payments, and, 4.446
jobseeker's allowance, and
generally, 1.71–1.72
prescribed income, 4.450–4.451
limitation period, 1.50–1.51
misrepresentation
fraudulently or otherwise, 1.57
generally, 1.53
material fact, 1.62
mental capacity, 1.61
misrepresents, 1.58
missing documents, 1.63
Northern Ireland, 1.90–1.91
offsetting, and
generally, 1.56
regulations, 4.447–4.448
recoverable amount
capital resources, diminution of, 4.462–4.463
deductions, 4.460–4.461
generally, 4.458–4.459

Overpayments of benefit—*cont.*
recovery of benefits, and
disregards, 1.227–1.231
generally, 1.225–1.226
recovery from earnings after trade dispute
cessation of employment, 4.477–4.478
deduction notices, 4.469–4.475
employer's duties, 4.476
generally, 4.467
increased awards, 4.472
protected earnings, 4.468
resumption of employment, 4.477–4.478
recovery procedure
couples, from, 4.466
deduction from benefits, from, 4.464–4.465
deduction from earnings after trade dispute, by, 4.467–4.478
relevant person
appointee, 1.55
generally, 1.54
spouses, 1.56
requirements
any person, 1.54
appointees, 1.55
automated credit transfers, 1.66
causation, 1.64
determination of amount, 1.65
disclosure, 1.60
failure to disclose, 1.59
fraudulently or otherwise, 1.57
generally, 1.53
material fact, 1.62
mental capacity, 1.61
misrepresents, 1.58
missing documents, 1.63
tax credits, 1.67
social fund, and
generally, 1.69–1.70
procedure, 1.85–1.89
supplementary benefits, and, 1.177
tax credits, 1.67
variation of benefit, 1.52

Payment of benefits
another natural person, to, 4.114–4.115
appointee, to, 4.112–4.113
attendance allowance, 4.96
child benefit
election, 4.162
generally, 4.94
constant attendance allowance, 4.96
death, and, 4.105–4.106
direct credit transfer, by
generally, 4.91–4.92
overpayment, 1.66, 4.457

641

Payment of benefits—*cont.*
direct payment, and
accommodation costs, 4.166
another natural person, to, 4.114–4.115
appointee, to, 4.112–4.113
funeral providers, to, 4.118–4.119
hostels, to, 4.120–4.121, 4.167
housing costs, 4.165
maternity expenses, 4.118–4.119
maximum amounts, 4.173
miscellaneous, 4.163–4.188
mortgage lenders, to, 4.116–4.117, 4.176–4.186
partner, to, 4.122–4.123
priority, 4.174
utility companies, to, 4.118–4.119, 4.168–4.170
disability living allowance
attendance allowance, 4.96
mobility component, 4.131–4.133
disabled persons' tax credit, 4.100
duplication of
maintenance payments, 4.454–4.455
prescribed income, 4.450–4.451
prescribed payments, 4.452–4.453
fractional sums, 4.101–4.102
funeral expenses, 4.118–4.119
guardian's allowance, 4.94
heating expenses, 4.118–4.119
hostels, to person in, 4.120–4.121
incapacity benefit, 4.95
income support, 4.97
industrial injuries gratuities, 4.107
information required, 4.108–4.111
instruments of payment
generally, 4.134–4.135
presentation, 4.89–4.90
interim payments
bringing into account, 4.445
generally, 4.443–4.444
overpayment, 4.446
jobseeker's allowance, 4.98–4.99
long term benefits, 4.93
maternity allowance, 4.95
maternity expenses, 4.118–4.119
method of payment
generally, 4.87–4.88
miscellaneous, 4.148–4.161
presentation of instrument, 4.89–4.90
mortgage payments, 4.116–4.117
Motability, to
generally, 4.131
restriction, 4.133
termination, 4.132
off-setting
exceptions, 4.448
generally, 4.447

Payment of benefits—*cont.*
partner, to, 4.122–4.123
pending appeals, 4.389
person aged 17 or under, 4.103–4.104
residential accommodation, to person in, 4.120–4.121
severe disablement allowance, 4.95
supplementary benefits, and, 1.177
third parties, and
accommodation costs, 4.166
another natural person, to, 4.114–4.115
appointee, to, 4.112–4.113
funeral providers, to, 4.118–4.119
hostels, to, 4.120–4.121, 4.167
housing costs, 4.165
maternity expenses, 4.118–4.119
maximum amounts, 4.173
miscellaneous, 4.163–4.188
mortgage lenders, to, 4.116–4.117, 4.176–4.186
partner, to, 4.122–4.123
priority, 4.174
utility companies, to, 4.118–4.119, 4.168–4.170
time of payment
generally, 4.87–4.88
long term benefits, 4.147
miscellaneous, 4.149
presentation of instrument, 4.89–4.90
working families' tax credit, 4.100
Payments into court
recovery of benefits
generally, 1.214–1.216
regulations, 4.489
Pending appeals
payment of benefit, 4.389
Persons aged 17 or under
payment of benefit, 4.103–4.104
notice of decision, 4.296–4.298
Pilot schemes
generally, 1.388–1.389
Prisoners
disqualification from benefit, 4.382–4.383
suspension of benefit, 4.384
Private life, right to respect for
human rights, 3.71–3.74
Property, protection of
human rights, 3.85–3.86
Public authorities, acts of
generally, 3.15–3.16
judicial acts, 3.27–3.28
judicial remedies, 3.24–3.26
proceedings, 3.17–3.23
remedial action, 3.29–3.30
Punishment without law, prohibition on
human rights, 3.70

Index

Reciprocal arrangements with other systems
Northern Ireland, 1.154–1.157
outside UK, 1.158–1.159
Record of proceedings
appeals procedure, 4.345–4.346
Recovery from compensation
adjustments, 4.492
appeals to Commissioners, 1.207–1.209
appeals to tribunal
  generally, 1.200–1.203
  reference of questions, 1.204–1.206
  supplementary, 1.210–1.211
assessment of damages, and, 1.218–1.219
certificate of recoverable benefits
  appeals, 1.200–1.211
  applications, 1.186–1.187
  contents, 1.188–1.189
  regulations, 4.488
  review, 1.197–1.199
court orders, 1.212–1.213
disregarded payments, 1.227–1.231
exemptions, 4.483
income support, and
  diversion of arrested earnings, 1.107–1.108
  generally, 1.95–1.98
  recovery of benefit, 1.99–1.100
  recovery of income support, 1.101–1.104
information, provision of
  compensator, by, 4.484
  employer, by, 4.486
  generally, 1.233–1.237
  injured person, by, 4.485
  procedure, 4.487
introduction, 1.94, 1.181
liability of compensator
  generally, 1.190–1.191
  overpayments, and, 1.225–1.226
  recovery procedure, 1.192–1.193
  wrongly-made payments, 1.227–1.231
overpayments
  disregards, 1.227–1.231
  generally, 1.225–1.226
payments into court
  generally, 1.214–1.216
  regulations, 4.489
recoverable benefits, 1.182–1.183
recoverable payments
  exempt payments, 1.248
  generally, 1.182–1.183
  list, 1.251–1.253
  small payments, 1.249–1.250
reduction of compensation payment
  complex cases, 1.220–1.224
  generally, 1.194–1.195
  lump sum payments, 1.220–1.222
  more than one person, payments by, 1.223–1.224

Recovery from compensation—*cont.*
reduction of compensation payment—*cont.*
  periodical payments, 1.220–1.222
  supplementary, 1.196
reference of questions, 1.204–1.206
relevant cases, 1.180–1.181
relevant payments
  exempt payments, 1.248, 4.483
  generally, 1.182–1.183
  list, 1.251–1.253
  small payments, 1.249–1.250
relevant period, 1.184–1.185
review of certificates
  generally, 1.197–1.199
  supplementary, 1.210–1.211
structured settlements, 4.491
Recovery from couples
generally, 4.466
Recovery from deduction from benefits
generally, 4.464–4.465
Recovery from earnings after trade dispute
cessation of employment
  failure to notify, 4.478
  generally, 4.477
deduction notices
  contents, 4.469
  duration, 4.470
  effect, 4.471
  further, 4.474
  service, 4.469
  variation, 4.472–4.473
employer's duties
  failure to notify, 4.478
  generally, 4.476
generally, 4.467
increased awards, 4.472
protected earnings, 4.468
resumption of employment
  failure to notify, 4.478
  generally, 4.477
Re-determination of appeals
generally, 1.306–1.308
Reduced earnings allowance
imprisonment, 4.382–4.383
incapacity for work, 4.396–4.397
Reduction of benefit
complex cases
  generally, 1.220–1.224
  lump sum payments, 1.220–1.222
  more than one person, payments by, 1.223–1.224
  periodical payments, 1.220–1.222
  regulations, 4.490
generally, 1.194–1.195
income support, and, 1.105–1.106
supplementary, 1.196

Index

References of forfeiture rule question
acknowledgment, 4.224
decisions
  correction of errors, 4.238
  forfeiture rule questions, 4.237
  generally, 4.236
  setting aside, 4.239
  supplementary, 4.240
directions, 4.228
Forfeiture Act 1982, under, 4.223
generally, 4.22
medical evidence, 4.230
response to notice or reference,
  generally, 4.226
  reply, 4.227
withdrawal, 4.234
Reference of issues to Revenue
appeals, 1.339–1.340
generally, 1.294–1.295
Religion, freedom of
human rights, 3.75–3.76
Residential accommodation, person in
payment of benefit, 4.120–4.121
Retirement pensions
claims for benefit
and see **Claims for benefit**
  advance claim, 4.67–4.68
  generally, 4.16–4.17
imprisonment, 4.382–4.383
Revision of decisions
appeals, 4.300–4.301
definitions, 4.268
effective date, 4.255–4.256
extension of time limits, 4.253–4.254
generally, 1.283–1.288
procedure, 4.246–4.252

Secretary of State, decisions by
appeals, 1.299–1.315
  dependant upon appeal in other cases, 1.341–1.345
  generally, 1.279–1.282
industrial injuries benefit, 4.276–4.277
reference of issues to Revenue, 1.294–1.295
regulations, 1.296–1.298
review of decisions, 1.283–1.288
superseding earlier decisions, 1.289–1.293
Security, right to
human rights, 3.58–3.59
Self-certification
medical evidence, 4.430
Service of notices
Commissioners procedure, 4.216
Setting aside decisions
generally, 1.360–1.362

Setting aside decisions—*cont.*
regulations
  appeals procedure, 4.349–4.350
  generally, 4.239
Severe disablement allowance
claims for benefit
and see **Claims for benefit**
  generally, 4.56
imprisonment, 4.382–4.383
payment of benefit, 4.95
Slavery, prohibition of
human rights, 3.56–3.57
Social fund
adjustment, 1.151–1.152
allocations, 1.149–1.150
claims for benefit
and see **Claims for benefit**
  generally, 1.32–1.35
decisions
  appropriate officers, 1.375–1.376
  review of determinations, 1.380–1.383
  social fund Commissioner, 1.378–1.379
generally, 1.147–1.148
overpayment of benefits
  generally, 1.69–1.70
  procedure, 1.85–1.89
Social Security Act 1998
arrangement of sections, 1.265
citation, 1.399–1.400
commencement, 1.399–1.400
definitions, 1.384, 1.396–1.398
general provisions
  appeal tribunals, 1.270–1.278
  Christmas bonus, 1.372–1.373
  contributions, 1.386
  decision-making, 1.266–1.269
  error correction, 1.353–1.362
  incapacity for work, 1.367–1.369
  industrial accidents, 1.363–1.366
  industrial diseases, 1.370–1.371
  Inland Revenue appeals, 1.339–1.340
  medical examinations, 1.325–1.330
  other decisions, 1.385
  procedure, 1.316–1.324
  Secretary of State appeals, 1.341–1.352
  social fund payments, 1.375–1.383
  social security appeals, 1.299–1.315
  social security decisions, 1.279–1.298
  suspension of benefits, 1.331–1.338
miscellaneous provisions
  pilot schemes, 1.388–1.389
  recitals, 1.265
  regulations and orders, 1.390–1.392
  reports by SoS, 1.393–1.395
schedules
  appeal tribunals, 1.401–1.410
  appealable decisions, 1.422–1.423
  Commissioners, 1.424–1.431

Index

Social Security Act 1998—*cont.*
schedules—*cont.*
excluded decisions, 1.411–1.421
procedure, 1.432–1.434
Social Security Administration Act 1992
arrangement of sections, 1.1
citation, 1.174
commencement, 1.174
definitions, 1.172–1.173
general provisions
adjudication, 1.46
adjustment of benefit, 1.74–1.93
claims for benefit, 1.2–1.45
computation of benefit, 1.129–1.145
enforcement, 1.109
failure to maintain, 1.95–1.108
information, 1.110–1.128
overpayment of benefit, 1.47–1.73
payment of benefit, 1.2–1.45
reciprocal arrangements with other systems, 1.154–1.159
recovery of benefit, 1.94
social fund, 1.146–1.153
miscellaneous provisions, 1.160–1.167
schedules
claims for benefit, 1.175–1.176
supplementary benefit, etc., 1.177–1.178
subordinate legislation, 1.168–1.171
Social Security (Claims and Payments) Regulations 1979
arrangement of regulations, 4.1
citation, 4.2
commencement, 4.2
definitions, 4.3–4.5
general provisions,
industrial injuries, benefits for, 4.6–4.9
schedules,
accident particulars, 4.10–4.12
Social Security (Claims and Payments) Regulations 1987
arrangement of regulations, 4.13
citation, 4.14
commencement, 4.14
definitions, 4.15
general provisions
claims for benefits, 4.16–4.86
disability living allowances, 4.128–4.133
extinguishment of benefits, 4.124–4.127
payment of benefit, 4.87–4.111
third parties, 4.112–4.123
miscellaneous provisions
payment of benefit, 4.134–4.135
revocations, 4.136–4.138
schedules
child benefit, 4.162
claims for benefits, 4.139–4.140

Social Security (Claims and Payments) Regulations 1987—*cont.*
deductions from benefit, 4.163–4.188
jobseeker's allowances, 4.141–4.142
payment of benefit, 4.147–4.161
time limits, 4.143–4.146
Social Security (Claims and Payments) Regulations 1999
arrangement of regulations, 4.189
citation, 4.190
commencement, 4.190
definitions, 4.191
general provisions, 4.192–4.207
Social Security Commissioners
and see **Commissioners**
appeals, 4.220–4.221
applications for leave to appeal, 4.217–4.219
decisions, 4.236–4.240
delegation of functions, 4.215
further appeal, 4.241
powers, 4.213
procedure, 4.225–4.235
references, 4.222–4.224
service of notices, 4.216
transfer of proceedings, 4.214
Social Security Commissioners (Procedure) Regulations 1999
arrangement of regulations, 4.208
citation, 4.209
commencement, 4.209
definitions, 4.212
general provisions,
appeals, 4.220–4.221
applications for leave to appeal, 4.217–4.219
decisions, 4.236–4.240
further appeal, 4.241
generally, 4.213–4.216
procedure, 4.225–4.235
references, 4.222–4.224
revocation, 4.210
transitional provisions, 4.211
Social Security, etc. (Decisions and Appeals) Regulations 1999
arrangement of regulations, 4.242
citation, 4.243
commencement, 4.243
definitions, 4.243
general provisions
capacity for work, 4.272–4.273
certificates of recoverable benefits, 4.271
revision of decisions, 4.246–4.256
supersession of decisions, 4.257–4.270
schedule
service of notices, 4.244–4.245

645

Index

Social Security (General Benefit) Regulations 1982
arrangement of regulations, 4.380
citation, 4.381
commencement, 4.381
definitions, 4.381
general provisions
  disqualification for benefits, 4.408–4.410
  industrial injuries benefit, 4.391–4.407
  non-industrial injuries, benefits for, 4.389–4.390
  prisoners, benefits for, 4.382–4.388
miscellaneous provisions, 4.411–4.412
schedules
  industrial injuries benefit, 4.414–4.423
  non-industrial injuries, benefits for, 4.413

Social Security (Medical Evidence) Regulations 1976
arrangement of regulations, 4.424
citation, 4.425
commencement, 4.425
definitions, 4.425
general provisions, 4.426–4.430
schedules, 4.431–4.440

Social Security (Payments on Account, Overpayments and Recovery) Regulations 1988
arrangement of regulations, 4.441
citation, 4.442
commencement, 4.442
definitions, 4.442
general provisions
  calculation of recoverable amount, 4.458–4.463
  duplication of payments, 4.449–4.456
  interim payments, 4.443–4.446
  offsetting, 4.447–4.448
  overpayments, 4.457
  recovery procedure, 4.464–4.478
  revocation, 4.479
  transitional provisions, 4.480

Social Security (Recovery of Benefits) Act 1997
application, 1.239–1.240
arrangement of sections, 1.179
citation, 1.247
commencement, 1.247
definitions, 1.241
general provisions
  appeals, 1.200–1.211
  certificates of recoverable benefits, 1.186–1.189
  complex cases, 1.220–1.224
  courts, 1.212–1.219
  liability of payer, 1.190–1.193
  reduction of payment, 1.194–1.196
  references, 1.204–1.211

Social Security (Recovery of Benefits) Act 1997—*cont.*
  reviews, 1.197–1.211
introductory provisions, 1.180–1.185
miscellaneous provisions, 1.225–1.246
schedules
  compensation payments, 1.248–1.253

Social Security (Recovery of Benefits) Act 1997
arrangement of regulations, 4.481
citation, 4.482
commencement, 4.482
definitions, 4.482
general provisions
  adjustments, 4.492
  application for certificate, 4.488
  complex cases, 4.490
  exemptions, 4.483
  information, provision of, 4.484–4.487
  payments into court, 4.489
  structured settlements, 4.491
transitional provisions, 4.493

Social Security, etc., (Transfer of Functions, etc.) Act 1999
arrangement of sections, 1.254
citation, 1.263
commencement, 1.263
definitions, 1.262
general provisions
  decisions and appeals, 1.255–1.260
miscellaneous provisions, 1.261
recitals, 1.254

State maternity allowance (SMA)
claims for benefit
  and see **Claims for benefit**
  advance claim, 4.66
  generally, 4.57–4.59
payment of benefit, 493

Statement of reasons
appeals procedure
  generally, 4.342–4.343
  late application, 4.344

Statements of compatibility
human rights, 3.46–3.47

Statutory maternity pay
claims for benefit
  and see **Claims for benefit**
  generally, 1.40–1.41

Statutory sick pay
claims for benefit
  and see **Claims for benefit**
  generally, 1.38–1.39

Striking out
appeals procedure
  generally, 4.332
  misconceived applications, 4.334
  reinstatement, 4.333

Structured settlements
recovery of benefits, 4.491